HBJ
LANGUAGE

7

Dorothy S. Strickland
Richard F. Abrahamson
Roger C. Farr
Nancy R. McGee
Nancy L. Roser

7

Karen S. Kutiper
Patricia Smith

HBJ
LANGUAGE

 HARCOURT BRACE JOVANOVICH, PUBLISHERS

Orlando   San Diego   Chicago   Dallas

Acknowledgments

For permission to reprint copyrighted material, grateful acknowledgment is made to the following sources:

Atheneum Publishers, an imprint of Macmillan Publishing Company: From "Summer—First the Good News" in *Pieces of My Mind* by Andrew A. Rooney. Copyright © 1984 by Essay Productions, Inc. From *Dicey's Song* by Cynthia Voigt. Copyright © 1982 by Cynthia Voigt.

Bantam Books, a division of Bantam, Doubleday, Dell Publishing Group, Inc.: From pp. 250–254 in *20,000 Leagues Under the Sea* by Jules Verne, translated by Anthony Bonner, with an introduction by Ray Bradbury. Copyright © 1962 by Bantam Books, Inc.

Cobblestone Publishing, Inc., Peterborough, NH 03458: "The Man Who Stopped Traffic" by Virginia Calkins from *Cobblestone* Magazine, July 1987. © 1987 by Cobblestone Publishing Inc.

Don Congdon Associates, Inc.: From *Dandelion Wine* by Ray Bradbury. Copyright © 1953 by Ray Bradbury, renewed 1981 by Ray Bradbury.

Victor Hernández Cruz: "The Latest Latin Dance Craze" from *Tropicalization* by Victor Hernández Cruz. © 1976 by Victor Hernández Cruz. Published by I. Reed Books.

Delacorte Press: From "The All—American Slurp" by Lensey Namioka in *VISIONS: Nineteen Short Stories by Outstanding Writers for Young Adults,* edited by Donald R. Gallo. Copyright © 1987 by Lensey Namioka. All rights reserved.

Mr. and Mrs. Frank Finn, on behalf of Kevin Finn: "Smoking in Public Buildings" from the *Lewenberg Literary Journal,* Volume II, June 1987.

Harcourt Brace Jovanovich, Inc.: From p. 112 in *Babbitt* by Sinclair Lewis. Copyright 1922 by Harcourt Brace Jovanovich, Inc., renewed 1950 by Sinclair Lewis. "Dog At Night" from *Stars to Steer By* by Louis Untermeyer. Copyright 1941 by Harcourt Brace Jovanovich, Inc., renewed 1968 by Louis Untermeyer. "Study Steps to Learn a Word" from *HBJ Spelling,* Signature Edition, Level 7 (Silver) by Thorsten Carlson and Richard Madden. Copyright © 1988, 1983 by Harcourt Brace Jovanovich, Inc.

Short pronunciation key and entries from *HBJ School Dictionary.* Copyright © 1985 by Harcourt Brace Jovanovich, Inc.

Harper & Row, Publishers, Inc.: From pp. 3–6 in *Cheaper by the Dozen* by Frank B. Gilbreth, Jr. and Ernestine Gilbreth Carey. Copyright © 1948, 1963 by Frank B. Gilbreth, Jr. and Ernestine Gilbreth Carey.

Henry Holt and Company, Inc.: From "Stopping by Woods on a Snowy Evening" in *The Poetry of Robert Frost,* edited by Edward Connery Lathem. Copyright 1923 by Holt, Rinehart and Winston, renewed 1951 by Robert Frost.

Leland B. Jacobs: From "What a State" by Lee Blair in *Poetry for Chuckles and Grins,* selected by Leland B. Jacobs. Copyright © 1968 by Leland B. Jacobs.

Alfred A. Knopf, Inc.: "African Dance" from *Selected Poems of Langston Hughes* by Langston Hughes. Copyright 1926 by Alfred A. Knopf, Inc., renewed 1954 by Langston Hughes.

Lothrop, Lee and Shepard Books, a division of William Morrow and Company, Inc.: "How We Dance" from *The Break Dance Kids* by Lillian Morrison. Text copyright © 1985 by Lillian Morrison.

Harold Ober Associates Incorporated: "The Case of the Missing Will" in *Poirot Investigates* by Agatha Christie. Copyright 1923, 1924, 1925 by Dodd, Mead & Company, Inc.; copyright renewed 1953 by Agatha Christie Mallowan.

Oxford University Press: From "The Rescue" in *Tomorrow is My Love* by Hal Summers. © 1978 by Hal Summers.

The Reader's Digest Association, Inc.: Text from "Caring for a baby bird" in *Back to Basics: How to Learn and Enjoy Traditional American Skills.* Copyright © 1981 by The Reader's Digest Association, Inc.

Richard Rieu, as Executor of the Estate of Dr. E. V. Rieu: From "The Castaways" in *Cuckoo Calling* by E. V.

continued at the end of the book

Contents

1 Relating Personal Experiences   8

Reading ◄► Writing Connection

Composition Focus: Personal Narrative

Language Focus: Sentences

Persuading Others 154

5 **Comparing and Contrasting**

6 Creating Images 248

8 Creating Stories

Reading ◀▶ Writing Connection

Composition Focus: Mystery Story

Language Focus: Complex Sentences and Verbals

Reporting Information 404

Extra Practice   1

Dear Student,

  Have you ever told a story to entertain young children or tried to persuade classmates to vote for you in an election? Have you ever informed others about how to play a new game or expressed your feelings about a television show? Then you were using your language to communicate your thoughts and ideas.

  Communication is a two-way process. You need to be able to communicate your ideas to other people, but you also need to be able to understand other people when they speak or write. HBJ Language will help you use English effectively when you listen, speak, read, and write.

  We hope that you will enjoy learning more about your language and how to use it to communicate exactly what you mean.

Sincerely,
The Editors

Understanding the Writing Process

Writing a story, a poem, or an essay is like going on a long hike. A hiker must plan carefully, gather and organize the necessary equipment, and keep his or her goal in mind in order to reach it. A good writer also follows a plan in order to reach a goal. This plan is called the **writing process.** The writing process includes five stages:

1. Prewriting
2. Drafting
3. Responding and Revising
4. Proofreading
5. Publishing

A writer, like a hiker, may change his or her plans. The writer, like a hiker who gets lost and has to backtrack, may also have to go back and make changes in his or her writing before going on. The following diagram shows how a writer might make the journey through the writing process.

| Prewriting | Drafting | Responding and Revising | Proofreading | Publishing |

1 Prewriting

Sometimes it is not easy to begin writing. That is why prewriting is such an important stage of the writing process. During the prewriting stage, you

- identify your reading audience, the person or people for whom you are writing.
- define your purpose, or reason for writing, and choose a form for your writing.
- decide what you want to write about by brainstorming a list of ideas.
- choose one topic to focus on in your writing.
- gather and organize information about your topic.

Examples of various writing forms, audiences, and purposes are listed in this chart.

Writing Form	Audience	Purpose
how-to paragraph	teacher	**to inform** about a skill
description	self	**to express** feelings about a work of art
friendly letter	pen pal	**to entertain** with an anecdote
essay	classmates	**to persuade** others to act

Graphic Organizers

Graphic organizers help writers to choose their topics and also to gather and organize material.

Inverted Triangle   Use an inverted triangle when you need to narrow your topic. An inverted triangle is especially useful when you are planning to write an essay or a research report.

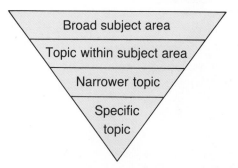

Venn Diagram   Use a Venn diagram when you want to identify the similarities and differences between two items. A Venn diagram is useful when you need to organize information for a comparison/contrast composition.

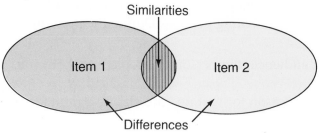

Cluster   Use a cluster to note ideas and details about your topic. A cluster is useful for planning a description.

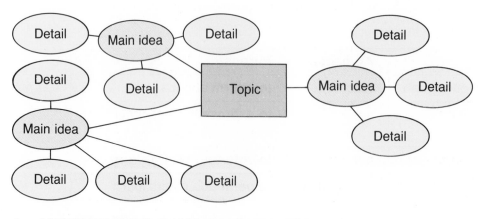

Diagram Use a diagram to help you visualize a sequence of steps or events in time order. A graphic organizer of this type helps you plan a how-to paragraph or a personal narrative.

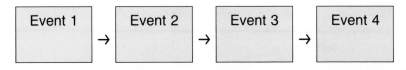

Story Map Use a story map to help you plan a story. A story map reminds you to begin a story by introducing the characters, the setting, and the problem. It helps you remember to include the complication, bring your story to a climax, and end it with the resolution.

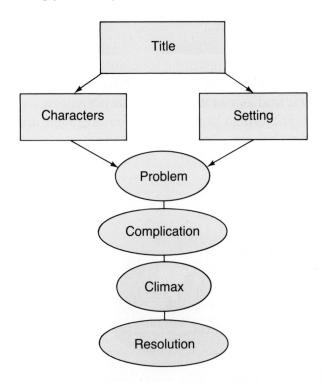

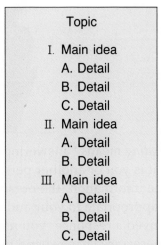

Outline Use an outline when you want to organize a large amount of information into a logical order, paragraph by paragraph. An outline can be helpful when you are preparing material for a long composition presenting many facts, such as a research report or a persuasive essay.

2 Drafting

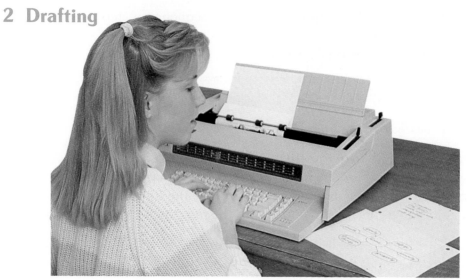

At the drafting stage you begin to turn your prewriting ideas into a smoothly flowing work of writing. At this time it is best to write freely, not worrying about errors in grammar or mechanics. If you find as you write that your prewriting plan doesn't work as you had hoped, you can go back to the prewriting stage and collect more information or make other changes in your plan.

3 Responding and Revising

Responding means "answering." When someone responds to your first draft, whether it is you or another person, he or she reviews it. The person responding checks the information, the organization, and the language in the draft to see if they are appropriate to your audience and your purpose for writing. After you have received a response, you *revise* your draft by looking back over it and making necessary changes and improvements.

4 Proofreading

Proofreading is a printer's term for the final check given to material before it is published in book form. In the writing process it is the stage at which you correct errors in capitalization, punctuation, grammar, and spelling.

5 Publishing

Publishing means "making work public." This is the final stage of the writing process, when you present your work to the audience for whom you wrote it. Publishing can be oral or written. It can be a private sharing of a composition between two people or a group activity during which you and many of your classmates share your compositions. Thinking about your purpose and your audience will help you determine the best way in which to publish your work.

UNIT

1

Relating Personal Experiences

◆ **COMPOSITION FOCUS:** **Personal Narrative**
◆ **LANGUAGE FOCUS:** **Sentences**

Anyone who hears the words "Once upon a time" knows what will follow—a story! One of the most interesting story forms is the **personal narrative**—a story in which the teller takes a part.

Personal narrative is a writing form that appeals to a variety of people. Lensey Namioka (na•mi•ō′kə), an immigrant from China, is writing an autobiography about her family's adjustment to life in America. In her book, she includes several brief stories of events in which she takes part from beginning to end. In each narrative, she focuses on one event or on a series of related events. She includes the action of an event from beginning to end and adds details that tell who was involved, what happened, when and where the event occurred, and how things turned out.

In this unit you will record something that happened to you. You will write a personal narrative.

Lensey Namioka writes about her personal experiences *to entertain* her audience and *to share* a part of her cultural heritage.

Reading with a Writer's Eye
Personal Narrative

There are many aspects of American culture that surprise
newcomers to our country. Lensey Namioka has vivid memories of her
family's first encounter with raw celery. As you read the narrative,
think about how telling the story from her point of view captures the
audience's interest and holds their attention.

from **The All-American
Slurp**

by Lensey Namioka

The first time our family was invited out to dinner in America,
we disgraced ourselves while eating celery. We had emigrated to this
country from China, and during our early days here, we had a hard
time with American table manners.

In China we never ate celery raw, or any other kind of vegetable raw. We always had to disinfect the vegetables in boiling water first. When we were presented with our first relish tray, the raw celery caught us unprepared.

We had been invited to dinner by our neighbors, the Gleasons. After arriving at the house, we shook hands with our hosts and packed ourselves into a sofa. As our family of four sat stiffly in a row, my young brother and I stole glances at our parents for a clue as to what to do next.

Mrs. Gleason offered the relish tray to Mother. The tray looked pretty, with its tiny red radishes, curly sticks of carrots, and long, slender stalks of pale green celery. "Do try some of the celery, Mrs. Lin," she said. "It's from a local farmer, and it's sweet."

Mother picked up one of the green stalks, and Father followed suit. Then I picked up a stalk, and my brother did too. So there we sat, each with a stalk of celery in our right hand.

Mrs. Gleason kept smiling. "Would you like to try some of the dip, Mrs. Lin? It's my own recipe: sour cream and onion flakes, with a dash of Tabasco sauce."

Most Chinese don't care for dairy products, and in those days I wasn't even ready to drink fresh milk. Sour cream sounded perfectly revolting. Our family shook our heads in unison.

Mrs. Gleason went off with the relish tray to the other guests, and we carefully watched to see what they did. Everyone seemed to eat the raw vegetables quite happily.

Mother took a bite of her celery. *Crunch.* "It's not bad!" she whispered.

Father took a bite of his celery. *Crunch.* "Yes, it *is* good," he said, looking surprised.

I took a bite, and then my brother. *Crunch, crunch.* It was more than good; it was delicious. Raw celery has a slight sparkle, a zingy taste that you don't get in cooked celery. When Mrs. Gleason came around with the relish tray, we each took another stalk of celery, except my brother. He took two.

There was only one problem: long strings ran through the length of the stalk, and they got caught in my teeth. When I help my mother in the kitchen, I always pull the strings out before slicing celery.

I pulled the strings out of my stalk. *Z-z-zip, z-z-zip.* My brother followed suit. *Z-z-zip, z-z-zip, z-z-zip.* To my left, my parents were taking care of their own stalks. *Z-z-zip, z-z-zip, z-z-zip.*

Suddenly I realized that there was dead silence except for our zipping. Looking up, I saw that the eyes of everyone in the room were on our family. Mr. and Mrs. Gleason, their daughter Meg, who was my friend, and their neighbors the Badels—they were all staring at us as we busily pulled the strings of our celery.

That wasn't the end of it. Mrs. Gleason announced that dinner was served and invited us to the dining table. It was lavishly covered with platters of food, but we couldn't see any chairs around the table. So we helpfully carried over some dining chairs and sat down. All the other guests just stood there.

Mrs. Gleason bent down and whispered to us, "This is a buffet dinner. You help yourselves to some food and eat it in the living room."

Our family beat a retreat back to the sofa as if chased by enemy soldiers. For the rest of the evening, too mortified to go back to the dining table, I nursed a bit of potato salad on my plate.

Next day Meg and I got on the school bus together. I wasn't sure how she would feel about me

after the spectacle our family made at the party. But she was just the same as usual, and the only reference she made to the party was, "Hope you and your folks got enough to eat last night. You certainly didn't take very much. Mom never tries to figure out how much food to prepare. She just puts everything on the table and hopes for the best."

I began to relax. The Gleasons' dinner party wasn't so different from a Chinese meal after all. My mother also puts everything on the table and hopes for the best.

Respond

1. Would the story have been as interesting if it hadn't been told from Lensey Namioka's point of view? Explain your answer.

Discuss

2. What do you think is Lensey Namioka's purpose for recording this event?
3. What is the strongest image that comes to your mind when you read the story? What specific words does the writer use to help you form this image?

Thinking As a Writer
Analyzing a Personal Narrative

Writer's Guide

To write a personal narrative, good writers

♦ tell a story about an event they witnessed or participated in.

♦ use the first-person point of view.

♦ include a beginning, a middle, and an ending.

A narrative tells a story. A personal narrative tells a story about you. In a personal narrative, you write from your own point of view about an experience you had or witnessed. Like all stories, a personal narrative has a beginning, a middle, and an ending. Read these passages from "The All-American Slurp."

The first time our family was invited out to dinner in America, we disgraced ourselves while eating celery. We had emigrated to this country from China, and during our early days here, we had a hard time with American table manners.

* * *

Suddenly I realized that there was dead silence except for our zipping. Looking up, I saw that the eyes of everyone in the room were on our family. Mr. and Mrs. Gleason, their daughter Meg, who was my friend, and their neighbors the Badels—they were all staring at us as we busily pulled the strings of our celery.

* * *

I began to relax. The Gleasons' dinner party wasn't so different from a Chinese meal after all. My mother also puts everything on the table and hopes for the best.

The **beginning** of the story identifies the problem the main character or characters will face.

The **middle** of the story relates what happens as the problem develops.

The **first-person point of view** uses first-person pronouns (*I, our, we*) to show that this is a personal narrative.

The **ending** of the story shows how the problem is resolved.

Discuss

1. Look at the beginning, the middle, and the ending of the personal narrative. How is the information in each part different?
2. Why should a personal narrative be written from the first-person point of view?

Try Your Hand

A. Analyze the Point of View   Read the following passages from personal narratives. Identify whether either is written from the first-person point of view, and explain how you know.

1. My team entered the comic strip competition in the "Odyssey of the Mind" contest. We met every Saturday to plan our skit and costumes. Each of us was responsible for part of the preparation. I was in charge of "Garfield" posters.

2. Around harvest time some people in New England put stuffed mannequins near their houses and barns. These figures represent various character types and are usually placed in humorous poses. Some lounge in lawn chairs; others are poised on rooftops.

B. Analyze Story Parts   Read each part of a narrative. Identify whether it is the beginning, the middle, or the ending.

3. When I was in the saddle, I encouraged the bird to move, but it stood stock still and then buried its head in the sand. I decided to stick to horses.

4. You might expect spring vacation at my uncle's ostrich ranch to be restful. Not a chance! I am exhausted.

C. Read a Personal Narrative   Look in a book of short stories for another personal narrative. Read the narrative and identify the beginning, middle, and ending. Determine how the point of view affects the telling of the narrative.

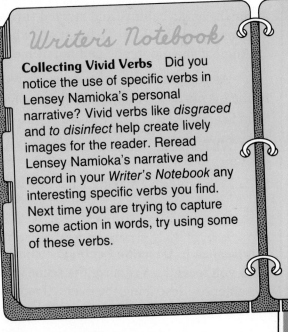

Writer's Notebook

Collecting Vivid Verbs   Did you notice the use of specific verbs in Lensey Namioka's personal narrative? Vivid verbs like *disgraced* and *to disinfect* help create lively images for the reader. Reread Lensey Namioka's narrative and record in your *Writer's Notebook* any interesting specific verbs you find. Next time you are trying to capture some action in words, try using some of these verbs.

Thinking As a Writer
Visualizing Events and Feelings

To write a vivid personal narrative, a writer first pictures events and recalls feelings. The writer then uses these mental images as the basis for describing what happened. Here is what one writer visualized.

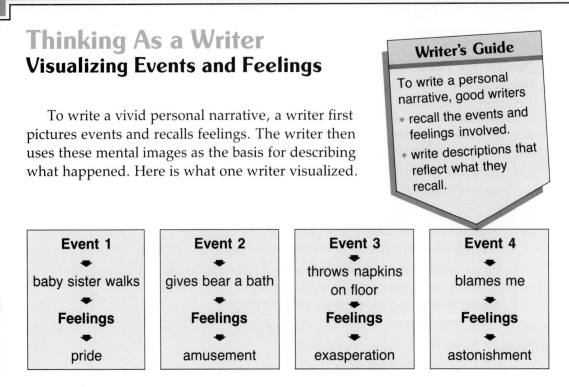

Event 1	Event 2	Event 3	Event 4
baby sister walks	gives bear a bath	throws napkins on floor	blames me
Feelings	**Feelings**	**Feelings**	**Feelings**
pride	amusement	exasperation	astonishment

Here's the way the writer used the mental images to write about the event.

    The day my baby sister Angie learned to walk was unforgettable. First, she gave her teddy bear a bath in the bathtub. Then she headed for the china cabinet and started throwing all the tablecloths and napkins on the floor. To top it off, when Father came in and asked Angie if she did it, she pointed at me!

    As you plan your personal narrative, be sure that you first visualize the events and recall your feelings about them.

Discuss

1. What specific features from her visualizing did the writer actually use?
2. Why wouldn't making a list of what Angie did be as useful as visualizing it?

Try Your Hand

Visualize to Describe Feelings Think about something that happened to you recently. Visualize the scene and recall your feelings. Write three sentences describing the event. Trade with a partner and compare your descriptions.

Developing the Writer's Craft
Capturing the Reader's Interest

Because writers want to capture and hold the reader's attention, their narratives must be interesting, even riveting. Writers use different techniques to do this in the title, the beginning, and the ending of their compositions.

Writers often begin with a puzzling, eye-catching, or humorous title. Lensey Namioka's title, "The All-American Slurp," is puzzling because the meaning is unclear and funny because of the silly word "slurp."

Writers use techniques called *hooks* to capture the reader's interest. Three popular hooks are listed here:

- A **startling statement** that readers don't expect piques curiosity about what will happen next.
- A **question** gets readers involved as they begin to think about possible answers.
- A **hint** about what will happen later in the story helps involve readers in the story line right away.

Lensey Namioka's first sentence is startling and hints at what will happen later in the story.

Writers craft a satisfying ending when they tie up the loose ends of the story effectively. Lensey Namioka does this by relating the girls' next meeting and emphasizing their similarities rather than their differences.

When you write your personal narrative, try to capture and maintain your reader's attention by using a good title, a catchy beginning, and a satisfying ending.

Discuss

What might happen if a writer did not have a good title and a good beginning?

Try Your Hand

Write a Catchy Beginning   Use one of the hooks mentioned to write a different beginning for Lensey Namioka's narrative.

1 Prewriting
Personal Narrative

Prewriting Checklist
☑ Make a list to select an event to use.
☑ Visualize the event and recall your feelings about it.
☑ Make a chart to show how the event progresses.

Yvonne, a student at Oscar M. Chute Junior High School, wanted to write to her older sister who was away at college. She used the checklist in the **Writer's Guide** to help her plan her narrative. Look at what she did.

◆ Brainstorming and Selecting a Topic

First, Yvonne made a list of events from which to choose. Then she visualized each event and tried to recall her feelings about each one. Here is her list.

> winning the sack race on
> Field Day
> adopting our cat from the shelter
> trying out for a part in
> children's theater
> being elected captain of the
> soccer team
> cooking the family dinner

Yvonne reviewed her list. She thought about her older sister's interests and decided to write about her children's theater audition. She had always wanted to be in a play, and she thought her sister would enjoy hearing about it.

Discuss

1. Look at each note Yvonne wrote. Did she fully describe each event in complete sentences? Why do you think she wrote her list the way she did?
2. Do you think this list might provide a good start for a personal narrative? Explain your answer.

◆ Gathering Information and Organizing the Facts

Since Yvonne was working from a very general list, she knew that she needed more details before she could begin her narrative. First, she made a list of things that happened in connection with the tryouts. Then she arranged them in a chart. This is what she did.

Beginning— Waiting	1. Very nervous 2. Nobody there—wrong place? 3. Director announces parts for tryouts
Middle— Trying Out	1. I decide I want rooster 2. Try out for queen 3. Try out for rooster
Ending— After Audition	1. Miss Hall heard me crow. 2. Wait for phone call. 3. Hurray! I made it!

Discuss

1. In what part of her personal narrative did Yvonne plan to include the fact that she got the part? Why did she include it in that section?
2. Yvonne separated trying out for the queen and trying out for the rooster in her chart. Why do you think she did this?

Try Your Hand

Now plan a personal narrative of your own.

A. Brainstorm and Select a Topic   If you have a journal, look over your journal entries. Choose one that is important to you that also will be interesting to your audience. If you do not have a journal, think of an event to write about that has happened in the last few days.

B. Gather and List Facts   Write down as many facts about the event as you can remember.

C. Organize the Facts   Plan the facts that will go in the beginning, the middle, and the ending of your personal narrative. You may want to make a chart like this one.

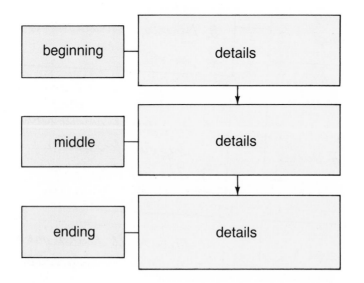

 Save your list and chart in your *Writer's Notebook*. You will use them when you draft your personal narrative.

2 Drafting
Personal Narrative

Before Yvonne started to draft her narrative, she thought about a way to tell her sister about her successful audition. Yvonne followed the checklist in the **Writer's Guide.** Look at what she did.

> Last week there were tryouts for the children's theater production of a play. I was so nervous that my knees were shaking. I was the first one there, and I was afraid that I'd come to the wrong place. Then everyone else showed up and we went into the auditorium.

Discuss

Did Yvonne capture the reader's interest with her beginning sentence? Explain your answer.

Try Your Hand

Now you are ready to write a personal narrative.

A. Review Your Information   Think about the details you gathered and organized in the last lesson. Decide whether you need more information. If so, gather it.

B. Think About Your TAP   Remember that your task is to write a personal narrative. Your purpose is to inform your audience about the event you selected.

Task: What?
Audience: Who?
Purpose: Why?

C. Write Your First Draft   Use the **Drafting Checklist** to write your personal narrative. Choose an interesting way to begin that captures your readers' attention.

When you write your draft, just put all your ideas on paper. Do not worry about spelling, punctuation, or grammar. You can correct the draft later.

Save your first draft in your *Writer's Notebook*. You will use it when you revise your personal narrative.

3 Responding and Revising
Personal Narrative

Yvonne used the checklist in the **Writer's Guide** to revise her narrative. Look at what she did.

◆ Checking Information

When Yvonne read over her draft, she realized that she needed a catchy beginning. To show this, she used this mark ∧ .

◆ Checking Organization

Yvonne saw that one sentence was out of place and another sentence was unnecessary. She used this mark ◯ to move the copy and this mark ℓ to cut the unnecessary sentence. She used the same mark ℓ to cut part of a sentence.

◆ Checking Language

When Yvonne checked the sentences in her second paragraph, she noticed she had switched from first-person point of view to third-person point of view. She used this mark ‿ to replace third-person pronouns with first-person pronouns.

Add —

Move —

Cut —

Cut —

Replace —

I never dreamed I could be a rooster – until recently, that is !
∧Last week there were tryouts for the children's theater production of a play. ↑I was so nervous that my knees were shaking. ⟨I was the first one there, and I was afraid that I'd come to the wrong place.⟩ Then everyone else showed up, and we went into the auditorium ~~to have the tryouts there~~. When the director, Mr. Jonas, told us about the play and the available parts, I immediately wanted to play the part of the rooster. (And I got it!)ℓ

Mr. Jonas wanted me to be the pompous queen. *I*/She huffed and sneered and stuck *my*/her nose in the air. Then I tried out for the rooster. *I*/He leapt up on a platform, flapped *my*/his wings, and gave a loud crow—ERK—ERK—ERK—ERK—ERRRRR! The rooster is bold and proud. The part had to be mine!

Discuss

1. What effect will Yvonne's new first sentence have?
2. How does the switch to third-person point of view change the narrative?

Try Your Hand

Now revise your first draft.

A. Read Your First Draft As you read your narrative, think about your audience and your purpose. Read your narrative silently or to a partner to see if it is complete and well organized. Ask yourself or your partner the questions in the box.

Responding and Revising Strategies

✔ **Respond** Ask yourself or a partner:	✔ **Revise** Try these solutions:
• Have I included all the details that tell about the event?	• Check the items on your list, and, if necessary, **add** some to your personal narrative.
• Did I write my personal narrative from my point of view?	• **Add** personal pronouns to show first-person point of view.
• Does my personal narrative tell the story from beginning to end?	• **Move** any sentences that are out of place.
• Did I include information that will capture my reader's attention?	• **Add** a catchy beginning or an interesting detail.
• Does each word in my personal narrative add something to its meaning?	• **Cut** unnecessary words or **replace** them with words that add to the meaning. See the **Revising Workshop** on page 24.

B. Make Your Changes If the answer to any question in the box is *no,* try the solution. Use the **Editor's Marks** to show your changes.

C. Review Your Personal Narrative Again Decide whether there is anything else you want to revise. Keep revising your narrative until you feel it is well organized and complete.

EDITOR'S MARKS

∧ Add something.

✗ Cut something.

⟳ Move something.

∧ Replace something.

Save your revised personal narrative in your *Writer's Notebook.* **You will use it when you proofread your narrative.**

Revising Workshop
Using a Thesaurus

Good writers use vivid descriptions to create rich mental images for their readers. If they find that their description isn't bringing their ideas to life, they sometimes replace some words they have used with words that are more colorful. A **thesaurus** is a resource book that gives groups of words with similar shades of meaning. It is a valuable tool that helps writers choose just the right word to use. Look at the underlined word in this sentence from Yvonne's narrative.

> I leapt up on a platform, flapped my wings, and gave a <u>loud</u> crow—ERK-ERK-ERK-ERK-ERRRRR!

Yvonne wasn't satisfied with the word *loud* at the end of her sentence. She decided that looking in a thesaurus might give her some ideas for a more vivid word. Here is the entry Yvonne found:

> **loud** *adj.* Not quiet; noisy. The carpet reduces **loud** noises.
> *boisterous* Wild and noisy. The students were told not to be *boisterous* on the bus.
> *resounding* Making a loud sound; echoing. *Resounding* applause filled the theater.
> *thunderous* Making a loud sound like thunder. His *thunderous* voice boomed out a stern command.

Yvonne decided to change her sentence. She changed the word *loud* to *resounding* to suggest a great echoing sound.

Practice

Rewrite each sentence. Replace the colorless word that is underlined. Your **Writer's Thesaurus** may help you.

1. I was <u>happy</u> to go to clown school.
2. We <u>learned</u> juggling.
3. The juggling instructor was <u>nice</u>.
4. We practiced a <u>funny</u> skit.
5. Putting on make-up is very <u>hard</u>.
6. I still have my <u>old</u> costume.
7. I learned an <u>unusual</u> magic trick.
8. I have <u>many</u> memories.

Listening and Speaking
Tips on How to Speak and Listen in a Response Group

There are several ways you can respond to your own and your classmates' writing.

Decide whether you want to read your material aloud or have each member of the group read it silently. Often, listening to your work can help you experience it objectively.

Speaking in a Response Group

1. If you read your work aloud, read it twice. Allow at least a minute of silence between readings so that your audience can organize their thoughts.
2. When responding to someone's work, you may want to use one of the following methods:
   a. List the main points and feelings it conveys.
   b. Summarize the work in one sentence that tells what it is about.
   c. Choose one word from the writing that describes the content.
   d. Choose one word that is not in the writing to summarize it.
3. Give specific reactions to specific parts.
4. Never quarrel with someone else's reaction.

Listening in a Response Group

1. Be quiet and listen while someone else's work is read.
2. After reading your own work, ask for specific feedback, but do not defend the work.
3. Do not reject what people tell you.
4. Try to understand the reasons for people's comments.

4 Proofreading
Personal Narrative

Writer's Guide

Proofreading Checklist

☑ Check for errors in capitalization.

☑ Check for errors in punctuation.

☑ Be sure that all your paragraphs are indented.

☑ Check for errors in grammar.

☑ Circle any words you think are misspelled. Find out how to spell them correctly.

⇒ For proofreading help, use the **Writer's Handbook.**

After Yvonne revised her personal narrative, she used the checklist in the **Writer's Guide** and the **Editor's Marks** to proofread it. Look at what she did.

⁋I walked out of the tryouts feeling numb. I saw

Miss Hall, who smiled ⟨encourageingly⟩ *encouragingly* she said

she had heard me crow all the way across the

school! the phone call didn't come until

Saturday afternoon. By that time I was wild with

anticipation ⟨anticipasion⟩. from the moment I picked up the

phone, I knew I'd gotten the part. now I'm a real

actor, just like you.

Discuss

1. Look at Yvonne's proofread narrative. What kinds of mistakes did she make?
2. Why did she indent the first line of her paragraph?

Try Your Hand

Proofread Your Personal Narrative Now use the checklist in the **Writer's Guide** and the **Editor's Marks** to proofread your personal narrative.

Save your corrected personal narrative in your *Writer's Notebook.* You will use it when you publish your personal narrative.

EDITOR'S MARKS

≡ Capitalize.

⊙ Add a period.

∧ Add something.

⋀ Add a comma.

ᐯᐯ Add quotation marks.

✂ Cut something.

⋀ Replace something.

↝ Transpose.

◯ Spell correctly.

⁋ Indent paragraph.

╱ Make a lowercase letter.

5 Publishing
Personal Narrative

Yvonne made a clean copy of her personal narrative and checked it to be sure she had not left anything out. You can see her completed narrative on page 48 of the **Writer's Handbook** at the back of this book. Yvonne and her classmates published their narratives by making tape recordings and mailing them to relatives.

Here's the way Yvonne published her personal narrative.

1. First, Yvonne practiced reading her narrative aloud so that she could make a clear recording.

2. Then she made her tape. Yvonne held the microphone a few inches from her mouth and spoke slowly and distinctly. She tried to sound enthusiastic and friendly. She used her voice to emphasize key words and phrases.

3. After she had finished recording, she played back the tape to check it. Then she prepared a mailing envelope. She checked with the post office to be sure she mailed it correctly.

Discuss

What might happen if Yvonne didn't speak clearly and distinctly when recording?

Try Your Hand

Publish Your Personal Narrative Follow the checklist in the **Writer's Guide.** Then tape-record your personal narrative, or try this idea for sharing it.

• Start a scrapbook in which you collect stories about yourself (and other members of your family, if you wish). Include your personal narrative and an illustration to accompany it.

COMPOSITION: PUBLISHING Personal Narrative **27**

Writing in the Content Areas

Use what you learned to write another personal narrative. You can write about something that happened to you or about something you observed.

Science

Write a personal narrative focusing on a particular science lab experiment or field trip. You might describe how you took part in the activity. Be sure to include the steps from beginning to end and your part in the outcome of the activity.

Literature

Tell the story of how you encountered your favorite book for the first time, and describe the effect it had on you as you first read it. Include in your narrative the important details about how you felt. Use your point of view to stress how you feel about the book and why it is important to you.

Fine Arts

Describe something that happened one day in drama class or music class. Make your retelling very dramatic. In your narrative, describe your feelings in relation to the drama or the music.

Physical Education

Write a real or imaginary personal narrative telling how you saved the day in an intramural sports event at your school. You may choose a sport that you know well or one that you don't. Relive the action of the moment. If possible, enliven the narrative with play-by-play details.

CONNECTING
WRITING ↔ LANGUAGE

Personal narratives help us to recapture events that are important to us or that we think about often. Notice the variety of sentences in this section from a personal narrative.

Whenever I think of my sister as a child, I picture her as a skinny kid with spindly arms and legs and curly, squirrel-colored hair pulled severely back behind her ears. She always got special attention, even though she wasn't the youngest child. What made her so special? It was the fact that she had asthma and couldn't run around wildly like the other kids at play.

I remember that she usually hung around the fringes of an active group, glancing wistfully at the running, shouting children who were her friends. Every now and then, when she couldn't stand being on the sidelines, she'd join the group. Picture the result if you can. After only a few moments, her face would redden, and she would begin gasping for breath. If I happened to be there, I'd lead her, choking and wheezing, back to our house.

Years later, when my sister's asthma was under control and she could join others in mild exercise, she became almost a new person. Now, seeing her play with her own children, I wonder whether she remembers those difficult days. Sometimes, noting a gleam in her eye, I almost think she's trying to even the score!

◆ **Sentences in a Personal Narrative** The groups of highlighted words are examples of types of sentences. Each serves a different purpose: makes a statement, asks a question, states a command or request, or expresses emotion. A personal narrative will contain these different types of sentences.

◆ **Language Focus: Sentences** The following lessons will help you use different kinds of sentences in your own writing.

1 Sentences

◆ **FOCUS**   A **sentence** is a group of words that expresses a complete thought.

Every complete thought is a sentence. It can be long or short. A sentence always begins with a capital letter and ends with a punctuation mark.

1. Students read.
2. These students are using a computer for information.

Every sentence has two parts. The **subject** part names whom or what the sentence is about.

3. These two students

The **predicate** part tells something about the subject.

4. are using a computer in a library for information.

A sentence must contain a subject and a predicate. If it doesn't, it will not make sense. If either the subject or the predicate is missing, the group of words is not a sentence. It is an incomplete thought.

5. the resources in a library   incomplete thought
6. are available to everyone   incomplete thought
7. The resources in a library are available to everyone.   complete thought

Guided Practice

A. Identify whether each group of words is a *complete thought* or an *incomplete thought*.

1. The Harvard University library is the oldest in the United States.
2. Established in 1638.
3. Thirty-one years after English settlers landed in Jamestown.
4. John Harvard donated money and 400 books.
5. The first public library began 100 years later.

THINK AND REMEMBER

• Remember that a **sentence** expresses a complete thought.
• Remember that a capital letter begins a sentence and a punctuation mark ends it.

Independent Practice

B. Identifying Complete and Incomplete Thoughts   Write *complete* or *incomplete* to indicate whether each group of words is a complete thought or an incomplete thought.

6. Ancient Rome had many public libraries.
MODEL> complete
7. Were copied onto parchment and rolled around sticks.
8. Replaced parchment for most writing.
9. A hanging tag on each manuscript showed the title.
10. Great religious libraries in the Middle Ages.
11. Free American lending libraries opened more than a century ago.
12. The Chinese invented paper.
13. Left a collection of 400 books.
14. The printing press.
15. Ancient Egyptians wrote on papyrus.

C. Making Incomplete Thoughts into Sentences   Write each group of words as a sentence. Add a subject or a predicate to make a complete thought. Underline the part you add.

16. Our school librarian
MODEL> Our school librarian is very helpful.
17. Books and magazines
18. belong in the card catalogue
19. My first book report
20. listed the authors and titles
21. are my favorite books
22. Dictionaries and encyclopedias
23. Sometimes high-school students
24. are recorded on cassettes
25. Medical and law libraries
26. Microfilm
27. provide filmstrips and videotapes
28. My classmates
29. are all enthusiastic readers

Application — Writing

A Secret Message   Imagine that you and the students in the photograph are experts at writing computer messages. Use an alphabet code to write a secret message. Be sure each sentence in your message is a complete thought. Give your message to a partner to decode.

2 Four Kinds of Sentences

◆ **FOCUS** There are four kinds of sentences: declarative, interrogative, imperative, and exclamatory.

You can express your thoughts with four different types of sentences: declarative, interrogative, imperative, and exclamatory. A **declarative** sentence makes a statement. An **interrogative** sentence asks a question. An **imperative** sentence gives a command or makes a request. An **exclamatory** sentence expresses strong emotion.

Read each sentence. Notice the punctuation that ends each one.

1. Charlie bought a hat at the rummage sale.   declarative
2. Did you see the colors in that coat?   interrogative
3. Tell me what you think of these hats.   imperative
4. Wow, this bicycle looks new!   exclamatory

Link to Speaking and Writing

Sometimes you may want to turn a declarative, an interrogative, or an imperative sentence into an exclamation. Say each sentence as an exclamation. How does the meaning change as the tone of your voice changes?

I surprised him.
Is he surprised?
Surprise him.
I surprised him!
Is he surprised!
Surprise him!

Guided Practice

A. Identify each sentence as *declarative, interrogative, imperative,* or *exclamatory.* Identify the punctuation mark to end each sentence.

1. Can we buy new team uniforms
2. How great the team will look in them
3. Everyone donated at least one item
4. Come to our sale on Saturday

THINK AND REMEMBER

* Use declarative, interrogative, imperative, and exclamatory sentences in your writing.
* Use a period to end a declarative or imperative sentence. Use a question mark to end an interrogative sentence. Use an exclamation point to end an exclamatory sentence.

Independent Practice

B. Identifying Sentence Types and Adding Punctuation   Write the
sentences and identify each one as *declarative, interrogative, imperative,*
or *exclamatory.* Add the correct punctuation mark at the end of each.

   5. My sister and I bought a telephone

MODEL⟩   My sister and I bought a telephone.
         declarative

   6. Have you ever played a game called telephone
   7. Whisper a message in someone's ear
   8. That person whispers the message in another
          person's ear
   9. Send the same message through several people
   10. The people can be standing in a long line
   11. Please stay where you are
   12. Do you think it will remain the same
   13. Why might the message change
   14. Everything will stay the same
   15. What a silly game this is

C. Writing Sentence Types   Write four types of sentences about each
topic. Identify each type. Use the correct end punctuation.

   16. computers

MODEL⟩   I bought a computer.   declarative
         Do you have a computer?   interrogative
         Please lend me a diskette.   imperative
         Computers are great fun!   exclamatory

17. television	**22.** radio	**27.** magazines
18. books	**23.** movies	**28.** telegrams
19. gestures	**24.** paintings	**29.** music
20. sign language	**25.** handshakes	**30.** friendly letters
21. illustrations	**26.** smiles	**31.** stage shows

Application — Writing and Speaking

A Persuasive Paragraph   Imagine that your class wants to encourage
people to attend a rummage sale. Write a paragraph to persuade
people to come. Your paragraph could be taken home by your
classmates or read over the school sound system. Use the four kinds of
sentences. Be sure to use correct punctuation.

3 Complete and Simple Subjects

◆ **FOCUS**   The **subject** of a sentence names someone or something.

The **complete subject** contains the topic of the sentence and any words that tell about the topic.

1. The seventh-grade class visited a local television station.

The **simple subject** is the main word or words in the complete subject. The simple subject is usually a noun or a pronoun.

2. The seventh-grade class visited the local television station.

3. We spoke to several newspeople about our school magazine.

If the simple subject is a proper noun, it may include more than one word.

4. Maria Lopez interviewed several people.

Sometimes the complete subject is a single word. Then the complete subject is also the simple subject.

5. Television is fascinating!

Guided Practice

A. Identify the complete subject in each sentence.

1. Our school magazine is published four times a year.
2. Even the younger students in the school enjoy the magazine.
3. Maria wrote a feature story about our trip to the television station.
4. Several local businesses bought advertising space.
5. The magazine committee spends the money.
6. We have a full staff of reporters.
7. The editorial staff is excellent.
8. Many students contribute articles.
9. Other students do the illustrations.

B. 10.–18.   Use the sentences in **A.** Identify the simple subjects.

THINK AND REMEMBER

+ Remember that a **complete subject** tells whom or what the sentence is about.
+ Remember that a **simple subject** is the main word or words in the complete subject.

Independent Practice

C. Identifying Complete Subjects   Write the complete subject.

19. Jennifer started <u>Words</u>, a school magazine.
MODEL> Jennifer

20. The monthly magazine contains poetry, drawings, features, and stories.
21. Students from all grades contribute their work.
22. The next issue's theme is communication.
23. It will be published tomorrow.
24. The entire school enjoys the magazine.
25. The journalism teacher praised Jennifer.
26. He entered the magazine in a contest.
27. Magazines from hundreds of schools were judged.
28. Jennifer's magazine won an honorable mention.

D. 29.–38. Identifying Simple Subjects   Use the sentences from **C**. Write the simple subject in each sentence.

MODEL> 29. Jennifer

E. Creating Sentences with Complete Subjects   Add a complete subject to each phrase to make a complete sentence. Underline each complete subject.

39. reads our magazine
MODEL> My older brother reads our magazine.

40. graduated last year
41. writes for the newspaper
42. knows the secret code
43. contains historical facts
44. likes humorous articles
45. won a journalism award
46. wrote a great editorial
47. praised public officials
48. interested everyone
49. contains colorful artwork
50. has good sports coverage
51. is educational and fun
52. supports school issues
53. praises students' efforts
54. printed the class schedules
55. raises valid questions

Application — Writing

A Journal Entry   Imagine that you and your classmates were interviewed on the evening news. Write a journal entry about your experience. Tell what the interview was about, what you said, and how you felt about being interviewed. If you need help writing a journal entry, see page 47 of the **Writer's Handbook** at the back of this book.

4 Complete and Simple Predicates

◆ **FOCUS** The **predicate** of a sentence tells what the subject is or does.

In a sentence, the **whole predicate,** or **complete predicate,** contains the verb and any words that tell about the verb.

1. Our basketball team plays well .

The **simple predicate** is the main word or words in the complete predicate. The simple predicate is always a verb or a verb phrase.

2. Liz has scored the most points this season.

Sometimes the complete predicate is just one verb or verb phrase. Then the complete predicate is also the simple predicate.

3. The crowd cheered .

Link to Speaking and Writing
When a word interrupts a verb phrase, that word is not part of the verb.

Our team was quickly scoring points.

From now on in this text, the word *verb* will refer to the simple predicate. The word *subject* will refer to the simple subject.

Guided Practice

A. Identify the complete predicate in each sentence.

1. Our basketball team won the city tournament.
2. The school newspaper printed a full-page story about it.
3. Mayor Callihan presented the trophy to our coach.
4. Liz was selected as the most valuable player.
5. She gave a speech at an assembly in the gymnasium.

B. 6.–10. Identify the verb in each sentence in **A.**

THINK AND REMEMBER
◆ Remember that a **verb** is the main word or words in the complete predicate.

Independent Practice

C. Identifying Complete Predicates Write the complete predicate.

11. Our class is conducting a poll about sporting events.
MODEL> is conducting a poll about sporting events
12. A small group created a questionnaire.
13. Students ask other students about their interests.
14. We have already collected eighty-seven questionnaires.
15. The group is tallying the answers.
16. The students are very interested in sports.

D. 17.–22. Identifying Verbs Write the verb in each sentence in **C.**
MODEL> 17. is conducting

E. Finding Subjects and Verbs Read each sentence. Write the subject and the verb. Underline the subject once and the verb twice.

23. Our school newspaper covers all our sporting events.
MODEL> newspaper covers
24. Marsha is a sportswriter for the school newspaper.
25. She writes all of the sports articles.
26. Marsha's story was late.
27. Editor Carl Levin listened carefully to her problems.
28. The seventh-grade team should have played at noon.
29. Rain had delayed the game.
30. The article about the track team was late, too.
31. Marsha's column will be in next week's paper.

F. Writing Sentences Use each subject and verb in a sentence.

32. coach shouts
MODEL> The coach shouts during practice.

33. tickets sell	35. star players demand	37. crowd stands
34. television is	36. cheerleaders dance	38. people shout

Application — Writing

A News Story Imagine that you are the sportswriter for the school newspaper and you are assigned to cover the championship basketball game. Write a news story that describes the game. Write complete predicates. If you need help writing a news story, see page 55 of the **Writer's Handbook.**

5 Word Order in Sentences

◆ **FOCUS** Words in a sentence can be in natural or inverted word order.

In most declarative sentences, the subject appears first and the verb follows. This is **natural word order.**

1. The most important news is on the front page of a newspaper.

Imperative sentences are in natural word order. The subject of an imperative sentence never appears in the sentence. The subject is always *you* (understood).

2. (*you*) Please hand me the business section.

Some sentences are in **inverted,** or **reverse, word order.**

3. On the front page is the most important news.

Sentences that begin with *here* or *there* use inverted word order. *Here* and *there* are never the subjects of sentences. When *here* or *there* begins a sentence, the subject always follows the verb.

4. Here is the photo of the inauguration.
5. There are the names of the world leaders.

Most interrogative sentences are in inverted word order. The verb is a verb phrase, and the subject comes between the parts of the verb.

6. May I read the sports section after you finish?

To find the subject of a sentence in inverted word order, change it to natural word order. Write a question as a statement.

7. Are the scores from last night's game in the paper?   inverted
8. The scores from last night's game are in the paper.   natural

Guided Practice

A. Identify the order in each sentence as *natural* or *inverted.*

1. There is a new section in today's paper.
2. This section is on weather in North America.
3. The headline reports a storm in the Gulf of Mexico.
4. Where is the storm located?
5. Look at the map on page 2.

B. 6.–10.   Identify the subject and the verb in each sentence in **A.**

Independent Practice

C. Identifying Word Order in Sentences   Write each sentence. Then write *natural* or *inverted* to describe the word order of each sentence.

11. Did you read the article about Louis Braille?

MODEL⟩ inverted

12. Louis Braille lost his sight at an early age.

13. There was a need for a reading system for the blind.

14. Louis Braille developed his reading system in 1824.

15. There is a pattern of words and numbers in Braille's system of raised dots.

16. Run your fingers along the dots.

17. How do the dots form letters, numbers, and punctuation marks?

18. Each group of dots is a letter or a number.

19. Braille taught his new "language" to many students.

20. How much happiness did his system bring to the blind?

D. 21.–30.   Identifying the Subject and Verb   Use the sentences in **C.** Write the subject and verb. If the sentence is imperative, write *you.*

21. Did you read the article about Louis Braille?

MODEL⟩ subject—you   verb—Did read

Application — Writing and Speaking

An Opinion   Imagine that you feel strongly about a community issue. Write a paragraph that expresses your feelings. Present it as a television message. Use inverted word order in at least one of your sentences. If you need help writing a paragraph, see page 39 of the **Writer's Handbook.**

6 Compound Subjects and Predicates

FOCUS

◆ A **compound subject** is two or more subjects that have the same verb.

◆ A **compound predicate** is two or more verbs that have the same subject.

Sentences can have compound elements. A **compound subject** is two or more subjects that have the same predicate. Compound subjects are usually joined by *and* or *or.* These words are called **conjunctions.**

1. Juan , Matt , *and* Debbi led a discussion at a recent assembly.

A **compound predicate** is two or more verbs or verb phrases that tell what the subject is or does. The verbs are also joined by the conjunction *and, or,* or *but.*

2. Some listeners opposed *and* rejected a few ideas *but* still enjoyed the discussion.

A sentence can have a compound subject and a compound verb.

3. The panelists and the audience liked the discussion and found it helpful.

Guided Practice

A. Decide whether each sentence has a *compound subject,* a *compound predicate,* or *both.* Identify the subjects or the verbs in each compound.

1. Panelists listen and speak.
2. Parents and teachers planned the event.
3. A guest speaker displayed several magazines and spoke for twenty minutes.
4. The books and magazines were chosen by the PTA.
5. The cleanup crew and several PTA members folded chairs and stacked tables.

THINK AND REMEMBER

• Combine two or more subjects to make a **compound subject.**

• Combine two or more verbs to make a **compound predicate.**

• Use the conjunction *and, but,* or *or* to join compound elements.

Independent Practice

B. Identifying Compound Subjects and Predicates   Write the sentences. Underline the subjects once and the verbs twice. Write *compound subject, compound predicate,* or *both* after each sentence.

6. Books or magazines make good gifts.

MODEL⟩ <u>Books</u> or <u>magazines</u> <u><u>make</u></u> good gifts.   compound subject

7. Jim and Tina have written letters to me.
8. Letters convey feelings and show good manners.
9. The stationery and envelopes are on the shelf.
10. Do you and your mom write letters or send postcards?
11. Joe enjoys letters but will not write them.

C. Revising: Writing Compound Subjects and Compound Predicates   Write each set of sentences as one sentence with a compound element. Use *and* to join the subjects or predicates.

12. News shows were the subject of the talk. Cartoons were the subject of the talk.

MODEL⟩ News shows and cartoons were the subject of the talk.

13. Aña wrote a script. Aña sent it to a studio.
14. Her mom encouraged her. Her dad encouraged her.
15. The producer liked Aña's script. He made Aña an offer.
16. The producer made revisions. The director made revisions.
17. A show was filmed. It was later released.

D. Creating Sentences with Compound Subjects or Compound Predicates   Use *and, or,* or *but* and one or more simple subjects or predicates to make the kind of compound shown in parentheses.

18. Aña will sign a contract.   (compound predicate)

MODEL⟩ Aña will sign a contract and begin work on another script.

19. Our class will write a screenplay.   (compound subject)
20. Yesterday we planned our plot.   (compound predicate)
21. Mrs. Nelson will choose the best outline.   (compound subject)
22. Mr. Avery will help us.   (compound subject)
23. Perhaps a studio will produce it.   (compound predicate)

Application — Writing and Speaking

An Introduction   Imagine that you are a discussion leader. You must introduce the members of your panel to your classmates. Write a short paragraph of introduction. Use compound subjects and predicates.

7 Simple and Compound Sentences

FOCUS

◆ A **simple sentence** contains one subject and one predicate.

◆ A **compound sentence** contains two or more related simple sentences.

A simple sentence can be long or short.

1. Traffic lights control the flow of traffic on city streets.
2. Lights change.

Some simple sentences may have compound elements.

3. Automobiles , trucks , and pedestrians obey the signals.
4. The signals regulate , warn , and guide traffic.
5. Both commuters and city dwellers want and support traffic control.

A compound sentence contains two or more simple sentences. Use the conjunction *and, or,* or *but* to join simple sentences. A comma is placed before the conjunction.

6. Traffic signs are placed along the roads, and laws are enforced.
7. Today computers set traffic lights, or traffic flow can set them.
8. Traffic can be dangerous, but signals are helping to make it safe.

Guided Practice

A. Identify each sentence as *simple* or *compound*.

1. Many cities have severe traffic problems.
2. New roads are built, and transit systems are developed.
3. Problems occur during rush hours, and some cities have them often.
4. Many highways are too crowded for safe travel.
5. More control is needed, or the problem will get worse.

B. 6.–10. Name the simple subject and verb in each sentence in **A.**

THINK AND REMEMBER

• Remember that a **simple sentence** has one complete subject and one complete predicate.

• Remember that a **compound sentence** contains two or more simple sentences.

• Use the conjunctions *and, or,* or *but* in compound sentences.

• Use a comma before a conjunction.

Independent Practice

C. Identifying Simple and Compound Sentences   Write *simple* or *compound* for each sentence below.

11. Laney had mixed feelings about her trip to Chicago.

`MODEL`〉 simple

12. Her bus stalled on Lake Shore Drive.

13. She listened to her radio, and her friends played games.

14. She and her friends were on the way to a Cubs game.

15. They were upset, but they could do nothing.

16. No one stopped and offered help.

D. 17.–22. Identifying Subjects and Verbs   Write each subject and verb in **C**. Draw one line under the subjects and two under the verbs.

17. Laney had mixed feelings about her trip to Chicago.

`MODEL`〉 <u>Laney</u> <u><u>had</u></u>

E. Revising: Writing Compound Sentences   Write each sentence pair as a compound sentence. Use the conjunction in parentheses ( ).

23. The traffic was awful. It made us late for school. (and)

`MODEL`〉 The traffic was awful, and it made us late for school.

24. All the traffic lights were broken. They were all stuck on red. (and)

25. We tried a side street. It was just as crowded. (but)

26. Susie rode by. Tim walked past us. (and)

27. We arrived late. Our teachers were annoyed. (and)

28. We told our friends. No one gave us sympathy. (but)

F. Revising: Using Conjunctions Correctly in Compound Sentences   Use an appropriate conjunction to make each sentence pair compound.

29. Our traffic has gotten worse. We can solve it.

`MODEL`〉 Our traffic has gotten worse, but we can solve it.

30. The mayor computerized the signals. The voters agreed.

31. Computers will run the traffic lights. This will help.

32. Traffic will improve. People will relax.

33. This will happen. My family will move.

34. Traffic cannot get worse. It can get better.

Application — Writing and Speaking

A Traffic Bulletin   Imagine that you are caught in rush-hour traffic. Write a traffic bulletin for other drivers. Then deliver your bulletin as an announcer would. Use simple and compound sentences.

8 Avoiding Sentence Fragments and Run-on Sentences

♦ **FOCUS** Two common sentence errors are sentence fragments and run-on sentences.

A **sentence fragment** is a word group that makes an incomplete thought.

    1. need fast mail service   **2.** because we are busy

A sentence fragment is missing a subject, a verb, or both. To correct a fragment, decide which sentence part is missing, and add it.

    3. We need fast mail service.   **4.** We need it because we are busy.

A **run-on sentence** is a group of words that contains more than one complete thought and lacks the correct punctuation.

    5. Facsimile machines send messages they travel from coast to coast.

To correct run-on sentences, add punctuation to separate the complete thoughts into simple sentences or turn the run-on sentence into a compound sentence. Use a semicolon or the conjunction *and, or,* or *but* to join the simple sentences. Put a comma before the conjunction.

    6. Facsimile machines send messages they travel from coast to coast.   **run-on sentence**
    7. Facsimile machines send messages; they travel from coast to coast.   **compound sentence**
    8. I want a computer it is too expensive.   **run-on sentence**
    9. I want a computer, but it is too expensive.   **compound sentence**

Guided Practice

A. Identify each word group as a *fragment*, a *run-on*, or a *sentence*.

    1. Iris likes computers she uses them often.
    2. People working on computers.
    3. Computers to organize information.
    4. My computer talks.

B. 5.–8. Make sentences from the incomplete groups in **A.**

> **THINK AND REMEMBER**
> • Never write a fragment or a run-on as a complete sentence.

Independent Practice

C. Identifying Fragments, Sentences, and Run-on Sentences   Write whether each group of words is a *fragment*, a *run-on sentence*, or a *sentence*.

   9. Bought a computer.

MODEL▷ fragment

   10. Do you know how computers talk to each other?

   11. Can send a message by telephone from one computer to another with a modem.

   12. An article goes from Miami to Chicago, it takes six minutes.

   13. Can send a magazine article to the printer by phone.

   14. Busy signal on the telephone.

   15. Is the computer talking?

D. Revising: Correcting Fragments   Add words to correct these sentence fragments. Write the new sentences.

   16. Mailing a letter.

MODEL▷ I am mailing a letter.

   17. Send by phone.   **19.** Rainy day.   **21.** Letters from home.

   18. At the office.   **20.** Computerized service.   **22.** During thunderstorms.

E. Revising: Correcting Run-on Sentences   Correct each run-on sentence. Write the new sentences.

   23. Have you ever had a pen pal I have.

MODEL▷ Have you ever had a pen pal? I have.

   24. My pen pal lived in South America her name was Juno.

   25. We both wrote our letters on computers, and we wrote about school and home, we described our friends.

   26. Juno and I corresponded for nearly three years, we stopped.

   27. That was a long time ago I still think of Juno.

   28. Now I have a pen pal from England he visited me last year.

   29. He spent three weeks at our house, he came to school with me and met all my friends.

   30. This year I'm going to see him in England his parents have asked me to stay with them and they've promised to show me all the sights.

Application — Writing

A Message   Imagine that you are away from home and must send an important message to your family. Write your message as briefly as you can. Check to be sure you have corrected sentence fragments or run-on sentences. Exchange messages with a partner for proofreading.

Building Vocabulary
Context Clues

What do you do when you read an unfamiliar word in a story? Do you look up the word in a dictionary? There are other ways to learn the meaning of an unfamiliar word. You can identify it by using context clues.

Context clues are the words surrounding an unfamiliar word. They give you hints about a word's meaning. Read the chart. It describes five of the most common types of context clues. The unfamiliar words are underlined once and the context clues twice.

Type of Context Clue	Signal Word	Example
Synonym	or	The two governments held a summit, or meeting, to communicate their ideas.
Antonym	rather than, although	To everyone's surprise, the opposing leader's behavior was affable rather than unfriendly.
Definition	in other words, that is	The translator had to enunciate, that is, carefully pronounce, each word of the ambassador's speech.
Example	for example, for instance, such as	The entire convention was made public through various media, such as television, radio, and newspapers.
Situation	because, since	Because the meeting was so portentous, the story was on the front page of all of the local newspapers.

Remember, context clues can help you to understand the meaning of an unfamiliar word. They will also help you to make your writing and language clear.

Reading Practice

Read each sentence. Write the meaning of each underlined word. Identify the context clues that helped you determine the meaning.

Example: Grace did not want to give in, but she finally acquiesced and helped her brother with his homework. (Meaning: *gave in*. Context clues: *did not want to give in, but she finally*)

1. Although the candidate tried to appear friendly and warm, he could not hide his aloofness.
2. Even his acceptance speech conveyed, or communicated, an air of snobbishness.
3. The voters manifested their disapproval by showing an overwhelming preference for his opponent.
4. The defeated candidate offered many pretexts for his poor showing, for example, poor voter turnout, bad publicity, and lack of campaign funds.

Writing Practice

Rewrite each sentence. Add a context clue to explain each underlined word. If necessary, use a dictionary to find the meaning. The chart on the previous page may help you.

5. The school's audio equipment is available to students.

MODEL⟩ The school's audio equipment (radios, compact disk players, and tape recorders) is available to students.

6. Since teenagers seem to be loquacious, many telephone bills are exceedingly high.
7. Perhaps teenagers should find alternative means of communication and reduce their phone bills.
8. How many teenagers contemplate writing a letter to a friend rather than calling on the phone?
9. It is, however, unfair to surmise that all teenagers spend excessive amounts of time on the phone.

Project

Read the next chapter in your social studies text. Choose four unfamiliar or difficult words. Use the context clues to determine their meaning. Write the words, clues, and your definitions. Then check a dictionary to see if your meanings are correct.

Language Enrichment
Sentences

Use what you know about sentences to do these activities.

 Scrambled Scraps

Putting words in order in sentences can be tricky. Write an interesting sentence on a sheet of paper. Then write each word on a separate scrap of paper and exchange the scraps with those of a partner. See how many versions of each other's sentences you can write.

 You Said It!

Communication can be funny at times. Write the best caption you can think of for the main character in this cartoon. Use one declarative, one imperative, one interrogative, and one exclamatory sentence. Share your captions with your class.

Dog

Dog barked.

The big dog barked.

The big black dog barked.

Pssst! Pass It On!

A good memory is important to good communication. How good is *your* memory? Find out by playing this sentence-building game. The first person begins by saying a simple subject. The next person adds a simple predicate. Each person in turn adds a word to the subject or predicate to form an increasingly elaborate sentence. When no one can repeat the sentence from memory, begin a new sentence.

CONNECTING

LANGUAGE ⟷ WRITING

In this unit you learned that a sentence is the most basic combination of words to communicate a complete thought. Sentences are used to state a fact, ask a question, give a command, or express an emotion. Every sentence begins with a capital letter and ends with a form of punctuation.

◆ **Using Sentences in Your Writing**   Knowing how to write complete sentences will allow you to share your ideas with others. It also will help you to make ideas clear to yourself. Pay special attention to the sentence-building skills you use as you do these activities.

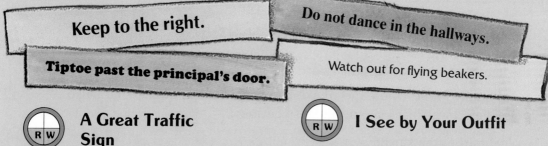

Keep to the right.

Do not dance in the hallways.

Tiptoe past the principal's door.

Watch out for flying beakers.

A Great Traffic Sign

Imperative sentences are used frequently to tell people what they should or should not do. Think of an imperative sentence that would make a great "traffic sign" for your school hallways. Design your sign on a separate sheet of paper. Then write a paragraph explaining why you think people should obey it. Display your traffic sign in class and share your paragraph.

I See by Your Outfit

On the **Building Vocabulary** page you learned to use context clues to determine word meaning. Read this paragraph. Write the meaning of each underlined word. Check your meanings in a dictionary.

The pony express was an <u>audacious</u> attempt at carrying mail. Although the <u>venture</u> failed, it brought glory to the <u>lithe</u> riders and <u>sinewy</u> equines.

Unit Checkup

Think Back	Think Ahead
◆ What did you learn about writing a personal narrative in this unit? What did you do to write one?	◆ How will what you learned about a personal narrative help you when you read about something that has happened to someone? ◆ How will what you have learned about visualizing help you write a personal narrative?
◆ Look at the writing you did in this unit. How did sentences help you express your ideas?	◆ What is one way you can use sentences to improve your writing?

Analyzing a Personal Narrative   *pages 14 – 15*

Read the following excerpt from a personal narrative. Then write the letter of the item that best answers the question.

> I finally found where the smoke had been coming from. What I also discovered was that I shouldn't be so curious.

1. What part of the narrative is this?
   a. beginning   b. middle   c. ending
2. How do you know what part of the personal narrative this is?
3. The point of view is
   a. first person.   b. second person.   c. third person.
4. What word signals the point of view?
5. What suggests that this is part of a personal narrative?

Visualizing Events and Feelings   *page 16*

Write whether each statement is *true* or *false*.

6. Visualizing means "drawing" a picture in one's mind.
7. Visualizing means finding photographs of a scene.
8. Visualizing provides details for a personal narrative.
9. People who visualize must close their eyes.

Capturing the Reader's Interest   *page 17*

Write the letter of the item that correctly completes each sentence.

10. A good title
   a. must be a sentence.
   b. identifies the characters.
   c. must be catchy.
11. To open a personal narrative, a question
   a. can be very effective.   b. is usually weak.
12. To close a personal narrative, a good ending
   a. wraps up the story.   b. leaves the reader hanging.
13. Involve a reader
   a. at the beginning.   b. in the middle.   c. at the ending.

The Writing Process   *pages 18 – 27*

Write the letter of the item that correctly answers each question.

14. When you plan a personal narrative, what should you do first?
   a. Organize the material.
   b. Gather information.
   c. Record possible topics.
15. When organizing facts, which should you do?
   a. Decide on a beginning, a middle, and an ending.
   b. Write a topic sentence.   c. Keep a journal.
16. What topic is most appropriate for a letter to your grandparents?
   a. your softball team   b. a play you heard about   c. the weather
17. Suppose you are revising, and you see that you forgot to tell
   important details about the middle of the event. What should you do?
   a. Recopy the narrative and include them.
   b. Use editor's marks to show where to insert them.
   c. Add them at the end with an explanation.

Sentences   *pages 30 – 31*

Write *complete* or *incomplete* to indicate whether each group of words is a complete thought or an incomplete thought.

18. Janine understands five languages.
19. Speaks to her mother in German.

20. Singing to her in Swedish.
21. Her father is Italian.
22. Growing up in a New England city.
23. Of course, she speaks English too.

Four Kinds of Sentences   *pages 32 – 33*

Write each sentence. Write *declarative, interrogative, imperative,* or *exclamatory.* Add the correct punctuation mark at the end of each.

24. Have you ever visited the United Nations
25. People from nearly every country are there
26. We took a school trip to New York
27. Tell me about what you did and what you saw
28. What a lot of fun it was

Complete and Simple Subjects   *pages 34 – 35*

Write the complete subject and underline the simple subject.

29. Roy Rogers and his horse understood each other.
30. People with pets often feel very attached to their animals.
31. They and their animals communicate.
32. My aunt and uncle communicate well.
33. My aunt and the cat seem to talk!

Complete and Simple Predicates   *pages 36 – 37*

Write the complete predicate. Underline the verb.

34. Postage stamps have beautiful colors.
35. I buy attractive stamps at a window in the post office.
36. The recipient of my letter sees the address and the stamp.
37. My sister matches her stamps, her stationery, and her ink!
38. My brother will not use anything but flag stamps.

Word Order in Sentences   *pages 38 – 39*

Write *natural* or *inverted* to describe the word order of each sentence.

39. Do you see that smoke in the sky?
40. Black smoke means fire.
41. There is only white smoke over there.
42. An incinerator makes that smoke.
43. In that direction is a large apartment complex.

Compound Subjects and Compound Predicates   *pages 40–41*

Write the sentences. Underline the subjects once and the verbs twice.
Write *compound subject, compound predicate,* or *both* after each sentence.

44. My little brother and sister like this toy mailbox.

45. Gina draws and scribbles on a piece of paper.

46. She opens the door and drops it in.

47. Jake goes to the mailbox and opens it.

48. He opens his mail and reads it.

49. Gina and Jake sit and laugh over their mail.

Simple and Compound Sentences   *pages 42–43*

Write *simple* or *compound* for each sentence below.

50. Lester designed the program for the school play.

51. Mark helped, and Judy took it to the printer.

52. I have collected and saved programs from plays.

53. The collection is colorful; programs line my walls.

54. I look at the programs and remember the events.

Avoiding Sentence Fragments and Run-on Sentences   *pages 44–45*

Write *fragment, run-on sentence,* or *sentence* for each word group.

55. Sending the telegram.

56. Jack wanted to send a telegram he got it ready.

57. Received a telegram for her birthday.

58. Have you ever sent a telegram?

59. I received a telegram it brought good news.

Context Clues   *pages 46–47*

Read each sentence. Write the meaning of each
underlined word. Identify the context clues that
suggested its meaning.

60. Last summer, Siu thought a job working at the newspaper office
would be an enjoyable <u>diversion</u>, that is, an activity different from
what she normally did.

61. After she began the job, she realized she had <u>misgivings</u>, or regrets,
about a summer job that kept her indoors.

62. Siu discovered that she disliked the <u>confinement</u> of working at a
desk in an office, especially on sunny days.

63. Rather than quit the job, Siu made <u>inquiries</u> at the office trying to
find out what other kinds of work might be available.

UNIT

Capturing an Impression

◆ **COMPOSITION FOCUS:** **Character Sketch**
◆ **LANGUAGE FOCUS:** **Nouns**

Have you ever watched a sidewalk portrait artist at work? With a few deft strokes, the artist makes the subject spring to life on paper. Writers, too, bring people to life on paper. When a writer captures a personality in words, we call the piece of writing a **character sketch.**

Character sketches can describe real or imaginary people. They can stand alone or be part of a larger work such as a novel or a biography. For example, Frank B. Gilbreth, Jr., and Ernestine Gilbreth Carey included a character sketch of their father in their family biography called *Cheaper by the Dozen*. Like most character sketches, theirs combines narration and description.

In this unit you will learn how to bring a personality to life in a character sketch.

Frank B. Gilbreth, Jr., and his sister wrote their family biography *to entertain* their readers and *to express* their love for their father.

Reading with a Writer's Eye
Character Sketch

Life at the Gilbreth home in Montclair, New Jersey, was never dull. Joyful noise and activity abounded—not surprising in a house with 12 children, their mother, and their father, Frank Gilbreth, who was a dedicated efficiency expert. Mr. Gilbreth practiced efficiency in his own life. For example, he buttoned his vests from the bottom up because it saved him four seconds. He also practiced efficiency techniques on his children. He had them listen to foreign-language instruction records while they took their baths, so that there wouldn't be wasted time or, as he called it, "unavoidable delay." As you read this character sketch of Frank Gilbreth, notice the kinds of information his son and his daughter include to give you a vivid picture of their father.

from Cheaper by the Dozen

by Frank B. Gilbreth, Jr., and
Ernestine Gilbreth Carey

Dad was happiest in a crowd, especially a crowd of kids. Wherever he was, you'd see a string of them trailing him—and the ones with plenty of freckles were pretty sure to be Gilbreths.

He had a way with children and knew how to keep them on their toes. He had a respect for them, too, and didn't mind showing it.

He believed that most adults stopped thinking the day they left school—and some even before that. "A child, on the other hand, stays impressionable and eager to learn. Catch one young enough," Dad insisted, "and there's no limit to what you can teach."

Really, it was love of children more than anything else that made him want a pack of his own. Even with a dozen, he wasn't fully satisfied. Sometimes he'd look us over and say to Mother:

"Never you mind, Lillie. You did the best you could."

We children used to suspect, though, that one reason he had wanted a large family was to assure himself of an appreciative audience, even within the confines of the home. With us around, he could always be sure of a full house, packed to the galleries.

Whenever Dad returned from a trip—even if he had been gone only a day—he whistled the family "assembly call" as he turned in at the sidewalk of our large, brown home in Montclair. The call was a tune he had composed. He whistled it, loud and shrill, by doubling his tongue behind his front teeth. It took considerable effort and Dad, who never exercised if he could help it, usually ended up puffing with exhaustion.

The call was important. It meant drop everything and come running—or risk dire consequences. At the first note, Gilbreth children came dashing from all corners of the house and yard. Neighborhood dogs converged for blocks around. Heads popped out of the windows of near-by houses.

Dad gave the whistle often. He gave it when he had an important family announcement that he wanted to be sure everyone would hear. He gave it when he was bored and wanted some excitement with his children. He gave it when he had invited a friend home and wanted both to introduce the friend to the whole family and to show the friend how quickly the family could assemble. On such occasions, Dad would click a stopwatch, which he always carried in his vest pocket.

Like most of Dad's ideas, the assembly call, while something more than a nuisance, made sense. This was demonstrated in particular one day when a bonfire of leaves in the driveway got out of control and spread to the side of the house. Dad whistled, and the house was evacuated in fourteen seconds—eight seconds off the all-time record. That occasion also was memorable because of the remarks of a frank neighbor, who watched the blaze from his yard. During the height of the excitement, the neighbor's wife came to the front door and called to her husband:

"What's going on?"

"The Gilbreths' house is on fire," he replied, "thank God!"

"Shall I call the fire department?" she shouted.

"What's the matter, are you crazy?" the husband answered incredulously.

Anyway, the fire was put out quickly and there was no need to ask the fire department for help.

Dad whistled assembly when he wanted to find out who had been using his razors or who had spilled ink on his desk. He whistled it when he had special jobs to assign or errands to be run. Mostly, though, he sounded the assembly call when he was about to distribute some wonderful surprises, with the biggest and best going to the one who reached him first.

So when we heard him whistle, we never knew whether to expect good news or bad, rags or riches. But we did know for sure we'd better get there in a hurry.

Sometimes, as we all came running to the front door, he'd start by being stern.

"Let me see your nails, all of you," he'd grunt, with his face screwed up in a terrible frown. "Are they clean? Have you been biting them? Do they need trimming?"

Then out would come leather manicure sets for the girls and pocket knives for the boys. How we loved him then, when his frown wrinkles reversed their field and became a wide grin.

Or he'd shake hands solemnly all around, and when you took your hand away there'd be a nut chocolate bar in it. Or he'd ask who had a pencil, and then hand out a dozen automatic ones.

"Let's see, what time is it?" he asked once. Out came wrist watches for all—even the six-week-old baby.

"Oh, Daddy, they're just right," we'd say.

And when we'd throw our arms around him and tell him how we'd missed him, he would choke up and wouldn't be able to answer.

Respond

1. What part of the character sketch gives you the most vivid picture of Frank Gilbreth?

Discuss

2. What different kinds of information do the writers include about their father?

3. How do they make this character sketch personal?

Thinking As a Writer
Analyzing a Character Sketch

A character sketch presents details that reveal a subject's memorable character traits. It also reveals the writer's attitude toward the subject. Read these passages from *Cheaper by the Dozen*.

Dad was happiest in a crowd, especially a crowd of kids. Wherever he was, you'd see a string of them trailing him—and the ones with plenty of freckles were pretty sure to be Gilbreths.

He had a way with children and knew how to keep them on their toes. He had a respect for them, too, and didn't mind showing it.

*   *   *

Sometimes, as we all came running to the front door, he'd start by being stern.

"Let me see your nails, all of you," he'd grunt, with his face screwed up in a terrible frown. "Are they clean? Have you been biting them? Do they need trimming?"

Then out would come leather manicure sets for the girls and pocket knives for the boys. How we loved him then, when his frown wrinkles reversed their field and became a wide grin.

*   *   *

And when we'd throw our arms around him and tell him how we'd missed him, he would choke up and wouldn't be able to answer.

The **introduction** identifies the subject and his or her memorable character traits, and sometimes includes a setting in which a particular trait is revealed.

The **body** gives details about the subject's physical appearance and about how he or she moves, dresses, acts, talks, and treats others.

The **conclusion** tells how others respond to the subject and, if the sketch is nonfiction, includes a personal response.

Discuss

1. Look at the introduction, the body, and the conclusion of the character sketch. How is the information in each part different?
2. What is Frank Gilbreth's most memorable character trait?

Try Your Hand

A. Analyze Introductions to Character Sketches   Read the following introductions. Identify each character's most memorable trait.

1. The Great Wizwham was a failure at magic. Try as he might, he couldn't pull off a single spell, tame one itsy-bitsy dragon, or grant any wish, no matter how trivial. His valiant efforts were touching but ineffective. He tried hard, but he didn't have the gift.

2. Wanda Wallingcraft, the famous movie actress, smiled faintly at the crowd and bowed. As always, Wanda got away without signing any autographs. Nobody ever got near her, and it's probably just as well. If her fans had actually met her, she might not have had any fans left.

3. Sitting in the library behind stacks of magazines, Herman Munch spent day after day hunched in his chair. His brow was wrinkled in fierce concentration. No one seeing Herman's rapt expression would have been surprised to discover that his reading material was historical journals.

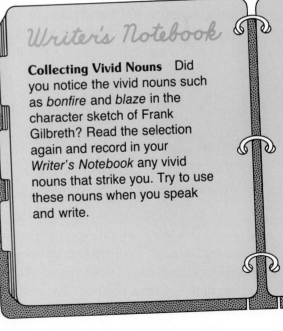

B. Add Information to the Body
Write five sentences for the body of a character sketch of one of the three characters in **A**. Give details about appearance, movements, and attitude.

C. Add Information to the Conclusion Pretend you know one of the subjects. Write two sentences to end the sketch of the person you know. State your feelings about the subject.

D. Read a Character Sketch Find another character sketch. Read it aloud to a partner, identifying the introduction, the body, and the conclusion and the type of information included in each part.

Writer's Notebook

Collecting Vivid Nouns Did you notice the vivid nouns such as *bonfire* and *blaze* in the character sketch of Frank Gilbreth? Read the selection again and record in your *Writer's Notebook* any vivid nouns that strike you. Try to use these nouns when you speak and write.

Thinking As a Writer
Classifying Information into Categories

To prepare to write a character sketch, a writer first chooses the subject's most memorable character trait. Then the writer chooses categories that will best reveal the trait. After choosing the categories, the writer classifies the information about the subject under the appropriate category. Look at this part of a cluster diagram about Frank Gilbreth.

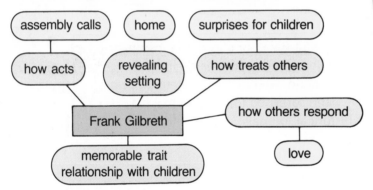

Each category in the diagram helps to reveal Frank Gilbreth's most memorable trait—his warm relationship with his children. As you prepare to write your character sketch, choose appropriate categories and classify details about your subject that reveal his or her memorable trait.

Discuss

1. Why might different character sketches concentrate on different categories?
2. Why didn't the authors of the model refer to how their father dressed or what he looked like?

Try Your Hand

Classify Details   Write down 10 details about an imaginary character. Decide in what category each detail would fit. Trade details with a partner. Try to classify the details your partner wrote into appropriate categories. Check each other's answers.

Developing the Writer's Craft
Using Vivid Language

Because writers of character sketches want their readers to get a vivid mental picture of the subject, they use vivid language to describe the person. Read these sentences from the selection.

> He whistled it, <u>loud</u> and <u>shrill</u>, by doubling his tongue behind his front teeth. It took considerable effort and Dad, who never exercised if he could help it, usually ended up <u>puffing with exhaustion</u>.

The writers carefully chose the underlined words to describe their father and the way he called them to assembly.

When you write your character sketch, try to capture your subject's most memorable characteristic by using vivid words to describe him or her.

Discuss

1. To which senses did the writers appeal with the vivid language they used in the example?
2. Look back at the selection. Find another passage that has vivid language. Describe the image it creates in your mind.

Try Your Hand

Use Vivid Language   Look at the picture of the magician. Write three sentences describing how he is dressed. Use vivid language. Trade sentences with a partner and compare your two descriptions.

1 Prewriting
Character Sketch

Carlos, a student at St. John's School, wanted to write a character sketch to entertain his classmates. He used the checklist in the **Writer's Guide** to help him plan his character sketch. Look at what he did.

◆ Brainstorming and Selecting a Topic

First, Carlos brainstormed a list of possible subjects for his character sketch. Look at Carlos's list.

Next, Carlos crossed off the names of people whom he couldn't write about in an amusing way or people whom he didn't know well. He also crossed off Oliver's name because he realized that Oliver might not want to be the subject of a sketch that their classmates would read.

Last, Carlos circled the name of the person that he felt most comfortable writing about—Elizabeth, his younger sister. He found her amusing, and he was sure his classmates would too. Carlos also knew that he could think of a lot to say about Elizabeth because he knew her so well.

Doctor Mary Benson
Elizabeth (little sister)
Aunt Amelia
Oliver (best friend)
Dad

Discuss

1. Why is a family member a good choice for a character sketch?
2. If Carlos were writing a biography, whom might he have chosen as a subject? Why?

◆ Gathering and Organizing Information

After Carlos selected his subject, he gathered information for his character sketch. He began by choosing Elizabeth's most memorable character trait. Elizabeth impressed Carlos with her stubborn resolve—her ability to hold out against everyone.

Next, Carlos made a list of categories for a character sketch. He circled the ones that would help his readers picture Elizabeth.

Then, he made a cluster diagram of his categories and added details that fit each category.

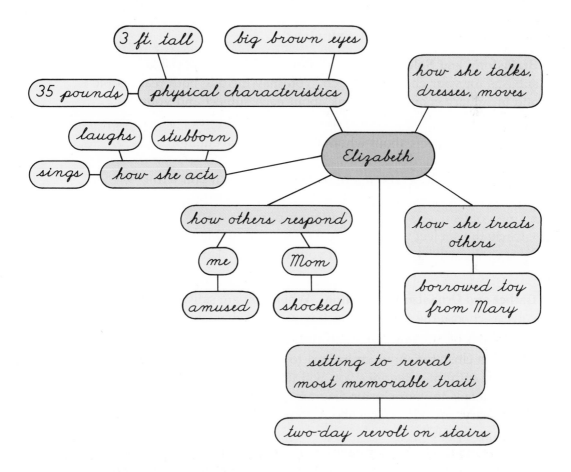

Carlos thought about his introduction, body, and conclusion. He decided to include the memorable trait and the setting in his introduction. He knew he would put his reactions in the conclusion and all the other details in the body of the character sketch.

WRITING PROCESS

Discuss

1. Why did Carlos gather and organize his information at the same time, rather than gathering first and organizing later?
2. Why do you think Carlos decided not to include details on how Elizabeth dresses, talks, and moves?
3. Why do you think Carlos didn't include a complete physical description of Elizabeth in his cluster diagram?

Try Your Hand

Now plan a character sketch of your own.

A. Brainstorm and Select a Topic   Brainstorm a list of possible subjects for your character sketch. You may include both real people and imaginary characters. Think about each subject and your audience.

- Cross out subjects about whom you don't have enough information.
- Cross out subjects who might feel embarrassed if you wrote about them.
- Cross out subjects who don't fit your purpose.
- Circle the subject whom you feel most comfortable writing about. He or she will be the subject of your character sketch.

B. Gather and Organize Information   When you are satisfied with your subject, choose the subject's most memorable character trait.

- Plan which categories will help you show this trait.
- Make a cluster diagram or a chart to help you record details that fit into the categories you will use.
- Add details to your cluster diagram. Make it as detailed as necessary. Include details about your subject's appearance, if they are appropriate.
- Think about which information goes into the introduction, the body, and the conclusion of your character sketch. You may want to mark this on your cluster diagram or your chart.

 Save your cluster diagram or chart in your *Writer's Notebook*. You will use it when you draft your character sketch.

Listening and Speaking
Tips on How to Interview

1. You may not always write a character sketch about someone you know well. Often, in magazine and newspaper articles, people write about someone who is well known but who is not someone they know personally. If you are called on to write about someone you do not know well, you may want to interview that person before you write your sketch.

2. Before the interview, find out as much as you can about the person. Talk to people who know the person. If the person attends your school, talk to his or her classmates and teachers. If the person lives in your community, try to talk to people who work or play with that person.

3. Make a list of questions you would like to ask. Leave a large space after each question to fill in the answer. Also leave space for extra information or answers to questions that occur to you as the interview progresses.

4. Call or write for an appointment for the interview. Be sure to make a note of the correct date and time. Arrive promptly for the interview. Be sure you are dressed appropriately.

5. Begin by introducing yourself. Explain the purpose of the interview.

6. Be friendly and respectful. Use polite language, such as "Excuse me" and "Would you repeat that, please?"

7. After you ask a question, listen carefully to the answer. Take notes carefully and precisely. You may think of another question that is not on your list. If the person strays from the topic, ask a question to bring him or her back to your topic.

8. Besides taking notes, you may want to use a tape recorder. However, never record an interview without first obtaining permission from the person you are interviewing.

9. Ask the person you interview whether you can quote him or her. Also ask for a telephone number. You may need to call to check facts or to ask for more details.

10. Thank the person for the interview.

2 Drafting
Character Sketch

Writer's Guide

Drafting Checklist
- ☑ Use your cluster diagram for ideas.
- ☑ Write the introduction first.
- ☑ Write the body next.
- ☑ Write the conclusion last.

Using his cluster, Carlos followed the **Writer's Guide** to draft his sketch. Look at what he did.

> When I think of Elizabeth, I think of our stairs--not that they are unusual. They are narrow and covered with mottled green carpeting. It was on these stairs that Elizabeth staged her big revolt at the tender age of three. At age three, this child weighed only 35 pounds, but 34½ of those pounds were pure stubbornness.

Discuss

1. How did Carlos connect the memorable trait with the setting he chose?
2. Why do you think Carlos chose to use Elizabeth's weight in his character sketch?

Try Your Hand

Now you are ready to write a character sketch.

A. Review Your Information Think about the information you gathered and organized in the last lesson. Decide whether you need more information. If so, gather it.

B. Think About Your TAP Remember that your task is to write a character sketch. Your purpose is to tell your audience about the subject you have selected.

C. Write Your First Draft Use the **Drafting Checklist** to write your character sketch. Be sure to arrange the facts to reveal the memorable character trait.

Task: What?
Audience: Who?
Purpose: Why?

When you write your draft, just put all your ideas on paper. Do not worry about spelling, punctuation, or grammar. You can correct the draft later.

 Save your first draft in your *Writer's Notebook.* **You will use it when you revise your character sketch.**

3 Responding and Revising
Character Sketch

Carlos used the checklist in the **Writer's Guide** to revise his sketch. Look at what he did.

◆ Checking Information

Carlos decided to cut some information because it was irrelevant. To show his change, Carlos used this mark ℰ.

◆ Checking Organization

Carlos moved a sentence to the end of the paragraph. To show this, he used this mark ⌇.

◆ Checking Language

In the first sentence of the first paragraph, Carlos combined two sentences by making part of one sentence an appositive. He used this mark ∧. He used this mark ⌢ to change the form of a name.

Writer's Guide

Revising Checklist

☑ Read your character sketch to yourself or to a partner.

☑ Think about your audience and your purpose. Add or cut information.

☑ Check to see that your character sketch is organized correctly.

☑ Check to see whether you can combine any sentences.

Replace/ Add/Cut

Cut

Move

Cut

This is what happened. ∧Elizabeth's Elizabeth has a friend named Mary. Mary lent Elizabeth her stuffed yellow duck. When Elizabeth went to Mary's house to play, she returned the duck, but she refused to say <u>thank you</u>. (The battle had begun.) Mom explained that we should show our appreciation when someone lends us something. Elizabeth was silent. Mary watched with interest. Mom warned Elizabeth that if she refused to thank Mary she would have to go straight home. Elizabeth shrugged. Mom took Elizabeth home and told her to sit on the stairs until she was ready to say <u>thank you</u>.

Discuss

1. Why did Carlos think that the sentence he moved made more sense in its new position?
2. Is there other information that you think Carlos should have included in the body of his sketch? Explain your answer.

Try Your Hand

Now revise your first draft.

A. Read Your First Draft   As you read your character sketch, think about your audience and your purpose. Read your character sketch silently or to a partner to see if it is complete and well organized. Ask yourself or your partner the questions in the box.

Responding and Revising Strategies

✔ **Respond**	✔ **Revise**
Ask yourself or a partner:	**Try these solutions:**
• Have I clearly identified the subject and the trait I find most memorable?	• Find the answers in your diagram and **add** them to the introduction. If necessary, **move** this information to the introduction.
• Have I classified all of the information that reveals the memorable trait and added details ?	• Find the details in your diagram and **add** them to the body. **Cut** details that do not help reveal the trait.
• Have I included my own reaction in the conclusion?	• Think about your own feelings and **add** an explanation of them.
• Have I used vivid words to add to my description?	• **Replace** colorless words with vivid words. See the **Writer's Thesaurus** at the back of this book.
• Are all of my sentences as clear and as concise as they could be?	• Combine sentences with appositives to rename or identify the character and his or her traits. See the **Revising Workshop** on page 73.

B. Make Your Changes   If the answer to any question in the box is *no*, try the solution. Use the **Editor's Marks** to show your changes.

C. Review Your Character Sketch Again   Decide whether there is anything else you want to revise. Keep revising your sketch until you feel it is well organized and complete.

EDITOR'S MARKS

∧ Add something.

‿ Cut something.

◯ Move something.

∧ Replace something.

Save your revised character sketch in your *Writer's Notebook.* You will use it when you proofread your sketch.

WRITING PROCESS

Revising Workshop
Combining Sentences with Appositives

An appositive is a noun or a pronoun set beside another noun or pronoun to explain or identify it. Good writers combine short, related sentences by using appositives or appositive phrases. In this way they avoid repetition. Look at the underlined words in these sentences.

1. Uncle Henry likes to play practical jokes. Uncle Henry is my mother's brother.
2. Uncle Henry, my mother's brother, likes to play practical jokes.

In the first example, the writer used two sentences to convey information about Uncle Henry. In the second example, the writer used an appositive to identify Uncle Henry. The appositive replaced the second sentence from example 1.

Practice

Combine each pair of sentences to make one sentence. Use the information in one sentence to make an appositive in the other. You may change a few words if necessary to make your new sentence flow more smoothly.

1. Roger Hammer works as a zookeeper. Roger Hammer tells wonderful elephant jokes.
2. Cindy Monmouth lives in Stinking Water Branch. Cindy Monmouth is a collector of humorous place names.
3. Dr. Patricia Gagnon owns lots of Mickey Mouse paraphernalia. Dr. Patricia Gagnon is a friend of my father's.
4. *The BFG* is a very funny novel by Roald Dahl. *The BFG* is the tale of a "big friendly giant" who invents wonderful dreams.
5. Don Rickles is a popular comedian. Don Rickles makes people laugh with his pointed, sarcastic humor.
6. The Great Dynamo is a juggler. The Great Dynamo can keep a number of objects in the air continuously.
7. The Ringling Brothers Circus Clown School is located in Florida. The Ringling Brothers Circus Clown School is a place where some of the best clowns in the world are trained.

4 Proofreading
Character Sketch

After revising his character sketch, Carlos used the **Writer's Guide** and the **Editor's Marks** to proofread it. Look at what he did.

¶It wasn't until the next day that Elizabeth finally gave in. By that time I was begging mom to let up. I told her that I would have cracked after one boring half hour. Wasn't it cruel to treat a baby this way? Mom pointed out that Elizabeth enjoyed her own company more than I did mine. She predicted that Elizabeth would not be so stubborn in the future and would learn to be courteous. i, for one, didn't believe it. But you know what? Mom was right. It was a memorable lesson. When Elizabeth is asked to say thank you now, she says it. We are all glad she learned her lesson, and we learned to respect her toughness.

Discuss

1. Look at Carlos's proofread sketch. What kinds of mistakes did he make?
2. Why did Carlos capitalize the word *mom* in the second sentence?

Try Your Hand

Proofread Your Character Sketch   Now use the **Writer's Guide** and the **Editor's Marks** to proofread your character sketch.

Save your corrected character sketch in your *Writer's Notebook.* You will use it when you publish your sketch.

EDITOR'S MARKS

≡	Capitalize.
⊙	Add a period.
∧	Add something.
⋏	Add a comma.
ⱽⱽ	Add quotation marks.
✂	Cut something.
⌃	Replace something.
∿	Transpose.
◯	Spell correctly.
¶	Indent paragraph.
∕	Make a lowercase letter.

WRITING PROCESS

5 Publishing
Character Sketch

Carlos made a clean copy of his character sketch and checked it to be sure he had not left anything out. Then he and his classmates published their character sketches in individual booklets. You can find Carlos's sketch on page 54 of the **Writer's Handbook.**

Here's how Carlos and his classmates published their booklets.

Writer's Guide

Publishing Checklist

☑ Make a clean copy of your character sketch.

☑ Check to see that nothing has been left out.

☑ Make sure there are no mistakes.

☑ Share your character sketch in a special way.

1. First, Carlos took a picture of Elizabeth looking stubborn— showing her most memorable character trait.

2. Next, he designed a cover for his booklet. He wrote the title in large letters. He decorated the cover appropriately.

3. He arranged his photo and text in order. Then he put the booklet together.

4. He shared his booklet with others and let them "meet" the person he wrote about.

Discuss

1. How can a photo help the reader of a character sketch?
2. What could happen if the pages weren't securely fastened to the cover?

Try Your Hand

Publish Your Character Sketch   Follow the checklist in the **Writer's Guide.** If possible, create a booklet, or try this idea for sharing your character sketch.

♦ Read your character sketch aloud to a group of students who know the subject, but don't mention the subject's name. Let the group guess the name of the person you wrote about.

Writing in the Content Areas

Use what you learned to write about another person. You could write a sketch of someone in your school or city. Use one of these ideas or an idea of your own.

Writer's Guide

When you write, remember the stages of the Writing Process.
- Prewriting
- Drafting
- Responding and Revising
- Proofreading
- Publishing

Literature

Who is your favorite literary character? Sherlock Holmes? Anne of Green Gables? Write a character sketch telling about a memorable character from literature. Before you begin, reread at least one book in which the character appears.

Music

Performers in opera and ballet often portray characters as being larger than life. Try to capture such a character in a character sketch. You can get your information from a recording, a television or radio broadcast, a videotape, or a movie of an opera or a ballet.

Science

Is there a scientist whose life and work you admire? Share your knowledge of this person with your classmates through a character sketch. Read a biography of your subject, but make sure that you don't write a biography yourself. Just focus on a single memorable trait.

Mathematics

Archimedes would be a great subject for a character sketch—he made his discovery while in a bathtub! Or how about Isaac Newton, who made his discovery under an apple tree?

Write a sketch about one of these men or about some other historical figure in the field of mathematics.

CONNECTING

WRITING ⬌ LANGUAGE

Writing a character sketch is one way to describe a person. Some character sketches just describe how a person looks. Others tell you how a person thinks and acts and how other people relate to him or her. Read this character sketch from *Dicey's Song* by Cynthia Voight and try to picture the character.

"Conflict," was written on the board in Mr. Chappelle's square printing . He couldn't write on a straight line . He was young and skinny and had carroty red hair that he kept trying to brush flat with his hands , but it always popped back up. He always wore a suit and tie . He had a pale face : pale blue eyes , pale skin , even his freckles were pale brown. He was one of those teachers who taught standing up, but he didn't move around much, just stood in front of the chalkboard . He pushed the big teacher's desk over to the side of the room , so there was a clear space in front of the board . He always rolled a piece of chalk in his fingers . On the first day of class , he had introduced himself as the English and Drama teacher . In Dicey's opinion , he wasn't very dramatic.

◆ **Nouns in a Character Sketch** The highlighted words are nouns. Nouns name persons, places, things, and ideas. Nouns can show number and relationship. They can be singular or plural and can show ownership.

◆ **Language Focus: Nouns** The following lessons will help you use different kinds of nouns in your own writing.

1 Nouns

FOCUS
◆ A **noun** names a person, a place, a thing, or an idea.
◆ Two kinds of nouns are common nouns and proper nouns.

Everything you can think of is named by a noun. A noun can be one word or more than one word. The words in color are nouns.

David Atkins is an actor in the city of Philadelphia. His work shows great talent.

Common nouns name things in general. **Proper nouns** name particular things. Proper nouns always begin with capital letters.

	Common
Person	actor
Place	city
Thing	work
Idea	talent

	Proper
Person	David Atkins
Place	Philadelphia
Thing	
Idea	

Link to Writing
Use a proper noun in place of a common noun whenever you can. It will make your writing more specific. Why is the revised sentence more interesting? How do proper nouns make your writing clearer?

                                            Amy
        ~~The girl~~ went to the
                   Roxy   Willow
        ~~theater~~ to see a ~~movie.~~

Guided Practice

A. Identify each noun as *common* or *proper*.

1. Buster Keaton was a famous comedian.
2. He made movies of fine quality in Hollywood.
3. Most of his early movies were silent.

B. 4.–6. Tell if each noun in **A** is a *person*, a *place*, a *thing*, or an *idea*.

THINK AND REMEMBER
• Remember that a **noun** names a person, place, thing, or idea.
• Use a **common noun** to name any person, place, thing, or idea.
• Use a **proper noun** to name a particular person, place, or thing.
• Always capitalize a proper noun.

Independent Practice

C. Identifying Nouns   Write each noun. Identify it as *common* or *proper*.

    7. Groucho Marx was a famous comedian.
MODEL Groucho Marx—proper; comedian—common

    8. Groucho Marx and his brothers are well known to people throughout the world.

    9. These four men began their careers in vaudeville.

  10. Their careers spanned stage, screen, and radio.

  11. During the 1950's, Groucho hosted a show on television.

  12. In later years, a play called <u>Minnie's Boys</u> was written about them.

  13. Groucho spent his free time as a writer of letters.

  14. Many of his letters are in the care of the Library of Congress.

D. 15.–22. Identifying Nouns as Persons, Places, Things, or Ideas   Set up a chart. Identify each noun from **C** as a *person, place, thing,* or *idea.*

MODEL **15.** *Persons*   *Places*   *Things*   *Ideas*
        Groucho Marx
        comedian

E. Revising: Replacing Common Nouns with Proper Nouns   Choose proper nouns to replace the common nouns in parentheses ( ). Write the sentences in the form of a paragraph.

  23. I live in (city), which I feel is not the movie capital of the world.
MODEL I live in Boise, which I feel is not the movie capital of the world.

  24. Last (weekday) I read in the paper that (movie star) was coming to town.

  25. I thought it said he would sign autographs in (video store).

  26. We decided to get there early and have lunch at (restaurant) before the autograph session.

  27. (Classmate) and I were surprised to find out that the ad said "movie sale," not "movie star."

Application — Writing

A Review   Imagine that you are a theater or movie critic. Write a brief review of a recent stage production, movie, or television program you have seen. Choose your nouns carefully.

2 Kinds of Nouns

◆ **FOCUS**   Nouns are concrete, abstract, or collective.

As you know, nouns can be proper or common. Nouns can also be concrete or abstract. **Concrete nouns** name things that you can see, hear, smell, or touch. The words in color are concrete nouns.

   1. Laughter echoed throughout the room.

Abstract nouns name things the senses cannot recognize. Qualities or ideas are recognized by your mind. The words in color are abstract nouns.

   2. He is planning a career in magic.

Collective nouns name a group of persons or things. The words in color are collective nouns.

   3. The flock of doves flew into the crowd.

Concrete Nouns	
see:	room
hear:	laughter
smell:	odor
touch:	ice

Abstract Nouns	
career	happiness
time	patriotism
magic	truth
beauty	courage

Collective Nouns	
people:	crowd
	team
animals:	herd
	flock
things:	fleet
	cluster

Guided Practice

A. Identify the nouns in each sentence. Decide whether each noun is *concrete* or *abstract*.

   1. Magic Melvin amused the group with his collection of tricks.
   2. He wore an orange cape, and he communicated an air of enthusiasm to his audience.
   3. A multicolored bunch of flowers flew out of his handkerchief.
   4. For the crowd, he pulled rabbits from a hat.
   5. The audience applauded the colorful show.

B. 6.–10.   Identify the collective nouns in **A.**

THINK AND REMEMBER
* Remember that a **concrete noun** names an object that can be recognized by at least one of the senses.
* Remember that an **abstract noun** names a quality or an idea that cannot be recognized by the senses.
* Remember that a **collective noun** names a group with more than one member.

Independent Practice

C. Identifying Nouns   Write each noun. Identify the noun as *concrete* or *abstract* and as *common* or *proper*.

11. People laugh at jumping beans.

MODEL▷ People—concrete, common
beans—concrete, common

12. Some people don't believe that jumping beans really jump.

13. The jumping bean is a seed that grows in Mexico.

14. A caterpillar gets inside the seed.

15. There it spins its cocoon and causes movement.

16. Our imagination makes us think the seed jumps.

D. Identifying Collective Nouns   Write each noun. Put a C after each collective noun.

17. audience

MODEL▷ audience—C

| **18.** family | **20.** troupe | **22.** chorus |
| **19.** musicians | **21.** bunch | **23.** students |

E. Revising: Using Nouns   Choose a noun to take the place of the underlined words. Write each new sentence. Underline the nouns you choose.

24. The clowns juggled things people eat from and things people drink from.

MODEL▷ The clowns juggled plates and glasses.

25. The people who were watching laughed.

26. The young boys and girls in the crowd really enjoyed the show.

27. Their mothers, fathers, aunts, and uncles also applauded the clowns' antics.

28. Sounds of people enjoying themselves filled the room.

29. I plan to come to the place where clowns entertain next year.

Application — Writing

A Job Description   Imagine that you are the owner of a magic store. You want to hire a student to help out on weekends. Write a paragraph that describes the job. Include all the duties you will expect your employee to perform. Use as many concrete, abstract, and collective nouns as you can.

3 Capitalization of Proper Nouns

◆ **FOCUS**   Each important word in a proper noun begins with a capital letter.

A **proper noun** names a particular person, place, or thing. A proper noun always begins with a capital letter. Use a dictionary if you are not sure whether a word should be capitalized.

people	Evan White, Olive Adams
titles	Mayor Gray, Dr. Sarah Miles, Senator Beadsley
months, days	July, Monday
streets, roads	Lombard Street, Interstate 80
cities, states	San Antonio, Texas
countries	United States of America
continents	Africa, Europe
planets	Pluto, Earth
areas, regions	New England, North Pole, the West
documents	Declaration of Independence, Bill of Rights
natural features	Grand Canyon, Atlantic Ocean, Lake Erie, Rio Grande
buildings, landmarks	White House, Empire State Building, Hoover Dam
institutions, clubs, corporations	Conway Middle School, Civitan Club, General Motors
organizations	Federal Bureau of Investigation, Red Cross
events, holidays	World Series, New Year's Eve, Independence Day
languages	Arabic, Spanish, French
titles of works	*A Wrinkle in Time,* ''The Star-Spangled Banner''

Guided Practice

A. Identify the words that should be capitalized.

1. sen. sam nunn
2. north carolina
3. natural features
4. elks club
5. treaty of verdun
6. dr. kiko omori
7. snake river
8. high school
9. boston
10. south america
11. august
12. school holiday
13. buckingham palace
14. tuesday
15. independence day
16. neptune
17. continents

THINK AND REMEMBER

* Always begin a proper noun with a capital letter.
* Use a dictionary to find correct capitalization.

Independent Practice

B. Capitalizing Proper Nouns   Capitalize each proper noun correctly.

18. Is this pecos plaza?

MODEL⟩ Pecos Plaza

19. Suzanne went to the carnegie library last saturday.
20. She read about charles stratton, who was forty inches tall and was better known as tom thumb.
21. Tom thumb, who joined p. t. barnum's circus, married another little person, lavinia warren.
22. On tom and lavinia's honeymoon, they met president abraham lincoln.
23. The strattons lived happily in connecticut when they were not traveling around the world.

Application — Writing and Speaking

An Advertisement   Design a product of the future and write a slogan for it. Give it a brand name. Write an advertisement that will appear in magazines and newspapers. Capitalize nouns correctly. Read your advertisement aloud.

4 Abbreviations

An abbreviation is a shortened form of a word. Many abbreviations stand for nouns. Many common abbreviations are forms of proper nouns and are written with capital letters. Use periods with most abbreviations; do not use periods with the postal abbreviations for the names of states.

When you write, use a dictionary to find the correct spelling, meaning, capitalization, and punctuation of most abbreviations. The following guidelines will help you form abbreviations.

• Some abbreviations are formed from the first letter or letters or the first and last letters of the word to be shortened.

Days	Mon. (Monday)	Tues. (Tuesday)
Months	Feb. (February)	Sept. (September)
Titles	Dr. (Doctor) Jr. (Junior)	Mr. (Mister) Rev. (Reverend)
Addresses	St. (Street) Apt. (Apartment)	Blvd. (Boulevard) Mt. (Mountain or Mount)
Time	A.M. (midnight to noon)	P.M. (noon to midnight)
Postal Abbreviations	TX (Texas) CA (California)	MT (Montana) FL (Florida)

• Proper nouns made up of more than one word are usually abbreviated by using the first letter of each word. Periods are placed after each letter.

P.O. (Post Office)   Kennedy H. S. (Kennedy High School)

• Abbreviations for large organizations may be written like state abbreviations—in capital letters and without periods.

GE (General Electric)   CIA (Central Intelligence Agency)

• Abbreviations for measurements are written in lowercase letters. Some abbreviations use periods and some do not. Check your dictionary if you are unsure of the punctuation.

gal. (gallon)   tsp. (teaspoon)   mph (miles per hour)   m (meter)
ft. (foot)   in. (inch)   hp (horsepower)   qt. (quart)

Guided Practice

A. Identify the meaning of each abbreviation.

1. Dr.   4. ft.   7. Wed.   10. Mrs.
2. Ave.   5. FBI   8. Mt.   11. Rev.
3. Mr.   6. Jr.   9. P.M.   12. Dec.

> **THINK AND REMEMBER**
> ◆ Use abbreviations to shorten some words.
> ◆ Use a dictionary to find the correct spelling, meaning, capitalization, and punctuation of most abbreviations.

Independent Practice

B. Writing Abbreviations   Shorten the appropriate words with abbreviations. Use a dictionary or the **Writer's Handbook** in this book for help.

13. Connecticut
MODEL▷ CT

14. Governor Bailey   18. Max Singer, Junior
15. January   19. Lincoln High School
16. quart   20. Florida
17. Thursday   21. Sunset Boulevard

C. Proofreading: Using Abbreviations   Rewrite the sentences. Use abbreviations where appropriate. Spell out all other words.

22. Please come to 211 West 66th Street this Fri. at 4 in the afternoon.
MODEL▷ Please come to 211 W. 66th St. this Friday at 4:00 P.M.

23. The class is giving a party for Mister Blake.
24. A former pupil of Mister Blake's, Senator Alan Fairchild, will be a surprise guest.
25. Even little Jonathan Blake, Junior, will be there.
26. Senator Fairchild is on a committee to help the North Atlantic Treaty Organization.
27. Mister Blake was always the senator's favorite teacher.

Application — Writing

An Invitation   Imagine that you are having a party. Write an invitation that tells your friends the place, date, and time. Use abbreviations. If you need help writing an invitation, see page 61 of the **Writer's Handbook**.

5 Singular and Plural Nouns

FOCUS

◆ A **singular noun** names one person, place, thing, or idea.

◆ A **plural noun** names more than one person, place, thing, or idea.

Use the following rules to make singular nouns plural.

• Add *s* to most nouns.
waiter   waiters   napkin   napkins

• Add *es* to nouns ending in *s, ss, z, x, sh*, or *ch*.
dish   dishes   boss   bosses

• Add *s* to nouns ending in *o* preceded by a vowel. Usually add *s* when the *o* is preceded by a consonant.
zoo   zoos   cello   cellos

• Add *es* to some nouns ending in *o* preceded by a consonant.
tomato   tomatoes   potato   potatoes

• Add *s* to nouns ending in *y* preceded by a vowel.
joy   joys   key   keys

• Change *y* to *i* and add *es* to nouns ending in *y* preceded by a consonant.
pantry   pantries   lady   ladies

• Add *s* to most nouns ending in *f, ff,* or *fe.*
chef   chefs   puff   puffs
safe   safes   belief   beliefs

• Change *f* to *v* and add *es* to some nouns ending in *f* or *fe.*
knife   knives   shelf   shelves
loaf   loaves   thief   thieves

Guided Practice

A. Spell the plural of each noun.

1. clown   4. party   7. chief
2. comedy   5. hero   8. costume
3. actress   6. couch   9. self

THINK AND REMEMBER

• Follow the rules on this page to spell the plural forms of most nouns.

Independent Practice

B. Making Nouns Plural   Write the plural form of each noun.

10. laugh
`MODEL` laughs

11. leaf	**13.** sigh	**15.** potato	**17.** cuff
12. hoax	**14.** key	**16.** stress	**18.** bow

C. Using Plural Nouns   Write each sentence, using the correct plural form.

19. (Comedys, Comedies) are plays that amuse us.
`MODEL` Comedies are plays that amuse us.

20. They were introduced at ancient Greek (festivals, festivales).
21. Things like (autos, autoes) moving backward fast make us laugh.
22. Proper (ladys, ladies) and gentlemen sometimes look funny.
23. Keys that stick on (pianos, pianoes) might produce a giggle.
24. The Keystone Cops, a comedy team from many years ago, delighted (audiencies, audiences) at early motion-picture shows.

D. Completing Sentences with Plural Nouns   Write the plural form of each noun in parentheses ( ).

25. I could hear _____ in the next room.   (chuckle)
`MODEL` chuckles

26. Henry knows how to draw comic _____.   (hero)
27. The seventh-grade _____ help him.   (student)
28. They make up new _____ each week. (story)
29. In today's story, four _____ run loose in the gym. (monkey)
30. They manage to break most of the piano _____.   (key)
31. Finally two _____ wave red _____ at them and chase them away.   (boy, scarf)
32. Next week's story will involve two _____ who want to marry a princess.   (serf)
33. They will undergo many hilarious _____.   (test)
34. At the end they will both marry _____.   (princess)

Application — Writing and Speaking

A Thank-You Note   Imagine that you have just been a guest at a very unusual party. Write a thank-you note to the host or hostess, mentioning some of the strange and wonderful things you enjoyed about the party. Use some plural nouns and be sure you form them correctly. Share your thank-you note with the class. If you need help writing a note, see page 62 of the **Writer's Handbook**.

6 More Plural Nouns

◆ **FOCUS** Some nouns form their plurals in special ways.

Here are more ways to form noun plurals.

* Some noun plurals are formed by changing a vowel sound or by adding a syllable.
  foot   feet   mouse   mice   child   children

* Some nouns stay the same in the singular and plural forms.
  deer   species   fish

* Some nouns have only a plural form.
  scissors   clothes   savings

* Some nouns appear to be plural but are singular in meaning.
  molasses   news   economics

A **compound noun** is two or more words used as one noun. Use the following rules to make compound nouns plural.

* When compound nouns are spelled as one word, you usually make the last part plural.
  eyelid   eyelids   grandmother   grandmothers

* When compound nouns are hyphenated or spelled as two words, make the most important word plural.
  mother-in-law   mothers-in-law   runner-up   runners-up
  New Mexican   New Mexicans   track meet   track meets

* Add *s* to compound nouns that end in *ful.*
  spoonful   spoonfuls   cupful   cupfuls

Guided Practice

A. Spell the plural of each noun.

1. court-martial   4. goose   7. trousers
2. brother-in-law   5. pliers   8. series
3. ox   6. civics   9. woman

> **THINK AND REMEMBER**
> * Use a dictionary to check the correctness of noun plurals in your writing.

Independent Practice

B. Making Nouns Plural   Write the plural form of each noun. Use a dictionary if you wish.

10. man

MODEL〉 men

11. rice   **14.** grapefruit   **17.** division of labor
12. Iroquois   **15.** moose   **18.** mouthful
13. pants   **16.** berry   **19.** sergeant at arms

C. Using Plural Nouns   Write the plural form of each noun in parentheses ( ).

20. The _____ fell into the pot.   (mouse)

MODEL〉 mice

21. Add two _____ of stones to the soup.   (handful)
22. Stir in five _____ of chicken broth.   (teacup)
23. Add two _____ of _____.   (cupful) (daisy)
24. I broke two _____ on this soup.   (tooth)
25. It should be served with _____, not _____.   (pliers) (spoon)

D. Using Collective Nouns with Plural Nouns   Use each noun in a phrase. If the noun is collective, add a plural noun. If the noun is plural, add a collective noun. Underline each collective noun.

26. flock

MODEL〉 a <u>flock</u> of pigeons

27. girls   **28.** herd   **29.** boys   **30.** musicians   **31.** bunch   **32.** army

E. Proofreading: Correcting Plural Nouns   Correct each plural noun that is formed incorrectly in the sentences.

33. My doctor works for all of the board of healths.

MODEL〉 boards of health

34. She keeps rubber mices to play with in the office.
35. Dr. Stone used the scissors to cut off my cast.
36. Then she tapped my kneescap to test my reflexes.
37. My foots almost hit her in the mouth!
38. Mom clenched her tooths during the whole thing.

Application — Writing

A Narrative   Write a short personal narrative about a funny incident. It can be something that happened to you or to someone else. Be sure to use precise nouns for the people and the place. If you need help in writing a narrative, see page 48 of the **Writer's Handbook.**

7 Possessive Nouns

◆ **FOCUS**   A **possessive noun** shows ownership or possession.

A noun can be singular or plural. It can also show ownership. Most nouns have four forms: singular, plural, singular possessive, and plural possessive.

girl   girls   girl's   girls'

Use these guidelines to form possessives.

- To form the possessive of a singular noun, add an apostrophe (') and *s*.

    student's books   Chris's dog   Mr. Young's report

- To form the possessive of a plural noun that ends in *s*, add only an apostrophe.

    girls' lockers   parents' questions   the Perrys' house

- To form the possessive of a plural noun that does not end in *s*, add an apostrophe and *s*.

    children's pictures   people's voices   women's clothes

- To form the possessive of a compound noun, add an apostrophe or an apostrophe and *s* to the end of the compound.

    country club's members   postcards' messages

> **Link to Writing**
> Do not confuse a possessive noun with a plural noun. A possessive noun shows ownership. The name of the possession usually follows the possessive noun.

Our class officers are excellent.
Our class officers' speeches are excellent.

Guided Practice

A. Identify each noun as *singular possessive* or *plural possessive*.

1. men's	4. assignments'	7. boards of trustees'
2. pupils'	5. Luis's	8. witness's
3. custodian's	6. classroom's	9. student council's

B. Rephrase each group of words to include a possessive noun.

10. orders of the president
11. graduation of the students
12. books of the professor
13. records of the computer
14. report card of Jonas
15. opinion of the class

THINK AND REMEMBER

- Use **possessive nouns** to show ownership or possession.
- Form the possessive of a singular noun by adding an apostrophe and *s*.
- Form the possessive of a plural noun that ends in an *s* by adding only an apostrophe.
- Form the possessive of a plural noun that does not end in *s* by adding an apostrophe and *s*.

Independent Practice

C. Identifying Nouns   Label each noun *singular possessive* or *plural possessive*.

16. dictionaries'
MODEL> plural possessive

17. women's
18. book's
19. novel's
20. Charles's
21. friends'
22. customers'
23. Joneses'
24. country's
25. animals'

D. 26.–35. Using Possessive Nouns and Singular and Plural Nouns   Write sentences using the nouns in **C.** Be sure a noun follows each possessive noun to show the thing possessed.

26. dictionaries'
MODEL> I used the three dictionaries' definitions in our explanation.

Application — Writing

A Wish   Think about things you have always wanted. Imagine that a genie has given you three wishes. Write a "wish" paragraph describing your wishes. Be imaginative. Use as many possessive nouns in your paragraph as you can. If you need help writing a paragraph, use page 39 of the **Writer's Handbook.**

8 Appivositives

◆ **FOCUS** An **appositive** is a noun that identifies or renames the noun or pronoun that precedes it.

An appositive can be a single word or a group of words. Commas are often used to set off appositives from the rest of the sentence. The words in color are appositives.

1. Jen and Jim, the new comedy team, are trying out for the comedy competition.

Although commas are used to set off some appositives, do not use a comma to set off an appositive that is part of a proper name.

2. Jen the Joker and Jim the Juggler took first place.

When an appositive is necessary to identify the word or words it follows, do not use commas to set off the appositive.

3. My friend Dena saw them perform.

Link to Speaking and Writing
Often appositives can help you explain your subject to your listener or reader. How does the appositive in this sentence help the reader or listener? When will you use appositives in your writing?

Star Search, the talent show, has helped many new performers begin their careers.

Guided Practice

A. Identify the appositive and the word or words to which it refers.

1. My favorite jokes, elephant stories, are usually silly.

2. Louise, my younger sister, always laughs.

3. My brother Ike hates them, but my brother Joe loves them.

4. Each morning my classmate Oscar tells me a new joke.

5. Now I can tell Oscar a joke every day from my favorite birthday present, a new joke book.

Independent Practice

B. Identifying Appositives Write the sentences. Underline the appositive once. Underline twice the word or words it explains.

6. My friend Elisa dyed her hair green.

MODEL⟩ My friend Elisa dyed her hair green.

7. Elisa, a clown, works for the circus.
8. Emmett Kelly, a famous clown, had a sad face, his trademark.

C. Combining Sentences with Appositives Combine each set of sentences by using an appositive. Use commas where needed.

9. Fanny Brice was an actress. She appeared in the Ziegfeld Follies.

MODEL⟩ Fanny Brice, an actress, appeared in the Ziegfeld Follies.

10. Fanny Brice was a comedian. Fanny Brice was born in 1891.
11. Fanny learned many accents. Fanny was a budding actress.
12. Fanny won first prize in a contest. The prize was $10.00.

D. Proofreading: Punctuating Appositives Correct each sentence. Add commas wherever necessary. Underline the appositives.

13. Greeks celebrated festivals religious events with plays.

MODEL⟩ Greeks celebrated festivals, religious events, with plays.

14. They saw a tetralogy a group of four plays.
15. The first three plays formed a trilogy a group of three.
16. Often a series a sequence of movies is made on the same theme.
17. Star Trek one film series has five individual movies.
18. Even the movie Cocoon has a sequel.

Application — Writing

A Fan Letter Imagine that you have just enjoyed a performance by a famous comedy team. Write a fan letter telling them what you enjoyed. Use at least one appositive in your letter. If you need help writing a friendly letter, see page 59 of the **Writer's Handbook**.

Building Vocabulary
Synonyms and Antonyms

Read the paragraph. Decide what is wrong with it.

Marge said that Harry was her friend. Harry said that Marge was his friend. They both said that Bill was their friend. Bill said that he was Harry's friend, but he said that Marge was not his friend.

One way writers avoid boring, repetitive writing is to use synonyms and antonyms. **Synonyms** are words that have similar meanings. **Antonyms** are words that have opposite meanings. Read the paragraph below. Notice how the writer uses synonyms and antonyms.

Marge said that Harry was her friend. Harry claimed that Marge was only an acquaintance. They both insisted that Bill was their buddy. Bill agreed that he and Harry were pals, but he explained that Marge was his enemy.

The words *acquaintance, buddy*, and *pal* are synonyms for *friend*. The last sentence contains an antonym. *Enemy* means the opposite of *friend*. Notice that the word *but* signals that you will read something in contrast to what is in the rest of the sentence.

As you write, use a thesaurus to help you add variety to your sentences. A thesaurus, like a dictionary, is a reference book that contains words and their synonyms and antonyms. It lists the words in alphabetical order and gives their parts of speech. Read the thesaurus entries below. Use them to rewrite these sentences.

The courageous knight was to fight the courageous dragon. When the courageous knight saw the size of the courageous dragon, he became less courageous.

The orange pumpkin sat on the porch of the orange house. Orange flames flickered from the orange candle inside it, casting orange lights on the passersby.

courageous *adj.* brave, fearless, intrepid, valorous, gallant, spirited, heroic, stouthearted, resolute, bold, rugged, dashing, doughty, mettlesome, manly, indomitable, audacious. **ant.** cowardly, timid, fainthearted, fearful, skittish.

orange *adj.* coppery, ginger-colored, flame-colored, golden, coral, apricot, cinnamon-colored, rust, ruddy, persimmon, salmon, fiery, glowing.

Reading Practice

Read each sentence. Find the two words that are either synonyms or antonyms. Write each word pair. Label each pair *synonyms* or *antonyms*.

1. The comic told a joke that he thought was hilarious, but the audience did not think it was funny.
2. Some people find slapstick comedy entertaining, although others find it boring.
3. To make the audience laugh, circus clowns will trip over things and stumble around the ring.
4. Practical jokes are often nothing more than dangerous tricks.
5. Sometimes I am in a humorous mood, while at other times I feel more serious.
6. That movie was more tragic than comic.

Writing Practice

Write a friendly letter that tells about a funny experience. Include as many of the following synonyms and antonyms as you can.

	Synonym	Antonym
funny	comical	serious
unusual	odd	typical
friend	companion	enemy
enjoyable	pleasant	miserable
laugh	giggle	cry
huge	gigantic	tiny
messy	rumpled	neat
colorful	flamboyant	dull
run	race	plod

Project

Read a short newspaper article. Rewrite the article by replacing as many words as you can with synonyms. Use a thesaurus for help. Then read your rewritten article to see if the synonyms have changed the meaning of the article. Share the articles in class, and discuss the differences in meaning.

Language Enrichment
Nouns

Use what you know about nouns to do these activities.

 **Make It Short**

Shorten this letter by using abbreviations wherever possible. List the abbreviations by line number.

January 21, 1990

Dear Lieutenant Ortega,

At Captain Donohue's request, move your troops to Middletown Forks, Michigan, to sandbag the Whatachacallee River. It is 6 feet (approximately 2 meters) above flood stage. Then, report to City Hall, 100 Main Street at 2:30 in the afternoon, on Saturday, January 23.

Sincerely,

Commander Elliot Liu

 Applied Appositives

Can you name the proper nouns that these appositives describe?

1. Bambi's rabbit friend
2. Sherlock Holmes's assistant
3. Tom Sawyer's aunt
4. the President's Washington home
5. Captain Kirk's spaceship

Write five appositives that describe famous proper nouns. Take turns with your classmates, reading aloud the appositives and calling on volunteers to give the proper nouns.

 What's in a Name?

"Fireplace" is a common noun that allows the reader to picture the object named and suggests its function.

Working in a small group, brainstorm or make up common nouns that describe the appearance or function of common items. Then share your work with the class.

CONNECTING

LANGUAGE ↔ WRITING

In this unit you learned that nouns can be singular or plural. They can also name whole groups of things as well as specific persons, places, things, and ideas. You know that proper nouns are always capitalized and that possessive nouns are used with an apostrophe to show to whom or to what they are related.

◆ **Using Nouns in Your Writing** You always use nouns when you write. Using them correctly will make you a more effective writer. Pay attention to the nouns you use in these activities.

 Diamond Dazzlers

Use what you learned about synonyms and antonyms on the **Building Vocabulary** page to write diamond-shaped poems, seven-line poems that begin and end with nouns that are synonyms or antonyms. The middle line is the longest. Read the example. Then write your own poem!

morning
expectant, hushed
waking, chirping, calling
sun, climbing – shadows, stretching
fading, darkening, sighing
draining, huddled
night

 Comedy Cookbook

Imagine that your class is publishing a cookbook to raise money. Write the directions for a favorite recipe. In place of the usual ingredients, use abstract and concrete nouns that describe qualities of your fellow classmates. Read this example.

Comic Cake
Take 1 cup of Susan's smile; add 2 tablespoons of Jorene's laughter, a dash of John's snicker, and a dollop of Jed's jokes. Add two of Paul's puns and a pinch of José's zaniness. Stir well with fifth period's energy and bake for one class period.

Unit Checkup

Think Back	Think Ahead
◆ What did you learn about writing a character sketch in this unit? What did you do to write one?	◆ How will what you learned about a character sketch help you when you read one? ◆ How will classifying information help you write a character sketch?
◆ Look at the writing you did in this unit. How did nouns help you express your ideas?	◆ What is one way that you can use nouns to improve your writing?

Analyzing a Character Sketch   *pages 62 – 63*

Write whether each statement is *true* or *false*.

1. A character sketch is always humorous.
2. A setting is often included in a character sketch because it helps reveal the character.
3. Focusing on several outstanding traits gives the reader a clearer picture of a person.
4. What a person looks like is not important; how the person behaves *is* important.
5. How the writer feels about the subject belongs in a character sketch.

Classifying Information into Categories   *page 64*

In what categories would you put the following pieces of information about your favorite teacher?

6. taught in Japan for two years
7. just under five feet tall
8. received "Teacher of the Year" award
9. enjoys traveling
10. likes crossword puzzles

Using Vivid Language   *page 65*

Write the following sentences. Use vivid words that appeal to the senses to complete each description.

11. When she was happy, her face _____.
12. His hair was really striking, for it _____.
13. If you saw her coming, you'd recognize _____.
14. When the baby saw her, he usually _____.
15. When she told a joke, she _____.

The Writing Process   *pages 66 – 75*

Write the letter of the correct ending for each sentence.

16. When you plan a character sketch, the best candidate is
    a. someone you know well.
    b. someone you want to know.
    c. a pen pal in Argentina.
17. As part of an interview, you should
    a. do research before the interview.
    b. do research after the interview.
    c. take notes or tape the interview.
18. As you write the first draft, you should
    a. check spelling in a dictionary.
    b. do more prewriting if you find you need it.
    c. worry about purpose and audience later.
19. To cut a worn-out word and replace it with a more vivid one, you should use the mark
    a. ⌒̂   c. ⋏
    b. ∧   d. ⌒
20. Use the **Editor's Marks** to
    a. indicate where you want to make changes.
    b. show the reader your corrections on your final draft.
    c. show your revising partner what is wrong in your draft.

Nouns   *pages 78 – 79*

Write each noun. After each word, write *common* or *proper*.

21. Raúl lent Jennifer a book, a collection of cartoons.
22. The book has a bright cover.
23. The cover is orange, blue, and pink!

24. Jennifer put the book on her dresser at home.
25. The book stayed there for three weeks.

Kinds of Nouns   *pages 80 – 81*

Write each noun. Then write *concrete* or *abstract* and *common* or *proper* after each noun.

26. The new movie showing at the local theater is very funny.
27. The Bloopers, who act in comedies, star in the film.
28. Kelly and Wanda saw the movie and described the plot.
29. The new theater, the Laughorama, shows only funny movies.
30. Most of the families are happy about the policy.

Capitalization of Proper Nouns   *pages 82 – 83*

Write each proper noun using correct capitalization.

31. A juggler from houston visited the library on jamison street wednesday.
32. Most of my classmates read about the appearance in the daily news, our local newspaper.
33. The juggler has a course he calls jack's juggling jesters, and he teaches others to juggle.
34. The course begins in may, and marsha mason has received permission from her mother to take it.
35. Our family doctor, dr wilram, can juggle five oranges at a time!

Abbreviations   *pages 84 – 85*

Use abbreviations to shorten the appropriate words.

36. Texas
37. 47 West Elm Street
38. Reverend Matthews
39. Mr. Jack Green
40. Doctor Luis Lopez
41. Lincoln Avenue
42. Mike Malone, Senior
43. Mrs. Adrian Lampes
44. ounce
45. gallon

Singular and Plural Nouns   *pages 86 – 87*

Write the plural form of each noun.

46. cello
47. shelf
48. pantry
49. soprano
50. sigh
51. tomato
52. chef
53. auto
54. lady
55. city

More Plural Nouns   *pages 88 – 89*
Write the plural form of each noun.

56. deer

57. savings

58. mouse

59. molasses

60. civics

61. eyelid

62. child

63. news

64. scissors

65. woman

Possessive Nouns   *pages 90 – 91*
Label each noun *singular possessive* or *plural possessive*.

66. studios'

67. Jonah's

68. officer's

69. monkeys'

70. children's

71. speeches'

72. libraries'

73. computer's

74. men's

75. mess's

Appositives   *pages 92 – 93*
Write each sentence. Underline once the appositive or appositives in each sentence. Underline the word it modifies twice.

76. Teresa, my classmate, can speak double-talk.

77. Double-talk, nonsense that sounds like language, is funny.

78. Everyone, each of my classmates, has tried to speak double-talk.

79. The "language" sounds like a real language, Chinese or Hebrew.

80. When Teresa speaks, we are sure she is making sense, completely logical conversation.

81. The more we listen to the words, the syllables coming out of her mouth, the more we laugh.

Synonyms and Antonyms   *pages 94 – 95*
Read each sentence. Find the two words that are either synonyms or antonyms. Write each word pair. Label each pair *synonyms* or *antonyms*.

82. Marta laughs at the sight of Tilly, our Great Dane, although nobody else finds the spectacle of Tilly amusing.

83. Marta and Tilly have a special sympathy, and this understanding baffles and amuses everyone.

84. When Tilly wants to romp but Marta wants to rest, Tilly makes a soft dog sound that almost sounds like "please."

85. The two of them often play ball outside, with Marta throwing the ball and Tilly catching it in her mouth.

1-2 Cumulative Review

Four Kinds of Sentences   *pages 32–33*

Add the correct punctuation mark at the end of each sentence. Write *declarative, interrogative, imperative,* or *exclamatory* to identify each sentence.

1. Martha wrote a letter to her cousin
2. Do you know whether he received it
3. The letter was seventeen pages long
4. Ask Martha what she wrote
5. She kept a copy of the letter
6. Have you ever received a long letter
7. What is the longest letter you have written
8. Read Martha's letter
9. Be sure to save an afternoon to read it
10. Perhaps one day Martha will write a book

Complete Subjects and Complete Predicates   *pages 34–37*

Write the sentences. Underline the complete subject once. Underline the complete predicate twice.

11. Body language is fun to watch.
12. A huge yawn might suggest boredom.
13. Leila had no sleep last night.
14. She yawns from tiredness.
15. Mark sometimes taps his foot on the floor.
16. He seems impatient.
17. Mark is worried about the basketball game.
18. Tapping can indicate nervousness.
19. A big grin sends my favorite message.
20. It says "Hello."

Word Order in Sentences   *pages 38–39*

Write the sentences. Underline the simple subject once. Underline the verb twice. Write *natural* or *inverted* to describe the word order of each sentence.

21. Do you have long conversations with your friends?
22. My sister talks for hours on the telephone.
23. There are many subjects to discuss.

24. Have they been apart for days?

25. Here is the amazing part.

26. They spend all day together in school.

27. How those two can talk!

28. What a problem it is!

29. All evening long they converse.

30. Will I ever get my call?

31. How does my sister do it?

Compound Subjects and Predicates *pages 40–41*

Write the sentences. Underline the subjects once and the verbs twice.
Write *compound subject* or *compound predicate* after the sentence.

32. Dogs and cats make good pets and protective
friends.

33. Often a dog barks and runs in circles at unusual
sounds.

34. Sometimes a pet's noise and movements are
bothersome.

35. Good watchdogs yelp and stare at strangers.

36. Aunt Sally's dog howls and cries at the moon.

37. Her dog sounds and looks like a wolf.

38. Its personality and character are those of a
friendly puppy.

39. Cats and kittens are usually quiet.

40. However, felines and canines can be equally noisy.

41. Goldfish, hermit crabs, and garter snakes are quiet pets.

42. They wait, watch, or sleep silently.

Simple and Compound Sentences *pages 42–43*

Write *simple* or *compound* for each sentence below.

43. A handshake and a nod can seal an agreement.

44. Lauren helped her brother clean the garage, and
he helped her rake the leaves.

45. They sealed their agreement with a handshake;
they knew they could trust each other.

46. Sometimes a written contract or letter spells out terms.
47. Mr. Stuber has an agreement with Mrs. Solomon; he is building her new porch.
48. The cost, the time period, and the job are described in writing.
49. Mr. Stuber and Mrs. Solomon have both signed the agreement, and they each have a copy.

Avoiding Sentence Fragments and Run-on Sentences *pages 44–45*

Write whether each word group is a *fragment*, a *run-on sentence*, or a *sentence*. Rewrite each fragment and run-on sentence correctly.

50. Ellen's desk with all the papers on it.
51. What does your desk?
52. The desk looks neat the drawers are messy.
53. Spends a lot of time at her desk.
54. Can never find anything.
55. Lots of papers and letters.
56. Give these folders to Lisa.
57. Does your desk say anything about you?
58. Pencils in cups, papers in trays.
59. She works all day her desk is well organized.
60. Does everything?
61. Do it now.

Nouns *pages 78–79*

Write each noun. Identify it as *common* or *proper*.

62. Youngsters always enjoy games.
63. Scavenger hunts are enjoyed by the children.
64. When a child finds unusual items in funny places, the guests have a good laugh.
65. Even "Hide and Seek" is fun.
66. Chasing friends across the yard makes people giggle.
67. On Saturday there was a wonderful party.
68. Although Liu was thirteen, the games at his birthday party were children's games.
69. The neighbors up and down Elm Street heard the laughter.

Singular and Plural Nouns   pages 86–89

Copy each noun and write its plural form. If there is no plural form,
write *none*.

70. physics
71. New Zealander
72. wharf
73. lady
74. inch
75. moose
76. grocery
77. turkey
78. tax
79. country

80. lottery
81. aunt
82. blueberry
83. handkerchief
84. zigzag
85. senator
86. goose
87. tomato
88. auto
89. fox

90. tragedy
91. piano
92. loss
93. leaf
94. monkey
95. foot
96. twenty
97. melon
98. cupful
99. chief of police

Possessive Nouns   pages 90–91

Label each noun *singular possessive* or *plural possessive*.

100. monkeys'
101. men's
102. children's
103. animals'
104. zoo's
105. Henry's
106. student's
107. week's

108. Morrises'
109. professor's
110. consumers'
111. communities'
112. magazine's
113. classrooms'
114. crowd's
115. nieces'

Appositives   pages 92–93

Write the sentences. Draw one line under the appositive in each
sentence. Draw two lines under the word or words it explains.

116. The Famous People Players, a group of puppeteers, use black light.

117. Black light, a Japanese invention, is made up of ultraviolet rays.

118. Fluorescent colors, shades of special intensity, cover puppets.

119. The puppeteers wear black, a color invisible under black light.

120. Puppets, the center of attention, seem to come alive.

121. The puppeteers, true professionals, must practice their routines.

122. At the finale, the end of the show, the audience applauds loudly.

123. The Famous People Players, performers from Canada, make their
    audiences happy.

UNIT

3

Giving Instructions

If you had lived in the year 450 B.C. and had wanted to catch a crocodile, you could have followed the instructions in the "best-seller" of that time—a book by the Greek historian Herodotus (hi·räd'ə·təs). Today you could read a translation of that very same book and follow the same instructions.

The rules for writing good instructions are the same today as they were in ancient times. Instructions and directions have to be clear, complete, accurate, and useful to the people who will use them. When you read instructions, you expect them to be in a logical order. You want to know what materials or tools you will need.

When the editors of *Reader's Digest* decided to publish instructions on how to care for a baby bird that has fallen from its nest, they had to be sure to explain the entire process. They knew it was important to list all of the materials a person would need in order to provide the necessary care. They had to determine which tasks should be carried out immediately and which could be performed after the primary care was completed. Then they had to put the steps in a logical order.

Think about something you know how to do well or about a place where, even if blindfolded, you could find your way. In this unit you will learn to write a how-to paragraph that explains something you know well.

Reading with a Writer's Eye
How-to Paragraph

In everyday life we often need to follow instructions to complete a task or follow directions to get from one place to another. Instructions and directions are important sets of information that relate processes. Both good instructions and good directions have two important elements: specific order and precise language.

This selection explains how to care for a baby bird that has fallen from its nest. As you read, pay close attention to the order and the language of the explanation. Notice the importance of order and clear details in giving instructions.

Caring for a Baby Bird

by the editors of *Reader's Digest*

Occasionally a fledgling falls from its nest or is orphaned. If you find a young bird on the ground, try to return it to its nest or a nearby perch. Should this prove impossible, the first thing to provide is warmth—tiny birds are very susceptible to pneumonia. A small box of the type in which strawberries are sold, lined with tissues, makes a good emergency nest. If the bird's feathers have not come in yet, place the box on a heating pad set to *Low*. Begin feedings as soon as the chick is set up in its new nest. Start with warm milk sweetened with a bit of sugar and thickened with baby cereal. Feed with a medicine dropper at 15-minute intervals until the bird regains its strength, then about once each hour. Night feeding is not necessary. When the bird is old enough to swallow easily, change the diet to bits of mashed fruit, hard-boiled egg yolk, and lean ground beef. Never feed a young bird water—it could choke. When the bird can eat on its own, set a little water nearby in a saucer.

Respond

1. Briefly describe how you would care for a bird that has fallen from its nest.
2. What is the purpose of a set of instructions?

Discuss

3. What two types of information does the writer include in a set of instructions?
4. Why is order important in writing instructions? Why is the language in good instructions clear and precise?

Thinking As a Writer
Analyzing a How-to Paragraph

A **how-to paragraph** explains how to do something or how to get somewhere. Good instructions list materials and tools necessary to complete a process. Good directions tell both direction and distance. In both kinds of explanation, it is necessary to arrange the steps in the proper sequence. Often, words called transitional expressions will connect steps.

Begin feedings as soon as the chick is set up in its new nest. Start with warm milk sweetened with a bit of sugar and thickened with baby cereal. Feed with a medicine dropper at 15-minute intervals until the bird regains its strength, then about once each hour. Night feeding is not necessary. When the bird is old enough to swallow easily, change the diet to bits of mashed fruit, hard-boiled egg yolk, and lean ground beef.

A **topic sentence** names a process to be explained. A **list of materials** may be included as part of the topic sentence.

Detail sentences list steps in the process in chronological order. Time-order words are used.

Discuss

1. What process does the paragraph explain?
2. What materials would someone need to carry out these instructions?
3. Are the instructions easy to follow? What makes them easy or difficult to understand?

Try Your Hand

1. Name the Process Write a topic sentence for each how-to paragraph.

First, collect several grains—such as cornmeal, rice, and millet—some peanut butter, and a pine cone. Then, mix the grains into the peanut butter and smear the mixture on the pine cone. Finally, tie a strong string around the pine cone and attach it to a tree branch. Soon, you will see many birds enjoying what you have made.

2. First, put on heavy gloves to protect your hands from the spines. Next, gather some prickly-pear pads (the big, flat, paddle-shaped parts). Ask a parent or another adult to burn off the spines. He or she can use a sharp knife to slice through the outer husk. The pulpy inside is good to eat raw or cooked.

3. First, look at the sky on a clear night to find the Big Dipper. Then, identify the front lip of the cup. Trace an imaginary line through those two stars. Start with the bottom of the dipper, and, using the front edge of the dipper as a guide, move along about five times the length of the front edge of the dipper. At the end of this line you will find Polaris, the North Star.

B. List Materials   Look back at the three sets of directions. Make a list of the materials you would need for each activity.

C. Check Transitional Expressions   Find the transitional expressions in the three paragraphs. If necessary, use the *Writer's Notebook* to identify them. How do they improve the instructions?

D. Read and Talk About a How-to Paragraph   Read another how-to paragraph. Identify each part. Briefly restate the directions. Tell whether they are easy or difficult to follow.

Writer's Notebook

Collecting Transitional Expressions
Did you notice the transitional expressions *first* and *then* and the direction word *start* in the paragraphs? Transitional expressions help writing move smoothly from one point to another. Some words, such as *finally* and *next,* show order. Others, like *start, trace,* and *move,* give commands or directions. Reread all the models and record transitional expressions in your *Writer's Notebook.* Try to use these kinds of words to connect sentences when you write.

Thinking As a Writer
Connecting Ideas in Sequence

In a good how-to paragraph, a writer presents events in chronological, or time, order. After writing the topic sentence, the writer visualizes, or pictures, the process in his or her mind, like a kind of movie.

Here are the five steps of the writer's "movie" about how to dry flowers.

Step 1 Begin on dry day.	Step 2 Cut the flowers.	Step 3 Strip leaves.	Step 4 Tie in bunches.	Step 5 Hang downward in dry place.

Read the paragraph below. The writer added time-order words to the five steps to make the ideas flow smoothly.

> Drying flowers for long-lasting bouquets is simple if you begin on a dry day. First, cut the flowers you wish to dry, leaving the stems at least 10 inches long. Second, strip the leaves from the lower part of the stem. Then, tie the flowers firmly in medium-size bunches. Finally, hang the bunches head downward in a warm, dry place with good air circulation.

As you write your how-to paragraph, be sure to arrange events in chronological order and to link them with transitional expressions.

Writer's Guide

To write a how-to paragraph, good writers

- identify the process in a topic sentence.
- make a "movie" in their minds, showing the steps of the process.
- write the steps in the order in which they "see" them.
- make sure the sequence is complete from beginning to end.
- use time-order words to make the sequence clear.

Discuss

Why is proper sequencing important in a how-to paragraph?

Try Your Hand

Identify Sequence Reread the selection about the baby bird. Draw the sequence as the writer might have visualized it, using the step-by-step method shown above. Compare your sequence with that of a partner.

Developing the Writer's Craft
Using Precise Language

Because writers of how-to paragraphs are giving instructions that others must follow, they must record accurately the proper sequence of events. To give an exact set of instructions, a good writer uses precise words. Read the paragraph again on how to dry flowers. Notice the underlined phrases.

Drying flowers for long-lasting bouquets is simple if you begin on a dry day. First, cut the flowers you wish to dry, leaving the stems at least 10 inches long. Second, strip the leaves from the lower part of the stem. Then, tie the flowers firmly in medium-size bunches. Finally, hang the bunches head downward in a warm, dry place with good air circulation.

The writer carefully chose the underlined words to instruct the reader. The information tells exactly how to act to make the process successful. Each precise phrase gives the reader a clear mental picture of what to do and how to do it.

When you write your how-to paragraph, try to capture on paper exactly what should happen. Use precise words to help readers picture the process.

Discuss

1. Look at sentences four and five in the paragraph. What precise words did the writer use? What mental picture or pictures do you get when you read the two sentences?
2. Why is it important for a how-to paragraph to be clear and accurate?

Try Your Hand

Use Precise Words   Imagine that you are going on a canoe trip. Write a topic sentence and four detail sentences for a how-to paragraph about preparing for the trip. Use precise words.

1 Prewriting
How-to Paragraph

Writer's Guide

Prewriting Checklist
- ☑ Brainstorm topics.
- ☑ Select a topic.
- ☑ Think about your audience and your purpose.
- ☑ List the materials and steps in the process. Put the steps into sequence.
- ☑ Connect the steps with time-order words.

Leah, a student at Pike's Peak Middle School, wanted to write a how-to paragraph for her classmates. She used the checklist in the **Writer's Guide** to help her plan her paragraph. Look at what she did.

◆ Brainstorming and Selecting a Topic

First, Leah brainstormed and listed processes with which she was familiar. Then, she looked down her list and crossed off topics that might not interest her audience or that her audience might already know about. Next, she asked her dad's advice about the two topics that remained. He helped her to consider some facts she had not thought about before.

Finally, Leah decided to write about how to estimate the temperature according to the frequency of insect noises. She chose this topic because few people would know how to do it and her classmates would probably find it interesting and fun. Leah knew she could easily describe this process because she had used it during her last vacation.

1. making blueberry muffins
2 giving directions to Grandmother's house
3. telling temperature by insect activity
4. making hand-printed greeting cards

Discuss

1. Look at each topic Leah crossed off her list. Why do you think she didn't choose it?
2. If Leah had been writing a how-to paragraph for her art class, which topic do you think she might have chosen? Why?

◆ Gathering Information

After Leah selected her topic, she gathered information for her writing. She made two lists, one of materials and the other of steps.

Steps

count the number of times the
   cricket chirps in 14 seconds

add 40 to total, result is
   degrees Fahrenheit

find a chirping cricket make
   sure it's not a grasshopper

listen to katydid's call

check chart to find
   temperature Fahrenheit

listen carefully

Materials

chirping cricket or singing
   katydid

watch with second hand

Kate = 58 degrees

Kay-tee = 65 degrees

Katy-did = 72 degrees

Katy-did-it = 78 degrees or more

look for katydids

Discuss

1. Why do you think Leah recorded her information this way?
2. Is Leah's information well organized? Explain your answer.
3. What other information might be important to Leah's explanation?

◆ Organizing Information

After Leah had gathered her information, she organized her lists. First she made a three-part chart, seen below and on the next page. Next she filled in the "Topic" and "Materials" sections.

Topic

How to estimate the temperature according to the frequency of insect noises.

Then she pictured the process in her mind as she listed the steps in chronological order.

> ## Materials
> chirping cricket or singing katydid
>
> a watch with a second hand
>
> ## Steps
> find a chirping cricket—make sure it's not a grasshopper
>
> count the number of times the cricket chirps in 14 seconds
>
> add 40 to total—result is in degrees Fahrenheit
>
> ### Or
> find a katydid
>
> listen to syllables of
>
>   katydid's call
>
> check chart to find the
>
>   temperature Fahrenheit
>
> | | |
> |---|---|
> | Kate—58 degrees | |
> | Kay-tee—65 degrees | |
> | Katy-did—72 degrees | |
> | Katy-did-it—78 degrees or more | |

Discuss

1. How did Leah change the order of the steps?
2. Why did Leah separate the steps for the cricket from the steps for the katydid?

Try Your Hand

Now plan a how-to paragraph of your own.

A. Brainstorm and Select a Topic   Brainstorm a list of interesting topics that you know well. Think about each topic and your audience.

- Cross out topics that are processes everyone knows how to do.
- Cross out topics that will not interest your audience.
- Cross out topics that you do not know enough about.
- Circle the best topic left as the topic of your paragraph.

B. List Materials and Steps   List the materials and the steps necessary for your process. Do not stop to arrange them in a particular order.

C. Organize the Information   Make a chart to organize your information. Picture the process in your mind, and put the steps in sequence. Check to be sure you have left nothing out.

 Save your lists and your chart in your *Writer's Notebook*. You will use them when you draft your how-to paragraph.

WRITING PROCESS

2 Drafting
How-to Paragraph

Writer's Guide

Drafting Checklist

☑ Use your lists and chart for ideas.

☑ Name the process in your topic sentence.

☑ Write detail sentences, listing the materials and putting the steps in chronological order.

☑ Use time order words.

Before Leah started to draft her how-to paragraphs, she thought about a way to explain the process she had chosen. Using her chart, Leah followed the checklist in the **Writer's Guide** to draft her paragraphs. Look at what she wrote.

> There are two easy ways to estimate the temperature by listening to insects. One way uses a cricket; the other uses a singing katydid. Katydids may be found in long grass or fields, anyplace you might expect to find grasshoppers. Crickets may be found in damp, dark places.

Discuss

1. Look at Leah's topic sentence. What process is she describing?
2. Did Leah write a good introduction to her explanation? Explain. What is another way she could have introduced her explanation?

Try Your Hand

Now you are ready to draft a how-to paragraph.

A. Review Your Information Think about the information you gathered and organized in the last lesson. Decide whether you need more information. If so, gather it.

B. Think About Your TAP Remember that your task is to write a how-to paragraph. Your purpose is to explain the process you selected to your audience.

C. Write Your First Draft Use the **Drafting Checklist** to write your how-to paragraph. If you think it will help make your explanation clearer, include a chart or a diagram with your paragraph.

When you write your draft, just put all your ideas on paper. Do not worry about spelling, punctuation, or grammar. You can correct the draft later.

Task: What?
Audience: Who?
Purpose: Why?

Save your first draft in your *Writer's Notebook*. You will use it when you revise your how-to paragraph.

3 Responding and Revising
How-to Paragraph

Writer's Guide

Revising Checklist

☑ Read your how-to paragraph to yourself or to a partner.

☑ Think about your audience and your purpose. Add or cut information.

☑ Be sure that your how-to paragraph is in chronological order.

☑ Be sure your words are as clear and precise as possible.

Leah used the checklist in the **Writer's Guide** to revise her how-to paragraphs. Look at what she did in the first part.

◆ Checking Information

Leah decided to add a word describing the cricket. To show this, she used the mark ∧ . She also decided to cut a sentence because it didn't explain the process. To take it out, she used this mark ℓ .

◆ Checking Organization

Leah wanted to move a sentence that was out of place. She used this mark ⌃ to move it.

◆ Checking Language

When Leah checked her second paragraph, one sentence was not very precise. She used this mark ⌒ to correct it.

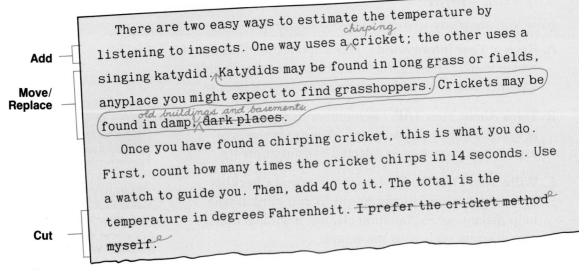

Add — There are two easy ways to estimate the temperature by listening to insects. One way uses a ⌄*chirping* cricket; the other uses a singing katydid. ∧Katydids may be found in long grass or fields, anyplace you might expect to find grasshoppers. Crickets may be

Move/Replace — found in damp, *old buildings and basements.* ∧dark places.

Once you have found a chirping cricket, this is what you do. First, count how many times the cricket chirps in 14 seconds. Use a watch to guide you. Then, add 40 to it. The total is the temperature in degrees Fahrenheit. ~~I prefer the cricket method~~

Cut — ~~myself.~~

Discuss

1. In what way do Leah's replacement words make her work more precise?
2. How does the new order of the sentences improve the paragraph?

Try Your Hand

Now revise your first draft.

A. Read Your First Draft   As you read your how-to paragraph, think about your audience and your purpose. Read your how-to paragraph silently or to a partner to see if it is complete and well organized. Ask yourself or a partner the questions in the box.

Responding and Revising Strategies

✔ Respond
Ask yourself or a partner:

- Have I included all the information that should be in the explanation?

- Is all the information important?

- Are all details precise and clear?

- Are the steps arranged in chronological order? Did I use transitional expressions to indicate the order of steps?

- Does each sentence in my explanation add something to its meaning?

✔ Revise
Try these solutions:

- Scan your chart and **add** any missing information.

- **Cut** information that is not important.

- **Replace** vague details with ones that are more precise. See the **Revising Workshop** on page 120.

- **Move** any material that is out of the proper sequence. **Add** transitional expressions. See the **Writer's Thesaurus** at the back of the book.

- **Cut** unnecessary information or **add** information to complete the explanation.

B. Make Your Changes   If the answer to any question in the box is *no*, try the solution. Use the **Editor's Marks** to show your changes.

C. Review Your How-to Paragraph Again   Decide whether there is anything else you want to revise. Keep revising your how-to paragraph until you feel it is well organized and complete.

EDITOR'S MARKS

∧ Add something.

✂ Cut something.

↻ Move something.

∧ Replace something.

Save your revised how-to paragraph in your *Writer's Notebook*. You will use it when you proofread your how-to paragraph.

Revising Workshop
Avoiding Wordy Language

In a how-to paragraph good writers use as few words as possible to relate their message. They avoid using wordy language. The following sentences are from a set of directions for making a special kind of clock. Notice the underlined phrases in the first sentence.

1. To make a <u>potato-powered</u> clock <u>that runs on power from two potatoes,</u> begin by inserting an electrode into each potato.
2. To make a potato-powered clock, begin by inserting an electrode into each of two potatoes.

In the first sentence the writer used wordy language. The second underlined phrase is a long-winded repetition of the first underlined phrase. In the second sentence the writer says the same thing in fewer words.

Practice

A. Read each sentence. Write the wordy language that you find.

1. If you want to get to the restaurant called Deedee's Diner from Central Middle School, follow these directions.
2. First, begin by walking south on Elm Street, watching for the R & J Gas Station that you will see on the left.
3. Walk past the gas station, continuing straight on your way for three blocks.
4. You will pass a restaurant called Pizza Patio on the first corner and a dance studio called Lindy's Dance Studio on the second.
5. Use the special pedestrian walkway labeled Pedestrian Walkway to avoid the construction work in the last block.
6. You will be standing on a corner near a grocery store that is called Ken's Food Market.
7. Turn right and continue to walk past three buildings until you come to Number 407. You will be at Deedee's Diner.

B. Revise the sentences in **A**. Take out the words you underlined, or replace them with fewer words that mean the same thing. Write the directions in paragraph form.

4 Proofreading
How-to Paragraph

After Leah revised her how-to paragraphs, she used the checklist in the **Writer's Guide** and the **Editor's Marks** to proofread them. Look at what she did.

Writer's Guide

Proofreading Checklist

- ☑ Check for errors in capitalization.
- ☑ Check for errors in punctuation.
- ☑ Check to see that all your paragraphs are indented.
- ☑ Check for errors in grammar.
- ☑ Circle any words you think are misspelled. Find out how to spell them correctly. See **How to Use a Dictionary** in the *Study Skills* section at the back of this book.
- ⇒ For proofreading help, use the **Writer's Handbook.**

temperature
¶ Katydids only tell the (tempurtor) in a certain
katydid
range. first, listen to the chirp of the (kaydid.)

Note the syllables of its song carefully. Next,

find them on the chart. Then, read the
temperature
(temperatour) in degrees fahrenheit.

Discuss

1. Look at Leah's proofread how-to paragraph. What kinds of mistakes did she make?
2. Why did she capitalize the word *Fahrenheit?*
3. What do Leah's spelling errors tell you about the importance of proofreading?

EDITOR'S MARKS

- ≡ Capitalize.
- ⊙ Add a period.
- ∧ Add something.
- ⋏ Add a comma.
- ⋁⋁ Add quotation marks.
- ✄ Cut something.
- ⋀ Replace something.
- ～tr Transpose.
- ◯ Spell correctly.
- ¶ Indent paragraph.
- ／ Make a lowercase letter.

Try Your Hand

Proofread Your How-to Paragraph   Now use the checklist in the **Writer's Guide** and the **Editor's Marks** to proofread your how-to paragraph.

Save your corrected how-to paragraph in your *Writer's Notebook.* You will use it when you publish your how-to paragraph.

5 Publishing
How-to Paragraph

Leah made a clean copy of her how-to paragraph and checked it to be sure it was complete. You can find Leah's how-to paragraph on page 40 of the **Writer's Handbook.** Then she and her classmates published their how-to paragraphs by reading them aloud to their classmates. Here's how Leah and her classmates published their how-to paragraphs.

1. They practiced reading their how-to paragraphs aloud so that they were prepared to present them to the class. Students who planned to use charts or other visual aids practiced pointing to them at appropriate times.
2. They read their how-to paragraphs, speaking slowly and distinctly. They used their voices to emphasize key words and phrases. They pointed to their charts, diagrams, or illustrations when appropriate.
3. Leah and her classmates answered questions. Then each student invited a partner to repeat the instructions. This let the writer know how well he or she had spoken and how well the audience had listened.

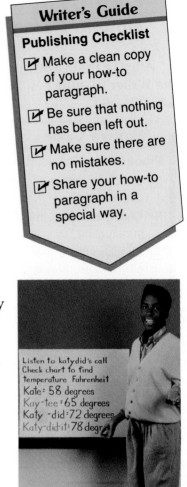

Listen to katydid's call
Check chart to find
temperature Fahrenheit
Kate = 58 degrees
Kay-tee = 65 degrees
Katy -did = 72 degrees
Katy-did-it = 78 degrees

Discuss

What might happen if the instructions in a how-to paragraph were not clear, accurate, complete, and in chronological order?

Try Your Hand

Publish Your How-to Paragraph   Follow the checklist in the **Writer's Guide.** Then read your how-to paragraph aloud to the class, or try one of these ideas for sharing how-to paragraphs.

- Collect the paragraphs, including any charts or illustrations. Use them as a class resource.
- Trade paragraphs with a partner. Try to follow each other's explanation. Talk with your partner about the results.
- Make the paragraphs into a booklet to display in the school library.

WRITING PROCESS

Listening and Speaking
Tips on How to Give and Listen to Directions

Giving Directions

1. Plan what you are going to say. Make sure your directions are complete, accurate, clear, and in chronological order. Do not pause too often; your listener may have a more difficult time following the sequence that way.
2. If you are giving directions on how to get to a certain place, present the simplest route even if it isn't the shortest.
3. Use key words. In giving directions, use direction words (*right*, *left*, *north*, *south*). Include distances (*3 blocks*, *¼ mile*). Mention visual landmarks (*the large brick church, Route 144*). Emphasize important words with your voice. Use words that indicate time order—*first*, *second*, *next*, *last*, and so on.
4. If possible, use a map when you give directions. If you don't have a map, draw one. Include roads and important landmarks. Always start with your current location, pointing it out clearly.
5. Be sure your listener understands the directions. If he or she does not, speak more slowly and review the directions once more.
6. If you are unsure of the directions, tell the person where he or she might get more help (a local gas station, a store, or a church, for example).

Listening to Directions

1. When you request directions, state clearly:
   * exactly where you want to go.
   * how you are traveling (by bicycle, on foot, by car or bus).
   * whether or not you know the area.
2. Listen carefully. Pay close attention to key distances, direction words, and landmarks. If possible, write down the directions.
3. Repeat the directions to make sure you understand them.
4. Thank the person for his or her help. If you are still unsure of the directions, you might try to find a gas station that has a local map.

Writing in the Content Areas

Use what you learned to write another how-to paragraph.

Writer's Guide

When you write, remember the stages of the Writing Process.

* Prewriting
* Drafting
* Responding and Revising
* Proofreading
* Publishing

Health

Write down your favorite healthful recipe and share it with your classmates. List all of the necessary ingredients and utensils needed to follow the recipe. Write the steps of explanation clearly and in order. If you wish, and if your teacher approves, prepare the food and bring it to class.

Art

Write an explanation of how to draw a certain popular comic strip character (or make up a character). Explain the process from creating the character to drawing the finished cartoon we see in a newspaper. List the creative as well as the practical steps in the process. If possible, find out from a professional cartoonist whether your explanation is accurate.

Physical Education

Write clear instructions for playing a simple game. It can be a game everyone knows or a game you make up. Then, have your friends play the game using your instructions. Are the instructions clear and accurate? If not, ask the players to help you revise them. Play the game again with the rewritten instructions. Is it easier to play now?

Social Studies

Write directions on how to get from your school to the nearest museum. Draw a map to show the route. Include all geographic landmarks—schools, churches, parks. If convenient, send out a scouting party to see if they can find the museum by using the map. Estimate the amount of time it should take. When the party returns, find out whether the directions were satisfactory.

CONNECTING

WRITING ⬌ LANGUAGE

One of the best ways to learn how to do something is to read or listen to a "how-to" explanation. Read the poem "To Become an Archer," by José Garcia Villa. Decide whether you could follow these instructions.

> To become an archer,
> You should be for two
> Years under a loom and not blink
> Your eyes when the shuttle
> Shoots back and forth:—
>
> Then for three years
> With your face turned
> To the light, make a louse climb
> Up a silk thread: When the
> Louse appears to be
>
> Larger than a wheel,
> Than a mountain; when
> It hides the sun: you may then
> Shoot . You will hit it right
> In the middle of the heart.

◆ **Verbs in a How-to Explanation**   The highlighted words are verbs. They describe a series of actions. Showing action and being are important functions of verbs. When you write a how-to explanation, your choice of verbs may determine how well your audience understands you.

◆ **Language Focus: Verbs**   The following lessons will help you use different kinds of verbs in your own writing.

1 Verbs

◆ A **verb** expresses action or being.
◆ A **linking verb** connects the subject to a word or words in the predicate.

Verbs tell what the subject of a sentence does or is. The verb is the most important word in the predicate. Two types of verbs are action verbs and being verbs.

1. Mr. Martinez coaches our team.   action verb

2. He is a wonderful coach.   being verb

Most verbs are action verbs. **Action verbs** express physical or mental action. Physical action can be seen. Mental action occurs only in the mind.

3. Mia hit a home run.   physical action

4. I believed she could do it.   mental action

Some verbs express a state of being. These verbs do not indicate action. They tell what the subject is, not what it does. Being verbs are often linking verbs. A **linking verb** links, or connects, the subject to words in the predicate that identify or describe it.

Some Forms of *To Be*
am, is, are, was, were, will be, has been, have been, can be

Other Linking Verbs
seem, appear, grow, become, look, feel, stay, smell, taste, sound

5. Mia is excited.   linking verb

6. Everyone seems a little overwhelmed.   linking verb

The chart shows some common linking verbs.

Some verbs can be used both as action verbs and as linking verbs. To determine whether a verb is a linking verb, replace it with a form of the verb *be*. If it makes sense, the verb is a linking verb.

The juice *tastes* sweet.   The juice is sweet.   linking verb
She *tastes* the juice.   She is the juice.   action verb

Link to Speaking and Writing
You can paint a vivid picture if you use strong action verbs. Why is *bunted* more vivid than *hit lightly*? What other verbs could you use?

bunted
Mia hit the ball lightly.
Mia bunted.

Guided Practice

A. Identify the verb in each sentence.

1. Today Miguel ran home quickly.
2. He hurried with his good news.
3. The coach selected him for the team.
4. Suddenly Miguel appears taller!
5. He is proud of himself.

B. 6.–10. Identify the verbs in **A** as action verbs or linking verbs.

THINK AND REMEMBER

• Remember that **verbs** express action or being.

• Remember that **action verbs** express physical or mental action.

• Remember that **linking verbs** connect the subject with words in the predicate that identify or describe it.

Independent Practice

C. Identifying Verbs Write the verb. Write *action* or *linking* after it.

11. Mildred ("Babe") Didrikson lived in Texas.

MODEL⟩ lived—action

12. Young Babe Didrikson earned her nickname with home runs.
13. In the 1930's, Babe became an All-American basketball player.
14. During the off-season she trained in track-and-field events.
15. She appeared successful beyond belief.
16. Babe's accomplishments are legendary.

D. Revising: Replacing Verbs Use your **Writer's Thesaurus** to help replace each underlined word or phrase with a stronger verb. Write the new sentences.

17. Connie's skiing will surprise you.

MODEL⟩ Connie's skiing will astonish you.

18. Last year she broke her leg.
19. How did she harm herself?
20. The crowd looks at her tricks.
21. She explains her technique.
22. Her brothers play in the snow.

Application — Writing

A Character Sketch As a spectator at an athletic event, you may often wonder about the qualities that make a good athlete. Write a character sketch that describes the attributes you admire in an athlete. Use vivid verbs to bring these qualities to life. If you need help writing a character sketch, see page 54 of the **Writer's Handbook.**

2 Main Verbs and Helping Verbs

FOCUS

◆ The **main verb** is the most important verb in a verb phrase.
◆ A **helping verb** works with the main verb to express action or being.

A **verb phrase** is made up of a main verb and helping verbs. The main verb is the most important verb in the phrase. Other verbs in a verb phrase are helping verbs. They help the main verb make its statement. A helping verb always comes before the main verb.

1. Brad is hanging his campaign posters.   **verb phrase**

A verb phrase can have more than one helping verb.

2. The election will be held on Tuesday.   **verb phrase**

Some Common Helping Verbs				
am	be	had	did	have
is	was	can	will	might
are	been	has	should	do

A verb or verb phrase can act as a main verb in one sentence and as a helping verb in another.

3. Janine is here today.   **main verb**

4. She is speaking at the assembly.   **helping verb**

Link to Writing

Sometimes such words as *not, never, finally,* or *already* interrupt a verb phrase. An *interrupter* separates the verbs, but it is not a verb.

Guided Practice

A. Identify each verb phrase.

  1. Bella has been campaigning for class president.
  2. She might forget her lines during speeches.
  3. Sometimes her voice will fail.
  4. This year could have been her third misfortune.
  5. Bella, however, has been elected!

B. 6.–10.   Identify the main verb and the helping verbs in each verb phrase in **A.**

THINK AND REMEMBER

◆ Remember that **main verbs** and **helping verbs** go together to express action or being.

Independent Practice

C. Identifying Verb Phrases   Write each verb phrase. Do not include interrupters.

11. Tom has not held a class office.
MODEL▷ has held

12. Tom's sister, Sara, has already completed high school.
13. Sara is now applying to colleges.
14. She has been visiting colleges on her vacations.
15. You may have noticed the college catalogues at their house.
16. For her applications, Sara must write several essays.
17. The schools will finally send their decisions this spring.
18. Will the results be worth the effort?

D. 19.–26. Identifying Main Verbs   Write the main verbs in **C.**
MODEL▷ **19.** held

E. Adding Helping Verbs   Complete these sentences by adding helping verbs to each verb in parentheses ( ) in order to make a verb phrase. Use a variety of helping verbs.

27. You _____ for a class office. (run)
MODEL▷ You can run for a class office.
28. First, you _____ if you want to run for office. (decide)
29. Then, you _____ your goals for the office. (list)
30. Next, you _____ your beliefs to your classmates. (relate)
31. You _____ posters and flyers to distribute. (create)
32. During the campaign you _____ your staff carefully. (manage)
33. You _____ not _____. (win)
34. You _____, however, _____your talents well. (use)

Application — Writing and Speaking

A Persuasive Essay   Imagine that you are running for a school or class office. Write a campaign speech telling what office you seek and why your classmates should vote for you. Read your speech aloud. Use verb phrases. If you need help writing a persuasive essay, see page 44 of the **Writer's Handbook.**

3 Principal Parts of Regular Verbs

◆ **FOCUS** The principal parts of a verb are the **present,** the **present participle,** the **past,** and the **past participle.**

Each verb has four principal parts: the present, the present participle, the past, and the past participle. You use the principal parts of a verb to form the tenses. The principal parts express the time of a particular action or state of being. Notice that the present participle and the past participle are used with helping verbs, as shown on this chart.

Principal Parts of Regular Verbs

Present	Present Participle	Past	Past Participle
play(s)	(is, are) playing	played	(have, has, had) played
march(es)	(is, are) marching	marched	(have, has, had) marched
live(s)	(is, are) living	lived	(have, has, had) lived
shop(s)	(is, are) shopping	shopped	(have, has, had) shopped

Many verbs are regular. The past and past participle forms of regular verbs are the same, as in *played.*

- Make the past and past participle of regular verbs by adding *ed* to the present form, as in *marched.* Add *d* if the present form already ends in *e,* as in *lived.*
- Make the present participle of regular verbs by adding *ing* to the present form, as in *playing* and *marching.*
- Sometimes you need to double a final consonant or drop a final *e* before adding an ending, as in *shopped* or *living.*

Guided Practice

A. Tell whether the underlined verb or verb phrase is in the *present,* the *present participle,* the *past,* or the *past participle* form.

1. Pablo Casals <u>played</u> the cello most of his life.
2. He <u>had started</u> lessons at age ten in Spain.
3. People still <u>enjoy</u> his music.
4. His reputation <u>is living</u> on.
5. Casals <u>has appeared</u> in theaters worldwide.

Independent Practice

B. Identifying Principal Parts of Verbs   Write each verb or verb phrase. After the verb, write *present, present participle, past,* or *past participle* in parentheses ( ).

6. Music has existed throughout history.

MODEL⟩ has existed   (past participle)

7. Ancient Egyptians played stringed instruments.
8. Pictures of the instruments decorate Egyptian tombs.
9. Today's traditional orchestra uses woodwinds, strings, and percussion instruments.
10. Modern musicians are adding electronic instruments.

C. Writing Verb Forms   Copy each verb and write its present form.

11. whistling

MODEL⟩ whistle

12. created	16. deciding	20. hoping	24. amusing
13. picked	17. humming	21. dancing	25. fixing
14. strummed	18. hopped	22. composing	26. saving
15. rehearsing	19. searched	23. called	

D. Writing Principal Parts of Verbs   Make four columns. Under each column, write the principal parts of each verb.

27. MODEL⟩

Present	Present Participle	Past	Past Participle
whistle	(is, are) whistling	whistled	(have, has, had) whistled

28. listen	31. close	34. stop	37. create
29. work	32. rain	35. live	38. snow
30. laugh	33. love	36. move	39. thrill

Application — Writing

A Record Jacket   Imagine that your school orchestra has signed a recording contract. Write a paragraph for the record or tape cover. Tell the listeners about the musical achievements of the orchestra. Use the principal parts of each verb correctly.

4 Principal Parts of Irregular Verbs

◆ An **irregular verb** does not have *ed* or *d* added to the present to form the past or the past participle.

◆ The principal parts of some irregular verbs are formed according to certain patterns.

Many irregular verbs follow a pattern to form their principal parts. To form the present participle of most irregular verbs, add *ing* to the present form. Sometimes you must double the final consonant or drop the final *e* before adding the ending. Notice that the present participle and the past participle are used with helping verbs on this chart.

Present	Present Participle	Past	Past Participle
Group 1			
come(s)	(is, are) coming	came	(have, has, had) come
go(es)	(is, are) going	went	(have, has, had) gone
run(s)	(is, are) running	ran	(have, has, had) run
(Note the vowel change in the past form. The past participle and the present forms are the same or similar.)			
Group 2			
begin(s)	(is, are) beginning	began	(have, has, had) begun
drink(s)	(is, are) drinking	drank	(have, has, had) drunk
ring(s)	(is, are) ringing	rang	(have, has, had) rung
sing(s)	(is, are) singing	sang	(have, has, had) sung
swim(s)	(is, are) swimming	swam	(have, has, had) swum
(Note that the *i* in the present form changes to *a* in the past and *u* in the past participle.)			
Group 3			
bring(s)	(is, are) bringing	brought	(have, has, had) brought
catch(es)	(is, are) catching	caught	(have, has, had) caught
say(s)	(is, are) saying	said	(have, has, had) said
sell(s)	(is, are) selling	sold	(have, has, had) sold
think(s)	(is, are) thinking	thought	(have, has, had) thought
(Note that the past and the past participle forms are the same.)			
Group 4			
burst(s)	(is, are) bursting	burst	(have, has, had) burst
hit(s)	(is, are) hitting	hit	(have, has, had) hit
(Note that present, past, and past participle forms are the same.)			

Guided Practice

A. Tell whether each verb is in *present, present participle, past,* or *past participle* form.

1. bursts	**6.** had rung
2. sold	**7.** had hit
3. rang	**8.** thinks
4. go	**9.** have caught
5. burst	**10.** are beginning

B. 11.–20. Use each verb or verb phrase from **A** in a sentence.

THINK AND REMEMBER

♦ Remember that verbs have four principal parts: present, present participle, past, and past participle.

♦ Use a dictionary to see whether a verb is regular or irregular.

Independent Practice

C. Identifying Verb Forms Write *present, present participle, past,* or *past participle* after each verb.

21. hits

MODEL⟩ present

22. has sold	**25.** was hitting	**28.** drank
23. rang	**26.** had sung	**29.** catches
24. go	**27.** is swimming	**30.** have begun

D. Revising: Writing the Correct Verb Forms Choose the correct verb in parentheses ( ). Write each verb.

31. Liza's telephone (has rang, has rung) often since she left.

MODEL⟩ has rung

32. Last fall Liza (goed, went) to visit her cousin in Vermont even though she (catchs, catches) a cold as soon as the cool weather (begins, begun).

33. Her visit (began, beginned) with a tour of the fall foliage.
34. Liza (had went, had gone) at a beautiful time of year.
35. Later Liza (said, sayed), "I should (have brung, have brought) some canvas to paint the colorful trees."

E. Using Verb Forms   Write each sentence. Use the past or past participle form of the verb in parentheses ( ). Underline the verb or verb phrase in your answer.

36. Stephanie (bring) a notebook to our meeting.
MODEL⟩ Stephanie brought a notebook to our meeting.
37. She had (say) she would interview Liza about her trip to Vermont.
38. Stephanie (think) about what to ask.
39. She wondered if she had (swim) in any lakes or had (run) through any meadows.
40. These ideas had just (burst) into her mind.
41. She (begin) to ask Liza about her trip.

F. Writing Correct Forms of Appropriate Verbs   Write these sentences. Complete each one with an irregular verb from page 132 that fits the sentence. Use the correct form of each verb.

42. Amy _____ to our local animal shelter every day.
MODEL⟩ Amy goes to our local animal shelter every day.
43. Every day she _____ the animals a special treat.
44. At first she _____ the dogs to give them exercise.
45. She would _____ fast just to keep up with them.
46. Then she _____ giving the animals their dinner.
47. Now she _____ to learn grooming.
48. Sometimes while she grooms them, she _____ softly.
49. Lately her joy and enthusiasm _____ to spread.
50. Today three of Amy's classmates _____ their volunteer work at the shelter.

Application—Writing, Listening, and Speaking

An Interview   Suppose that you are able to interview a teacher about his or her career and interests. Write a list of questions that interest you. Use some irregular verbs. Then conduct your interview.

5 More Irregular Verbs

◆ **FOCUS**   Some irregular verbs do not follow a pattern when they change form.

This chart shows more irregular verbs.

Present	Present Participle	Past	Past Participle
Group 5			
eat(s)	(is, are) eating	ate	(have, has, had) eaten
give(s)	(is, are) giving	gave	(have, has, had) given
grow(s)	(is, are) growing	grew	(have, has, had) grown
know(s)	(is, are) knowing	knew	(have, has, had) known
ride(s)	(is, are) riding	rode	(have, has, had) ridden
take(s)	(is, are) taking	took	(have, has, had) taken
write(s)	(is, are) writing	wrote	(have, has, had) written
(Note that the present and past participle forms are similar.)			
Group 6			
break(s)	(is, are) breaking	broke	(have, has, had) broken
choose(s)	(is, are) choosing	chose	(have, has, had) chosen
freeze(s)	(is, are) freezing	froze	(have, has, had) frozen
speak(s)	(is, are) speaking	spoke	(have, has, had) spoken
tear(s)	(is, are) tearing	tore	(have, has, had) torn
wear(s)	(is, are) wearing	wore	(have, has, had) worn
(Note that the past and the past participle forms are similar.)			

Guided Practice

A. Tell whether each verb is in *present*, *present participle*, *past*, or *past participle* form.

1. broke
2. have worn
3. is taking
4. has written
5. have frozen
6. had done
7. flies
8. rode
9. grow
10. have known

B. 11.–20.   Use each verb or verb phrase from **A** in a sentence.

> **THINK AND REMEMBER**
> ◆ Remember that the principal parts of irregular verbs are formed in various ways.

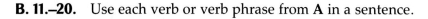

Independent Practice

C. Identifying Verb Forms Write *present*, *present participle*, *past*, or *past participle* after each verb or verb phrase.

21. growing

MODEL present participle

22. wears	**25.** wrote	**28.** are swimming
23. has chosen	**26.** eats	**29.** are growing
24. have frozen	**27.** gave	**30.** had ridden
		31. ate

D. Revising: Correcting Verbs Rewrite each sentence with the correct verb in parentheses ( ).

32. Marie (taked, took) the picture.

MODEL Marie took the picture.

33. Marie (gived, gave) up many movies and snacks to buy her camera.

34. She (has took, has taken) beautiful photographs around school.

35. We students (has spoken, have spoken) about her special talent.

36. Ollie (rode, rided) his horse on a scenic trip, and he borrowed Marie's camera.

37. Marie's camera broke when the horse (throwed, threw) Ollie.

38. The class (had chosed, has chosen) to have a bake sale and buy a new camera for Marie.

E. Using Verb Forms Write the past or past participle form of the verb in parentheses ( ).

39. Mike had (speak) about a similar problem.

MODEL spoken

40. Everyone (write) about an experience he or she had had.

41. Mike (know) what to write about.

42. Recently he (wear) his brother's sweater and (tear) it.

43. Mike has not yet (give) the sweater back to his brother.

44. He had not (speak) to him about the damage.

45. Mike (write) about whether or not to point out the tear.

46. "I have (choose) to tell my brother what I (do)," he said.

Application—Writing

An Apology Imagine that you accidentally ruined something that belonged to a relative or a classmate. Write a note of explanation and apology to give to that person. Use irregular verbs correctly. If you need help writing a friendly letter, see page 59 of the **Writer's Handbook.**

6 Simple Verb Tenses

◆ **FOCUS**   The simple tenses are the present, the past, and the future.

Verb tenses tell when the action of the verb occurs. Verbs express time in the present tense, the past tense, or the future tense.

The **present tense** expresses an action that takes place now. The **past tense** expresses an action that took place at some time in the past. The **future tense** expresses an action that will take place in a time to come.

1. Benny talks to Rob about a history test.   present tense

2. This morning he talked to Carol on the school bus.   past tense

3. Later, Benny will talk about the test with Ed.   future tense

Use these spelling rules to form the present, past, and future tenses.

Present Tense	
• For most verbs, add *s* to the present form.	talk—talks
• When a verb ends in *s, x, z, ch,* or *sh,* add *es.*	switch—switches
• When a verb ends in a consonant plus *y,* change the *y* to *i* and add *es.*	spy—spies
Past Tense	
• For most verbs, add *ed* to the present form.	talk—talked
• When a one-syllable verb ends in a single consonant and that consonant is preceded by a single vowel, double the final consonant before adding *ed.*	hum—hummed
• When a verb ends in *e,* drop the *e* and add *ed.*	serve—served
• When a verb ends in a consonant plus *y,* change the *y* to *i* before adding *ed.*	fry—fried
Future Tense	
• Add the helping verb *will* (or *shall*) to the present form of the verb.	join—will join
	hope—shall hope

Link to Speaking and Writing
If you are in doubt about verb tense, ask yourself these questions:

Is it happening now?
Did it already happen?
Will it happen later?

Guided Practice

A. Tell whether each verb is in the *present, past,* or *future* tense.

1. marched
2. will fly
3. applauded
4. uses
5. whirred
6. will scramble

THINK AND REMEMBER

◆ Remember that **tenses** show time.

◆ Use verb tenses to express time in the present, past, or future.

Independent Practice

B. Identifying Tense   Write each verb or verb phrase. Write the tense in parentheses ( ).

7. will gather

MODEL ⟩ will gather (future)

8. elects
10. will wink
12. chews
9. beeped
11. banished
13. will read

C. Writing Verb Tenses   Write sentences using each verb in the tense shown in parentheses ( ). Use *he* or *she* as the subject.

14. write (future)

MODEL ⟩ She will write a story.

15. shop (past)
17. hope (past)
19. arrive (present)
16. bake (future)
18. reach (present)
20. slip (future)

D. Writing Sentences Using Given Verb Tenses   For each sentence, write the verb using the tense shown in parentheses ( ).

21. New inventions constantly _____. (appear—present)

MODEL ⟩ appear

22. Alexander Graham Bell _____ the telephone in 1876. (invent—past)
23. Today, robots _____ at dangerous jobs in industry. (work—present)
24. In the future we _____ food from the ocean. (produce—future)
25. Centuries ago people _____ of going to the moon. (dream—past)

Application — Writing

A Friendly Letter   Write a letter to a relative. Describe something you did a few days ago and explain how it will affect something you hope to do in the future. Check your verb tenses. If you need help writing a friendly letter, see page 59 of the **Writer's Handbook.**

7 Perfect Verb Tenses

◆ **FOCUS** The perfect tenses are the present perfect, the past perfect, and the future perfect.

Besides the simple tenses, there are also perfect tenses. The **present perfect tense** expresses action that happened at some indefinite time in the past. Form this tense with the helping verb *have* or *has* and the past participle.

1. The Nobel Committee has awarded prizes in literature and physics.

The **past perfect tense** expresses action that started and ended before another action in the past. Form this tense with the helping verb *had* and the past participle.

2. Alfred Nobel had established the prize long before the first one was awarded.

The **future perfect tense** expresses an action that will begin and end before a particular time in the future. Form this tense with the helping verb phrase *will have* and the past participle.

3. By year's end, new winners will have received their awards.

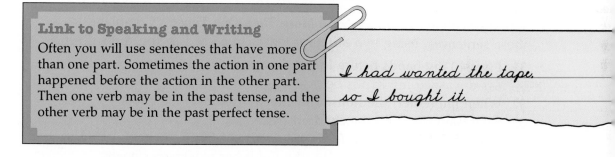

Link to Speaking and Writing
Often you will use sentences that have more than one part. Sometimes the action in one part happened before the action in the other part. Then one verb may be in the past tense, and the other verb may be in the past perfect tense.

I had wanted the tape, so I bought it.

Guided Practice

A. Identify the tense of each verb as *present perfect, past perfect,* or *future perfect.*

1. will have worked
2. had investigated
3. has experimented
4. have voted
5. will have looked
6. has checked

B. 7.–12. Use each verb phrase from **A** in a sentence.

- Use the **present perfect tense** to express an action that occurred at an indefinite time in the past and may still be going on.
- Use the **past perfect tense** to express an action that happened before another past action.
- Use the **future perfect tense** to express an action that will be completed before a stated time in the future.

Independent Practice

C. Identifying Tense   Write the tense of each verb phrase.

13. will have written
MODEL〉 future perfect

14. will have gathered
15. had researched
16. has considered
17. have computed

18. have mastered
19. will have tried
20. has formulated
21. had completed

D. 22.–30. Using Verbs   Use each verb phrase from **C** in a sentence.

22. will have written
MODEL〉 I will have written my essay by next Friday.

E. Writing Sentences with Verbs in More Than One Tense   Complete these sentences, using two different tenses in each. Use the verbs given.

31. I (wash) my hands before I (eat) dinner.
MODEL〉 I had washed my hands before I ate dinner.

32. When Jim (enter) the house, he already (remove) his boots.
33. Sally (say) she (call) the children twice.
34. Mom (expect) stew, but Dad (prepared) spaghetti.
35. Before Mom (go) to the table, she (fold) her newspaper neatly.
36. By the time we (eat) dinner, Rachel already (finish) her homework.
37. When the guests (arrive), I had not even (start) mine.

Application—Writing and Speaking

A Proposal   Imagine that, like Alfred Nobel, you can leave a legacy to future generations. Write a statement that sets down the purpose of your foundation. Use perfect tenses to explain how recipients of your award will be chosen. Read aloud your proposal to your classmates.

8 Be, Have, Do

◆ **FOCUS**   The verbs *be, have,* and *do* are irregular.

In English the verbs *to be, to have,* and *to do* are used more often than any others. These verbs are irregular. You should memorize the forms of irregular verbs. The charts below and on the next page list the tenses of *be, have,* and *do.* A list of all the forms of a verb is a **conjugation.** When you list a verb in this way, you conjugate it.

Conjugation of the Verb *Be*			
Principal Parts: *be, being, was, been*			
	Present	**Past**	**Future**
I	am	was	will be
you	are	were	will be
he, she, it	is	was	will be
we, they	are	were	will be
	Present Perfect	**Past Perfect**	**Future Perfect**
I	have been	had been	will have been
you	have been	had been	will have been
he, she, it	has been	had been	will have been
we, they	have been	had been	will have been

Conjugation of the Verb *Have*			
Principal Parts: *have, having, had, had*			
	Present	**Past**	**Future**
I	have	had	will have
you	have	had	will have
he, she, it	has	had	will have
we, they	have	had	will have
	Present Perfect	**Past Perfect**	**Future Perfect**
I	have had	had had	will have had
you	have had	had had	will have had
he, she, it	has had	had had	will have had
we, they	have had	had had	will have had

Conjugation of the Verb *Do* Principal Parts: *do, doing, did, done*			
	Present	**Past**	**Future**
I	do	did	will do
you	do	did	will do
he, she, it	does	did	will do
we, they	do	did	will do
	Present Perfect	**Past Perfect**	**Future Perfect**
I	have done	had done	will have done
you	have done	had done	will have done
he, she, it	has done	had done	will have done
we, they	have done	had done	will have done

Always use the third-person singular form of the verb (ending in *s*) after *he, she, it,* or a singular noun.

1. He is in class today.

Always use a helping verb with the present or past participle. Never use a helping verb with the simple past tense.

2. They are having a discussion about democracy.

3. Our class has done that, too.

4. We did that already.

Link to Speaking and Writing

Many commonly used contractions are forms of *be, have,* and *do.* To form a contraction, combine two words by leaving out one or more letters. An apostrophe replaces the missing letters.

doesn't
Sam does not want an apple.
Sam doesn't want an apple.

Guided Practice

A. Use the correct form of the verb in parentheses ( ) in the sentence. Give the person, number, and tense of each form you choose.

1. Democracy (be) government by the people and for the people.
2. Some early societies (have) a form of democracy.
3. New England town meetings (be) once ideal democracies.

Independent Practice

B. Identifying Verbs   Write the correct form of the verb in parentheses ( ). Give the person, number, and tense of each form you choose.

4. Our class (have) morning meetings.
MODEL〉 has (third person, singular, present tense)

5. In our class we (have) a democratic process.
6. Sometimes our daily meetings (be) long.
7. We have stayed until everyone (have) a chance to be heard.
8. Sometimes we (do) so much talking that we (have) to stop to take a break.
9. The democratic process (be) sometimes tedious.

C. Using Verbs   Write the correct form of each verb in parentheses ( ).

10. Early Greeks (have) the first word for *democracy*.
MODEL〉 had

11. Modern democracy (have) different forms here and in England.
12. Americans always (have) an elected President and a Congress.
13. Great Britain (be) a monarchy with an elected Parliament.
14. The governing party in some countries (have) complete power.
15. Democracies (be) not perfect, but the ideals (be) just.

D. Writing Sentences   Use each phrase in a sentence. Use contractions where you can.

16. he is not
MODEL〉 He isn't late.

17. they are	**21.** I will be	**24.** they will have had
18. we have done	**22.** we have had	**25.** I am
19. you have been	**23.** they do not	**26.** he has not been
20. they will have done		

Application — Writing

An Opinion   Imagine that your class is voting on the destination for the next class field trip. Write a paragraph that states your choice. Give three reasons. Use forms of *be*, *have*, and *do* correctly. If you need help writing a paragraph, see page 39 of the **Writer's Handbook**.

9 Subject-Verb Agreement

◆ **FOCUS**   A subject and its verb must agree in number.

A verb must agree with its subject in number. **Number** refers to whether a word is singular or plural. In a sentence both subject and verb must be singular or both must be plural. The words in color show agreement.

1. A spacecraft orbits the earth.

2. Astronauts ride in the module.

Remember that in inverted word order, the subject comes after the verb.

3. Where are the rocket motors ?

Use a plural verb with most compound subjects joined by *and*.

4. Power and speed are required to reach the moon.

Use a singular verb with compound subjects that are normally thought of as a unit.

5. Rest and sleep is far from our thoughts.

If a compound subject contains both a singular and a plural subject and uses a conjunction other than *and*, make the verb agree with the subject closer to the verb.

6. The photographs or a headline grabs the public's attention.

When a collective noun stands for one unit, it takes a singular verb.

7. The crowd waits for the lunar landing.

A noun plural in form but singular in meaning takes a singular verb.

8. Today's news is wonderful!

Link to Speaking and Writing

When a phrase separates a subject from a verb, the number of the subject or verb is not affected.

The astronauts, with Mars in view, remain calm.

Guided Practice

A. Make each verb agree with the word in parentheses ( ). Use the present tense.

1. (he) contemplate	**4.** (he) wonder	**7.** (he) speak
2. (she) observe	**5.** (he) note	**8.** (she) look
3. (they) think	**6.** (she) talk	**9.** (they) listen

> **THINK AND REMEMBER**
> ◆ Remember that subjects and verbs must agree in **number.**

Independent Practice

B. Writing Verb Forms Write each verb in the third-person singular present tense and in the third-person plural present tense.

10. do

MODEL⟩ he, she, it does; they do

11. congregate	**14.** pay	**17.** go
12. make	**15.** mix	**18.** move
13. spy	**16.** receive	**19.** come

C. Choosing Verb Forms Write the correct form of the verb in parentheses ( ).

20. She (win, wins) every award.

MODEL⟩ wins

21. Careful scientists (use, uses) the scientific method.

22. A team of researchers always (observe, observes) carefully.

23. The chief scientist and her assistants (create, creates) a theory; then they (test, tests) it.

24. Experiments (prove, proves) or (disprove, disproves) the theory.

25. Mice (help, helps) scientists even more than monkeys (do, does).

26. Scientists (collect, collects) information to reach scientific conclusions.

27. Scientific achievements, whether major or minor, (depend, depends) on the knowledge of atoms.

28. The power of atoms (concern, concerns) the scientific community.

Application — Writing

A Narrative Space travel fires people's imaginations. Write a paragraph that tells why you would or would not like to travel in space. Share it with a classmate.

Building Vocabulary
Homophones and Homographs

Homophones are words that sound the same but have different meanings and different spellings. Find the homophones in the following sentences. Say each sentence aloud to hear which words sound the same. Decide what each word means.

1. Tired of war, the people hoped for peace.
2. Marsha needs a piece of string to finish her project.

Did you notice that *peace* and *piece* sound the same? *Peace* means "quiet order"; *piece* means "a part of something."

Homographs are words that are spelled the same but have different meanings. They are often pronounced differently. Read these sentences.

3. In the army, you never refuse an order.
4. The barge carried the refuse down the river.

Refuse appears in both sentences. In sentence 3 *refuse* means "to decline to do something." In sentence 4 *refuse* means "trash." In your reading, pay close attention to homographs. If you do not know the pronunciation and meaning of these words, you will misunderstand what you read.

As you write, try to use homophones and homographs. Some examples are listed below.

Homophone	Definition	Sample Sentence
close	to shut	Please *close* the door.
clothes	things you wear	All of my *clothes* are in the closet.
coarse	rough	*Coarse* wood can give you splinters.
course	route	The ship was blown off *course*.

Homograph	Definition	Sample Sentence
hide	to conceal	You can *hide* your diary here.
hide	animal skin	A buffalo has a tough *hide*.
present	a gift	I appreciate my birthday *present*.
present	to give	We are proud to *present* this award.

Reading Practice

Read each pair of sentences. Write each homograph and its definition. Then write *same* or *different* to tell how the words are pronounced.

1. a. Horace lost the race by one minute.
   b. Although the issue seems minute, I am upset.
2. a. The wind blew his hat two blocks away.
   b. Wind the kite string around this spool.
3. a. This spoke is so damaged it cannot be repaired.
   b. The audience was silent when Matt spoke.
4. a. The explorer asked his men not to desert him.
   b. Alone in the desert, he managed to reach safety.
5. a. Please record this on tape for me.
   b. This should go on the class record.
6. a. Kim will lead this group of scouts.
   b. This cannon is made of lead.

Writing Practice

Use homophones and homographs to complete the sentences. Some will appear in the chart on the previous page.

7. I took a computer _____ last summer.
8. The score was _____, but we still lost.
9. Before it is refined, grain is very _____.
10. All of the winter _____ are on sale.
11. Our _____, Mrs. Callahan, received a special _____ from the faculty.
12. King Arthur has _____ the battle _____.
13. There was _____ way for him to _____ the outcome.
14. He seemed _____ understand _____ things: winning and losing.
15. The king uttered a _____ when he saw how large the enemy force had _____.

Project

Start a notebook. Divide it into two sections: *Homophones* and *Homographs.* Whenever you read a new book or story, list any homophones or homographs you find. Also, list their meanings and use each word in a sample sentence. Share your entries.

Language Enrichment
Verbs

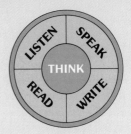

Use what you know about verbs to do these activities.

 Action-word Anagram

Write your first and last names vertically down the left-hand side of a sheet of paper. Then write an action verb that begins with each of the letters. Complete the predicates with phrases that describe you.

Example: J ams at dances
E njoys reading
D evours pizza

S lides in baseball
M asters bass fishing
I nteracts with algebra
T errorizes younger brother
H ugs Grandma

 Call a Lifeguard

You have just fallen into an enormous vat of your favorite soup while touring the McHenry Soup Factory. Use the following linking verbs to help you write your impressions of your experience. Then use the present tense to describe to your classmates what happened.

Linking verbs:
am is are seem appear look
become taste feel smell sound

 And in This Corner...

Write an "eyewitness" description of an important moment in a championship football game, tennis match, ice skating competition, or sport of your choice. Be sure to use plenty of action verbs. Then give your broadcast aloud while one or two of your classmates act out the event.

CONNECTING
LANGUAGE ↔ WRITING

In this unit you learned that verbs show action and link a subject to a predicate. You also discovered that verbs can be regular or irregular and can tell you when the action takes place. You learned to follow certain patterns to write the correct verb tense forms and to check that your subjects and verbs agree.

◆ **Using Verbs in Your Writing**   Knowing how to use verbs effectively will help you make your writing interesting. Pay special attention to the verbs you use as you do these activities.

 Listen Closely!

On the **Building Vocabulary** page you studied homophones and homographs. Use that knowledge in these activities.

   1. Write a sentence that contains at least one example of a homophone. Dictate your sentence to your classmates and have them write it.
   2. Try to use two homographs in a single sentence. Before you begin, use a dictionary to check the word meanings.

 Up, Up, and Away!

Make a paper airplane of your own design. Begin with a square sheet of paper. Then write a "how-to" explanation for each step. Pay special attention to your verbs. Take turns with a partner in reading and revising instructions until they are clear.

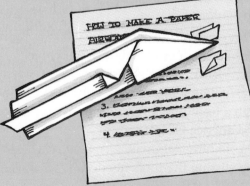

Unit Checkup

Think Back	Think Ahead
◆ What did you learn about writing a how-to paragraph in this unit? What did you do to write one?	◆ How will what you learned about a how-to paragraph help you when you read instructions? ◆ How will knowing how to connect ideas in a sequence help you write instructions?
◆ Look at the writing you did in this unit. How did verbs help you express your ideas?	◆ What is one way you can use verbs to improve your writing?

Analyzing a How-to Paragraph *pages 110 – 111*

Write whether each statement is *true* or *false*.

1. A how-to paragraph does not need a topic sentence.
2. Transitional expressions help a reader connect steps.
3. The list of materials is placed at the end.
4. Steps in a how-to paragraph need to be numbered.
5. Chronological order explains the logical sequence of events.

Connecting Ideas in Sequence *page 112*

Write the letter of the item that correctly completes each sentence.

6. Prepare for writing a how-to paragraph by
   a. seeing a movie about your topic.
   b. picturing the steps.
   c. taking a photo of the finished product.
7. In a how-to paragraph, the writer makes the sequence clearer by
   a. joining commas.
   b. listing the tools needed.
   c. using transitional expressions.

8. The *process* in the paragraph refers to

a. the words chosen.   b. the steps taken.   c. the results given.

9. *Time order* is defined as

a. various appointments.

b. moving left to right or right to left.

c. the order in which things happen.

Using Precise Language   *page 113*

Replace the underlined words with precise words.

10. Bake the cake in a <u>pan</u>.

11. Clean up the <u>place</u> after you have finished.

12. Wear <u>a covering</u> to protect your clothes.

13. Add <u>some</u> salt.

14. Let it boil for <u>a while</u>.

The Writing Process   *pages 114–123*

Write the letter of the item that answers each question.

15. When you plan a how-to paragraph, what should you do first?

a. Choose your audience.

b. List possible topics.

c. Learn something new.

16. How do you choose a topic to write about?

a. Choose something you know nothing about.

b. Choose a topic most people know how to do.

c. Choose a topic interesting to your readers.

17. What might be a good aid when organizing facts?

a. a picture   b. a chart   c. a story map

18. Suppose you are revising, and you find that everything is in correct order, but there are no transitional expressions. What do you do?

a. Don't worry.

b. Use **Editor's Marks** to add transitional expressions.

c. Insert numbers to show order of steps.

Verbs   *pages 126 – 127*

Write the verb. Write *action* or *linking* after it.

19. Lester carves buildings out of balsa wood.

20. His collection resembles the buildings in our town.

21. Last week we had an exhibition of Lester's work.

22. Everyone seemed amazed at its accuracy.

23. In art class Lester gave the students carving lessons.

Main Verbs and Helping Verbs *pages 128–129*

Write each verb phrase. Underline the main verb.

24. Victoria has read a book or a play each week during the summer vacation.

25. She will be an invaluable resource for reading recommendations.

26. Oscar's hobby, photography, has kept him busy.

27. He has been taking photographs of every shop in his area.

28. He will show each photograph to the shop owners.

Principal Parts of Regular Verbs *pages 130–131*

Write each verb or verb phrase. After the verb, write *present, present participle, past,* or *past participle* in parentheses ( ).

29. Pablo Picasso, an artist, painted in France.

30. He had lived in Spain as a child.

31. Picasso's work appears in many museums in the world.

32. Leonard studied Picasso's work.

33. He especially admires Picasso's sculptures.

34. Leonard is studying art history.

Principal Parts of Irregular Verbs *pages 132–134*

Write each verb, identifying it as *present, present participle, past,* or *past participle*.

35. sells
36. are running
37. had swum
38. goes
39. had come
40. is catching
41. has run
42. swam
43. have drunk
44. had gone

More Irregular Verbs *pages 135–136*

Write each verb, identifying it as *present, present participle, past,* or *past participle*.

45. is riding
46. are wearing
47. grew
48. speaks
49. have taken
50. had torn
51. have chosen
52. had hidden
53. have eaten
54. had grown

Simple Verb Tenses *pages 137–138*

Write each verb or verb phrase. After it write the tense.

55. will walk
56. jogged
57. named
58. naps
59. see
60. will melt

61. divides

62. ducked

63. clicked

64. drips

Perfect Verb Tenses   *pages 139 – 140*

Write each verb phrase. Write its tense in parentheses ( ).

65. had attached

66. have managed

67. had mailed

68. will have seemed

69. have trapped

70. has bathed

71. will have met

72. have nibbled

73. had run

74. have waited

Be, Have, Do   *pages 141 – 143*

Use the correct form of the verb in parentheses ( ) in the sentence. Give the person, number, and tense of each form you choose.

75. John (have) been a chess player from the age of three.

76. He (be) the champion of his state.

77. His parents (do) a lot to help him for many years.

78. They (be) his first teachers.

79. John (have) trophies all over his shelves.

Subject-Verb Agreement   *pages 144 – 145*

Write the correct form of the verb in parentheses ( ).

80. Taka and Elena (have, has) different ideas about food.

81. Taka (like, likes) sweet foods such as honey and oranges.

82. Elena (prefer, prefers) spicy foods.

83. Although salt (is, are) not good for you in large quantities, sometimes your body (need, needs) it.

84. A bit of extra salt (is, are) necessary for hard-working athletes.

Homophones and Homographs   *pages 146 – 147*

Use the list of homophones to fill in the sentences.

85. Will you hike with us if you aren't _____ busy?

86. Meet us _____ at seven A.M., and be sure to eat a hearty breakfast.

87. When _____ going to hike a long way, you need a lot of energy.

88. I keep track of the miles I hike, and I record the _____ in my hiking journal.

Homophones
sum, some
to, two, too
hear, here
you're, your

UNIT

Persuading Others

◆ **COMPOSITION FOCUS:** **Persuasive Essay**
◆ **LANGUAGE FOCUS:** **Verbs**

The great Roman poet Horace once wrote, "If a better system is thine, impart it." In other words, if you have a good idea about how things should be done, share it. Throughout time new ideas have been responsible for much of the world's progress. To spread their ideas, people use a technique called *persuasion*.

Everyone uses persuasion. Advertisers, politicians, and community and social activists all try to persuade you to buy something, to vote for somebody, or to take a particular stand.

You are going to read a persuasive essay by Kevin Finn. Kevin, a seventh-grader at Solomon Lewenberg Middle School in Mattapan, Massachusetts, feels strongly about whether people should be allowed to smoke in public buildings. In his essay Kevin explains an important concern and gives reasons to support his argument.

In this unit you will learn to use persuasive writing convincingly.

Kevin Finn used several appeals in his essay *to persuade* his audience.

Reading with a Writer's Eye
Persuasive Essay

Crucial choices about public policy are certainly worth thinking about, arguing about, and doing something about. In this persuasive essay, Kevin Finn states and supports his views about smoking in public places. As you read this essay, notice what kind of information Kevin uses to support his views.

Smoking in Public Buildings

by Kevin Finn

Should people be able to smoke whenever or wherever they want? Cities and states across the United States have been saying, "No!" In New York as of May 7, 1987, smoking has been outlawed in subways, stores, banks, hospitals, and many other public buildings. In Cambridge, Massachusetts, smoking was banned as of March 9, 1987, in just about all public buildings. The Chamber of Commerce in Beverly Hills, California, passed a law on February 17, 1987, that disallows smoking in restaurants, schools, taxis, theaters, public meetings, and most retail stores. The General Services Administration now restricts 890,000 federal employees from smoking in their workplaces.

Dr. C. Everett Koop, former surgeon general of the United States, released a report that says: "Today only 19.9 percent of the population smokes and of

Thank You For Not Smoking

No Smoking in This Area

those people 87 percent want to quit." The report also stated, "Nonsmokers are placed at an increased risk for development of disease as the result of exposure to environmental tobacco smoke."

Although I realize that smokers have rights too, I think that Dr. Koop's point that a minority is putting the rest of us at risk is important. Even if smokers want to risk the hazards of smoking themselves, why should they be allowed to put others in danger? The law should be expanded to protect everyone.

I feel that if an employer adopted this policy, it would be a rule like any other rule in the workplace. If an employee disobeyed the rule, he or she would be subjected to a fine. I also think that if someone disobeyed the rule in a restaurant, then he or she would be asked to stop smoking or to leave. The rule would be enforced just like any other rule is enforced.

The trend in the United States is to limit smokers to certain rights and to enlarge nonsmokers' rights. I believe that the government and the people it represents should encourage smokers to stop smoking and prevent children from starting to smoke.

Respond

1. Does Kevin's argument convince you? Explain your answer.

Discuss

2. What kind of information does Kevin use to support his point of view?
3. In your own words, restate the evidence Kevin cites to support his stand.

Thinking As a Writer
Analyzing a Persuasive Essay

A **persuasive essay** convinces a specific audience to do or to believe something. It includes a **thesis statement** and **facts** to support the thesis. It usually includes one or more of the three basic appeals: the appeal to reason, the appeal to emotion, and the ethical appeal.

The appeal to reason uses facts, figures, and other evidence to support a stand. A writer may state, for example, "Seventy-eight percent of the graduates of Nonesuch School go on to college." An appeal to emotion plays upon the reader's feelings. A statement like this one, for example, appeals to a Northeasterner's feelings of regional pride: "The Northeast is the most desirable part of the country because it offers the best schools, the most popular cultural events, and the best-paying jobs." Finally, an ethical appeal influences by portraying the writer as fair, community-minded, and dedicated. Someone using this appeal may write, "I am the most qualified person for this office because I love my city and will give my every minute to its concerns." Note that such appeals are not always logical, and it is your job to decide whether they are worth your attention.

Writer's Guide

A persuasive essay

• includes a thesis statement and reasons to support the thesis.

• may use three types of appeals: appeal to reason, appeal to emotion, and ethical appeal.

• has an introduction, a body, and a conclusion.

Dr. C. Everett Koop, surgeon general of the United States, released a report that says: "Today only 19.9 percent of the population smokes and of those people 87 percent want to quit." The report also stated, "Nonsmokers are placed at an increased risk for development of disease as the result of exposure to environmental tobacco smoke."

Although I realize that smokers have rights too, I think that Dr. Koop's point that a minority is putting the rest of us at risk is important. Even if smokers want to risk the hazards of smoking themselves, why should they be allowed to put others in danger? The law should be expanded to protect everyone.

Reasons that support the opinion with evidence are often given in increasing or decreasing order of importance.

An **appeal to reason** gives facts that support a position.

An **ethical appeal** recognizes that there is another side to the issue. The **thesis** states an opinion.

An **appeal to emotion** tries to use emotion to influence judgment.

Discuss

1. Look back at the thesis statement. Where in the model does it appear?
2. What is Kevin trying to convince people to believe? How does each of the appeals he uses add to his argument?

Try Your Hand

A. Add Information to the Essay Look back at the essay. Write three sentences that could be inserted somewhere in it.

B. Change the Thesis Statement Think about your own attitudes toward smoking. Restate the thesis of this essay to reflect your views. Remember that the thesis is your opinion.

C. Reorganize the Reasons Review the reasons that Kevin used to support his opinion. List the reasons in a different order. Be ready to explain the reasons for your choice.

D. Add a Persuasive Appeal Add another persuasive appeal to the essay. It can be an appeal to reason, an appeal to emotion, or an ethical appeal. Tell which kind you used.

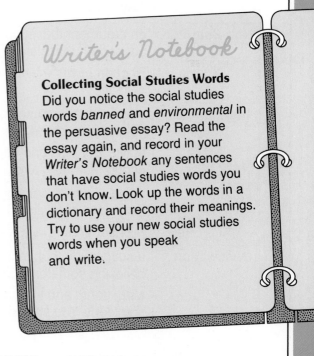

Writer's Notebook

Collecting Social Studies Words
Did you notice the social studies words *banned* and *environmental* in the persuasive essay? Read the essay again, and record in your *Writer's Notebook* any sentences that have social studies words you don't know. Look up the words in a dictionary and record their meanings. Try to use your new social studies words when you speak and write.

E. Read and Talk About a Persuasive Essay Read a persuasive essay. You might look in the "Letters to the Editor" section of a newspaper or magazine. Identify the thesis statement and the reasons that the author gives to support his or her opinion. State the author's stand in your own words. See if the three kinds of appeals are used.

Thinking As a Writer
Evaluating Reasons to Support an Opinion

Writer's Guide

To write a persuasive essay, good writers

- use legitimate arguments to persuade readers.
- avoid using faulty reasoning.

In a good persuasive essay, a writer tries to convince readers by using legitimate arguments. The use of faulty reasoning to convince readers is a form of propaganda. It is something good writers avoid.

There are seven common kinds of faulty reasoning that writers who are trying to persuade should avoid.

Hasty Generalization	a conclusion that is drawn without enough support
	This gorilla won't come out in the sun after noon. It is clear that gorillas do not like hot weather.
Faulty Cause and Effect	an argument that assumes that an event that follows another event was also caused by it
	Acid rain became a problem here after that paint plant opened.
Begging the Question	the statement that something is true because it is true
	Soft drinks are not as good for you as fruit juices, because they are less healthful.
Non Sequitur	an argument that supports a claim with information that has no bearing on that claim
	Rhonda Lewis will make a good treasurer because she loves animals.
Testimonial	a technique that uses a well-known person's reputation to bolster the writer's belief or proposal
	Mayor Burgess and I agree on this proposal, and if it's good enough for the mayor, isn't it good enough for you?
Labeling	a use of emotional language to label someone good or bad, instead of discussing his or her true qualifications
	Michael Waters is a weakling with no backbone.
Bandwagon	a suggestion that implies that if many people are doing or believing something, you should be doing or believing it too
	Meg, John, and I are all voting for Hilary for student council president. You should as well.

When you write your persuasive essay, a good way to evaluate possible supporting reasons for your argument is to ask questions. Read these questions.

1. Am I misusing the appeal to reason by
    a. concealing information while seeming to state all the facts?
    b. drawing conclusions from insufficient evidence?
    c. making statements that are based on faulty reasoning?
    d. using unrelated information to support my argument?

2. Am I misusing the ethical appeal by linking my argument with a well-known person simply to make my position look better?

3. Am I misusing the appeal to emotion by
    a. manipulating the reader's emotions rather than presenting facts?
    b. making the reader feel uncomfortable rather than using reason?

When you write your own persuasive essay, be sure you have avoided faulty reasoning.

Discuss

1. Explain each propaganda technique in your own words.
2. Why should you avoid propaganda techniques in a persuasive essay?

Try Your Hand

Evaluate the Best Support   For each example, choose the best supporting statement, and then explain why the others are weak.

1. Position: Mayor Jones has been a good mayor despite overspending.
    Reason a: You say Mayor Jones is careless with money, but have you never spent more than you budgeted?
    Reason b: The overspending in Mayor Jones's term was partially due to the city council's financing a new sewer system this year rather than over five years.
    Reason c: Mayor Jones can make up the deficit in one more term because he has a Ph.D. and is really smart.

2. Position: More Holstein cattle than Jerseys should be bred.
    Reason a: Holsteins produce more milk per cow than Jerseys.
    Reason b: I had a Jersey that kicked me, so I know that Jerseys are difficult to handle.
    Reason c: 75 percent of the Vermont farmers I know prefer Holsteins.

Developing the Writer's Craft
Using Quotations from Oral and Written Sources

Writers of persuasive essays want to gather the best support for their opinions. They read books and interview people. An effective way to make use of a special point someone discovers in research is to quote the source.

Read these sentences from Kevin's persuasive essay. Notice how Kevin made these quotations from a well-known authority an important and effective part of his argument.

> Dr. C. Everett Koop, surgeon general of the United States, released a report that says: "Today only 19.9 percent of the population smokes and of those people 87 percent want to quit." The report also stated, "Nonsmokers are placed at an increased risk for development of disease as the result of exposure to environmental tobacco smoke."

When you write your persuasive essay, find information that you want to quote in order to make your argument more effective. Then follow these guidelines.

1. Write all the information—don't try to rely on your memory.
2. Quote your source accurately, using the source's exact words.
3. Transcribe your notes correctly, and double-check your final copy.

Discuss

Why might quoting a fact from a source be more effective in a persuasive essay than simply stating that same fact?

Try Your Hand

Using Quotations from Oral and Written Sources   Imagine that you are writing a persuasive essay about a matter of public concern. Find three sources and write a quotation from each one that supports your viewpoint. Exchange papers with a partner. Talk about how effectively each quotation supports your position.

1 Prewriting
Persuasive Essay

Ralph wanted to persuade the mayor that seventh-grade students can make a worthwhile contribution to the community. Ralph used the checklist in the **Writer's Guide** to help him plan his persuasive essay. Look at what he did.

Writer's Guide

Prewriting Checklist
- ☑ Brainstorm topics.
- ☑ Select a topic and an audience.
- ☑ Formulate your opinion.
- ☑ Gather information.
- ☑ Evaluate your supporting reasons.
- ☑ Organize your appeals in a logical order.

◆ Brainstorming and Selecting a Topic

First, Ralph looked for topics of interest to the community and thought about ways his Young Detectives' Club could contribute.

Next, Ralph looked down his list and crossed out jobs that were obviously too complex for students his age. He eliminated topics that named tasks he knew adults wouldn't want students to undertake. Finally, Ralph chose to have his group become members of a junior crimestoppers' league because he felt strongly about such a commitment.

> 1. Set up detective agency for students like Encyclopedia Brown's.
> 2. Become junior crimestoppers with the police.
> 3. Try to solve a real crime.

Discuss

1. Look at each idea that Ralph didn't use. Explain why you think it is not practical.
2. Consider Ralph's topic. Do you think the mayor is Ralph's best audience?

◆ Gathering and Organizing Information

Ralph felt he could take a stand on his topic, but he still needed to gather information to be able to use all three appeals. Ralph wrote his facts in a three-part chart.

Ethical Appeal	Appeals (Reasons) Appeal to Reason	Appeal to Emotion
Ralph—four years in club, two as president (dedication) wants to donate services (community minded)	plan has been successful elsewhere gets students into community service helps community keeps students out of trouble	helps create good citizens provides an additional resource for community protection city will have the first group of this kind

Ralph evaluated his reasons and decided to use the ethical appeals to begin his essay. He avoided writing any points that could lead to faulty reasoning.

Then, Ralph decided to combine his appeals of reason and emotion. He rearranged them in **order of importance.** Ralph knew that in persuasive writing, the appeals are listed in either increasing or decreasing order of importance. This is how he ordered his appeals.

1. Helps the community and has been successful elsewhere (reason and emotion)
2. Keeps students occupied and out of trouble, thereby creates better citizens (reason and emotion)
3. Gets young people interested in community service (reason)
4. Makes our city the first in the area to have such a group (emotion)

Discuss

1. What other emotional or ethical appeal could Ralph use?
2. What other kinds of facts or evidence could Ralph include?
3. How does Ralph's list differ from his chart?
4. Did Ralph begin his final list with the appeal that is the most important or the least important? How do you know?

Try Your Hand

Now plan a persuasive essay of your own.

A. Brainstorm and Select a Topic Brainstorm a list of topics that are both serious and important and that require persuasion. As you select your topic, be sure it is something you can cover in a few paragraphs.

+ Cross out topics that involve impractical ideas.
+ Cross out topics that you don't know enough about.
+ Cross out topics that will take more than three paragraphs.
+ Of the remaining topics, circle the one that you feel most strongly about and on which you can take a stand. This will be the topic of your persuasive essay.

B. Take a Stand State your topic as an opinion that you intend to persuade people to accept.

C. Select an Audience Use these questions to help you choose an audience for your topic.

+ Whom or what group do you want to persuade?
+ Who can give you the most support (money, time, whatever you need)?

D. Gather and Organize Information List as many facts as you can think of that will support your appeals. Put the facts in a chart. Organize them by the appeal to which they apply. Then add material to support each appeal. Be sure to use logical, not faulty, reasoning. List the appeals in order of importance. You may put your most important appeal either first or last.

Save your chart and your lists in your *Writer's Notebook*. You will use them when you draft your persuasive essay.

Listening and Speaking
Tips on How to Recognize Motive and Bias

Speakers, like writers, present information in a particular way to persuade you to adopt their point of view. **Motive** is the speaker's purpose for saying something. **Bias** is an attitude about a subject that is based on feelings rather than facts. As you listen to a speaker, you might want to ask yourself questions to determine his or her motive for speaking. Also, pay attention to ways in which a speaker signals bias toward a subject.

1. Does the speaker have a clear objective? Is he or she trying to establish a fact, change a belief, or move you to action?
2. Does the speaker present legitimate reasons and support them with valid evidence?
3. Does the speaker support his or her evidence with facts and expert opinions? Are the experts people who have gained experience in the subject being discussed or in an unrelated field?
4. Does the speaker use only emotional appeals to convince you of his or her opinion?
5. Do you believe in the speaker's credibility? Is he or she believable and trustworthy?
6. Is the speaker ethical? Does he or she lie, distort, or resort to name-calling?
7. Does the speaker have a personal stake in the outcome? Will the speaker or someone close to that person gain from the outcome?

2 Drafting
Persuasive Essay

Before Ralph started to draft his persuasive essay, he decided how to present his ideas about the Young Detectives' Club. Using his chart, Ralph followed the checklist in the **Writer's Guide.** Look at what he did.

> I believe that a group of seventh–grade students can benefit our city. I am serving my second term as president of the Young Detectives' Club. We meet in the science lab. In the four years since we started, under the sponsorship of our science teacher, Ms. Christie Hubbard, we have shown unflagging interest in learning the techniques of crime detection. Our guide is The Young Detective's Handbook by William Vivian Butler. We are a bunch of 53 kids.

Writer's Guide

Drafting Checklist

☑ Use your chart and your lists.

☑ Write an introduction that states your opinion on a topic.

☑ Write a body that includes appeals (reasons) to convince your audience.

☑ Present your appeals in order of importance.

Discuss

What might Ralph add to his essay? Why?

Try Your Hand

Now you are ready to draft a persuasive essay.

A. Review Your Information Think about the information you gathered and organized in the last lesson. Decide whether you need more information. If so, gather it.

B. Think About Your TAP Remember that your task is to write a persuasive essay. Your purpose is to persuade your audience to agree with your opinion.

C. Write Your First Draft Use the **Drafting Checklist** to write your persuasive essay.

When you write your draft, just put all your ideas on paper. Do not worry about spelling, punctuation, or grammar. You can correct the draft later.

TAP

Task: What?
Audience: Who?
Purpose: Why?

Save your first draft in your *Writer's Notebook.* You will use it when you revise your persuasive essay.

3 Responding and Revising
Persuasive Essay

Ralph reread his draft. He used the checklist in the **Writer's Guide** to revise his work. Look at what he did.

◆ Checking Information

Ralph wanted to identify himself and his group. To add the name of his school, he used the mark ∧. He used the mark ✗ to cut an unnecessary detail.

◆ Checking Organization

Ralph used this mark ⌇ to put his most important appeal last. Then he used the ᵛ mark to change a statement into a quotation.

◆ Checking Language

When Ralph checked his sentences, he noticed that some were monotonous and needed variety. He used this mark ∧ to replace some words in a sentence.

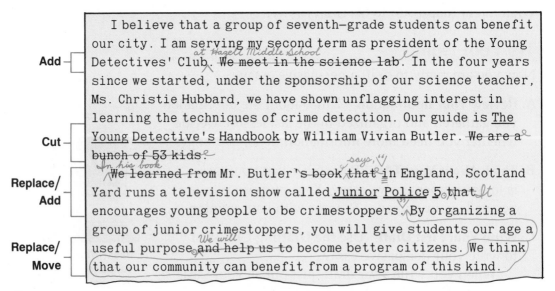

Add — I believe that a group of seventh-grade students can benefit our city. I am serving my second term as president of the Young Detectives' Club. *at Hazett Middle School* ∧ ̶W̶e̶ ̶m̶e̶e̶t̶ ̶i̶n̶ ̶t̶h̶e̶ ̶s̶c̶i̶e̶n̶c̶e̶ ̶l̶a̶b̶. In the four years since we started, under the sponsorship of our science teacher, Ms. Christie Hubbard, we have shown unflagging interest in learning the techniques of crime detection. Our guide is <u>The Young Detective's Handbook</u> by William Vivian Butler.

Cut — ̶W̶e̶ ̶a̶r̶e̶ ̶a̶ ̶b̶u̶n̶c̶h̶ ̶o̶f̶ ̶5̶3̶ ̶k̶i̶d̶s̶.

Replace/Add — *In his book* ̶W̶e̶ ̶l̶e̶a̶r̶n̶e̶d̶ from Mr. Butler's book *says, "* that in England, Scotland Yard runs a television show called <u>Junior Police 5</u> that *It* encourages young people to be crimestoppers. By organizing a group of junior crimestoppers, you will give students our age a useful purpose

Replace/Move — *We will* ̶a̶n̶d̶ ̶h̶e̶l̶p̶ ̶u̶s̶ to become better citizens. ̶W̶e̶ ̶t̶h̶i̶n̶k̶ ̶t̶h̶a̶t̶ ̶o̶u̶r̶ ̶c̶o̶m̶m̶u̶n̶i̶t̶y̶ ̶c̶a̶n̶ ̶b̶e̶n̶e̶f̶i̶t̶ ̶f̶r̶o̶m̶ ̶a̶ ̶p̶r̶o̶g̶r̶a̶m̶ ̶o̶f̶ ̶t̶h̶i̶s̶ ̶k̶i̶n̶d̶.

Discuss

1. Do you agree that Ralph should change the order of the sentences in the second paragraph? Explain your answer.
2. Why did Ralph shorten some sentences and lengthen others?

WRITING PROCESS

Try Your Hand

Now revise your first draft.

A. Read Your First Draft   As you read your persuasive essay, think about your audience and your purpose. Read your draft silently or to a partner to see if it is complete and well organized. Ask yourself or your partner the questions in the box.

Responding and Revising Strategies

✔ **Respond**
Ask yourself or a partner:

- Have I begun with an opinion?

- Does all the information in my persuasive essay support my opinion? Is it free from bias and faulty reasoning?

- Is my persuasive essay organized with the appeals (reasons) in order of importance?

- Do I use quotations and oral sources to support my opinion?

- Do I use a variety of sentence lengths to add interest to my essay?

✔ **Revise**
Try these solutions:

- **Add** your opinion on the topic. **Cut** extra or inappropriate information.

- **Cut** information that is not helping the argument.

- **Move** any sentences that are out of place.

- **Replace** quotations that are not useful in your appeals.

- **Cut** or **add** words to sentences to provide variety. See the **Revising Workshop** on page 170.

B. Make Your Changes   If the answer to any question in the box is *no,* try the solution. Use the **Editor's Marks** to show your changes.

C. Review Your Persuasive Essay Again   Decide whether there is anything else you want to revise. Keep revising your essay until you feel it is well organized and complete.

EDITOR'S MARKS

∧ Add something.

⚡ Cut something.

◯ Move something.

∧ Replace something.

Save your revised persuasive essay in your *Writer's Notebook.* You will use it when you proofread your essay.

Revising Workshop
Varying Sentence Length

Good writers vary the length of their sentences. They avoid placing too many short, choppy sentences or too many long, complicated sentences together. Sometimes, short, choppy sentences need to be combined to make longer, smoother sentences. Also, some complicated sentences may need to be shortened or divided. Look at these examples.

1. **a.** I like to baby-sit. I do it often on weekends. I get paid by the hour.
    b. I like to baby-sit, and I often do on weekends. I get paid by the hour.
2. **a.** Our trio, the Triangles, has recently been hired to play at a number of local parties, and since this happened, we have made enough money to buy new equipment. We purchased a set of speakers, and we also upgraded our synthesizer.
    b. Our trio, the Triangles, has recently been hired to play at a number of local functions and parties. Since this happened, we have made enough money to buy new equipment. We purchased a set of speakers. We also upgraded our synthesizer.

In the first example, the writer started out with three short, choppy sentences. Two sentences were combined, and the wording was changed slightly to flow better. In the second example, the writer started out with two long, complex sentences. They were both divided, leaving four sentences of varying lengths.

Practice

Rewrite this paragraph. Combine some short, choppy sentences to create a smoother, more flowing style. Also, divide longer sentences when necessary. Change the wording if it will make the piece flow better.

> Last week our girls' club went camping. The site we chose was in the state forest. Several parents supervised us. A sudden storm came up. Tree branches flew. Several girls were injured. Alicia, who has Red Cross certification, gave expert care to the injured girls, and when they were taken to the hospital, the emergency-room physician complimented her on her first-aid technique. For this reason, I think Alicia's action should be publicly recognized.

4 Proofreading
Persuasive Essay

After Ralph revised his persuasive essay, he used the **Writer's Guide** and the **Editor's Marks** to proofread it. Look at what he did.

Writer's Guide

Proofreading Checklist

- ☑ Check for errors in capitalization.
- ☑ Check for errors in punctuation.
- ☑ Check to see that all your paragraphs are indented.
- ☑ Check for errors in grammar. Be sure to use correct verb tenses.
- ☑ Circle any words you think are misspelled. Find out how to spell them correctly.
- ⇨ For proofreading help, use the **Writer's Handbook.**

---

evidence
There is good (evidince) that such a program can really help a community. Our city would be the first in this part of the state to (sponser) *sponsor* such a program. All of us ∧needless to say∧ are willing to undertake any training that is required. We *you require* hope you will consider our idea and will support us in our desire to donate our time to our community. We hope that soon we will be *detectives* junior (detectiffs).

Discuss

1. Look at Ralph's proofread essay. What kinds of mistakes did he make?
2. Why did Ralph change *that is required* to *you require*?

Try Your Hand

Proofread Your Persuasive Essay   Now use the checklist in the **Writer's Guide** and the **Editor's Marks** to proofread your essay.

Save your corrected persuasive essay in your *Writer's Notebook.* You will use it when you publish your essay.

EDITOR'S MARKS

- ≡ Capitalize.
- ⊙ Add a period.
- ∧ Add something.
- ⋀ Add a comma.
- ⱽⱽ Add quotation marks.
- ✐ Cut something.
- ⌒ Replace something.
- ⤮ Transpose.
- ◯ Spell correctly.
- ¶ Indent paragraph.
- / Make a lowercase letter.

---

5 Publishing
Persuasive Essay

Ralph made a clean copy of his persuasive essay and checked it to be sure he had not left out anything. Then he and his classmates published their persuasive essays by presenting mock television public service announcements. You can find the completed essay that Ralph submitted to the mayor on page 44 of the **Writer's Handbook.**

Here's how Ralph and his classmates published their persuasive essays.

Writer's Guide

Publishing Checklist

☑ Make a clean copy of your persuasive essay.

☑ Be sure that nothing has been left out.

☑ Make sure there are no mistakes.

☑ Share your essay in a special way.

1. They divided into groups. Students who had persuasive essays on the same or similar topics were in the same group.
2. Each group decided who would introduce the speakers and their topics. That person would sit at a desk in the center of the classroom and be the moderator. Each group member wrote an introduction for the moderator to use. The introduction stated the student's name, school, and any special interests.
3. Each student practiced giving his or her public service message until the reading was smooth. Students discussed as a group the props they wanted to use. They made a sign that said *Moderator* and one for each student with his or her name on it.

4. They presented their messages to their classmates.
They tried to be serious and convincing and to
speak clearly and distinctly.

Discuss

1. What would have happened if Ralph had not included a proper
introduction for the moderator?
2. What might have happened if students had not spoken clearly and
distinctly?

Try Your Hand

Publish Your Persuasive Essay   Follow the checklist in the **Writer's
Guide.** Then present your essay as a public service announcement, or
try one of these ideas for sharing your persuasive essay.

- Show it to your parents for their opinion.
- Send a copy of it to be used as an editorial on a television or a radio
  program.
- Send copies of it to other interested parties.

Writing in the Content Areas

Use what you learned to write another persuasive essay.

Writer's Guide

When you write, remember the stages of the Writing Process.

- Prewriting
- Drafting
- Responding and Revising
- Proofreading
- Publishing

Social Studies

Write a persuasive paragraph in a letter to the editor of your local paper. Choose a subject of concern to seventh-graders in your community, for example, bicycle traffic, the local bus service, the hot lunch program, the recreation department programs, and so on. Use an emotional appeal in your letter.

Science

Write a persuasive essay to convince the principal and the teachers at your school that there should be an after-school science club that focuses on chemistry, astronomy, model rocketry, or zoology.

Health

Write a persuasive essay attempting to convince fellow students to practice a health measure that they currently ignore, such as getting enough exercise or eating more healthful snacks and less sugar. Use appeals to reason in your argument.

Physical Education

Write a persuasive essay to convince school officials to have a sporting day at your school in which students participate in a variety of sports and games. In your paragraph, attempt to convince them to invite students from another community. Use an ethical appeal in your persuasion.

CONNECTING
WRITING ↔ LANGUAGE

A well-written persuasive business letter is a valuable tool for anyone in the business world. Often through the use of such letters, potential providers of certain goods and services are reached quickly and efficiently. Suppose this letter had been addressed to you. Would you have invested in this venture? See the **Writer's Handbook** for other examples of effective letters.

La Rabida
Palos, Spain
February, 1485 A.D.

Their Royal Highnesses
Isabella and Ferdinand of Spain
Segovia, Spain

Your Royal Majesties:
    I propose to sail to the west to discover new trading routes that will provide riches from the Orient for commerce for Spain. You, as my major benefactors and investors, will control access to any new routes.
    For a small investment these benefits could be yours. All I request is three ships, a share of the trade, the title of admiral, and a noble rank. Please, your highnesses, think about it. I will anxiously await your reply.

        Your humble servant,
        Christopher Columbus

◆ **Verbs in a Persuasive Paragraph** The highlighted words are transitive verbs—they send the action from the subject to an object, or receiver of the action. An effective business letter makes use of many transitive verbs, because it speaks to the reader in the active voice.

◆ **Language Focus: Verbs** The following lessons will help you use verbs in different forms and different voices.

1 Progressive Forms of Verbs

◆ **FOCUS**   A **progressive verb** expresses action that continues.

   Progressive forms of verbs show action that continues over time. Verbs have a progressive form for each tense. To make the progressive form of a verb, you always use the present participle as the main verb with a form of *to be* as a helping verb.

Present Progressive	He is making friends now.
Past Progressive	He was making friends this morning.
Future Progressive	He will be making friends tomorrow.
Present Perfect Progressive	He has been making friends since September.
Past Perfect Progressive	He had been making friends since childhood.
Future Perfect Progressive	He will have been making friends all year long.

Guided Practice

A. Identify each verb phrase and give the tense of its progressive form.

1. Marty has been teasing Leila for days.
2. He had been annoying her until yesterday.
3. Yesterday, Leila was studying in the library.
4. Marty said, "I have been teasing you on purpose."
5. By tomorrow, they will have been laughing about it for hours.

THINK AND REMEMBER
- Use **progressive forms** of verbs to express action that continues over time.
- Always use the present participle with a form of *to be* as a helping verb in progressive forms.

Independent Practice

B. Identifying Progressive Forms   Write each verb phrase. In parentheses ( ), write its tense.

6. I am thinking about friendship.

MODEL⟩ am thinking   (present progressive)

7. I have been thinking about my friends.

8. Today as I was walking to the bus, I saw my friend Teddy.

9. He had been talking to someone I did not know.

10. Teddy said that John is moving here.

11. Soon we three were planning a Sunday afternoon hike.

C. Writing Progressive Forms   Write each verb in the tense indicated in parentheses ( ).

12. they speak (present progressive)

MODEL⟩ are speaking

13. they shake (past perfect progressive)

14. they agree (future progressive)

15. they share (future perfect progressive)

16. they enjoy (past progressive)

17. they joke (present perfect progressive)

D. 18.–23. Using Progressive Forms   Use each verb from **C** in a sentence.

MODEL⟩ **18.** They are speaking at the convention this morning.

E. Revising: Writing Sentences   Write the sentences. Change each underlined verb or phrase into a progressive form. After each sentence, write the form you used.

24. Lisa <u>visits</u> often.

MODEL⟩ Lisa <u>is visiting</u> often.   present progressive

25. Recently Marsha's new computer <u>beeped</u> with activity.

26. Lisa <u>visited</u> Marsha often to use it.

27. Lisa <u>has appreciated</u> Marsha's generosity.

28. By Wednesday, Marsha <u>will write</u> a long term paper.

29. Lisa, a fine typist, <u>has thought</u> about inputting it for her.

Application — Writing

A Definition   Throughout your life you will probably make many friends and acquaintances. Write a paragraph for your classmates that sums up your definition of a good friend. Use progressive verb forms. If you need help writing a paragraph, see page 39 of the **Writer's Handbook**.

2 Direct Objects

◆ FOCUS   A **direct object** receives the action of the verb.

In a sentence, the subject tells whom or what the sentence is about. The predicate tells what the subject does. Sometimes a sentence needs a complement. A **complement** completes the thought of a sentence. A direct object is a sentence complement. The direct object is usually a noun or pronoun that receives the action from an action verb. To find the direct object, always ask who or what receives the action.

1. The quarterback throws the ball .   throws what?
2. He always watches his receivers . watches whom?

A direct object can be compound.

3. The crowd watches the receiver and the pursuers .

Guided Practice

A. Identify the subject, the verb, and the direct object in each sentence.

1. My oldest brother plays football for his school.
2. This year his team entered the state finals .
3. The team lost the championship in a close game.
4. Their opponents received the trophy .
5. Afterward my brother had a different feeling about the season.

> **THINK AND REMEMBER**
> • Remember that a **direct object** receives the action of a verb.

Independent Practice

B. Identifying Sentence Parts   Write each sentence. Underline the subject once and the verb twice. Box each direct object.

6. Jerry plays the game as well as Marvin.

MODEL〉 Jerry plays the game as well as Marvin.

7. Many students enjoy the competition .
8. The coach always chooses a play with several options.
9. During recent practices the offense practiced each part .

10. Excellent athletic ability does not always bring a victory.

11. The team had talented players and coaches.

C. Identifying Direct Objects Write each direct object.

12. Mary loves basketball.
MODEL⟩ basketball

13. Some students enjoy team sports and games.
14. Others lack the skill for a school team.
15. They do not join varsity or intramural teams.
16. Many students prefer individual sports such as jogging or skating.
17. Still others hit a ball against a backboard.
18. Real sports lovers have desire and determination.
19. They do not really need athletic ability.

D. Completing Sentences with Direct Objects Write these sentence beginnings. Add endings that include direct objects to make each one a sentence.

20. My cousin Dino enjoys
MODEL⟩ My cousin Dino enjoys hockey during the winter months.

21. From December through February he spends
22. Only Dino can lead
23. The other members of his team value
24. Unlike Dino, my cousin Andrea enjoys
25. During the summer months, Andrea spends

E. Using Direct Objects Use each of these nouns as the direct object in a sentence about sports or games. Be sure to use an action verb in each sentence.

26. baseball
MODEL⟩ I play baseball every day during the summer.

27. fast ball	31. swimming	35. jackknife
28. gymnastics	32. laps	36. tennis
29. vault	33. diving	37. net
30. uneven bars	34. platform	38. backhand

Application — Writing

A Pep Talk Imagine that you are a coach for one of the teams at your school. Write a pep talk to encourage your players. Use direct objects correctly.

3 Indirect Objects

◆ **FOCUS** An **indirect object** tells to whom or for whom the action of the verb is done.

All sentences have a subject and a predicate. In a sentence with an action verb, a direct object receives the action. An indirect object tells *to* or *for whom* or *to* or *for what* the action is done. The words in color are indirect objects.

   1. Clara feeds the dogs high-protein food.

A sentence must have a direct object to have an indirect object. The indirect object is a noun or a pronoun. It is always placed after the verb and before the direct object in a sentence.

   2. Clara gives pets obedience lessons.

Indirect objects can be compound.

   3. Clara gives the dogs and their owners clear instructions.

Link to Writing

If a noun or pronoun follows the word *to* or *for*, it is not an indirect object but part of a prepositional phrase. Which sentence contains an indirect object? How do you know?

She gives kitty treats to the cats.
She gives the cats kitty treats.

Guided Practice

A. Identify the *direct object* and the *indirect object* in each sentence.

   1. Clara had given her dog obedience training.

   2. Clara showed her neighbor her dog-training ability.

   3. Mr. Ramirez offered Clara a job training his dog.

   4. Mr. Ramirez has been telling friends his high opinion of Clara's skills.

   5. Now Clara teaches many dogs basic obedience skills.

   6. She is building herself a bank account for college.

Independent Practice

B. Identifying Direct and Indirect Objects   Write each sentence. Underline the direct object once and the indirect object twice.

   7. Julio gives others the benefit of his experience.
MODEL⟩ Julio gives <u>others</u> the <u>benefit</u> of his experience.

   8. Julio has always bought himself supplies at Dr. Potter's office.
   9. Recently he wrote Dr. Potter a letter requesting a part-time job.
   10. Julio offered Dr. Potter his familiarity with animals.
   11. Dr. Potter gave Julio a job at his veterinary office.
   12. As the "information expert," Julio gives customers advice on pet care.
   13. Through this job, Julio gives others valuable information.
   14. His job gives him excellent experience for later life.

C. Revising: Writing Indirect Objects   Rewrite each sentence. Use the information in the underlined phrase to write an indirect object.

   15. Mrs. Ames assigned a project about pets <u>to the class</u>.
MODEL⟩ Mrs. Ames assigned the class a project about pets.
   16. Mrs. Ames gave the assignment <u>to everyone</u>.
   17. We made lists <u>for ourselves</u> of at least six interesting pet facts.
   18. Next, we told our favorite ideas, interests, and skills <u>to our classmates</u>.
   19. We listened and offered several valuable ideas <u>to individuals and groups</u>.
   20. Finally, a guest speaker gave great inspiration <u>to us</u> on the humane treatment of all animals.
   21. We made a promise <u>to ourselves</u> to adopt all our future pets from animal shelters.

Application — Writing

A Dialogue   Imagine that you meet a friend who is taking her dogs for an obedience training session in the park. Write a dialogue that you and she might have about dog training. Use indirect objects.

4 Predicate Nominatives

◆ **FOCUS** A **predicate nominative** is a noun or a pronoun that follows a linking verb and renames the subject.

A predicate nominative always follows a linking verb. It is a noun or pronoun that renames or identifies the subject of the sentence.

1. Mr. Cohen is a man with much to tell.   renames subject
2. Mr. Cohen has been a shop owner for years.   identifies subject
3. That man in the blue suit is he .   identifies subject

Do not confuse predicate nominatives and direct objects. Direct objects follow action verbs. Predicate nominatives follow linking verbs.

4. Mr. Cohen tells stories about the neighborhood.   direct object

5. He is the oldest person on our block.   predicate nominative

A predicate nominative can be compound.

6. Mr. Cohen is a storekeeper and a friend .

Link to Writing
Remember that predicate nominatives never follow action verbs. To decide whether a noun or a pronoun is a predicate nominative, use the verb *is* to connect the subject to the predicate.

Mr. Cohen is my friend.
Mr. Cohen is stories about the neighborhood.

Guided Practice

A. Identify the predicate nominative and the word in the subject to which it refers.

1. Mr. Cohen's shop has been a gathering place for more than fifty years.
2. Even my great-grandparents were his customers and friends.
3. Mr. Cohen is a wonderful storyteller.
4. When he was young, his life was a challenge.
5. I am a fortunate person to know Mr. Cohen.

Independent Practice

B. Identifying Predicate Nominatives   Write the sentences. Underline each predicate nominative once. Underline twice the word to which it refers.

6. According to Mr. Cohen, life was a hardship fifty years ago.

MODEL> According to Mr. Cohen, life was a hardship fifty years ago.

7. In summer the stores were hothouses.

8. Today, with air-conditioning, they are almost iceboxes.

9. For a visitor to a faraway state, the train trip was a challenge.

10. Today, after a speedy plane trip, you are a happy person.

11. Thirty years ago, the owner of a stereo was a lucky person.

12. Today, the lucky one is he or she with a compact disc player.

C. Distinguishing Between Predicate Nominatives and Direct Objects   Write whether each underlined word is a *predicate nominative* or a *direct object*.

13. When Mr. Cohen was a child, this town was farmland.

MODEL> child—predicate nominative; farmland—predicate nominative

14. In 1935 manufacturing was a major industry.

15. This area became a center for electronics.

16. Electronics, chemicals, and rockets helped Texas greatly.

17. He remembers when nearly everyone was a farmer.

18. Each homeowner had many fields.

19. The fields were an inheritance for the farmers' children.

20. Those who did not become farmers sold farm equipment.

21. These people made their own wares.

22. After a while manufacturing became the dominant industry.

Application — Writing

A Friendly Letter   Imagine that Mr. Cohen lives in your neighborhood. Write a letter to a relative who also knows him but who has moved away. Retell some of Mr. Cohen's stories. Use predicate nominatives. If you need help writing a friendly letter, see page 59 of the **Writer's Handbook.**

5 Transitive and Intransitive Verbs

FOCUS
◆ A transitive verb has a direct object.
◆ An intransitive verb does not have a direct object.

A verb that has a direct object is a **transitive verb.**

1. Emma makes funny faces for the baby.   transitive

A verb that does not have a direct object is an **intransitive verb.**

2. The baby laughs .   intransitive

Trans means "across." A transitive verb sends the action across to a receiver. An intransitive verb does not direct action to a receiver. Although action verbs can be either transitive or intransitive, linking verbs are always intransitive. Moreover, a verb can be transitive in one sentence and intransitive in another.

3. Flo bounced the baby on her knee.   transitive

4. The baby bounced high.   intransitive

To determine whether a verb is transitive or intransitive, ask *whom* or *what* after the verb. (Whom or what did Flo bounce?) If you can answer with a noun or pronoun, the verb is transitive. If you cannot, it is intransitive.

Guided Practice

A. Identify the action verb in each sentence. Tell whether the verb is *transitive* or *intransitive.*

   1. Jason, Emma's younger brother, crawled toward a dog.
   2. Jason smiled and cooed.
   3. Emma grabbed Jason away.
   4. Babies experience emotions.
   5. For many years babies require attentive, constant care.

> **THINK AND REMEMBER**
> ◆ Remember that a **transitive** verb has a direct object.
> ◆ Remember that an **intransitive** verb does not have a direct object.

Independent Practice

B. Identifying Transitive and Intransitive Verbs Write each sentence. Underline the verb. After the sentence, write *transitive* or *intransitive*.

6. People can have different emotions at once.

MODEL〉 People <u>can have</u> different emotions at once.   transitive

7. People look happy and sad at the same time.
8. Jason's baby-sitter arrives at the house.
9. Later, the baby-sitter leaves a sad Jason.
10. Two different emotions cause ambivalence.
11. Have you experienced ambivalence?

C. 12.–17. Identifying Direct Objects Write each direct object in **B**. If a verb does not have a direct object, write *none*.

12. People can have different emotions at once.

MODEL〉 emotions

D. Using Transitive and Intransitive Verbs Change each sentence. If an underlined verb is transitive, write another sentence using it as an intransitive verb. If it is intransitive, use it as a transitive verb. After your new sentence, write *transitive* or *intransitive*.

18. Lily <u>drives</u> the toy car.

MODEL〉 Lily drives well.   intransitive

19. My little sister, Lily, <u>learns</u> very quickly.
20. Lily also <u>hears</u> extremely well.
21. This child <u>repeats</u> everything!
22. She <u>remembers</u> something after one time.
23. She <u>sings</u> happily in her sandbox.
24. Lily <u>builds</u> castles and forts out of sand.
25. Terry, my little nephew, <u>likes</u> blocks.
26. He <u>can build</u> wonderful towers and bridges with them.
27. He <u>builds</u> very well for such a young child.
28. Lily and Terry <u>may</u> someday <u>earn</u> degrees in engineering.

Application — Writing

Instructions Perhaps you or someone you know has a baby brother or sister. Write a list of instructions for a new baby-sitter that tells him or her ways to calm the baby when he or she cries. Use transitive and intransitive verbs. If you need help writing instructions, see page 40 of the **Writer's Handbook.**

6 Active and Passive Voice

◆ A transitive verb is in the **active voice** when the subject performs the action.

◆ A transitive verb is in the **passive voice** when the subject receives the action.

Tense	Active Voice
Present	she sees
Past	she saw
Future	she will see
Present perfect	she has seen
Past perfect	she had seen
Future perfect	she will have seen

Tense	Passive Voice
Present	she is seen
Past	she was seen
Future	she will be seen
Present perfect	she has been seen
Past perfect	she had been seen
Future perfect	she will have been seen

When the subject of a sentence performs the action and the object receives the action, the verb is in the active voice.

1. Gillian rode her bicycle.   active voice

When the action of the verb returns to the subject, the verb is in the passive voice. Note that in the passive voice, the verb changes from the past to the past participle form. A form of *to be* precedes the verb.

2. It was ridden by Gillian.   passive voice

There are other ways in which sentences change when the verb is in the passive voice. The object of a verb in the active voice becomes the subject in a sentence with a verb in the passive voice.

3. Joel drove the family car .   active voice

4. The family car was driven by Joel.   passive voice

The subject of a sentence with a verb in the active voice comes after the word *by* in a sentence with the verb in the passive voice.

5. Gillian saw Joel in the car.   active voice

6. Joel was seen by Gillian .   passive voice

Guided Practice

A. Identify the verb or verb phrase in each sentence. Tell whether each one is in the *active* voice or *passive* voice.

1. Jeremy has been riding a bicycle since early childhood.
2. Many such skills are stored in his memory.
3. Memory also stores verbal and emotional responses.
4. Jeremy's emotional memory includes the fear of large dogs.
5. In his verbal memory all kinds of information can be found.

Independent Practice

B. Identifying Active and Passive Voice Write each verb in these sentences. After each, write *active voice* or *passive voice*.

6. Last night Ana memorized material for a test.

MODEL⟩ memorized—active voice

7. This morning, most of the answers were remembered.
8. Later, Ana's time was used to review new formulas for math class.
9. By math class, the formulas had been forgotten by Ana.
10. But she had remembered the dates and events for the first test.
11. Why had she forgotten the formulas?
12. The formulas had been studied before science class.
13. In science class, Ana was taught new material.
14. The newly learned formulas had been pushed out of Ana's memory.
15. Ten hours of sleep had not erased the social studies facts from Ana's memory.

C. Revising: Writing Sentences Change each verb to the active voice. Write the sentences. Create appropriate subjects.

16. Memory can be greatly affected by experience.

MODEL⟩ Experience can greatly affect memory.

17. Sometimes something extremely unpleasant is experienced.
18. Perhaps all memories of the experience are forgotten.
19. Even earlier memories will have been erased.
20. Yet new information is remembered as usual.
21. This phenomenon has been named "amnesia."

Application — Writing

A Summary Think about something you can do such as ride a bicycle. Write a paragraph that describes the experience. It can be something you have done recently or something that you remember doing. Use verbs in the active voice.

7 Easily Confused Verb Pairs

◆ **FOCUS**   Sometimes a verb is confused with another verb.

In your reading and speaking, be careful when you use these verbs.

Verb	Meaning	Use in Sentence
lay	"to place or to put something down" transitive	**Lay** your jackets over there, and let the dog **lie** here.
lie	"to recline or remain at rest" intransitive	
set	"to put or place something down" transitive	**Set** the food down; then **sit** next to me.
sit	"to seat oneself or to rest" intransitive	
leave	"to go away or to cause to remain behind" transitive or intransitive	My parents **leave** early, but they **let** me stay late.
let	"to allow or to permit" transitive	
learn	"to gain knowledge of something" transitive or intransitive	Jaime **learns** patience as he **teaches** us soccer.
teach	"to show someone how to do" transitive or intransitive	
take	"to carry something away from a place" transitive	Please **take** this basket out to the shed and **bring** back some wood for the fireplace.
bring	"to carry something to a place" transitive	

Guided Practice

A. Read each sentence. Choose the correct verb in parentheses ( ).

1. Mrs. Burns (taught, learned) the class to appreciate poetry.
2. Maria (laid, lay) a book of sonnets on the table for Carol.
3. Carol (brought, took) the book and went home with it.
4. She (set, sat) in her favorite chair and began to read.
5. Dudley, her dog, (lay, laid) happily by her side.

Independent Practice

B. Choosing Verbs   Write the correct verb in each set of parentheses ( ).

6. In the kitchen Carol's mom (brought, took) cookies from the oven.

MODEL⟩ took

7. Later she (sat, set) a plate next to Carol's chair.
8. The scene (took, brought) Carol a feeling of cheerfulness.
9. As Carol munched, she (lay, laid) back and closed her eyes.
10. She (let, left) herself see, hear, smell, and "touch" the scene.
11. Carol had (learned, taught) herself to observe carefully.

C. Using Verbs   Write the correct form of an appropriate verb from the chart on page 188.

12. The modern Spanish poets have _____ us a legacy.

MODEL⟩ left

13. In the 1950's and 1970's Spanish poets _____ the highest honor in literature, the Nobel Prize.
14. Fine translations of Spanish poetry _____ on shelves in libraries and bookstores.
15. Readers can _____ for themselves the beauty of Spanish poetry.
16. _____ yourself enjoy García Lorca's poetry.
17. Many hours of pleasure _____ before you once you discover the Spanish writers.

D. Revising: Writing Sentences   Rewrite these sentences using verbs correctly.

18. Modern American poets bring some inspiration from other lands.

MODEL⟩ Modern American poets take some inspiration from other lands.

19. Oriental poets, for example, learned us how to write haiku.
20. Reading haiku lets much to the imagination.
21. When reading haiku, you can't just lay back and be entertained.
22. You must set quietly but leave your imagination run free.
23. Your active participation in the poem is what takes you much enjoyment.

Application — Writing

A Greeting Card   Imagine that you have spent a relaxing afternoon either by yourself or with your friends. Compose a greeting card that conveys the mood of the day. Use some of the verbs from the lesson.

Building Vocabulary
Prefixes, Base Words, and Roots

A **base word** is a word that can stand on its own. The word *spell* is an example of a base word. A **root** is the main part of a word that cannot stand on its own. The word part *script* is an example of a root. A **prefix** is a word part that is added to the beginning of a base word or a root to make a new word. A prefix changes the meaning and sometimes the spelling of the base word or the root. In the word *misspell, mis* is a prefix and *spell* is the base word. *Misspell* means "to spell incorrectly."

Use the meanings of roots and prefixes to help you determine the meanings of unfamiliar words.

Prefix	Meaning
anti	against
bi	two
circum	around
de	off, from, down
in, im, ir	not, opposite of, into
inter	between
mid	middle

Prefix	Meaning
pre	before
post	after
re	again
sub	under
trans	across
un	not, opposite of

Root	Meaning
aud, audi	hear
dic, dict	say, speak
fac, fact	make, do
ject	throw

Root	Meaning
port	carry
scrib, script	write
spect	examine
vis	see

Prefix + Root	Meaning
interject	throw between
transport	carry across
circumscribe	write around
predict	tell before
subject	undergo

Prefix + Base Word	Meaning
preview	look before
misunderstand	understand wrongly
rewrite	write again
bilingual	able to speak two languages
inability	not having ability

Reading Practice

For each word, write the prefix, the root, or the base word as well as its meaning. For example, you may write *im—into; port—carry*. Then write the correct meaning below each word. You may use a dictionary.

1. antitoxin
   a. a poison
   b. a remedy to fight against poison
   c. a wrong remedy

2. invisible
   a. able to be seen
   b. not able to be seen
   c. not able to be helped

3. predict
   a. to say after
   b. to see before
   c. to say before

4. semicircle
   a. a quarter circle
   b. an oval
   c. a half circle

5. propose
   a. to set forth for acceptance or rejection
   b. to serve dinner
   c. to stand in front of something

6. misguide
   a. to lead in the wrong direction
   b. to tell the wrong answer
   c. to not understand

7. unaltered
   a. to change beforehand
   b. not changed at all
   c. changed in the wrong way

Writing Practice

Use each pair of words in a sentence. Tell about something you do now that you could not do when you were younger. Underline each prefix.

1. possible—impossible
2. approve—disapprove
3. weekly—biweekly
4. selfish—selfless
5. predict—mistake
6. interject—reject
7. irresponsible—responsible
8. active—inactive

Project

Reread the essay from this unit to find any words that have prefixes and roots or prefixes and base words. List the words on a sheet of paper. Next to each word, write the word parts and their definitions. Volunteers can share their lists aloud with the rest of the class.

Language Enrichment
Verbs

Use what you know about verbs to do these activities.

 Curse of the Pharaoh

The explorers are about to open the long-lost tomb of Pharaoh Keepouttadis. A curse inscribed on the door threatens dreadful punishment to anyone who disturbs the tomb. Nevertheless, the explorers are going ahead. As a reporter you are on the scene to report live for *Whirled News.* Using the present progressive tense, describe for your eager readers and listeners what is happening.

 What's the Difference?

Choose a pair of commonly confused verbs that you studied in the unit lesson. Divide a sheet of notebook paper in half. Write one verb at the bottom of each half. Then illustrate the meaning of each verb. Combine your work with the class's in a picture dictionary that can be shared with other students.

 Say That Again!

What happens if you reverse the order of the direct object and indirect object in a sentence?

Example: Give the elephant a peanut.
Give the peanut an elephant.

Work in a small group to brainstorm funny examples of direct object/indirect object reversals. Write the original sentence; then reverse it. Have someone in your group illustrate the second example. Share your work with the rest of the class.

CONNECTING
LANGUAGE ↔ WRITING

In this unit you studied how verbs can describe an action that is taking place in the present and how verbs are used in the active and passive voices. You also learned that some pairs of verbs are confused with others.

◆ **Using Verbs in Your Writing** Understanding verb tense and active and passive voice will give flexibility to your writing. The correct use of direct and indirect objects will ensure that your writing is clear. Being able to use commonly confused verbs correctly will help you present your ideas well. Pay special attention to the verbs you use as you do these activities.

 Funny Phobias

You learned about prefixes, roots, and base words on the **Building Vocabulary** page. One interesting root is *phobia*, which means "an exaggerated and continuous dread of something." Use your dictionary to discover and write down the meanings of the following phobias. Then choose one phobia and write a paragraph that vividly describes your imaginary symptoms. Let a classmate guess the phobia.

acrophobia   ailurophobia
agoraphobia   astrophobia
autophobia   haptephobia
taphephobia

 A Great Idea

Ralph Waldo Emerson remarked that if you could build a mousetrap better than anyone else, the world would beat a path to your door. Design the ultimate mousetrap. Be sure the trap does not harm the mouse. Draw and label your invention. Then write a persuasive paragraph convincing people to buy it. Trade your paragraph with a classmate who will act as a customer and decide whether or not to purchase the trap. Good luck!

Unit Checkup

Think Back	Think Ahead
◆ What did you learn about persuasive essays in this unit? What did you do to write one?	◆ How will what you learned about persuasive essays help you when you read other materials that persuade? ◆ How will evaluating reasons to support an opinion help you write a persuasive essay?
◆ Look at the writing you did in this unit. How did verbs help you express your ideas?	◆ What is one way you can use verbs to improve your writing?

Analyzing a Persuasive Essay   *pages 158–159*

Write the type of appeal each statement uses: *appeal to reason, appeal to emotion,* or *ethical appeal.*

1. If you don't clean your room, Mom will be very upset.
2. A stitch in time saves nine.
3. Keep our community beautiful—don't litter.
4. Smoking can cause cancer.
5. If you do that, I'll never speak to you again!

Evaluating Reasons to Support an Opinion   *pages 160–161*

Write *legitimate* or *faulty* to identify the type of reasoning in each statement.

6. Everyone must buy pink grapefruit because the one I ate was excellent.
7. Dr. Smith is not a good doctor because she attended a medical school I never heard of.
8. Mary is a redhead, and since redheads are sensitive to the sun, Mary probably sunburns easily.
9. He's very careful, so he'll make an excellent accountant.

Using Quotations from Oral and Written Sources   *page 162*

Write the letter for the answer to each question.

10. Why is it important to quote accurately?
a. It's not really important. b. Quotes are exact words. c. It's just good manners.

11. Use quotes when
a. you want to support a special point.
b. you can't make your point as well.
c. both a and b.

12. Use quotes when
a. you're not exactly sure of the author's meaning.
b. a quote from a respected source will strengthen your argument.
c. neither a nor b.

13. A weak quote is better than no quote.
a. true   b. false   c. depends on situation

The Writing Process   *pages 163 – 173*

Write the letter for the answer to each question.

14. When you plan a persuasive essay, which topic is best?
a. one of historical interest
b. one that interests you
c. one that requires a lot of research

15. When gathering information, what should you consider?
a. how current your sources are
b. length of written sources
c. whether the sources support your opinion

16. Which topic is most appropriate for the current events club?
a. what caused World War I
b. who was the best United States President
c. why sixteen-year-olds should be allowed to vote

17. Suppose you are proofreading, and you realize you left out a line.
What should you do?
a. Don't bother adding it.
b. Write the line, and use an arrow to show where it should be inserted.
c. Rewrite the page.

18. What is a major consideration for sending a persuasive letter?
a. the receiver agrees with the position
b. both sides are stated fairly and fully
c. topic is of national interest

Progressive Forms of Verbs   *pages 176–177*

Write each verb phrase. In parentheses ( ), write its tense.

19. Everyone had been catching the flu for months.
20. I am thinking about all the absences!
21. Alicia, for example, had been leaping ahead in her mathematics this semester.
22. She has been missing many classes.
23. She is receiving the homework at home.
24. When she returns, she will have been making progress.

Direct Objects   *pages 178–179*

Write the subject, the verb, and the direct object in each sentence.

25. Without knowing why, we sometimes do things.
26. Sometimes instinct guides us.
27. With good instincts people make wise decisions.
28. Of course instinct alone does not provide answers.
29. Thoughts about an issue add important input.

Indirect Objects   *pages 180–181*

Write each sentence. Underline the direct object once and the indirect object twice.

30. Reading materials give us ideas for conversations and thoughts.
31. Linda offered me an interesting magazine yesterday.
32. It had given her valuable insights into the acid rain problem.
33. My parents tell me information they have read in the newspaper.
34. I bought myself a local newspaper today.

Predicate Nominatives   *pages 182–183*

Write the sentences. Underline each predicate nominative once and the word to which it refers twice.

35. Civil rights are important issues for every American.
36. People are equals in the eyes of the law.
37. Whether a person is a child or an adult, civil rights apply.
38. Education, freedom of religion, and the right to vote are civil rights.
39. Citizens are recipients of these privileges.

Transitive and Intransitive Verbs   *pages 184 – 185*

Write each sentence. Underline the verb. After the sentence, write
transitive or *intransitive* in parentheses ( ).

40. Music often gives people strong feelings.
41. Ed enjoys fast rock and roll.
42. The music makes him energetic.
43. Slow music is relaxing.
44. At the end of a long day, I sit quietly and listen.

Active and Passive Voice   *pages 186 – 187*

Write each verb in these sentences. After each, write *active* or *passive* in
parentheses ( ).

45. Martha enjoys spring weather.
46. Few people like winter best.
47. Many are kept indoors by the cold.
48. Summer is preferred by many little children.
49. Long days offer more playtime.

Easily Confused Verb Pairs   *pages 188 – 189*

Write the verb in parentheses ( ) that is correct.

50. After years of hating it, Bob (taught, learned) himself not to mind
    waiting in lines.
51. One day when he (took, brought) an overdue book back to the
    library, he had to wait in a long line.
52. He (let, left) himself browse through the book as he waited for his turn.
53. Then he (set, sat) down and closed his eyes.
54. Bob wished he could (lay, lie) down and take a nap.

Prefixes, Base Words, and Roots   *pages 190 – 191*

For each word below, write the prefix and the root or the base word.
Then write the meaning of the whole word. You may use a dictionary.

55. unbelievable
    a. not probable   b. not alive   c. very possible
56. submarine
    a. underwater   b. secretive   c. on the surface of the sea
57. prenatal
    a. after birth   b. before birth   c. during Christmas
58. intercede
    a. to come before   b. to come after   c. to come between

1-4 Cumulative Review

Compound Subjects and Predicates   *pages 40–41*

Write the sentences. Underline the subjects once and the verbs twice. Write *compound subject, compound verb,* or *both* after the sentence.

1. Leslie takes nature photographs and prints them.
2. Photos and paintings can present a scene.
3. Green, brown, and gold are some colors in this tree.
4. That photograph distorts the tree and gives it an eerie look.
5. The drawing and the sketch suggest different moods and feelings about the tree.
6. A story and a poem can also describe and picture a tree.
7. The leaves and flowers on trees amaze and delight me.
8. Bark and leaves have distinctive textures.

Simple and Compound Sentences   *pages 42–43*

Write *simple* or *compound* for each sentence below.

9. Gary watches television and listens to the radio.
10. Television news can show you what happens, but radio news can suggest events.
11. Marvin and Sandra want to be journalists.
12. They both write for the school paper, and they read a lot.
13. Sandra wants to cover news, but Marvin prefers cultural events.
14. Marvin reviewed the school play and the new movie downtown.
15. Sandra wrote about the school elections, and she gave a talk about the differences among political parties.

Avoiding Sentence Fragments and Run-on Sentences   *pages 44–45*

Write whether each group of words is a *fragment,* a *run-on sentence,* or a *sentence.* Rewrite the fragments and run-on sentences to correct the errors.

16. Is my favorite magazine.
17. The best article in a recent issue.
18. I learned many new things about the subject I would like to learn even more.
19. Illustrations may be drawings or photographs I prefer drawings.
20. The length of an article.

Possessive Nouns   *pages 90–91*

Label each noun *singular possessive* or *plural possessive*.

21. women's
22. Charles's
23. actors'
24. audience's
25. writer's
26. joke's
27. friends'
28. storyteller's
29. comedians'
30. families'

31. shows'
32. laughter's
33. stories'
34. props'
35. tale's
36. refreshments'
37. soda's
38. act's
39. smiles'
40. men's

Verbs   *pages 126–127*

Write whether the underlined verb is an *action verb* or a *linking verb*.

41. Liz passed the advanced swimming test.
42. She seems eager for the lifesaving course.
43. The swimming instructor really teaches well.
44. A lifesaving certificate is valuable.
45. The certificate qualifies you for an unforgettable summer job.
46. The local lifeguards love their work.
47. Swimmers respect them.
48. To some, a lifeguard's job appears easy.
49. A lifeguard's mind never strays from the job.
50. Paying careful attention at all times is a real challenge.

Principal Parts of Verbs   *pages 130–131*

Write each verb. After the verb, write *present, present participle, past,* or *past participle*.

51. Our class is painting a mural for the hall.
52. Chiu decided on the theme "work and play at school."
53. A small group of students has worked on the design.
54. Everyone is helping in some way.
55. The mural looks good already.
56. We have tried to make the mural lifelike.
57. The best classroom artists sketched the outlines in pencil.
58. My classmates are working many hours each week on the project.
59. We had planned to work only on Friday mornings.
60. Plans changed.

Verb Tenses   *pages 137–140*

Write each verb or verb phrase. After it, write its tense.

61. mumbles
62. has flipped
63. will have crushed
64. had managed
65. noticed
66. have counted
67. have promised
68. will jog
69. applauded
70. will have marched

71. sees
72. had followed
73. have listened
74. will have played
75. will cherish
76. manufactured
77. counted
78. had cleaned
79. has argued
80. have cooked

Irregular Verbs   *pages 132–134*

Write *present, present participle, past,* or *past participle* after each verb to show which principal part is used.

81. does
82. is being
83. has thought
84. is beginning
85. have sung
86. swam
87. is having
88. has drunk
89. have swum
90. had sold

91. have been
92. has said
93. have caught
94. has rung
95. is teaching
96. are running
97. has done
98. drank
99. has burst
100. is bringing

Direct and Indirect Objects   *pages 178–181*

Write each sentence. Underline direct objects once and indirect objects twice.

101. Miguel gave his classmates little gifts before he moved last month.

102. He gave me this drawing.

103. I showed my classmates the picture.

104. They gave me a way to thank Miguel.

105. I wrote him a poem.

106. My gift shows Miguel my feelings.

107. Miguel left us keepsakes and memories.

108. The class wrote and asked Miguel questions about his new life.

109. Miguel sent the class a long reply.

Transitive and Intransitive Verbs   *pages 184–185*

Write each sentence. Underline the verb. After the sentence, write *transitive* or *intransitive*.

110. Mountains fascinate most people.
111. Have you climbed a mountain?
112. From the top the view is usually beautiful.
113. Mountain air feels cold because of the altitude.
114. No trees grow on top of high mountains.
115. My family visited the Rocky Mountains last summer.
116. We hiked for days.
117. At first I became very tired.
118. The mountain air gave us energy.
119. A city person at heart, I also love mountains.
120. I draw the line, however, at climbing Mount Everest.

Active and Passive Voice   *pages 186–187*

Write each verb in these sentences. After each, write *active voice* or *passive voice*.

121. The art room was given a new coat of paint.
122. Everyone helped paint the walls and ceiling.
123. Colors were chosen by several students.
124. The final choices were selected by the whole class.
125. One wall has been made bright yellow, the rest white.
126. We painted the ceiling blue and added white clouds.
127. Wonderful feelings are experienced in the room.
128. Color influences mood.
129. We need a pleasant environment.
130. Everyone has been given a lift by the change.

Easily Confused Verb Pairs   *pages 188–189*

Write each correct verb in parentheses ( ).

131. Sports can (learn, teach) everyone something.
132. Don't just (lie, lay) back and ignore them.
133. I (sit, set) and watch, and I still have fun.
134. When you (take, bring) your best efforts with you to a game, you feel good whether you win or lose.
135. Don't (let, leave) losing get you down.
136. (Sit, Set) your mind on a goal and work to achieve it.
137. My sports interests now (lie, lay) in the area of team sports.

UNIT

5

Comparing and Contrasting

◆ **COMPOSITION FOCUS:** **Comparison/Contrast Composition**
◆ **LANGUAGE FOCUS:** **Pronouns**

Are word processors better than typewriters? Would you rather spend your vacation in the mountains or by the ocean? Is a cat or a dog a better choice for your family? How can you decide?

Sometimes it is useful to compare and contrast the similarities and the differences or the advantages and the disadvantages of two different ideas, objects, or places. When people compare and contrast, they usually begin by classifying—deciding what attributes of each thing they will use to make a comparison.

Andy Rooney, a nationally syndicated columnist and television personality, thinks that summer has both advantages and disadvantages. In his short essay he compares and contrasts them. In this unit you will learn to write a comparison/contrast composition.

Andy Rooney writes about a variety of subjects *to inform* and *to entertain* his readers.

Reading with a Writer's Eye
Comparison/Contrast Essay

We wait all year for summer to come, but when it finally arrives, some of us find fault with it. Read this essay and see which view of summer is yours. As you read, decide whether summer has more advantages or more disadvantages.

Summer: First the Good News

by Andy Rooney

There are good things and bad things about summer and you can just about divide them in half. I've made a list.

GOOD THINGS ABOUT SUMMER: It's nice and warm.
BAD THINGS ABOUT SUMMER: It's too hot.
GOOD: Corn on the cob and real, ripe, red tomatoes.
BAD: Disappointingly hard peaches and tasteless melons.
GOOD: A swim in water that feels too cold when you first get in and so good after you've been in a while that you don't want to get out.
BAD: So many people at the lake or beach that going in the water is no fun.
GOOD: Waking up on vacation and realizing you don't have to go to work.
BAD: Waking up on vacation and realizing you only have four days of vacation left.
GOOD: Visiting places you've always wanted to go to.
BAD: Driving forever to get someplace you didn't want to go to anyway.
GOOD: An air-conditioned car on a hot day.
BAD: Getting into a car that's been closed up and parked in the sun.
GOOD: Being out in the sun and getting a tan that makes you look great.
BAD: The nervous feeling you ought not be out in the sun so much because it's bad for your skin and will make you look old sooner.

GOOD: The long hours of sunlight in July.

BAD: The realization in August that the days are getting shorter and it'll be all downhill from now on.

GOOD: Friends you don't see any other time of year.

BAD: People you can't avoid because everything's so open in summer.

GOOD: The satisfying feeling mowing the lawn can give you.

BAD: Realizing the grass is so long you have to mow it even though you don't feel like mowing the lawn today.

GOOD: Cooking outdoors. It can make tough meat taste good.

BAD: Cooking outdoors. It can make good meat taste tough.

GOOD: No snow.

BAD: No snow.

Respond

1. Which ideas most reflect your view of summer—the advantages or the disadvantages that Andy Rooney mentions? Explain why you feel the way you do.

Discuss

2. What is Andy Rooney's conclusion about summer?

3. What do you think was Andy Rooney's purpose in recording these contrasts?

Thinking As a Writer
Analyzing a Comparison/Contrast Composition

A comparison/contrast composition can point out similarities and differences between two ideas, objects, or places. It can also show the advantages and the disadvantages of each. Each paragraph includes a topic sentence and detail sentences. The composition as a whole contains an introduction and a conclusion.

In comparison/contrast compositions, the topics can be explained in separate paragraphs, or they can be handled within one paragraph.

There are two ways of organizing the paragraphs. You can treat your material **point by point,** as Andy Rooney did, or you can deal with it one subject at a time, using the **block method.**

This paragraph contrasts summer and winter, using the block method.

> There are many differences between summer and winter. In summer the climate is hot. People enjoy warm-weather activities such as swimming and tennis. Many prefer to eat light meals or to barbecue their food. In winter, on the other hand, the climate is cold. Activities such as sledding and skating are popular, and people enjoy hot stews and casseroles.

The **topic sentence** states the two subjects to be contrasted.

Detail sentences show the differences—in this case by using the block method and treating first one subject and then the other.

Read this paragraph that uses the point-by-point method.

> We don't often think about it, but there *are* similarities between winter and summer. Both winter and summer are vacation times for many people. Because students have holidays from school, both seasons are often times for families to go away together. Also, winter and summer are both times for family gatherings. Independence Day and the winter holidays are both occasions for get-togethers and visiting.

The **topic sentence** states the two subjects to be compared.

Detail sentences show the similarities—in this case using the point-by-point method, discussing first one similarity and then the next.

Writer's Guide

A comparison/contrast composition

♦ establishes a common denominator.

♦ discusses points of similarity and difference or of advantage and disadvantage.

♦ often has an introduction and a conclusion.

Discuss

In your own words, explain the block method and the point-by-point method of developing comparison/contrast compositions.

Try Your Hand

A. **Identify Topics**   Read each paragraph. Decide what things are being compared or contrasted.

> 1.   That was the year I went to a great new school. I was able to play in the town's softball league, and I finally got to have a room of my own. On the other hand, I also had increased responsibilities. I had to start helping my father work in his vegetable garden and helping my mother take care of our pet goats.

> 2.   Mother and Father both grew up in Puerto Rico. They went to the same college, and both majored in biology. They both play the flute and enjoy cooking and tennis.

B. **Write Topic Sentences**   For each paragraph, write a possible topic sentence.

C. **Add Detail Sentences**   For each paragraph, add a detail sentence that fits the topic.

D. **Read a Comparison/Contrast Composition**   Find a comparison/contrast composition. Read it to a partner. Tell whether it shows similarities and differences or advantages and disadvantages. Tell whether it uses the point-by-point method or the block method.

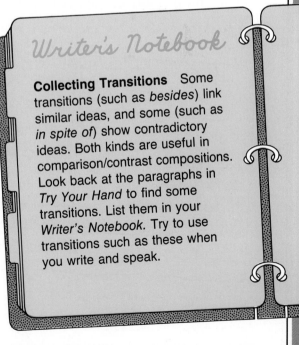

Writer's Notebook

Collecting Transitions   Some transitions (such as *besides*) link similar ideas, and some (such as *in spite of*) show contradictory ideas. Both kinds are useful in comparison/contrast compositions. Look back at the paragraphs in *Try Your Hand* to find some transitions. List them in your *Writer's Notebook.* Try to use transitions such as these when you write and speak.

Thinking As a Writer
Evaluating for Comparison and Contrast

To write a good comparison/contrast composition, a writer begins by choosing two subjects that are similar or different and then identifying the similarities and differences. Here are three examples.

1. Hammers and saws are both *tools*.
2. Gloves are for *hands*, but socks are for *feet*.
3. Dogs and cats are both *animals*.

Next, the writer chooses categories that show the characteristics of the group to which both subjects belong. These categories will be different for each group. For example, tools can be categorized by purpose, appearance, power source, efficiency, and so forth. You would not use the same categories to analyze the similarities and the differences between two animals.

Once the writer has established the categories, it is time to fill them in with information for the two chosen subjects. Read this chart.

	Dogs	Cats
class	mammal	mammal
personality	responsive and playful	reserved and quiet
relationship to owner	companionable	independent
how show anger	growl and bite	hiss and scratch
diet	carnivorous	carnivorous

In order to see clearly the similarities and the differences, the writer next makes a Venn diagram. With it the writer shows the characteristics that dogs and cats have in common and those that are unique to each animal. Then he or she is ready to begin a first draft. Study the Venn diagram below.

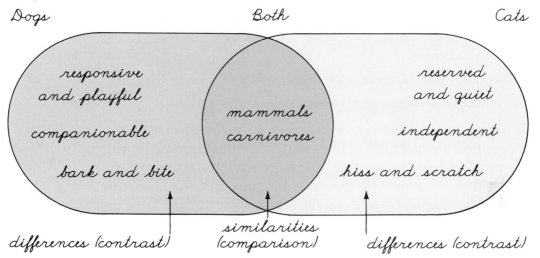

Dogs   *Both*   *Cats*

responsive and playful

companionable

bark and bite

mammals carnivores

reserved and quiet

independent

hiss and scratch

differences (contrast)   *similarities (comparison)*   *differences (contrast)*

When you write a comparison/contrast composition, follow these steps to help you identify similarities and differences.

Discuss

1. Why wouldn't you use *purpose* as a category to classify animals?
2. What other category could you use to classify animals?

Try Your Hand

A. Match Items and Classifications   Match each item to the set of classifications that fits it.

A. Australia   B. dishwasher   C. dictionary   D. building

1. purpose, materials, date constructed, location
2. size, location, population, resources, type of government
3. color, capacity, price, source of power
4. copyright date, intended audience, length, number of words

B. Add Items to Classifications   Add one item to each list in **A**. Tell why the item fits the category.

C. Make a Venn Diagram   Choose two items to compare and contrast. Create a Venn diagram for the two items to show their similarities and their differences.

Developing the Writer's Craft
Writing for an Audience and Purpose

The purpose and the intended audience always guide a writer's choices in what to say and how to say it. Read these examples. They are intended for two different audiences.

A lion is like a big kitty–cat.
Lions, like domestic cats, belong to the family *Felidae*.

Since a comparison/contrast composition can be persuasive or informative, a writer must define clearly his or her purpose for writing. In a persuasive piece, the focus is on convincing the audience. In an informative piece, the writer analyzes the subject in order to decide what information to present and how to organize it. Read these examples.

1.
> High-school seniors are much like adults. They have many of the responsibilities of adulthood. Thus, it is clear that all high-school seniors, regardless of age, should be allowed to vote.

2.
> High-school seniors are much like adults. Many, especially girls, have reached their adult stature. They have formed many of the interests that they will carry into adulthood.

When you write your comparison/contrast composition, remember your purpose for writing and your audience.

Discuss

1. Look at the sentences about lions. Identify the approximate ages of the intended audiences. Tell for what purpose they were written.
2. Do you think the paragraphs about high-school seniors are effective? Explain your answer.

Try Your Hand

Write for an Audience and a Purpose Choose an audience and a purpose for writing. Then write two sentences comparing a cat and a lion. Trade papers with a partner. See whether you can identify the purpose and the intended audience for your partner's sentences.

1 Prewriting
Comparison/Contrast Composition

Writer's Guide

Prewriting Checklist
- ☑ Choose two items to compare and contrast.
- ☑ Think about your audience and your purpose.
- ☑ Gather information.
- ☑ Organize information.

Vijaya wanted to write a comparison/contrast composition that showed similarities and differences for other students. She used the checklist in the **Writer's Guide** to help her plan her comparison/contrast composition. Look at what she did.

◆ Brainstorming and Selecting a Topic

First, Vijaya brainstormed a list of suitable topics for a comparison/contrast composition. She decided she would write about a topic with which she was personally familiar.

Next, Vijaya looked down her list and crossed out topics that would be of little interest to students, that would be too difficult to explain, or that would be too complicated to cover in two or three paragraphs.

Finally, Vijaya decided to compare and contrast middle school and elementary school for an audience of fifth-graders, because she knew that this was a topic of immediate concern to students who were about to make the transition. Since she had entered middle school just a few months before, the similarities and differences were fresh in her mind and would be easy to recall. Here is the list she used.

1. life in India and life in America
2. pet cats and pet dogs
3. elementary school and middle school
4. 9-month school year and year-round school

Discuss

1. Look at each topic Vijaya crossed off her list. Why do you think she didn't choose it?
2. If Vijaya had wanted to write a comparison/contrast composition for a social studies class, which topic might she have chosen? Why?

◆ Gathering and Organizing Information

After Vijaya selected her topic, she gathered information for her comparison/contrast composition. She made a list of categories to use to classify the two kinds of schools.

Categories for Schools	
classes	homework
teachers	extracurricular activities
schedule	student council
dress	field trips

Next, Vijaya used these categories and filled in information for elementary school and for middle school.

	Elementary	Middle
1. classes	math	math
	science	science
	physical education	physical education
	social studies	social studies
	language arts	language arts
	reading	reading
	art	art
	music	music
		industrial arts/ home economics
		computer
		band
		homeroom

WRITING PROCESS

After completing both lists, Vijaya entered her information on a Venn diagram. The Venn diagram shows the similarities and the differences between the two types of schools.

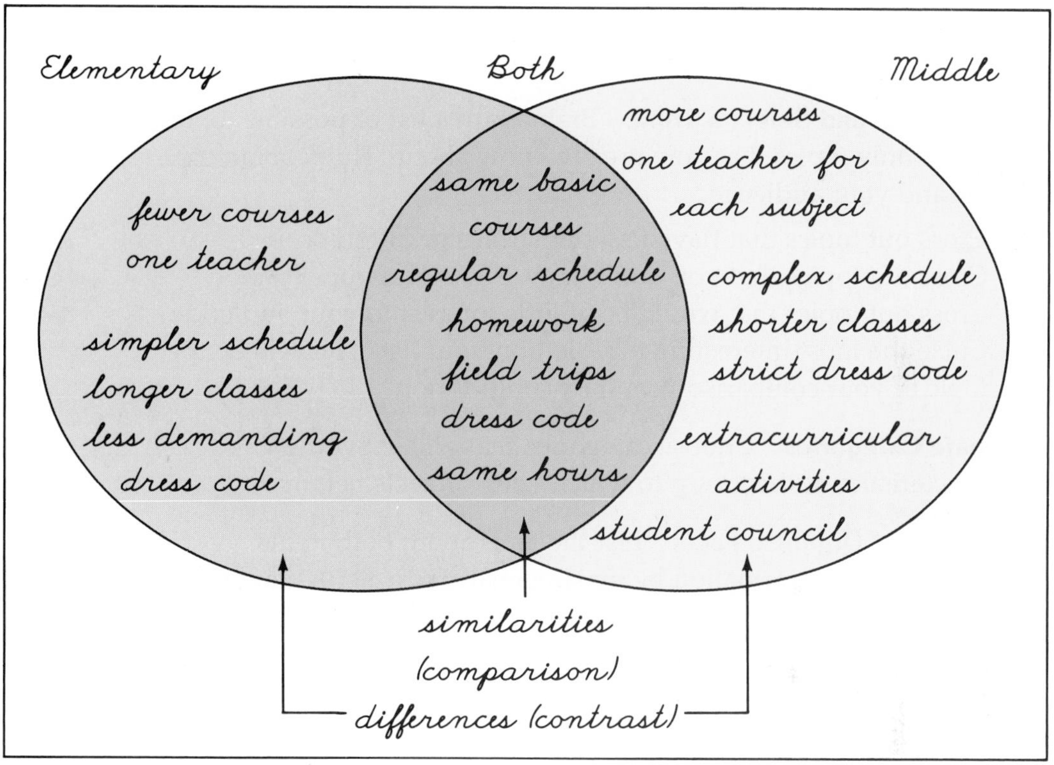

Elementary

Both

Middle

same basic courses
regular schedule
homework
field trips
dress code
same hours

fewer courses
one teacher

simpler schedule
longer classes
less demanding
dress code

more courses
one teacher for each subject

complex schedule
shorter classes
strict dress code
extracurricular activities
student council

similarities
(comparison)
differences (contrast)

Vijaya wanted to write her paragraph of comparison first, and she planned to use the point-by-point method. However, she realized that she might change her mind when she began her first draft.

Discuss

1. What categories did Vijaya use to classify the characteristics of elementary school and middle school? What are others she could have used?
2. Why does Vijaya's Venn diagram present her information more clearly than her lists do?

3. Why would Vijaya want to use her lists and her diagram as she writes her paper?

4. If Vijaya were contrasting the advantages and the disadvantages of elementary school and middle school, what categories might she use? Why?

Try Your Hand

Now plan a comparison/contrast composition of your own.

A. Brainstorm and Select a Topic   Brainstorm a list of possible topics. Include only topics that you already know about. Think about each topic and your audience.

   ◆ Cross out topics that have few similarities or differences.
   ◆ Cross out topics that you don't know enough about.
   ◆ Cross out topics that would be of little interest to your audience.
   ◆ Circle the most interesting topic left on your list. This will be the topic of your comparison/contrast composition.

B. Create Categories   Choose categories that will show the characteristics of the group to which your subjects belong.

C. Gather and Organize Facts   List the facts about both items. Organize your information by making charts or a Venn diagram as Vijaya did. Check to see that you have covered all the major points that should be compared and contrasted. Then decide the order in which you will organize your facts. Decide if you want to use the point-by-point method or the block method in your composition. You may want to use this Venn diagram as a model.

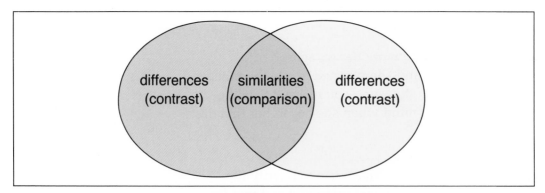

differences (contrast)   similarities (comparison)   differences (contrast)

 Save your lists and your charts or diagram in your *Writer's Notebook.* You will use them when you draft your comparison/contrast composition.

WRITING PROCESS

2 Drafting
Comparison/Contrast Composition

Before Vijaya started to draft her comparison/contrast composition, she decided to use the point-by-point method on which she had planned. She used her lists and her diagram and followed the checklist in the **Writer's Guide** to draft her composition. Look at what she did.

Middle school is like elementary school in many ways. In both schools you study the same basic subjects: math, science, social studies, language arts, art, music, and physical education. There are field trips in middle school once a month, just like elementary school. The schools begin and end at the same time. In both you have a regular schedule of classes. By the way, the middle school is on Central Street.

Writer's Guide

Drafting Checklist

☑ Use your lists and diagram for ideas.

☑ Write a paragraph to show comparisons and another to show contrasts.
Or

☑ Write a paragraph telling the advantages and the disadvantages of one subject and another paragraph telling the advantages and the disadvantages of another subject.

☑ Add a conclusion, if necessary.

Discuss

1. Where did Vijaya get her information? Why didn't she use it all?
2. Look at Vijaya's topic sentence. What is she comparing?

Try Your Hand

Now draft your comparison/contrast composition.

A. Review Your Information Think about the information you gathered in the last lesson. Decide whether you need more. If so, gather it.

B. Think About Your TAP Remember that your task is to write a comparison/contrast composition. Your purpose is to compare and contrast your two subjects.

C. Write Your First Draft Use the **Drafting Checklist** to write your comparison/contrast composition.

When you write your draft, just put all your ideas on paper. Do not worry about spelling, punctuation, or grammar. You can check them later.

Task: What?
Audience: Who?
Purpose: Why?

Save your first draft in your *Writer's Notebook*. You will use it when you revise your comparison/contrast composition.

3 Responding and Revising
Comparison/Contrast Composition

Vijaya read over her draft. Then she used the checklist in the **Writer's Guide** to revise her composition. Look at what she did.

◆ Checking Information

Vijaya saw that she had forgotten a school subject that showed an important similarity. To indicate the addition, she used this mark ∧ .

◆ Checking Organization

Vijaya realized that she had mentioned field trips early in her composition. Since they were not a major point, she decided it would make better sense to mention them later. To move the sentence, she used this mark ⌒ .

◆ Checking Language

When Vijaya checked the sentences in her first paragraph, she found that one of the detail sentences was not necessary to her subject. For the sake of unity, she took the sentence out using this mark ℓ .

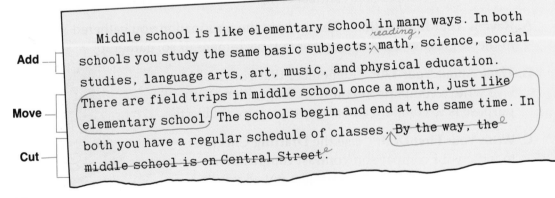

Add — Middle school is like elementary school in many ways. In both schools you study the same basic subjects: reading, math, science, social studies, language arts, art, music, and physical education. There are field trips in middle school once a month, just like elementary school. The schools begin and end at the same time. In both you have a regular schedule of classes. By the way, the middle school is on Central Street.

Move —

Cut —

Discuss

1. Why did Vijaya remove the comment about the location of the middle school?
2. Why did she move the sentence about field trips?

Try Your Hand

Now revise your first draft.

A. Read Your First Draft As you read your comparison/contrast composition, think about your audience and your purpose. Read your composition silently or to a partner to see if it is complete and well organized. Ask yourself or your partner the questions in the box.

Responding and Revising Strategies

✔ Respond **Ask yourself or a partner:**	✔ Revise **Try these solutions:**
◆ Have I included the basic information that should be in the composition?	◆ Find the information in your list or Venn diagram, and **add** it to your composition.
◆ Have I written an introduction and a conclusion, if appropriate?	◆ If necessary, **add** these to your composition.
◆ Does the topic sentence adequately identify the main idea of each paragraph?	◆ **Change** the wording to make it clearer.
◆ Does each detail sentence support the main idea of the paragraph?	◆ **Cut** unnecessary ideas. See the **Revising Workshop** on page 218.
◆ Did I follow my plan of organization from Prewriting?	◆ **Move** any material that is out of its proper sequence.
◆ Does my writing suit my audience and purpose?	◆ **Change** any words that may not be relevant to them.

B. Make Your Changes If the answer to any question in the box is *no*, try the solution. Use the **Editor's Marks** to show your changes.

C. Review Your Composition Again Decide whether there is anything else you want to revise. For example, you might decide to change from the block method to the point-by-point method of showing similarities and differences. Keep revising your composition until you feel it is well organized and complete.

EDITOR'S MARKS

- ∧ Add something.
- Cut something.
- Move something.
- Replace something.

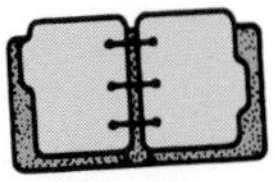

Save your revised comparison/contrast composition in your *Writer's Notebook*. You will use it when you proofread your composition.

Revising Workshop
Keeping to the Topic

   Good writers make their writing focused and unified. Every
sentence in their paragraphs directly supports the main idea. Look
at the underlined sentences in the following paragraph.

> Both summer and winter vacations can be wonderful family times.
> In my family this is certainly so. We use our vacation time to see new
> places and meet new people. We spend extra time together as a family.
> <u>My brother Peter says he would rather be with his best friend, Brian,
> but then he is only five.</u> We try to do special activities during
> vacation time that we don't do the rest of the year. Sometimes we go
> camping. Occasionally we eat out. <u>My favorite restaurant meal is
> lamb chops with mint jelly.</u>

   This paragraph is not unified, because the writer included
information that has nothing to do with the comparison being made. If
you delete the two underlined sentences, the paragraph is unified.

Practice

Read the comparison/contrast paragraph. Underline the sentences
that do not contribute to the main idea and should be removed for
unity. Then rewrite the paragraph so that it is unified. Add two
contrasts or comparisons that support the main idea.

> Staying home on vacation can be as attractive as going away.
> When you go away you eat out every day, but when you stay home you
> barbecue and go to neighborhood potluck suppers. Chicken is what we
> usually serve. Away on vacation you usually meet new people, but at
> home you have time to enjoy your longtime friends. My best friend is
> Wendy Russell. On vacation you see beautiful scenery you have never
> seen before. At home you have the pleasure of watching the seeds you
> planted develop into beautiful flowers or vegetables. Did you ever try
> growing rhubarb?

4 Proofreading
Comparison/Contrast Composition

After Vijaya revised her comparison/contrast composition, she used the checklist in the **Writer's Guide** and the **Editor's Marks** to proofread it. Look at what she did.

Writer's Guide

Proofreading Checklist

- ☑ Check for errors in capitalization.
- ☑ Check for errors in punctuation.
- ☑ Check to see that all your paragraphs are indented.
- ☑ Check for errors in grammar. Be sure that you have not written any sentence fragments or run-on sentences.
- ☑ Circle any words you think are misspelled. Find out how to spell them correctly.
- ⇒ For proofreading help, use the **Writer's Handbook.**

In some ways of course, middle school differs from *elementary* (elementery) school. There are new courses such as computer, industrial arts, and home economics, and this makes your schedule a little more complicated. You have more homework. Each day than you did in elementary school. The student *council* (counsel) in middle school, allows students to have more of a voice in school (affares) *affairs* than they did in elementary school. And it is more fun!

Discuss

1. Look at Vijaya's proofread comparison/contrast composition. What kinds of mistakes did she make?
2. Why did she take out the period after the word *homework* and begin *each* with a lowercase letter?

EDITOR'S MARKS

- ≡ Capitalize.
- ⊙ Add a period.
- ∧ Add something.
- ⩟ Add a comma.
- ⱽ ⱽ Add quotation marks.
- ✀ Cut something.
- ⋀ Replace something.
- ∼ Transpose.
- ◯ Spell correctly.
- ꓨ Indent paragraph.
- / Make a lowercase letter.

Try Your Hand

Proofread Your Comparison/Contrast Composition Now use the checklist in the **Writer's Guide** and the **Editor's Marks** to proofread your comparison/contrast composition.

Save your corrected comparison/contrast composition in your *Writer's Notebook.* You will use it when you publish your composition.

5 Publishing
Comparison/Contrast Composition

Writer's Guide
Publishing Checklist

- ☑ Make a clean copy of your comparison/contrast composition.
- ☑ Check to see that nothing has been left out.
- ☑ Make sure there are no mistakes.
- ☑ Share your composition in a special way.

Vijaya made a clean copy of her composition and checked it to be sure she had not left out anything. Then she and her classmates published their compositions by reading them aloud to the class. You can find Vijaya's completed composition on pages 41 and 42 of the **Writer's Handbook.**

Here's how Vijaya took the Publishing stage one step further.

1. Vijaya practiced reading her composition aloud so that she would be prepared to present it to an audience.
2. Vijaya shared her composition when she spoke before a group of elementary school students. She spoke slowly and distinctly, using her voice to emphasize key words and phrases. She used facial expressions and gestures to help communicate her message to her audience. She found the **Tips on How to Signal Ideas While Speaking**, on page 221, helpful.
3. She listened to the students and responded to their questions.

Discuss

1. What might have happened if the comparison part and the contrast part of the composition were not clearly separated?
2. Why was it important for Vijaya to use the **Tips on How to Signal Ideas While Speaking** when she spoke?

Try Your Hand

Publish Your Comparison/Contrast Composition   Follow the checklist in the **Writer's Guide.** Then read your composition aloud to a class, or try this idea for sharing it.

• Share your composition with your family. Ask for their views on the same topic. Discuss the various points you mentioned.

Listening and Speaking
Tips on How to Signal Ideas While Speaking

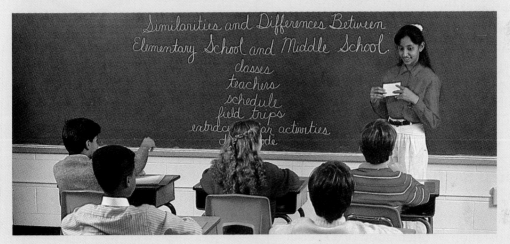

Voice

1. In general, speak slowly, loudly, and clearly. Mumbled or rushed speech is difficult to comprehend.
2. Your voice can get louder or softer and higher- or lower-pitched. During your talk, let your voice change in ways that help emphasize the important points. A monotone bores the audience.

Body

Stand comfortably, with feet apart and knees slightly bent. A speaker who shifts from foot to foot distracts the audience.

Face

Relax your facial muscles, and assume a natural expression. Let your expression reflect the content of your talk.

Writing in the Content Areas

Use what you learned to write another comparison/contrast composition for your classmates. Use one of these ideas or an idea of your own.

Writer's Guide

When you write, remember the stages of the Writing Process.

* Prewriting
* Drafting
* Responding and Revising
* Proofreading
* Publishing

Science

Compare and contrast two plants or two animals that are in the same class or family, such as pumpkins and squash or blue jays and grackles. Research the attributes of the class or the family. Then decide which categories to use to classify the subjects. After you have completed your composition, make an illustration that points out the similarities and the differences.

Fine Arts

Compare and contrast two works of art that have the same subject, such as two still lifes that show flowers, or a painting and a sculpture of a dancer. Decide on categories to use in your comparison/contrast composition. Determine whether you are more interested in what is the same about the works or what is different.

Social Studies

Compare and contrast a custom in two different cultures, such as food preparation or celebration of a special holiday. You might want to compare how birthdays are celebrated in different parts of the world. How are the celebrations the same, and how are they different? Maybe you would like to celebrate your next birthday the way a student would in another country.

Physical Education

Compare and contrast two similar sports, such as two racket sports or two sports played with balls moved only by the human body, such as football and basketball. They can be sports you have played or sports that you have seen played. To be able to describe the contrasts between the two, try to visualize the way you would play each game.

CONNECTING

WRITING ◄► LANGUAGE

A well-written comparison/contrast composition helps the reader understand the points that the writer makes. Read the following paragraphs. What similarities and differences between butterflies and teenagers can you discover?

Metamorphosis is a Greek word that means "a change from one form to another." In biology, it is used to describe the changes that occur in the form and structure of some animals between their birth and their maturity. The term *metamorphosis* also has been used to describe a significant change in an individual's attitudes, beliefs, or behavior. Parts of both meanings can be seen in people whom we know as *teenagers*.

Although a teenager does not display the four separate stages of growth that characterize the life cycle of a butterfly, he or she nevertheless clearly passes through physical, emotional, and intellectual changes. Just ask a parent or teacher!

◆ **Pronouns in a Comparison/Contrast Composition**   The highlighted words are pronouns. Pronouns take the place of nouns in writing and speaking. For example, the pronoun *it* in the second sentence replaces the noun *metamorphosis*, whereas the pronoun *their* in the same sentence refers to *some animals*. In paragraph two the words *he/she* refer to *a teenager*. Using pronouns can help you avoid repetition.

◆ **Language Focus: Pronouns**   The following lessons will help you use different types of pronouns in your own writing.

1 Pronouns

◆ **FOCUS**   A **pronoun** takes the place of a noun or nouns.

A pronoun can be used to take the place of a noun. Pronouns are used to avoid repetition. The pronouns that are used most frequently are personal pronouns. The word in color is a personal pronoun.

Alex notices how he changes from day to day.

Personal Pronouns		
	Singular	**Plural**
First person (speaker)	I, me	we, us
Second person (person spoken to)	you	you
Third person (person spoken about)	he, she, it him, her	they, them

Pronouns show number and gender. **Number** refers to whether a pronoun is singular or plural.

> **Singular:** I, me, you, he, she, him, her, it
> **Plural:** we, us, you, they, them

Gender indicates whether a word is masculine, feminine, or neuter. Something that is neuter is neither masculine nor feminine. Neuter pronouns do not refer to people but to things, places, or ideas. Only third-person singular pronouns are classified by gender.

Masculine: he, him   **Feminine:** she, her   **Neuter:** it

Guided Practice

A. Identify the personal pronoun or pronouns in each sentence.

1. Janet was blonde as a child, but now she has brown hair.
2. Janet says, "When I was five, we moved here from Utah."
3. Henry remembers when she came, for he had just moved in.

B. 4.–6. Identify the person, number, and gender (if appropriate) of each pronoun in **A.**

Independent Practice

C. Identifying Personal Pronouns   Write the personal pronouns in each of the following sentences.

   7. When Janet was young, she was mischievous, and the family says she kept them busy.

MODEL⟩ she, she, them

   8. When Janet was ten, she enjoyed playing outside, and the exercise seemed to give her a huge appetite.

   9. When she received new toys or games, she raced to show them to me.

   10. She and I loved to tell silly jokes, but I doubt that those jokes would make us laugh today.

   11. Janet collected seashells, and she displayed them on the wall next to a dozen trophies.

   12. We built a clubhouse and created a secret password that members had to say before they could enter it.

   13. Now Janet and I are twelve, and she and I laugh about what we were like when we were in fifth grade.

D. 14.–20. Identifying Person, Number, and Gender   For each different pronoun in the sentences in **C,** write the person, number, and, where possible, gender.

MODEL⟩ 14. she—third person, singular, feminine
       them—third person, plural

Application—Writing

A Description   Remember a happy event you experienced as a child. It may have been something you did alone, with your friends, or with your family. Write a description of the event for your classmates. Use personal pronouns correctly. If you need help writing a description, see page 45 of the **Writer's Handbook.**

2 Pronouns and Antecedents

◆ **FOCUS** A pronoun should agree with its antecedent in number and gender.

You know that a pronoun can take the place of a noun or nouns. The word that a pronoun replaces is its **antecedent.** The antecedent usually comes before the pronoun and names the person, place, thing, or idea to which the pronoun refers. A pronoun must agree with its antecedent in number and gender. For example, if the antecedent is masculine and singular, the pronoun must be masculine and singular.

1. The boy is building a treehouse so he can enjoy it .
   boy—he masculine, singular   tree house—it neuter, singular

In the sentence, *boy* and *tree house* are the antecedents of *he* and *it.* An antecedent is usually one word, but it can be more than one. Here are some ways in which pronouns and antecedents are used.

An antecedent can be one word.

2. Jake thinks he can build a tree house.

3. Jake thinks the experience will help him .

4. Jake will use his tools.

An antecedent can be more than one word.

5. Jake and four friends begin work on their treehouse.

An antecedent can be in another sentence.

6. Esther walks past the unfinished tree house .

7. She asks when it will be finished.

An antecedent can follow the pronoun.

8. "We did it!" the boys shout.

Guided Practice

A. Name the pronoun and antecedent in each sentence or sentence pair.
1. The carpenter said he would help the boys.
2. Brian asked Mr. Brooks if he had the tools.
3. The toolbox was heavy. It held about thirty tools.
4. "I can't wait to get started!" shouted Mark.
5. When the boys saw Mr. Brooks, they led him away.

Independent Practice

B. Identifying Antecedents   Write the pronoun and its antecedent in each of the following sentences. The antecedent may be in a different sentence.

   6. People seldom think about how much they depend on trees.

   MODEL⟩ they—People

   7. Ron decided to write about trees in his report.
   8. "I found surprising information," Ron said.
   9. Trees are extremely important; they are used in many industries.
   10. Paper is made from trees; it is used everywhere.
   11. Does a woman think of trees when she dabs on perfume?
   12. When babies need medicine, from where does it come?
   13. Trees need help if they are to survive.

C. Using Pronouns and Antecedents   Choose and write the correct pronoun to complete each sentence. Be sure that the pronoun agrees with the antecedent.

   14. Floyd and Jenny are building a doghouse for _____ dog.   (his, their)

   MODEL⟩ their

   15. They asked a lumber salesman if _____ could help them.   (he, they)
   16. Mr. Bailey showed _____ doghouse blueprints.   (him, them)
   17. Jenny said they looked pretty hard to _____.   (her, them)
   18. "I used _____ last year," Mr. Bailey said.   (it, them)
   19. "Did the plans cause _____ any problems?" Floyd asked.   (you, him)

Application — Writing and Speaking

A How-to Paragraph   Think of something you can do that you might teach to someone else. Write the procedure step by step. Be sure to use clear pronouns and antecedents. Either explain the steps to a classmate, or trade papers and read each other's instructions. Then try to follow the instructions. If you need help writing a how-to paragraph, see page 40 of the **Writer's Handbook.**

3 Subject and Object Pronouns

◆ **FOCUS** Pronouns can be in the **nominative case** or the **objective case**.

Pronouns can be subjects or objects. A **subject pronoun** can be the subject of a sentence, or it can be a predicate nominative. Subject pronouns are in the nominative case.

Nominative	
Singular	**Plural**
I	we
you	you
he, she, it	they

1. I boarded a plane for the East Coast.   subject
2. It was I who went.   predicate nominative

An **object pronoun** can be a direct object or an indirect object or can be used after words such as *to*, *with*, and *from*. Object pronouns are in the objective case.

Objective	
Singular	**Plural**
me	us
you	you
him, her, it	them

3. Todd called me from Pittsburgh.   direct object
4. Sarah brought me flowers.   indirect object
5. I rode home with them .   after the word *with*

Pronouns change form to show whether they are in the nominative case or the objective case.

Notice that *you* never changes form. The pronoun *it* keeps the same form in both the nominative and the objective cases.

It is important to use the correct pronoun in compound subjects and objects. To test yourself, separate the compound into two parts.

6. Sonny called home. I called home.
7. Sonny and I called home. (not me called)
8. Cheri sent Ray a card. Cheri sent her a card.
9. Cheri sent Ray and her a card. (not sent she)

Guided Practice

A. Identify the case of each underlined pronoun as *nominative* or *objective*.

1. Will you go on the flight with Myra?
2. I will take it to Rome.
3. George and I want him to come with us to the Grand Canyon.

Independent Practice

B. Using Subject Pronouns   Write a subject pronoun to replace the noun or phrase in parentheses ( ). Write whether it is used as a subject or as a predicate nominative.

  4. (People) first flew in hot-air balloons.
MODEL They first flew in hot-air balloons.   subject

  5. In 1785 (a balloon) crossed the English Channel.
  6. It was (the Wright brothers) who built an airplane of wood and cloth.
  7. (The plane) flew for nearly a minute.

C. Using Object Pronouns   Write an object pronoun to replace the noun in parentheses ( ). Write whether it is used as a direct object or an indirect object.

  8. People use (airplanes) in different ways.
MODEL them   direct object

  9. A crop duster spreads (fertilizer).
  10. Forest rangers give (pilots) responsibility for fighting fires.
  11. All my friends like (air travel) except Martha.

D. Revising: Writing Correct Pronouns in Compounds   Choose and write the correct pair of pronouns in each sentence.

  12. (He and I, Him and me) read about the history of aviation.
MODEL He and I

  13. Andy lent a book on flight to (he and she, him and her).
  14. (He and they, Him and them) and other airplane buffs can enjoy the exhibits at the Smithsonian.

Application — Writing

A Postcard   Imagine that you are about to take your first jet trip. Write a postcard that describes your trip. Use subject and object pronouns correctly. Try to use pronouns in one compound subject or object.

4 Possessive Pronouns

◆ **FOCUS** A **possessive pronoun** is a pronoun that shows ownership or possession.

A possessive pronoun takes the place of a possessive noun. Like a possessive noun, a possessive pronoun shows ownership. It must agree in number and gender with the possessive noun it replaces. The words in color are possessive pronouns.

1. The students pick up their books and belongings.
2. They are collecting their coats and scarves.
3. Julie's book seems to be her prized possession.
4. It certainly holds her attention.

Possessive pronouns have one form when they are used before a noun or phrase and another form when they are used alone.

Possessive Pronouns			
Before Nouns		**Alone**	
Singular	**Plural**	**Singular**	**Plural**
my	our	mine	ours
your	your	yours	yours
his, her, its	their	his, hers	theirs

5. Shyness is her problem.
6. It used to be mine , too.
7. What is yours ?

Never use a pronoun with an apostrophe to show possession. Apostrophes are used when a pronoun and verb are combined to form a contraction; apostrophes are not used with possessive pronouns.

Confusing Homophone Pairs	
Contractions	**Pronouns**
you're (you are)	your
it's (it is)	its
there's (there is)	theirs
they're (they are)	their

Guided Practice

A. Identify the pronouns in each sentence.

1. I had difficulty overcoming my shyness.
2. You helped when you told me about your shy feelings.
3. Nearly every student in our class has had his or her problems with shyness.
4. The others' problems with shyness, however, seemed less obvious than mine.

B. 5.–8. Tell whether each pronoun in **A** is personal or possessive.

THINK AND REMEMBER

+ Remember that a **possessive pronoun** can be used to take the place of a possessive noun that shows ownership.
+ Remember that a possessive pronoun can be used with a noun or by itself in a sentence.
+ Never use an apostrophe with a possessive pronoun.

Independent Practice

C. Identifying Possessive Pronouns Write each possessive pronoun in the sentences.

9. Alexander is shy, and so is his younger brother.

MODEL⟩ his

10. Since his father and his grandmother also have shy feelings, has Alexander perhaps inherited their shyness?
11. Scientists do believe that a parent's personality traits can be passed on to his or her children.
12. However, not all of their traits will come from their parents.
13. If we choose, we can almost always change our ways.
14. Alexander has been making a conscious effort to overcome his shyness.
15. He walks up to his new classmates and shakes their hands.
16. Alexander and his younger brother Robert fight their shyness every day.
17. They say proudly, "Our shyness is only temporary; we will overcome it soon."

D. Using Possessive Pronouns   Choose and write the correct possessive pronoun in each sentence.

18. That idea was (your, your's) idea.
`MODEL` your

19. Julie and Marcie have solidified (theirs, their) friendship.

20. Julie's shyness was more noticeable than Peter thought (his, him) was.

21. She and (her, her's) sister Ila spoke to nobody when they arrived.

22. We mistook (their, their's) ways for unfriendliness or snobbishness.

23. As (they're, their) friendliness increased, so did (ours', ours).

24. Now I know that the first steps toward friendship could have been (my, mine).

E. Proofreading: Distinguishing Between Possessive Pronouns and Contractions   Choose and write the correct possessive pronoun(s) for each sentence.

25. What is (its, it's) solution?
`MODEL` its

26. (Theirs, There's) was one good way to confront the problems of shyness.

27. Build (you're, your) courage, and for a week say hello to three different people.

28. The next week share your interests, and ask them about (theirs, there's).

29. Remember to listen carefully to (their, they're) answers and ask some questions of (your, you're) own.

30. Although (its, it's) problems are real, (your, you're) extreme shyness can be overcome.

31. If thousands of others can change (their, they're) lives, so can you.

32. Do not measure (your, you're) achievement by anyone else's, however; measure it by how much you have improved.

Application — Writing and Speaking

A Conversation   Imagine that you have a very shy friend. Write a conversation in which you try to help that friend overcome his or her shyness. Use possessive pronouns correctly.

5 Reflexive, Intensive, and Demonstrative Pronouns

FOCUS

◆ A **reflexive pronoun** refers to the subject.
◆ An **intensive pronoun** emphasizes a noun or a pronoun.
◆ A **demonstrative pronoun** points out a particular person, place, or thing.

Reflexive and intensive pronouns have the same forms but different functions. Both reflexive and intensive pronouns end in *self* and *selves.* A reflexive pronoun reflects or refers to the subject of the sentence. It is necessary to the sentence's meaning and cannot be left out. An intensive pronoun is used with a noun or another pronoun for emphasis. It can be left out without changing the meaning of the sentence.

1. I find myself fascinated by this project.   **reflexive**

2. Geoffrey himself held one of the white mice.   **intensive**

The antecedent of a reflexive pronoun is the subject of the sentence. The antecedent of an intensive pronoun is the word it emphasizes. Both reflexive and intensive pronouns must agree with their antecedents in person, number, and gender.

Reflexive and Intensive Pronouns		
	Singular	**Plural**
First person	myself	ourselves
Second person	yourself	yourselves
Third person	himself, herself, itself	themselves

A demonstrative pronoun is a pronoun that points out a particular person, place, or thing. Demonstrative pronouns are *this, that, these,* and *those. This* and *these* point out persons and things that are nearby. *That* and *those* point out persons and things farther away. *This* and *that* are singular; *these* and *those* are plural.

3. This is my white mouse.   5. These are the oldest white mice.

4. That is your white mouse.   6. Those are the youngest white mice.

When *this, that, these,* and *those* are used before nouns, they are adjectives, not pronouns.

Guided Practice

A. Identify each reflexive pronoun and its antecedent.

1. In multiple-response learning, a subject teaches himself.
2. You do this when you teach yourself a new skill.
3. When we give ourselves rewards, we reinforce learning.
4. I gave myself an hour's break after I finished that task.
5. Sometimes Dr. Kim gives himself a day off.

B. Identify each demonstrative pronoun and its antecedent.

6. This is an experiment in multiple-response learning.
7. Is that a difficult maze?
8. These are mazes with many twists and turns.
9. Those are even more complex mazes.
10. These must be very clever animals!

THINK AND REMEMBER

- Remember that a **reflexive pronoun** refers to the subject in the sentence.
- Use an **intensive pronoun** with a noun or pronoun for emphasis.
- Be sure a **demonstrative pronoun** points out its antecedent.

Independent Practice

C. Identifying Reflexive and Intensive Pronouns   Write each reflexive or intensive pronoun and its antecedent.

11. We might get ourselves what we want by "accident."
MODEL⟩ ourselves—We
12. Our cat once got herself a treat by meowing at the table.
13. I myself said, "Just this once," as I slipped her a tidbit.
14. Later, she opened a cabinet and got a tidbit herself.
15. I should have told myself not to offer her "people food."
16. Mom said, "You have no one to thank for that but yourself!"

D. Identifying Demonstrative Pronouns   Write each demonstrative pronoun and its antecedent.

17. That was an example of insight learning.
MODEL⟩ That—example

18. This was the experiment: Bananas were out of reach.
19. That was a real challenge for the chimpanzee!
20. Looking at the bananas, the chimp wondered, "How can I get those?"
21. Finally, the animal piled up all the boxes in his cage, climbed out, and ate the fruit; this was his reward.
22. Unlike learning a series of steps, that was a problem requiring the animal to understand a solution all at once.

E. Identifying Demonstrative, Reflexive, and Intensive Pronouns   Write the correct pronoun in each sentence. Identify it as reflexive, intensive, or demonstrative.

23. Pavlov (himself, hisself) created an experiment.

MODEL> himself—intensive

24. Hungry people find (theirselves, themselves) salivating when they see food.
25. (This, That) means that digestive juices start flowing in the mouth.
26. When Pavlov fed his laboratory dogs, he and his assistant set off signals at the same time (theirselves, themselves).
27. (These, Them) included lights, buzzers, or bells, called stimuli.
28. Then Pavlov observed for (hisself, himself) that a bell or a light alone, without food, made a hungry animal salivate.
29. (This, These) became evidence of conditioned learning.

F. Using Demonstrative, Reflexive, and Intensive Pronouns   Write the correct type of pronoun to complete each sentence.

30. White mice teach _____ tricks.   (reflexive)

MODEL> themselves

31. "Is _____ a white mouse over there?" ask visitors to our classroom.   (demonstrative)
32. _____ are clever white mice.   (demonstrative)
33. Most of us find _____ disgusted by rats and mice, for they can be harmful animals.   (reflexive)
34. Once I _____ asked how I could work with mice.   (intensive)
35. Now _____ is the best hobby I can think of.   (demonstrative)

Application — Writing

An Explanation   Design a maze. Practice it until you can easily complete it. Then write instructions for the maze. Use reflexive, intensive, and demonstrative pronouns correctly. If you need help writing an explanation, see the **Writer's Handbook.**

6 Indefinite Pronouns

◆ **FOCUS** An **indefinite pronoun** is a pronoun that does not refer to a particular person, place, thing, or idea.

An indefinite pronoun may not need an antecedent. The person or thing to which it refers may be unknown. An indefinite pronoun can be the subject of a sentence. The words in color are indefinite pronouns.

1. Nothing happened this morning.   no antecedent

Indefinite pronouns that are singular take singular verbs.

2. Neither of my parents drives to work.

Indefinite pronouns that are plural take plural verbs.

3. Both travel by public transportation.

Some indefinite pronouns can be singular or plural. To determine whether to use a singular or a plural verb, check the word to which the pronoun refers.

4. Most of the class is present. singular

5. All of the students are well behaved.   plural

The chart at the right shows the most common indefinite pronouns.

When indefinite pronouns are used before nouns, they are adjectives, not pronouns.

6. Some parents work odd hours.   adjective

7. Some are doctors or businesspeople.   pronoun

Guided Practice

A. Identify each indefinite pronoun and its antecedent. If there is no antecedent, write *none*.

1. Some of the parents take turns driving.
2. Our car pool works well for everybody.
3. The car pool pleases most of the parents.
4. My father would like everyone to be on time.
5. Both of my best friends are in our car pool.

Singular
no one
either
another
nothing
neither
nobody
somebody
someone
something
one
each
much
such
anyone
anybody
anything
whatever
whichever
whoever
everybody
everyone
everything

Plural
both
few
many
several

Singular or Plural
all
more
most
some
any
none

Independent Practice

B. Using Indefinite Pronouns Write an indefinite pronoun to fill in each blank.

6. Work has become important in the lives of _____.

MODEL〉 many

7. Over the years life has changed for _____.
8. _____ of our writers note that women have always worked.
9. Until recently, _____ worked in certain professions.
10. Until _____ began to pay close attention to these differences, only 7 of every 100 doctors were women.
11. Now, when _____ leaves in the morning, she might be going to her job as an auto mechanic, a lawyer, or a police officer.
12. _____ would be surprised!

C. Revising: Replacing Nouns with Indefinite Pronouns Write the sentences. Replace the underlined nouns or phrases with various indefinite pronouns. Add words if necessary.

13. The lives of <u>women</u> have changed over the years.

MODEL〉 The lives of many have changed over the years.

14. In 1848, American women wanted equality for <u>men and women</u>, including the right to vote.
15. <u>People</u> believed women were too ignorant to vote.
16. Not until 1920 did the Nineteenth Amendment give <u>citizens</u> over 21 the right to vote.
17. Now if <u>a person</u> wants to run for office, it makes little difference if <u>she</u> is female.
18. Since 1960, a half-dozen women have headed their countries, and <u>every woman</u> has become an important role model.

Application — Writing

A Paragraph Imagine that you have completed your education and are about to begin your first job. Write a paragraph that describes what you expect. Include details that tell where you will work and what kind of work you will do. Use indefinite pronouns correctly.

7 Interrogative Pronouns

♦ **FOCUS** An **interrogative pronoun** is used to ask a question.

The five interrogative pronouns are *who, what, whose, which,* and *whom*. It is easy to remember them because they all begin with *wh*.

1. Who is speaking on that telephone?
2. What is she doing to make it work?
3. Which is she using?
4. Whose is it?
5. Whom can she call?

The pronouns *who* and *whom* can be tricky. *Who* is a subject pronoun, and *whom* is an object pronoun. To check your choice, answer the question by using the pronouns *he* or *she, him* or *her*. If the answer is a subject pronoun, use *who*. If it is an object pronoun, use *whom*.

6. (Who, Whom) is the operator? She is the operator.   **Who**
7. (Who, Whom) did Mary call? Mary called her.   **Whom**

Link to Writing
Avoid confusing *whose* with *who's*. *Who's* is a contraction that means "who is."

Whose is that?
(interrogative pronoun)
Whose telephone is that?
(possessive pronoun)
Who's taking class notes?
(contraction)

Guided Practice

A. Identify the interrogative pronoun in each sentence. Tell whether the pronoun is a subject or an object.

1. What do you know about telephones?
2. Alex, who invented the telephone?
3. Which would you rather have, a car phone or a videophone?
4. Whom would you call on a videophone?
5. Liz, whose is this telephone message?

Independent Practice

B. Identifying Interrogative Pronouns Write each interrogative pronoun. In parentheses ( ), write whether the pronoun is a subject or an object.

6. Who wants to visit the telephone company?

<u>MODEL</u>〉 Who (subject)

7. What does a telephone operator do?
8. From whom does he learn his skills?
9. Which is the most modern telephone?
10. Who feels he learned something from the visit?
11. Whom have you told about the field trip?

C. Using Interrogative Pronouns Choose and write the correct pronoun to complete each sentence.

12. (What, Which) do you know about telephones?

<u>MODEL</u>〉 What

13. (Who, Whom) uses a cordless telephone?
14. (Who, Whom) has made a phone call from a plane or a train?
15. (What, Which) is the latest development in communications?
16. (Whose, Who's) idea was it to use communications satellites?

D. Using *Who* and *Whom* Write *who* or *whom* to complete each sentence.

17. _____ knows how to make a simple telephone?

<u>MODEL</u>〉 Who

18. To _____ do the two tin cans and string belong?
19. _____wants to make a hole in the bottom of each can?
20. _____ will you ask to take a can and stand over there?
21. _____ do you want to talk to on your "telephone"?
22. _____ will try this next?

Application — Writing

A List of Questions Imagine that you and your classmates are touring the telephone company. Make a list of questions to ask your tour guide. Use several interrogative pronouns.

Building Vocabulary
Denotation and Connotation

Suppose you are writing about an extremely intelligent person. Which word would you use to describe him or her?

intellectual   thinker   egghead

Each of these words has the same dictionary definition: "an intelligent person." The dictionary definition of a word is called its **denotation.**

Besides dictionary definitions, words also have connotations. A **connotation** is the feeling that a word suggests when someone uses it. Words can be positive, negative, or neutral.

Read the three words above again. Most often when you read about someone who is an *intellectual*, your reaction is positive. If he or she is described as a *thinker*, your reaction is probably neutral, neither good nor bad. However, when a person is labeled an *egghead*, the word receives a negative reaction.

Read these sentences. Decide whether the connotation is positive, negative, or neutral.

a. Use Sudsy Soap to get your dishes clean.
b. Use Sudsy Soap and your dishes will sparkle.

Clean is neutral and *sparkle* is positive. Advertisers and politicians use words with strong connotations to encourage people to form positive or negative impressions of a person, a thing, or an idea. People in other professions do this, too. As you read and listen, pay close attention to the connotations of words.

In your writing, connotations can play an important role. When you write a persuasive letter or paragraph, choosing the correct word can be important. Read these sentences.

a. As I unpacked my new bike, I noticed the chain was broken.
b. As I unpacked my new bike, I noticed the chain was mangled.

Why is the word *mangled* stronger and more negative than the neutral word *broken*? Which of the two words would probably be used in a letter of complaint to the bicycle company? Why?

Reading Practice

Write each pair of sentences. Write *positive, negative,* or *neutral.* If the sentence is positive or negative, underline which word or words elicit that response.

1. a. Sometimes Miller's Toy Store is in disarray.
b. Sometimes Miller's Toy Store is a mess.

2. a. The new puzzles they sell are engrossing.
b. The new puzzles they sell are challenging.

3. a. I can't complete a simple puzzle, and I am made to feel like a featherbrain.
b. I can't complete a simple puzzle, and I feel uncomfortable.

4. a. Mr. Miller convinces a customer to buy a toy.
b. Mr. Miller humiliates a customer until he or she buys a toy.

5. a. Palmer's store, however, is uncluttered.
b. Palmer's store is usually spotless.

6. a. The merchandise is captivatingly attractive.
b. The merchandise is attractively arranged.

7. a. Many toy stores sell action figures.
b. Many toy stores sell toys depicting violence.

8. a. I prefer tamer toys, such as games.
b. I prefer entertaining board games.

Writing Practice

Imagine that you bought a new pair of blue jeans. Decide whether you are satisfied or dissatisfied with your purchase. Write a business letter to the jeans company, either praising or complaining about your new jeans. In your letter, use one word from each pair to indicate your feelings.

9. lightweight–flimsy

10. tasteful–gaudy

11. confining–snug

12. overpriced–reasonable

13. compliments–criticisms

Project

Look through magazine and newspaper advertisements. Find three ads that use words with positive connotations. Cut out each advertisement and mount it on a sheet of paper. Under each one, rewrite the ad using words with neutral connotations. Discuss how the ads are different after the wording has been changed.

Language Enrichment
Pronouns

Use what you know about pronouns to do these activities.

 What's Behind the Door?

Our hero must decide his fate by choosing whatever is behind one of these four unexciting doors. Replace each pronoun with a drawing of the surprise behind the door. Jot down a brief description of each drawing. Then invite a partner to choose one of the doors. Stand back!

 Double Standards

People do not always apply the same standards to themselves that they do to others. Test this idea by completing each comparison. Change the noun to a pronoun and finish each sentence. Then write five more comparisons of your own.

Sylvia says she is slender.
Actually, *she* is skinny.
Mark claims to be sensitive.
Actually, _____ is _____.
Ann says that she is generous.
Actually, _____ is _____.

 Replacement Therapy

Have you ever realized just how useful pronouns are? Try this activity. Working in a small group, brainstorm ideas for a short short story or anecdote. Choose an idea, and decide how the story will progress. Have one person in the group write the words to the story as the group dictates it. Then, as the final copy of the short short story is made, be sure that only nouns are used for the names of persons, places, things, and ideas. Then exchange stories with another group. As a group, replace the repetitive nouns with appropriate pronouns, and return the story to the group it came from. Which version of each story reads more smoothly?

The king is hungry.
The ^He king wants to eat breakfast.

CONNECTING
LANGUAGE ⟷ WRITING

In this unit you learned that a pronoun takes the place of a noun. Personal pronouns are the most common, and the way they are used in sentences determines their case. Other pronouns ask questions, point something out, stand for an indefinite number, or refer to themselves.

◆ **Using Pronouns in Your Writing** Being able to use pronouns correctly will help you make your writing more concise. Pay special attention to the pronouns you use as you do these activities.

 Johnny-on-the-Spot

You are the roving reporter for WWCM, and you are the first on the scene of an accident. Think of as many questions as you can that begin with the interrogative pronouns *what*, *which*, *who*, *whom*, and *whose*. Write the questions and use them to interview one of your classmates, who was an eyewitness to the accident. Then use your questions and his or her answers to give an on-the-spot report for the evening news.

 That Makes Me Think of...

You learned about denotation and connotation when you read the **Building Vocabulary** page. Use a dictionary to help list the denotative meaning for each word listed below. Then list the feelings and ideas you associate with each one.

skunk	king	snake
house	rose	school

Unit Checkup

Think Back	Think Ahead
◆ What did you learn about comparing and contrasting in this unit? What did you do to write a comparison/contrast composition?	◆ How will what you learned about comparing and contrasting help you when you read a comparison/contrast composition? ◆ How will evaluating two subjects help you write a comparison/contrast composition?
◆ Look at the writing you did in this unit. How did pronouns help you express your ideas?	◆ How can you use pronouns to improve your writing?

Analyzing a Comparison/Contrast Composition   *pages 206 – 207*

Read the excerpt from the comparison/contrast composition. Then answer these questions.

> A lot of thought went into deciding whether to buy a Labrador retriever or a poodle. We considered how much exercise each dog would need, what kind of temperament each is noted for, and the average intelligence of each one.

1. What subjects are compared?
2. What are the points of comparison?
3. Is this the beginning, middle, or ending of a comparison/ contrast composition?
4. How do you know which part of the composition this is?
5. Which will be emphasized, similarities or differences?

Evaluating for Comparison and Contrast   *pages 208 – 209*

Write the category that does not belong in each set.

6. countries: population, location, leaders, state flower
7. cars: cost, repair records, two-door, upholstery type

8. friends: physical stature, special skills, creativity, hobbies
9. books: type of book, length, availability, weight
10. sleeping bags: zipper, stuffing, fabric, washability

Writing for an Audience and Purpose   *page 210*

Write four versions of a topic sentence that compares two classes you have taken. Base each version of the sentence on one of the following.

11. a letter to your best friend, to amuse
12. an article for your local newspaper, to inform
13. an essay for your class, to persuade
14. an article for the second-grade class newsletter, to inform

The Writing Process   *pages 211 – 221*

Write the letter of the answer to each question.

15. When you plan a comparison/contrast paragraph, what should you do first?
    a. Choose two items to compare.
    b. List characteristics that are the same or different.
    c. Write a first draft.
16. What is a helpful way to choose categories for a comparison/contrast composition?
    a. Ask strangers.   b. Brainstorm a list.   c. Do research.
17. What is the purpose of a topic sentence?
    a. to let readers know what your purpose for writing is
    b. to make the audience feel welcome
    c. to begin telling about one of the items being compared or contrasted
18. Why should a composition be revised for unity?
    a. to check punctuation and capitalization
    b. to eliminate irrelevant information
    c. to be sure new paragraphs are started

Pronouns   *pages 224 – 225*

Write the personal pronouns in each of the following sentences.

19. We painted the fence in the backyard last week.
20. Maurice and I worked all day Saturday.
21. I showed him the way to paint, and we worked together.
22. My mother made us lemonade to drink while we painted.
23. With Maurice and me helping, the job went quickly.

Pronouns and Antecedents   *pages 226 – 227*

Write the antecedent for each underlined pronoun.
The antecedent may be in a different sentence.

24. As Florida townspeople, <u>we</u> live in a rapidly growing town.
25. When people walk down the main street, <u>they</u> see new buildings in the town all the time.
26. Not everyone thinks construction brings good fortune with <u>it</u>.
27. <u>My</u> mother says <u>her</u> office is so noisy that <u>she</u> can hardly think!
28. In addition, <u>we</u> have more dust in the area than <u>we</u> have ever had before.

Subject and Object Pronouns   *pages 228 – 229*

Write each pronoun. Then write *subject* or *object* to indicate the type of pronoun it is.

29. From the window, I can see a nest with five baby birds in it.
30. The birds chirp for us in the morning while we have breakfast.
31. The mother searches for food for them.
32. When she brings it to them, they chirp even louder.
33. Jeanne and I watch the birds grow, and we know that soon they will be flying off alone.

Possessive Pronouns   *pages 230 – 232*

Write each possessive pronoun in the sentences.

34. Now that my sister has gone off to college, the bedroom is mine.
35. I thought I would be happy to have our room become just mine.
36. However, I miss her, and her things remind me that she is gone.
37. When people are living their lives one way, they notice changes.
38. Our family hears from Janine often, but it's not the same as when she was here.

Reflexive, Intensive, and Demonstrative Pronouns   *pages 233 – 235*

Write each reflexive, intensive, and demonstrative pronoun and its antecedent.

39. This is going to be a great season for the girls' softball team.
40. Our best players are back, and that means a terrific team!

41. In addition, I myself have seen the new players.
42. We are going to have ourselves a winning combination.
43. The girls are already getting themselves in shape.

Indefinite Pronouns   *pages 236 – 237*
Write an indefinite pronoun to fill in each blank.

44. _____ has been sweeping the sidewalks in front of the shops.
45. The neighborhood looks better, and _____ are pitching in.
46. Until recently _____ cared, and things were looking run-down.
47. The Scouts began the campaign, and now _____ comments on it.
48. If _____ continue, we'll win the "Clean Neighborhood" award!

Interrogative Pronouns   *pages 238 – 239*
Write each interrogative pronoun. Then write whether the pronoun is a *subject* or an *object*.

49. To whom do you report on your job?
50. Who else works there?
51. Which of the jobs do you most enjoy?
52. What will you be doing next week?
53. With whom will you be working?
54. Who trains you for your work?
55. With whom do you drive to work?
56. With whom will you go tomorrow?
57. When you leave, who will replace you?

Denotation and Connotation   *pages 240 – 241*
Write the sentences. After each sentence write *positive, negative,* or *neutral.* If a sentence is positive or negative, underline which word elicits that response.

58. a. When he was little, he was thin.
    b. When he was little, he was skinny.
59. a. Now that he is older, he has filled out.
    b. Now that he is older, he has fattened up.
60. a. My sister was a healthy baby.
    b. My sister was a big baby.
61. a. Liza had frizzy red hair when she was small, but now it is wavy.
    b. Liza had curly red hair when she was small, but now it is wavy.

UNIT

6

Creating Images

◆ **COMPOSITION FOCUS:** Poem
◆ **LANGUAGE FOCUS:** Adjectives and Adverbs

Look at the picture. The photograph of the ice skater captures movement. A movement takes only a short moment to perform, and then it is gone. However, this particular movement was captured and preserved by a photographer. Photography is one way to preserve a special moment. Another way is to write a poem.

Ordinary people as well as established poets write poetry, and different poets write different types of poetry. Some choose to write narrative poems—long poems that tell a story. Others express their thoughts and feelings in lyric poems such as haiku, limericks, and sonnets.

Although poems can have different forms, they have common elements. Poets use words economically and always for a reason.

Poets use comparisons and sensory images rather than long explanations. Through rhythm and rhyme the poet emphasizes the poem's meaning. Every poet uses these elements to create his or her poetry. In this unit you will learn how to create a poem.

Victor Hernández Cruz

Lillian Morrison

Langston Hughes

Reading with a Writer's Eye
Poem

Dance is a favorite topic for poets. Its grace, style, and character are fun to try to capture in a word picture. Three poets—Victor Hernández Cruz, Langston Hughes, and Lillian Morrison—each used his or her imagination to capture brief moments of dance. As you read, concentrate on the images that emerge from each poem.

The Latest Latin Dance Craze

by Victor Hernández Cruz

First
You throw your head back twice
Jump out onto the floor like a
Kangaroo
Circle the floor once
Doing fast scissor work with your
Legs

Next
Dash towards the door
Walking in a double cha cha cha
Open the door and glide down
The stairs like a swan
Hit the street
Run at least ten blocks
Come back in through the same
Door
Doing a mambo-minuet
Being careful that you don't fall
And break your head on that one
You have just completed your first
Step.

African Dance

by Langston Hughes

The low beating of the tom-toms,
   The slow beating of the tom-toms,
   Low . . . slow
   Slow . . . low—
Stirs your blood.

       Dance!
A night-veiled girl

Whirls softly into a
   Circle of light.
Whirls softly . . . slowly,
Like a wisp of smoke around the fire—
   And the tom-toms beat,
   And the tom-toms beat,
And the low beating of the tom-toms
   Stirs your blood.

How We Dance

by Lillian Morrison

Jimmy dances like a jittery
   mannekin,
Debbie like a limp rag doll,
Heather like an ocean wave with
   deep undulation,
Betty like a bird in thrall.
Charles dances like a benevolent
   serpent,
Bonnie like a beach ball floating on
   the sea,
Steve like a volcano, all sudden
   smooth eruptions,
Penny like a pendulum that suddenly
   has conniptions.

Respond

1. Which poem or which part of a poem caught your imagination the most? Explain your choice.

Discuss

2. Why do you think each poet wrote his or her poem?
3. In your own words, describe the images created by each poem.

Thinking As a Writer
Analyzing a Poem

Writer's Guide

A poem
- contains the elements of imagery, rhythm, and rhyme.
- may include patterns in the rhythm (meter), in the sound (which may include rhyme), and in the repeated words.
- usually has a title.

A **poem** is an expression of a poet's perceptions of the world. A poem uses elements such as imagery, rhythm, and rhyme to convey the poet's perceptions in a vivid but compact way.

Imagery is a special use of words that makes them suggest more than they mean in ordinary speech. By using imagery the poet helps the reader form mental pictures. In "The Latest Latin Dance Craze," for example, the lines "Jump out onto the floor like a/Kangaroo" suggest a picture of someone jumping. In the reader's mind a merged image of people and kangaroos hopping conveys the precise jumping style that Victor Hernández Cruz envisioned.

Rhythm is the pattern of accented and unaccented syllables in a line of poetry. This pattern gives a poem its *beat*. Many years ago most poems had regular rhythmic patterns and were arranged in a verse, or stanza, form. Modern poets, however, seem to favor an irregular style. In "African Dance," for example, few lines follow a regular pattern; in fact, because the line "Dance!" is a single word, it has no pattern at all. Yet this strong imperative is the one accented syllable around which the entire poem revolves.

Rhyme is a regular pattern of similar sounds. You are probably familiar with *end rhyme*, in which sequential or alternate lines end in words such as *fan* and *ran*. Any regular pattern of vowel sounds, however, no matter where it occurs in a poem, qualifies as rhyme. Notice that in "African Dance" Langston Hughes rhymes *low* and *slow* in the first two lines and then repeats them in lines three and four, as if to emphasize their sounds. In the second part of the poem, he rhymes *whirls* and *circle*. Related to rhyme and sound is **onomatopoeia,** the use of words that imitate sounds. In "African Dance" the word *tom-tom*, repeated throughout the poem, is an example of onomatopoeia.

Reread the poem "How We Dance" by Lillian Morrison. Notice how it makes use of the elements of poetry.

How We Dance

Jimmy dances like a jittery mannekin,
Debbie like a limp rag doll,
Heather like an ocean wave with deep undulation,
Betty like a bird in thrall.
Charles dances like a benevolent serpent,
Bonnie like a beach ball floating on the sea,
Steve like a volcano, all sudden smooth eruptions,
Penny like a pendulum that suddenly has
  conniptions.

The **title** defines or adds something to the poem.

Imagery creates pictures in the reader's mind.

Strong rhythm moves the poem along, since it has no regular meter.

Repetition of the word *like* creates a pattern of comparisons.

Rhyming *doll* and *thrall* and *eruptions* and *conniptions* gives the poem its pace.

Discuss

1. How does the repetition of the word *like* help you to visualize the poet's message?
2. Does the title of the poem fit the images the poet has created? Explain your answer.

Try Your Hand

A. Analyze Poems for Imagery, Rhythm, and Rhyme Explain how you can recognize imagery, rhythm, and rhyme in the poems on pages 250 and 251.

B. Read and Talk About a Poem Find a poem and read it to a partner. Point out the poet's use of imagery, rhythm, and rhyme.

C. Create Images Select a paragraph from a textbook or magazine. Make a list of images you might use if you changed the paragraph into a poem.

Writer's Notebook

Collecting Unusual Words Did you notice the unusual words *thrall*, *undulation*, and *conniptions* in the poem you just read? Poets often use unusual words in order to catch the reader's attention or to convey a special meaning. Reread the other two poems on pages 250 and 251. Record in your *Writer's Notebook* any unusual words you find there. Look up and record definitions for any words you don't know. Try to use unusual words when you write poetry.

Thinking As a Writer
Visualizing Comparisons

Poets often use comparisons to help describe their subjects. First the poet visualizes the subject in his or her mind and then makes a mental picture of something else that is similar to it. Then the poet phrases this comparison as a simile or a metaphor. A **simile** uses the word *like* or *as* to express the comparison. A **metaphor** says that one thing *is* another. Read this example from "How We Dance." Then read the next line, which paraphrases it.

> Jimmy dances *like* a jittery mannekin.   simile
> Jimmy *is* a jittery little mannekin when he dances.   metaphor

In the first sentence, the word *like* is used to make the comparison between Jimmy and a jittery mannekin. This comparison is a simile. In the second sentence, the linking verb *is* identifies Jimmy as a jittery mannekin. This comparison is a metaphor.

As you write your poem, decide whether a simile or a metaphor will help you express what you want to say about your subject.

Discuss

1. In two or three sentences, describe what you think Lillian Morrison means when she says, "Jimmy dances like a jittery mannekin." What is similar about the two things she compares? What is different?
2. Reread all three poems on pages 250 and 251. What similes or metaphors have been used in these poems? How do these similes or metaphors help you to visualize the action in the poems?

Try Your Hand

Write Comparisons   Write four comparisons—two metaphors and two similes—about a place or object with which you are familiar. Trade sentences with a partner. Identify which of your partner's sentences contain similes and which contain metaphors. Talk about what each comparison means.

Developing the Writer's Craft
Avoiding Clichés

Writer's Guide

Good poets
- avoid clichés.
- use effective, fresh words to create vivid images.

Because poets want to convey their vivid mental images to their readers through words, the words they choose are very important. Good poets avoid clichés. A **cliché** is an overused expression. Many clichés are descriptive phrases. *Clear as glass* and *cold as ice* are examples of similes that have become clichés.

Clichés may describe what the poet visualizes, but they do not convey vivid impressions to the reader. Because they have been used so often, they have lost their power to convey ideas. This is why poets should choose fresh, even unusual, words to communicate their own mental pictures to their readers.

When you write poems, try to use fresh, vivid words and avoid clichés.

Discuss

1. How would Lillian Morrison's poem be different if she had used a cliché for each comparison rather than a fresh, vivid image?
2. Why do you think Victor Hernández Cruz used an invented compound word, *mambo-minuet,* in his poem?

Try Your Hand

A. Avoid Clichés   Finish each of the common expressions below with your own new, fresh comparison. Avoid the cliché that is usually used to complete the phrase.

1. As fresh as _____
2. As quick as _____
3. As pretty as _____
4. Growing like _____
5. As busy as _____
6. As old as _____
7. As snug as _____
8. As sweet as _____

B. Use Vivid Imagery   Write a fresh comparison for each pair.

9. a desert and a snowstorm
10. a lake and a calm, tranquil person

1 Prewriting
Poem

Sean, a student at Riverside Middle School, was asked to use rhythm and rhyme to write a poem for younger students. He used the checklist in the **Writer's Guide** to help him plan his poem. Look at what he did.

Writer's Guide

Prewriting Checklist

☑ Brainstorm topics.

☑ Select a topic.

☑ Think about your audience and your purpose.

☑ Gather words and images.

☑ Make decisions about rhythm and rhyme.

☑ Organize your material.

◆ Brainstorming and Selecting a Topic

First, Sean decided that his poem would be about something he really liked—music. Then, he brainstormed and listed for his poem suitable topics having to do with music.

Next, Sean looked at his list. He liked all the topics and knew enough about each one to write a poem about it. He circled his favorite topic. He decided to write about his sister Suzanne, who was a percussionist in the school jazz band.

1. *my sister — percussionist*
2. *marches*
3. *the piano*
4. *the fife and bugle*
5. *operas*

Discuss

1. How is the topic for Sean's poem suitable for his audience and purpose?
2. Why do you think it is important to choose a topic that you know well and about which you have strong feelings?

◆ Gathering Information

After Sean selected his topic, he gathered information for his poem. He used words that show sensory details (especially sounds) and precise, vivid words in a cluster centered around the word *Percussionist*. He visualized comparisons between the percussion instruments and the sounds they make. Sean was not sure whether he would use the comparisons, but he knew he would need the words as examples of different sounds.

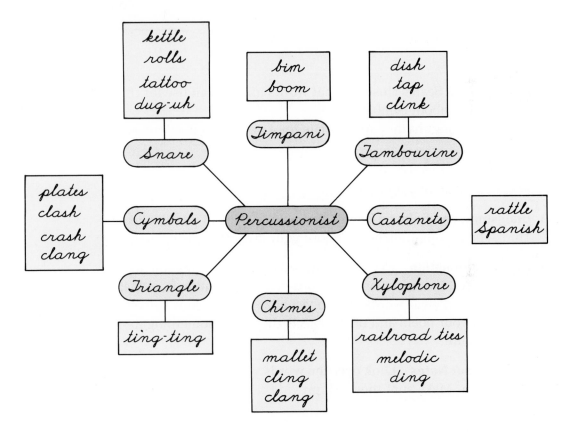

Discuss

1. Sean's diagram isn't complete. Identify three more words he could add to it.
2. Do you think Sean will use every word from his diagram for his poem? Explain your answer.
3. Why did Sean focus on the "images" of sounds?

◆ Organizing Information

Before Sean started to draft his poem, he thought about a way to organize his material. He decided that he would consider form, rhyme, and rhythm. He made a chart and filled in his plan.

Form and length	*four stanzas. five lines each*
Rhyme	*line 2 and line 4 of each stanza will rhyme.*
Rhythm	*Begin with "percussionist verbs." Keep a strong beat.*

Discuss

1. Look again at Sean's cluster. What words might Sean use for rhyming words in the stanza about cymbals?
2. Why is a strong rhythm appropriate for a poem about a percussionist?

Try Your Hand

Now plan a poem of your own.

A. Brainstorm and Select a Topic   Brainstorm a list of possible topics. Think about your audience. Choose your favorite topic from the list.

B. Gather Information   Use your senses to gather information about your subject. You may wish to record your information in a cluster, using precise, vivid words. Try to visualize comparisons between objects in your poem and other objects they have something in common with.

C. Review Your Notes   Look over the words you gathered to use in your poem. Make sure they will provide rich, elaborate details and sensory images.

D. Organize Material for the Poem   Make some initial decisions about the form and length of your poem. Decide whether you want to use a regular rhyme and rhythm. Remember that these decisions may change as you write.

 Save your cluster and your notes in your *Writer's Notebook*. You will use them when you draft your poem.

WRITING PROCESS

2 Drafting
Poem

Writer's Guide

Drafting Checklist

☑ Use your diagram and your notes.

☑ Write your poem. Use images and sounds that will help the reader visualize the action. Use rhythm and rhyme if you wish.

☑ Write your title last.

Before Sean started to draft his poem, he thought about how to express his images of percussionists. Using his diagram and his chart, Sean followed the checklist in the **Writer's Guide** to draft his poem. Look at what he did.

> The Song of the Percussionist
>
> The percussionist plays
>   On the gigantic timpani,
> Being extra careful
>   When she tunes the key.
> Boom Bim Boom—Bim

Discuss

What are some additional details you might expect to find in Sean's poem? Where would you expect to find them? Why?

Try Your Hand

Now draft a poem.

A. Review Your Information Think about the information you gathered and organized in the previous lesson. Decide whether you need more information. If so, gather it.

B. Think About Your TAP Remember that your task is to write a poem. Your purpose is to create a vivid mental image for your audience.

C. Write Your First Draft Use the **Drafting Checklist** to write your poem.

Task: What?
Audience: Who?
Purpose: Why?

When you write your draft, just put all your ideas on paper. Do not worry about spelling, punctuation, or grammar, because you can check these details later.

Save your first draft in your *Writer's Notebook*. You will use it when you revise your poem.

3 Responding and Revising
Poem

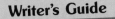

Sean read over his draft. Then he used the checklist in the **Writer's Guide** to revise his poem. Look at what he did.

Writer's Guide

Revising Checklist

☑ Read your poem to yourself or to a partner.

☑ Think about your audience and your purpose.

☑ Check to see that your poem is organized in a way that pleases you.

☑ Check to see that you have used vivid words and sensory images.

☑ Be sure you have avoided clichés.

☑ Replace uninteresting words with fresh ones.

◆ Checking Information

Sean thought that the word *gigantic* in line 2 threw off the rhythm. To cut this detail, he used this mark ℒ . He also added another *Boom* to make his rhythm come out right. He added it by using this mark ∧ .

◆ Checking Organization

Sean wanted to put the *clang* sound before the *ting-ting* sound of the cymbals. He used the mark ◡ to do this.

◆ Checking Language

When Sean checked the language in his poem, he used this mark ⌒ to replace an uninteresting verb and to change another verb to make its tense consistent.

Replace —	The percussionist plays	The percussionist ~~tapped~~ *taps*
Cut —	On the ~~gigantic~~ timpani,	On the cymbals of brass
Replace —	Being extra careful	And ~~hits~~ them together *clashes*
	When she tunes the key.	With a big resounding crash!
Add/ Move —	Boom Bim Boom–Bim ∧ *Boom*	∧Ting Ting–Ting–Ting (CLANG)

Discuss

1. Why did Sean add another *Boom* to the first sound line?
2. Sean thought that removing the word *gigantic* greatly improved the rhythm. Explain why you agree or disagree.

WRITING PROCESS

Try Your Hand

Now revise your first draft.

A. **Read Your First Draft** As you read your poem, think about your audience and your purpose. Read your poem silently or to a partner to see if it is complete and well organized. (See the **Tips on How to Read Poetry Aloud and Listen to Poetry,** page 265.) Ask yourself or your partner the questions in the box.

Responding and Revising Strategies	
✔ **Respond** **Ask yourself or a partner:**	✔ **Revise** **Try these solutions:**
◆ Have I used verb tenses consistently in my poem?	◆ **Replace** verb forms that are inconsistent. See the **Revising Workshop** on page 262.
◆ Have I followed the form I chose, or have I substituted another form with a pattern that fits my poem?	◆ **Move** any stanzas or lines that don't fit the pattern.
◆ Have I been consistent in my use of rhythm and rhyme?	◆ **Replace** any lines or rhyming words that confuse the patterns.
◆ Is my poem rich in detail, sensory images, comparisons such as similes and metaphors, and onomatopoeia? Is it free from clichés?	◆ **Cut** clichés and **replace** them with vivid, fresh words and images.

B. **Make Your Changes** If the answer to any question in the box is *no,* try the solution. Use the **Editor's Marks** to show your changes.

C. **Review Your Poem Again** Decide whether there is anything else you want to revise. Keep revising your poem until you feel it is complete and well organized.

EDITOR'S MARKS

⋀ Add something.

⌀ Cut something.

⟳ Move something.

⋀ Replace something.

Save your revised poem in your *Writer's Notebook.* You will use it when you proofread your poem.

Revising Workshop
Using Consistent Verb Tense

Good writers do not change the tenses of the verbs they are using unless they have a good reason. Changing tense without reason makes writing awkward and confusing to the reader. Look at the underlined verbs in these sentences.

1. The skater glides across the ice. She is about to do the jump called the triple lutz. Now, she has performed the jump flawlessly and glides once more.
2. The skater glided across the ice. She was about to do the jump called the triple lutz. Now, she has performed the jump flawlessly and glides once more.

In the first example, the writer is giving a moment-by-moment account of a skating routine in the present tense. The writer switches tenses in the last sentence to show that an action has just been completed, and then the writer returns to the present tense. This example shows effective use of tense change.

In the second example, the writer is giving a description of a completed routine, using the past tense. But in the last sentence, the writer switches tenses twice without a good reason. As a result, the writing seems clumsy and awkward.

To avoid problems with inconsistent use of tense, think about your choice of tense before you begin your writing. Because poetry sometimes omits complete sentences and may be broken into stanzas, it is sometimes hard to tell whether you have been consistent. By checking carefully and reading your work aloud, you will avoid unnecessary tense changes in poetry as well as in prose.

Practice

Look at the picture of the skater on this page. Write a paragraph of your own that describes the picture. Choose either the past tense or the present tense as the main tense of your paragraph. Have a good reason to switch to another tense in at least one sentence of your paragraph.

4 Proofreading
Poem

Writer's Guide

Proofreading Checklist

- ☑ Check for errors in capitalization.
- ☑ Check for errors in your use of apostrophes.
- ☑ Check for errors in grammar.
- ☑ Circle any words you think are misspelled. Find out how to spell them correctly.
- ⇨ For proofreading help, use the **Writer's Handbook.**

After Sean revised his poem, he used the checklist in the **Writer's Guide** and the **Editor's Marks** to proofread it. Look at what he did to the last part of the poem.

The percussionist rolls
On the drum called Snare,
And her wrists beat tattos ~~tattoos~~
As she ruffles the air
Dug-uh Dug-uh BRUM-BRUM-BRUM

The percussionist's melodic
On the Xylophone,
The marimba and the chimes
And the vibraphone.
La-Dee-Da-Dee Doo-Dee-Doe-Dee Ding-Dang-Dong!
And that's the end of my percussionists' song.

Discuss

1. Look at Sean's proofread poem. What kinds of mistakes did he make?
2. Why did he add one apostrophe before an *s* in one word and one after an *s* in another in the last line?

Try Your Hand

Proofread Your Poem   Now use the checklist in the **Writer's Guide** and the **Editor's Marks** to proofread your poem.

Save your corrected poem in your *Writer's Notebook.* You will use it when you publish your poem.

EDITOR'S MARKS

- ≡ Capitalize.
- ⊙ Add a period.
- ∧ Add something.
- ⋏ Add a comma.
- ⌄⌄ Add quotation marks.
- ✂ Cut something.
- ⌄⌃ Replace something.
- ∼ Transpose.
- ○ Spell correctly.
- ¶ Indent paragraph.
- / Make a lowercase letter.

5 Publishing
Poem

Sean made a clean copy of his poem and checked it to be sure he had not left anything out. Then he and his classmates published their poems in an illustrated book of poetry. You can find Sean's completed poem on page 53 of the **Writer's Handbook.**

Here's how Sean and his classmates published their poems.

1. Sean reread his poem and thought about an effective way to illustrate it. He finally decided to do an original drawing.
2. He drew his illustration, making sure that it fit the subject of his poem.
3. Finally, Sean and a group of classmates helped put the book together, while others designed the cover, decided on the order of poems, and wrote a table of contents.
4. Later they made copies of their book and shared them with younger students.

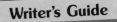

Writer's Guide

Publishing Checklist

☑ Make a clean copy of your poem.

☑ Be sure that nothing has been left out.

☑ Check to see that there are no mistakes.

☑ Share your poem in a special way.

Discuss

What might happen if students didn't cooperate as they compiled their poems?

Try Your Hand

Publish Your Poem   Follow the checklist in the **Writer's Guide.** Then add your poem to the class book, or try one of these ideas for sharing your poem.

+ Share your poem with your family.
+ Enter your poem in a poetry contest.
+ Send your poem to a literary magazine such as *Stone Soup.*

Listening and Speaking
Tips on How to Read Poetry Aloud and Listen to Poetry

Reading Poetry Aloud

1. Before you read the poem aloud, read the poem over to yourself several times. Note the following features:
   a. the rhythm
   b. the rhyme scheme, or sound
   c. where the stanzas end
   d. the words that are most important to the poet's ideas
   e. the relationship of these four things to the meaning of the poem
2. Practice using your voice to emphasize the rhythm and the rhymes. Don't exaggerate, though. Be careful not to overdo it.
3. Practice pausing slightly at the ends of lines that have punctuation. Pause slightly longer after complete stanzas.
4. Try to convey the poet's meaning with your voice.
5. Use gestures and facial expressions when appropriate.

Listening to Poetry

1. Listen carefully to the title so that you have an idea of what is to come.
2. Try to get an idea of the poem's form, rhythm, and rhyme scheme as you listen. Identify the topic. Listen for words that are repeated and emphasized.
3. If possible, listen to a poem several times.
4. Think about how the poet used the elements of poetry to express meaning.

Writing in the Content Areas

Use what you learned to write another poem. Use one of these ideas or an idea of your own.

Writer's Guide

When you write, remember the stages of the Writing Process.
- Prewriting
- Drafting
- Responding and Revising
- Proofreading
- Publishing

Fine Arts

Look in art books, or visit a museum in your area. Write a poem for your family about your favorite sculpture. Use vivid words to bring your poem to life. Use rhyme, rhythm, and a stanza form, if you wish.

Health

Write a poem about an incredible banquet. Use rhyme to tell what was served, why it was served, and what happened. Mention as many different foods in your poem as you can. Use precise, vivid words that create sensory images to describe the smell and texture of the food.

Literature

Write a poem about your favorite character from a childhood book. Describe the character and his or her actions. Use rhythm to make your character lively. Recite your poem to a group of young children. See if they can keep time with the rhythm of the poem.

Physical Education

Write a poem that captures an exciting moment of movement in a sport: a dunked basket in basketball, a grand slam in baseball, a flip in gymnastics, a kick in karate. Develop a rhyme scheme and meter that emphasizes the rhythm of the sport. Use onomatopoeia to capture the sound and movement of the action. Use similes or metaphors if appropriate.

CONNECTING
WRITING ↔ LANGUAGE

Read the poem "Dog at Night" by Louis Untermeyer.

At first he stirs uneasily in sleep
And, since the moon does not run off, unfolds
Protesting paws. Grumbling that he must keep
Both eyes awake , he whimpers; then he scolds
And, rising to his feet, demands to know
the stranger's business. You who break the dark
with insolent light, who are you? Where do you go?
But nothing answers his indignant bark.
The moon ignores him, walking on as though
Dogs never were. Stiffened to fury now ,
His small hairs stand upright , his howl comes fast ,
And terrible to hear is the bow-wow
That tears the night. Stirred by this bugle-blast,
The farmer's hound grows active ; without pause
Summons her mastiff and the cur that lies
Three fields away to rally to the cause.
And the next county wakes. And miles beyond
Throats ring themselves and brassy lungs respond
With threats, entreaties, bellowing and cries,
Chasing the white intruder down the skies.

◆ **Adjectives and Adverbs in Poetry** The highlighted words are adjectives and adverbs, which make writing more colorful and more exact.

◆ **Language Focus: Adjectives and Adverbs** The following lessons will help you use adjectives and adverbs in your own writing.

1 Adjectives

◆ **FOCUS**   An **adjective** modifies a noun or a pronoun.

Adjectives tell *what kind, which one, how many,* or *how much* about nouns and pronouns. Adjectives can come before or after the words they modify. More than one adjective can precede or follow a noun. The highlighted words are adjectives.

1. Tony flies a kite, bright and graceful .
   What kind?—bright, graceful

2. He wants four more kites!
   How many?—four   *How much?*—more

A, an, and *the* are called articles. **Articles** answer the question *which one. The* is a **definite article** because it names a particular thing. *A* and *an* are **indefinite articles** because they refer to any one of a group. The words in color are articles.

3. I want to fly the kite tomorrow.

4. Yesterday, Roland flew a box kite.

Proper adjectives can be made from proper nouns. *Chinese* and *American* are proper adjectives made from the proper nouns *China* and *America.* Capitalize proper adjectives.

> **Link to Speaking and Writing**
> You can paint a clear and vivid picture if you select adjectives carefully.

graceful
The ~~nice~~ kites fly high.

Guided Practice

A. Identify the adjectives in each sentence. Tell which ones are proper adjectives.

1. On her thirteenth birthday, Juanita received a dragon kite.
2. Shiny silver scales covered the colorful Japanese kite.
3. Juanita translated the Spanish assembly instructions.
4. She and a good friend spent the whole morning making the kite.
5. They had a long, happy afternoon to enjoy the lovely gift.

Independent Practice

B. Identifying Adjectives   Write the sentences. Underline each adjective. Underline proper adjectives twice.

6. Kites have a surprising history.

MODEL⟩ Kites have a surprising history.

7. Ben Franklin's famous experiment used a square kite, a key, and hemp string to prove that lightning is electricity.

8. Australian box kites were invented by Lawrence Hargrave.

9. The most popular kite in America is the Eddy kite.

C. Revising: Replacing Adjectives   Write the sentences. Replace each underlined adjective with a more vivid one.

10. Clear skies and a warm sun provided a beautiful spring day.

MODEL⟩ Clear skies and a warm sun provided a breathtaking spring day.

11. We found a large field for flying our kites.

12. After we flew the kites, we had a good picnic lunch.

13. I had a nice day.

14. It will be a favorite memory.

D. Adding Adjectives to Sentences   Write the sentences. Add a vivid adjective either before or after each underlined noun. Use your **Writer's Thesaurus.**

15. Allison made a kite.

MODEL⟩ Allison made an unusual kite.

16. Allison used paper and wood to make a kite.

17. She glued paper to the frame with adhesive.

18. Then she made a tail out of material.

19. Allison entered a contest and won a prize for the kite.

Application—Writing

A Poster   Imagine that you and your friends have planned a "Kite Day." Design a poster to announce a day of making and flying kites. Use adjectives to make the day sound inviting.

2 *This, That, These, Those*

◆ **FOCUS**   A **demonstrative adjective** points out the noun it modifies.

Demonstrative adjectives are more limiting than indefinite and definite articles. *This* and *these* point out something or someone nearby. *That* and *those* point out something or someone farther away. The words in color are demonstrative adjectives.

1. This aircraft looks peculiar.
2. That one is stranger.
3. Those planes are early models.
4. Look at these models!

When *this, these, that,* and *those* are used alone, they are demonstrative pronouns, not adjectives.

5. This is a flying balloon.   pronoun
6. This balloon is outstanding.   adjective
7. That is a wonderful one!   pronoun
8. That one is wonderful!   adjective

Guided Practice

A. Identify each demonstrative adjective.

1. These men learned to make things fly.
2. They began with these weapons.
3. With that feather attached, a small spear could travel farther.
4. This idea taught early people about floating objects.
5. Those weapons are some of the earliest bows and arrows.
6. People learned that this bow and others
   like it could propel arrows quite far.
7. This discovery kept hunters relatively safe.
8. With that bow they did not have to get too
   close to their prey.

B. 9.–16.   Identify the noun that each demonstrative adjective in **A** modifies.

THINK AND REMEMBER
 • Remember that a **demonstrative adjective** points out a specific noun.

Independent Practice

C. Identifying Adjectives   Write the demonstrative adjective. Write the noun it modifies.

17. That principle about floating objects helped us learn about propulsion.

MODEL〉 That—principle

18. Archimedes, an ancient Greek, learned why that object could float.

19. Later, these findings were used in building hot-air balloons.

20. People studied these earlier experiments.

21. The extraordinary ideas became the basis for this TV production.

22. These ideas were used much later to build airplanes.

23. Some of them went into inventing that glider.

D. Distinguishing Between Demonstrative Adjectives and Demonstrative Pronouns   Decide whether the underlined word is used as a demonstrative adjective or as a demonstrative pronoun. Write *adjective* or *pronoun*.

24. Orville and Wilbur Wright, <u>those</u> famous brothers, launched the Air Age.

MODEL〉 adjective

25. <u>That</u> had been their dream for years.

26. <u>These</u> men made a flight in a heavier-than-air flying machine.

27. <u>This</u> was a historical event.

28. After <u>that</u> remarkable feat, life changed throughout the world.

29. Aviation history has made <u>this</u> world smaller.

Application — Writing

A Description   Most people have a favorite method of transportation. Write a paragraph that describes how you like to get around. Do you prefer to ride a bicycle, walk, or be driven? Use demonstrative adjectives. If you need help writing a description, see page 45 of the **Writer's Handbook.**

3 Other Parts of Speech as Adjectives

♦ **FOCUS**   Other parts of speech can be used as adjectives.

Remember that any word that modifies a noun or a pronoun is an **adjective.** An adjective answers the question *what kind, which one, how many,* or *how much.*

Some words can be only adjectives.

1. People invent unusual objects.   adjective

Some words can be nouns or adjectives.

2. These objects are not found in every household .   noun
3. Look for these household objects.   adjective

Some words can be pronouns or adjectives.

4. What is this ?   demonstrative pronoun
5. This invention is outrageous.   adjective
6. Which is the most important invention?   interrogative pronoun
7. Which invention is here?   adjective
8. Few are this practical.   indefinite pronoun
9. Few inventions are this practical.   adjective

Guided Practice

A. Identify each underlined word as an *adjective* or as a *noun.*

1. Many inventions are for family use.
2. I use this invention with my family.
3. Do you know that someone invented paper?
4. Think about that inventor the next time you put your lunch in a paper bag.
5. The Egyptians were the first to make bricks.
6. Brick homes have been fashionable for centuries.

B. Identify each underlined word as an *adjective* or as a *pronoun.*

7. "Have you heard about that new computer program?" Brooke asked.
8. "Which do you mean?" Jim answered.
9. "Put in a list of words one at a time."

10. "That sounds easy," Jim said.
11. "The computer asks you if you need some help," Brooke said.

> **THINK AND REMEMBER**
> ◆ You use **adjectives** to modify nouns or pronouns.
> ◆ Remember that nouns and pronouns can be used as adjectives, for the way a word is used determines its part of speech.

Independent Practice

C. Identifying Parts of Speech   Write whether the underlined word is a *noun*, a *pronoun*, or an *adjective*.

12. The Wright brothers studied flight in their bicycle repair shop.
MODEL⟩ adjective

13. The bicycle is an example of an early improvement in transportation.
14. Many inventions in the past 100 years have aided the farming industry.
15. Everyone has been influenced by technology.
16. Most individual inventors are forward-thinking.
17. Some, however, are lonely individuals.

D. Using Adjectives   Write your own sentence, using the underlined noun or pronoun from each sentence as an adjective.

18. Long ago some inventions were looked upon as magic.
MODEL⟩ People thought inventors were performing magic tricks.

19. Ramona has a miniature radio shaped like a piano that she takes everywhere.
20. Barbara uses that to do her homework.
21. I am fascinated by these.
22. It is amazing that people still do this.
23. What could be more fun than designing new things!

Application — Writing

An Opinion   Think of an invention you could live without. Write a paragraph that tells why you think the invention is unnecessary. Use lively adjectives. If you need help in writing a persuasive paragraph, see page 44 of the **Writer's Handbook.**

4 Predicate Adjectives

◆ **FOCUS**   A **predicate adjective** is an adjective that follows a linking verb and describes the subject of the sentence.

A predicate adjective adds information about the subject of a sentence. Predicate adjectives always follow linking verbs. The most common linking verbs are forms of *be*. Others are *seem, taste, smell, look, sound,* and *feel*.

   1. These toys are almost lifelike .   predicate adjective

A sentence can have a compound predicate adjective.

   2. Young children seem amused and comforted by talking toys.

   3. Toys are fun and educational .

Remember that a predicate nominative is a noun that follows a linking verb and renames the subject of a sentence.

   4. The toys in the window are animals   predicate nominative

Guided Practice

A. Identify the predicate adjective(s) in each sentence.

   1. That toy bear is musical.
   2. I turn it on, and the baby becomes attentive.
   3. She tries to turn the knob, but her fingers are too weak.
   4. The baby coos with the music; everyone is content.
   5. No one is surprised that the music is soothing.

B. Identify each underlined word as a *predicate nominative* or a *predicate adjective*.

   6. A young child's favorite toy has always been a hobbyhorse.
   7. The horse may be large or small.
   8. Its mane curls, and its eyes are glass.
   9. As the child rides, the day becomes long and pleasurable.
   10. A hobbyhorse is an unforgettable gift.

> **THINK AND REMEMBER**
> • Remember that a **predicate adjective** follows a linking verb and modifies the subject of a sentence.

Independent Practice

C. Identifying Adjectives Write each sentence. Underline each predicate adjective. Draw an arrow from the predicate adjective to the word it modifies.

11. Leo is happy with empty plastic containers.

MODEL Leo is happy with empty plastic containers.

12. The kitchen is enchanting to a toddler.

13. It feels wonderful to bang one pot with another.

14. Benjy looks proud when he stacks plastic cups three high.

15. His games are noisy, active, and fun.

16. That area far from the stove seems perfect for Benjy and Leo to play in.

17. I keep an eye on them, and they stay content.

D. Distinguishing Between Predicate Adjectives and Predicate Nominatives Decide whether the underlined word or phrase is a predicate nominative or a predicate adjective. Write *nominative* or *adjective*.

18. Dolls have always been favorite toys.

MODEL nominative

19. In the Middle Ages, goldsmiths were toymakers.
20. Their detailed toy soldiers and horses are interesting and well made.
21. Later, inventions became ideas for new toys.
22. Toy balloons became popular in many countries after the first balloon flight.
23. Toy trains, automobiles, and airplanes are common.
24. Today, child-sized space capsules are modern hobbyhorses.

Application — Writing

Remembrances Think about the toys you enjoyed playing with as a child. Describe in a paragraph your experience with any single favorite toy. Sum up your paragraph with a generalization about toys. Use lively predicate adjectives. If you need help in writing a narrative, see page 48 of the **Writer's Handbook.**

5 Comparisons with Adjectives

◆ **FOCUS**   Adjectives can be used to compare nouns.

Many adjectives have forms called **degrees** that show comparison.

Positive Degree: 1. Norse myths are great stories.
                        no comparison is made

Comparative Degree: 2. Roman myths are greater than those.
                           compares two

Superlative Degree: 3. Greek myths are the greatest stories of all.
                           compares three or more

There are four common ways to form comparative and superlative degrees of comparison. Use these examples to help you. Notice that *more* and *less* are not used with the *er* forms and that *most* and *least* are not used with the *est* forms.

Positive	Comparative	Superlative
small	smaller	smallest
big	bigger	biggest
happy	happier	happiest
difficult	*more/less* difficult	*most/least* difficult

If an adjective ends in a single consonant preceded by a single vowel, double the consonant before adding the ending—as in *bigger* and *biggest*. For most adjectives that end in *y* preceded by a consonant, change *y* to *i* before adding *er* or *est*—as in *happier* and *happiest*.

Guided Practice

A. Tell whether each adjective is in the *positive, comparative,* or *superlative* form.

1. least accurate
2. rarer
3. more exciting
4. most beautiful
5. smaller
6. noisiest
7. oldest
8. new
9. largest
10. more colorful
11. less experienced
12. lightest

B. Correct each underlined adjective. Use the correct degree of comparison. Use a dictionary if necessary.

13. Greek and Roman mythologies are the populariest.

14. Egyptian myths are <u>least popular</u> than Hindu myths.

15. African myths are <u>difficulter</u> than Greek myths.

16. The myths of Scandinavia seem the <u>gloomier</u> of all.

17. Latin-American myths are not <u>funniest</u>.

THINK AND REMEMBER
- Use the **positive degree** when nothing is compared.
- Use the **comparative degree** when two things are compared.
- Use the **superlative degree** when three or more things are compared.

Independent Practice

C. Identifying Degrees of Comparison   Write each adjective. Then write in parentheses ( ) its degree of comparison. Use a dictionary.

18. tinier

MODEL › tinier (comparative)

19. handier   **23.** shiniest   **27.** hugest

20. more usual   **24.** noisiest   **28.** more costly

21. shortest   **25.** oldest   **29.** friendly

22. less gleaming **26.** most decorated **30.** unhappiest

D. Using Degrees of Comparison   Write the appropriate degree of comparison of the adjective in parentheses ( ) in each sentence. Use a dictionary if necessary.

31. This myth seems (strange) than that one.

MODEL › stranger

32. Greek mythological characters are (easy) to understand than Norse characters.

33. Gods and goddesses are the (common) of all mythological creatures.

34. Artemis and Aphrodite were (attractive) than the others.

35. Greek gods lived on Mount Olympus, which was the (high) mountain in the land.

36. People read mythology because it contains some of the (unusual) stories in literature.

Application — Writing

A Myth   Write a modern myth. Most myths present some sort of conflict between people and nature. Decide on a conflict. Use adjectives to make comparisons.

6 Irregular Comparisons with Adjectives

◆ **FOCUS**   Some adjectives have irregular forms of comparison.

Remember that many adjectives have positive, comparative, and superlative forms, called **degrees,** that show comparison. Some are compared in an irregular way. The words in color are irregular forms.

1. Our daily newspaper has good cartoons.

2. Sometimes the Sunday paper has better ones.

3. These cartoons are the best of all.

The following are some irregular forms of comparison.

Positive	Comparative	Superlative
good	better	best
bad	worse	worst
far	further	furthest
far (distance)	farther	farthest
little (quantity)	less	least
well (health)	better	best
much/many	more	most

Link to Speaking and Writing

Use *less* and *least, few* and *fewer, good* and *well,* and *farther* and *further* correctly. *Less* and *least* name things that cannot be counted. Use *few* and *fewer* with nouns that can be counted. Use *good* as an adjective. Use *well* as an adjective only when you mean "not sick." Use *farther* when discussing distance. Use *further* when discussing time, degree, or quantity.

Guided Practice

A. Identify the degree of comparison of each adjective: *positive, comparative, superlative.*

1. worse   2. most   3. least   4. far   5. fewer   6. better

B. 7.–12.   Tell the positive, comparative, and superlative forms of each of the adjectives in **A.**

Independent Practice

C. Identifying Adjective Forms   Make three columns: *Positive, Comparative,* and *Superlative.* List each adjective in its correct column. Complete all three columns for each adjective.

13. bad

MODEL	Positive	Comparative	Superlative
	bad	worse	worst

14. farther   **16.** many   **18.** noisiest   **20.** least

15. well   **17.** worst   **19.** good   **21.** furthest

D. Completing Sentences with Adjectives of Comparison   Write each sentence, using an irregular form of comparison in each blank. There may be more than one correct answer.

22. Explore art careers carefully, and you'll find the one _____ for you.

MODEL Explore art careers carefully, and you'll find the one best for you.

23. Because art is my _____ subject, I've thought about a career in graphic arts.

24. Even though some jobs require _____ college art courses, all of the jobs require some.

25. Cartoonists need imagination, ambition, and a sense of humor to make their careers the _____ they can be.

26. Political cartoonists have a _____ understanding of politics when they have a strong foundation in history and political science.

27. A friend was _____ than her brother in some ways, but she is now a cartoonist syndicated in 100 newspapers.

28. Maybe careers in art are the _____ of all careers!

Application — Writing

A Job Application   Suppose you are looking for a job as a cartoonist. Write a short description of your skills. Explain why you are the right person for the job. Use irregular adjectives to make comparisons.

7 Adverbs

◆ **FOCUS** An **adverb** modifies a verb, an adjective, or another adverb.

Adverbs can modify verbs, adjectives, and other adverbs.

1. Tina reads well . **modifies verb** *reads*

2. She is quite talented. **modifies adjective** *talented*

3. She speaks very dramatically. **modifies adverb** *dramatically*

An adverb can answer the question *how, when, where, how often,* or *to what extent.*

4. Tina walked calmly to the microphone. *How?*

5. She began promptly . *When?*

6. Tina stood there and entertained the audience for an hour. *Where?*

7. She does this frequently . *How often?*

8. She captivated the audience totally . *To what extent?*

Some Common Adverbs					
When?	today	next	promptly	early	never
	now	soon	late	then	tomorrow
Where?	in	near	out	around	outside
	up	here	there	inside	over
How?	calmly	neatly	nicely	happily	sadly
	slowly	quickly	hard	easily	fast
How Often?	weekly	daily	yearly	always	frequently
	twice	never	often	seldom	once
To What Extent?	slightly	quite	hardly	partly	greatly
	very	almost	nearly	too	terribly

Most adverbs that tell *how* should end in *ly.* To change adjectives into adverbs that tell *how,* follow these rules.

- To most words, add *ly.* quick—quickly
- To words ending in *ic,* add *ally.* magic—magically
- To words ending in *y* preceded by a consonant, change *y* to *i* and add *ly.* noisy—noisily

remarkably

She is a ~~very~~ good storyteller.

Guided Practice

A. Name the adverb or adverbs in each sentence.

1. "Do you remember how you always liked fairy tales?" asked Kit.
2. "Cinderella is often a favorite character," said Angela.
3. "Rapunzel is mine," said Kit. "I like it when the prince climbs up her hair."
4. Children seldom tire of fairy tales.
5. They hear them again and again.
6. My brother requests "The Three Bears" daily.
7. He responds quite happily each time.
8. As a youngster, I sat by the fireplace, and Dad read to me there.
9. I'm sure that's partly responsible for my love of reading.

B. 10.–18. Identify the word each adverb in **A** modifies, and tell whether the adverb answers *how, when, where, how often,* or *to what extent.*

C. Make adverbs that answer the question *how* from these adjectives. Change *y* to *i* when necessary.

19. easy	**22.** musical	**25.** lucky
20. stupendous	**23.** tragic	**26.** contrary
21. sympathetic	**24.** clear	**27.** typical

THINK AND REMEMBER

- Remember that **adverbs** modify verbs, adjectives, or other adverbs.
- Remember that adverbs answer the questions *how, when, where, how often,* and *to what extent.*

Independent Practice

D. Identifying Adverbs   Write each sentence. Underline the adverb once and the word it modifies twice.

28. *Grimm's Fairy Tales*, from the early 1800's, is still popular.

MODEL⟩ *Grimm's Fairy Tales, from the early 1800's, is still popular.*

29. The Brothers Grimm busily collected German fairy tales.

30. "Sleeping Beauty," "Hansel and Gretel," "Snow White," and "Cinderella" were once oral tales.

31. The Brothers Grimm wrote nearly 200 fairy stories.

32. Have you ever read any of *Grimm's Fairy Tales*?

33. Which one is really your favorite?

E. Revising: Changing Adverbs   Replace each underlined adverb with a more vivid adverb.

34. My brother believes the tooth fairy works <u>alone</u> at night.

MODEL⟩ *magically*

35. He believes the sandman <u>gently</u> puts sand in his eyes.

36. The "sand" <u>really</u> makes him sleep.

37. If he can't sleep, he says a <u>very</u> ugly creature scares him.

38. My brother has a <u>very</u> vivid imagination!

39. I <u>often</u> think he gets it from me!

F. Revising: Adding Adverbs   Revise the sentences by adding an adverb to modify each underlined word.

40. "The Ugly Duckling" <u>describes</u> its author's life.

MODEL⟩ *"The Ugly Duckling" actually describes its author's life.*

41. Hans Christian Andersen felt he was an <u>ugly</u> duckling.

42. He <u>collected</u> some of his 168 fairy tales and created others.

43. Andersen's Danish fairy tales <u>gained</u> worldwide popularity.

44. Adults and children <u>enjoy</u> "The Emperor's New Clothes."

45. The story is imagined, but its message is <u>real</u>.

46. We <u>enjoy</u> such imagined stories because of their truth.

Application—Writing and Speaking

A TV Commercial   Imagine that you have been asked to create a TV commercial using Cinderella to sell floor wax or a product of your choice. Write your commercial; share it aloud. Use adverbs to modify verbs, adjectives, and other adverbs.

8 Placement of Adverbs in Sentences

◆ **FOCUS**   The placement of an adverb in a sentence can vary.

An adverb that modifies an adjective or another adverb usually comes directly before the word it modifies.

1. Fantasy events are rarely possible.   *modifies adjective* **possible**

2. Science fiction events are very often possible.   *modifies adverb* **often**

An adverb that modifies a verb or a verb phrase can be put in various places in a sentence.

Before a verb:	3. I always enjoy Arthur Clarke's novels.
After a verb:	4. Clarke writes vividly .
Before a subject:	5. Maybe you know his work.
Between verb parts:	6. Clarke's characters are often threatened.
At the end:	7. I read science fiction frequently .

Correct placement of adverbs often depends on common sense. If a sentence containing an adverb sounds awkward, try putting the adverb in different places until the sentence sounds smooth.

Guided Practice

A. Decide where to place the adverb in parentheses ( ) to modify each underlined adjective.

1. Science fiction sometimes portrays <u>ideal</u> societies. (remarkably)
2. A <u>happy</u> society is called a *utopia*. (completely)
3. In a utopia, everybody is <u>strong</u> and healthy. (extremely)
4. All people are <u>equal</u> and wise in a utopian society. (truly)
5. Is a utopia science fiction, or is it a <u>wishful</u> fantasy? (foolishly)

THINK AND REMEMBER

• Place adverbs that modify adjectives or other adverbs just before them.

• Place adverbs that modify verbs
 • before a subject
 • between verbs in a verb phrase
 • at the end of the sentence
 • between a subject and verb
 • after a verb

Independent Practice

B. Using Adverbs to Modify Adjectives Write each sentence. Use the adverb in parentheses ( ) to modify an adjective.

6. My dreams can be lifelike. (truly)

MODEL⟩ My dreams can be truly lifelike.

7. I had a wonderful dream in which I traveled back in time. (quite)

8. It was 1871 in the thriving city of Dallas. (wildly)

9. Cowboys passed through, driving hardy cattle north. (extremely)

10. Peddlers sold plentiful stocks of household items. (remarkably)

11. If time travel were easy, to what year would you go? (so)

C. Using Adverbs to Modify Verbs and Other Adverbs Write each sentence. Place the adverb in parentheses ( ) so it modifies the underlined verb, verb phrase, or adverb.

12. Good science fiction <u>can predict</u> the future. (actually)

MODEL⟩ Good science fiction can actually predict the future.

13. Science fiction <u>appeared</u> more than a century ago. (first)

14. Jules Verne <u>had written</u> regular novels, but a publisher requested more imaginative, scientific writing. (initially)

15. Verne <u>wrote</u> about unseen space-age marvels. (accurately)

16. By 1870 Captain Nemo, a Verne character, <u>had traveled</u> the oceans in a submarine. (already)

17. Verne heroes even took <u>realistically</u> described trips to the moon! (quite)

D. Revising: Placing Adverbs Rewrite each sentence, placing the incorrectly placed adverb correctly.

18. Of all my classes I like science and writing especially.

MODEL⟩ Of all my classes I especially like science and writing.

19. I have taken recently up a hobby as a science fiction writer.

20. If I write well, I will make a career out of it perhaps.

21. Maybe someday internationally I will be well known.

22. I will be as famous as certainly Robert Heinlein.

23. I may write as well as Isaac Asimov possibly.

Application—Writing

A Friendly Letter Imagine that you have been on a space mission. Send a letter to your classmates that describes your mission. Use and place adverbs correctly. If you need help writing a friendly letter, see page 59 of the **Writer's Handbook.**

9 Comparisons with Adverbs

◆ **FOCUS** Some adverbs have three **degrees** of comparison: **positive**, **comparative**, and **superlative**.

Like adjectives, adverbs have forms called degrees of comparison.

Positive degree: 1. Tim's fish fought hard. no comparison

Comparative degree: 2. Bob's fish fought harder than Tim's. compares two

Superlative degree: 3. Albert's fish fought hardest of them all. compares three or more

To Form Degrees of Comparison of Adverbs			
Words with:	**Positive**	**Comparative**	**Superlative**
one syllable	soon near	soon*er* near*er*	soon*est* near*est*
two or three syllables	slowly accurately	*more* slowly *less* accurately	*most* slowly *least* accurately

To Form Degrees of Comparison of Irregular Adverbs		
Positive	**Comparative**	**Superlative**
well	better	best
badly	worse	worst
much	more	most
little	less	least

Link to Speaking and Writing

When you form comparative and superlative adverbs, never use *er* forms with *more* or *est* forms with *most*.

Tim saw his fish
~~more~~ sooner than Bob.

Guided Practice

A. Identify the degree of comparison of each adverb:
positive, comparative, or *superlative.*

1. less accurately
2. rarely
3. more quickly
4. soonest
5. best
6. little
7. most seldom
8. more recently
9. fastest
10. much
11. worse
12. lightly

B. Decide which adverb forms are incorrect, and use
them correctly.

13. I read stories more oftener than Tim.
14. Bob reads most oftenest of all.
15. Tim likes tall tales more better than novels.
16. I enjoy tall tales best.
17. I laugh more louder at the tall tales I read than at any other kind
of story.

> **THINK AND REMEMBER**
> - Use the **positive** degree when no comparison is made.
> - Use the **comparative** degree when two things are compared.
> - Use the **superlative** degree when three or more things are compared.

Independent Practice

C. Identifying Adverb Forms Make three columns: *Positive, Comparative,*
and *Superlative.* List each adverb in its correct column. Complete all
columns for each adverb.

18. sooner

	Positive	Comparative	Superlative
MODEL	soon	sooner	soonest

19. more noisily
20. most surely
21. less
22. well
23. badly
24. most rapidly
25. less quietly
26. farther
27. often

D. Using Adverbs Choose and write the correct adverb to complete each sentence.

28. Of all the lumberjacks, Paul Bunyan is the (more, most) famous.

MODEL〉 most

29. Nobody worked (more harder, harder) than Paul Bunyan and Babe, the Blue Ox.
30. His bunkhouse, with eighty tiers of bunks, was the (more impressively, most impressively) constructed of all the bunkhouses.
31. Once the 463 cooks had a (more difficult, difficult) time feeding all the men.
32. Paul handled this challenge (more easily, most easily) than his cooks.
33. He had a team of oxen leave a load of peas on a frozen lake, set the woods on fire around it, and cooked up a wonderful batch of pea soup which his men ate (more ravenously, ravenously).

E. Revising: Adding Adverbs to Make Comparisons Write the correct form of the adverb in parentheses ( ) to show the correct degree of comparison.

34. Tall tales are (much) entertaining than true stories.

MODEL〉 more

35. Tall tales depend (heavily) on imagination than on fact.
36. Davy Crockett was one of the (highly) esteemed tellers of tall tales.
37. He claimed he could "whip anything" (well) than the next man.
38. Davy Crockett certainly bragged (much) easily than the rest!
39. No one, however, can tell tall tales (well) than my little brother.
40. He once claimed that our cat could jump (high) than any other cat on earth.

Application — Writing, Speaking, and Listening

A Tall Tale People enjoy telling tall tales. Write your own tall tale about something you have done or always wanted to do. Use your imagination. Use adverbs that show comparison. Then tell your tall tale to the class. If you need help writing a narrative, see page 48 of the **Writer's Handbook.**

10 Negatives

◆ **FOCUS**   Two negative words should not be used together.

A **negative** is a word that means "no" or "not." Some negatives are modifiers. Contractions with *n't* for *not* are negative adverbs. The words *never, nowhere, barely, hardly,* and *scarcely* are also negative adverbs. The words in color are negatives.

1. Claude has never been able to concentrate.

2. He can't find his place because he is daydreaming.

Some Common Negative Words			
no	neither	nothing	hardly
none	nobody	nowhere	barely
not (n't)	no one	never	scarcely

A **double negative** is a statement that uses two or more negatives. Double negatives are incorrect.

3. Ms. Coleman reprimands him because he is not paying no attention.   double negative

4. Ms. Coleman reprimands him because he is not paying attention.   one negative

To eliminate double negatives, replace a negative word with a positive word.

5. He can't get nobody to go with him.   double negative

6. He can't get anybody to go with him.   one negative

Guided Practice

A. Identify the negative word in each sentence.

1. When Jessica concentrates, she hardly knows where she is!
2. She is scarcely aware of anything.
3. I don't know anyone with an imagination like hers.
4. She barely puts pen to paper, and she has a remarkable story or report.
5. Jessica never fails to dream up fascinating ideas.
6. She hardly knows when to stop.

7. I can scarcely write an acceptable report.

8. Somehow, my research is not apparent in my finished product.

9. Jessica, however, barely seems to exert herself.

THINK AND REMEMBER

• Remember that a **negative** word means "no" or "not."

• Never use a **double negative**—two or more negative words in the same sentence.

• When the word *not* is used as *n't* in a contraction, the statement is negative.

Independent Practice

B. Identifying Negatives   Write the negative from each sentence.

10. We each had to design a poster of our dreams, but I had scarcely thought about my dreams.

MODEL〉 scarcely

11. At first, I couldn't think of anything for the assignment.

12. Then, I could hardly contain myself!

13. I didn't have any trouble imagining forms for the poster.

14. The first two ideas sprang into mind quickly, but neither of them was as good as the third.

15. Everyone's ideas seemed to come from nowhere.

C. Revising: Correcting Double Negatives   Rewrite each sentence to correct the double negative.

16. Why isn't she not making her poster?

MODEL〉 Why isn't she making her poster?

17. You can't give your poster a name no more.

18. You shouldn't use no words on your poster, just pictures and colors.

19. Suddenly there isn't hardly anything in the world beyond your abilities; what do you plan to do?

20. My poster hasn't hardly clarified my dreams for me.

21. Maybe I've not never given them enough thought.

Application — Writing and Speaking

A Problem and a Solution   Imagine that you have unlimited money, time, and resources. Write and illustrate your solution to this challenge:

♦ Explain what you would and would not do with 3,000 inflated balloons. Tell why. Use negative words correctly.

11 Adverb or Adjective?

FOCUS
◆ An **adverb** modifies a verb, an adjective, or another adverb.
◆ An **adjective** modifies a noun or a pronoun.

Remember that adjectives and adverbs modify different parts of speech. Adjectives modify nouns and pronouns. Adverbs modify verbs, adjectives, and other adverbs.

1. Miguel describes the beautiful flowers.   adjective
2. He feels they are beautifully arranged.   adverb

Remember that adjectives sometimes follow linking verbs. Adverbs usually follow action verbs. Some words can be either adjectives or adverbs. When the word *well* means "healthy," it is an adjective.

3. This assignment about flowers was easy work.   adjective
4. I finished the assignment easily.   adverb
5. Miguel is feeling well today.   adjective
6. Marina did extremely well in the course.   adverb

Some pairs of adjectives and adverbs are troublesome.

Adjectives	Adverbs
good Is this good soil?	well The flowers planted there grow well.
bad It looks bad, but it isn't.	badly My vegetables turned out badly.
real (meaning *genuine*) This shows real imagination.	really (meaning *very*) Carlotta worked really hard on it.
sure (meaning *certain*) Are you sure you like it?	surely (meaning *certainly*) I'm surely going to try it myself.

Guided Practice

A. Decide whether each underlined modifier is an *adjective* or an *adverb*.

1. Figures of speech are <u>unexpected</u> comparisons.
2. Thinking up <u>good</u> comparisons requires imagination.

3. It's easy to grab at a cliché like "flat as a pancake."
4. What's a <u>really</u> new way of saying something is flat?
5. Can you <u>think</u> of a comparison that works <u>well</u>?

THINK AND REMEMBER

- You use **adverbs** to modify verbs, adjectives, or other adverbs.
- You use **adjectives** to modify nouns and pronouns.
- Never interchange adverbs and adjectives.

Independent Practice

B. Identifying Modifiers Write whether the underlined modifier is an *adjective* or an *adverb*.

6. Do you use your imagination <u>well</u> when you read?
MODEL⟩ adverb
7. You'll <u>surely</u> enjoy reading more if you use your imagination.
8. When a writer uses <u>good</u> descriptive language, read slowly.
9. Let each image and detail become <u>real</u> in your mind.
10. Don't feel <u>bad</u> if this isn't easy at first.
11. If a writer writes something <u>well</u>, it's worth reading.
12. Neither careful writing nor careful reading comes <u>easily</u>.

C. Choosing Modifiers Write the correct modifier to complete each sentence.

13. (Real, Really) look at your pencil.
MODEL⟩ Really
14. Have you ever looked at your pencil really (good, well)?
15. Imagine that you've never seen a pencil; what do you first notice when you take a (good, well) look at it?
16. Run a finger (easy, easily) over its surface; how does it feel?
17. Are you (sure, surely) you've described the whole pencil surface?
18. Tap it (light, lightly) on the desk; describe its sound.
19. Form an (unexpected, unexpectedly) comparison between a pencil and some other familiar object.

Application — Writing

A Description Choose an object in the room, and describe it for someone who has not really noticed that object before. Use your imagination to look freshly and write vividly. Use modifiers correctly. If you need help writing a description, see page 45 of the **Writer's Handbook.**

Building Vocabulary
Suffixes

A **suffix** is a word part that is added to the end of a base word. A suffix can change the meaning, the part of speech, and sometimes the spelling of a word. Suffixes can change nouns into verbs and verbs into nouns. They also can change nouns and verbs into adjectives, and adjectives into adverbs. Look at the examples.

Word	Part of Speech	Suffix	New Word	Part of Speech
beauty	noun	ful	beautiful	adjective
beauty	noun	ify	beautify	verb
farm	verb	er	farmer	noun
active	adjective	ity	activity	noun
happy	adjective	ly	happily	adverb

In descriptive writing, you will want to use suffixes to form adjectives. Some adjectives can be formed by adding certain suffixes to nouns, verbs, other adjectives, or roots. Read the chart.

Base Word	Suffix	Base Word + Suffix	Meaning
love	able, ible	lovable	able to be loved
comic	al	comical	funny
America	an, ian	American	related to America
metal	ic	metallic	like metal
child	ish	childish	like a child
help	less	helpless	without help
danger	ous	dangerous	having danger
worry	some	worrisome	having some worry
cheer	y	cheery	full of cheer, cheerful

- To add a suffix to form an adjective, use many of the same spelling rules that you use when adding to other parts of speech.
- To add a suffix to a word ending in *e*, drop the *e* and add the suffix.
- If a word ends with a consonant plus *y*, change the *y* to *i* and add the suffix.
- Often you drop more than one letter in adding a suffix.   terror + ify = terrify

Reading Practice

Read each sentence. Choose the word that has a suffix added to it. Write its meaning. Underline the suffix once and the base word twice. If the spelling changed when the suffix was added, write the base word.

1. Jessie felt foolish when she struck out for the third time.
2. Each time she tried, she seemed to become more nervous.
3. After the game Jessie's coach was still supportive.
4. "It's not hopeless," he said. "Everyone has a slump at some time."
5. Jessie answered, "You can't expect me to say everything is wonderful."
6. She sadly walked home, dragging her bat behind her.

Writing Practice

Use words with suffixes to replace the underlined words.

At first Chris's new job seemed able to be done with ease. He was supposed to take a package from one building and in a quick way deliver it to another building. Chris's first delivery went in a smooth way. He received a package at 10:00 and, fifteen minutes later, he had in an efficient way delivered it to its destination. At lunchtime Chris's job was giving him some trouble. Lunch hour traffic was heavy. Chris was not able to be beaten. He learned to maneuver in a crafty way through the crowd. Soon he was delivering packages with no effort during lunchtime.

Project

Brainstorm a list of descriptive words that contain suffixes. Use them to write a descriptive paragraph about a place that others in your class will recognize in your words. Don't actually name the place in your paragraph. Use as many words with suffixes as you can. Volunteers can read their paragraphs as the rest of the class tries to guess what place is being described.

Language Enrichment
Adjectives and Adverbs

Use what you have learned about adjectives and adverbs to do these activities.

 Champions and Non-Champions

Choose a partner to join you in providing the commentary for the All-Animal Track and Field Meet. Use comparative adverbs as you discuss the four-footed winners and losers of the events. In preparation for your broadcast, you may wish to write verbs that describe the activities and adverbs that can modify these verbs. If you like, enlist additional classmates to help you carry out personal interviews with the "athletes."

 Switch Arounds

You cannot always tell whether a word is an adjective or an adverb by looking at it. Sometimes you must look at the way it is used in a sentence. Working in a small group, write two sentences for each of the following words. Use each word as an adjective and as an adverb.

best   clean   direct   friendly   high

Seconds for Synonyms

Working in a small group, brainstorm and record as many synonyms as you can think of in 30 seconds for each of the following adjectives: *beautiful, generous, fast, small, large*. Share your work with the class. Then have each group list five words and exchange them. See how many synonyms each group can list.

CONNECTING

LANGUAGE ↔ WRITING

In this unit you learned that adjectives modify or describe a noun or a pronoun. Although most adjectives precede the word they describe, some may follow. Other parts of speech, such as common and proper nouns, may also act as adjectives. You also know that adverbs modify verbs, adjectives, and other adverbs. They tell *when*, *where*, *how*, *how often*, or *to what extent* something happened. Both adjectives and adverbs can be used to make comparisons.

◆ **Using Adjectives and Adverbs in Your Writing**   Knowing how to use adjectives selectively will help you make your writing both vivid and enjoyable for your reader. Pay special attention to the adjectives and adverbs you use as you do these activities.

 Grammar Grafting

On the **Building Vocabulary** page, you learned that suffixes can be attached to roots or base words to make new words. Choose four suffixes from the list on page 292, and make a noun, an adjective, a verb, and an adverb. Then write each word in a sentence, using each part of speech correctly.

 Use Your Imagination

Don't look now, but you have been captured by a UFO! Work in a small group to write about your adventures. To give your writing an extra boost, use the following adjectives and adverbs.

too	patriotic	usually
dazzling	definitely	confident
quite	extremely	surprisingly

Begin with this sentence: "One morning as I was sitting rather quietly at the breakfast table, I was captured by a UFO." Each person in your group should use at least one of the adverbs to add a sentence to the story. Record each sentence as you hear it. Then illustrate the story. Share the best written and illustrated version with the class.

Unit Checkup

Think Back	Think Ahead
◆ What did you learn about lyric poems in this unit?	◆ How will what you learned about a lyric poem help you when you read a poem? ◆ How will visualizing comparisons help you write a lyric poem?
◆ Look at the writing you did in this unit. How did adjectives and adverbs help you express ideas?	◆ What is one way you can use adjectives and adverbs to improve your writing?

Analyzing a Poem   *pages 252 – 253*
Identify what poetic device each of the following illustrates.

1. dum didee dum didee dum dum dum
2. Once there was a canary
   That was actually quite hairy.
3. Whoosh went the wind in the willow tree.
4. The spring rain tasted
   Fresh and sweet on my tongue.

Visualizing Comparisons   *page 254*
Write a comparison for each of the following topics.

5. how a squirrel sits with an acorn
6. how a toddler takes first steps across a room
7. how a snowman melts in the sun
8. how a living room looks after a birthday party

Avoiding Clichés   *page 255*
Rewrite the sentences, replacing the underlined phrases and clichés.

9. I was really wiped out.
10. You are as pale as a ghost!
11. Don't tell a soul!
12. She sings like an angel.

The Writing Process *pages 256 – 265*

Write the letter for the answer to each question.

13. When you plan a rhyming poem, what should you do first?
    a. Write rhyming words. b. Choose a topic you like. c. Choose a meter.
14. Which brainstorming technique won't help you find details?
    a. cluster map   b. Venn diagram   c. visualizing
15. When should you decide to improve the rhythm of a poem?
    a. when selecting   b. during   c. during
       a topic   revision   publishing
16. What might a literary magazine value most in a student's poem?
    a. an average topic   b. impressive vocabulary   c. vivid description
17. How should you handle rhyme and rhythm when reading a poem aloud?
    a. Exaggerate them.   b. Ignore them.   c. Emphasize them.

Adjectives *pages 268 – 269*

Write the sentences. Underline each adjective. Underline proper adjectives twice.

18. Thea has a Japanese computer.
19. Many people enjoy working on Korean computers.
20. Other people enjoy models of American or Soviet aircraft.
21. Our neighbor spends a lot of time creating unusual models.

This, That, These, Those *pages 270 – 271*

Write the demonstrative adjective. Write the noun it modifies.

22. This radio was built by my older sister, and that
    computer was built by me!
23. This family enjoys working with electronics.
24. These things are actually not difficult to put together.
25. Everyone in this family has gotten into the act.
26. That pile of pieces on the table was our alarm clock.

Other Parts of Speech as Adjectives *pages 272 – 273*

Write whether the underlined word is a *noun* or an *adjective*.

27. Leila has a warm <u>wool</u> vest she made herself.
28. Sometimes she uses cotton, and sometimes <u>wool</u>.
29. My favorite <u>birthday</u> gift is this <u>lap</u> blanket.
30. My cat loves to jump on my <u>lap</u>.
31. Our <u>house</u> is full of imaginative textiles.

Predicate Adjectives   *pages 274 – 275*

Write each sentence. Underline each predicate adjective once.
Underline the word it modifies twice.

32. The beach is beautiful in spring, before it becomes crowded.

33. The air seems crisp and fresh, and the sun shines warmly.

34. I usually write at the beach, where my ideas seem unending.

35. Some places are very different out of season.

36. Of course, some places are unpleasant out of season.

Comparisons with Adjectives   *pages 276 – 277*

Write each adjective. Then write in parentheses ( )
its degree of comparison. Use a dictionary.

37. handiest   **39.** less fussy   **41.** least scenic
38. beautiful   **40.** large   **42.** more portable

Irregular Comparisons with Adjectives   *pages 278 – 279*

Make three columns: *Positive, Comparative,* and *Superlative.* Write the
three forms of each adjective.

43. bad   **46.** farther
44. much   **47.** less
45. good   **48.** furthest

Adverbs   *pages 280 – 282*

Write each sentence. Underline each adverb once and the word it
modifies twice.

49. When he worked, Liu painted quickly.

50. I was truly amazed, for we were in a room without any windows!

51. An extremely vivid imagination can certainly help an artist.

52. Liu explained later that he had visited this scene.

Placement of Adverbs in Sentences   *pages 283 – 284*

Write each sentence. Place the adverb in parentheses ( )
so it modifies the underlined word or words in the sentence.

53. When I was <u>young</u>, my parents read me a bedtime story.   (very)
54. Knowing this, I <u>would look</u> forward to that part of my
day.   (always)

55. Ready for a new book, I would go to the library and <u>spend</u> hours choosing it.   (easily)

Comparisons with Adverbs   *pages 285 – 287*

Make three columns: *Positive, Comparative,* and *Superlative.* List each adverb in its correct column. Complete all the columns for each adverb.

56. busily
57. more successfully
58. most decoratively
59. vividly
60. much

Negatives   *pages 288 – 289*

Rewrite each sentence to correct the double negative.

61. Jim was so excited that he couldn't scarcely talk.
62. He made us promise that we wouldn't tell no one.
63. Neither my sister nor I would tell no one.
64. He couldn't barely get it out, but he told us the secret.
65. I have promised never to tell no one.

Adverb or Adjective?   *pages 290 – 291*

Write the correct modifier given in parentheses ( ).

66. Einstein had such a (good, well) imagination that his teachers called him a foolish daydreamer.
67. Although he looked (really, real) lazy, his mind worked quite (good, well).
68. Einstein did not turn out so (bad, badly) after all!
69. Einstein was especially (good, well) at making unusual connections between things.

Suffixes   *pages 292 – 293*

Read each sentence. Choose the word that has a suffix. Write the word and its meaning. Underline the base word once and the suffix twice. If the spelling changed when the suffix was added, write the base word.

70. Do you ever make up fantastic stories?
71. My classmates created a marvelous children's book.
72. Micky, who is artistic, drew pictures, and Liane wrote the story.
73. With skill and a whimsical touch, Micky's drawings capture the spirit of the story.

UNIT

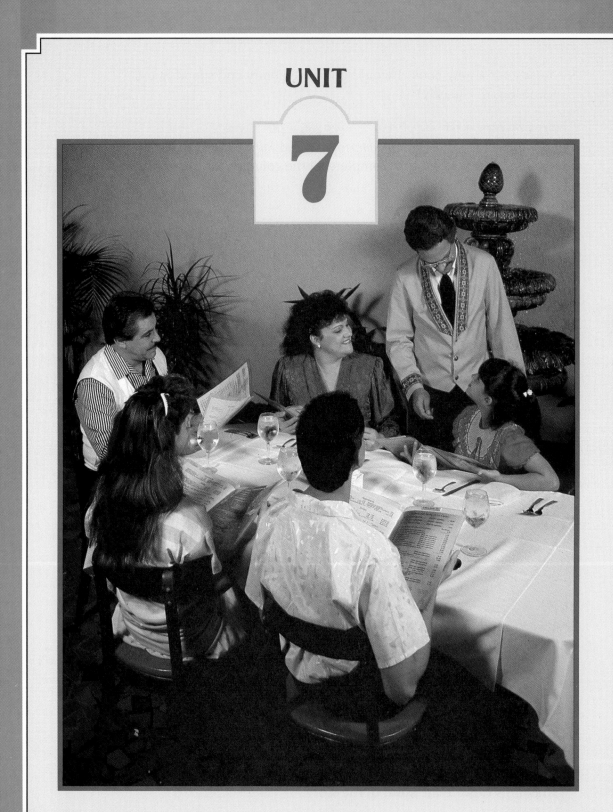

Painting Pictures
with Words

◆ **COMPOSITION FOCUS:** **Description**
◆ **LANGUAGE FOCUS:** **Prepositions, Conjunctions, Interjections**

If you found an unusual dish such as *pot-au-feu* listed on a menu and didn't know what it was, you would probably want a description before you ordered. A description gives the reader a single picture, like a snapshot, of the thing being described. It is used to inform, to persuade, to entertain, and to express. Novelist Jules Verne, for example, frequently uses description interspersed with narration in his novels.

Because he describes many different kinds of scenes, people, and objects, Verne uses various techniques in his description. He includes sensory words, colorful adjectives, and vivid verbs to help his readers imagine the things he is describing. He adds specific details to create images, and he provides apt comparisons to help the reader understand his description. In each passage, Verne chooses a consistent tone that gives a general impression of the place, person, or object described. In this unit you will learn how to create your own description.

Jules Verne (1825–1905) wrote
descriptions in his novels
to entertain readers.

Reading with a Writer's Eye
Description

In the 1860's a ship that could stay underwater for long periods of time was a scientist's dream. Jules Verne wrote a novel about just such a submarine that traveled *Twenty-Thousand Leagues Under the Sea*. In the story, Professor Arronnax (the narrator) and two others are shipwrecked. They are saved by the mysterious Captain Nemo and taken aboard Nemo's submarine, the *Nautilus*. In their four months on board, the companions see many wonders, which Verne describes in detail. As you read this portion of the novel, notice the techniques Verne uses to paint his word pictures.

from Twenty-Thousand Leagues Under the Sea
by Jules Verne

At about eleven o'clock at night I received a very unexpected visit from Captain Nemo. He asked me very politely if I was tired from having been up so late the previous night. I said I wasn't.

"Then, Monsieur Arronnax, I would like to invite you on a rather curious excursion."

"What sort of an excursion, Captain?"

"So far you have only seen the ocean depths during the day when the sun is out. How would you like to see them on a dark night?"

"Very much."

"This excursion will be tiring, I warn you. We'll have to do a lot of walking and mountain climbing. The roads aren't very well kept up."

"Your description only increases my curiosity. I'm ready to go."

"Splendid. Let's go put on our diving suits."

When I got to the dressing room, I saw that neither my companions nor any member of the crew were to go with us. Captain Nemo had made no mention of inviting Ned or Conseil.

It only took us a few minutes to put on our suits. The tanks, filled with considerable amounts of air, were put on our backs, but we weren't given our electric lamps. I mentioned this to the captain.

"We won't need them," he answered.

I thought I had not heard him correctly, but I could not repeat what I had said, for the captain's head had already disappeared inside the metal helmet. When I finished my preparations, I felt an iron-tipped stick being placed in my hand, and several minutes later, after the usual operations, we set foot on the floor of the Atlantic at a depth of a thousand feet.

It was almost midnight. The water was completely dark, but Captain Nemo showed me a reddish spot, a kind of large gleam shining about two miles away from the *Nautilus*. What this fire was, what was feeding it, why it was burning at all in the midst of the water, I had no idea. But in any case, it lit our way, dimly to be sure, but I soon became accustomed to the darkness and realized that the Ruhmkorff lamps had really not been necessary.

Captain Nemo and I, walking near each other, headed straight for the spot of light. The flat ground started to rise a bit. We took large strides, helping ourselves along with our sticks; but all the same our progress was slow, for our feet often sank in a kind of mud mixed with seaweed and strewn with flat stones.

As we walked I could hear a kind of crackling overhead, a continual pattern that would occasionally increase a bit in intensity. I soon understood what caused it. It was rain pounding on the surface of the ocean. I found myself worrying about getting soaked! Soaked by water in the midst of water! I could not help laughing at such a crazy idea. But to tell the truth, in a thick diving costume one has no sensation of being in water; it feels rather as if one were in the midst of a slightly denser atmosphere than that above the surface, and nothing more.

After we had walked for half an hour the ground became rocky. Jellyfish, microscopic shellfish and sea pens lit it up with their glimmers of phosphorescence. I could make out heaps of stones covered with masses of zoophytes and seaweed. I often slipped on this viscous bed of marine plants, and I would have fallen more than once had it not been for my stick. When I turned around I could still make out the whitish light from the *Nautilus* growing paler in the distance.

The heaps of rocks I have just mentioned were laid out on the ocean floor with a certain regularity of pattern that I could not explain. I noticed gigantic furrows which went off into the murky distance and whose length it was impossible to calculate. There were also other details which struck me as even more incredible. It seemed as if my heavy lead soles were trampling on a litter of bones, making them crack with a dry sound. What was this vast plain we were crossing? I wanted to ask the captain, but unfortunately I did not know the sign language he and his companions used under water.

Nevertheless, the reddish light guiding us was growing larger, and it now lit up the entire horizon. This source of light beneath the surface of the sea aroused my curiosity to the highest degree. Was it some electrical phenomenon? Was I about to see something unknown to scientists on land? Or was this thing—for the thought occurred to me—produced by the hands of man? Was I going to meet at these great depths companions or friends of Captain Nemo, living an existence as strange as his and whom he was now going to visit? Would I find there a whole colony of exiles who had grown weary of a miserable existence on earth and had sought and found freedom in the ocean depths? All these mad, inadmissible ideas raced through my brain, and with my mind constantly overstimulated by one wonder after another, I would not have been surprised to encounter one of those underwater cities of which Captain Nemo dreamed.

Our path grew lighter and lighter. The whitish gleam came from the top of a mountain about eight hundred feet high. But what I saw was only a reflection produced by the water itself; the source of this mysterious light was on the opposite side of the mountain.

Captain Nemo pushed on unhesitantly through the maze of rocks covering the floor of the Atlantic. He knew this dark route. He had undoubtedly been here often, and there was no danger of his getting lost. I followed him with unshakable confidence. He seemed like a spirit of the waters, and when he walked in front of me, I admired his tall build outlined in black against the lights on the horizon.

It was one in the morning. We had arrived at the foot of the mountain. But in order to climb it we had to go up difficult paths through a vast forest.

Yes, it was a forest of dead trees, without leaves or sap, trees petrified by the sea, with an occasional gigantic pine towering high into the water. It was like a coal field still standing, holding on to the furrowed soil with its roots, and its branches looking as if they had been delicately cut out of black paper. The reader might get some idea of it by trying to imagine the forest clinging to the sides of the Harz Mountains, but all under water. The paths were cluttered with seaweed and sea wrack, and among it crawled a whole world of shellfish. I climbed up rocks and stepped over fallen tree trunks, breaking the sea vines stretching from one tree to another and startling the fish flying from branch to branch. In my excitement I no longer felt any fatigue. I followed my guide, who never seemed to tire.

What a sight! How can I describe it? How can I depict the spectacle of these woods and rocks in the midst of the water, their undersides dark and forbidding, their upper sides tinted with the red light whose intensity was increased as it was reflected by the water? We would climb over rocks, enormous chunks of which would then fall down with the mute rumbling sound of an avalanche. On either side of the path were hollowed-out dark caves in which one could see nothing, and I occasionally wondered if some inhabitant of these underwater regions was not suddenly going to spring up before me.

Respond

1. What part of Verne's description creates the most memorable image for you? Explain what you think makes this part especially powerful.

Discuss

2. What does Verne describe in this passage?
3. How does Verne make his description come alive?

Thinking As a Writer
Analyzing a Description

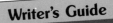
    A description creates a picture in words. It uses comparisons, images that appeal to the five senses (sensory images), descriptive language, and precise details to make the picture vivid. The topic sentence of each paragraph identifies what is being described or sets the mood to create a general impression. The detail sentences provide the vivid images that help you see the subject in your mind.

    When you read a description, pay special attention to the words the writer uses in the detail sentences. An experienced writer chooses words that will produce a specific tone, or mood. Study the paragraph below. Notice the words *petrified, gigantic, towering, clinging, cluttered, crawled, fallen, breaking, stretching, startling,* and *flying*. Together they suggest an alien world of gigantic proportions and frantic but decaying life forms.

    Yes, it was a forest of dead trees, without leaves or sap, trees petrified by the sea, with an occasional gigantic pine towering high into the water. It was like a coal field still standing, holding on to the furrowed soil with its roots, and its branches looking as if they had been delicately cut out of black paper. The reader might get some idea of it by trying to imagine the forest clinging to the sides of the Harz Mountains, but all under water. The paths were cluttered with seaweed and sea wrack, and among it crawled a whole world of shellfish. I climbed up rocks and stepped over fallen tree trunks, breaking the sea vines stretching from one tree to another and startling the fish flying from branch to branch. In my excitement I no longer felt any fatigue. I followed my guide, who never seemed to tire.

A **topic sentence** indicates what will be described. It may also suggest the tone, or mood, of the passage to follow.

Detail sentences contain comparisons, sensory images, concrete details, and phrases that show location.

Discuss

1. What is the function of the topic sentence in this descriptive passage?
2. What words would you use to give the passage a quiet, peaceful tone?
3. Why might the writer have wanted to set the eerie, frightening tone?
4. What aspects of descriptive writing are used in the detail sentences?

Try Your Hand

A. Analyze Topic Sentences Find other paragraphs of description in the selection. Identify the topic sentence in each paragraph. Tell what information it gives.

B. Analyze Detail Sentences Reread the other paragraphs of description you found in the selection. For each paragraph, tell whether Verne uses comparisons, sensory images, precise details, or phrases that show location. Explain how these techniques help you picture the scene.

C. Write a Topic Sentence and Descriptive Details Write a short paragraph that contains a topic sentence and three descriptive detail sentences.

D. Read and Talk About a Description Find a passage of description. Read it to a partner. Identify the topic sentence and the information it gives. Look for techniques the writer uses in the detail sentences.

Writer's Notebook

Collecting Specific Nouns Did you notice specific nouns such as *reflection, phosphorescence,* and *zoophytes* in the selection? Adjectives are not the only words that add color to descriptions. Specific, colorful nouns can help make description come alive. Reread the excerpt from Verne's novel, and record in your *Writer's Notebook* any other specific nouns you find. Look up the words in a dictionary and record their meanings. Try to use your new, specific nouns when you write and speak.

Thinking As a Writer
Observing Details

Writer's Guide

To write a description, good writers

• observe the subject and describe it with sensory words.

To write a good description, a writer first observes the subject to identify details. Good writers do not rely only on sight to identify details but make observations using touch, smell, taste, and hearing when appropriate.

After observing specific details, the writer records them, using precise, vivid words to capture each one. Study the chart. Then read the examples. Decide which senses were used for each one.

Sight	Touch	Smell	Taste	Hearing
size color material pattern	surface texture weight bulk	scent	sourness sweetness saltiness	pitch tone volume

1. It was a neatly painted white cottage, so tiny that it could have housed only one of the seven dwarfs.
2. The movie theater reeked of buttered popcorn and fruit punch and crackled with excitement.

When you write your description, use as many senses as possible to observe details.

Discuss

1. Look again at the opening selection. How does Verne's use of sensory details create exact images that you can visualize?
2. Which senses are not appealed to in Verne's description? Give an explanation for this.

Try Your Hand

Make Sensory Observations   Look again at the opening photograph on page 300. Pretend that you are present in the restaurant. Record as many sensory observations as possible. Trade observations with a partner. Identify which sense was used each time. Discuss how each of you could make your observations more vivid.

Developing the Writer's Craft
Writing from a Point of View

Your **point of view** is the vantage point from which you make observations. It includes where you are in relation to what you describe and also how you feel about it. Two people sitting side by side have different points of view. Their reactions, observations, and even locations are different.

The point of view you choose will have a great effect on your description. It will limit the kinds of observations you can make and will affect the way you organize them. It will help determine the general impression you convey. Unless there is a good reason to use more than one, a description should have only *one* distinct point of view. Read these examples.

1. As I glided along the high wire, smoothly performing my act, I looked down on a sea of upturned, open-mouthed, pale faces.
2. The lone tightrope artist paused in midstep, and the silence was so tense that I felt it would soon crack.

In the first example, the observation is made from the point of view of a performer on the high wire. In the second example, the observation is made from the point of view of a spectator in the audience. Neither observer is in a position to make the observation of the other. The tightrope artist conveys sureness, whereas the spectator conveys nervousness.

When writing a description, present a single, clear point of view.

Discuss

Even though Captain Nemo and Professor Arronnax were walking nearly side by side, their observations and descriptions of the scenes they passed through would have differed. Explain why this is so.

Try Your Hand

Use Point of View   Write six sentences describing a terrible thunderstorm. Write the first three sentences from the point of view of someone who is out in the storm. Write the last three from the point of view of someone who is safe inside a strong, comfortable house.

1 Prewriting
Description

Tony visited an art museum with his class and decided to write a description of a painting for his family. He used the checklist in the **Writer's Guide** to help him plan his description. Look at what he did.

◆ Brainstorming and Selecting a Topic

First, Tony brainstormed suitable paintings, and he listed the names of those he liked. Look at Tony's list.

1. *Water-lillies* by Claude Monet
2. *La Grenouilliere* by Auguste Renoir
3. *Starry Night* by Vincent van Gogh

Tony knew his family would like any painting he chose, so he selected his favorite painting, *Starry Night*.

Discuss

How was Tony's brainstorming for this writing assignment different from the brainstorming you have done for other assignments?

◆ Gathering and Organizing Information

After Tony selected his topic, he observed the details of the painting. He thought about his point of view, and he considered the general impression he wished to convey. Then he made a chart of his observations.

WRITING PROCESS

Observations of Details

Descriptive
Language: rolling hills, peaceful
                   countryside, gently lighted houses,
                   bushy trees
Sensory   sight—stars, moon, trees, hills,
Details: church, houses, color
Comparisons: stars like firecrackers
                   sky is the sea; the sea-sky
                   moon as brilliant as the sun
General   contrast between peaceful
Impression: countryside and violent sky

Tony wanted to use similes and metaphors to make his images vivid. Here is how Tony made his comparisons.

Stars burst in the sky like firecrackers. The waves of the sea-sky ripple through the night. A moon as brilliant as the sun lights the night sky.

Tony needed a way to organize the writing of his description. He used **spatial order** to show the relationship of each part of the painting to the others. To show spatial order, writers follow any of these plans.

1. bottom to top
2. left to right
3. background to foreground
4. center to outside

Tony started with the lower right-hand corner of the painting and worked his way up. Here's how he reorganized the details he observed.

Lower Right	Bottom to Top	Top

rolling hills
lines of trees
pattern of houses
—strong
   horizontals
	tall, greenish-black cypress
	church steeple pointing
	   skyward
		waves of sea-sky
		   blow through night
		contrast of violent
		   sky with peaceful
		   countryside

Discuss

1. Tony used comparisons to enhance three of his observations. Find each comparison. Identify whether each one is a simile or a metaphor.
2. How did Tony use spatial order to organize his details? In what other ways could he use spatial order to organize this description?

Try Your Hand

Now plan a description of your own.

A. Brainstorm and Select a Topic   Brainstorm a list of possible topics. Include only objects or scenes that you can readily observe. Think about each topic and about your audience.

 • Cross out topics that do not suggest strong images.
 • Cross out topics that won't interest your audience.
 • Circle the most interesting topic left on your list. This will be the topic of your description.

B. Gather and Organize Information   Write categories for your observations. Use your senses to gather information about your topic. Make a list of precise, vivid words, comparisons, and specific details to present rich images. Make a chart showing spatial order.

C. Define the General Impression   Decide what general impression your description will give. Try to think of a single word that names the impression you wish to convey. Keep this word in mind as you write.

 Save your list and your chart in your *Writer's Notebook*. You will use them when you draft your description.

WRITING PROCESS

2 Drafting
Description

Before Tony drafted his description, he thought about a way to describe *Starry Night*. Using his charts, Tony followed the checklist in the **Writer's Guide** to draft it. Look at what he did.

> I was struck when I first studied *Starry Night*, and I decided to give the picture more attention. I first noticed the beautifully lighted houses, their yellow lamps glowing like stars in the blue background. I was drawn into the peaceful countryside. Then, you let your eye travel up and to the right. This is a great picture, I thought.

Writer's Guide

Drafting Checklist

☑ Use your list and chart.

☑ Use spatial order to organize details about the object or scene.

☑ Write a topic sentence for each paragraph.

☑ Write detail sentences with descriptive language.

☑ Choose words that convey the general impression you have of your object or scene.

Discuss

1. What information does Tony's topic sentence offer in the paragraph?
2. Look back at the painting *Starry Night*. Does Tony's description give a good sense of the picture so far? Explain your answer.

Try Your Hand

Now write your own description.

A. Review Your Information Think about the details you gathered and organized. Decide whether you need more. If so, gather them.

B. Think About Your TAP Remember that your task is to write a description. Your purpose is to describe the object or scene you have selected.

Task: What?
Audience: Who?
Purpose: Why?

C. Write Your First Draft Use the **Drafting Checklist** to write your description.

When you write your draft, just put all your ideas on paper. Do not worry about spelling, punctuation, or grammar. You can correct them later.

Save your first draft in your *Writer's Notebook*. You will use it when you revise your description.

COMPOSITION: DRAFTING Description **313**

3 Responding and Revising
Description

Tony used the checklist in the **Writer's Guide** to revise his description. Look at what he did.

◆ Checking Information

Tony saw that he had not identified the artist who had painted the picture. He used this mark ∧ to add the information. He also cut a comment that did not belong. He used this mark ℓ .

◆ Checking Organization

Tony saw that his sentences were in the wrong order. To move a sentence he used this mark ♂ .

◆ Checking Language

Tony decided to replace one adjective to make his writing more vivid. He used this mark ⌒ . He used the same mark to correct an incorrect point of view.

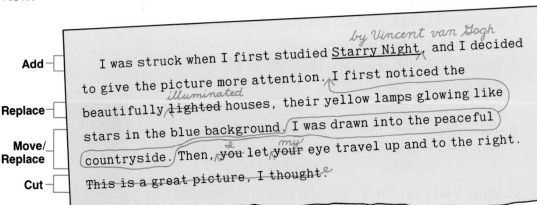

Add —

Replace —

Move/Replace —

Cut —

> *by Vincent van Gogh*
> I was struck when I first studied <u>Starry Night</u>, and I decided to give the picture more attention. I first noticed the
> *illuminated*
> beautifully ~~lighted~~ houses, their yellow lamps glowing like stars in the blue background. I was drawn into the peaceful countryside. Then, you let *my* your eye travel up and to the right.
> ~~This is a great picture, I thought.~~

Discuss

1. What was wrong with the point of view in sentence four until Tony corrected it?
2. Was it necessary for Tony to be specific about details in the painting when describing the scene? Explain your answer.

WRITING PROCESS

Try Your Hand

Now revise your description.

A. Read Your First Draft   As you read your description, think about your audience and your purpose. Read your description silently or to a partner to see whether it is complete and well organized. Ask yourself or your partner the questions in the box.

Responding and Revising Strategies

✔ Respond **Ask yourself or a partner:**	✔ Revise **Try these solutions:**
• Have I included a topic sentence and descriptive details in each paragraph?	• **Add** a sentence to each paragraph that introduces your topic and sets the mood. **Add** details that you have observed.
• Are all the details in the description important and interesting?	• **Cut** details that do not add interest to the description.
• Are the details arranged in a spatial order to help the reader visualize the scene?	• **Move** any material that is out of spatial order.
• Did I write from a single point of view?	• **Replace** any material that indicates an additional observer.
• Is my description rich in detail, sensory images, and comparisons?	• **Replace** tired or unclear descriptions with vivid, fresh words and phrases. See the **Revising Workshop** on page 316.

B. Make Your Changes   If the answer to any question in the box is *no*, try the solution. Use the **Editor's Marks** to show your changes.

C. Review Your Description Again   Decide if there is anything else you want to revise. Keep revising your description until you feel it is well organized and complete.

> **EDITOR'S MARKS**
>
> ∧ Add something.
> ⚋ Cut something.
> ⟲ Move something.
> ⋀ Replace something.

Save your revised description in your *Writer's Notebook.* **You will use it when you proofread your description.**

Revising Workshop
Expanding Sentences with Adjectives and Adverbs

Good writers use vivid description to create rich mental images for their readers. As they write, they sometimes expand their sentences to include additional descriptive details. One way to do this is to add lively, colorful adjectives and adverbs. Look at the underlined words in the second sentence.

1. The skeleton was displayed.
2. The <u>brittle</u> skeleton was displayed <u>prominently</u>.

The description in the first sentence is bare and general. In the second sentence, the addition of the adjective *brittle* and the adverb *prominently* gives the reader a much clearer idea of the scene described.

Sometimes a thesaurus can be helpful in expanding sentences. A **thesaurus** is a book that lists collections of words with similar shades of meaning. A thesaurus can help you choose the word you want.

Practice

Rewrite each sentence, expanding it with descriptive details. Use adjectives and adverbs.

1. This fossil was dug up.
2. That specimen arrived at the museum.
3. One display from an excavation was in the north wing.
4. An artifact stood on a pedestal.
5. The glass case was surrounded by ropes.
6. The lights were focused on a model.
7. Children were allowed to touch the replica.
8. An Egyptian exhibit is expected.
9. Artifacts from the lost civilizations will be on display.
10. Mummies, jewelry, and pottery will be part of the display.
11. Every museum in the country was interested.
12. I expect to stand in line to see it.

4 Proofreading
Description

After Tony revised his description, he used the checklist in the **Writer's Guide** and the **Editor's Marks** to proofread it. Look at what he did.

Writer's Guide

Proofreading Checklist

- ☑ Check for errors in capitalization.
- ☑ Check for errors in punctuation.
- ☑ Check to see that all your paragraphs are indented.
- ☑ Check for errors in grammar.
- ☑ Circle any words you think are misspelled. Find out how to spell them correctly.
- ⇨ For proofreading help, use the **Writer's Handbook.**

⊞ The violent movement of the night sky made a *makes*
sharp contrast with the calm village below the
stars burst out of the night like firecrackers.
A moon as brilliant as the sun lights. The
scene from the upper right-hand corner. Giant
waves--perhaps the blazing trail of a comet or
the movement of a great galaxy--blow across the
sea-sky. If the people in those (cosy) houses knew *cozy*
what this night was like, they would be out here
with me, gazing (breathles) at Starry Night. *breathless*

Discuss

1. Look at Tony's proofread description. What kinds of mistakes did he make?
2. Why did Tony change the verb *made* in the first sentence to *makes?*

Try Your Hand

Proofread Your Description   Now use the **Writer's Guide** and the **Editor's Marks** to proofread your description.

Save your corrected description in your *Writer's Notebook.* You will use it when you publish your description.

EDITOR'S MARKS

- ≡ Capitalize.
- ⊙ Add a period.
- ∧ Add something.
- ⩘ Add a comma.
- ∨∨ Add quotation marks.
- ✂ Cut something.
- ⋀ Replace something.
- ↝ Transpose.
- ◯ Spell correctly.
- ⊞ Indent paragraph.
- ╱ Make a lowercase letter.

WRITING PROCESS

5 Publishing
Description

Tony made a clean copy of his description and checked it to be sure he had not left anything out. Then he and his classmates published their descriptions in an illustrated book. You can find Tony's description on page 45 of the **Writer's Handbook.**

Here's how you and your classmates can publish your descriptions in an illustrated book.

1. Reread your description, and think about an effective way to illustrate it. You may use a photograph, a drawing, a painting, a collage, or any other medium of your choice.
2. Create your illustration. Make sure your illustration fits your description.

3. Compile your compositions in a book. As a group, decide the order of compositions, the cover design, and the title of the book.

4. Reproduce the book, and share it with your families.

Discuss

1. What might happen if students didn't check their descriptions while creating their illustrations?
2. Why is cooperation important in compiling the book?

WRITING PROCESS

Writer's Guide
Publishing Checklist

☑ Make a clean copy of your description.

☑ Be sure that nothing has been left out.

☑ Make sure that there are no mistakes.

☑ Share your description in a special way.

Try Your Hand

Publish Your Description   Follow the checklist in the **Writer's Guide.**
Then add your composition to the class book, or try one of these ideas
for sharing your composition.

- Share your description with your family. Ask whether they can
  picture the subject of your description. Have them tell you what parts
  of the description they like best.

- Include your description as part of a friendly letter to a relative or a
  pen pal.

Listening and Speaking
Tips on How to Listen for Details

Often you will listen to speakers who use detailed description as
part of their speech, broadcast, or address. This list may help you
follow the speaker more closely and help you recall what the speaker
had to say.

1. Begin by listening carefully to the topic sentence so that you can
   identify the subject. This will help you to listen for details that
   describe or support the subject.
2. Listen for key words to help you remember details. You might want
   to take notes of important words. If you are listening to narration
   or description, try to visualize the details. If you are listening to
   exposition, try to understand the order behind the arrangement
   of the detail sentences.
3. When the speaker is finished, review the speech in your mind. Try
   to write the main points. Go over the speech from beginning to end.
   Recall the details.
4. If the details are not easy to remember, the speaker may not have
   been clear. On the other hand, it may be that you need practice in
   listening to complex thoughts. Consider both possibilities before you
   comment on the speech.

Writing in the Content Areas

Use what you learned to write another description. Observe details. Use comparisons, sensory images, and a single point of view in your descriptions.

Fine Arts

Describe a particularly powerful or beautiful piece of music, such as "The Hall of the Mountain King" from *Peer Gynt* or "The Dance of the Sugar Plum Fairy" from *The Nutcracker Suite*. Think of categories into which you will place the details of your observations. Use vivid words to describe sounds.

Literature

Imagine and describe the illustration on the cover of your favorite book. It can be a book you read in your childhood or a more recent choice. You might describe the cover from the point of view of the reader or from that of a character in the book. Include the general impression the illustration conveys.

Mathematics

Challenge yourself by trying to write a clear, accurate description of either a maze or a complex geometric design. Pay close attention to the spatial order of details. After you have completed the description, make an illustration showing your maze or your design.

Health

Describe your favorite meal. Use as much sensory description as possible. Concentrate on smell, taste, texture, and color. As you gather your details, visualize the food to help you describe it. Pay special attention to words that describe how the meal makes you feel as well as to words that describe how the food looks.

CONNECTING
WRITING ⟷ LANGUAGE

A well-written description paints a word picture for the reader. Read the description from *Babbitt* by Sinclair Lewis. How well can you "see" the people?

With them were six wives, more or less—it was hard to tell, so early in the evening, as at first glance they all looked alike, and as they all said, "Oh , *isn't* this nice!" in the same tone of determined liveliness. To the eye, the men were less similar: Littlefield, a hedge-scholar, tall and horse-faced; Chum Frink, a trifle of a man with soft and mouse-like hair, advertising his profession as poet by a silk cord on his eyeglasses; Vergil Gunch, broad, with coarse black hair *en brosse;* Eddie Swanson, a bald and bouncing young man who showed his taste for elegance by an evening waistcoat of figured black silk with glass buttons; Orville Jones, a steady-looking, stubby, not very memorable person, with a hemp-colored toothbrush mustache. Yet they were all so well fed and clean, they all shouted "Evening, Georgie" with such robustness, that they seemed to be cousins, and the strange thing is that the longer one knew the women, the less alike they seemed; while the longer one knew the men, the more alike their bold patterns appeared.

◆ **Prepositions, Conjunctions, and Interjections in a Description** The highlighted words are prepositions, conjunctions, and interjections. They add information and detail to a sentence, help to combine parts of a sentence, or express emotion.

◆ **Language Focus: Prepositions, Conjunctions, and Interjections** The following lessons will help you use prepositions, conjunctions, and interjections in your own writing.

1 Prepositions and Prepositional Phrases

FOCUS

◆ A **preposition** relates a noun or a pronoun to another word in a sentence.

◆ A **prepositional phrase** is made up of a preposition, the object of the preposition, and all the words in between.

Some Common Prepositions	
above	in
across	inside
after	into
along	near
among	next
around	of
at	on
before	out
behind	over
below	through
beside	to
between	toward
by	under
down	up
for	with
from	without

A preposition joins words in a sentence. It is always followed by a noun or pronoun known as the **object of the preposition.**

   1. The runner holds the torch above his head .

   above=preposition;   *head*=object

A **phrase** is a group of words that is used as a single word. It does not have a subject and a verb. A **prepositional phrase** begins with a preposition, can include modifiers, and ends with the object of the preposition, as shown in color below.

   2. A crowd waited in the enormous stadium .

Prepositional phrases occur anywhere in a sentence.

   3. I watched through my new binoculars .

   4. Below me , people craned their necks to see.

   5. Those seated behind the pillars cannot see.

Prepositional phrases can have compound objects.

   6. We sit behind the stage and the dignitaries .

Link to Speaking and Writing

Always use object pronouns, never subject pronouns, in prepositional phrases.

Between you and me, this is the best part. You and I can see well from here.

Guided Practice

A. Identify the preposition and the prepositional phrase in each sentence.

1. The earliest Olympic Games were held in Greece.
2. At first only men competed and watched.
3. The first games in 776 B.C. included only footraces.
4. In the eighth and seventh centuries B.C., new sports were added.
5. The Olympics were, at the beginning, ceremonies honoring Zeus.

B. Complete each prepositional phrase with an appropriate object pronoun.

6. Will you watch the Olympics with _____?
7. You can sit here between _____ and _____.
8. Please pass this down to _____.
9. I enjoy the Olympic Games, but I can't read with _____ on.
10. Will you watch the track events with _____?

THINK AND REMEMBER

- Remember that a **preposition** shows the relationship of a noun or pronoun to some other word or words in a sentence.

- Remember that a **prepositional phrase** begins with a preposition and ends with a noun or pronoun known as the **object of the preposition.**

Independent Practice

C. Identifying Prepositional Phrases   Write the sentences. Underline each prepositional phrase.

11. The first Olympics were held in the stadium of Olympia.

MODEL The first Olympics were held in the stadium of Olympia.

12. In the sixth century an earthquake ruined the Olympic stadium.
13. After thirteen centuries, archaeologists discovered the ruins.
14. This gave a Frenchman the idea of the modern Olympic Games.
15. In 1896 the first modern Olympics took place in Athens.
16. Now the games are held every four years in summer and winter.
17. Only highly skilled athletes compete in the modern games.
18. Relay runners bring a lighted torch from Olympia, Greece.

D. 19.–26. Identifying Objects   Write the object or objects in each prepositional phrase in **C.** Do not write adjectives and adverbs.

19. The first Olympics were held in the stadium of Olympia.

MODEL⟩ stadium, Olympia

E. Revising: Choosing Object Pronouns   Choose and write the correct pronoun in parentheses ( ).

27. The Summer Games are more popular with (we, us) than the Winter Games are.

MODEL⟩ us

28. To (I, me), the Summer Games and summer sports are my particular favorites.

29. Between (she, her) and (he, him), who is the better swimmer?

30. Perhaps you'll swim with (she, her) on the relay teams.

31. These students competed against (they, them) last year.

32. The Swedish team will play against (we, us) in the finals.

F. Expanding Sentences with Prepositional Phrases   Add a prepositional phrase to each sentence. Write the new sentences.

33. Have you seen the pentathlon?

MODEL⟩ Have you seen the pentathlon in the Olympics?

34. Come watch the pentathlon.

35. The ancient pentathlon included the discus throw, the javelin throw, the long jump, the sprint, and wrestling.

36. Look at the crowd gathering.

37. That man is standing.

38. He looks so strong.

39. Will he win?

40. Notice that Swedish athlete.

41. She has won several medals.

42. The Swedes excel.

43. The Norwegian team will be competing.

44. One team will win.

Application — Writing

Interview Questions   Imagine that you are interviewing for your school newspaper the youngest participant in the Olympic Games. Write several interview questions encouraging the athlete to share his or her feelings about being part of this competition. Use prepositional phrases correctly.

2 Prepositional Phrases Used as Adjectives

◆ **FOCUS** A prepositional phrase that modifies a noun or a pronoun is an **adjective phrase.**

Remember that an adjective gives information about a noun or a pronoun. An adjective phrase is a prepositional phrase that answers the question *what kind, which one, how much,* or *how many.*

1. Ancient Egyptians wore cotton clothing.   adjective

2. The fibers in cotton are light and cool.   adjective phrase

When a sentence contains more than one adjective phrase, the second phrase may modify the object of the preposition in the first phrase.

3. People from the land of Egypt used cotton often.

Guided Practice

A. Identify the adjective phrases and the nouns they modify.

1. Egyptians wore head cones of perfumed grease.
2. The heat of the day melted the cones.
3. Shiny grease with its perfume covered their shoulders.
4. These cones made their wearers slaves to high fashion.
5. A body with a glistening finish was fashionable.

THINK AND REMEMBER

• Remember that a prepositional phrase that modifies a noun or pronoun is an **adjective phrase.**

• Remember that adjective phrases tell *what kind, which one, how much,* or *how many.*

Independent Practice

B. Identifying Adjective Phrases   Write the sentences. Underline the adjective phrases. Draw arrows to the words they modify.

6. Clothes for Greek men and women were almost the same.

MODEL⟩ Clothes for Greek men and women were almost the same.

7. A tunic of classic simplicity was worn by the Greeks.

8. Tunics of wool or linen were popular.

9. Most fashionable were linen tunics with pleats.

10. The tunic for a man was shorter than a woman's tunic.

11. A border of flowers might decorate a tunic.

12. Men and women in fashionable circles wore jewelry of gold.

13. The jewelry with unusual designs is prized today.

C. Writing Prepositional Phrases   Reword the underlined adjectives as prepositional phrases. Write each noun and prepositional phrase.

14. <u>modern</u> dress

MODEL⟩ dress of modern times

15. <u>unruly</u> hair

16. <u>gold and silver</u> jewelry

17. <u>French</u> jeans

18. <u>most</u> students

19. <u>fast</u> running shoes

20. <u>three</u> brothers

D. Revising: Writing Sentences with Adjective Phrases   Rewrite the sentences, using information from the underlined adjectives to form prepositional phrases.

21. What will <u>future</u> clothing be?

MODEL⟩ What will the clothing of the future be?

22. Perhaps <u>nylon</u> or <u>metal</u> zippers will be replaced by bits of plastic or even cloth.

23. Can anyone invent a <u>no-wrinkle</u> fabric?

24. Washing and ironing might become <u>old-fashioned</u> tasks!

25. Maybe we'll have <u>comfortable</u> shoes.

26. How do you imagine <u>your</u> great-grandchildren's clothing?

27. Will <u>space station</u> workers wear plastic or metal?

28. Perhaps a new <u>plant</u> fiber will be discovered.

29. We may soon be wearing <u>leafy</u> clothing.

Application — Writing

A Description   Imagine that you have been asked to help design a display of American students' clothing of the twentieth century. Sketch a typical outfit for a boy or a girl. Write a detailed description of the clothing, so that someone centuries from today will have a clear idea of the fashion. Use both adjectives and adjective phrases in your work. If you need help writing a description, see page 45 of the **Writer's Handbook**.

3 Prepositional Phrases Used as Adverbs

◆ **FOCUS**   A prepositional phrase that modifies a verb, an adjective, or an adverb is an **adverb phrase.**

An adverb phrase is a prepositional phrase that acts as an adverb.

1. The shadow falls across the sundial .
2. A sundial works accurately to some degree .   modifies adverb
3. This one looks battered by the weather .   modifies adjective

Like adverbs, adverb phrases answer the questions *how, when, where, how often,* and *to what extent* about the words they modify.

4. The sundial is over there .   where
5. We read it in the morning and in the afternoon .   when
6. It tells time with accuracy and needs no care at all .   how, to what extent

Adverb phrases can be placed anywhere in a sentence.

7. In ancient Babylon sundials had fixed pointers at their centers .

Guided Practice

A. Identify the adverb phrases.

1. People first used sundials about 4,000 years ago.
2. Other ancient clocks marked time with water.
3. Water drains from a container.
4. After any time unit, you can measure water loss.
5. The water lost is always proportionate to the time passed.

B. 6.–10.   Name the word each phrase in **A** modifies; tell whether it answers *how, when, where, how often,* or *to what extent.*

THINK AND REMEMBER

• Remember that **adverbs** and **adverb phrases** modify verbs, adjectives, or other adverbs.

• Remember that **adverb phrases** answer the questions *how, when, where, how often,* and *to what extent.*

Independent Practice

C. Identifying Adverb Phrases   Write the sentences. Underline the phrases that act as adverbs. Draw an arrow to the word each adverb phrase modifies.

11. People used mechanical clocks during the 1700's.

> **MODEL** People used mechanical clocks during the 1700's.

12. Look closely at this antique clock.

13. This grandfather clock is encased in polished mahogany.

14. A heavy weight drives the clock's mechanism by gravity.

15. For five minutes the chimes ring with rich tones.

16. At a distance I watch the pendulum swing back and forth.

D. Distinguishing Between Adjective Phrases and Adverb Phrases   Write each prepositional phrase, indicating its use as an *adjective* or an *adverb*.

17. Even the best mechanical clocks are affected by wear and climate.

> **MODEL** by wear and climate—adverb

18. Are you the kind of person who is always prompt?
19. Consult a clock powered by atoms, and you cannot go wrong.
20. Atomic clocks measure time with remarkable accuracy.
21. About every 100,000 years, they gain or lose a few seconds.
22. These are the clocks of the future.

E. Revising: Replacing Adverbs with Adverb Phrases   Change each underlined adverb to an adverb phrase with approximately the same meaning.

23. Mia has a body clock that always gives her the time.

> **MODEL** Mia has a body clock that gives her the time without fail.

24. When it's time to wake up, her body clock gently wakes her.
25. Nightly she seems to know when nine o'clock arrives.
26. Does your body clock keep time well?
27. My body clock runs down speedily.
28. I am asleep early every night.

Application — Writing

A Journal Entry   Suppose all the watches and clocks in the world stop for a day, and sundials won't work because it is cloudy. Write a journal entry about your day. Use both adverbs and adverb phrases as modifiers. If you need help writing a journal entry, see page 47 of the **Writer's Handbook.**

4 Using Prepositions Correctly

◆ **FOCUS**   Some prepositions are frequently misused.

Several prepositions are often misused. Read the prepositions and their definitions. Notice how they are used in each sentence.

at, to

At indicates that someone or something is already in a certain place. *To* shows movement toward a place.

1. At the natural history museum, we saw a collection of fossils.
2. Students are always going to that exhibit.

in, into

In means "already inside." *Into* shows movement from the outside to the inside of something.

3. Scientists have a record of creatures that lived in past ages.
4. Scientists dig into cliffs to find them.

between, among

Between refers to two. *Among* refers to three or more.

5. Woolly mammoths fell between two mountains and into ice crevasses.
6. A woolly rhinoceros was among the most important finds.

beside, besides

Beside means "at the side of." *Besides* means "in addition to."

7. Often fragments of bone are found beside the buried animal.
8. Besides their tools, scientists use explosives to uncover a specimen.

Guided Practice

A. Identify the correct preposition in parentheses ( ).

1. Are you going (in, into) the dinosaur room?
2. (Beside, Besides) this exhibit, what else shall we see?
3. Can we choose from (among, between) all the exhibits?
4. We'll meet again (at, to) the drinking fountain.
5. Standing (beside, besides) the fossils, you look like a prehistoric student.

Independent Practice

B. Choosing Prepositions   Choose and write the correct preposition to complete each sentence.

6. The fossils (in, into) this display are especially interesting.

`MODEL` in

7. That fossil fern (among, between) the fossil magnolia and fossil palm is 250 million years old.

8. (Beside, Besides) being beautiful, fossils reveal what the climate was like millions of years ago.

9. We know that palm trees cannot grow (beside, besides) icebergs.

10. Yet fossil palms were found (in, into) what is now Greenland.

11. People (in, into) Greenland certainly have no palm trees now!

12. (Among, Between) the two rooms we have seen so far, I like this one better.

C. Writing Sentences with Prepositions   Use each word group correctly in a sentence.

13. besides the fossils

`MODEL` Besides the fossils, Sheila likes the gem displays.

14. beside the fossil display
15. choose between
16. choose among
17. went in
18. ran into
19. went to
20. stayed in
21. backed into
22. among the animals
23. between its eyes
24. sat beside
25. besides history class

Application—Writing

Directions   Imagine that a classmate is meeting you at the fossil exhibit at your local museum. Write directions telling him or her how to get from the museum entrance to the fossil display. Briefly describe two exhibits your classmate might enjoy looking at on the way to meet you. Use prepositions correctly.

5 Conjunctions

♦ **FOCUS** A **conjunction** connects words or groups of words in a sentence.

Conjunctions connect words that are equal in importance and share the same function in a sentence. Common conjunctions are *and*, *or*, and *but*. They are **coordinating conjunctions.** Use conjunctions in these ways.

To show similar ideas, use *and*.

1. The bride and groom had a huge outdoor wedding reception.
2. They walked out of the house and into the garden.

To show contrast between ideas, use *but*.

3. The party passed happily but much too quickly.
4. They will leave after teatime but before sundown.

To show a choice between ideas, use *or*.

5. We could dance on the lawn or listen to music on the patio.
6. We could leave now or later.

Some conjunctions are pairs of words called **correlative conjunctions.** The most common correlative conjunctions are these.

neither/nor 7. Neither the bride nor the groom has stopped smiling.
either/or 8. Either they are dancing, or they are greeting guests.
both/and 9. Both his family and her family are seated there.

> **Link to Speaking and Writing**
> When *and* joins words in a subject, the subject is always plural, and the verb must be plural to agree with the subject. When *or* or *nor* connects subjects, the verb always agrees in number with the noun or pronoun closest to it.

My cousins, my uncle, and my brother are arriving later.
My cousins, my uncle, or my brother is arriving later.
Neither he nor I am going to arrive on time.

Guided Practice

A. Identify the conjunction in each sentence.

1. Some older relatives, my sister, and I sit together.
2. The relatives talk, and we listen.
3. Neither my sister nor I have met these people before.
4. One uncle is especially funny and fascinating.
5. I laugh merrily but learn a lot at the same time.

B. 6.–10. Tell how each subject and verb in **A** agree.

> ### THINK AND REMEMBER
>
> ◆ Remember that a **conjunction** connects words or word groups.
>
> ◆ Use the **coordinating conjunctions** *and, but,* and *or* to join ideas that are similar.
>
> ◆ Use the **correlative conjunctions** *either/or, neither/nor,* and *both/and* to join pairs of ideas.
>
> ◆ Be sure the verb agrees in number with the noun or pronoun closest to it if *or* or *nor* joins words in a subject.

Independent Practice

C. Identifying Conjunctions   Write the conjunctions.

11. How do you begin to investigate recent or early ancestors?

MODEL〉 or

12. Ask at home, but also ask other relatives.
13. Either call or write to members of your family.
14. Make a family tree, and show how everyone is related.
15. In a library or bookstore, find books about making family trees.
16. Town records may exist in northern and southern Europe.
17. Birth or marriage records may hold valuable information.
18. Find the address or telephone number of the closest city hall.
19. Both telephone calls and letters can provide interesting leads.
20. Friends or relatives in nearby towns may be able to help you.
21. People of African and Asian descent may have greater difficulty in obtaining records.
22. Sometimes only a trip to Zaire or Hong Kong will furnish you with the records you need.

D. Checking Subject-Verb Agreement   Choose and write the correct verb to agree with the subject in these sentences.

23. Neither she nor I (know, knows) much about our grandparents.

MODEL〉 know

24. My sister and I (want, wants) to research our grandmother's life.

25. Either Saturday or Sunday (is, are) now spent in her kitchen.

26. She (cooks, cook), and we (eats, eat) and (talk, talks).

27. Both my sister and I (has, have) imagined such stories.

28. Grandmother and Grandfather constantly (surprises, surprise) us.

29. (Has, Have) you and your family shared tales?

E. Revising: Correcting Errors in Subject-Verb Agreement   Write correctly the words in each sentence that are incorrect. If a sentence has no errors, write *correct*.

30. Neither I nor the twins speaks Italian.

MODEL〉 speak

31. Both Ray and Rhonda wants to learn the language.

32. Either Rhonda or I will pay for the books and tapes.

33. Ray and I use them first.

34. Then Mom or Rhonda come into the room.

35. Either Ray or I stop reading.

36. Both Mom and Rhonda encourages us to continue.

37. Later, either Ray or I leaves the room.

38. Neither of us want to read aloud with an audience present.

39. Eventually, both Rhonda and I becomes less timid.

40. Rhonda and Ray read with no hesitation.

41. Mom and I am not yet sure of the right pronunciation.

42. After two weeks I speaks with a much better accent.

F. Writing Sentences with Correlative Conjunctions   Use each correlative conjunction in a sentence. Write each sentence.

43. either/or

MODEL〉 Either my sister or I will help you.

44. neither/nor   **45.** both/and

Application — Writing and Speaking

A Narrative   Project yourself into the future and describe an important day in your life to your grandchildren. Express your thoughts as if you were speaking into a tape recorder. Use conjunctions correctly. If you need help writing a narrative, see page 48 of the **Writer's Handbook.**

6 Interjections

◆ **FOCUS**   An **interjection** expresses feeling or emotion.

Interjections are often used in sentences to make them more lively. The words in color are interjections.

1. Oh , it is beautiful!   **2.** Wow ! Look at that!

Remember that an exclamation point shows feeling or emotion. When an exclamation point follows an interjection, the interjection shows strong feeling. When a comma separates an interjection from the sentence that follows, the interjection shows mild feeling.

3. Whew , I'm exhausted.   mild feeling

4. Whew ! I'm exhausted!   strong emotion

Some Common Interjections			
oh	sure	wow	hurray
great	ah	hey	oops
whew	say	well	you bet

Link to Speaking and Writing
Use interjections very rarely in essays. Use them sparingly in informal writing or dialogue.

Wow! The Statue of Liberty guards the harbor.
"Wow," he said,
"that's an amazing statue."

Guided Practice

A. Read aloud each sentence, supplying an interjection.
Use strong or mild emotion as indicated by the punctuation.

1. "_____, do you know about Ellis Island?" she asked.
2. "_____, about 16 million immigrants arrived there," he said.
3. "_____! When was that?" she asked.
4. "_____, Ellis Island had been used for a good many years by 1924."
5. "_____, where did everyone come from?" she continued.
6. "_____! Everywhere you can think of."

Independent Practice

B. Adding Interjections   Add an interjection to each sentence. Try not to repeat any.

7. "_____! That's amazing!" he said.

MODEL> Wow

8. "_____!" said Jerry. "You really arrived at Ellis Island?"
9. Uncle Dan answered, "_____, I didn't realize you knew about it."
10. "We read about it in school, but, _____, I'd like to know more."
11. "_____, tell me what you'd like to know," invited Uncle Dan.
12. "_____, were you scared?"
13. "_____!" said Uncle Dan. "I was terrified!"
14. Jerry asked, "_____, can you tell me what it was like?"
15. "_____! I remember it as though it were yesterday."

C. Writing Sentences with Interjections   Write a sentence that includes an appropriate interjection to describe each situation.

16. You're on a ship at sea, and the air is fresh.

MODEL> Say! This fresh ocean air is wonderful.

17. You're at sea, and the waves build threateningly.
18. You notice the sky darkening.
19. You're scared of the loud thunder.
20. You're very cold as the rain begins to fall.
21. As you walk to your cabin, you slip on the deck.
22. Suddenly the sky clears and you see the Statue of Liberty.

Application—Writing

A Dialogue   Imagine that you are an immigrant arriving on a ship at Ellis Island in New York Harbor. Write a conversation expressing your feelings and ideas about the journey and arrival. Use interjections.

Building Vocabulary
Idioms

Read these headlines.

Robots Take Over Assembly Lines
President Talks Up Latest Software Technology

Each of the headlines contains an idiom. An **idiom** is an expression that has a meaning different from the dictionary definition of the individual words. Many idioms begin or end with a preposition. What are the idioms in the headlines?

Take over and *talks up* are the idiomatic expressions. *Take over* means "to take charge of." *Talk up* means "to promote or push for." Idioms are part of our everyday language. Some idioms are so common that you probably don't realize they are idioms. One such is *How are you?* which means "What is the state of your health?" Other idioms are unfamiliar. If you are unsure of the meaning of an idiom, look it up in the dictionary under the main word.

Read the idioms in the chart.

Idiom	Meaning	Example
make believe	pretend	Children like to make believe they can fly.
not breathe a word	keep secret	Don't breathe a word of it to anyone.
play for time	stall	We played for time until the police arrived.
steal the show	be the center of attention	Children and animals often steal the show.
take cover	hide	During a tornado, take cover in a basement.
fed up	tired of	My father is fed up with his job and is looking for a new one.
how come	why	How come the run doesn't count?
run into	meet	I ran into Ann at the mall today.
bottle up	keep secret	He bottles up all his fears.
on the run	quickly	I'm late. I'll just eat on the run.
take up	begin learning	Tom wants to take up bowling.
sign off	stop talking	It's late, so I'll sign off now.

Reading Practice

Read the interview. Find the idioms. Rewrite each sentence, replacing the idiom with its meaning. Use a dictionary for help.

Reporter: Was it easy for you to join the Rockets as their lead singer?

Rock star: No, it took them forever to notice me.

Reporter: How did you get into the group?

Rock star: I begged the lead guitarist to take a chance on me. I sang for free. They saw at once that I was good.

Reporter: What's coming up for your band?

Rock star: We are going to take on a new keyboard player. Everything else is hush-hush. I have to be pretty tight-lipped about our other plans. We don't want anyone to get wind of anything.

Writing Practice

As an editor, you must edit this article. Replace each underlined idiom with a phrase from the box.

Today, Mayor Henderson admitted that the business community in the city is in a slump. However, she guarantees that her plan will help them pull through. Although many people take a dim view of it, the mayor is insisting that her plan is one that all citizens can sink their teeth into. At the press conference, Mayor Henderson said, "We aren't married to this plan. We'll try it, and if it doesn't work, we'll come up with another."

| underlying a decline |
| get involved in |
| disapprove |
| recover |
| committed to |
| think of |

Project

Make a list of idioms that contain the main words *through*, *take*, *touch*, *run*, and *put*. Then work in pairs to conduct interviews. One partner will act as the reporter and the other will be the person being interviewed. Make up questions and answers using idioms from the list. Rehearse your interview, and present it to the class. Ask classmates to identify and interpret your idioms.

Language Enrichment
Prepositions, Conjunctions, and Interjections

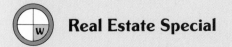

Use what you have learned about prepositions, conjunctions, and interjections to do these activities.

Real Estate Special

You are a super salesperson for Acme Realty Company. You have been put in charge of writing the feature advertisement for the Sunday paper. This is the featured property.

Describe the estate at the right in details that will set the office telephone ringing. Use prepositional phrases and conjunctions to add information about the property. Be sure to include the price—in small print.

Imagining Interjections

People of every generation use interjections, but the interjections change over the years. Working in a small group, brainstorm interjections from the past and the present, such as "Land sakes!" or "Fiddlesticks!" Also, think of interjections that may be in fashion in the next century. Appoint one person to record group members' suggestions under the headings *past*, *present*, *future*. Then share your list with the class.

My Favorite Monster

Draw a picture of your favorite monster. Then write an accurate description of the monster in your drawing. Use prepositions and prepositional phrases in your description. Your teacher can collect the original drawings and redistribute the descriptions so everyone receives someone else's paragraph. Now draw the monster in the description you received. When everyone has finished, compare the drawings based on the descriptions with the original drawings.

CONNECTING

LANGUAGE ⬌ WRITING

In this unit you learned to use connecting parts of speech called prepositions and conjunctions. You also practiced using words called interjections, which allow you to express emotion in your writing.

◆ **Using Prepositions, Conjunctions, and Interjections in Your Writing**
Knowing how to use these parts of speech correctly will help you sharpen your writing skills. Pay special attention to the prepositions, conjunctions, and interjections you use as you do the following activities.

Dynamic Duos

Throughout history, the conjunction *and* has joined the names of some very famous duos, both real and fictional. You probably have read books or seen TV shows and movies of famous pairs, for example, Batman and Robin and Laurel and Hardy. Working as a class, brainstorm famous pairs, and have one person write their names on the chalkboard. Then each of you may choose one pair and write a paragraph based on an imaginary interview with the famous duo.

Idiotic Idioms

On the **Building Vocabulary** page, you learned about colorful expressions called idioms. Choose one of the idioms from the lesson,

or think of another one that interests you. Make up a story to explain how the idiom began and what it means today. Share your story with the class. Afterward, refer to a book about idioms to learn the actual origin of the idiom you chose. See how close you came to the true origin.

Bill wrapped up his book report about seven o'clock.

Unit Checkup

Think Back	Think Ahead
◆ What did you learn about writing a description in this unit? What did you do to write one?	◆ How will what you learned about a description help you when you read a description of a person, place, or object? ◆ How will what you have learned about observing details help you write a description? a letter?
◆ Look at the writing you did in this unit. How did prepositions, conjunctions, and interjections help you express your ideas?	◆ What is one way you can use prepositions, conjunctions, and interjections to improve your writing?

Analyzing a Description   *pages 306–307*

Answer questions about the following journal excerpt.

> We went to the Union Square Greenmarket, where farmers brought vegetables to sell, calling out "Try my eggplant!" to passersby. The stacks of shiny eggplants were gorgeous—like purple pyramids. Beside them, peppers—orange, red, and green. They were lit up with deep, rich, fall colors. The fresh aroma of the vegetables overpowered city smells. What a terrific market!

1. What is described?
2. What is the general impression?
3. Identify one sensory image, and name the sense it applies to.
4. What is the topic sentence?
5. What detail shows location?

Observing Details *page 308*

For each sentence, list the sensory details. Then name the senses they apply to.

6. The red corduroy vest felt like velvet to her face.
7. The aroma of fresh bread welcomed the houseguests the minute they came.
8. I don't mind the traffic, but the horns honk constantly!
9. Lemon sherbet in a cantaloupe is just the right tongue-tingling flavor for a hot summer day.
10. Just thinking about poison ivy makes my skin itch!

Writing from a Point of View *page 309*

For each sentence tell whose point of view is described.

11. I saw her push the cart full of groceries down the aisle, so I put down the magazine and waited at my cash register.
12. I hope it won't take me all day to check out—that cashier looks unhappy to see me!
13. I'm not going to leave this theater until I get my money back!
14. My favorite shop is down the block, so let's look in after we finish our milk here in the booth.
15. Across the street is a school, next door to me is another apartment building, and on the left is a vacant lot.

The Writing Process *pages 310–319*

Write the letter for the answer to each question.

16. When you plan a description, why is a topic that cannot be observed a poor choice?
    a. Your reader won't believe it.
    b. It will be hard to gather information.
    c. It will have few details.

17. In gathering information, why should you use many senses?
    a. to help your audience visualize the subject
    b. to fill a page of prewriting
    c. to be able to write a long description

18. What description topic would be best for a four-year-old brother?
    a. a fire engine b. an oboe c. a coal mine

19. Why use a thesaurus when revising a description?
  a. to show off your vocabulary skills
  b. to help your readers learn new words
  c. to avoid stale language

Prepositions and Prepositional Phrases   *pages 322 – 324*
Write the sentences. Underline each prepositional phrase once.
Underline the object of the preposition twice.

20. If you live in a cold climate, you know that many animals disappear when the temperature drops.

21. Animals hibernate so that during the cold season they will not starve to death when the supply of food dwindles.

22. Frogs and snakes are a few of the animals that hibernate.

23. If the weather is especially mild on a particular day, some animals might awaken to have a romp and a snack.

24. If you walk in the woods and find little piles of acorns and nuts hidden here and there, do not disturb them.

Prepositional Phrases Used as Adjectives   *pages 325–326*
Write the sentences. Underline the adjective phrases once and the words they modify twice.

25. I saw bushels of apples today.

26. Fall apples have a crispness of texture that I love.

27. My mother and I bake pies of ripe fruit.

28. My father makes applesauce with cinnamon.

29. We pick delicious apples from the trees in our yard, but we usually have to buy more.

Prepositional Phrases Used as Adverbs   *pages 327–328*
Write the sentences. Underline the adverb phrase once. Underline the word it modifies twice.

30. A framed photograph of me is sitting on the shelf.

31. The teddy bear still lies on my bed today!

32. For a long time I thought the photograph was silly.

33. Now when I see it, I am glad it is on my shelf.

34. I gaze at family photographs.

Using Prepositions Correctly   *pages 329 – 330*
Write the preposition that is correct in parentheses ( ).

35. Later I am going (at, to) the movies with Stanley.

36. (Beside, Besides) going to the movies, we're doing some errands.

37. I'll take the bus (at, to) the theater.

38. For a snack I put some cheese (in, into) a plastic bag.

39. I chose (among, between) cheese and celery, and cheese is quieter.

Conjunctions   *pages 331 – 333*
Write the conjunctions.

40. Either today or tomorrow we should have our first snowstorm.

41. Neither Lucas nor Susanna has seen snow!

42. They have just moved here, and they are quite excited.

43. I enjoy snow, but it makes me want to be outside skiing.

44. Either the snow will be good for sledding or it won't.

Interjections   *pages 334 – 335*
Add an interjection to each sentence. Try not to repeat any.

45. "＿＿＿＿＿＿, that's a beautiful telephone!"

46. "＿＿＿＿＿＿, thanks. It's called the 'phone of the future.'"

47. "＿＿＿＿＿＿, why does it have a screen on it?"

48. "＿＿＿＿＿＿! Haven't you heard about videophones?"

49. "＿＿＿＿＿＿, I haven't. Tell me."

Idioms   *pages 336 – 337*
Read the sentences. Find the idioms. Rewrite each sentence, replacing the idiom with its meaning. Use a dictionary if you need help.

50. Before the invention of the telephone, how did
people keep in touch with their friends?

51. I never hesitate to give one of my friends a ring
whenever I feel like it.

52. Of course, in nice weather I always zip over to a
friend's house for a quick visit.

53. Staying on top of the news is, after all, important!

1-7 Cumulative Review

Four Kinds of Sentences   *pages 32–33*

Copy each sentence and add the correct punctuation mark at the end of each. Then write *declarative, interrogative, imperative,* or *exclamatory* to identify each sentence type.

1. What does your handwriting reveal about you
2. My letters slant to the right
3. Jan says that means I'm an optimist
4. Read a book on handwriting analysis
5. Do you believe what it says
6. Bring the book with you when you visit
7. Carl writes differently each day
8. I wonder if he has multiple personalities
9. Lou almost never uses handwriting because he has a computer
10. What do Lou's printouts reveal about him
11. Perhaps his mind is like a computer

Compound Subjects and Predicates
pages 40–41

Write the sentences. Underline the subjects once and the verbs twice. Write *compound subject, compound predicate,* or *both* after each sentence.

12. Frank and Murray collected travel brochures for the group project.
13. We researched and chose the project.
14. Our section and Mr. Field's section are working together.
15. They and we are planning a class trip around the world.
16. Of course, the plan and the trip are two different things.
17. Reading, reporting, and organizing are some of the tasks.
18. Joseph and Cathy have read and have sorted all the material so far.

Appositives   *pages 92–93*

Write each sentence. Underline the appositive in each sentence. Draw an arrow from the appositive to the noun it explains.

19. Many people contributed ideas to that skit, the best part of the show.

20. The actors, hardworking students, did a terrific job.

21. The laughter from the audience, friends and parents, showed everyone's enjoyment.

22. Humor, really funny material, is the hardest to create.

23. I don't know how Angel, the star of the show, managed to remember all of his lines and routines.

24. The funniest person in the show, Andrew, is very serious offstage.

25. I enjoy watching fine acting, a real gift.

Principal Parts of Verbs   *pages 130–133*

Write each verb. After the verb, write *present, present participle, past,* or *past participle* to show which principal part is used.

26. Autumn leaves are falling everywhere.

27. They gave me the idea for a nice surprise.

28. I just looked out the window, and the idea came to me.

29. My parents applauded my actions.

30. I have raked all the leaves from our yard.

31. My mother had asked my father about it.

32. He usually enjoys the work.

33. Lately, however, he has come home tired.

34. Through all my effort I discovered something.

35. Small kindnesses for others enrich me.

36. I am planning more surprises for this winter—efficient snow removal, for instance.

Verb Tenses   *pages 137–140*

Write each verb. After it, write its tense.

37. activates
38. has accused
39. will have tackled
40. had pouted
41. jested
42. have discounted
43. has discharged
44. will outwit
45. induced
46. will have recorded
47. suggests
48. will comply

49. portrayed
50. had extended
51. have rated
52. will have adjusted
53. will nourish
54. harassed
55. entrusted
56. had piloted
57. has coped
58. have erased
59. had appreciated
60. nourishes

Pronouns and Antecedents   *pages 226–227*

Write the correct pronoun in each set of parentheses. Be sure the pronoun agrees with the antecedent.

61. "Last year," Frieda said, "I wanted to wear jeans all the time to school, and (it, they) had to be stonewashed denim."
62. Why is it that students grab onto a fashion and stick to (them, it)?
63. When skirts are in style, (she, they) might be long or short.
64. Now students like T-shirts, and next year (they, you) might like jackets.
65. Mom and Dad wore this style when (it, they) were young.
66. I'll keep my clothes so my children can wear (them, it) later.

Possessive Pronouns   *pages 230–232*

Write the correct pronoun in parentheses ( ).

67. (Me, My) friend Donna and I love to study animals.
68. We went to the new zoo on (our, they're) field trip.
69. Perhaps you will get to go on (you're, yours).
70. The monkeys seem very happy on an island of (their, they're) own.
71. The monkeys certainly acted as if the island were (their, theirs).
72. Donna watched them through (hers, her) new binoculars.
73. I used (my, mine) turn to watch the giraffes running.
74. The city plans to use (its, it's) profits from the new zoo to build better animal habitats.

Reflexive, Intensive, and Demonstrative
Pronouns   *pages 233–235*
Make three columns labeled *Reflexive, Intensive,* and *Demonstrative.*
Write the appropriate pronouns and their antecedents in the correct
columns.

75. I myself cannot believe how quickly my brother grows.
76. My parents are always reminding themselves to take movies.
77. This is a picture I took of him with my own camera.
78. My books were on my desk, but Louie thought, "Those are mine!"
79. When Louie wants something for himself, he goes after it.
80. This has become a problem for everyone but Louie.

Subject–Verb Agreement   *pages 144–145*
Write the correct verb to complete each sentence.

81. My sisters and I often (watch, watches) the view from our window.
82. If anyone (look, looks) up, one of us is often there watching.
83. From our window we (see, sees) the park across the street.
84. In the spring everything (has, have) buds and bits of green.
85. By summer the trees and bushes (is, are) covered with leaves.
86. Autumn is my favorite season, and I (paint, paints) the view.
87. In winter almost nobody (play, plays) in the park.
88. The seasons are fun to watch, for all (has, have) their attractions.
89. Photographs and drawings (record, records) the view from a window.
90. However, nothing (capture, captures) the view as perfectly as memory.

Predicate Adjectives   *pages 274–275*
Write each sentence. Underline each predicate adjective once and the
word it modifies twice.

91. Tala looks content after her piano lesson.
92. The lessons are difficult, but she practices hard and learns quickly.
93. Are you musical at all?
94. Even if you are not truly artistic, you can still play an instrument.
95. Tala played the piano for our recital, and she was proud to participate.
96. Everyone becomes quiet when she plays.
97. A performer is always appreciative of a responsive audience.
98. Tala's performances never seem boring.
99. Her music sounds so lively.

Comparisons with Adjectives   *pages 276–277*

Make three columns: *Positive, Comparative,* and *Superlative.* List each adjective in its correct column. Then complete the other two columns for each adjective.

100. worst
101. dingy
102. more
103. ripe
104. small
105. best
106. further
107. most panicky
108. more private
109. hazier

110. fewest
111. luckier
112. farthest
113. least colorful
114. funny
115. angry
116. friendliest
117. less irritated
118. most painful
119. quickest

Adverbs   *pages 280 – 282*

Write the adverb or adverbs from each sentence.

120. Miranda lost her watch yesterday.
121. She checked with "lost and found" immediately, but they did not have it.
122. She retraced her steps very carefully.
123. When she had no luck, she thought long and hard about her day.
124. She posted signs everywhere describing the watch.
125. By nine o'clock, Miranda had completely lost hope.
126. Suddenly, she found it on a shelf in the kitchen.
127. She had put it there before washing the dishes.

Comparisons with Adverbs   *pages 285 – 287*

Make three columns: *Positive, Comparative,* and *Superlative.* List each adverb in its correct column. Complete all columns for each adverb.

128. most quickly
129. least handily
130. less easily
131. less boldly

132. worst
133. better
134. most angrily
135. more wickedly

136. more calmly	142. luckily
137. more fondly	143. least softly
138. least mildly	144. less kindly
139. most gently	145. loudly
140. timidly	146. more clearly
141. more miserly	147. far

Prepositions and Prepositional Phrases   *pages 322 – 323*
Write the sentences. Underline each prepositional phrase.

148. Soon my family is going to the jungle.
149. We are planning to camp along the legendary Orinoco River in Venezuela.
150. Our neighbor across the street has been telling us about the area.
151. He is a professor of anthropology at the university in Houston.
152. I stop by the library often for books about Brazil.
153. Every member of our family is studying something.
154. I am particularly interested in the animals along the river.
155. My sister is studying about Brazil's history.
156. During the journey we will hear lectures.
157. We'll move down the river in dugout canoes.
158. Looking toward the future, I am very excited.
159. Except for schoolwork, I think of little else.
160. When you see me next fall, you'll hear my stories about the trip.

Conjunctions   *pages 331 – 333*
Write the conjunction or conjunctions in each sentence.

161. I'd like to go walking or running.
162. Either she comes or I don't go.
163. Neither my aunt nor my uncle runs.
164. What terrific running shoes and shorts she bought!
165. Did you follow the Olympics on the news, or did you read about it in articles?
166. Both the runners and the swimmers interest me.
167. What fine coordination and good health those athletes have!
168. Do you prefer skating or gymnastics?
169. I like gymnastics, but I also enjoy track and field.
170. This week I will watch either the floor exercises or the relay races.

UNIT

8

Creating Stories

◆ **COMPOSITION FOCUS:** **Mystery Story**
◆ **LANGUAGE FOCUS:** **Complex Sentences and Verbals**

If you read the words *Leaping out of the shadows, he began the pursuit,* you would know that a tale of suspense was being told. Detectives, haunted ruins, stolen jewels—all are common to mystery stories. In addition, mystery story writers often combine a fanciful plot, interesting characters, and a problem that occurs in a domestic setting to provide their audience with an exciting reading experience.

Mystery story writers use the same techniques as writers of anecdotes, fairy tales, and westerns. When Agatha Christie sat down to write one of her dozens of mysteries, she did what any other story writer would do.

Like other story writers, Agatha Christie wrote a beginning, a middle, and an ending. She began by introducing her characters and involving them in a conflict. Then she moved the plot forward to a climax. At the end of her story, Agatha Christie resolved the conflict. In this unit you will learn how to develop a mystery story and will write one yourself.

Agatha Christie wrote mystery stories *to entertain* readers.

Reading with a Writer's Eye
Mystery Story

When a woman is challenged to find a missing will or else lose her inheritance, then, as Sherlock Holmes would say, "The game's afoot." This story is narrated by Hastings, the companion of the famous Belgian solver of mysteries, Hercule Poirot. Read this mystery story, and notice that Agatha Christie keeps you interested and entertained as you try to solve the mystery before Poirot does.

The Case of the Missing Will

by Agatha Christie

The problem presented to us by Miss Violet Marsh made rather a pleasant change from our usual routine work. Poirot had received a brisk and business-like note from the lady asking for an appointment, and he had replied asking her to call upon him at eleven o'clock the following day.

She arrived punctually—a tall, handsome young woman, plainly but neatly dressed, with an assured and business-like manner. Clearly a young woman who meant to get on in the world. I am not a great admirer of the so-called New Woman myself, and, in spite of her good looks, I was not particularly prepossessed in her favor.

"My business is of a somewhat unusual nature, Monsieur Poirot," she began, after she had accepted a chair. "I had better begin at the beginning and tell you the whole story."

"If you please, mademoiselle."

"I am an orphan. My father was one of two brothers, sons of a small yeoman farmer in Devonshire. The farm was a poor one, and the elder brother, Andrew, emigrated to Australia, where he did very well indeed, and by means of successful speculation in land became a very rich man. The younger brother, Roger (my father), had no leanings towards the agricultural life. He managed to educate himself a little, and obtained a post as a clerk with a small firm. He married slightly above him; my mother was the daughter of a poor artist. My father died when I was six years old. When I was fourteen, my mother followed him to the grave. My only living relation then was my Uncle Andrew, who had recently returned from Australia and bought a small place, Crabtree Manor, in his native county. He was exceedingly kind to his brother's orphan child, took me to live with him, and treated me in every way as though I was his own daughter.

"Crabtree Manor, in spite of its name, is really only an old farmhouse. Farming was in my uncle's blood, and he was intensely interested in various modern farming experiments. Although kindness itself to me, he had certain peculiar and deeply-rooted ideas as to the up-bringing of women. Himself a man of little or no education, though possessing remarkable shrewdness, he placed little value on what he called 'book knowledge.' He was especially opposed to the education of women. In his opinion, girls should learn practical housework and dairy work, be useful about the home, and have as little to do with book learning as possible. He proposed to bring me up on these lines, to my bitter disappointment and annoyance. I rebelled frankly. I knew that I possessed a good brain, and had absolutely no talent for domestic duties. My uncle and I had many bitter arguments on the subject, for, though much attached to each other, we were both self-willed. I was lucky enough to win a scholarship, and up to a certain point was successful in getting my own way. The crisis arose when I resolved to go to Girton. I had a little money of my own, left me by my mother, and I was quite determined to make the best use of the gifts God had given me. I had one long, final argument with my uncle. He put the facts plainly before me. He had no other relations, and he had intended me to be his sole heiress. As I have told you, he was a very

rich man. If I persisted in these 'newfangled notions' of mine, however, I need look for nothing from him. I remained polite, but firm. I should always be deeply attached to him, I told him, but I must lead my own life. We parted on that note. 'You fancy your brain, my girl,' were his last words. 'I've no book learning, but for all that, I'll pit mine against yours any day. We'll see what we shall see.'

"That was nine years ago. I have stayed with him for a weekend occasionally, and our relations were perfectly amicable, though his views remained unaltered. He never referred to my having matriculated, nor to my B.Sc. For the last three years his health had been failing, and a month ago he died.

"I am now coming to the point of my visit. My uncle left a most extraordinary will. By its terms, Crabtree Manor and its contents are to be at my disposal for a year from his death—'during which time my clever niece may prove her wits,' the actual words run. At the end of that period, 'my wits having proved better than hers,' the house and all my uncle's large fortune pass to various charitable institutions."

"That is a little hard on you, mademoiselle, seeing that you were Mr. Marsh's only blood relation."

"I do not look on it in that way. Uncle Andrew warned me fairly, and I chose my own path. Since I would not fall in with his wishes, he was at perfect liberty to leave his money to whom he pleased."

"Was the will drawn up by a lawyer?"

"No; it was written on a printed will-form and witnessed by the man and his wife who live in the house and do for my uncle."

"There might be a possibility of upsetting such a will?"

"I would not even attempt to do such a thing."

"You regard it, then, as a sporting challenge on the part of your uncle?"

"That is exactly how I look upon it."

"It bears that interpretation, certainly," said Poirot thoughtfully. "Somewhere in this rambling old manorhouse your uncle has concealed either a sum of money in notes or possibly a second will, and has given you a year in which to exercise your ingenuity to find it."

"Exactly, Monsieur Poirot; and I am paying you the compliment of assuming that your ingenuity will be greater than mine."

"Eh, eh! but that is very charming of you. My gray cells are at your disposal. You have made no search yourself?"

"Only a cursory one; but I have too much respect for my uncle's undoubted abilities to fancy that the task will be an easy one."

"Have you the will or a copy of it with you?"

Miss Marsh handed a document across the table. Poirot ran through it, nodding to himself.

"Made three years ago. Dated March 25; and the time is given also—11 A.M.—that is very suggestive. It narrows the field of search. Assuredly it is another will we have to seek for. A will made even half-an-hour later would upset this. *Eh bien,* mademoiselle, it is a problem charming and ingenious that you have presented to me here. I shall have all the pleasure in the world in solving it for you. Granted that your uncle was a man of ability, his gray cells cannot have been of the quality of Hercule Poirot's!"

(Really, Poirot's vanity is blatant!)

"Fortunately, I have nothing of moment on hand at the minute. Hastings and I will go down to Crabtree Manor to-night. The man and wife who attended on your uncle are still there, I presume?"

"Yes, their name is Baker."

The following morning saw us started on the hunt proper. We had arrived late the night before. Mr. and Mrs. Baker, having received a telegram from Miss Marsh, were expecting us. They were a pleasant couple, the man gnarled and pink-cheeked, like a shriveled pippin, and his wife a woman of vast proportions and true Devonshire calm.

Tired with our journey and the eight-mile drive from the station, we had retired at once to bed after a supper of roast chicken, apple pie, and Devonshire cream. We had now disposed of an excellent breakfast, and were sitting in a small paneled room which had been the late Mr. Marsh's study and living-room. A roll-top desk stuffed with papers, all neatly docketed, stood against the wall, and a big leather armchair showed plainly that it had been its owner's constant resting-place. A big chintz-covered settee ran along the opposite wall, and the deep low window seats were covered with the same faded chintz of an old-fashioned pattern.

"*Eh bien, mon ami,*" said Poirot, lighting one of his tiny cigarettes, "we must map out our plan of campaign. Already I have made a rough

survey of the house, but I am of opinion that any clue will be found in this room. We shall have to go through the documents in the desk with meticulous care. Naturally, I do not expect to find the will amongst them; but it is likely that some apparently innocent paper may conceal the clue to its hiding-place. But first we must have a little information. Ring the bell, I pray of you."

I did so. While we were waiting for it to be answered, Poirot walked up and down, looking about him approvingly.

"A man of method this Mr. Marsh. See how neatly the packets of papers are docketed; then the key to each drawer has its ivory label— so has the key of the china cabinet on the wall; and see with what precision the china within is arranged. It rejoices the heart. Nothing here offends the eye—"

He came to an abrupt pause, as his eye was caught by the key of the desk itself, to which a dirty envelope was affixed. Poirot frowned at it and withdrew it from the lock. On it were scrawled the words: "Key of Roll Top Desk," in a crabbed handwriting, quite unlike the neat superscriptions on the other keys.

"An alien note," said Poirot, frowning. "I could swear that here we have no longer the personality of Mr. Marsh. But who else has been in the house? Only Miss Marsh, and she, if I mistake not, is also a young lady of method and order."

Baker came in answer to the bell.

"Will you fetch madame your wife, and answer a few questions?"

Baker departed, and in a few moments returned with Mrs. Baker, wiping her hands on her apron and beaming all over her face.

In a few clear words Poirot set forth the object of his mission. The Bakers were immediately sympathetic.

"We don't want to see Miss Violet done out of what's hers," declared the woman. "Cruel hard 'twould be for hospitals to get it all."

Poirot proceeded with his questions. Yes, Mr. and Mrs. Baker remembered perfectly witnessing the will. Baker had previously been sent in to the neighboring town to get two printed will-forms.

"Two?" said Poirot sharply.

"Yes, sir, for safety like, I suppose, in case he should spoil one— and sure enough, so he did do. We had signed one—"

"What time of day was that?"

Baker scratched his head, but his wife was quicker.

"Why, to be sure, I'd just put the milk on for the cocoa at eleven. Don't you remember? It had all boiled over on the stove when we got back to the kitchen."

"And afterwards?"

"'Twould be about an hour later. We had to go in again. 'I've made a mistake,' says old master, 'had to tear the whole thing up. I'll trouble you to sign again,' and we did. And afterwards master give us a tidy sum of money each. 'I've left you nothing in my will,' says he, 'but each year I live you'll have this to be a nest-egg when I'm gone'; and sure enough, so he did."

Poirot reflected.

"After you had signed the second time, what did Mr. Marsh do? Do you know?"

"Went out to the village to pay tradesmen's books."

That did not seem very promising. Poirot tried another tack. He held out the key of the desk.

"Is that your master's writing?"

I may have imagined it, but I fancied that a moment or two elapsed before Baker replied: "Yes, sir, it is."

"He's lying," I thought. "But why?"

"Has your master let the house?—have there been any strangers in it during the last three years?"

"No, sir."

"No visitors?"

"Only Miss Violet."

"No strangers of any kind been inside this room?"

"No, sir."

"You forget the workmen, Jim," his wife reminded him.

"Workmen?" Poirot wheeled round on her. "What workmen?"

The woman explained that about two years and a half ago workmen had been in the house to do certain repairs. She was quite vague as to what the repairs were. Her view seemed to be that the whole thing was a fad of her master's and quite unnecessary. Part of the time the workmen had been in the study; but what they had done there she could not say, as her master had not let either of them into the room whilst the work was in progress. Unfortunately, they could not remember the name of the firm employed, beyond the fact that it was a Plymouth one.

"We progress, Hastings," said Poirot, rubbing his hands as the Bakers left the room. "Clearly he made a second will and then had workmen from Plymouth in to make a suitable hiding-place. Instead of wasting time taking up the floor and tapping the walls, we will go to Plymouth."

With a little trouble, we were able to get the information we wanted. After one or two essays, we found the firm employed by Mr. Marsh.

Their employees had all been with them many years, and it was easy to find the two men who had worked under Mr. Marsh's orders. They remembered the job perfectly. Amongst various other minor jobs, they had taken up one of the bricks of the old-fashioned fireplace, made a cavity beneath, and so cut the brick that it was impossible to see the join. By pressing on the second brick from the end, the whole thing was raised. It had been quite a complicated piece of work, and the old gentleman had been very fussy about it. Our informant was a man called Coghan, a big, gaunt man with a grizzled mustache. He seemed an intelligent fellow.

We returned to Crabtree Manor in high spirits, and, locking the study door, proceeded to put our newly acquired knowledge into effect. It was impossible to see any sign on the bricks, but when we pressed in the manner indicated, a deep cavity was at once disclosed.

Eagerly Poirot plunged in his hand. Suddenly his face fell from complacent elation to consternation. All he held was a charred fragment of stiff paper. But for it, the cavity was empty.

"*Sacré!*" cried Poirot angrily. "Someone has been before us."

We examined the scrap of paper anxiously. Clearly it was a fragment of what we sought. A portion of Baker's signature remained, but no indication of what the terms of the will had been.

Poirot sat back on his heels. His expression would have been comical if we had not been so overcome.

"I understand it not," he growled. "Who destroyed this? And what was their object?"

"The Bakers?" I suggested.

"Pourquoi? Neither will makes any provision for them, and they are more likely to be kept on with Miss Marsh than if the place became the property of a hospital. How could it be to anyone's advantage to destroy the will? The hospitals benefit—yes; but one cannot suspect institutions."

"Perhaps the old man changed his mind and destroyed it himself," I suggested.

Poirot rose to his feet, dusting his knees with his usual care.

"That may be," he admitted. "One of your more sensible observations, Hastings. Well, we can do no more here. We have done all that mortal man can do. We have successfully pitted our wits against the late Andrew Marsh's; but, unfortunately, his niece is no better off for our success."

By driving to the station at once, we were just able to catch a train to London, though not the principal express. Poirot was sad and dissatisfied. For my part, I was tired and dozed in a corner. Suddenly, as we were just moving out of Taunton, Poirot uttered a piercing squeal.

"Vite, Hastings! Awake and jump! But jump I say!"

Before I knew where I was we were standing on the platform, bareheaded and minus our valises, whilst the train disappeared into the night. I was furious. But Poirot paid no attention.

"Imbecile that I have been!" he cried. "Triple imbecile! Not again will I vaunt my little gray cells!"

"That's a good job at any rate," I said grumpily. "But what is this all about?"

As usual, when following out his own ideas, Poirot paid absolutely no attention to me.

"The tradesmen's books—I have left them entirely out of account! Yes, but where? Where? Never mind, I cannot be mistaken. We must return at once."

Easier said than done. We managed to get a slow train to Exeter, and there Poirot hired a car. We arrived back at Crabtree Manor in the small hours of the morning. I pass over the bewilderment of the Bakers when we had at last aroused them. Paying no attention to anybody, Poirot strode at once to the study.

"I have been, not a triple imbecile, but thirty-six times one, my friend," he deigned to remark. "Now, behold!"

Going straight to the desk, he drew out the key, and detached the envelope from it. I stared at him stupidly. How could he possibly hope to find a big will-form in that tiny envelope? With great care he cut open the envelope, laying it out flat. Then he lighted the fire and held the plain inside surface of the envelope to the flame. In a few minutes faint characters began to appear.

"Look, *mon ami!*" cried Poirot in triumph.

I looked. There were just a few lines of faint writing stating briefly that he left everything to his niece, Violet Marsh. It was dated March 25, 12:30 P.M., and witnessed by Albert Pike, confectioner, and Jessie Pike, married woman.

"But is it legal?" I gasped.

"As far as I know, there is no law against writing your will in a blend of disappearing and sympathetic ink. The intention of the testator is clear, and the beneficiary is his only living relation. But the cleverness of him! He foresaw every step that a searcher would take— that I, miserable imbecile, took. He gets two will-forms, makes the servants sign twice, then sallies out with his will written on the inside of a dirty envelope and a fountain-pen containing his little ink mixture. On some excuse he gets the confectioner and his wife to sign their names under his own signature, then he ties it to the key of his desk and chuckles to himself. If his niece sees through his little ruse, she will have justified her choice of life and elaborate education, and be thoroughly welcome to his money."

"She didn't see through it, did she?" I said slowly. "It seems rather unfair. The old man really won."

"But no, Hastings. It is *your* wits that go astray. Miss Marsh proved the astuteness of her wits and the value of the higher education for women by at once putting the matter in *my* hands. Always employ the expert. She has amply proved her right to the money."

I wonder—I very much wonder—what old Andrew Marsh would have thought!

Respond

1. Which part of the story do you find most exciting? Why?

Discuss

2. How can you tell that this story is intended to entertain?
3. If you were a newspaper reporter, how would your telling of this story be different from Agatha Christie's? Retell the story briefly as a reporter might.

Thinking As a Writer
Analyzing a Mystery Story

A mystery story, like any other short story, is written to entertain and has characters, a setting, a plot, and a conclusion that resolves the problem.

What makes a mystery different, however, is that there is more to the characters than meets the eye. Each must have an obvious good side and a hidden bad side, because, until the end, each is a suspect.

Another area in which mysteries differ from other stories is their setting. Although in the past many were set in eerie mansions, today the setting is usually quite ordinary. Modern plots seem much more effective when a ghastly crime occurs in the midst of peaceful surroundings.

Read these excerpts from "The Case of the Missing Will." They help to identify the parts of the story.

> ### Writer's Guide
>
> A mystery story
> - has a catchy title.
> - has characters that include a victim, a detective, witnesses, and suspects.
> - has a setting.
> - has a plot with a problem, complications, a climax, and a conclusion.
> - projects a mood of suspense or tension.

"My uncle left a most extraordinary will. By its terms, Crabtree Manor and its contents are to be at my disposal for a year from his death—'during which time my clever niece may prove her wits,' the actual words run. At the end of that period, 'my wits having proved better than hers,' the house and all my uncle's large fortune pass to various charitable institutions."

*In the first part of the **plot**, the **problem** or crime is revealed. In the **complication** the detective attempts to solve the mystery.*

*   *   *   *

"Look, *mon ami!*" cried Poirot in triumph.

I looked. There were just a few lines of faint writing stating briefly that he left everything to his niece, Violet Marsh.

*The **climax** is the point of highest interest, when the detective figures out the solution.*

*   *   *   *

"But no, Hastings. It is *your* wits that go astray. Miss Marsh proved the astuteness of her wits and the value of the higher education for women by at once putting the matter in *my* hands. Always employ the expert. She has amply proved her right to the money."

*In the **resolution** the problem is settled and the crime or problem is solved.*

A good way to organize a mystery story is to use a story map. Study this story map. Notice how it helps illustrate the action.

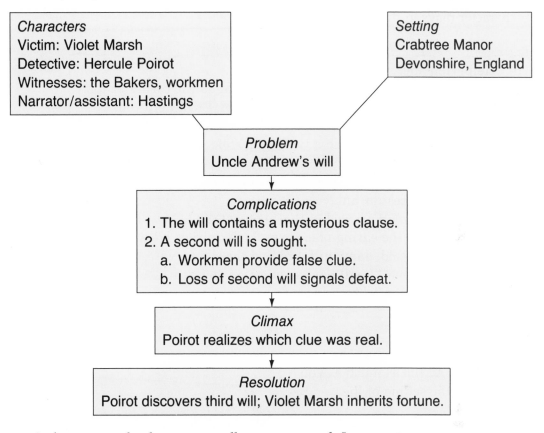

Characters
Victim: Violet Marsh
Detective: Hercule Poirot
Witnesses: the Bakers, workmen
Narrator/assistant: Hastings

Setting
Crabtree Manor
Devonshire, England

Problem
Uncle Andrew's will

Complications
1. The will contains a mysterious clause.
2. A second will is sought.
   a. Workmen provide false clue.
   b. Loss of second will signals defeat.

Climax
Poirot realizes which clue was real.

Resolution
Poirot discovers third will; Violet Marsh inherits fortune.

A short story also has an overall tone, or mood. In a mystery story, this mood reflects the suspense and tension involved in solving the problem. However, the mood can change from moment to moment.

> We examined the scrap of paper anxiously. Clearly it was a fragment of what we sought. A portion of Baker's signature remained, but no indication of what the terms of the will had been.
> Poirot sat back on his heels. His expression would have been comical if we had not been so overcome.

Discuss

1. How does each character move the action along?
2. How does the mood change at the end of the story?
3. Do you think the title is a good one? Explain your answer.

Try Your Hand

A. Identify Character Roles Read the following passage. Identify the role each character plays in the story.

> "Help! Help me!" shrieked Mrs. Simms.
> Constable Higgins appeared, chugging around the corner as fast as his rather plump form could move. "Madam, I will help you. What has happened?"
> "A man in a black coat and a tweed cap stole my purse! I couldn't see more; it's so dark now."
> "I saw him, too," said a passerby. "He did nab her purse. I think he went into that restaurant."
> Another policeman arrived at that moment, and Constable Higgins went into the eating place to make inquiries. He was not surprised, on this cold, damp night to find three men with black coats and tweed caps. "I will have to question you gentlemen in connection with a theft," he told them.

B. Identify Setting Reread the passage in **A**. Tell as much as you can about the setting of the mystery.

C. Identify Short Story Parts Look back at the story map. Tell which part of the plot is revealed by the passage.

D. Add Information to the Story Add two sentences that show complications in the plot of the passage.

E. Read a Mystery Read a short mystery story. Make a story map of it. Trade with a partner. Talk about the differences between the maps of your two stories.

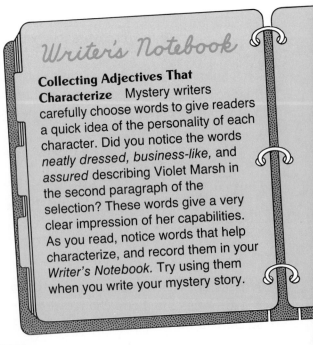

Writer's Notebook

Collecting Adjectives That Characterize Mystery writers carefully choose words to give readers a quick idea of the personality of each character. Did you notice the words *neatly dressed, business-like,* and *assured* describing Violet Marsh in the second paragraph of the selection? These words give a very clear impression of her capabilities. As you read, notice words that help characterize, and record them in your *Writer's Notebook.* Try using them when you write your mystery story.

Developing the Writer's Craft
Creating Mood Through Characterization and Dialogue

The **mood** of a story is the feeling that the author creates. In a mystery story, the mood reflects the suspense and the tension of solving the problem.

Writers rarely identify the mood that they are trying to create. Instead, they show the story's mood. Read this example from the opening selection. It occurs after Poirot has discovered the fragment of the burned will.

> "I understand it not," [Poirot] growled. "Who destroyed this? And what was their object?"

This example shows a mood of frustration. Notice that Agatha Christie used short, choppy sentences and the verb *growled* to illustrate it.

If you look back at the story, you will see that this example comes from a section of dialogue. **Dialogue** is conversation between characters. Writers often use dialogue to show a character's feelings and reactions to a situation.

Writers also use characterization to help create mood. A veiled or cloaked character may seem mysterious. One who refuses to speak above a whisper or moves in a sneaky way creates suspense.

When you write your mystery story, try to show, rather than tell, the mood. Use characterization and dialogue to help convey the mood.

Discuss

1. Find another passage in the selection in which Agatha Christie used dialogue or characterization for mood. Identify the mood.
2. Why is showing a mood better than telling what it is?

Try Your Hand

Create a Mood Choose a mood you want to convey. Write six sentences to illustrate it. Trade sentences with a partner. Have your partner identify the mood.

1 Prewriting
Mystery Story

Writer's Guide

Prewriting Checklist

☑ Brainstorm setting and characters.

☑ Think about your audience and your purpose.

☑ Gather information about the characters.

☑ Organize plot clues.

Ashley, a seventh-grader at Roosevelt Middle School, wanted to write a mystery story for a writing contest. She used the checklist in the **Writer's Guide** to help her plan it. Look at what she did.

◆ Brainstorming and Selecting a Topic

First, Ashley thought about places where mysteries often take place. She also considered mysteries she might want to write about, crime solvers, and means of discovery. She wrote her ideas in a chart.

Crime or Mystery	Setting	Crime solver	Means of Discovery
haunted house	Gobi desert	police officer	caught in the act
(theft)	yacht club	detective	confession
~~kidnapping~~	(mansion)	(amateur sleuth)	(deductive reasoning)
(lost valuable)	Mt. Everest	CIA agent	witness

Ashley reviewed her chart. She thought about the contest and tried to determine the interests of the judges. She also chose items she knew something about or could use her imagination to develop. She decided to write about the theft of a valuable coin from an elegant mansion because she thought that she could make the crime and the setting believable. She also decided that a teenage girl who would use logical thinking to solve the crime would be her amateur detective.

Discuss

1. Look at Ashley's chart. Why didn't she describe each detail in a complete sentence?
2. Some of Ashley's decisions were based on her own knowledge. Others were just a matter of personal choice. Which criteria do you think she used for which decisions? Support your answer.

◆ Gathering Information

After deciding on the main characters and the setting, Ashley knew she still needed more detailed information to develop the plot. She made another chart and filled it in.

	Criminal	Victim	Other Suspects
Name	Kevin (gardener)	Mr. Van der Horne	Maggie (cook)
Motive	needs cash	~~~~~~~	spite, blackmail
Opportunity	safe unlocked	~~~~~~~	safe unlocked
Alibi	~~~~~~~	stars	not given
Witness's	mentions		none
Clues	safe		

Ashley decided to use dialogue to reveal the mood. She also planned to use dialogue as the main way of moving the action along. She wanted her detective to infer information from the dialogue.

Discuss

1. Why would having many suspects make a story complicated?
2. If Ashley wanted to include false clues (such as lies by suspects), where might she place them on her chart?
3. What categories might you want to add to her chart?

◆ Organizing Information

Ashley wanted to develop the action of her story to build suspense. She also wanted to make sure that she put all her clues and her complications in the right order. She made a story map to help her decide how she wanted the plot to flow. With this map, she could begin to write her story.

Characters
Victim: Mr. Van der Horne
Detective: Jenny
Criminal: Kevin (the gardener)
Other suspect: Maggie (the cook)

Setting
Mr. Van der Horne's mansion

Problem
Mr. Van der Horne's valuable coin is stolen.

Complications

1. Two suspects
2. Misleading information about Maggie given by Mr. Van der Horne
3. Kevin's statement that he saw Maggie by the safe

Climax
Jenny's announcement that she has solved the crime

Resolution
Jenny's disclosure of how she solved the crime
Mr. Van der Horne calls police

WRITING PROCESS

Discuss

1. What complications lead Jenny to consider Maggie a suspect?
2. Why do you think Ashley doesn't reveal the criminal at the climax?

Try Your Hand

Now plan a mystery story of your own.

A. Choose an Audience   Decide for whom you want to write your mystery story.

B. Brainstorm and Select a Crime, a Setting, a Detective, and a Method of Solution   Make a chart, a list, or a diagram to show the topics you are considering. Choose elements that interest you, that you have some knowledge of, and that you think would interest your audience.

C. Gather Information   Record your decisions about the criminal, the victim, and the other suspects. Add as much information as you need in order to develop your plot.

D. Review Your Notes   Look over your charts. See whether your clues and your conclusions make sense. Take the time to change or eliminate any elements that don't work or that make your story plan too complicated.

E. Organize Information   Make a story map, another chart, or a diagram to show how you have handled the various plot elements. Make sure that you have included every important detail.

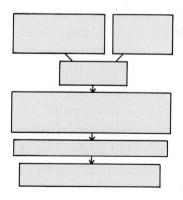

You may want to use a story map like this one to organize information for your mystery story.

  Save your charts and your story map in your *Writer's Notebook.* You will use them when you draft your mystery story.

2 Drafting
Mystery Story

Before Ashley started to draft her mystery story, she thought about a way to narrate it. Using her charts and her story map, Ashley followed the checklist in the **Writer's Guide.** Look at what she did.

Writer's Guide

Drafting Checklist

☑ Use your charts and story map.

☑ Write the introduction, the complication, and the resolution.

The Mystery of the Missing Coin

As Jenny pulled into the driveway, she wondered why Mr. Van der Horne had called her. When he greeted her at the door and escorted her into the elegant living room, Jenny knew at once that something was wrong.

"Jenny, I'm so glad to see you. I've been so upset since I found that my most valuable gold coin has been stolen," Mr. Van der Horne said.

"Exactly what happened?" Jenny asked anxiously.

Discuss

1. Which part or parts of Ashley's story are included here? How do you know?
2. What characters and information has Ashley introduced? Is she following her organization? How can you tell?

Try Your Hand

Now you are ready to write a mystery story.

A. Review Your Information Think about the information you gathered and organized in the last lesson. Decide whether you need more information. If so, gather it.

B. Think About Your TAP Remember that your task is to write a mystery story. Your purpose is to entertain your audience with a mystery story.

C. Write Your First Draft Use the **Drafting Checklist** to write your mystery story.

When you write your draft, just put all your ideas on paper. Do not worry about spelling, punctuation, or grammar. You can correct these later.

Task: What?
Audience: Who?
Purpose: Why?

Save your first draft in your *Writer's Notebook.* You will use it when you revise your mystery story.

3 Responding and Revising
Mystery Story

Ashley read over her draft. Then she used the checklist in the **Writer's Guide** to revise her story. Look at what she did.

◆ Checking Information

Ashley saw that she had included information that was unnecessary and irrelevant. To take it out, she used this mark ℮ . She also decided that some information seemed incomplete; therefore, she added a phrase using this mark ∧ .

◆ Checking Organization

Ashley decided that some information was fuzzy and unclear. She decided to reorder the information to make it clearer. To move the sentence, she used this mark ᴈ .

◆ Checking Language

When Ashley checked her sentences, she found a word that didn't set the mood she wanted. She used this mark ⌒‾ to replace the word with others.

Add ⌐
Move ⌐
Replace ⌐
Cut ⌐

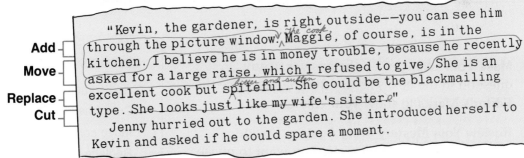

"Kevin, the gardener, is right outside——you can see him through the picture window. Maggie, *the cook*, of course, is in the kitchen. I believe he is in money trouble, because he recently asked for a large raise, which I refused to give. She is an excellent cook but spiteful. *bitter and sullen* She could be the blackmailing type. She looks just like my wife's sister."
        Jenny hurried out to the garden. She introduced herself to Kevin and asked if he could spare a moment.

Discuss

1. Why did Ashley reorganize this paragraph?
2. What did Ashley achieve by changing the word *spiteful* to the words *bitter and sullen?*

WRITING PROCESS

Try Your Hand

Now revise your first draft.

A. Read Your First Draft   As you read your mystery story, think about your audience and your purpose. Read your story silently or to a partner to see if it is complete and well organized. Ask yourself or your partner the questions in the box.

Responding and Revising Strategies	
✔ **Respond** **Ask yourself or a partner:**	✔ **Revise** **Try these solutions:**
◆ Do I include a title, a problem, complications, a climax, and a satisfying resolution?	◆ **Add, cut,** or **revise** as necessary.
◆ Did I include believable characters, an interesting setting, and an intriguing crime to be solved?	◆ **Add** any missing parts of the story.
◆ Is all the information in my narrative told in clear, well-written sentences?	◆ **Replace** unclear or rambling sentences. See the **Revising Workshop** on page 375.
◆ Do I tell the story in logical order?	◆ **Move** any sentences that are out of place.
◆ Do my characterization and dialogue reflect the mood I wish to convey?	◆ **Replace** words that do not reflect the proper mood.

B. Make Your Changes   If the answer to any question in the box is *no,* try the solution. Use the **Editor's Marks** to show your changes.

C. Review Your Mystery Story Again   Decide whether there is anything else you want to revise. Keep revising your story until you feel it is well organized and complete.

EDITOR'S MARKS

∧ Add something.

⸝ Cut something.

◌ Move something.

⌃ Replace something.

Save your revised mystery story in your *Writer's Notebook.* You will use it when you proofread your story.

WRITING PROCESS

Revising Workshop
Avoiding Rambling Sentences

Good writers make sure that their sentences do not run on and on. They avoid using the conjunction *so* to connect independent clauses, and they use the conjunction *and* sparingly. They revise rambling sentences by dividing them into two or more sentences. Look at these examples.

1. Detective Adler had a lead to follow, so he went to the alley behind the parking garage, and there he found Mort Savigley with a suitcase full of money that had been stolen earlier that morning, so he tried to arrest him, but Mort fled.
2. Detective Adler had a lead to follow that took him to the alley behind the parking garage. There he found Mort Savigley. Mort had a suitcase full of money that had been stolen earlier that morning. When Adler tried to arrest Mort, however, he fled.

In the first sentence, the writer used a rambling style, linking clause after clause. In the second example, the rambling sentence has been divided into four sentences, improving the coherence with no loss of meaning.

Practice

Rewrite each sentence to make it less monotonous. Revise it by dividing it into two or more sentences. Make sure that you do not leave out any important information. You may add a few words of your own if the words will help you to improve the sentences.

1. Detective Adler was determined not to let Mort escape, so he quickly called for reinforcements and followed Mort in a wild chase through the parking garage, and then Mort led him through a shopping mall, and he hid himself among the shoppers.
2. Detective Adler continued to hunt for Mort for quite a while, and then eventually gave up, and he called his chief so that he would know what happened, and went back to headquarters so that he could file his report.
3. Meanwhile, the airport police received an alert from Detective Adler's chief, and they quietly began searching the crowd, and after a long search they spotted Mort standing inconspicuously by the broom closet so he wouldn't be noticed, so they quietly moved in and arrested him.

4 Proofreading
Mystery Story

Writer's Guide

Proofreading Checklist

☑ Check for errors in capitalization.

☑ Check for errors in punctuation. Be sure that you have used quotation marks to show people's exact words.

☑ Be sure that all your paragraphs are indented.

☑ Check for errors in grammar.

☑ Circle any words you think are misspelled. Find out how to spell them correctly.

⇨ For proofreading help, use the **Writer's Handbook.**

After Ashley revised her mystery story, she used the checklist in the **Writer's Guide** and the **Editor's Marks** to proofread it. Look at what she did.

> "You said that (noone) *no one* besides you knew about the safe, but when I talked to Kevin he said that he saw Maggie heading toward it. Unless he knew where it was, he wouldn't have said that. He also knew when the theft (ocured) *occurred*. I think, while gardening, kevin saw you open the safe and glimpsed the gold coins. When you left, he saw the perfect chance to get the money he so desperately needed. He came into the house, took the coin, and was out before you returned." Jenny explained. "he carefully closed the safe and replaced the other coins. If you hadn't remembered leaving the safe open, it might have been weeks or months before you discovered the theft."

Discuss

1. Look at Ashley's proofread story. What kinds of mistakes did she make?
2. With what elements of punctuation in dialogue did Ashley have trouble?

Try Your Hand

Proofread Your Mystery Story   Now use the checklist in the **Writer's Guide** and these **Editor's Marks** to proofread your mystery story.

Save your corrected mystery story in your *Writer's Notebook.* **You will use it when you publish your story.**

EDITOR'S MARKS

≡ Capitalize.

⊙ Add a period.

∧ Add something.

⩘ Add a comma.

∨ ∨ Add quotation marks.

⤴ Cut something.

⋀ Replace something.

∿ Transpose.

◯ Spell correctly.

Ͱ Indent paragraph.

/ Make a lowercase letter.

WRITING PROCESS

5 Publishing
Mystery Story

Writer's Guide

Publishing Checklist

☑ Make a clean copy of your mystery story.

☑ Check to see that nothing has been left out.

☑ Share your story in a special way.

Once Ashley had made all her corrections, she sat down and read her mystery story once again. This time she tried to look at it from the point of view of the story contest judges. She reread the introduction to see whether her characters and setting were believable and were described in enough detail. She checked the complication to see whether the dialogue really revealed the personalities of the characters and helped the plot progress. Finally, she reread the resolution to make sure that she had written a satisfactory solution to the mystery.

1. Then Ashley sat down at her computer and input the story one more time. She checked the screen for typographical errors. Then she used her printer to make a final copy of her work.

2. Before Ashley mailed her story to the contest, she decided to make an original illustration for it. If her mystery story were chosen for publication in the magazine sponsoring the contest, she knew that artwork would give it a special touch. Then Ashley assembled her work.

3. Finally, Ashley found a large manila envelope. She addressed it to the contest sponsors and placed her story and her illustration inside. Then, with feelings of pride and satisfaction, she took it to the corner mailbox and sent her entry on its way.

Discuss

1. You have learned that you can go back to read or check your work at any stage in the writing process. Suppose that in rereading her proofread mystery story, Ashley decided that she needed more details in her setting. What should she do?
2. Ashley was lucky in that she had a computer to paginate her work. If she had used a typewriter or had copied her story in longhand, why would it be important for her to number the pages?
3. Why was it a good idea for Ashley to reread her story from the point of view of the contest judges?
4. Why is submitting your writing as a contest entry an excellent idea for publishing?

Try Your Hand

Publish Your Mystery Story   Follow the checklist in the **Writer's Guide.** Then submit your story to a story-writing contest, create a class mystery magazine, or try one of these ideas for sharing your story.

- Record your mystery story on an audio tape, along with sound effects. Make it as mysterious, suspenseful, and eerie as you can. Share the tape with your classmates, or send it to a pen pal.
- Have a class discussion and critique each other's mystery stories. You might want to start a mystery writer's club and share your writing on a regular basis.

WRITING PROCESS

Listening and Speaking
Tips on How to Speak and Listen in a Class Discussion

Speaking in a Class Discussion

1. Prepare for your part in the discussion. Know the subject you will be talking about. Do research, if necessary. Think about your audience and how to communicate what you want to say to them.
2. If you have done research, bring your notes with you to the discussion. You may have found a piece of information that no one else has or that no one else in the discussion was aware of.
3. Stick to the topic. Don't stray from the purpose of the discussion. Do this when you are giving information and when you are asking questions.
4. Participate fairly in the discussion. Don't take more than your share of the allotted time. Give others a chance to speak. Don't interrupt anyone.
5. If you feel that you can make an important point but someone else is still speaking, wait until the person is finished. Then indicate your interest by saying "I'd like to add to what Robert just said" or "I've read something that gives a different slant on that information."
6. Express disagreements in a tactful way. Give support for your views. It is much better to say "I have some information that disagrees with that point of view" than "Robert, you are totally wrong on that point."

Listening in a Class Discussion

1. Give other speakers your full attention. Listen carefully and critically to what others say. Think about their ideas and form an opinion. Ask questions if you don't understand something.
2. As you listen, try to separate the facts the speaker gives and his or her feelings about the topic. Your task will be to respond only to the facts.
3. Listen with an open mind. Don't prejudge the speaker or the topic. Wait to hear what is said. Be open to new information and new ideas. If you hear something that makes sense, be willing to consider changing your mind.

Writing in the Content Areas

Use what you learned to write another narrative. Use one of these ideas or an idea of your own.

Health

Some famous recipes, such as crepes suzette, chicken marengo, and peach melba, have real stories behind them. Find and retell a story or make up a story that explains the origin of a famous recipe or one of your own recipes. If it is an original recipe, give it a name that could appear in cookbooks for decades to come.

Fine Arts

Find a famous painting that you like. Make up a story that adds life to the people, the places, or the things in the picture. Write a narrative that tells about it. Imagine that you are writing for a museum catalogue. Your story will help a museum-goer approach the artwork with new interest.

Science

Write a science fiction narrative—a fictionalized story based on real scientific facts. For ideas, you might read "All Summer in a Day" or another short science fiction story by Ray Bradbury. Before you begin, you may want to read a few nonfiction science articles for background information.

Literature

Write a short sequel to your favorite novel. You might want to rewrite it from a different character's point of view. If the book was written for a particular audience, try to write it for a different audience. For example, if it is a story that appeals to boys, try to change it so that everyone will enjoy it.

CONNECTING
WRITING ↔ LANGUAGE

Everyone loves stories of adventure and suspense. We all like to be scared from time to time or challenged by a seemingly unsolvable mystery. One of the best ways to get a good dose of excitement is to read a kind of short story known as a *thriller*. Most thrillers are filled with the elements of both mystery and suspense. Read this opening passage from *The Adventures of the Beryl Coronet* by Sir Arthur Conan Doyle. Does it tempt you to read further?

"Holmes," said I as I stood one morning in our bow window looking down the street. "Here is a madman coming along . It seems rather sad that his relatives should allow him to come out alone ."

◆ **Complex Sentences and Verbals in a Mystery Story**   The highlighted groups of words are a complex sentence and verbals. Verbals are verb forms that are used as other parts of speech. The first sentence in the model above is a complex sentence. Some writers choose to use sentences with adjective clauses or adverb clauses. A complex sentence offers a way to add information to the sentence. The word groups *looking down the street* and *coming along* are participial phrases used as adjectives. The phrase *to come out alone* is an infinitive phrase that is used as a noun.

◆ **Language Focus: Complex Sentences and Verbals**   The following lessons will help you use different kinds of clauses and verbals in your own writing.

1 Phrases and Clauses

FOCUS

◆ A **phrase** is a group of words that is used as a part of speech.
◆ A **clause** is a group of words that has a subject and a verb.

You may recall that a phrase is a group of words that does not have a subject and a verb. A phrase is used as a single word is used in a sentence.

1. at the Round Table   **2.** bright, shining armor

A clause is a group of words that has a subject and a verb. There are two kinds of clauses. An **independent clause** expresses a complete thought and can stand by itself as a sentence.

3. King Arthur led his knights of the Round Table.

A **dependent,** or **subordinate,** clause does not express a complete thought. A dependent, or subordinate, clause cannot stand on its own.

4. although he was victorious

Subordinate clauses begin with **subordinating conjunctions** or with **relative pronouns,** such as *who, whom, whose, which,* and *that.* An independent clause can be turned into a subordinate clause by adding a subordinating conjunction.

5. When King Arthur married Guinevere

> ### Link to Writing
> Both phrases and subordinate clauses often begin with the words *after, since, until,* or *before.* You can easily distinguish between phrases and clauses. Clauses contain subjects and verbs; phrases do not.

Some Common Subordinating Conjunctions
after
although
as
as if
as soon as
as though
because
before
even though
if
in order that
since
so that
than
though
unless
until
when
whenever
where
wherever
while

Guided Practice

A. Identify each group of words as a phrase or a clause.

1. around the world
2. when the Round Table began
3. before brave Sir Gawain
4. Lancelot was champion
5. many wonderful stories
6. French literature exists

B. Decide whether each clause is independent or subordinate.

7. knights came from around the world
8. although the Round Table did not really exist
9. many stories have been written about the Round Table
10. since it existed during the Middle Ages
11. while Arthur was the king

THINK AND REMEMBER

* Remember that a **clause** is a group of words that has a subject and a predicate.
* Remember that an **independent clause** is a group of words that expresses a complete thought and can stand by itself as a sentence.
* Remember that a **dependent,** or **subordinate, clause** has a subject and predicate but does not express a complete thought.

Independent Practice

C. Distinguishing Between Phrases and Clauses Write whether each group of words is a phrase or a clause.

12. about Sir Lancelot
 MODEL⟩ phrase
13. if he is considered
14. the most virtuous

15. a wizard raised
16. an ancient legend
17. his foe was brave
18. a vicious villain

D. Identifying Clauses Write *independent* or *subordinate* for each underlined group of words.

19. Medieval knights were brave, and they fought hard.
 MODEL⟩ independent
20. At age seven a young boy began his knightly training.
21. Knights rode horses well, and they used lances skillfully.
22. If a knight was a coward, another knight broke his sword.
23. A knight had to be a gentleman, since he obeyed a code of honor.
24. However, some disobeyed the code of honor.

Application — Writing

An Announcement Imagine that you are a knight of the Round Table and that there is a shortage of qualified knights. Write an announcement asking knights to apply for membership. Use phrases and clauses correctly.

2 Complex Sentences

◆ **FOCUS** A **complex sentence** consists of an independent clause and at least one subordinate clause.

Remember that an independent clause has a subject and a verb and expresses a complete thought. A **simple sentence** consists of one independent clause.

1. Jason was an ancient Greek hero.

A **compound sentence** consists of two independent clauses. Remember that a coordinating conjunction or a semicolon joins the independent clauses.

2. Jason was an ancient Greek hero; he captured the Golden Fleece.

A **complex sentence** consists of an independent clause and a subordinate clause. Either clause can begin a sentence.

3. After Jason won the Golden Fleece, he sailed home with Medea.

Link to Writing

Remember to use a comma to separate a subordinate clause from an independent clause when the subordinate clause begins a sentence. Do not use a comma when the subordinate clause follows the independent clause.

When Jason returned home, he married Medea. Jason married Medea when he returned home.

Guided Practice

A. Identify each sentence as *simple, compound,* or *complex.*

1. Since ancient times, people have enjoyed listening to and reading myths.
2. Their heroes performed great deeds wherever they went.
3. Some heroes led great armies; others fought alone.
4. Although the hero Odysseus was a great fighter, he was also sly and crafty.
5. He seldom lost battles because he was able to outsmart his enemies.

Independent Practice

B. Identifying Kinds of Sentences   Write *simple, compound,* or *complex* to identify each sentence.

6. Everyone trembled; the deadly Minotaur ravaged the city.

MODEL⟩ compound

7. Since no one stopped him, the Minotaur devoured many children.

8. Because he was so very brave, Theseus battled the monster.

9. He killed the Minotaur with help from a princess.

10. Theseus was proclaimed a great hero, and the battle was won.

11. After he returned to Athens, Theseus became king.

C. Revising: Combining Sentences by Using Subordinating Conjunctions   Add a subordinating conjunction to an independent clause to create a complex sentence. Use commas correctly.

12. *The Odyssey* tells about Odysseus. He returns from the Trojan War.

MODEL⟩ *The Odyssey* tells about Odysseus as he returns from the Trojan War.

13. The war is over. Odysseus is delayed on his way home.

14. *The Odyssey* opens on an island. Odysseus is Calypso's prisoner.

15. Calypso keeps Odysseus on her island for seven years. She will not let him leave.

16. Finally Odysseus sets sail. The gods arrange his departure.

17. Finally the hero arrives home. His family awaits him.

Application — Writing and Speaking

A Paragraph of Thanks   Imagine that you are a Greek mythological hero who is about to retire. Write and deliver a speech thanking your faithful followers who have fought with you against dragons, monsters, and demons. Use complex sentences. If you need help writing a paragraph, see page 39 of the **Writer's Handbook.**

3 Adjective and Adverb Clauses

FOCUS

◆ An **adjective clause** is a subordinate clause that modifies a noun or a pronoun. It often begins with a relative pronoun.

◆ An **adverb clause** is a subordinate clause that modifies a verb, an adjective, or an adverb. It begins with a subordinating conjunction.

Remember that a dependent, or subordinate, clause has a subject and a verb but cannot stand on its own. Like a prepositional phrase, a subordinate clause can be used as an adverb or an adjective.

Like an adjective, an adjective clause answers the question *what kind, which one, how much,* or *how many* about a noun or a pronoun. The first word of an adjective clause is a **relative pronoun.** The relative pronouns are *who, whom, whose, that,* and *which.*

1. Everyone admires those who show great courage .   what kind

In a complex sentence, an adverb clause answers the question *how, when, where, why,* or *to what extent* about a verb, adjective, or adverb. The first word of an adverb clause is a subordinating conjunction.

2. The explorers rejoiced when they reached the North Pole .   when

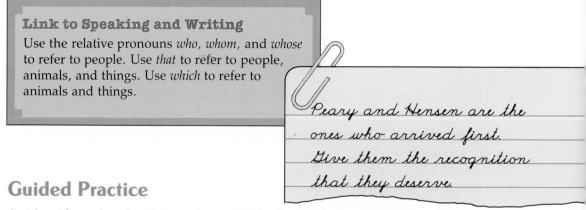

Link to Speaking and Writing
Use the relative pronouns *who, whom,* and *whose* to refer to people. Use *that* to refer to people, animals, and things. Use *which* to refer to animals and things.

Peary and Hensen are the ones who arrived first. Give them the recognition that they deserve.

Guided Practice

A. Identify each subordinate clause. Tell whether it is an adjective clause or an adverb clause.

1. Robert E. Peary, who reached the North Pole in 1909, was brave.
2. Peary was 52 when he left on his expedition.
3. Theodore Roosevelt, who was then President, saw him off.
4. Because the trip was dangerous, Peary took few with him.
5. Those who reached the pole hiked 150 miles in sub-zero weather.

Independent Practice

B. Identifying Adjective and Adverb Clauses   Write each subordinate clause. Write *adverb clause* or *adjective clause* to identify it.

6. Robert Scott pushed on until he reached the South Pole in 1911.

MODEL until he reached the South Pole in 1911   adverb clause

7. He discovered information about another explorer who had arrived there earlier.
8. As Scott began his return, he faced worse discoveries.
9. The weather, which had been extremely poor, became worse.
10. Visibility disappeared as blizzard winds blew.
11. He wrote a last journal entry that describes a man who maintained tremendous courage.

C. Revising: Combining Sentences by Using Relative Pronouns
Use a relative pronoun to combine each pair of sentences.

12. The *Nautilus* traveled under the Arctic ice cap. It was an atomic submarine.

MODEL The Nautilus, which was an atomic submarine, traveled under the Arctic ice cap.

13. Explorers often set new records. These become the new norm.
14. The *Nautilus* crew broke all records. Their trip covered 2,000 miles.
15. More records were broken by later submarines. They sailed during the 1970's.
16. New submarines are launched often. They are used in exploration.
17. Exploratory submarines give us new information about the world. They sail on peaceful missions.

Application — Writing

A Caption   Imagine that you have been asked to write a caption for a photograph of polar explorers. First, write a headline. Then, write a caption that describes the explorers. Use adjective and adverb clauses.

4 Misplaced Modifiers

◆ **FOCUS**   A modifier should be placed as close as possible to the word it modifies.

Remember that a **modifier** is a word, phrase, or clause that describes other words, phrases, or clauses. A **misplaced modifier** is a word or a phrase incorrectly placed in a sentence so that the meaning is unclear or distorted.

   1. The barbers discussed how to shave Joe aloud .   misplaced modifier

   2. The barbers discussed aloud how to shave Joe.   correct

To avoid misplacing modifiers, place the modifier and the word to be modified as close together as possible. Remember that prepositional phrases are used as adjectives and adverbs. Place a prepositional phrase near the word it modifies.

   3. Joe said on Tuesday he would get a haircut.   Joe mentioned the haircut on Tuesday.

   4. Joe said he would get a haircut on Tuesday .   Joe would get the haircut on Tuesday.

Adverb phrases should be placed near the modified word. They can come before or after the modified word.

   5. The barber shaved Joe's beard with a straight razor .

   6. With a straight razor the barber shaved Joe's beard.

> **Link to Writing**
> Sometimes a modifier is correctly placed, but the sentence still flows poorly. Rewrite choppy or awkward sentences.

Guided Practice

A. Correct the misplaced modifiers. Explain what is wrong with the sentences as they are.

   1. The people of Fitchburg saw a man smiling with a beard at them.

   2. Standing on the sidewalk with cruel words they mocked him.

3. The beard was worn by Joseph Palmer, which was long and flowing.
4. In the 1830's only men with whiskers appeared in the backwoods.
5. Joseph Palmer stood, with great courage, up for his rights.

THINK AND REMEMBER

♦ Remember that a misplaced modifier distorts or muddles sentence meaning.

Independent Practice

B. Revising: Rewriting Sentences with Misplaced Modifiers   Write the sentences. Correct and clarify misplaced modifiers. The sentences can be written several ways. Add words to each sentence if necessary.

6. The people attacked Joseph Palmer armed with shaving gear.
   MODEL⟩ Armed with shaving gear, the people attacked Joseph Palmer.
7. Thrown viciously to the ground, they seriously injured Palmer.
8. As he defended himself, his attackers failed to shave him.
9. Palmer was thrown, although his attackers were unharmed, into a jail cell.
10. For over a year Palmer was an irritant to the people of Fitchburg, Massachusetts, in solitary confinement.
11. By paying a very small fine he could have left simply at any time.
12. He insisted that he had been jailed for wearing a beard, not for assault loudly and clearly.
13. His heroic refusal gathered widespread attention to leave jail.
14. Sitting in a chair the jailers had to carry Palmer out.
15. Palmer inspired important questions about human rights who went from being a villain to a hero.
16. Today about hair or clothing people are generally more lenient.
17. For neat clothing and short haircuts the office is still one place, however.

Application — Writing

A Persuasive Essay   Imagine that you are a newspaper editor in Fitchburg, Massachusetts. Write an editorial supporting Joseph Palmer. Since your readers passionately disagree with you, write so they will listen to what you have to say. Use modifiers correctly. If you need help writing a persuasive essay, see page 44 of the **Writer's Handbook.**

5 Participles and Participial Phrases

◆**FOCUS** A **participle** is a kind of verbal, a verb form that is used as an adjective. A **participial phrase** consists of a participle and its related words.

A **verbal** is a verb form that is used as a noun, an adjective, or an adverb. One kind of verbal is a participle.

A **participle** is used as an adjective to modify a noun or a pronoun. It can be placed either before or after the word it modifies. Most participles end in *ing* or *ed*.

1. The waiting photographer adjusted his camera.   *modifies photographer*

Remember that a verb has two participle forms: present participle and past participle. Do not confuse a participle used as an adjective with the main verb of a verb phrase. A verb phrase contains a form of the verb *be* or another helping verb.

2. The photographer was waiting for the best shot.   **verb phrase**

3. The darkened landscape would not make a good photograph.   **participle**

A **participial phrase** is a group of words used as an adjective. A participle is the key part of a participial phrase.

4. Following the herd , the photographers set up camp.

5. They rested comfortably, tired after a long day .

Link to Writing
When a participial phrase introduces a sentence, use a comma after it.

Photographing the elephants, we became absorbed in our work.

Guided Practice

A. Identify each participle or participial phrase and the noun or pronoun it modifies.

1. Martin and Osa waited for arriving herds of animals.
2. Osa, thinking aloud, broke the silence.
3. "Martin," she said, "this is discouraging work."
4. Answering in a tired voice, he agreed.
5. Suddenly a startled zebra was staring right at them.

Independent Practice

B. Identifying Participles and Participial Phrases   Write the sentences. Underline each participle or participial phrase. Draw an arrow from each participle to the noun or pronoun it modifies.

6. Martin and Osa Johnson, skilled photographers, traveled to Africa.

MODEL⟩ Martin and Osa Johnson, skilled photographers, traveled to Africa.

7. Taking few risks the first year, they got few pictures.

8. The photographed animals were only seen under risky conditions.

9. Osa Johnson has described their exciting adventures in a book.

10. Once Martin was shooting movies of a beautiful advancing lion.

11. Suddenly the lion attacked, but Martin, enjoying the adventure, continued to crank the camera.

C. Writing Sentences with Participles and Participial Phrases   Use each word as a participle or participial phrase in a sentence. The sentence must use the participle as a verbal, not as part of a verb phrase.

12. visiting

MODEL⟩ Visiting dignitaries met the president.

13. spending	**15.** talking	**17.** thrilling	**19.** waited
14. explained	**16.** knowing	**18.** exciting	**20.** enjoyed

Application — Writing

A Business Letter   A team of photographers needs an assistant for their photo safari this summer. Although no experience is required, the assistant must be enthusiastic, reliable, and good-natured. Write a letter convincing them that you are the right person. Use participles correctly. If you need help writing a business letter, see page 60 of the **Writer's Handbook.**

6 Gerunds and Gerund Phrases

◆ **FOCUS** A **gerund** is a verbal, a verb form that is used as a noun. A **gerund phrase** consists of a gerund and its related words.

A gerund is a verb that ends in *ing*. A gerund is used as a noun and can act in several different ways in a sentence.

1. Rafting and canoeing are fun! subjects
2. We enjoy rafting . direct object
3. Our sport is canoeing . predicate nominative
4. After canoeing, we swim. object of preposition

A **gerund phrase** is made up of a gerund and its complements.

5. Sleeping by the side of a river is peaceful. subject

To determine whether an *ing* word is a gerund, a participle, or a verb, decide how the word is used in a sentence.

6. Pat's rowing skills are good. adjective—participle
7. Canoeing is challenging. subject—gerund
8. We are rowing to shore. part of verb phrase
9. Ivan likes rafting . direct object—gerund

Use the possessive form of a noun or pronoun to modify a gerund.

10. Mark's liking for water sports led to his summer job. possessive; gerund

Guided Practice

A. Identify each gerund. Tell whether it is used as a *subject, direct object, predicate nominative,* or *object of a preposition.*

1. We enjoyed canoeing as we laughed and sang.
2. Sunbathing is something we do as we row.
3. Even the birds seem to laugh at our playing.
4. A favorite pastime is splashing.
5. Rafting is even more fun.

THINK AND REMEMBER

- Use a **gerund** as a noun in a sentence.
- Use a gerund and its modifiers to create a **gerund phrase.**
- Do not confuse a gerund with a participle.

Independent Practice

B. Identifying Gerunds and Gerund Phrases Write the sentences. Underline each gerund or gerund phrase. Add an extra line under each gerund.

   6. When I fish, I enjoy catching catfish.

MODEL When I fish, I enjoy catching catfish.

   7. Fishing in the Rio Grande means big, blue catfish.

   8. Beavers, however, make fishing difficult.

   9. My father's frying of river catfish is worth the trip.

  10. A full moon provides lighting for our delicious meal.

  11. Later, the crackling of the fire makes me sleepy.

C. Identifying Word Use Write the gerund in each sentence. Write whether it is used as a *subject, direct object, predicate nominative,* or *object of a preposition.*

  12. Seeing the Grand Canyon is an experience.

MODEL Seeing—subject

  13. The Rio Grande, flowing calmly for miles, suddenly becomes wild.

  14. I enjoy kayaking on the white-water rapids.

  15. As a result, traveling the river is a lonely adventure.

  16. One of my favorite pastimes is watching for birds.

  17. Golden eagles soar high after swooping down at us.

  18. The howling of coyotes and the songs of swallows serenade us.

D. Distinguishing Among Gerunds, Participles, and Verb Phrases Write whether each underlined item is a *gerund, participle,* or *verb phrase.*

  19. Discovering a new place for rafting is wonderful!

MODEL gerund

  20. I have enjoyed every white-water trip we have taken.

  21. The first step is lifting the raft into the water.

  22. Assembling everything takes quite a bit of time.

  23. Watching beautiful scenery is such a peaceful experience.

  24. I am looking forward to our next trip.

Application — Writing

Story Imagine that you are rafting on a river. You round a bend and suddenly you come upon something that amazes you. Write about the experience for your friends back home. Use gerunds correctly. If you need help writing a narrative, see page 48 of the **Writer's Handbook.**

7 Infinitives and Infinitive Phrases

FOCUS

◆ An **infinitive** is a verbal, a verb form consisting of the present-tense form of a verb preceded by *to*.

◆ An **infinitive phrase** consists of an infinitive and its related words.

An infinitive is a verb form that is preceded by the word *to*. An infinitive can be used as a noun, as an adjective, or as an adverb. When an infinitive is used as a noun, it can be the subject, the predicate nominative, or the direct object in a sentence.

1. To fly was Amelia Earhart's love.   subject

2. She wanted to fly .   object

3. Her desire was to fly around the world.   predicate nominative

When an infinitive is a modifier, it can be an adverb or an adjective.

4. Amelia was eager to fly .   adverb modifying an adjective

5. She was the first woman to fly across America.   adjective modifying a noun

An **infinitive phrase** consists of an infinitive and its objects and modifiers. Don't confuse infinitive phrases with prepositional phrases that begin with *to*. An infinitive consists of *to* and a verb. A prepositional phrase consists of *to* and a noun or pronoun.

6. to travel everywhere   infinitive phrase
7. to Hawaii   prepositional phrase

To keep sentences smooth, avoid splitting infinitives. A **split infinitive** is an infinitive that contains an adverb after the word *to*. Place the adverb before the infinitive to improve your sentence.

Guided Practice

A. Identify each infinitive phrase and infinitive.

1. Amelia Earhart wanted to break flying records.
2. She was the first woman to fly solo across the Atlantic Ocean.
3. She decided to make history by flying from Hawaii to New Jersey.
4. While trying to circumnavigate the globe, Earhart went from Miami to the South Pacific.
5. Her greatest difficulty was to fly alone.

Independent Practice

B. Identifying Infinitives and Infinitive Phrases   Write the infinitive phrases and the infinitives in the sentences.

6. In 1930 Amy Johnson also wanted to break flying records.

MODEL⟩ to break flying records; infinitive = to break

7. She wanted to make a record-breaking solo flight.

8. Eager to begin, Johnson flew solo from England to Australia.

9. To do this was amazing.

10. In 1932 she managed to break her husband's speed record.

11. Next, Johnson began to ferry planes for the government.

C. Revising: Checking Infinitives   Rewrite each sentence to correct the split infinitive. Write *no change* if you wish it to remain as is.

12. All over America people flock to happily see air shows.

MODEL⟩ All over America people flock happily to see air shows.

13. An annual air show in Wisconsin invites more than 12,000 airplanes to impressively perform in exciting exhibitions.

14. Some pilots fly antique planes that they have worked to lovingly restore to their original conditions.

15. Others have chosen to carefully build planes from scratch.

16. One expects Earhart and Johnson to casually arrive at any time!

17. Someday I would like to bravely fly my own airplane.

D. Writing Sentences with Infinitives   Use each infinitive in a sentence. Use the infinitive as a noun, as an adjective, or as an adverb.

18. to carry

MODEL⟩ I tried to carry the luggage myself.

19. to make   **20.** to swim   **21.** to search   **22.** to arrive   **23.** to wander

Application — **Writing and Speaking**

A Description   Imagine that you are a radio announcer describing a historic flight for airplane buffs. Write your description. Then read it to a classmate. Use infinitives correctly.

Building Vocabulary
Compounds and Blended Words

A **compound word** is made up of two smaller words. The most common compound words are nouns called closed compounds. Read this sentence. Identify the closed compounds.

> Bob wanted to skate at the rink near the parkway, but he couldn't find one kneepad.

Parkway and *kneepad* are closed compounds. *Parkway* is made up of two words: *park* and *way*. *Kneepad* is made from the words *knee* and *pad*. Knowing the meanings of the two smaller words can help you determine the meaning of the longer word.

There are other types of compound words. *Open compounds* are written as separate words. They are also used as a single part of speech. *Life preserver* is an open compound.

Some words are *hyphenated compounds*. These words are not very common. *Right-of-way* and *jack-o'-lantern* are examples. If you are unsure about whether or not to use a hyphen in a compound, use your dictionary.

Writers often use a technique called compounding. **Compounding** is joining two words together to make a new word. Put the words *star* and *gazer* together. What about *ear* and *ring*?

Another way you can make your writing interesting is to blend words. **Blending** is similar to compounding except that you use parts of words. Look at these blended words: *smoke + fog = smog; breakfast + lunch = brunch.*

Smog is smoky fog. Brunch is a meal that is part breakfast and part lunch and is usually eaten sometime between breakfast time and lunchtime. What word can you make by blending *twist* and *whirl?* What does your new word mean?

Read the blended words in the chart.

helicopter + airport	=	heliport
television + broadcast	=	telecast
situation + comedy	=	sitcom
motor + hotel	=	motel

Reading Practice

Read each sentence. Write the compounds or blended words. If the word is a compound, write *open*, *closed*, or *hyphenated*. If it is a blended word, write the two words from which it is made.

1. The police officer was not sure a crime had been committed.
2. When she arrived at the scene, the homeowner reported a robbery.
3. "They took my new computer. It is the model described as state-of-the-art."
4. Detective Carter noticed a large splotch on the floor. "Is that where you kept your computer?" she asked.
5. "No, I kept my computer in an out-of-the-way place."
6. The detective stood in the open doorway.
7. "It sounds like a run-of-the-mill robbery to me," she said, writing down the details.
8. "I'll contact the district attorney when I get back," she thought.

Writing Practice

Brainstorm a list of compound words. Include open, closed, and hyphenated compounds. Use the words in your list to write a short story about an adventure in outer space. Use the following questions to help you develop your story.

1. Who invited you on the mission?
2. Where are you going?
3. Who is going with you?
4. For how long will you be there?
5. How did you feel during blast-off?
6. What unusual sights did you see?
7. Did you meet any alien creatures? If so, describe them briefly.
8. What work did you do while you were there?
9. What happened when you returned?

Project

Use a dictionary to help you find 10 compound words about one of the following: school, food, home, sports. Use graph paper to make a crossword puzzle. Provide clues, and write the answers on a separate sheet of paper. Exchange puzzles with a classmate, and try to solve each other's puzzles.

Language Enrichment
Complex Sentences and Verbals

Use what you have learned about complex sentences and verbals to do these activities.

 Subordinate Sense

You just found a newspaper article written in the early 1900's. Unfortunately, the story has fallen apart and only fragments are left. Write five subordinate clauses and five independent clauses on separate slips of paper. Put all the slips into a bag. Take turns drawing a slip and completing the sentences.

 Crime Fighters' Catalogue

You and your classmates have been hired to write advertisements to accompany crime-fighting equipment. Work in a small group. Choose five items, and use verbals to tell why each piece of equipment would be useful to detectives. Use at least three verbal phrases to describe it. For example, isn't a pogo stick handy for *escaping from tight places* or for *interviewing a highly placed witness*? Illustrate your descriptions, and compile them in a catologue to share with your classmates.

 **Move Over!**

You have stopped at an inn for the night. The landlord tells you that the inn is crowded and everyone will have to share a room with someone else. Rewrite the five pairs of sentences so that each pair becomes one complex sentence. Then use the sentences to write a paragraph that describes your adventure at the inn. Sweet dreams!

Our arrival looked like a circus.
We arrived in a variety of carts.

We could hear the patrons of the inn making merry.
The inn was bursting at the seams.

Pedro headed for the kitchen.
His belly was complaining as loudly as he was.

Three familiar figures glared at us.
They caused me to grab my sword.

We fought up and down the stairs.
Guests scattered like squawking chickens.

CONNECTING
LANGUAGE ↔ WRITING

In this unit you learned that a complex sentence is made up of an independent clause and a subordinate, or dependent, clause. You also learned that verb forms may act as nouns, adjectives, and adverbs. Participles are verb forms that are used as adjectives, while gerunds are verb forms ending in the suffix *ing* that act as nouns. Infinitives are verbals made from the infinitive forms of verbs. They act as nouns, adjectives, or adverbs. Verbals will make your writing more interesting and will also add variety to your sentences.

◆ **Using Complex Sentences and Verbals in Your Writing** Knowing how to use complex sentences and verbals is important because they are sophisticated forms of writing. As you do these activities, pay special attention to the structure of your sentences and the verb forms you use.

 ### Thriller Competition

Hold a contest to see who can write the best original first paragraph of a mystery story. Begin with a spellbinding first sentence. Use exciting and mysterious verbals, of course. Work in a small group, taking turns reading sentences aloud. Choose the best beginning sentence from your group. Then complete the first paragraph of the mystery individually. Read your work aloud.

 ### Two for One

On the **Building Vocabulary** pages, you learned that a blended word is a combination of two separate words. For example, *smog* is a combination of *smoke* and *fog*. Make up blended words for these words. Then share them with your class.

lion + tiger   = _____
airplane + boat = _____
mud + snow   = _____
house + office   = _____
fox + dog   = _____

8 Unit Checkup

Think Back	Think Ahead
◆ What did you learn about a mystery story in this unit? What did you do to write one?	◆ How will what you learned about a mystery story help you when you read a mystery story?
◆ Look at the writing you did in this unit. How did complex sentences and verbals help you express your ideas?	◆ What is one way that you can use complex sentences and verbals to improve your writing?

Analyzing a Mystery Story   *pages 364–366*
Read this synopsis of a mystery. Then answer the questions.

> In this story, "Morning at the Opera," two voice students, a boy and a girl, attend an opera rehearsal in a fancy opera house. The scenery falls on the performers, and the female lead is killed. Unsure that this was an accident, the police call Detective Smyth. Since the girl is the understudy for the dead star, she and her boyfriend are suspects. They claim innocence.

1. Who are the characters?
2. What is the setting?
3. What is the overall mood?
4. What is the problem?
5. What complication occurs?

Creating Mood Through Characterization and Dialogue   *page 367*
Rewrite each sentence to convey the mood indicated. Use dialogue, characterization, and details to show rather than to tell what the mood is.

6. The child was unhappy when his playmate pushed him.
7. The mood in the room was sad.
8. The class liked the poem she read.
9. The child was happy to be able to walk.
10. Her grandmother was pleased to see her.

The Writing Process   *pages 368 – 379*
Write the letter for the answer to each question.

11. When you plan a mystery story, what should you do first?
   a. Make a chart to gather and organize information.
   b. Proofread an existing mystery story.
   c. Create dialogue.
12. Before deciding on a beginning, what might you consider?
   a. setting   b. dialogue   c. an ending
13. Suppose you are revising, and you find that you have used very little dialogue. What should you do?
   a. Let it remain as it is.
   b. Add dialogue.
   c. Ask your teacher if you should add dialogue.
14. What is a major consideration for a mystery story's being published in a journal or a magazine?
   a. that the characters be familiar
   b. that the plot be clear and intriguing
   c. that an excellent detective be the hero

Phrases and Clauses   *pages 382 – 383*
Write whether each group of words is a *phrase* or a *clause*.

15. when she climbed the mountain
16. to the mountaintop
17. with very heavy equipment
18. although the temperature was perfect
19. with the wind blowing all around her
20. the view was fantastic
21. until she had seen it herself

Complex Sentences   *pages 384 – 385*
Write *simple, compound,* or *complex* to identify each sentence.

22. Lin looked all day for a weekend job, but she could not find one anywhere.
23. After dinner one evening, she had a telephone conversation with her best friend.
24. Lin had not been looking for a job working with children, but her friend suggested it.
25. She thought of speaking to the librarian, who had long been her friend.

26. For years Lin had attended story hours every weekend.
27. Now perhaps she was old enough to participate in the story hour.
28. When the librarian heard Lin's idea, she asked her to come on Saturday.
29. Lin chose a book for the children.
30. When she got home, she practiced reading it aloud.
31. After an hour, she called her friend and read it to her.
32. Molly had a few suggestions about different parts.
33. When she read the story the next day, all the children paid attention.
34. The librarian was delighted, and she asked Lin to work there on weekends as her assistant storyteller.

Adjective and Adverb Clauses   *pages 386 – 387*

Write each subordinate clause. Write *adverb clause* or *adjective clause* to identify it.

35. Pilots who are working with hurricane trackers develop their skills every day.
36. Because few pilots work near hurricanes, most must work alone.
37. During hurricanes, the pilots who have been researching and studying throughout the year are needed.
38. Sometimes a deadly hurricane comes when it is least expected.
39. Because the pilots are trained and ready, they can fly directly into the hurricane to gather research data.

Misplaced Modifiers   *pages 388 – 389*

Write the sentences. Correct and clarify misplaced modifiers. The sentences can be written several ways. Add words to each sentence if necessary.

40. Ann's teammate passed while pretending to look the other way the ball to her.
41. If you are clever when you play for your side, you can gain important advantages.
42. In your favor the element of surprise can be if you use it carefully.
43. Sports involve the mind as well as for most players the body.
44. The spectators enjoy a game well played cheering in the bleachers.

Participles and Participial Phrases *pages 390 – 391*

Write the sentences. Underline each participle or participial phrase once. Underline the noun or pronoun it modifies twice.

45. Nancy Drew, a disciplined detective, is a fictional heroine.

46. Her thrilling adventures helped readers learn to love books.

47. At the end of every novel was a solved crime.

48. Many readers, hoping to become detectives, read every book.

49. They trade their finished books with friends.

Gerunds and Gerund Phrases *pages 392 – 393*

Write the sentences. Underline each gerund phrase once. Underline each gerund twice.

50. Riding on horseback is Isabel's hobby.

51. She has been riding since arriving in Texas.

52. Taking lessons once a week got her started.

53. Progressing to jumping and showing soon followed.

54. Developing her natural talent required patience and discipline.

Infinitives and Infinitive Phrases *pages 394 – 395*

Write the infinitives in the sentences.

55. One of my classmates is going to be in a movie.

56. Recently two men from a studio came to scout a location.

57. They were also trying to find young actors.

58. Several of my friends were asked to come to an interview.

59. They were given a short speech to prepare in advance.

Compounds and Blended Words *pages 396 – 397*

Read each sentence. Write the compounds or blended words. If the word is a compound, write *open*, *closed*, or *hyphenated*. If it is a blended word, write the two words from which it is made.

60. After brunch I loaded the dishwasher.

61. Then I folded the clothes in the clothes dryer
   while I watched a sitcom on TV.

62. The other day I dropped a watermelon.

63. My mother was double-parked in the car outside
   the supermarket.

UNIT

9

Reporting Information

◆ **COMPOSITION FOCUS:** Research Report
◆ **LANGUAGE FOCUS:** Mechanics Wrap-up

How did the invention of the printing press change the world? What steps enabled someone finally to invent television? If you wanted to know the answers to these questions, you could write a research report. A research report answers complex questions and explains them to an interested audience.

People in different walks of life write research reports. Science, archaeology, history, and education are just a few of the fields in which people do research as a part of their everyday lives.

Virginia Calkins is a professional writer who finds out the answers to historical questions. She was hired by a magazine to write an article on the inventor of the traffic signal. To answer questions about the inventor, Virginia Calkins began her research in the library. She used books, reference materials, and magazine articles. She wanted to find as much information as she could about the invention as well as about the inventor. Then she organized the information into a chain of events that clearly shows the steps that led to the invention. In this unit you will learn how to explain a cause-and-effect chain, and then you will incorporate a cause-and-effect relationship into a research report.

Virginia Calkins writes *to inform* readers about the reasons that an event took place and the effects of that event on our lives.

Traffic signals—it's hard to imagine life without them. But until 1923, there were no such things. You can imagine the trouble drivers of horse-drawn carriages and early automobiles had deciding who had the right of way! Then along came Garrett Morgan, the man who changed all that. Read this research report by Virginia Calkins to find out what event caused Morgan to invent the traffic light and what some of the effects of his invention are.

The Man Who Stopped Traffic

by Virginia Calkins

In the early days of the automobile, efforts to regulate traffic were not very successful. Sometimes a stop-and-go signal would be placed at a busy intersection with a police officer assigned to turn it at intervals. If the officer delayed turning the signal, or if no officer was available, drivers would become confused and do as they pleased. Accidents were common.

An accident that took place in Cleveland, Ohio, in the early 1920's changed this. When an automobile collided with a horse and carriage, two people were thrown from the carriage and the driver of the car was knocked unconscious. The horse was injured and had to be shot.

A black businessman named Garrett Morgan witnessed this accident. Born on a farm in Kentucky to a very poor family, he had left home when he was only fourteen years old. First he went to Cincinnati and then to Cleveland. He had a natural talent for working with machinery and held several jobs in this field. Eventually, Morgan ran his own tailor

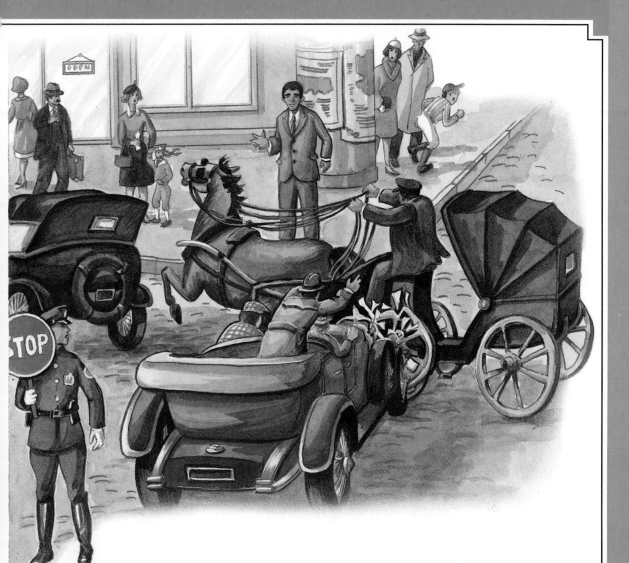

shop and had thirty-two employees. He had designed and built much of the equipment for the shop himself.

Garrett Morgan also was an inventor. Among other things, he had invented a breathing device that provided clean air for firefighters, police officers, and others who did rescue work in areas where there was heavy smoke or fumes. This Safety Hood, as it was later called, was adapted for use as a gas mask in World War I. It earned Morgan many honors and awards.

After witnessing the collision between the automobile and the horse and carriage, Morgan could not get the accident out of his head. "Something should be done to make driving safer," he said to himself.

Putting his inventive mind to work on the problem, Morgan finally devised a three-way traffic signal. It consisted of a pole with arms that were operated by electricity. The word "stop" appeared on the arms. The word "go" appeared on the edge of the arms and on the pole so that it could be read by those traveling in the opposite direction. Colored lights illuminated the words, the familiar red for stop and green for go. There was also a yellow "caution" light.

The signal had other useful features. The arms could be put in a half-mast position at night, when traffic was lighter, to indicate that all drivers should use extra caution. (We now use a blinking yellow light for this purpose.) The signal also could be adjusted to stop traffic in all directions to allow pedestrians to cross the street.

In February 1922, Morgan applied for a patent on his invention. It was issued to him in November 1923. He also secured the British and Canadian rights to the device. Cleveland was the first city to use the new signal, but soon many other cities followed suit. After a short time, Morgan sold his rights to the traffic signal to General Electric. He received forty thousand dollars, a huge sum in those days.

Through the years, Morgan's traffic signal has been modified to meet changing needs. Now we have "walk" lights for pedestrians, and where streets have several lanes, turning arrows have been added.

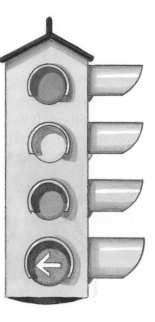

In August 1963, the one-hundredth anniversary of the Emancipation Proclamation, an Emancipation Centennial was held in Chicago to pay tribute to the accomplishments of black people over the past century. Although he was eighty-six years old, sick, and nearly blind, Morgan had planned to attend. Sadly, he died a month before it took place, but his work received much recognition at the celebration.

Garrett Morgan's traffic signal stopped confusion and allowed traffic to go in an orderly way. The world is a safer place because of this creative and talented man.

Respond

1. What interests you most in this report? What information does the writer include that catches your attention?

Discuss

2. *Cobblestone* printed this article in July 1987. Why is the topic Virginia Calkins chose one that would interest any audience at any time?
3. In your own words, tell what led Morgan to invent the traffic signal and what the results were.
4. What recognition did Morgan receive for his invention?

Thinking As a Writer
Analyzing a Research Report

A **research report** gives information that answers a complex question. It has a title, an introduction, a body of several paragraphs, and a conclusion. Read the excerpts from "The Man Who Stopped Traffic."

In the early days of the automobile, efforts to regulate traffic were not very successful. Sometimes a stop-and-go signal would be placed at a busy intersection with a police officer assigned to turn it at intervals. If the officer delayed turning the signal, or if no officer was available, drivers would become confused and do as they pleased. Accidents were common.

* * *

After witnessing the collision between the automobile and the horse and carriage, Morgan could not get the accident out of his head. "Something should be done to make driving safer," he said to himself.

Putting his inventive mind to work on the problem, Morgan finally devised a three-way traffic signal. It consisted of a pole with arms that were operated by electricity. The word "stop" appeared on the arms. The word "go" appeared on the edge of the arms and on the pole so that it could be read by those traveling in the opposite direction. Colored lights illuminated the words, the familiar red for stop and green for go. There was also a yellow "caution" light.

* * *

Garrett Morgan's traffic signal stopped confusion and allowed traffic to go in an orderly way. The world is a safer place because of this creative and talented man.

The **introduction** states the subject of the paper. In a cause-and-effect paper, it may state the initial cause or explain the situation that existed before the causal chain began.

The **body** answers the question posed by the writer. Often it is three paragraphs long, but it may be longer, depending on the topic.

The **conclusion** sums up the paper. It may briefly restate the topic or identify the points that the writer has made.

Discuss

1. Look back at the title, the introduction, the body, and the conclusion of Virginia Calkins's report. How is the information in each part different?
2. How is the article organized? Why do you think she organized it this way?
3. What characteristics of Garrett Morgan did Virginia Calkins bring out as she told about his invention?
4. Virginia Calkins discusses events in Garrett Morgan's life from birth through death. Why has the report not been called a biography?

Try Your Hand

A. Write Research Report Questions   Write one question that Virginia Calkins's report answers.

B. Select Appropriate Titles   Read these titles for research reports. Write the ones that would be appropriate for Virginia Calkins's report.

- ◆ Garrett Morgan, Troubleshooter
- ◆ Traffic Problems
- ◆ Hand-Operated Traffic Signals
- ◆ The Life-Saving Signal
- ◆ The Traffic Wizard

C. Add to the Body   Write another sentence that could appear in the body of this report.

D. Read and Talk About a Research Report   Find a research report. Read it to a partner. Identify these parts:

- ◆ title
- ◆ introduction
- ◆ body
- ◆ conclusion

Discuss whether the report adequately covers what it indicates in the introduction.

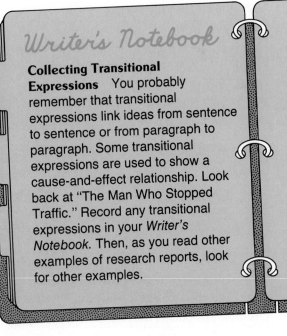

Writer's Notebook

Collecting Transitional Expressions   You probably remember that transitional expressions link ideas from sentence to sentence or from paragraph to paragraph. Some transitional expressions are used to show a cause-and-effect relationship. Look back at "The Man Who Stopped Traffic." Record any transitional expressions in your *Writer's Notebook.* Then, as you read other examples of research reports, look for other examples.

Thinking As a Writer
Connecting Cause and Effect

Writer's Guide

To show causes and effects in a research report, writers

- make a flow chart.
- write in a way that shows the relationships between causes and effects.
- use time order.
- use transitional expressions.

To write a good cause-and-effect paragraph, a writer begins by establishing in his or her mind the links between the causes and the effects. Good writers often make flow charts to show the relationship between the causes and the effects they want to write about. There are several different possible cause-and-effect relationships, and each kind can be shown in its own flow chart. The writer thinks about the relationship and then decides which chart expresses it best. Look at these three flow charts.

1. multiple causes with one effect

cause ⟍
cause ———————————————————— effect
cause ⟋

2. one cause with multiple effects

effect
cause ⟨——————————— effect
effect

3. causal chain—each effect becomes the cause of another effect

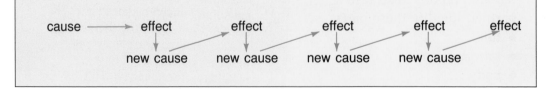

To transform the flow chart into the paragraphs of a report, writers arrange the events in time order so that it is clear which elements cause which effects. Writers add transitional expressions such as *then,*

therefore, *as a result*, *because of*, and *in spite of* to link causes to effects. Look at the chart and the resulting paragraphs from *The Automobile* by Barbara Ford. Her treatment of causes and effects is much like what you will do in your research report.

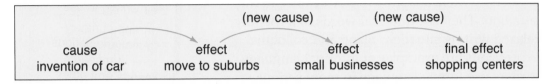

One of the biggest changes was in the places people lived. As soon as cars were readily available, many city residents who could afford to buy houses moved to the suburbs. The car made it possible for them to drive to their work in the city.

As residents moved to the suburbs, shops and other small businesses followed them. A new kind of shopping area, the shopping center, first appeared in a suburb of Kansas City, Missouri, in the 1920's. Customers, most of whom arrived by car, parked in special areas. Shops in many cities lost customers to the shopping centers.

The writer of these paragraphs used time order, putting the causes before the effects. The writer used the transitional expression *as soon as* to show the change that the cause brought about.

When you write your research report, be sure that causes and effects are always explained clearly.

Discuss

1. Look back at the report on pages 406–409. What type of chart describes the cause-and-effect relationship in Virginia Calkin's article?
2. Did she put all the events in time order? How do you know?

Try Your Hand

Make a Flow Chart   Make a flow chart to show the cause-and-effect relationships in your own life, such as those involved in learning to ride a bike, taking care of a pet, or having a new brother or sister.

Developing the Writer's Craft
Using Formal and Informal Language

Writer's Guide

Good writers change their writing to use

♦ an appropriately formal and serious tone in research reports and other formal compositions.

♦ an informal and casual tone in less serious writing.

Good writers adapt their word choice to the situation. They use informal words in a friendly, relaxed writing situation. Slang and colloquial expressions are examples of informal language. Writers use formal language in more serious, impersonal situations. Formal language is used in business and research reports. Look at the underlined words and phrases in these sentences from a research report on the history of jazz.

1. Some of the <u>hottest</u> jazz <u>hits</u> <u>saw first light</u> at <u>jam</u> sessions.
2. Some <u>famous</u> jazz <u>pieces</u> <u>arose</u> out of <u>informal improvisation</u> sessions.

The words in the first sentence are informal and casual. This sentence would be appropriate in casual speech. In the second sentence, the informal language is replaced with words and phrases in a tone that is appropriate to the writing task.

When you write your research report, be sure to use formal language.

Discuss

1. How can you recognize the difference between informal and formal language?
2. Why should a research report be written in formal language?

Try Your Hand

Adapt Your Language Look at this picture of a famous jazz group. Write two descriptions, one using formal language and one using informal language. Trade descriptions with a partner. Talk about how the formal and informal descriptions are different.

1 Prewriting
Research Report

Mercy had to write a research report for her final grade in social studies. She used the checklist in the **Writer's Guide** to help her plan her report.

Writer's Guide

Prewriting Checklist

☑ Brainstorm topics.

☑ Select and limit a topic.

☑ Think about your audience and your purpose.

☑ Gather information.

☑ Organize the facts.

◆ Brainstorming and Selecting a Topic

First, Mercy thought of possible subjects. Her report was to contain causes and effects. She looked through books for ideas. Then she listed broad subjects.

Next, Mercy crossed out inappropriate subjects and those that would be hard to research. She circled *horses* because she had read an interesting account in her science book about them.

> 1. the beginning of civilization
> 2. ancient Greek and Roman architecture
> 3. Mickey Mouse
> 4. (horses)

Then Mercy began to limit her subject. Here is what she did.

Horses		
Types	**History**	**Current Uses**
saddle horses	carried knights	riding
draft horses	drew plows	plowing
harness horses	drew farm wagons	pulling parade wagons

After reviewing her chart, Mercy decided to limit her topic to draft horses. She thought they would make an interesting and unusual topic.

Finally, Mercy wrote a question about draft horses that her paper would answer. Her question had to include cause and effect. It also had to be answered in a maximum of five paragraphs. Here is Mercy's question: What events led to the development of the draft horse?

Discuss

1. Why did Mercy have to do research before she could limit her topic?
2. How will Mercy's question involve cause and effect?

◆ Gathering and Organizing Information

After Mercy selected her topic, she used the library reference section to locate and gather information. She looked in an encyclopedia, an atlas, and an almanac. She also looked for general information in nonfiction books. Then she made bibliography cards for her sources. (For more help in using reference materials, see page 472 of the Study Skills section at the back of this book.)

Draft Horses

Origin of draft horses
descended from great war horses of Crusades
tallest, heaviest, strongest horses include
Shire, Clydesdale, Belgian,
Percheron, and Suffolk

"Horses." The World Book Encyclopedia. 1986 ed.

Patent, Dorothy Hinshaw. Draft Horses.
New York. Holiday House. 1986.

"The First Draft Horse." The Draft Horse
Journal. April 1987. pp. 322-326.

Mercy took notes from each source. Then she used her information to make a flow chart. The chart would show how historical events led to causes and effects in the development of the draft horse.

small Mongolian—original horse
(cause)   (effect)
change in environment ————→ horse grew larger
(new cause) ←——————————————————————   (effect)
horse grew larger ——————————→ bred to carry knights
(new cause) ←——————————————————————   (effect)
bred to carry knights ——————→ became "Great Horses"
(new cause) ←——————————————————————   (effect)
became "Great Horses" ——————→ bred to pull loads
(new cause) ←——————————————————————   (effect)
bred to pull loads ——————————→ became largest draft
                                 horses

After Mercy filled in her causal chain, she was sure she had enough information to write her report.

Mercy used her notes and chart to make an outline. Here, each main heading represents the main idea of a paragraph. Each subheading represents a detail sentence to support the main idea. Here is part of her outline.

```
              The Development of the Draft Horse
   I.   Introduction--definition of draft horse
        A. Meaning of name
        B. General description
   II.  Origin of modern horse
        A. Mongolian wild horse
        B. Migrated to Europe and changed
   III. Changes in horses for war
        A. For war chariots
        B. For carrying armored knights--"Great Horses"
```

Discuss

1. Why did Mercy use a cause-and-effect flow chart to decide whether she had enough information?
2. In which part of the research report will Mercy explain what a draft horse is? Why will she put the information there?
3. Why isn't Mercy's outline exactly like her cause-and-effect chart?

Try Your Hand

Now plan a research report of your own.

A. Brainstorm and Select a Topic Brainstorm a list of possible topics. Include several different topics that interest you and your audience.

- Cross out topics on which you cannot get enough information.
- Cross out topics that are not of interest to you.
- Cross out topics that are too complicated.
- Circle the most interesting topic left on your list. This will be the topic of your research report.

B. Limit Your Topic Use categories to help you limit your topic. If a category does not work, do not use it. Do some initial research if necessary. If you find that you have few useful ideas, try another topic from your original list.

C. Create a Question Use your topic to create a question. Make sure that your question involves cause and effect. Be sure that your question is suitable for the length of your paper.

D. Gather Information Use the library to locate reference sources. Try to find books, encyclopedia entries, articles in periodicals, and other references. Identify each source on a bibliography card. Then note briefly the important information in each source.

E. Review Your Notes Study your cards. Make sure that they contain the necessary details to explain the cause-and-effect chain in your report. Use a causal flow chart to check whether your chain is complete. If you need more information, do more research.

F. Organize the Facts Organize your information in an outline. Be sure it shows which facts you wish to include in the introduction, the body, and the conclusion. You should have a Roman numeral for each paragraph you plan to write.

 Save your note cards, your flow chart, and your outline in your *Writer's Notebook*. You will use them when you draft your research report.

WRITING PROCESS

2 Drafting
Research Report

Before Mercy started to draft her research report, she decided how to explain the development of the draft horse. Using her cards, her flow chart, and her outline, Mercy followed the checklist in the **Writer's Guide.** Look at what she did.

Writer's Guide

Drafting Checklist

☑ Use your note cards, your flow chart, and your outline for ideas.

☑ Write a topic sentence for each paragraph.

☑ Write detail sentences to support each main idea.

☑ Include a clear cause-and-effect chain.

☑ Write a title.

The Development of the Draft Horse

<u>Draft</u> means "used for pulling." Because draft horses are the strongest, heaviest, and tallest of all horses, they are especially suited to pulling loads. They are short-legged and heavily muscled work animals with big hooves. These horses were first bred in the Middle Ages after the Crusades ended. They are still used today. This is the story of how they were developed.

Discuss

1. What is good about Mercy's introductory paragraph?
2. What cause-and-effect relationship has Mercy mentioned?

Try Your Hand

Now you are ready to write a research report.

A. Review Your Information   Think about the information you gathered and organized. Decide whether you need more information. If so, gather it.

B. Think About Your TAP   Remember that your task is to write a research report. Your purpose is to explain a cause-and-effect chain of relationships to your audience.

C. Write Your First Draft   Use the **Drafting Checklist** to write your research report.

When you write your draft, put all your ideas on paper. Do not worry about spelling, grammar, or punctuation. You can correct the draft later.

Task: What?
Audience: Who?
Purpose: Why?

Save your first draft in your *Writer's Notebook*. You will use it when you revise your research report.

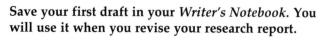

3 Responding and Revising
Research Report

Mercy read over her draft; then she used the checklist in the **Writer's Guide** to revise her research report. Look at what she did.

Writer's Guide
Revising Checklist
- ☑ Read your report to yourself or to a partner.
- ☑ Think about your audience and your purpose. Add or cut information.
- ☑ Check to see that your facts are organized according to your outline.
- ☑ Check for transitional expressions.
- ☑ Check to see that your report is unified and coherent.

◆ Checking Information

Mercy saw that she had left out an important detail. To add it, she used the mark ∧ . She also noticed that one comment did not belong in a research report. She used the mark ℓ to cut it.

◆ Checking Organization

Mercy saw that she had mentioned causes and effects in a confusing order. She felt a change in the order would make the paragraph more coherent. She used this mark ♪ to move the information.

◆ Checking Language

When Mercy checked her sentences, she saw that some words were too informal. She used this mark ∧‾ to replace them.

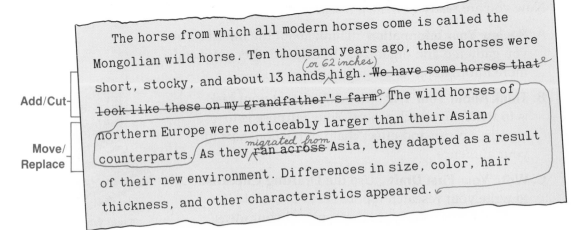

Add/Cut —

Move/ Replace —

The horse from which all modern horses come is called the Mongolian wild horse. Ten thousand years ago, these horses were short, stocky, and about 13 hands high *(or 62 inches)*. ~~We have some horses that look like these on my grandfather's farm.~~ The wild horses of northern Europe were noticeably larger than their Asian counterparts. As they *migrated from* ~~ran across~~ Asia, they adapted as a result of their new environment. Differences in size, color, hair thickness, and other characteristics appeared.

Discuss

Why did it help the organization of the paragraph to move the sentence about the size of the horses?

Try Your Hand

Now revise your first draft.

A. Read Your First Draft As you read your research report, think about your audience and your purpose. Read your report silently or to a partner to see if it is complete and well organized. Ask yourself or your partner the questions in the box.

Responding and Revising Strategies	
✔ **Respond** **Ask yourself or a partner:**	✔ **Revise** **Try these solutions:**
◆ Have I shown the cause-and-effect relationship that answers my question?	◆ Find additional details in your outline, and **add** them to your explanation.
◆ Is all the information in the report relevant and interesting?	◆ **Cut** information that is not relevant or interesting.
◆ Are all the details related?	◆ **Cut** unrelated details.
◆ Are the details arranged logically and in a coherent manner?	◆ **Move** any material that would fit better elsewhere. See the **Revising Workshop** on page 422.
◆ Have I used formal language in my report?	◆ **Cut** informal words or **replace** them with more formal language.
◆ Did I use transitional expressions to show the cause-and-effect relationships between ideas?	◆ **Add** expressions that show relationships.

B. Make Your Changes If the answer to any question in the box is *no,* try the solution. Use the **Editor's Marks** to show your changes.

C. Review Your Research Report Again Decide whether there is anything else you want to revise. Keep revising your research report until you feel it is well organized and complete.

> **EDITOR'S MARKS**
>
> ∧ Add something.
> ⌿ Cut something.
> ◯ Move something.
> ∧ Replace something.

Save your revised research report in your *Writer's Notebook.* You will use it when you proofread your report.

Revising Workshop
Checking for Unity and Coherence

Good writers strive for unity and coherence to make their ideas flow smoothly and clearly. They achieve unity by writing only sentences that support their main idea. They achieve coherence in two ways. They organize their ideas to make them connect clearly, and they use transitional expressions to link ideas within sentences and between paragraphs.

When writers write material with cause-and-effect relationships, they use time order to arrange the events and connect what happened first with what came next. Read this example.

> For many centuries in Europe, trees were one of the most important resources. They were used for building, for heating, and for cooking. Later, they also provided the fuel for making iron. All this use of wood gradually depleted the forests. Forests were also cleared to make room for more farmland. Eventually wood became scarce. Consequently, by the 1600's, wood and wood products had become very expensive.

In the paragraph the writer used time order and the transitional expressions *later*, *also*, *all this*, *eventually*, and *consequently* to help you relate the causes to the effects.

Practice

Organize these sentences into a paragraph. Add transitional expressions to put them in a logical order.

1. Whatever they wanted, they had to provide for themselves. People had to be self-reliant and capable.
2. Men hunted animals, cut and cured the meat, and prepared the skins for clothes.
3. They farmed the land and built whatever buildings, furniture, or vehicles they needed.
4. American pioneer families were often far from neighbors or stores.
5. Women prepared and canned food, wove cloth, made clothing, and educated their children.
6. They also made necessary items such as soap and candles.
7. Together, a pioneer husband and wife provided nearly all of their family's needs.

4 Proofreading
Research Report

After Mercy revised her research report, she used the checklist in the **Writer's Guide** and the **Editor's Marks** to proofread it. Look at what she did.

Writer's Guide

Proofreading Checklist

- ☑ Check for errors in capitalization. Be sure you have written proper nouns correctly.
- ☑ Check for errors in punctuation.
- ☑ Check that all your paragraphs are indented.
- ☑ Check for errors in grammar.
- ☑ Circle any words you think are misspelled. Find out how to spell them correctly.
- ⇨ For proofreading help, use the **Writer's Handbook**.

Horses were bred to a large size to pull war chariots. Large horses became desirable to carry knights in armor in the crusades. A large, *muskular* (muskular) breed called great horses was bred to carry enormous weights. Only a large, strong horse could carry a knight and armor weighing 400 pounds.

After the crusades it was natural to look for another occupation for the Great Horses. As a result of the invention of horseshoes and of a new kind of horse collar, these strong horses could plow the damp clay soil of Northern europe. Consequently, their use led to great improvements in agriculture.

EDITOR'S MARKS

- ≡ Capitalize.
- ⊙ Add a period.
- ∧ Add something.
- ⋀ Add a comma.
- ⱽⱽ Add quotation marks.
- ✄ Cut something.
- ∧ Replace something.
- ∼ Transpose.
- ◯ Spell correctly.
- ⊬ Indent paragraph.
- / Make a lowercase letter.

Discuss

1. Look at Mercy's proofread research report. What kinds of mistakes did she make?
2. Why did she capitalize certain words within the report?

Try Your Hand

Proofread Your Research Report   Now use the checklist in the **Writer's Guide** and the **Editor's Marks** to proofread your research report.

Save your corrected research report in your *Writer's Notebook.* You will use it when you publish your report.

COMPOSITION: PROOFREADING   Research Report   **423**

5 Publishing
Research Report

Writer's Guide

Publishing Checklist

☑ Make a clean copy of your research report.

☑ Be sure that nothing has been left out.

☑ Make sure there are no mistakes.

☑ Share your research report in a special way.

Mercy made a clean copy of her report and checked it to be sure she had not left out anything. Then she and her classmates published their research reports by making a history book. You can find Mercy's completed report on pages 57 and 58 of the **Writer's Handbook.**

Here's how Mercy and her classmates published their reports.

1. First, Mercy reread her research report and thought about an effective way to illustrate it. She knew she could use a photograph, a drawing, a painting, a collage, or any other medium. She thought about including a map, a chart, a time line, a diagram, or another device that would make the subject easier for her audience to understand. Finally she chose to make a drawing and a map.

2. Then the class took the reports and laid out the pages to make up a book. They separated the written work with illustrations. Some pages had illustrations on the same page as the text and other pages had illustrations on facing pages.

3. Next, they put their research reports and illustrations into a book. They used divider pages to separate the students' work. They designed an attractive cover to let their readers know what kind of material the book included.

4. Then they gave their social studies teacher their history book.

Discuss

1. What might happen if students didn't plan their layouts carefully?
2. Why is the cover of a book so important?

Try Your Hand

Publish Your Research Report Follow the checklist in the **Writer's Guide.** Then create a history book, or try one of these ideas for sharing your research report.

♦ Give an oral presentation of your report, using large-size illustrations of the same types suggested for the book. Follow the guidelines in **Tips on How to Give an Explanation Using an Illustration.**

♦ With your classmates, make copies of your book and share them with members of a local senior citizens' center. Ask the senior citizens to relate stories about their heritage to your class.

Listening and Speaking
Tips on How to Give an Explanation Using an Illustration

1. A chart, a diagram, a graph, a time line, an illustration, or a photograph can enhance an audience's understanding of a research report.
2. Make sure that the illustrations you make or select are large enough to be seen easily by everyone in the audience. Make drawings and lettering large enough to be read easily.
3. Include only major details or important points. Your illustrations are not supposed to cover every fact completely.
4. Plan your illustrations to correlate with the organization of your report. Decide when you will refer to them and exactly where you will point.
5. Be sure that your words give the basic information. Your illustrations should help, not tell the whole story.
6. Do not display your illustrations when you are not using them. They may distract your audience from what you are saying.

Writing in the Content Areas

Use what you learned to write another research report. Use one of these ideas or an idea of your own.

Writer's Guide

When you write, remember the stages of the Writing Process.

- Prewriting
- Drafting
- Responding and Revising
- Proofreading
- Publishing

Science

Find an interesting science article in a local newspaper. Do research to find out more about the subject, and write a report about it. If you can, contact a specialist in that field to add the most recent data to your report.

Mathematics

Write a report about a famous mathematician and his or her contribution to the field of mathematics. You might write about Lewis Carroll (the author of *Alice in Wonderland*) and his system of logic, or about someone who invented a famous brainteaser.

Literature

Throughout history, certain themes have been explored by many writers. Research and write a report about a theme common in children's literature—for example, dragons, giants, or elves. Then present your report to a group of young children.

Social Studies

Choose a custom from any culture. Find out more about it, and write a report for classmates who do not know about it. You might want to interview someone who has grown up in that culture. If possible, mention dress, food, and special holidays in your report.

CONNECTING
WRITING ⬌ LANGUAGE

Often, you cannot write about a topic without first finding out more about it. Read the information about the Texas Rangers. What possible sources did the writer use to write these paragraphs? What kind of organization did the writer use?

In the early 1800's, Stephen Austin recruited bands of men to protect the American settlers along the Brazos River from attack. This handful of mounted men, who never had uniforms or regular pay, became the legendary Texas Rangers.

The Texas Rangers were successful in keeping the peace on the frontier. They practiced riding, shooting, and tracking skills until they were experts. According to legend, they were the best fighters in all of Texas. You could say their motto was "Be prepared!"

According to a Ranger uncle of mine, the Rangers have not changed that much over the years. He still patrols and uses his own horse. He doesn't wear a particular uniform. He is proud to be part of a special group of police officers.

◆ **Mechanics in a Research Report**   The highlighted parts of this report belong to the mechanics of writing. They include capitalization and punctuation marks.

◆ **Language Focus: Mechanics Wrap-up**   The following lessons will help you polish the mechanics of English in your own writing. Not only will you learn to place commas correctly in sentences, but you will also discover how to use them in letters and in bibliography entries. You will even learn to use hyphens, dashes, and parentheses correctly.

1 Capitalization and End Punctuation in Sentences

◆ **FOCUS** Every sentence begins with a capital letter and ends with a punctuation mark.

A sentence can do the following things.

Make a statement.	**1.** We will polka tonight.
Ask a question.	**2.** Can you dance a merengue?
Give a command.	**3.** Come to the dance.
Exclaim.	**4.** Those costumes are lovely!

Link to Writing and Speaking

Questions can be direct or indirect. A direct question is an interrogative sentence and ends in a question mark. An indirect question is a declarative sentence and ends in a period.

Will he dance?
I wonder if he will dance.

Guided Practice

A. Tell whether each sentence is *declarative, interrogative, imperative,* or *exclamatory.* Tell how each sentence should end.

1. Did you know that the tango is a ballroom dance
2. The tango began in South America
3. Many people saw *Tango Argentina* when it came to America
4. Did the tour come to your city
5. To dance a tango you need special tango music
6. Get a record
7. Let's tango

B. Tell whether each sentence asks a direct or an indirect question. Tell which punctuation each one should have.

8. Have you ever seen Spanish flamenco dancing
9. Lee asked his friend how flamenco began
10. How do dancers learn the steps so easily
11. I wonder if all of the gypsies in Spain dance flamenco
12. What instruments besides the guitar accompany flamenco

THINK AND REMEMBER

- Remember that sentences can be declarative, interrogative, imperative, or exclamatory.
- Remember that a period, a question mark, or an exclamation point can end a sentence.

Independent Practice

C. Adding Punctuation to Sentences   Write the sentences. Capitalize and punctuate each one correctly. Write which kind of sentence each one is.

13. folk dances can tell stories

MODEL> Folk dances can tell stories.—declarative

14. japanese dances are especially dramatic

15. have you heard of Japanese Kabuki

16. it is a form of dance-drama that is more than three centuries old

17. in Kabuki men usually dance all the roles

18. have you ever heard the Japanese music that accompanies Kabuki

19. the instruments include flutes, gongs, drums, and a kind of banjo

20. please bring me that tape of Kabuki music

21. many art books have illustrations of Kabuki

22. what a wonderful performance that was

D. Changing Sentence Types   Change each direct question into an indirect question.

23. Can Caroline square dance?

MODEL> He'd like to know if Caroline can square dance.

24. Did you teach Fred how to do the do-si-do?

25. Can you show us how to promenade?

26. Are there any square-dance clubs in your area?

27. How many dances do you really know?

28. Is square dancing really American folk dancing?

Application — Writing, Speaking, and Listening

A Radio Commercial   Create a radio commercial to let your community know about the food and festivities in an upcoming folk festival. Use all four sentence types. Read your commercial to a classmate.

2 Commas Within Sentences

◆ **FOCUS**   A **comma** is used to separate one part of a sentence from another to make the meaning clear.

Use commas in your sentences to show a pause in thought. Commas are used in a variety of ways. First, commas are used to separate three or more words, phrases, or clauses in a series.

1. The meal, planned, cooked, and eaten, was superb!
2. I went to the dairy, to the butcher, and to the bakery.
3. I steamed fish, Yuki stir-fried vegetables, and Jim made dessert.

Second, commas are used before a coordinating conjunction that joins two simple sentences.

4. The church supper is tomorrow, and I am making Irish stew.

Third, commas are used after an introductory word or phrase. This can be a noun of direct address or a mild interjection.

5. Gustavo, do you eat octopus?   6. Oh my, this is delicious!

Finally, commas are used to set off interrupters. Interrupters are nouns of direct address, appositives, or expressions that are added to a sentence for emphasis or clarity. An interrupter can be removed from a sentence without changing the meaning of the sentence. An interrupter can be placed almost anywhere in a sentence.

7. Please, everyone, remember your belongings.
8. Jim, my best friend, will take me home.
9. In my opinion, we should make this dinner a tradition.

Guided Practice

A. Indicate where commas belong in each sentence.

1. Mexican food delicious and healthful is often based on corn.
2. Tacos tostadas and enchiladas are made with cornmeal tortillas.
3. Pedro do tamales usually contain cornmeal and meat?
4. Some Mexican dishes are spicy and other dishes are mild.
5. Red-hot chili peppers of course add necessary spice!

THINK AND REMEMBER
• Follow the rules above to use commas correctly in sentences.

Independent Practice

B. Using Commas Write each sentence. Add commas where necessary.

6. Curry a popular dish in India is very tasty.

> MODEL ▷ Curry, a popular dish in India, is very tasty.

7. Gene have you ever had food from India?
8. Rice a flat bread or a puffy bread accompanies most dishes.
9. Many Indians eat no meat and Indian vegetable dishes are especially good.
10. What people eat is after all important to them.
11. My neighbors a family from New Delhi invited me for dinner.
12. Of course we had many different dishes but very few of the flavors were familiar.
13. Indian food hot and savory has strong flavors.
14. I especially enjoyed the cucumbers in yogurt the bread stuffed with potatoes and peas and the spinach stew.

C. Proofreading: Deleting Commas Rewrite each sentence. Take out unnecessary commas.

15. Sharing foods, from different countries, is fun.

> MODEL ▷ Sharing foods from different countries is fun.

16. We had an international supper, and the turnout, was impressive.
17. Julie's mother made Swedish meatballs, and smoked herring.
18. Lin's father, made dumplings, and we helped stuff them.
19. The new German, family brought savory pig's knuckles, and cabbage.
20. Oh my, how will we ever, top this year's dinner?
21. Well, Gene, we could have a barbecue, a picnic, or a formal dinner, here.
22. This year's event, exciting and fun, will be difficult, to forget.

Application — Writing

A Description Imagine that someone from another country has asked you to describe a typical American meal. Write a description. Use commas correctly. If you need help writing a description, see page 45 of the **Writer's Handbook.**

3 Other Punctuation Within Sentences

◆ **FOCUS**   Semicolons, colons, hyphens, dashes, and parentheses are used as punctuation within sentences.

Every punctuation mark performs a specific function in a sentence. A **semicolon** joins two independent clauses to make a compound sentence.

1. Computer jobs are much alike; so are farming jobs.

Use a **colon** to set off a list of items when the list is preceded by a noun or phrase to which the list refers.

2. These people are from the following countries: India, Saudi Arabia, Jamaica, and Pakistan.

A colon is also used to separate the hour and minutes in numerals to indicate time.

3. The workday begins at 8:00.

A **hyphen** is used to separate syllables at the end of a line. A hyphen never comes at the beginning of a new line.

4. We had an extremely early appointment at the American Embassy.

A hyphen can also separate parts of compound words.

5. I bought a city map at the drive-up window.

A **dash** is used to signal a sudden break in thought.

6. We rented a European car—it was an unusual red color—to tour the region.

Parentheses are used to add an explanation of secondary importance to the sentence.

7. On any trip (and this trip was no different) anything can occur.

Guided Practice

A. Indicate where a semicolon belongs in each sentence.

1. Kimonos are a tradition in Japan both men and women wear them.
2. A kimono is long and loose it is made of cotton, silk, or rayon.
3. Around the waist is a sash this is called an *obi*.
4. Traditional Japanese shoes are sandals slippers are worn indoors.
5. Clothing for work is different suits are worn in offices.

B. Indicate where a colon belongs in each sentence.

6. Traditional farmer's clothing in the Netherlands includes these items wooden shoes, baggy trousers, and a wool cap.

7. Dutch women also have traditional clothing wooden shoes, a full skirt, an apron, and a lace cap.

8. In northern Scandinavia the Lapp women wear these items black woolen dresses with bright red borders, bright red woolen hats, and sturdy black boots.

9. Most Lapp men wear the following outer clothing black trousers, heavy flannel shirts, blue or black woolen sweaters with bright red borders, and sturdy black boots.

10. On St. Lucia's day Swedish girls wear this traditional costume white dresses, red sashes, and a crown of evergreens and candles.

THINK AND REMEMBER
- Follow the rules in the text to use semicolons, colons, hyphens, dashes, and parentheses correctly.

Independent Practice

C. Using Semicolons   Write the sentences. Add semicolons where necessary.

11. Traditional Mexican clothing is handwoven it is quite beautiful.
MODEL> Traditional Mexican clothing is handwoven; it is quite beautiful.

12. Men might wear leather sandals these are called *huaraches*.

13. A *poncho* is a blanket with a slit for the head a *serape* is a colorful blanket draped over the shoulders.

14. The covering worn by a woman is different she wears a *rebozo*.

15. For special occasions Mexicans might dress in their national costumes these are quite elegant and colorful.

16. Mexicans have a warm climate their colorful clothing suits their weather.

D. Using Colons   Write these sentences using colons correctly.

17. I expected to be at the airport at 900 in the morning, but I was late.
MODEL> I expected to be at the airport at 9:00 in the morning, but I was late.

18. To make me late, the cab driver did the following things ran out of gas, stopped for breakfast, and got stuck in traffic.

19. My desk was covered with these items mail, packages, and messages.

20. It took me until 600 P.M. to sort it all out.

21. Then I did these things ate, showered, and fell into bed.

E. Using Hyphens Break each word into syllables and insert hyphens between syllables. Use a dictionary for help.

22. Amish

MODEL> Am-ish   **25.** textiles   **28.** religious
23. parka   **26.** uniform   **29.** Mexican
24. kimono   **27.** ceremonial   **30.** national

F. Using Dashes Write these sentences using dashes correctly.

31. Mrs. Li travels with one suitcase an old, battered piece of luggage.
32. She uses a trick learned over many years to pack quickly and well.
33. Rolling things up socks, underwear, and sweaters really saves space.
34. She also packs small objects cosmetics and medication, for example, in shoes.
35. She travels widely all over Europe, in fact with the same bag.

G. Using Parentheses Write these sentences using parentheses correctly.

36. Having just returned from Scandinavia this being her first trip there , Mrs. Li has many wonderful memories.
37. The forests and lakes of Norway she says she can still see them in her mind's eye were breathtaking.
38. On one high mountain peak the natives call it *Finste,* meaning "end of the world" she saw snow in August.
39. The boat trip across the Orësund this narrow body of water separates Norway from Sweden lasted from evening to morning.
40. She shudders to remember the damp, dark passageways under the castle at Helsingborg it is thought to be the castle Hamlet owned in the Shakespearean play.

H. Proofreading: Using Various Punctuation Add semicolons, colons, hyphens, dashes, and parentheses to the following paragraph.

Last summer my family and I went to Europe on our summer vacation. We traveled to the following picturesque coun tries England, France, Spain, Portugal, Italy, and Switzerland. I really had a good time however, I did have trouble getting used to all the time changes. We left home at 300 P.M. and arrived in London at 1100 A.M. which was 600 A.M. our time. I really believe and my parents feel the same way that this was no problem. I would go back tomorrow.

Application — Writing

A Design Imagine that you have been inspired by the fashions of another country. Design an article of clothing for a boy or girl your age. Draw it and describe it in a paragraph. Use punctuation correctly.

4 Capitalization of Proper Nouns, Proper Adjectives, and *I*

◆ **FOCUS** A proper noun, a proper adjective, and the pronoun *I* are always capitalized.

The charts on this page and the next illustrate common capitalization. **Proper nouns,** which name particular persons, places, and things, are always capitalized. The pronoun *I* is also always capitalized.

	Capitalize	Don't capitalize
pronouns	*I*	all other pronouns
names, initials	Tories, I. M. Pei	political party
titles, abbreviations of titles	President Lincoln Mr. Roger Wilson, Jr.	a company president my uncle
streets, highways	New Jersey Turnpike	the avenue, the road
days, months	Tuesday, December	a month ago
seasons	(never capitalized)	summer, fall, winter
planets	Mercury, Earth	planet, solar system
events, periods	Boer War, Dark Ages	birthday, holiday, war
city, state, country, U.S. region	Jamestown, Texas, Vietnam, the South	city, state, country, continent, northern
documents	Bill of Rights	treaty, will, bylaws
natural features	Grand Canyon	canyon, desert, butte
bodies of water	Atlantic Ocean	sea, lake, river
buildings, bridges, monuments	Mount Rushmore, Lincoln Memorial	monument, dam, fort, memorial
clubs, businesses, organizations	National Park Service, Elks Club	club, university (when not part of name)
languages, races	Inuit, Asian	black, white, mestizo
religious terms	God, Bible, Quaker	a god, rules, religion

Proper adjectives are adjectives formed from proper nouns. Proper adjectives must always be capitalized.

America—American flag; China—Chinese New Year

	Some Abbreviations of Proper Nouns			
titles	Dr. Claire Stratton		Doctor	
	Mr. James Jackson, Jr.		Mister, Junior	
months	Jan.	January	Sept.	September
	Feb.	February	Nov.	November
days of the week	Mon.	Monday	Thurs.	Thursday
	Wed.	Wednesday	Fri.	Friday
addresses	St.	Street	Apt.	Apartment
	Ave.	Avenue	Mt.	Mount or Mountain
	Blvd.	Boulevard	Rte.	Route
	Rd.	Road	Dr.	Drive
businesses	Inc.	Incorporated	Co.	Company
	Corp.	Corporation	Ltd.	Limited (British)

Guided Practice

A. Identify words that should be capitalized and those that could be abbreviated.

1. The first permanent american settlement was jamestown, virginia.
2. Important leaders were captain john smith and sir thomas dale.
3. In 1619 the house of burgesses met there.
4. Visitors to jamestown today see colonial national historical park.
5. President and mistress Thomas Jefferson would be surprised to see it today.

> **THINK AND REMEMBER**
> * Begin proper nouns and proper adjectives with capital letters.
> * Use a dictionary to check correct capitalization.
> * Use a dictionary to check abbreviations.

Independent Practice

B. Capitalizing Proper Nouns and Proper Adjectives   Write each
sentence. Capitalize words correctly.

6. We visited charleston, south carolina, last year.

MODEL We visited Charleston, South Carolina, last year.

7. There we learned about the first shots fired in the american civil war.

8. It was 1861, and abraham lincoln was our president.

9. The worst battle of the war was fought in gettysburg, pennsylvania.

10. The union army defeated general robert e. lee's confederate troops.

11. At thanksgiving, president lincoln delivered the gettysburg address.

C. Writing Proper Nouns   Use this information to write proper nouns.

12. a street in your community

MODEL Main Street

13. the proper name of a building   **16.** a park in your community
14. any business organization   **17.** the principal of your school
15. a body of water in your state

D. Writing Proper Adjectives   Change each proper noun into a proper
adjective. Use the proper adjective in a sentence.

18. Italy

MODEL Italian—We went to our favorite Italian restaurant.

19. Mexico   **21.** Korea   **23.** India
20. America   **22.** France   **24.** Ireland

E. Writing Abbreviations   Abbreviate proper nouns correctly.

25. Governor Chester Bailey

MODEL Gov. Chester Bailey

26. Monday, November 6, 1990
27. Random Access Locksmith Company
28. Mount Rushmore
29. Wilshire Boulevard
30. Wednesday, March 2
31. Captain Regina Carlson

Application — Writing

A Historical Description   Think of an event that has happened in your
community that you feel future generations should know about. Describe
the event. Capitalize proper nouns and proper adjectives correctly.

5 Letters and Envelopes

The parts of a letter and the addresses on an envelope follow rules of capitalization and punctuation.

Read this letter that Fay, visiting her cousins, sent to her mother. Notice which words she capitalized and where she placed commas.

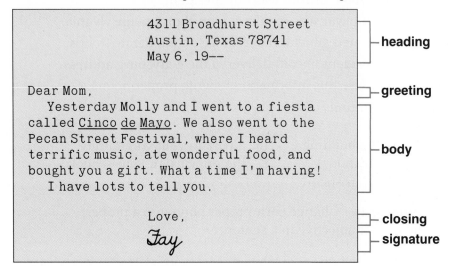

4311 Broadhurst Street
Austin, Texas 78741
May 6, 19-- — **heading**

Dear Mom, — **greeting**
    Yesterday Molly and I went to a fiesta called <u>Cinco de Mayo</u>. We also went to the Pecan Street Festival, where I heard terrific music, ate wonderful food, and bought you a gift. What a time I'm having!
    I have lots to tell you. — **body**

Love, — **closing**

Fay — **signature**

Read this business letter Fay wrote after her visit to Austin. Pay attention to the capitalization and punctuation.

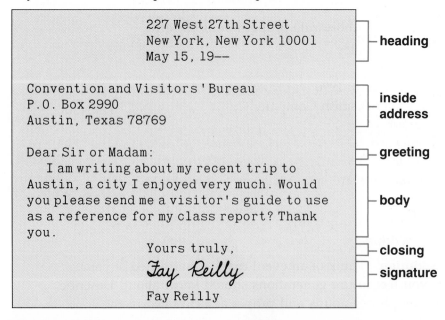

227 West 27th Street
New York, New York 10001
May 15, 19-- — **heading**

Convention and Visitors' Bureau
P.O. Box 2990
Austin, Texas 78769 — **inside address**

Dear Sir or Madam: — **greeting**
    I am writing about my recent trip to Austin, a city I enjoyed very much. Would you please send me a visitor's guide to use as a reference for my class report? Thank you. — **body**

Yours truly, — **closing**

Fay Reilly — **signature**
Fay Reilly

Look at the way Fay addressed her envelope.

```
227 West 27th St.                    return
New York, NY 10001                   address


      Convention and Visitors' Bureau    mailing
      P. O. Box 2990                      address
      Austin, TX 78769
```

Use these postal abbreviations on envelopes for your friendly and business letters.

Alabama	AL	Kentucky	KY	Ohio	OH
Alaska	AK	Louisiana	LA	Oklahoma	OK
Arizona	AZ	Maine	ME	Oregon	OR
Arkansas	AR	Maryland	MD	Pennsylvania	PA
California	CA	Massachusetts	MA	Puerto Rico	PR
Colorado	CO	Michigan	MI	Rhode Island	RI
Connecticut	CT	Minnesota	MN	South Carolina	SC
Delaware	DE	Mississippi	MS	South Dakota	SD
District of		Missouri	MO	Tennessee	TN
Columbia	DC	Montana	MT	Texas	TX
Florida	FL	Nebraska	NE	Utah	UT
Georgia	GA	Nevada	NV	Vermont	VT
Hawaii	HI	New Hampshire	NH	Virginia	VA
Idaho	ID	New Jersey	NJ	Washington	WA
Illinois	IL	New Mexico	NM	West Virginia	WV
Indiana	IN	New York	NY	Wisconsin	WI
Iowa	IA	North Carolina	NC	Wyoming	WY
Kansas	KS	North Dakota	ND		

Guided Practice

A. Identify the words that should be capitalized and where punctuation should be placed in each letter part. Name the punctuation.

1. dear mr murray
2. 2440 tipperary road
3. los angeles california 90010
4. sincerely yours
5. dear mr president
6. august 30 1991

Independent Practice

B. Writing and Punctuating Letter Parts Correctly

Write each letter part correctly. Add correct punctuation.

7. american medical association

MODEL⟩ American Medical Association

8. dear sirs   **10.** 237 east 14th street   **12.** february 28 1992

9. sincerely yours   **11.** miami florida   **13.** dear madam

C. Writing Parts of a Letter   Use this information to write parts of friendly or business letters. Use correct capitalization and punctuation.

14. Write a greeting for a letter to your aunt Belle.

MODEL⟩ Dear Aunt Belle,

15. Write a closing for a letter to your pen pal in Great Britain.

16. Write an inside address for a business letter to your principal.

17. Write a closing for a business letter to an official of your city.

18. Write a greeting for a letter to your favorite relative.

19. Write a heading for a business letter to the publisher of this book.

20. Write a greeting for a business letter to the President of the United States.

21. Write your return address as it would appear on an envelope.

Application—Writing

A Business Letter   Write a letter to your local automobile club requesting maps and informational brochures on sightseeing and on hotel accommodations. Be sure to mention where you plan to travel. Capitalize and punctuate your letter correctly. If you need help writing a business letter, see page 60 of the **Writer's Handbook.**

6 Titles

◆ **FOCUS** The title of a written work follows rules of capitalization and punctuation.

As in proper nouns, most important words in titles are capitalized. When you write titles, do not capitalize short or unimportant words unless they occur at the beginning of the title.

1. My father read *Our Town*.   **2.** I read *The Hobbit*.

In most books and publications, titles are printed in italics. Italics are slanted letters. If you are writing or typing, underline titles.

Use underlining or italics with the following kinds of titles:

Books	*The Captive*	*Indian Chiefs*
Magazines	*National Geographic*	*Penny Power*
Newspapers	*Los Angeles Times*	*Atlanta Constitution*
Plays	*Peter Pan*	*Fences*
Movies	*Who Framed Roger Rabbit*	*E.T.*
TV series	*The Cosby Show*	*Masterpiece Theatre*
Works of art	*Starry Night*	*Pietà*
Musical pieces	*Moonlight Sonata*	*An American in Paris*
Planes, trains, ships	*Spirit of St. Louis*, *Andrea Doria*	*Sunset Limited*, *Apollo 12*

Write the titles of short works or parts of longer works in quotation marks.

Short stories	"The Disappearing Man"	"The Necklace"
Poems	"The Raven"	"Foul Shot"
Songs	"Songbird"	"Maria"
Articles	"I Hate Mornings"	"Drought Worsens"
Book chapters	"Childhood"	"Westward Ho!"

Guided Practice

A. Identify which words should be capitalized and underlined or capitalized and placed in quotation marks.

1. We went to see indiana jones and the temple of doom last night.
2. I read the poem annabel lee in class.
3. My parents have the washington post delivered to our house.
4. The sinking of the titanic is still discussed today.
5. Do you like the old phantom of the opera or the new one?

Independent Practice

B. Writing Titles   Rewrite each sentence. Capitalize and punctuate correctly.

6. In a recent issue of traveler, I read about the museums of Europe.

MODEL⟩ In a recent issue of Traveler, I read about the museums of Europe.

7. If I go to the Louvre, I'll see the discus thrower.

8. When my parents were in Milan, they heard the opera madama butterfly.

9. Mom recently read an article in the theater section of the new york times.

10. It discussed the new musical called chess.

11. At school we heard a recording of Martin Luther King's i have a dream speech.

12. In our history books we read a chapter called the new technology.

13. A song called new wave is all electronic music.

14. The concorde provides a look at transportation of the future.

15. What can we expect when a poem is entitled television?

C. Writing Sentences with Titles   Use the information below to write sentences. Capitalize and punctuate correctly.

16. a favorite musical composition

MODEL⟩ My first piano recital piece was Tarantella.

17. a movie	**22.** a newspaper
18. a song	**23.** a work of art
19. a poem	**24.** a play or musical
20. a book	**25.** a television show
21. a plane or train	**26.** a magazine

Application — Writing

A Summary   Write a critical opinion of a book, movie, play, television show, or record album. Include an evaluation and support for your opinion. You may add a recommendation if you wish. Write your titles correctly.

7 Outlines and Bibliographies

◆ **FOCUS**   An outline and a bibliography follow rules of capitalization and punctuation.

A **topic outline** organizes main ideas and details. Roman numerals indicate main topics; capital letters indicate subtopics; and Arabic numerals indicate supporting details. Outline titles should be centered at the top of the page. The first letter of each topic or subtopic is capitalized.

I.
  A.
  B.
    1.
    2.
II.

Here is the beginning of an outline on the history of Texas.

I. Early explorations of Texas
   A. Sixteenth-century exploration by the Spanish
      1. Alonso Álvarez de Piñeda
      2. Alvar Núñez Cabeza de Vaca
      3. Francisco Vásquez de Coronado
      4. Hernando de Soto
   B. Sixteenth-century exploration by others

A **bibliography** gives information about sources used in a research report. A source may be a book, magazine article, or encyclopedia entry. As you do your research, record each bibliography entry on a separate index card. Pay special attention to placement of commas, periods, colons, quotation marks, and underlining.

Book

Hagan, William T. <u>American Indians in Texas</u>. Chicago: University of Chicago Press, 1961.

Place a comma between the author's last name and first name and between the publisher's name and the year of publication. Underline the title of the book. Insert a colon after the place of publication. Indent every line after the first line.

Magazine Article

LaFay, Howard. "Texas!" <u>National Geographic</u>, 157 (1980): 440–483.

Place a comma between the author's last name and first name. The title of the article is in quotation marks. The name of the magazine in which the article appears is underlined. Commas separate the name of the magazine from the information naming the volume, volume number, date of publication, and page numbers. Place periods after abbreviations. Place a colon after the year of publication.

Encyclopedia Entry

Frantz, Joe B., and others. "Texas History." <u>World Book Encyclopedia</u>, Vol. 19, pp. 161–164. Chicago: World Book–Childcraft International, 1980.

Place a comma between the author's last name and first name and before "and others." If there is no author, begin with the title of the article. Put the title of the article in quotation marks. Underline the name of the encyclopedia. Identify the volume and the page numbers. Identify the place of publication and put a colon after it; then give the name of the publishing company followed by a comma and the year of publication.

Guided Practice

A. Add this information to the outline on the previous page. Identify where each heading should be placed. Name the appropriate capitalization and punctuation.

1. II settlement of Texas by the Spanish a spanish
   missions established b forts built to guard
   missions c san Antonio became seat of Spanish government

B. Use the bibliography information to answer these questions.

2. In a bibliography, how is the title of a book, magazine, or encyclopedia identified?
3. How is the title of a magazine article or encyclopedia entry identified?
4. Where does the publisher's location go in a bibliography entry for a book?
5. Where do you write the date of publication for a magazine?
6. Where do authors' names appear in a bibliography?

THINK AND REMEMBER

♦ Follow the rules in the text to make outlines and bibliographies.

Independent Practice

C. Completing an Outline   Use this information to complete the outline on the history of Texas. Use correct capitalization and punctuation.

7. III texas part of Mexican empire in 1824 a good Mexican-American relations b american colony thrives 1 stephen f. Austin organizer 2 mexicans fear increasing number of americans IV texas revolution for independence 1835–1836 a battle of the Alamo b battle of San Jacinto

D. Writing Bibliography Entries   Write bibliography entries from the following information.

8. Book title: America
   Publisher: Alfred A. Knopf
   Place: New York
   Date: 1973
   Author: Alistair Cooke
9. Title: The Real Texas
   Magazine: Texas Monthly, Vol. 7, no. 8
   Date: August 1987
   Pages: 26–29
   Author: Marlene Flowers
10. Title: Texas Economy
    Book: World Book Encyclopedia, Vol. 19, pp. 175–180
    Place: Chicago
    Date: 1984
    Author: none
    Publisher: World Book–Childcraft International

Application—Writing

A Research Topic   Write an outline and bibliography cards for a subject of your choice. Make a bibliography card for three different types of sources. Write one for a biography, one for a magazine article, and one for an encyclopedia article. Trade with a classmate to proofread each other's outlines and cards.

8 Direct Quotations and Dialogue

♦ **FOCUS** A **direct quotation** follows rules of capitalization, and quotation marks are used to indicate a speaker's exact words.

When a speaker's exact words are written, they are enclosed in quotation marks. Quotation marks are placed before and after continuously quoted material, except for long quotations, which are set off as blocks of text. Always place a period inside closing quotation marks.

1. Midge said, "Danny, you and your father have the same sense of humor."
2. "Oh, no, you can't mean that," Danny replied.

A direct quotation can be divided into parts. When the quotation continues, begin the second part with a lowercase letter.

3. "Danny," Midge said, "you and your father have the same sense of humor."

When a quotation is divided but the continuation begins with a new sentence, begin that sentence with a capital letter.

4. "Oh, no, you can't mean that," Danny replied. "I have never thought so."

When a quotation contains several sentences that are not interrupted, use one set of quotation marks.

5. "In what other ways are we alike? Do we have the same nose, eyes, chin, and hairline?" Danny inquired.

When a quotation ends with an exclamation point or question mark, the end punctuation is placed inside the quotation marks unless the sentence containing the quotation is itself the question or exclamation.

6. Danny asked, "How long have you been aware of our similarities?"
7. Was Danny's actual statement "You can't mean that"?

A quotation that is a declarative or imperative statement can be set off from the rest of a sentence with commas.

8. "Don't laugh," said Midge, chuckling.

An indirect quotation gives information about what another person said. It does not use the person's exact words. No quotation marks are used in indirect quotations.

9. Midge told Danny that he resembled his father.

Dialogue is a conversation between two or more people. When you write a dialogue, begin a new paragraph every time the speaker changes.

Guided Practice

A. Tell how each sentence should be written.

1. my sister has a special talent for music said Marie.
2. arnold asked does she play an instrument
3. well said Marie she plays the piano. Her real talent, though, is singing.
4. oh replied Arnold does she sing in a regular group?
5. yes she does answered Marie proudly she is the lead soprano in our city chorus.

> **THINK AND REMEMBER**
> ◆ Follow the rules in the text to punctuate dialogue.

Independent Practice

B. Writing Dialogue   Write the sentences as direct quotations.

6. Mr. Lee said an aptitude is a special talent.

MODEL⟩ Mr. Lee said, "An aptitude is a special talent."

7. He explained perhaps someone paints well or can fix things well.
8. Often Mr. Lee added an aptitude is inherited.
9. Well Marc said why am I the only one in my family who can't sing?
10. Mr. Lee answered an aptitude isn't necessarily passed on. In fact, even if it is, aptitude also depends on environment.
11. Marc asked Mr. Lee what do you mean by environment.
12. Did you hear Liane said Mr. Lee say that environment is everything around us—home, community, and school?

Application — Writing

A Dialogue   Write an imagined dialogue in which you and a classmate discuss the special talents of two of your classmates. Use direct quotations correctly.

Building Vocabulary
History of Words

You might find the history of words interesting. Some words we use today are words from other languages that remain unchanged. *Chipmunk, squash,* and *Miami* are Indian words. Look at this dictionary entry. It shows the **etymology,** or history, of the word *hamburger.*

ham·burg·er (ham′bûr′gər) *n.* **1** Ground beef. **2** A sandwich made with a broiled or fried patty of this meat. (from German)

Hamburg is a large city in Germany, and perhaps the hamburger originated there. As you begin studying the etymology of words, why not start with food names? You might be surprised at the food names that come from other languages.

We know that English has also been influenced by people. For example, the word *sandwich* comes from England. It described the meal the Earl of Sandwich often ate—meat between slices of bread.

Read the charts. They list English words and names and their origins.

English Words Derived from Other Languages			
English Word	**Place of Origin**	**English Word**	**Place of Origin**
ballet	France	novel	Italy
banana	Africa	ranch	Spain
boomerang	Australia	ski	Norway
coach	Hungary	slogan	Scotland
kindergarten	Germany	tomato	Mexico

Words from People's Names		
Word	**Name**	**Place of Origin**
sideburn	Ambrose Burnside	United States
Ferris wheel	George Ferris	United States
maverick	Samuel Maverick	United States

Reading Practice

Read the selection. Match each underlined word with the correct etymology. Use the list. Write the word and the letter of the etymology after it.

a. Greek for "black"
b. Greek for "to lose control"
c. English for "artistic"
d. English for "from the friendly field"
e. Spanish for "a place where horses are raised"
f. Spanish that names a kind of horse
g. French for "an open area of grass"

The mustang was one of the wildest horses on the ranch. Emily knew this, but she insisted on trying to tame him. She even named him Winfield in the hope that he would take after his name. His color, a rich ebony, added to his stature.

Today they would go for their first ride. When she opened the gate, Winfield charged. Emily was calm. She didn't panic. She quickly slammed the gate shut.

Emily worked all day. By sundown, Emily and her mustang were riding across the prairie.

Writing Practice

Write a story using English words taken from French and Spanish. You may use a foreign language dictionary and any French and Spanish words in the charts in the lesson. In your story describe a heroic event that could have taken place in the United States. The information below will help you get started. Your story can be as long as you wish.

Josh was riding home to his _____ with his _____ when suddenly his horse began to buck. At first, _____. Then, _____.

Project

Work in pairs to make a word map with English words taken from foreign languages. Use a dictionary to help you find your words. Create one large map. You may want to begin with words from Italy, England, Germany, France, Greece, and Spain.

Language Enrichment
Mechanics

Use what you have learned about the mechanics of English to do these activities.

 Comma Commotion

Someone at the Sentence Factory spilled a box of commas into the sentence-making machine. Help workers repair the damage by copying the following sentences. Remove all the *unnecessary* commas.

1. She leaped, from the window, overlooking the garden and, darting among the guests, escaped through the open gate.

2. Many animals, such as beaver, mink, and muskrat, have become known to Europeans, only through their beautiful pelts.

3. "Open this door immediately, Daughter," he thundered, beating on the innocent wood, with his pipe.

4. Observe a boy, who is a slow runner, such as Chuck or James, and someone, who is a fast runner, such as, Paulie.

5. Why, do you think, all of the guests, have gone, when, to listen to them talking, one would have been convinced of their intention to stay?

 Inquiring Reporter

Do research for a possible report about the heritage of Americans by interviewing five of your classmates. Ask each one, "What's the best thing about being an American?" Write a direct quotation from each person. Write the question and the five responses on a sheet of paper. If possible, include a photograph of each person you interview. Display the interviews in the classroom or compile them into a classroom booklet.

Says Who?

Uh-oh! It looks as if we are about to have a classic Old West duel. Work in a small group. Write a dialogue between two characters from the Old West. You can determine the situation and the characters. Then choose two members of your group to read the dialogue aloud to the class.

CONNECTING

In this unit you learned many of the mechanics of writing. Knowing how to use capitalization at the beginning and punctuation at the end of a sentence as well as within the sentence will help you make your writing clearer for your readers.

◆ **Using Correct Mechanics in Your Writing** Knowing what forms to use for letters, outlines, and bibliographies will help you develop your communication and research skills. Pay special attention to the mechanics of English when you do these activities.

 ### Pen in Hand

You and your friends want the right to sell handmade merchandise at your school's fall festival. You decide to write a letter to the chairperson. In your letter, state your request and describe your merchandise. Since the chairperson is a classmate and friend, you don't know whether you should write a friendly letter or a business letter. Write two letters. Pay attention to the mechanics and tone. Then choose one of the letters to "send." Choose a classmate to act as a chairperson. He or she will write back to you in the same format as your letter, granting or denying your request.

 ### The Name's the Thing

On the **Building Vocabulary** pages, you learned about word origins. Often, names have an original meaning that is significant. For example, the name *Pedro* means "rock" and the name *Fletcher* means "arrow-maker." Your name may also have an interesting meaning. From what language did it come? Do research to find out. Then compile a class list of names and their meanings.

I hope I find a Margaret in this oyster.

Unit Checkup

Think Back	Think Ahead
◆ What did you learn about a research report in this unit?	◆ How will what you learned about a research report help you when you read a researched article or book? ◆ How will connecting cause and effect help you when you write a research report?
◆ Look at the writing you did in this unit. How did mechanics help you express your ideas?	◆ What is one way you can use mechanics to improve your writing?

Analyzing a Research Report   *pages 410 – 411*

Write the answer to each question.

1. What part of a research report develops the main ideas?
2. How are the title and the introduction different?
3. How are the title and the introduction similar?
4. How are the conclusion and the introduction similar?

Connecting Cause and Effect   *pages 412 – 413*

Chart the causes and effects in these statements.

5. She called home late at night and awakened her father.
6. Our move to Albuquerque was brought on by the noise, crowds, and pollution in New York City.
7. I was hungry, so I went into the kitchen.
8. Having used the Writing Process, I find my writing has improved.

Using Formal and Informal Language   *page 414*

Rewrite a formal language sentence as an informal sentence, and vice-versa. Use a thesaurus if necessary.

9. If you don't keep quiet, you're going to be in trouble!

10. What a fortunate coincidence that we met at the music club!
11. Give me a ring when you're ready, and I'll pick you up.
12. Without having had extensive training, he still sang well.

The Writing Process   *pages 415 – 425*
Write the letter of the answer to each question.

13. When you plan a research report, what should you do first?
    a. Limit your subject.   b. Do research.   c. Create a bibliography.
14. If you choose too difficult a topic, what should you do?
    a. Consider another topic from your original list.
    b. Find another resource book.
    c. Seek help in reading the information.
15. What advantage is there in creating a question that a research report
    will answer?
    a. It gives a purpose to your report.
    b. It shows that you have been thinking about the topic.
    c. It provides material for a conclusion.
16. Suppose you are organizing your information, and you realize you
    need more. What should you do?
    a. Change your outline to omit that topic.
    b. Do more research.
    c. Try to get along without it.

Capitalization and End Punctuation in
Sentences   *pages 428 – 429*
Write the sentences. Capitalize and punctuate
each one correctly.

17. let's go to the slide show about Iceland
18. everyone has asked for a repeat show
19. have you met the new Icelandic student
20. we asked which island Jean came from
21. did you find the island on the world map

Commas Within Sentences   *pages 430 – 431*
Write each sentence. Add commas where necessary.

22. Florence what do you know about Florence Italy?
23. That city a beautiful one has some wonderful art.
24. Classical sculpture unlike modern art is often
    found in churches as well as in museums.

25. Florence's family named her after the city for they have family in Florence.
26. Florence her brother and her sister will visit there.

Other Punctuation Within Sentences

pages 432 – 434

Write the sentences. Add a semicolon, colon, hyphen, or parentheses as needed.

27. My aunt styles long hair she makes braids.
28. I'll see her at 400, when she'll braid my hair.
29. At the recital my sister in law will play the piano.
30. The recital an annual tradition at the school highlights the dances of other countries.

Capitalization of Proper Nouns, Proper Adjectives, and *I* *pages 435 – 437*

Write each sentence. Capitalize words correctly.

31. On tuesday there is a speaker at carnegie library.
32. Next week she will talk about france.
33. The library is on carnegie avenue.
34. The speaker, miss lopez, appears every week.
35. She will describe french monuments.

Letters and Envelopes *pages 438–440*

Write each letter part correctly. Add correct punctuation.

36. yours truly
37. march 5 1989
38. dear miss jones
39. new york, new york
40. dear sir
41. dear mel

Titles *pages 441 – 442*

Rewrite each sentence. Use capitalization, punctuation, and underlining correctly.

42. My favorite magazine is national geographic.
43. Have you read the play othello?
44. I saw the movie raiders of the lost ark.
45. Look at the headline in the new york times.
46. She's taking the crescent, an Amtrak train, from New York to Chicago.

Outlines and Bibliographies   *pages 443 – 445*

Use the information on writing a research report to complete this section of an outline correctly.

47. I prewrite
    a brainstorm and select a topic
    b organize information
    1 make a cluster diagram of possibilities
    2 use a chart to divide the subject into parts

Write a bibliography entry with this information.

48. Book title: A Wider World
    Publisher: Harper & Row Perennial Library
    Place: New York
    Date: 1986
    Author: Kate Simon

Direct Quotations and Dialogue   *pages 446 – 447*

Write the sentences as direct quotations.

49. are you ready shirley asked.
50. when are we leaving Zach asked.
51. The last bus Shirley said leaves at 4:00.
52. I wonder said Zach if your dad will meet the bus.
53. Knowing my dad Shirley laughed he certainly will!

History of Words   *pages 448 – 449*

Match each underlined word with the correct etymology below. Write the word and the letter of its etymology.

54. Years after my grandmother came to America, her underline{tenacious} efforts to learn English paid off.

55. She got a job in a Hungarian underline{restaurant}.

56. Sometimes the customers would underline{gesticulate} when describing what they wanted to eat.

57. Every evening my grandmother would underline{cycle} home.
    a. a French word that means "a place to get refreshed"
    b. a Latin word that means "to make gestures"
    c. a Greek word that means "to go round and round"
    d. a Latin word that means "held fast"

1-9 Cumulative Review

Simple, Compound, and Complex Sentences

pages 32–33, 42–43, 384–385

Write *simple*, *compound*, or *complex* to identify each sentence.

1. Although many heroes are famous, not all are.
2. People do heroic things every day, and nobody even knows about it.
3. Imagine a child about to run into a street full of traffic.
4. If someone grabs that child, perhaps the child's life has been saved.
5. Do you consider the person a hero?

Avoiding Sentence Fragments and Run-on Sentences *pages 44–45*

Write whether each group of words is a *fragment*, a *run-on sentence*, or a *sentence*. Rewrite the fragments and run-on sentences to correct the errors.

6. Do you judge a book by its cover?
7. Usually not a good way.
8. Sometimes buying a book.
9. Children's books especially.
10. Bright pictures on the cover.
11. I enjoy reading with my little sister she can only
    look at the pictures.

Kinds of Nouns *pages 78–79*

Write each noun. After each, write *common* or *proper*.

12. Marissa and her family went to the Ringling Brothers Circus.
13. The family drove there in their new station wagon.
14. Marissa, her parents, and her eight brothers and sisters
    live in the green house on Austin Boulevard.
15. When the Joneses left their car in the Keystone Parking Lot,
    they erupted into laughter.
16. The Joneses felt like a parade of clowns getting out of a car!

Possessive Nouns *pages 90–91*

Label each noun *singular possessive* or *plural possessive*.

17. scripts'	**19.** pageants'	**21.** bushels'	**23.** erasers'	**25.** cat's
18. tweezers'	**20.** hermit's	**22.** comets'	**24.** gazelle's	**26.** dogs'

Verbs   *pages 126–127*
Write the verb. Write *action* or *linking* after it.

27. Courtney has become a fine photographer.
28. Her family gave her a camera for her birthday last year.
29. She takes excellent black-and-white photographs.
30. Soon she learned developing and enlarging at college.
31. As a part-time job, Courtney takes photographs at weddings.

Irregular Verbs   *pages 132–136*
Write *present, present participle, past,* or *past participle* after each verb form.

32. done	**36.** seen	**40.** given	**44.** drive
33. being	**37.** knew	**41.** brought	**45.** went
34. eaten	**38.** is	**42.** freeze	**46.** running
35. catches	**39.** swum	**43.** worn	

Subject-Verb Agreement   *pages 144–145*
Write the correct form of the verb in parentheses ( ).

47. Someone (has, have) bought the winning ticket.
48. Our library raffle and our bake sale (raise, raises) funds.
49. This time Fred and Anna (is, are) running the events.
50. Everybody (know, knows) the effort involved.
51. Some (draw, draws) posters for the sale.
52. Most (sell, sells) raffle tickets.
53. Marcie and I (has, have) sold four books of tickets!

Direct and Indirect Objects   *pages 178–181*
Write each sentence. Underline the direct object once and the indirect object twice.

54. The shapes of clouds usually give me ideas for pictures.
55. I gave my sister this photograph of a cloud in the sky.
56. She showed me a cloud that looked like a unicorn with a flowing tail.
57. We showed our classmates the same photograph.
58. They told us their interpretations of the formations.
59. "These clouds show me the shape of a cow," said Yoko.
60. Ron wrote us a long list of animals and objects.
61. Our teachers, too, gave Marsha and me their impressions.
62. We made ourselves a chart of the responses.

Pronouns and Antecedents   *pages 226–227*

Write the correct pronoun in parentheses ( ) that completes each sentence. Be sure the pronoun agrees with the antecedent.

63. Taro went on a camping trip last summer with (his, its) scout troop.
64. When Taro visited me, he was very talkative about (his, its) trip.
65. "What was the high point of (your, his) trip?" I asked.
66. He said that (his, our) group experienced an emergency.
67. The counselors had to rush a boy to a hospital because (he, they) had suffered an attack of appendicitis.
68. (They, He) left Taro in charge of the group.
69. Taro's reassuring leadership showed a part of (his, their) character that he had not demonstrated before.

Subject and Object Pronouns   *pages 228–229*

Write the pronoun in each sentence. Write *subject* or *object* to indicate what type of pronoun it is.

70. Marty Tran spoke to us in assembly last week.
71. His family brought him to the United States from Vietnam.
72. They sailed from Vietnam to Thailand in a fishing boat.
73. Marty has a Vietnamese name, but he prefers the name Marty.
74. Hearing from him about the dangers of the trip, the students were shocked.
75. Huge waves and terrible winds tossed the tiny fishing boat and almost sank it.
76. When Marty was finished, the audience gave him a huge round of applause for telling the story so well.

Indefinite Pronouns   *pages 236–237*

Write the verb that agrees with each indefinite pronoun.

77. Anyone can (write, writes) poetry.
78. If anyone (ask, asks) about it, we share it.
79. Many (is, are) reluctant to show their poetry.
80. When someone (share, shares) personal writing, a response is important.
81. If anyone (like, likes) something in a poem, he or she should be specific when talking about it.
82. One also (do, does) a writer a favor by pointing out weak spots that might be made stronger.
83. If anyone (help, helps) you, she or he should be thanked.

Comparisons with Adjectives and Adverbs   *pages 276–277, 285–287*

Make three columns: *Positive, Comparative,* and *Superlative.* List each form in its correct column. Complete all three columns for each word.

84. badly
85. thoughtful
86. well
87. joyfully
88. further
89. lovely
90. more politely
91. secretive
92. tired
93. much
94. awful
95. more lovingly
96. most enjoyably
97. less kindly
98. badly
99. least sincerely
100. powerful
101. reddest
102. thorough
103. late

Prepositional Phrases   *pages 322–323*

Write the sentences. Underline the prepositional phrases. Draw an arrow to the words they modify.

104. Newspapers are delivered to the homes of many people.

105. Perhaps in the future their computers will display the daily news.

106. More and more people are using computers in their homes.

107. In schools students become skillful computer operators.

108. At this moment people are using computers for airline reservations.

109. Across the country furniture stores are selling designer computer desks.

110. My mother and father have been banking by computer.

111. I could send homework to my teacher electronically.

112. Without any problem I could receive the lessons I had missed.

113. What new computer will arrive on the scene?

114. Scientists' minds race with energy when they consider the possibilities!

Adjective and Adverb Phrases   *pages 325 – 328*

Write the sentences. Draw one line under the prepositional phrases that act as adjectives or adverbs. Draw two lines under the word or words each modifies. Write *adjective phrase* or *adverb phrase* to identify the underlined prepositional phrase.

115. Can you imagine cars of the year 2020?
116. Will they run on gasoline?
117. A car powered by the sun already exists.
118. Perhaps manufacturers will put electric engines in cars.
119. Will a battery-powered car run for years?
120. Conserving the energy in the world remains a challenge.
121. Will gasoline engines become things of the past?
122. New cars seem smaller in size each year.
123. Most large cars use a lot of fuel.
124. If the cost of fuel goes down, will cars of the future be larger?
125. People are safer in large cars.
126. In the next century cars will protect riders more effectively.

Conjunctions and Interjections   *pages 331 – 335*

Write the sentences. Add an interjection. Try not to repeat the same interjections. Underline the conjunctions.

127. Are you busy with something now, or are you free?
128. I was thinking about my future, and I'd like advice.
129. What are the pros and cons of going to college?
130. How can I find out about universities and colleges?
131. Perhaps I won't get in anywhere, but at least I will try.

Adjective and Adverb Clauses   *pages 386 – 387*

Write the subordinate clause. Write *adverb clause* or *adjective clause* to identify it.

132. My brother wants to be a veterinarian when he is older.
133. He has loved animals since we had our first dog.
134. As he learns more about animals, John becomes even more determined.

135. John, who is an excellent student, will probably succeed.
136. He works with animals when he is not in school.
137. Since he hopes to go to veterinary school, John has applied to three good schools.
138. Even if he does not gain admission, John will work with animals.
139. Someone who is as determined as John does not give up.

Misplaced Modifiers *pages 388 – 389*
Write the sentences. Correct and clarify misplaced modifiers. The sentences can be written several ways. Add words and punctuation if necessary.

140. The child swam too far out in the blue swimsuit.
141. The lifeguard saw the struggling child sitting on her lifeguard chair.
142. Jumping to the rescue which was filled with swimmers, she ran into the water.
143. Using her techniques fortunately, the lifeguard saved the child.
144. The mother could not thank the lifeguard enough watching the rescue.

Participles, Gerunds, and Infinitives *pages 390 – 395*
Write each sentence. Underline the participles, gerunds, and infinitives. Identify what each is.

145. I have to hurry!
146. Larry, waiting for us patiently, felt cold.
147. Having a treasure hunt is fun.
148. This is an ideal way to spend an afternoon!
149. It is also a great way to get to know your class.
150. Planning this picnic was fun too.
151. Half of our classmates made an illustrated map for the other half.
152. We have been studying mapmaking in school.
153. I wonder what buried treasure awaits us.
154. The treasure-seekers, waiting to begin the hunt, talked excitedly.
155. I'd like to do this more often.
156. Even losing will be fun.

STUDY SKILLS

Contents

1 Finding Words in a Dictionary

A **dictionary** is a reference book that lists words, along with their definitions, their pronunciations, and sometimes their origins. The words in a dictionary are listed in **alphabetical order** from *A* to *Z*. Words that begin with the same letter are arranged according to their second letter. If the first two letters are the same, then the third letter is used, and so on through the last letter.

racket   reckon   reference   robin   robot   rutabaga

One way to use the dictionary quickly is to think of the alphabet as divided into three parts, like this.

front: abcde   middle: fghijklmnop   back: qrstuvwxyz

Words beginning with *a* through *e* will be in the front of the dictionary; *f* through *p* will be in the middle; and *q* through *z* will be in the back.

Each word listed in the dictionary is called an **entry word. Guide words** at the top of each page help you find the entry word you want. The guide word at the top left shows the first entry word on that page. The one at the top right shows the last entry word on the page. All the entry words on the page appear in alphabetical order between them.

guide words

entry word

pitch-dark   place

pitch-dark [pich′därk′] *adj.*   **piv·ot** [piv′ət]   **1** *n.* Something, as a
   Extremely dark.   pin or short shaft, on which a part
pitch·er[pich′ər] *n.*   **1** A container   turns: The needle of a compass
with a handle and either a lip or   rests on a *pivot.*
spout, used for holding liquids.

Some entry words are made up of more than one word. These words are **compound words.** Sometimes a compound word has a hyphen, as in *pitch-dark.* Sometimes it is written as one word, as in *pitchfork.* Sometimes it is written as two separate words, as in *pitch pipe.*

Practice

Write these words in alphabetical order. Underline those found on a page with the guide words *scoot* and *screaming.*

1. scope, scoot, spare
   MODEL⟩ scoot, scope, spare
2. scour, scare, scout
3. simple, scrape, scrap
4. scrawl, scrawny, soon
5. salamander, salad, salt
6. simmer, scream, scuttle
7. scoundrel, scrod, scholar
8. scow, sentence, scraper
9. soothe, soft, sew
10. Scottie, sound, scratch
11. scrapbook, scrappy, script
12. scowl, scoot, sort
13. seem, seam, scoreboard
14. seahorse, scale, soft-shoe
15. Scotland Yard, scrub, scuba

2 Using a Dictionary Entry

A dictionary gives a great deal of information about each word entry. One type of information is the **definition,** or the meaning, of the word. Words with **multiple meanings** appear in numbered lists. The most common meaning is given first, followed by the next most common, and so on.

> **pine¹** [pīn] *n.* **1** Any of a number of trees bearing cones and needle-shaped evergreen leaves in clusters. **2** The wood of any of these trees.
> **pine²** [pīn] *v.* **pined, pin·ing** **1** To grow thin or weak, as with longing or grief: The imprisoned captive *pined* away. **2** To have great desire or longing: to *pine* for one's homeland.

Some dictionaries give **example sentences** to show how a word may be used. In the entry above, the example sentence is *The imprisoned captive* pined *away.*

When two words have different meanings but are spelled the same, they are called **homographs.** Dictionaries list these words as two separate entries, followed by numbers. The model above shows *pine* as a homograph.

Dictionaries also tell what **part of speech** a word is. Notice the abbreviation *n.* in the first meaning for *pine.* This means the word is a *noun.* The homograph is followed by *v.,* which stands for *verb.* A key at the beginning of the dictionary explains the abbreviations for the parts of speech.

If a word has two spellings, or **variant spellings,** both should be listed. The entry will also tell you whether a word's spelling changes as its use changes. Here is an example of an entry for a variant spelling.

> **pin·ey** [pī′nē] *adj.* **pin·i·er, pin·i·est**
> Another spelling of PINY.

Finally, a dictionary entry may give the **etymology,** or history, of a word as well as information about whether it is **standard usage, informal usage,** or **slang.**

Practice

Use the entry for *piney,* above, to write answers to these questions.

1. What phrase illustrates the second meaning of **pine²**?
   MODEL〉 *to* pine *for one's homeland*
2. What is the more common meaning of **pine¹**?
3. How do you know what part of speech the second meaning of **pine¹** is?
4. Are any variant spellings given? How do you know?
5. What is the less common meaning of **pine¹**?

3 Using a Dictionary for Pronunciation

One way in which a dictionary is useful is in helping you to pronounce words correctly. Study this model entry word.

> **dem·o·li·tion** [dem′ə·lish′ən] *n.* The act or result of demolishing; destruction.

A **phonetic respelling**, which shows how a word is pronounced, appears after most entry words. In a phonetic respelling, each sound is represented by a letter or symbol. A **pronunciation key,** like the one shown below, is used to interpret the symbols in the phonetic respelling. This key usually appears on alternate pages of the dictionary.

a	add	i	it	o͝o	took	oi	oil
ā	ace	ī	ice	o͞o	pool	ou	pout
â	care	o	odd	u	up	ng	ring
ä	palm	ō	open	û	burn	th	thin
e	end	ô	order	yo͞o	fuse	th	this
ē	equal					zh	vision

ə = { a in *above*   e in *sicken*   i in *possible*
      o in *melon*   u in *circus*

The phonetic respelling also shows the **syllabication,** or divisions, of each entry word. A **syllable** is a word part that has only one vowel sound. A dot or a space is usually used to separate the syllables in a word.

Finally, the phonetic respelling shows where the **accents,** or stresses, are in a word. In *demolition*, the primary accent, or main stress, is on the third syllable; the secondary accent is on the first syllable. A syllable with a primary accent is pronounced with more force than one with a secondary accent.

Practice

Look up these words. Write answers to the questions below.

librarian   radiology   crustacean   sophisticated

1. Which words have five syllables?

    MODEL⟩ sophisticated, radiology

2. In which word is the primary accent on the third syllable?

3. Which phonetic respelling contains the symbol /â/?

4. Write the phonetic respelling for *crustacean*.

5. Which words have both primary and secondary accents?

6. Which word ends in /jē/?

7. Which word has the same pattern of accented syllables as *gymnasium*?

4 Using a Title Page, a Copyright Page, a Table of Contents, and an Appendix

The first few pages of a book give a great deal of information about its contents and organization. The **title page,** for example, lists the title, author, publisher, and city in which the book was published.

The **copyright page** tells when the book was first published. It also gives the date of the latest printing so readers know how up-to-date it is. The copyright page may also list the titles of other books from which material was reproduced by permission.

The **table of contents** lists each unit, chapter, or story in the order in which it appears in the book. If the book is made up of chapters, the table of contents will list each **chapter title.** It will also list the **page number** on which each chapter begins.

Sometimes a nonfiction book includes an **appendix** at the back. This may contain maps, charts, diagrams, and tables that could not conveniently be placed in the body of the book. Statistics found in the appendix could be valuable for writing a detailed paper or a research report.

PIONEER OF FREEDOM A Biography of Harriet Tubman by Moses Robinson Bedrock Publications Chicago, Boston	Copyright © 1986 by Bedrock Publications, Boston, MA Acknowledgments Noteworthy Books, "Bright Song," from *African Folk Songs,* ed. by John Davies Printed in the United States of America	**CONTENTS** The Child .... 1 Growing Up .... 14 Lessons Learned ... 25 The First Step ..... 33 "The Old Man" ..... 75 Appendix A: The Civil War ....115 Appendix B: The War Ends .... 120 Index 144
title page	**copyright page**	**table of contents**

Practice

Use the model pages to write answers to these questions.

1. Which page shows when and where *Pioneer of Freedom* was published?

   MODEL▷ the copyright page

2. Which two pages give the name of the publisher?
3. How would you learn the name of a book's author?
4. What information appears in the table of contents?
5. Which sections contain charts, tables, and diagrams?
6. From which book did the publisher borrow a song?

5 Using Footnotes, a Bibliography, and an Index

The title page, the copyright page, and the table of contents tell what a book contains and how it is organized, but other parts tell where the information comes from. For example, if you read that 50 inches of rain fell in Tibet in 1985, a small number above the line at the end of the sentence may alert you to this footnote at the bottom of the page.

[3]Harris, John. *Rain Forests and Jungles.* Chicago: Reindeer Press, 1986, p. 4.

Footnotes give the source of particular information. Since many footnotes may appear on a page, you must match the raised number in the text with the number of the footnote. Sometimes footnotes are listed at the end of a chapter or at the end of a book, where they may be called *End Notes* or just *Notes*.

A book may also include a **bibliography,** which lists the sources from which the writer borrowed material. Bibliography entries, which appear at the back of the book, are arranged in alphabetical order by the source writer's last name.

Raymond, Elizabeth. *Tales of Early Greece.* Boston: Harpoon Publishers, 1988.

An **index** also appears at the back of a book. It lists each topic in a book in alphabetical order and gives the page numbers on which each topic appears. Some topics are divided into **subtopics,** which are smaller divisions of the topic. **Cross-references,** noted by the words *See also,* are provided whenever related information can be found under other topic heads.

Greece, ancient, 65, 109, 146, 152, 236	Holidays
government of, 243, 244	in the Middle Ages, 174
trade with Italy by, 142	Roman, 154, 158
See also Athens	Hyksos, 56 – 57

Practice

Use the models above to write answers to these questions.

1. What is the footnote number? What does it tell you?

MODEL⟩ 3; it means that two other footnotes have come before it

2. Who published *Tales of Early Greece*?

3. From what book was information about rainfall used?

4. What pages deal with ancient Greek government?

5. Name the two subtopics for *Holidays*.

6. What cross-reference is given in the index?

6 Using the Dewey Decimal System

In the library all the books about real people or events are arranged by number. One system, used in many college and private libraries, is the **Library of Congress system.** The one your school or public library probably uses, however, is the **Dewey Decimal System.** In this system, books are numbered and organized into ten main subject areas. The chart shows the subject headings, the range of numbers assigned to each one, and the kinds of books in each category.

```
000–099 General works (encyclopedias, atlases, newspapers)
100–199 Philosophy (ideas about the meaning of life, psychology)
200–299 Religion (world religions, mythology)
300–399 Social science (education, law, business, government)
400–499 Language (dictionaries, grammar books, books on language)
500–599 Pure science (mathematics, chemistry, biology, botany)
600–699 Applied science (engineering, radio, how-to books)
700–799 Arts and recreation (music, sports, art)
800–899 Literature (poems, plays, essays, criticism)
900–999 History (biography, geography, travel)
```

Within the numbered range of a subject, each subtopic is given one specific number—its **call number.** When you know a book's call number, you scan the library shelves until you reach the call number of the book you want.

Practice

Use the Dewey Decimal System chart to write the answers to these questions.

1. Under what numbers and subject would you find a book on space travel?
   MODEL⟩ 600–699, Applied science
2. Under which numbers and subject would you find a book of myths?
3. Where might you find a book about laws for people under 18?
4. Where would you find books about calculus?
5. What subject and range of numbers includes the *Encyclopaedia Britannica?*
6. Where would you find a play by Tennessee Williams?
7. Under which numbers and subject is a book on Chinese philosophy?
8. Where would you find *The World Book Atlas?*
9. Where would you find a book on baseball?
10. Which section has a biography of Dr. Martin Luther King, Jr.?
11. Under which numbers and subject is a book on TV repair?

7 Using the Card Catalogue

Another resource that will help you find the library books you want is the **card catalogue.** It is usually a cabinet of small drawers. Every book in the library is listed on a card in one of the drawers. The cards are arranged alphabetically. Guide letters on each drawer tell what cards are inside.

There are three types of cards in a card catalogue. The **title card** lists the title of the book first. The **author card** lists the author's last name first. The **subject card** lists the subject of the book first. The subject card is useful when you want a book on a subject but do not have a particular book in mind. However, the most important piece of information on every card is the book's call number. When you know the call number, you know where to find the book you want.

800.011
  W   **Williams, Leonie**
       Literature through the ages / Leonie Williams;   **author card**

800.011   Literature through the ages
  W   **Williams, Leonie**
       Literature through the ages / Leonie Williams;   **title card**

800.011   LITERATURE
  W   **Williams, Leonie**
       Literature through the ages / Leonie Williams;
designed by Terry Casey. New York: Harrison
Publishers, 1976.

CONTENTS: English literature, A.D. 900 –
present; American literature, 1600 – present;
selected titles from World literature,
500 B.C. – present. 864 pp.: ill.   **subject card**

1. Literature I. Title
Library of Congress

Practice

Use the model catalogue cards to write the answers to the following questions.

1. Who is the author of the book?
MODEL▷ Leonie Williams
2. What is the book's complete title?
3. What span of years is covered in English literature?
4. Does the book probably contain some literature
from ancient Greece? How do you know?
5. When was the book published?
6. Where would you look for more books by this author?
7. Where would you look for more books on this subject?

8 Identifying Kinds of Books

As you probably know, libraries have separate sections for the different kinds of books they own. One large section contains all of the books of **fiction.** Fictional works include novels and short stories. They are arranged on the shelves alphabetically by the authors' last names. Some libraries have special sections for science fiction, mystery, or romance.

In another area are nonfiction books. **Nonfiction,** as you already know, includes books about real people, things, and events. Nonfiction represents all the categories in the Dewey Decimal System except literature.

A **biography** is a nonfiction book that tells about the life of a real person. Usually, biographies are organized by the Dewey Decimal System in the 900 range of nonfiction books. Some libraries, however, have a special section for them. Libraries also have a reference section for nonfiction books that cannot be checked out. **Reference** books include encyclopedias, dictionaries, and atlases.

Periodicals, or works such as magazines that are published daily or monthly, are often located in the reference section. In some libraries, however, they have a section of their own where people can browse.

Practice

Write which section of the library would have these books. Some books may be in more than one section.

1. a biography of Eleanor Roosevelt

MODEL⟩ nonfiction section or biography section

2. a mystery about a detective and her trained cat
3. a collection of funny poems
4. an atlas
5. a biography of Frederick Douglass
6. a book on the history of your state
7. *Star Chores,* the story of an imaginary Martian colony
8. *Jane Eyre,* a novel about a young orphan
9. a book about animal languages
10. the *Encyclopaedia Britannica*
11. *The Friends,* a novel
12. a book about the history of the Chippewa tribe
13. a book on child psychology
14. *Webster's Dictionary*
15. a biography of Javier Pérez de Cuellar, secretary-general of the United Nations
16. *Horse Trails,* a western novel
17. a book on stamp collecting
18. a book of arts and crafts

9 Using Reference Works

A library contains many kinds of reference books. Each kind provides a different type of information.

An **atlas** is a book of maps. A world atlas has maps of every country or region in the world, and a United States atlas has a map of every state. Most atlases include maps and charts that show the size, the climate, the population, and the natural features of the regions. They may also give information on industry, agriculture, and natural resources. Atlas maps usually show country or state capitals as well as other important cities.

An **almanac** gives information on a great many subjects. This information is often listed as statistics. For example, an almanac may list the major-league records of champion baseball players, the average rainfall of all the countries in the world, the speeds at which different animals run, or the dates of all the terms of the U.S. Presidents. Almanacs include articles, lists, charts, and tables on such topics as sports, weather, history, politics, and literature.

A **biographical reference** offers brief biographies, or life stories, of many kinds of people. Biographical references are usually organized by topic, such as "the most powerful people in the United States today" or "African Americans in history."

An **encyclopedia** is a collection of articles on a wide variety of subjects. Encyclopedias often include such information as maps, statistics, and biographies that can also be found in other reference books.

A **dictionary** is a book that gives the meaning and pronunciation of many words. Some dictionaries tell you how to translate words from one language into another. A Spanish-English dictionary, for example, will list a word in Spanish, tell how to pronounce it, and then tell what the word means in English. Single-language dictionaries may include articles about the history of language, as well as charts of weights and measures, lists of well-known abbreviations, and other useful information.

Practice

Write which type of reference book would include the following information. Give two books if both would have the information.

1. biographies of famous musicians
   MODEL⟩ biographical reference or encyclopedia
2. pronunciation of the word *reference*
3. a list of the Olympic winners for the last 20 years
4. a map of your state, showing the state's natural resources
5. information about the history of mountain climbing
6. information about the discovery of radium
7. the English meaning of the French term *le chapeau*

10 Using Newspapers

A newspaper is an important reference because it is published often, usually daily or weekly. **Newspapers** carry articles about events that happened the day or the week before. Most carry international, national, and local news. Others print news only for one city or neighborhood.

All newspapers use eye-catching **headlines,** short titles that give some idea of what a particular article is about. Most sections in a newspaper also have **photographs.** These are pictures that tell a story by themselves or accompany an article. Photos almost always have **captions,** words that identify the people in the picture and explain what they are doing.

Newspapers have several different sections. The **news section,** which is usually the first part of the paper, carries news stories about the latest world, national, and local events. As a rule, these articles are objective, or unbiased. This means that they contain only documented facts, not opinions.

In a newspaper the place for opinions is the **editorial section.** Many of the articles express the thoughts of the newspaper staff on important issues, such as those having to do with national, state, and local government. This section also contains space for readers' letters to the editor.

Large newspapers usually carry sections on special interests, such as sports, the arts, family topics, or business. You may find comics, reviews, advice columns, contests, and puzzles in these sections as well.

Finally, most newspapers carry **advertisements.** They may have a special section for advertising, called the **classified section,** where goods for sale, jobs, and real estate are listed. Many also print advertisements throughout the paper.

Practice

Write what each newspaper item is and where it may be found.

1. A report on last night's basketball game
   MODEL〉 an article—sports section
2. An article supporting a candidate for city council
3. A listing of a job opening at a local hospital
4. A description of a hurricane that destroyed several homes
5. A few words about a photo of a blizzard on Main Street
6. The title *Mayor Announces New Parking Regulations*
7. A picture of a cake mix, with the words *Try Tastee Mix*
8. A letter from a reader expressing an opinion on the rights of nonsmokers
9. Photos and descriptions of homes for sale
10. A report on the death of a prominent local politician
11. A report on stock market trends in the computer industry

11 Using the *Readers' Guide to Periodical Literature*

STUDY SKILLS

Magazines and other publications appearing at regular intervals are called **periodicals.** They may be printed weekly, monthly, every few months, or, in some cases, once a year.

Because periodicals take so much less time to publish than books, they usually contain more up-to-date information. However, even back issues of periodicals are interesting. For a report on an election, for example, you may want to read what the magazines of the time were saying, even if there is also a book on the topic.

To locate articles on the topics you want, use the reference book called the *Readers' Guide to Periodical Literature.* The *Readers' Guide* is published every week. At the end of each month, the weekly *Guides* are organized into one *Guide* for the month, which is later organized into a *Guide* for the whole year.

The *Readers' Guide* is organized alphabetically by topic. You may want to look under more than one topic to find all the information you want. For example, for a report on elections, you should check the names of the candidates as well as the topics *elections, government,* and *politics.* Study this section of the *Readers' Guide to Periodical Literature.*

COMPACT DISCS
    See also
    CD-ROM (Compact disc-Read
      only memory)
    Compact disc interactive
    Compact disc video
Born again [classical releases on RCA
  Red Seal] P. G. Davis. il *New York*
  21:64+ Je 6 '88
The CD spread. See issues of *High
Fidelity* (New York, N.Y.)

        Popular music
Berlin on CD: they say it's wonderful [I.
  Berlin] R. Hoffman. il por *Business
  Week* p142 My 16 '88
Cole, Nat King: Complete "After
  midnight" sessions; Very thought of
  you; Cole sings/George Shearing plays.
  T. Teachout. *High Fidelity* (New
  York, N.Y.) 38:71-2 Je '88

Practice

Use the model *Readers' Guide.* Write answers to the questions.

1. Under what topic are the articles listed?

MODEL⟩ *COMPACT DISCS*

2. What other topics are suggested in the cross-references?

3. On what page does the first article appear?

4. What is the name of the first publication listed under Popular Music?

5. Which artist is featured on the compact disc mentioned under *Popular Music?*

12 Using Audiovisual Aids

Most libraries contain other kinds of reference sources besides printed materials. Record albums and cassettes allow people to listen to various types of music, speeches, poetry, and plays. Many classic radio broadcasts as well as foreign language instruction and other kinds of information are available only on cassettes. They can either be checked out or listened to in the library.

Many libraries now have videotapes, films, filmstrips, and slide-tape shows. A popular movie or a documentary, a sort of nonfiction film, may be on videotape. There may even be a recording of a television program.

A **filmstrip** is a series of still pictures, sometimes with captions or other writing and sometimes with sound. It is shown with a special kind of projector. A **slide-tape show** also contains a series of still pictures along with a tape that provides sound. The slides are shown with a slide projector while the tape is played on a tape recorder. Videocassettes, films, cassette tapes, filmstrips, and slide-tape shows are usually found in the audiovisual aids section of the library.

Important information from the past can often be found on **microfilm** and **microfiche.** Instead of providing magazines and newspapers so old that they might fall apart if you handled them, libraries have photographed them on special film. Many libraries offer free use of microfilm and microfiche projectors to their patrons. Sometimes even fairly recent papers and magazines are put on microfilm just to save space.

Practice

A. Match each audiovisual aid with its definition. Write the letter of the definition.

  1. cassette tape
  MODEL⟩ e.
  2. videotape
  3. film
  4. filmstrip
  5. slide-tape show

  a. moving picture shown with projector
  b. still pictures, usually without sound
  c. still pictures with sound
  d. moving pictures shown on a VCR
  e. sound recording

B. Complete these sentences by writing the correct response for each blank.

  6. _____ and _____ are photographed onto microfilm.
  MODEL⟩ Magazines, newspapers

  7. The greatest advantage of microfilm and microfiche is _____.

  8. Documentaries might be recorded on _____ or _____.

  9. Three items that might be on records or cassettes are _____, _____, and _____.

  10. Foreign language instruction is most commonly found on _____.

13 Using the Encyclopedia

An **encyclopedia** is a set of books that contains information on a wide range of topics. Each book in an encyclopedia is called a **volume.** Each volume contains many topics listed in **alphabetical order.** Letters on the **spine,** or bound side, of each volume show that articles beginning with those letters can be found in that volume.

On each page of a volume are **guide words** indicating the first and last articles found on that page. **Key words** that explain important ideas on a page are also frequently given. Each topic in an encyclopedia is called an **entry.** An entry usually includes the name of a topic and an article on that topic. Sometimes, however, an entry consists only of a topic with a suggestion on where to find information.

For example, suppose you looked up the word *cars* in the encyclopedia. That entry might consist only of the word *cars* plus the suggestion that you look under the word *automobile.* In this case, *automobile* would be a key word. The suggestion to look under *automobile* is called a **cross-reference.** Cross-references may also be found at the ends of articles.

In every encyclopedia there is an index, which is usually the last volume. The **index** lists the number or letter of the volume and the pages on which information on a subject can be found. Each subject is listed in the index in alphabetical order. The index usually includes cross-references to related entries as well.

Practice

Write answers to the following questions.

1. What is a volume?

MODEL⟩ a book in a set of encyclopedias

2. What is an entry?

3. How do you know which entries are listed on a page?

4. How do you know which entries are listed in a volume?

5. Suppose you want information about mapmaking. You look up *mapmaking* and find the words *See also: cartography.* What kind of encyclopedia feature would *cartography* be?

6. What is the suggestion *See also: cartography* called?

7. In what order are encyclopedia volumes organized?

8. Where is the index usually found?

9. Where can you find the page numbers and the volume number that show where a topic can be found?

10. Name three places where cross-references might be found in an encyclopedia.

14 Taking Notes

Taking notes is a very important skill. By taking notes, you can keep a record of the information in the books and magazines you read. If you want to use some of that material in a speech or report, you don't have to go back and read the source again. The information you want will be in your notes!

As you take notes, you **paraphrase,** or write the material in your own words. Many people use abbreviations in notes and write in phrases rather than in sentences. Read this paragraph, and then look at the paraphrased notes that follow.

> Annie Sullivan was able to help Helen Keller because she understood what it was like to be an isolated child. When Annie was young, her eyes were very bad, and for many years she was almost blind. After her parents died, she and her little brother went to live in the Tewksbury poorhouse. Not until she went to the Perkins Institute for the Blind did Annie Sullivan receive a decent education.

```
—Annie could see but was almost blind.
—parents died; went to poorhouse with brother
—educated at Perkins Institute for the Blind
```

One good way to organize your notes is to use **note cards.** Start a separate card each time you use a new book or magazine. Write the title, the author's name, and the page number on the card so you know the source of each piece of information. It is also useful to start a new card for each new topic. Write the name of the topic at the top of each card so you can easily find the card you want.

Practice

Use the passage to write answers to these questions.

> The Greeks used myths to explain the events in their world. They believed that Apollo, the sun god, drove the sun across the sky in a chariot. They also believed that sea storms were caused by the god Poseidon's stirring up the waves with his spear, or trident.

1. What is one note you might take from this passage?

MODEL⟩ The Greeks believed in myths.

2. What is another note?

3. What is a third note?

4. What title might you give the note card with these notes?

5. What else should you always write on a note card?

15 Writing an Outline

Once you have taken all your notes, it is useful to organize them into an **outline.** An outline shows the main ideas and the most important details in your report. It shows the order in which the ideas will appear. It also helps make clear which items are the most important and which are details. Study this section of an outline.

The Life of a Star

I. Introduction: Old myths vs. new theories
II. A star's birth
   A. Dense cloud of gas forms
   B. Gas heats up
      1. Atoms' energy increases
      2. Temperature—20 million degrees F
   C. Nuclear reactions begin

Practice

Use this outline to write answers to the questions.

Australia

I. Geography
   A. Continent plus island of Tasmania
   B. Very large
      1. As big as U.S. without Alaska or Hawaii
      2. 50% bigger than Europe without U.S.S.R.
II. Government
   A. Queen of England—head of state
   B. Federal Parliament
      1. House of Representatives—elected every 3 years
      2. Senate—elected every 6 years

---

1. What is the first main idea in this outline?
MODEL⟩ Australia's geography
  2. What is the second main idea?
  3. Which idea under *Geography* has two details under it?
  4. What is the second idea under *Government*?
  5. What would you do about an entry under *Government* that read *C. Farming*?
  6. What topics might be suitable for a *C* entry under *Geography*?

16 Writing a Bibliography

A **bibliography** is the part of your report that tells what books, magazines, and other research sources you have used. It gives credit to the writers and others whose work has helped you. It also allows readers to see which sources you have used, so if they are interested in the subject, they can use them too. A bibliography is usually organized alphabetically, although some are arranged by type of source. Study this bibliography for a report on UFO's.

"A UFO Stopped Here—or Did It?" *Harrison Daily News*, May 5, 1988, p. 7.

Mason, John. *UFOs: Fact or Fiction?* New York: Ferguson Publishing Company, 1986.

"More Sightings, More Questions." *News Magazine*, Vol. XXXV, No. 26 (May 7, 1988): 56–58.

Patterson, Patricia. *The Texas Mystery*. Boston: Martin-Jason Press, 1985.

Richardson, Leonie. "What's Next for UFO Research?" *Scientific Studies*, Vol. XVI, No. 8 (June, 1987): 43–44.

Notice that books are always listed by the last name of the author. Other sources are listed by the last name of the author if there is one given; otherwise they are listed by the first letter of the title of the article.

A bibliography entry for a book also includes the title, the place of publication, the publisher, and the date. An entry for a magazine includes the title of the article, the name of the magazine, the volume and the number, the date, and the page numbers of the article. Newspaper entries do not usually include a volume number. Notice that each type of entry has a different format, with commas, periods, and parentheses in certain places.

Practice

Use the model bibliography to write these sources in correct form.

1. *Drought*, a book by Ed James, Paragon Press, 1985, New York.

   MODEL⟩ James, Ed. *Drought*. New York: Paragon Press, 1985.

2. "Farmers in Crisis" by Jo Taylor, March 1, 1986, *Iola Daily News*, pages 2 and 3.

3. Lily Anderson's book, *Waiting for the Rain*, Apple Bough Publishers, Minneapolis, 1984.

4. "No Rain Yet," *Weekly World News*, pp. 11–12, July 5, 1986, Vol. XLII, No. 30.

17 Skimming and Scanning

STUDY SKILLS

People read for information in different ways. Some read every word in a book. Some skim or scan the material to see if they need to read further.

To **skim** material is to look at it quickly in order to take in the general subject, the divisions, and the major headings. You might skim a table of contents to see if the chapters in a book have the information you want. You might also skim a magazine, checking article titles to see if you want to read any selections.

To **scan** material is to glance over a passage to find a piece of information that you want. For example, if you were looking for the latest census figures on your town, you might scan a list of state figures, looking for your town's name.

If you were skimming the table of contents (below left), the topic of the book—astronomy—would be immediately apparent. You would notice that the book contains information about our solar system and our galaxy. You would also notice that it does *not* include any chapters on space travel, constellations, or UFO's. If you were scanning the chart (below right), you might not look at all the names. Instead, you might just scan to see which star is farthest from Earth or which star is the closest.

Unit I Our Solar System	
Chapter 1 Planets	15
Chapter 2 The Sun	68
Chapter 3 Asteroids	79
Unit II Our Galaxy	
Chapter 4 Origins	90
Chapter 5 Major Stars	110
Chapter 6 Other Planets	125

Distance of Stars from Earth	
Star	*Light-Years*
Sirius	8
Canopus	650
Alpha Centauri	4
Vega	23
Capella	42
Arcturus	32

Practice

Write the answers to these questions.

1. What are the two main topics covered in the table of contents?
MODEL our solar system and our galaxy
2. What does the title of the last chapter suggest?
3. Which star is farthest away from Earth?
4. Which star is closest to Earth?
5. How far is Capella from Earth?
6. Would you skim or scan to find your name in the telephone directory?
7. Would you skim or scan to find the name of your school in a list of schools?
8. Would you skim or scan to find whether there are any chapters on feudalism in your history book?

18 Summarizing

Summarizing material is often useful. To **summarize** is to put the ideas of a long piece of writing into short form. If you read a 100-page book about the Revolutionary War, you might write a one-page summary of it. The summary could let others know what you have learned from the book, or it could help you remember its main points.

You can also summarize an article, a chapter, or even someone else's report. A good summary tells what the book or article is about and describes the information that can be found there. It might give one or two examples of details, but if it gives too many, it ceases to be a summary. Read this student's summary of a book about the Revolutionary War.

> *New Nation in the New World* is a history of the Revolutionary War. It begins with the first grievances of the colonists and ends with the ratification of the Constitution's Bill of Rights. The central idea is that the United States formed a type of government that had never been seen before.

Notice that the summary tells only the author's main idea. Whoever reads the summary will probably know whether he or she needs to read the whole book. You can also write a summary of a piece of fiction. Again, this summary should not tell the whole story. Only the main idea is necessary.

> *Jane Eyre* is the story of an orphaned young woman who marries the man she loves. Before she does so, however, she faces many hardships, first from her relatives, then at school, then from the man for whom she works. The main idea is that Jane must be true to herself to be happy.

Practice

Write whether each sentence belongs in a summary. If not, give a reason.

1. The date of the first Continental Congress was Sept. 5, 1774.
MODEL〉 No—this would be too much detail.

2. The main idea is that it took a long time to write the Constitution.

3. The book starts with the Emancipation Proclamation and ends when Lincoln is shot.

4. Here are the names of all the characters in the book: Jane, Mr. Rochester, Diana, Mary, St. John, Adela, Bertha.

5. The author describes several important Civil War battles.

6. Mr. Rochester is not a very good-looking man.

7. The Rochester mansion burns to the ground.

19 Writing Friendly Letters

Read this letter Gail wrote to a friend who had moved away.

629 West 115th Street
New York, New York 10025
December 2, 19—

— heading

Dear Janet,
   How I miss you since you moved to Chicago! It
still seems strange not to see your smiling face
at school each day!

— greeting

   Seventh grade has been a big change for me. The
teachers seem to take both our work and their own
more seriously. We've been responding in the same
way. The homework is even longer than last
year's!
   Last week the band played its first concert of
the year. We really sounded good, I think, but we
missed your clarinet. The program included the
Sousa march we worked on last year.
   Is life in Chicago much different from New
York? Please write me soon with some details.
   I hope you'll be able to come and visit during
your winter or spring vacation. Any time should
be all right--just let me know a week or two in
advance.

— body

                Love,
                Gail

— closing
— signature

   A **friendly letter** is a letter written to a friend or a relative in order to exchange greetings and news. Friendly letters have five parts. The **heading** gives the sender's address and the date on which the letter was written. The **greeting** addresses the person to whom the letter is being sent. The **body** of the letter contains the questions, news, and comments that the letter writer wants the receiver to know. The **closing** is the "sign-off," or the writer's way of saying that the letter has come to an end. The **signature,** as a rule, consists only of the sender's first name.

Tips on the Friendly Letter Format
1. Write a **heading,** which includes your address and the date, in the upper right corner of the page.
2. Write the **greeting** under it and to the left.
3. Write the **body** in paragraph form.
4. Write your **closing** and **signature** in line with the heading.
5. Prepare an envelope with your address in the upper left corner and the receiver's address in the lower middle.

Practice

A. Use the model letter on page 482 to write answers to the following questions.

1. To whom is the letter addressed?

MODEL▷ to Janet, Gail's friend who moved away

2. Why might the writer have sent a letter instead of called on the telephone?
3. Where does the writer live? How do you know?
4. What event gave the writer a reason to send her letter?
5. Name some news that is included in the body of the model letter.
6. If you were the person who received Gail's letter, what news might you give her in response?
7. Why might Gail's next letter to Janet be an invitation?
8. What does Gail say to indicate that she is a real friend to the receiver of the letter?

B. Write this letter in the correct form.

North Haven, Connecticut 07463
27 Barnes Road August 13, 19--
Dear Tony
I am really enjoying my vacation in the country. The hills, the fields, and the woods are wonderful places to explore. The sun is warm, and there is always a cool breeze. I don't miss the city a bit! Tomorrow we're going swimming in Long Island Sound, and the next day we've planned a picnic. Maybe you can join me here next year. It would be fun!
Your friend Allan

C. Imagine that a relative has gone away to college. Write a letter to him or her. Make sure each part of your friendly letter is in the correct position on the paper.

20 Writing a Business Letter

Suppose you did not receive the item you sent for when you ordered it by mail. You would be correct in sending a letter of adjustment to the company. Read Jon's letter below.

547 Elm Street
Roanoke, Virginia 24001
December 8, 19--

— heading

Customer Service Department
Treat's of Lansing
414 South Main Street
Lansing, Michigan 48924

— inside address

Dear Sir or Madam:

— greeting

As the enclosed copy of my order form indicates, on November 23, 19—, I ordered two pairs of men's pajamas, size M, in <u>cotton</u>. The catalogue number was PM-943-C, and the items were billed to credit card 64-81048.

When I received the items on December 7, I noted that the pajamas were 60% <u>polyester</u>, 40% cotton. I am returning the package and ask that you send me the items as ordered.

If the items are not in stock, please cancel my order.

— body

Sincerely yours,
Jon Grant
Jon Grant

— closing
— signature

There are various kinds of business letters. Most of them are written to companies to order merchandise, to ask for information, to complain about faulty or late delivery, or to request a refund of money sent. The letter written by Jon Grant to Treat's of Lansing is a **letter of adjustment.**

Notice that the writer includes the six parts of a business letter: **heading, inside address, greeting, body, closing,** and **signature.** Notice, too, that he is very careful to give the company the information they will need to correct his order. Moreover, his tone is polite but firm, and his language is businesslike. These tips on writing business letters may help when you need to write a letter of adjustment.

1. Write your address and the date in the upper right corner of the page.
2. Write the inside address below and to the left of the heading.
3. Write the greeting under the inside address.
4. Write the body in paragraph form. Make your tone polite but firm. Ask only for something the company can reasonably do.
5. Write your closing and signature in line with the heading.
6. Prepare an envelope with your address in the upper left corner and the receiver's address in the lower middle.

Practice

A. Write the answers to these questions.

    1. Why did Jon write this letter?

MODEL〉 *The company did not send him the items he ordered.*

    2. What does Jon ask the company to do about his problem?

    3. Is Jon's request reasonable? Why or why not?

    4. Besides the fact that Jon follows business letter format, what about the letter makes it correct?

    5. What is especially good about the way Jon describes the items he ordered?

B. Rewrite this letter to correct its tone as well as its form. Add your own wording for any details that are missing.

To someone sane at Artifacts Alley, New York, New York
Three weeks ago I ordered a print of a field of daisies from your catalogue to give to Mom on her birthday. What do you think I got in the mail yesterday? You may not believe this, but it was a huge stuffed fish on some kind of wooden plaque. Now I ask you, is that a gift that a guy gives his mom on her birthday? For that matter, why would anyone want to give anyone else a stupid stuffed fish?
Now, fellas, get on your toes and send me the right gift. You have exactly five days until Mom's birthday.
Get your act together,
Jim

C. Write a letter of adjustment to Audiovisual Helps, Inc., 38 Main Street, Portland, Maine 04101. Request replacement of a slide set called *Birds of America*, which arrived badly scratched. The set costs $8.95. Use business letter format.

21 Writing Social Notes

Friendly letters written for a specific purpose include letters of thanks, apology, and invitation. Such friendly letters are called **social notes.** Here are two examples. The first one is a thank-you note, and the second is a letter of apology.

```
                          2060 Broad Street
                          Bethesda, Maryland 20815      — heading
                          July 15, 19--
Dear Mr. and Mrs. Nelson,                               — greeting
    Ever since I got back from Lake Dunmore, I've
been thinking of the happy times I had with you. I
will always remember your dock as the place I          — body
caught my first fish.
    Thanks very much for inviting me to stay with
you.
                          Sincerely,                    — closing
                          Alex Robinson                 — signature
```

```
                          144 Whitmore Street
                          Chicago, Illinois 60610       — heading
                          June 6, 19--
Dear Mr. and Mrs. Johnson,                              — greeting
    I know I've already said this in person, but I
feel that I have to apologize again in writing.
I'm very sorry that I broke your kitchen window
last Friday. Since I've just been learning to          — body
bat, I had no idea that I could hit a baseball
that far!
    Of course, I will pay for a new window out of my
weekly allowance. Meanwhile, our baseball
practices have been relocated to Brandon Park.
I'm sure I'll never break your window again.
Thank you for being so understanding.
                          Your neighbor,                — closing
                          Lawanda Jackson                — signature
```

Social notes, like other friendly letters, have five parts. Study these tips for writing social notes with correct content and format.

Tips for Writing Social Notes
1. The **heading** goes in the upper right corner. It includes the writer's address, which includes city, state, and ZIP code. It also includes the date.
2. The **greeting** goes at the left margin. Add a comma after the person's name.
3. Write the **body** of the letter in indented paragraphs. Be sure that you mention something especially memorable about your visit if you are thanking people for their hospitality. Use a tone suitable for the age group of the person to whom you are writing.
4. Put the **closing** in line with the heading. Capitalize the first word of the closing. Put a comma after the last word in the closing.
5. Write your **signature** under the closing.

Practice

A. Rewrite this thank-you note to reflect proper form. Change its tone to one suitable for Abe's grandparents.

> 88 Lexington Avenue
> New Castle, Pennsylvania 16101
> January 3, 19--
>
> dear Grandma and Granddad
> Thanks outrageously for the two <u>rad</u> computer programs you sent me for the holidays. <u>Paint Me</u> is awesome! I can think of two zillion different things to draw & color with it. <u>Dark Castle</u> just blows me away—it's so <u>rad</u>! Thanks again. your grandson Abe.

B. Write a letter to your friend's parents, thanking them for taking you on their family's winter trip. You visited Montreal, Quebec, and saw the famous ice festival there.

22 Writing a Book Report

You have probably written many book reports on novels. Reports on books of nonfiction such as biographies, however, require some changes in format. Study this book report.

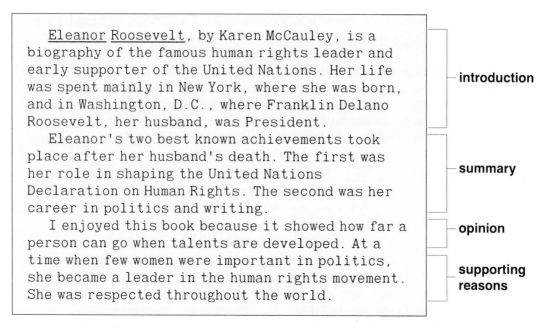

Eleanor Roosevelt, by Karen McCauley, is a biography of the famous human rights leader and early supporter of the United Nations. Her life was spent mainly in New York, where she was born, and in Washington, D.C., where Franklin Delano Roosevelt, her husband, was President. — **introduction**

Eleanor's two best known achievements took place after her husband's death. The first was her role in shaping the United Nations Declaration on Human Rights. The second was her career in politics and writing. — **summary**

I enjoyed this book because it showed how far a person can go when talents are developed. At a time when few women were important in politics, she became a leader in the human rights movement. She was respected throughout the world. — **opinion** / **supporting reasons**

Notice that the writer begins with an **introduction**. A short **summary** of the person's life follows, and the report ends with an **opinion** on the book and **supporting reasons** for the opinion.

Practice

A. Write the answers to these questions.

1. Why isn't it necessary to include the main characters and the setting when writing a book report on a biography?
   MODEL〉 because the emphasis is on the subject of the book and only incidentally on the other characters and the setting

2. In what ways is a nonfiction book report like a book report on a fictional book?

3. Why does a report on a nonfiction book include a summary of the book's contents?

B. Write a book report on another book of nonfiction, such as a science book (not a textbook) or a book on nature. Follow the format given above.

23 Studying for Tests

One way to take a test with more confidence is to study for it effectively. The first thing to remember about studying for a test is to relax. Sometimes people are so nervous about tests that they cannot concentrate. Fortunately, there are some good habits that you can develop to study well for tests.

First of all, study a little every day. This tactic seems to help because you do not have to face all the material at once. When you do sit down to study, however, try to organize your time. Do not get bogged down in any one part of the material. Instead, put that part aside for the time being, and ask your teacher about it the next day!

One good way to review is to ask yourself questions like the ones you expect on the test. Write each question on a separate sheet of paper. Then make brief notes on each sheet to answer the question. If you have to look up the answers, take clear, precise notes. Review your notes the next evening.

You may also want to make a set of study notes. Write short, specific notes from a passage, including the main ideas and the most important details. Again, review your notes instead of the book.

Practice

A. Rewrite the following study tips to make them helpful.

1. Always review every word in your book.
   MODEL▷ Take study notes from your book and review those.
2. Spend the most time on difficult sections of the material.
3. Do all of your studying the day before the test.
4. If you have questions, try to find the answers in your text.
5. Do not try to anticipate questions that will be on the test.
6. Before you start studying, remind yourself how hard the test is.

B. Use your own paper to take five study notes on the following passage.

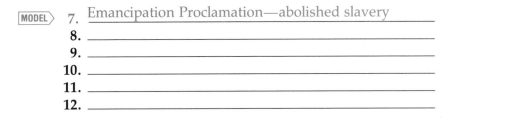

The Emancipation Proclamation was the executive order that abolished slavery in the Confederacy. It was signed by President Lincoln on January 1, 1863. It did not free all slaves—it freed only those in the Confederate states. The proclamation helped strengthen the North by allowing blacks to join the Union Army.

MODEL▷ 7. Emancipation Proclamation—abolished slavery

8. _____
9. _____
10. _____
11. _____
12. _____

24 Taking Tests

The first thing to do when taking a test is to be sure you understand the directions. Read them well. Notice whether there are special instructions about marking your answers. If instructions are given orally, listen carefully. If there is anything you do not understand, ask the person giving the test.

A test can have various kinds of questions. Some tests ask you to solve analogies. An **analogy** is a kind of comparison.

bird : air :: fish : water

This analogy says that a *bird* has the same relationship to the *air* as a *fish* has to *water*. Analogy questions usually leave one of the four parts blank. It may help to put the analogy into words: A *bird* flies through the *air*; a *fish* swims through the *water*.

A **multiple choice question** requires you to choose one of three, four, or five answers. Sometimes you will know the answer right away. In that case, just find the answer among the choices, mark it, and go on to the next question. If you are not sure of the answer, look at the answer choices. One or two may seem to be clearly wrong. If so, forget about them and study the choices that seem right. If you still can't decide on the answer, you may want to take your best guess. Be careful, however. Some tests subtract points for wrong answers.

Try to leave time for checking your answers before you finish the test. Be sure you have written them in the form and in the place specified. Remember that some tests are scored by computers. If your answers are not marked carefully, all your correct answers can be counted as incorrect.

Practice

A. Write on your own paper the correct order for these test-taking steps.

MODEL⟩ ___4___ **1.** Eliminate any answers that are obviously wrong.
_____ **2.** Read directions carefully.
_____ **3.** Choose the correct answer.
_____ **4.** If necessary, guess between two answers.
_____ **5.** Read each test question carefully.
_____ **6.** Ask about directions you do not understand.
_____ **7.** Try to leave time to check your answers.

B. Rewrite these test-taking tips to make them more helpful.

8. It is always better to guess than not to give an answer.
MODEL⟩ It is sometimes better to guess than not to give an answer.
9. Skim directions quickly to save more time for the test.
10. Never put an analogy into your own words.
11. It doesn't matter how or where you write your answers.
12. Don't bother to check your answers.

STUDY SKILLS

25 Taking Essay Tests

Essay tests require thoughtful, well-organized answers. The first thing to do is to read the essay question and to determine how to organize your response. Look for words in the question that tell you what kind of answer is needed. Study these key words and expressions.

1. Give an opinion (Tell how you feel about something and give good reasons to support your answers.)
2. Compare (Show how two things are alike.)
3. Contrast (Show how two things are different.)
4. Explain (Give reasons to show *why* or *how*; give causes and effects.)
5. Describe (Tell how something looks or how it works.)
6. Trace (Show how something began and developed.)

Tips for Taking an Essay Test

1. Read the question carefully.
2. Use key words to interpret the question.
3. Recall what you know about the topic.
4. Organize ideas for your answer. Then write your response.
5. Read the question again. Be sure you have answered completely.

Read one student's answer to this essay question: *The earth is rich in natural resources. What are some of these resources, and why are they valuable to us?*

The earth gives us many valuable resources. One important resource is water. We need water for drinking, cooking, and watering crops. Water is also a source of power. Power plants near rivers or waterfalls use water to run the machines that produce electricity.

We also find natural resources in the earth's crust. Coal, natural gas, and oil are fuels that we use to run machinery and heat and cool our homes.

Practice

Write the answers to these questions.

1. What key words in the question tell the topic of the essay?
   MODEL〉 "What are some resources; why are they valuable?"
2. What is good about the way the writer begins the answer?
3. What examples does the writer give to support the topic?
4. What ideas must the writer consider to answer the question?
5. How did the student organize ideas to answer the question?
6. Which kind of question is this essay question?

26 Using Bar Graphs, Line Graphs, and Pie Charts

Often a book or an article will include visual information instead of only words. **Visual aids** can help you to understand complicated material, especially numbers and statistics.

Two common visual aids are **graphs** and **charts**. A **bar graph** has two axes, or sides, one horizontal and one vertical. A scale of some kind usually occupies the vertical axis. Labels at the bottom of the horizontal axis tell what is being measured. The vertical axis is always on the left.

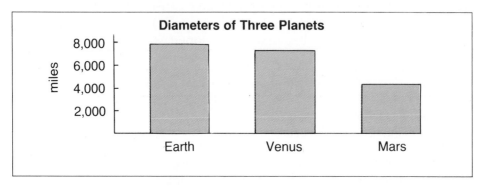

By looking at the bar graph, you can see about how many miles in diameter each planet is. You can also easily compare their sizes, which would be harder to do if you were just reading the figures in words.

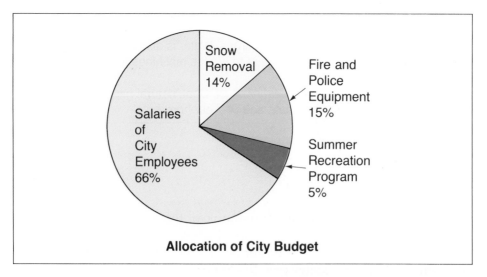

The **pie chart** shows how a city budget is divided. Each portion of the budget gets a piece of the "pie," so that just by looking you can compare the sizes of the allocations.

The axes of a **line graph** are set up like those of a bar graph; however, lines connect the points to which the bars would extend. The lines show relationships over time. They allow the reader to see increases and decreases.

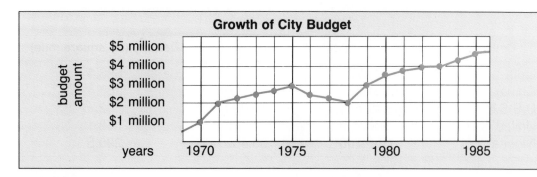

Growth of City Budget

Practice

A. Use the bar graph to help you write the answers to these questions.

1. Which planet is the biggest in diameter?

MODEL⟩ Earth

2. Which planet is the smallest in diameter?
3. About how many miles bigger in diameter than Venus is Earth?
4. About how many miles smaller in diameter than Venus is Mars?
5. About how many miles smaller in diameter than Earth is Mars?

B. Use the pie chart to help you write the answers to these questions.

6. Which part of the city budget gets the most money?

MODEL⟩ salaries of city employees

7. Which part of the city budget gets the least money?
8. Which parts of the budget need about the same allocation?
9. About how many times bigger is the allocation for fire and police equipment than for the summer recreation program?
10. List the parts of the budget and their allocations in order from smallest to largest.

C. Use the line graph. Write the answers to the questions.

11. In what year was the city budget the highest?

MODEL⟩ 1985

12. In what year labeled on the graph was the city budget the lowest?
13. In which years was the city budget between $3 and $4 million?
14. By how much did the budget grow between 1970 and 1975?

27 Using Tables and Diagrams

Tables are helpful when you want to organize statistics. In a **table,** figures from many different sources are assembled in one place. Study this table.

Country	Size (in square miles)	Population	Density (by square mile)
India	1,229,737	785,000,000	638.3
China	3,691,521	1,050,000,000	284.4
U.S.S.R.	8,649,489	280,000,000	32.4
United States	3,540,939	241,000,000	68.1
Nigeria	356,700	105,400,000	295.5

This table of population density tells you three things about each country: its size, its population, and its density, or the number of people per square mile. Notice the information in parentheses that tells units of measurement.

A **diagram** is a type of visual aid that shows you the names of the different parts of something. It can also show you how something works. Study this diagram.

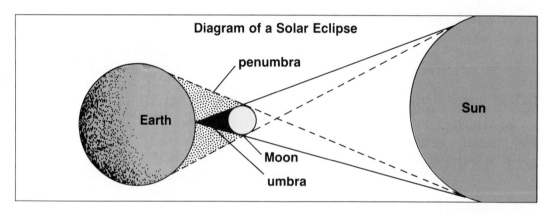

Diagram of a Solar Eclipse

Practice

A. Use the table and the diagram to write answers to these questions.

1. Which country has the largest population?
MODEL> China
2. Which country has the smallest population?
3. Which country has the highest density per square mile?
4. How many people live in Nigeria?
5. What is the name of the smaller shadow cast by the moon?

B. Make a table showing the time it takes you to do several things over a period of five days.

STUDY SKILLS

28 Using Maps

Maps give you information about various countries, regions, states, and even the moon's surface. If you know how to read a map, you can be a world explorer—at least from behind a desk.

Most maps include a **compass rose,** which shows north, east, south, and west. Some compass roses also show the in-between compass points, such as northeast and southwest. On most maps, north is at the top of the map, but this is not always the case.

On most maps, you can also find a distance scale. A **distance scale** shows how to measure distances on the map. By using the scale you can figure out how far one place is from another.

Maps also include **symbols,** or marks, that indicate different parts of a country's or state's geography. For example, on this map a thin line is the symbol for a river. You can also see the symbol for mountains.

Each map should include a legend. A **legend** explains the codes and symbols used on the map. On this map, for example, the legend illustrates a capital city with a circled star.

Practice

Use the map to answer the following questions.

1. Which two states are pictured in the map?
   MODEL> California and Nevada
2. Name a river in California.
3. Which compass direction points to the left edge of the map?
4. Name a mountain range in northern California.
5. What is the capital of Nevada? How do you know?
6. Name another important city in Nevada.
7. Name the capital and two other cities in California.
8. In which direction do you go to travel from San Francisco to Carson City?
9. About how many miles is it from Sacramento to Carson City?

29 Taking Messages and Using the Telephone Directory

An important telephone skill is **taking a message**—that is, writing down the important information from a telephone call so that another person can receive it.

The most important parts of a telephone message are usually the caller's name and phone number. Be sure that you understand the caller's name clearly and that you know how to spell it. If you aren't sure, ask!

A **telephone directory** is a useful source of information. It lists in alphabetical order the name of everyone who has a published phone number. The White Pages list names of people and businesses. Individuals are listed last name first. Businesses are listed by the name of the business. The Yellow Pages also list businesses and their advertising. Listings in a telephone directory usually include an address.

Have you ever been unable to find the name of a person or a business in the telephone directory because you weren't sure how to look it up? Then these tips may help.

Tips for Using Telephone Directories	
1. Entries beginning with initials come before entries beginning with first names.	*Lynds, M.* is before *Lynds, Martin*
2. Other abbreviations are listed as if they were spelled out.	*St. Jude's Hospital* is listed as *Saint Jude's Hospital.*
3. Names that begin with initials are listed first in their alphabetical sections.	*TT Travel Agency* is listed before *Town Travel Agency.*
4. Numbers in names are alphabetized as if the numbers were spelled out.	*65 Club* is alphabetized as *Sixty-Five Club.*

Practice

A. 1.–5. Write five important points about this phone call.

"Hi, this is Lou Cameron. Please ask your sister Angela to call me by 5:00 P.M. at (707) 555-1928 to tell me when she's arriving. She may leave a message."

MODEL⟩ **1.** Lou Cameron called.

B. Use your own paper to write the correct response for each blank.

6. A telephone directory has listings in _____ order.

MODEL⟩ alphabetical

7. Only businesses are listed in the _____ Pages.

8. Individuals are listed _____ name first.

30 Completing Forms

People fill out magazine subscription forms, job applications, order forms in catalogues, library card applications, and many other forms. Each form is different, and some are hard to read. However, if you read forms carefully, it is not usually difficult to complete them.

It is a good idea to look over the entire form before you start to fill it out. Some forms require your last name first, and others require your first name first. Some forms have separate spaces for the different parts of your address. If you have looked over the whole form first, you will be able to put the information in the correct place.

Jenkins		Lupe		V.
Last Name		First Name		Initial
4789	Camino Blvd.	Jersey City	NJ	07806
Number	Street	City	State	ZIP code

Item Ordered: Blue Sweater Number: 1 Price: $25.00

Please include 6% tax and $1.50 for shipping and handling.
Total Amount Enclosed: $28.00

Please print in blue or black ink. Allow 6 weeks for delivery.

Note that the directions to print and to use blue or black ink appear at the bottom of the form. If Lupe had started to fill out the form without reading the whole thing, she might not have done it correctly.

Practice

Make a copy of this magazine subscription form. Imagine that you want to order a two-year subscription to the magazine. Then fill out the form.

Last Name	First Name	Initial
House Number	Street Name	Apartment
City	State	ZIP code
Phone: Area Code	Number	

Subscription for (Check one) Amount enclosed:

_____ _____ _____ _____
1 year—$10.00 2 years—$17.50 3 years—$25.00

EXTRA PRACTICE

Contents

UNIT 1

1 Sentences *pages 30 – 31*

A. Identifying Complete Sentences and Sentence Fragments   Write *complete* or *incomplete* to describe each word group.

1. The staff of the school newspaper.
   MODEL〉 incomplete
2. The school newspaper staff met Monday afternoon.
3. They discussed plans for the next edition of the paper.
4. Liz, the sports editor, and Tod, the editor in chief.
5. The Special Olympics on school grounds next month.
6. The sports editor wanted to include a background story.
7. The editor supported the idea enthusiastically.
8. Pictures of the events and of the participants.
9. Plans for a two-page spread with pictures and stories.
10. Provided feature stories about the participants.
11. Decided not to write a history of the Special Olympics.

B. Rewriting Sentence Fragments   If a sentence is complete, write *complete*. Rewrite the fragments to make sentences.

12. The editor in chief.
    MODEL〉 The editor in chief was pleased with our work.
13. The entertainment editor described plans for a feature.
14. The school play was scheduled for a week in May.
15. Interviews with the drama coach and the cast.
16. Pictures taken at tryouts and at the dress rehearsal.
17. Scenery, props, costumes, lighting, and sound effects.
18. Announced the date and encouraged the sale of tickets.
19. The photographer promised action photos for a feature.
20. Referred to the feature stories in previous editions.
21. Rejected the idea of a critical review of the play.
22. Everyone in the cast and everyone in the audience.

C. Writing Complete Sentences   Write a sentence about a school newspaper for each group of words and phrases.

23. asked, article
    MODEL〉 The editor asked a reporter for her article.
24. some, more experienced
25. wanted, reporters, feature articles
26. assigned, reporter, photographer
27. editor in chief, planning
28. additional reporters, staff

UNIT 1

2 Four Kinds of Sentences *pages 32–33*

A. Identifying the Four Kinds of Sentences Write whether each sentence is *declarative, interrogative, imperative,* or *exclamatory*.

1. Turn on the radio.
MODEL⟩ imperative

2. The traffic helicopter flew over the highways.

3. Which roadways are congested today?

4. Did you ever drive into the city during rush hour?

5. What an aggravation that can be!

6. Some highways are always crowded in the morning.

7. Avoid them if you possibly can.

8. Listen to the traffic report on the radio.

9. You may be very glad you did!

B. Punctuating the Four Kinds of Sentences Rewrite each sentence, using correct punctuation and capitalization.

10. a news bulletin flashed on the radio
MODEL⟩ A news bulletin flashed on the radio.

11. some stations carry only news programs

12. do you get your news from radio or from television

13. please turn to the news now

14. would you like to be a radio reporter

15. what an exciting job that would be

16. radio commentators are often popular personalities

17. who are the major commentators in your area

18. talent and luck combine to create many radio careers

C. Changing Sentence Formats Make each declarative sentence into an interrogative, exclamatory, or imperative sentence. Vary the kinds of sentences you write.

19. The news report was exciting.
MODEL⟩ Was the news report exciting?

20. The radio reported a fire in Chicago.

21. Various stations carried different information.

22. The fire began in a downtown hotel.

23. It spread to several old buildings nearby.

24. Firefighters fought the blaze for hours.

25. Some firefighters were treated for smoke inhalation.

3 Complete and Simple Subjects *pages 34 – 35*

A. Identifying Complete and Simple Subjects   Write each complete subject, underlining it once. Then underline each simple subject twice.

1. Modern conveniences have changed society.
MODEL⟩ <u>Modern <u>conveniences</u></u>
2. Television gives people instant communication.
3. People the world over can witness the same event.
4. Millions watch the launch of a space shuttle.
5. Boston citizens see the President's arrival in Mexico.
6. Londoners watch the Olympic games from Canada or Korea.
7. A flaming torch in New York shines bright in California.
8. Television has made the world a global village.
9. Can you imagine your life without television?

B. Expanding Simple Subjects   Use each simple subject to help you write a complete subject that fits each sentence.

10. Children decided to watch cartoons.
MODEL⟩ The four young children decided to watch cartoons.
11. Children watch television at home.
12. Programs can be instructive and entertaining.
13. Children confuse commercial messages with the programs.
14. Hosts should never be allowed to endorse products.
15. Characters seem real to children.
16. Fantasy is as believable as reality.
17. Viewers may imitate the actions of cartoon characters.
18. Puppets come to life for children.

C. Writing Complete Subjects to Make Sentences   Add a complete subject to each word group to form a sentence. Use correct punctuation and capitalization.

19. provides jobs
MODEL⟩ Cable television provides jobs.
20. need talented writers
21. has jobs for camera crews
22. formed a television writers' guild
23. appear on cable stations
24. are expensive to make
25. can be seen late at night

4 Complete and Simple Predicates *pages 36 – 37*

A. Identifying Complete and Simple Predicates   Write each complete predicate. Underline it once. Then underline the simple predicate twice.

1. The teacher gave an assignment to the class.
   MODEL⟩ gave an assignment to the class

2. Term papers always present a challenge.
3. The seventh-grade class approached the task anxiously.
4. The teacher carefully provided step-by-step guidance.
5. Each student chose a topic of interest.
6. That topic was too broad for a short term paper.
7. The students narrowed their topics.
8. One student chose water transportation as her topic.
9. She narrowed the topic with the help of her teacher.

B. Expanding Simple Predicates   Expand each simple predicate to make a complete sentence.

10. The research began
    MODEL⟩ The research began in the school library.
11. The card catalogue provided
12. The index of each book listed
13. The library's shelves held
14. The nonfiction books belonged
15. The table of contents identified
16. Magazines and journals offered
17. The *Readers' Guide to Periodical Literature* listed

C. Adding Complete Predicates to Sentences   Add a complete predicate to each subject to form a sentence.

18. Each student
    MODEL⟩ Each student took notes.
19. The notes
20. The outline
21. The first draft
22. Students and their partners
23. Some changes
24. The second draft

EXTRA PRACTICE

UNIT 1

5 Word Order in Sentences *pages 38–39*

A. Identifying Word Order in Sentences   Write *natural* or *inverted* to identify the word order in each sentence.

1. Computers have altered communication forever.
MODEL〉 natural
   2. From computer technology comes an information explosion.
   3. Computers handle many tasks for a variety of purposes.
   4. Businesses use computers for accounting and bookkeeping.
   5. Do supermarkets use scanners in their checkout systems?
   6. How good is the new checkout system?
   7. Computers bill customers and track inventory for stores.
   8. Does your library locate information through computers?
   9. How they contribute to the explosion of information!
   10. Have you seen computers at work for airplane travelers?
   11. What a problem it is when the computers are down!

B. Changing Sentence Formats   Rewrite each sentence. Change natural order to inverted order.

   12. A computer terminal stood inside the classroom.
MODEL〉 Inside the classroom stood a computer terminal.
   13. Computers can solve complex problems.
   14. Radar defense systems depend on sophisticated computers.
   15. A rapid analysis of data comes from a computer.
   16. Computers process photographic images for astronomers.
   17. Vast amounts of data are available with computers.
   18. Many computers work in private homes.

C. Writing Sentences in Natural and Inverted Order   Complete each sentence. Then write *natural* or *inverted* to identify its word order.

   19. In our class   ·
MODEL〉 In our class we have a new computer.   natural
   20. From computers come
   21. With limited instruction students
   22. After their training, programmers
   23. A computer terminal in the classroom
   24. How do computers
   25. With computers students
   26. A computer presents

UNIT 1

6 Compound Subjects and
Predicates *pages 40 – 41*

A. Identifying Compound Subjects and Predicates   Write the compound subject or compound predicate and the joining word in each sentence. Identify each compound element.

   1. People speak or write in ordinary communication.
   MODEL⟩ speak or write—predicate
   2. Phone calls or letters provide personal communication.
   3. Speech and gestures are used in ordinary conversations.
   4. Sometimes people write letters or send telegrams.
   5. Teachers and students share ideas in the classroom.
   6. In large or small groups people talk and listen.
   7. Personal communication and mass communication differ.
   8. Books and television are forms of mass communication.

B. Writing Compound Subjects and Predicates   Add words to form a compound subject or predicate. Write each sentence.

   9. Radio and _____ broadcast news reports.
   MODEL⟩ Radio and television broadcast news reports.
   10. CB radios and _____ are available for cars.
   11. Television can inform or _____.
   12. Newspapers and _____ are sources for news.
   13. Students read and _____ textbooks.
   14. Commercials and _____ can provide information.
   15. The teacher may assign and _____ a film.
   16. Films depict and _____ historical events.
   17. Actors and _____ portray historical figures.

C. Punctuating Sentences Correctly   Write each sentence. Add commas where they are needed.

   18. Books magazines and newspapers spread the news.
   MODEL⟩ Books, magazines, and newspapers spread the news.
   19. Danes Germans and Britons experimented with telegraph systems.
   20. Morse developed perfected and introduced the telegraph.
   21. Cities states and nations were linked by telegraph.
   22. Heliographs daguerrotypes and calotypes preceded photos.
   23. Inventors conceived developed and improved photography.

EXTRA PRACTICE

7 Simple and Compound Sentences *pages 42 – 43*

A. Identifying Simple and Compound Sentences Write *simple* or *compound* to identify each sentence.

1. I sent two letters, and I received one.
[MODEL] compound
2. Friendly letters remain a popular form of communication.
3. Some people send cards, but others prefer letters.
4. Students send letters to pen pals around the world.
5. Jay and Anna have pen pals in Hawaii, Peru, and Brazil.
6. I can ask questions in a letter, or I can answer them.
7. A letter can be brief, or it can be long and newsy.
8. Whenever possible, I send photographs with my letters.

B. Changing Sentence Formats Rewrite each pair of simple sentences as a compound sentence. Use the conjunction or semicolon in parentheses ( ).

9. I read the letters. I enjoyed them. (and)
[MODEL] I read the letters, and I enjoyed them.
10. Some letters have merit. They are published in books. (and)
11. Vincent van Gogh wrote many letters. He often wrote several in a day. (;)
12. He wrote to his brother Theo. Theo saved his letters. (and)
13. The letters describe van Gogh's struggles. They illuminate his paintings. (;)
14. He made many sketches. He included these in his letters. (and)
15. Vincent lived in Arles, France. He painted constantly. (and)

C. Writing Compound Sentences Change each simple sentence to a compound sentence by adding a related simple sentence. Use the conjunction in parentheses ( ).

16. Tim wrote a letter. (and)
[MODEL] Tim wrote a letter, and he waited for an answer.
17. I sent a birthday card to my friend. (but)
18. People wait eagerly for the letter carrier. (and)
19. Will the cost of postage increase? (or)
20. I save postcards from around the world. (;)
21. My friends don't write letters. (but)
22. You can write a long letter. (or)
23. I read my letter aloud to my family. (and)

8 Avoiding Sentence Fragments and Run-on Sentences *pages 44–45*

A. Identifying Sentences, Fragments and Run-on Sentences   Read each group of words. Identify each by writing *sentence, sentence fragment,* or *run-on sentence.*

1. A laboratory in New Jersey.
    MODEL⟩ sentence fragment
2. Patented over 1,000 inventions.
3. Researchers at Edison's laboratories worked together.
4. Edison learned to operate a telegraph he managed a telegraph office when he was fifteen.
5. He invented a transmitter and a receiver for the automatic telegraph.
6. What was Edison's first major invention?
7. It was a stock ticker for printing stock quotations.
8. A manufacturing shop in Newark, New Jersey.

B. Rewriting Sentence Fragments   Rewrite each fragment as a complete sentence. Add a subject, a predicate, or both. Write *complete* if a sentence is complete.

9. Revolutionized communication.
    MODEL⟩ The telephone revolutionized communication.
10. Could not imagine life without the telephone.
11. Every business and many homes.
12. Often conduct business meetings with conference calls.
13. Can order anything from flower seeds to concert tickets.
14. In busy offices telephones constantly ringing.
15. Use the telephone to check the time or get a weather report.

C. Correcting Run-on Sentences   Correct each run-on sentence. Add punctuation to separate the complete thoughts into simple sentences, or turn run-on sentences into compound sentences.

16. I chose a topic I wrote a report on it.
    MODEL⟩ I chose a topic, and I wrote a report on it.
17. Many businesses communicate information with reports employees in these businesses must write well.
18. Class reports are a way of sharing information they provide valuable experience.
19. Writing skills are important they do not ensure success.
20. Everyone can learn public speaking it is not difficult.

UNIT 2

1 Nouns *pages 78 – 79*

A. Identifying Nouns Write the nouns in each sentence. Write whether each noun names a *person*, a *place*, a *thing*, or an *idea*.

1. Will had a happy childhood.
MODEL> Will—person   childhood—idea
2. Will Rogers was born in Oklahoma.
3. His first pony was a mare he loved very much.
4. Will accepted his responsibilities and did his chores.
5. All the children played in the woods and fields.
6. Will roped steers by the horns.
7. He took lessons and could throw a lasso.
8. The children packed a lunch and fished in the river.
9. The boys and girls had grasshoppers and worms for bait.
10. In his childhood he had few worries.
11. He received his education in the town of Drumgoole.

B. Substituting Proper Nouns for Common Nouns Write each sentence. Substitute proper nouns for the underlined words.

12. A comedian performed on television.
MODEL> Bill Cosby performed on television.
13. The woman is a famous comedian.
14. She appeared on a popular show.
15. Some of the jokes were about our country.
16. The comedian came to our school.
17. She arrived in the morning one day.
18. Our teacher took the class to the auditorium.
19. My friend and I sat in the first row.
20. Our principal introduced the comedian to us.
21. The comedian lives in a nearby city.
22. She told us to be proud of our town.

C. Using Nouns in Sentences Write a proper noun for each common noun. Use the pairs in original sentences.

23. comic strip
MODEL> Starlight, Starbright
My favorite comic strip is Starlight, Starbright.
24. host
25. sponsor
26. parent
27. character
28. day
29. fantasy
30. school
31. television show
32. child
33. program

2 Kinds of Nouns *pages 80–81*

A. Identifying Concrete and Abstract Nouns Make two lists entitled *Concrete Nouns* and *Abstract Nouns*. Write nouns from each sentence in the appropriate column.

1. Many people enjoy satire.

MODEL> Concrete Nouns   Abstract Nouns
       people   satire

2. Comedians amuse us with their wit.

3. Dick Gregory showed his humor in many performances.

4. His shows brought him wide success for many years.

5. Gregory avoided stereotypical material in his skits.

6. He used his performances to advance important causes.

7. Bill Cosby is an entertainer.

8. People identify with his characters and their problems.

B. Using Collective Nouns in Sentences Write each sentence, substituting a collective noun for the underlined noun. You may change other words if necessary for sense.

9. Many people came to see the show.

MODEL> A large crowd came to see the show.

10. The teenagers wanted to see the comedians.
11. Reviewers had encouraged the students to attend.
12. The workers at the theater had made arrangements.
13. The advertisers had worked hard on publicity.
14. People knew it would be a spectacular show.
15. Several reporters filmed each performer.
16. The performers included newcomers and oldtimers.

C. Writing Concrete, Abstract, and Collective Nouns in Sentences Use each noun in a funny sentence about a show or performance. Identify it as *concrete* or *abstract*. Then, label appropriate concrete nouns *collective*.

17. team

MODEL> The team went to Austin instead of Houston. *concrete, collective*

18. flock	21. group	24. laughter
19. audience	22. herd	25. amusement
20. comic	23. intelligence	26. popularity

EXTRA PRACTICE

3 Capitalization of Proper Nouns *pages 82 – 83*

A. Identifying the Correct Forms of Proper Nouns   Write the correct form of each proper noun in parentheses ( ).

1. My little sister is reading (*Harry The Dirty Dog, Harry the Dirty Dog*).

   MODEL ⟩ *Harry the Dirty Dog*

2. Tom's little brother likes the book (*Green Eggs and ham, Green Eggs and Ham*).

3. I wrote to (Harold n. Barrett, Harold N. Barrett), who lives in (newtown, Connecticut; Newtown, Connecticut).

4. We are going to visit the (Department of the Treasury, Department Of The Treasury) on our trip to the capital.

5. Next year we will travel to (the Columbia River Valley, The Columbia River valley).

6. Cleon and I do volunteer work for (Friends of Animals, Friends Of Animals) in (New jersey, New Jersey).

7. (St. Louis, Missouri; St. louis, Missouri) is often called the (Gateway to the West, Gateway To The West).

8. Would you like to join our singing club, the (New south Wails, New South Wails)?

9. Chen and Andre went to see a performance of the comedy (Blithe spirit, Blithe Spirit).

B. Capitalizing Proper Nouns   Capitalize each proper noun correctly.

10. house of representatives

   MODEL ⟩ House of Representatives

11. the thurber carnival

12. chrysler building

13. st. patrick's day

14. orlando humane society

15. sea world of texas

16. great smoky mountains

17. jenny swanson lorenson

18. "the night the bed fell"

19. laurel junior high school

20. treaty of paris

C. Proofreading Sentences with Proper Nouns   Write ten sentences about amusing people you know, places you have visited, or things you have read. Then proofread and correct any errors you have made in capitalizing proper nouns.

UNIT 2

4 Abbreviations *pages 84 – 85*

A. Identifying Abbreviations   Write the word or words that each abbreviation stands for.

1. Dec.
MODEL> December

2. oz.	**7.** Mt.	**12.** mph
3. ft.	**8.** Jr.	**13.** NJ
4. Nov.	**9.** Tues.	**14.** Blvd.
5. h.p.	**10.** A.M.	**15.** UN
6. Gov.	**11.** cm	**16.** USSR

B. Writing Abbreviations   Write each word, and next to it write its correct abbreviation.

17. Avenue
MODEL> Avenue—Ave.

18. Saturday	**23.** Senior	**28.** August
19. Doctor	**24.** October	**29.** Mister
20. Reverend	**25.** Wednesday	**30.** Drive
21. Street	**26.** Apartment	**31.** Senator
22. quart	**27.** December	**32.** Alabama

C. Writing Abbreviations   Rewrite each item using abbreviations for whole words where appropriate.

33. Kai's address is 8 Lee Road, Waco, Texas 76710.
MODEL> Kai's address is 8 Lee Rd., Waco, TX 76710.

34. The envelope was addressed to Mister Lars Nelson, 627 Lotus Lane, New Castle, Pennsylvania 16101.

35. Allan's birth certificate reads March 1, 1986, instead of March 1, 1976.

36. That sign reads "High Point, North Carolina, 20 miles."

37. The advertisement in the paper says "Four gallons of gas for the price of three."

38. The map says "Take Route 4 West to Santa Cruz."

39. That letter to the editor in the paper is signed *Governor Kean.*

40. Mister Frank Smith, Junior, is my dad.

41. The party will begin about 6:30 in the evening.

EXTRA PRACTICE

UNIT 2

5 Singular and Plural Nouns *pages 86 – 87*

A. Writing Plural Nouns   Write the plural form of each word.

  1. hiss

MODEL hisses

   2. buzz   **6.** safe   **10.** box

   3. baby   **7.** tomato   **11.** glass

   4. flash   **8.** loaf   **12.** worry

   5. gas   **9.** zoo   **13.** chef

B. Writing Plural Forms of Singular Nouns   Write the singular nouns in each sentence. Then write their plurals.

  14. The show was held in an outdoor theater.

MODEL show—shows   theater—theaters

  15. The boy sat on the bench.

  16. The comedian appeared on stage.

  17. A spotlight centered directly on him.

  18. A fan edged forward on her chair.

  19. The actor told a funny story.

  20. An elderly lady laughed very hard.

  21. A baby cried softly.

  22. The comedian made a joke about the baby.

  23. One listener fell off his chair laughing.

  24. Each ticket was well worth its price.

C. Writing Nouns in Sentences   Write the plural nouns in each sentence. Write each singular form, and then use them in a sentence of your own.

  25. Bright flashes came from the strobe light in the wings.

MODEL flashes—flash   wings—wing

     The flash of a hummingbird's wing is too fast for the eye to see.

  26. Many families watch comedies together.

  27. Years ago radios brought comedy into the home.

  28. I like hearing about the early comics.

  29. My grandfather liked the ventriloquists and their dummies.

  30. Some comedy teams featured husbands and wives.

  31. George Burns and Gracie Allen performed for many years.

  32. Gracie was one of the funniest of the funny ladies.

  33. George Burns continues to delight his fans.

6 More Plural Nouns *pages 88 – 89*

A. Identifying Singular and Plural Nouns   Write the underlined noun in each sentence, and identify it as *singular* or *plural.*

1. One comedian discussed kinds of <u>fish</u> in his act.
MODEL> fish—plural
2. Another made jokes about the <u>news</u> of the day.
3. The network realized a <u>savings</u> in its costs.
4. Several television <u>series</u> were canceled in midseason.
5. Several <u>people</u> were asked their opinions of TV sitcoms.
6. Some <u>species</u> of sitcoms, they said, were just too silly.
7. A sitcom with a talking <u>moose</u> was canceled.
8. A <u>team</u> of comedy writers was hired to try to improve it.
9. They knew the show was in trouble the day the design <u>crew</u> got more laughs than the comedian.

B. Writing Noun Plurals   Write the plural form of each noun.

10. mailbox
MODEL> mailboxes

11. bookmark	15. spoonful	19. brother-in-law
12. foot	16. tooth	20. track meet
13. child	17. eyelash	21. great-grandmother
14. cupful	18. economics	22. salesperson

C. Writing Sentences with Plural Nouns   Write each sentence, using the plural form of the noun in parentheses ( ).

23. A flock of (sheep) grazed on the hillside.
MODEL> A flock of sheep grazed on the hillside.
24. The comedian made jokes about several (species) of animals.
25. She imitated the movement of schools of (fish).
26. She said the frogs were (runner-up) in a jumping contest.
27. She imitated a flock of (goose) flying overhead.
28. Does the plural word (*moose*) rhyme with *goose*?
29. Why did all the (elk) cross the mountain?
30. How many (sheep) ate all the grass on the hillside?
31. She asked why the (reindeer) were not at the North Pole.
32. She asked why the (ox) crossed the road.
33. Do (mouse) live in the house?

UNIT 2

7 Possessive Nouns *pages 90 – 91*

A. Identifying Possessive Nouns   Write the possessive nouns in these sentences.

1. The crowd's response to the performance of the comedian was electrifying.
   `MODEL` crowd's
2. The audience's applause was overwhelming.
3. The comedian had made comments about women's rights.
4. She had won her bosses' approval for the act long ago.
5. In rehearsal, her sister's comments had helped her to judge how the women would respond.
6. Chita's point had been that the element of truth in her jokes would be appreciated.
7. The comedian eventually realized that a clown's antics were not necessary to get her message across.
8. The previous act, a man in a sailor's outfit, had not been well received.

B. Writing Possessive Forms   Write these singular nouns in a list. Then write the singular possessive, the plural, and the plural possessive. You will have four columns.

9. act

Singular	Singular Poss.	Plural	Plural Poss.
`MODEL` act	act's	acts	acts'

10. year	13. child	16. knife
11. sheep	14. ox	17. tooth
12. loaf	15. cameo	18. bus

C. Rewriting Sentences with Possessives   Write seven sentences. Include a possessive form of one of the following phrases in each sentence.

19. the fame of Eddie
    `MODEL` Eddie's fame surprised no one more than himself.
20. a movie with Lily Tomlin
21. a performance by Whoopi Goldberg
22. a role made famous by Jackie Gleason
23. a review published this morning
24. the affection of the audience
25. a reward for a comedian
26. seats for the ticket holders

UNIT 2

8 Appositives *pages 92 – 93*

A. Identifying Appositives Write the appositive in each sentence. Then write the noun that the appositive explains or describes.

1. Marla, my friend, watches old movies on TV.
MODEL> friend—Marla

2. Woody Allen, a filmmaker, began his career as a writer.
3. Allen admired Mort Sahl, a stand-up comedian.
4. Letty, his sister, became his friend and companion.
5. Willie Mays, star of the N.Y. Giants, was Allen's hero.
6. Woody, an avid reader, took charge of his own education.
7. Allen directed *Take the Money and Run,* his first success.
8. *Sleeper,* a big hit, appealed to many people.
9. Comedy, Woody's specialty, is difficult to write.

B. Combining Sentences with Appositives Rewrite each pair of sentences using an appositive.

10. We all like Carol Burnett. Carol Burnett is a popular comedian.
MODEL> We all like Carol Burnett, a popular comedian.
11. Carol Burnett wrote her memoirs. The book is called *One More Time*.
12. Carol Burnett is a talented woman. She wrote her memoirs for her children.
13. Her first visit to the circus impressed her. It had been a scary experience.
14. As a young woman, Carol was an aspiring actress. She studied theater arts.
15. People respond well to her. She is a veteran actress.

C. Rewriting Sentences with Appositives Rewrite each sentence, using an appositive.

16. Rita Moreno is a performer who won four major awards.
MODEL> Rita Moreno, a performer, won four major awards.
17. Rita Moreno was born in Humacao, which is a town in Puerto Rico.
18. Jerome Robbins was a director and choreographer, and he cast Rita Moreno in *West Side Story*.
19. Rita, who is a talented singer and actress, won an Oscar for Best Supporting Actress in that film.
20. The film won ten Academy Awards in 1962, and it was a success.
21. Rita Moreno acted in *The Electric Company,* which is an educational program.

UNIT 3

1 Verbs *pages 126 – 127*

A. Identifying Verbs   Write the verb in each sentence.

  1. Today we honor Matthew Henson.
MODEL⟩ honor
  2. Robert Peary studied a report about Greenland.
  3. The study aroused his interest in the Arctic.
  4. He learned the survival skills of the Eskimos.
  5. Matthew Henson accompanied Peary into Greenland.
  6. Peary explored the coastline of Greenland.
  7. Peary and Henson reached the North Pole in 1909.
  8. Frederick Cook also made a similar claim.
  9. His claim was questionable.

B. Identifying Action and Linking Verbs   Write the verb in each sentence. Write *action* or *linking* to identify the kind of verb used.

  10. Explorers seem very brave.
MODEL⟩ seem—linking
  11. Richard Byrd became an Antarctic explorer.
  12. He attended the United States Naval Academy.
  13. He flew over the North Pole in 1926 with Floyd Bennett.
  14. Congress gave Byrd the Medal of Honor for his flight.
  15. Private donors appeared enthusiastic.
  16. Byrd's expedition established a base in Antarctica.
  17. Little America appeared on the Ross Ice Shelf.
  18. Byrd and his group flew to the South Pole and back.

C. Writing Sentences with Linking Verbs   Write each sentence and add a linking verb to complete it.

  19. Byrd _____ an explorer.
MODEL⟩ Byrd was an explorer
  20. He _____ famous.
  21. His family and friends _____ proud of him.
  22. He _____ an explorer with a good reputation.
  23. He _____ dedicated to becoming truly great.
  24. Byrd's talent _____ special.
  25. He _____ always a serious student.
  26. His career _____ a credit to his dedication.
  27. He _____ thrilled by the establishment of a base.
  28. He _____ humble in spite of all the attention.
  29. In every expedition he _____ brave and enthusiastic.

2 Main Verbs and Helping Verbs *pages 128 – 129*

A. Identifying Verb Phrases   Write the verb phrase in each sentence.

    1. I have been reading a book by Maya Angelou.
    MODEL⟩ have been reading
    2. Maya Angelou has written her autobiography.
    3. I did enjoy her book *I Know Why the Caged Bird Sings.*
    4. I will be reading other books as well.
    5. Angelou has been a popular and successful writer.
    6. She does write both fiction and poetry.
    7. Her creativity has flowed into other areas as well.
    8. You can see her work in the theater and on film.

B. Writing Verb Phrases   Write each sentence, using a verb phrase for each verb in parentheses ( ).

    9. I (enjoy) these poems by Maya Angelou.
    MODEL⟩ I am enjoying these poems by Maya Angelou.
    10. Our class (read) collections of Angelou's poetry.
    11. My friend (prepare) a presentation for the class.
    12. Angelou (performed) on stage.
    13. Our teacher (tell) us about one performance.
    14. Maya Angelou (create) musical compositions.
    15. She (comment) on the work of black artists.
    16. Angelou (praise) the writer's persistence.
    17. Writers (give) a legacy to the next generation.

C. Completing Sentences with Verb Phrases   Complete each sentence with an appropriate verb phrase.

    18. Our class _____ the play.
    MODEL⟩ Our class was enjoying the play.
    19. Plays _____ excitement for the players.
    20. The audience _____ the mood of the play.
    21. An appreciative audience _____ the performers.
    22. A dull audience _____ the players.
    23. Some actors _____ no matter what happens.
    24. Theater-goers _____ tickets this year.
    25. The cost of producing a play _____.
    26. Local theaters _____ larger and larger audiences.
    27. Good publicity _____ a play.
    28. Bad publicity, on the other hand, _____ a play.

UNIT 3

3 Principal Parts of Regular Verbs *pages 130–131*

A. Identifying Principal Parts of Verbs in Sentences Write the verb or verb phrase in each sentence. Identify it as the *present, present participle, past,* or *past participle* form.

  1. Simón Bolívar lived in Venezuela.
  MODEL〉 lived—past
   2. The class is studying about young Simón Bolívar.
   3. Bolívar's family owned a mansion in Caracas, Venezuela.
   4. For generations the family had possessed great wealth.
   5. Spanish authorities had banned revolutionary books.
   6. Rodriguez Carreno entered Bolívar's life as his tutor.
   7. Spanish monks had instructed the young Bolívar before.
   8. Rodriguez based his lectures on theory and fact.
   9. Our class is learning new facts about Bolívar.

B. Writing Principal Parts of Regular Verbs Write four headings on a sheet of paper: *Present, Present Participle, Past,* and *Past Participle* and complete the chart for each verb in the list.

  10. look

Present	Present Participle	Past	Past Participle
look	looking	looked	looked

MODEL〉

   11. love   **15.** flap   **19.** match
   12. persuade   **16.** call   **20.** hate
   13. climb   **17.** touch   **21.** stop
   14. receive   **18.** charm   **22.** watch

C. Writing the Correct Principal Part of a Verb Write each sentence, using the given principal part of each verb in parentheses ( ).

  23. Bolívar had (learn) a lesson.   past participle
  MODEL〉 Bolívar had learned a lesson.
   24. Bolívar had (desire) independence.   past participle
   25. In 1810 he is (emerge) as a leader.   present participle
   26. He (establish) the second republic in 1813.   past
   27. Setbacks (force) his retreat into Jamaica.   present
   28. Bolívar (achieve) a major victory in Colombia.   past
   29. Then he was (elect) president.   past
   30. Resentment is (thrive).   present participle
   31. Bolívar had (work) for liberty.   past participle

4 Principal Parts of Irregular Verbs *pages 132 – 134*

A. Choosing the Correct Verb Form Write the verb form in parentheses ( ) that completes each sentence correctly.

   1. We have (come, came) for field day.

   MODEL〉 come

   2. Field day is (begun, beginning) in an hour.
   3. Tamara and I are (run, running) in one race.
   4. I had never (run, ran) in a race before.
   5. My friends are (coming, came) for the race.
   6. The race is (beginning, begun) now.
   7. I have (catching, caught) Tamara and have won the race.

B. Writing the Correct Verb Form Write each sentence, using the correct past or past participle form of the verb in parentheses ( ).

   8. The modern Olympic Games (begin) in 1896.

   MODEL〉 The modern Olympic Games began in 1896.

   9. Pierre de Coubertin (think) about the games.
   10. He (bring) the games back to Greece.
   11. In 1896 athletes (come) from 11 countries.
   12. The games have (bring) great attention to athletes.
   13. New athletes have (burst) on the scene.
   14. Matt Biondi (swim) for seven medals in 1988.
   15. In 1936 Jesse Owens (run) four winning races.

C. Writing Verb Forms Rewrite each sentence. Change each verb from the past to the past participle form, adding an appropriate helping verb. Change each past participle form to the past, omitting the helping verb. Label each new verb correctly.

   16. The bells rang throughout the city.

   MODEL〉 The bells have rung throughout the city.—past participle

   17. The Lions won the championship.
   18. The fans threw confetti into the air.
   19. People have come from all over the state.
   20. Parents brought their children to the city.
   21. Souvenir shops have sold all their souvenirs.
   22. People have begun to fill the stadium.
   23. They have sung together outside.
   24. Everyone came for the same reason.

EXTRA PRACTICE

UNIT 3

5 More Irregular Verbs *pages 135 – 136*

A. Writing Past Participles of Verbs   Rewrite each sentence. Change each verb from the past form to the past participle form. Add helping verbs.

  1. Characters in myths did amazing things.
MODEL〉 Characters in myths have done amazing things.
  2. Daedalus gave wings to his son Icarus.
  3. Father and son flew on wings made of feathers and wax.
  4. Prometheus chose to help the humans.
  5. The gods became angry.
  6. Phaëthon rode in the chariot of the Sun.
  7. The horses took control of the chariot.

B. Writing the Past Forms of Verbs   Rewrite each sentence. Change each past participle form to the simple past form.

  8. Geniuses have given us new and important ideas.
MODEL〉 Geniuses gave us new and important ideas.
  9. Benjamin Franklin has written an almanac.
  10. The assembly line has grown since its creation.
  11. Alfred Nobel has known how to manufacture dynamite.
  12. Lavoisier has given an explanation of combustion.
  13. Albert Einstein has spoken his last words in German.
  14. Thomas Edison had chosen to start an invention factory.

C. Changing Verb Forms   Rewrite each sentence. Change each verb from the past form to the past participle form, and add an appropriate helping verb. Change each past participle form to the past form, and omit the helping verb. Label each new form.

  15. Riders have brought their best horses to the show.
MODEL〉 Riders brought their best horses to the show.—past
  16. The contestants had ridden around the field twice.
  17. They knew how their horses would behave.
  18. The riders wore traditional riding gear.
  19. The organizers have spoken with each of the riders.
  20. They have done their best to prepare carefully.
  21. The horses have eaten special foods to nourish them.
  22. Some riders flew in on Friday.
  23. The ground had frozen late in the season.
  24. The riders had ridden over rough terrain before.
  25. A beautiful mare won the grand prize.

UNIT 3

6 Simple Verb Tenses *pages 137 – 138*

A. Identifying Verb Tenses Write each verb or verb phrase, and identify the tense as *present*, *past*, or *future*.

1. changed

MODEL〉 changed—past

2. asked	**6.** want	**10.** will play
3. open	**7.** will see	**11.** agree
4. expect	**8.** watched	**12.** anticipated
5. will go	**9.** cancel	**13.** will pay

B. Identifying Verbs and Their Tenses Write the verb from each sentence. Write *present*, *past*, or *future* to identify its tense.

14. We study American Indian cultures.

MODEL〉 study—present

15. We will study several American Indian tribes.
16. Groups first lived in New Mexico 20,000 years ago.
17. The Anasazi developed an advanced culture.
18. The people lived in communal dwellings, or pueblos.
19. Today people visit the sites in the American Southwest.
20. One name for the early Anasazi is *Basket Makers*.
21. You will find woven baskets from early tribes.
22. The dry climate preserved bags, sandals, and nets.

C. Writing the Correct Tense Write the correct form of the verb in parentheses ( ) to complete each sentence correctly. Use the tense shown.

23. We _____ a vacation. (want—present)

MODEL〉 want

24. Our family _____ west this summer. (travel—future)
25. I _____ information from Arizona. (request—past)
26. My family _____ places of interest. (select—future)
27. Earlier we _____ parks and monuments. (visit—past)
28. Soon we _____ pueblos in Arizona. (see—future)
29. The animals _____ elk and bear. (include—present)
30. If time _____, we will go north. (permit—present)
31. We may _____ the Grand Canyon. (see—present)
32. I _____ rafting on the river. (go—future)
33. We _____ the Anasazi ruins. (see—future)
34. Our family always _____ together. (travel—present)

EXTRA PRACTICE

7 Perfect Verb Tenses *pages 139–140*

A. Identifying the Perfect Tenses   Write each verb, and identify its tense.

1. had wanted
MODEL⟩ had wanted—past perfect

2. has walked   **5.** had planned   **8.** have called
3. had eaten   **6.** has planned   **9.** will have waited
4. had hoped   **7.** has stayed   **10.** will have talked

B. Identifying the Perfect Tenses   Write the verb in each sentence. Be sure to include the helping verbs. Identify each as *present perfect, past perfect,* or *future perfect.*

11. Nilda has played the piano for five years.
MODEL⟩ has played—present perfect
12. The students have prepared for the school play.
13. The drama coach had chosen a musical comedy last fall.
14. After this year's play, the drama coach will have directed the school plays for 10 years.
15. The students have planned a special presentation.
16. They had hoped for a full house on opening night.
17. They will not have hoped in vain.
18. Family and friends have purchased all the tickets.
19. Everyone has anticipated this performance for months.
20. From the start the drama coach had created a fine show.
21. Prior to opening night, the cast will have received excellent training.

C. Writing Verb Tenses   Complete each sentence with the verb in parentheses ( ). Use the tense shown. Write the sentence.

22. All clubs (conduct—present perfect) meetings.
MODEL⟩ All clubs have conducted meetings.
23. The Careers Club (plan—present perfect) an assembly.
24. They (invite—past perfect) many speakers in advance.
25. Dr. Smith (decline—past perfect); she later accepted.
26. She (prepare—present perfect) her talk carefully.
27. The invitation (delight—past perfect) her.
28. She (complete—future perfect) her talk by noon.
29. Dr. Smith (request—present perfect) a question period.
30. The members (discuss—past perfect) the idea already.
31. Several students (prepare—present perfect) questions.
32. Amy (submit—future perfect) questions in advance.

UNIT 3

8 Be, Have, Do pages 141–143

A. Identifying Forms of Be, Have, and Do Write the form of *be*, *have*, or *do* in each sentence.

1. Joe has done it.

MODEL> has done

2. My classmates are participants in a contest.
3. It is an essay contest sponsored by our town.
4. The theme of the essay is patriotism.
5. We have been contestants in other meets before.
6. I was happy with the results of the other meets.
7. I have had luck in the past.
8. I will do my best in this contest.

B. Writing Verb Tenses Complete each sentence, using the tense and the verb in parentheses ( ). Write the sentence.

9. I (do—present perfect) my homework.

MODEL> I have done my homework.

10. Our school (have—present) a special awards assembly.
11. It (be—present) an honor to receive an award.
12. Parents and friends (be—future) present.
13. The judges (have—future perfect) a difficult time.
14. They (do—present perfect) a good job in the past.
15. By tomorrow we (have—future) the results.
16. I (do—present) not know who the winners will be.
17. Perhaps you (be—future) one of the winners.

C. Writing Verbs Complete each sentence with an appropriate form of the verb in parentheses ( ). Write the sentence. Identify the tense of the verb in each new sentence.

18. I (do) not see the yearbook before.

MODEL> I did not see the yearbook before.—past

19. I (have) old school yearbooks from the library.
20. This (be) the yearbook from 1980.
21. How funny the clothes (be)!
22. (Do) you find the scholarship winners in the book?
23. I (do) not believe I know any of these people.
24. This winner (be) my neighbor.
25. She (have) never told me she won a scholarship.
26. (Be) you interested in seeing other yearbooks?
27. I (do) tell the librarian I would return the book.

UNIT 3

9 Subject-Verb Agreement *pages 144 – 145*

A. Using Verb Forms Write each verb in the third-person present tense. Use *he, she,* or *it* and *they.*

1. apply
MODEL⟩ she applies; they apply

2. talk	**6.** search	**10.** go
3. pass	**7.** try	**11.** fix
4. buzz	**8.** climb	**12.** flash
5. fry	**9.** practice	**13.** desire

B. Writing Verb Forms in Sentences Write each sentence, using the present-tense form of the verb in parentheses ( ).

14. Jahid and Damon (be) here for the games.
MODEL⟩ Jahid and Damon are here for the games.
15. The contestants (arrive) for the Special Olympics.
16. The committee (work) to make the day a success.
17. Runners (gather) at the starting line.
18. The race (provide) a challenge and an opportunity.
19. Ella (compete) for the first time ever.
20. Her mother and father (watch) from the sidelines.
21. Where (be) the judges?
22. There (go) the starting gun.

C. Rewriting Sentences for Agreement Rewrite each sentence, keeping it in the present tense. Correct any verb that does not agree with its subject. If a sentence is correct, write *correct.*

23. Sandy and Carlos reads about the Special Olympics.
MODEL⟩ Sandy and Carlos read about the Special Olympics.
24. The Special Olympics is an athletic competition.
25. Entrants compete in various events.
26. What make the Special Olympics so special?
27. The participants compete despite their handicaps.
28. Over one million people participates.
29. Gymnastics are a popular event.
30. A recent addition are winter sports.
31. A committee organize the games in our town.
32. Every contestant receive encouragement.
33. The awards ceremony is a proud moment for all.
34. Raeann win an award in the long jump.

1 Progressive Forms of Verbs *pages 176–177*

A. Identifying the Progressive Tenses of Verbs   Write whether each verb is in the *present progressive, past progressive,* or *future progressive* tense.

1. is carrying
> [MODEL] present progressive

2. am thinking	**5.** was wishing	**8.** will be asking
3. will be telling	**6.** am considering	**9.** were feeling
4. are pleasing	**7.** is repeating	**10.** will be calling

B. Recognizing Progressive Forms in Sentences   Write the verb phrase in each sentence. Identify it as *present progressive, past progressive,* or *future progressive.*

11. Summer is coming.
> [MODEL] is coming—present progressive

12. The weather is turning warmer.
13. Schools are closing for the summer.
14. Soon we will be celebrating Independence Day.
15. Our school was sponsoring a July Fourth essay contest.
16. Students were writing essays about patriotism.
17. They were giving the subject much thought.
18. The teachers were discussing patriotism in class.
19. The committee will be announcing the winners tomorrow.
20. The winners will be reading their essays aloud.

C. Changing Simple Tenses to Progressive Forms   Rewrite each sentence. Change the simple tense of each verb to the corresponding progressive form.

21. My favorite holiday comes soon.
> [MODEL] My favorite holiday is coming soon.

22. Tamara plans a picnic for the Fourth of July.
23. She makes a list of the food for the party.
24. She will go to the grocery store for the food.
25. She did not wait until the last minute.
26. She learned from her previous mistakes.
27. Her guests look forward to the party.
28. They will enjoy the food and the companionship.
29. Tamara will make all her guests feel comfortable.
30. The guests will find new friends at the party.

UNIT 4

2 Direct Objects *pages 178 – 179*

A. Identifying Direct Objects   Write the direct object in each sentence.

1. I received a letter.
MODEL> letter
2. The students sent invitations for their graduation.
3. The school was holding the ceremony outdoors.
4. Students could invite their families.
5. The boys and girls rented caps and gowns.
6. Students had a sense of accomplishment.
7. Everyone congratulated the graduates.

B. Supplying Direct Objects   Add a direct object to each sentence.

8. At the museum Theo saw a _____.
MODEL> At the museum Theo saw a painting.
9. The museum exhibit featured a _____.
10. The displays inspired _____ in the viewers.
11. Some creative artists made these _____.
12. Viewers studied the _____ in the great hall.
13. Everyone likes the _____.
14. Guides gave _____ through the museum.
15. Some visitors bought _____.
16. People gave _____ to the cashier.
17. I can carry the _____ home on the bus.

C. Writing Direct Objects   Rewrite each sentence. Replace the direct object with another that makes sense.

18. I eat bread with every meal.
MODEL> I eat fruit with every meal.
19. I like spinach better than any other vegetable.
20. I always make pasta for dinner.
21. People eat more bread than ever before.
22. No one ever wants desserts after dinner.
23. Before dinner I serve appetizers.
24. Everyone in my family wants fish on Sundays.
25. Put the dishes on the table, please.
26. Did you take the rolls out of the oven?
27. Who will wash the dishes for us?
28. Next week we will eat dinner at your house.

UNIT 4

3 Indirect Objects *pages 180 – 181*

A. Identifying Direct and Indirect Objects Identify the direct object and the indirect object in each sentence.

1. Please give me your answer.

MODEL> answer—direct object; me—indirect object

2. My grandmother tells me stories about her childhood.
3. Once she had told my mother the same stories.
4. It gives me a good feeling to hear about my family.
5. Her father had built his family a large house.
6. He left his children a legacy of his handiwork.
7. I have sent my cousins copies of the pictures.

B. Recognizing Indirect Objects in Sentences Write the indirect objects in the sentences. If a sentence has no indirect object, write *no indirect object*.

8. Kennedy sent voters a message.

MODEL> voters

9. John Kennedy left us a legacy.
10. He promised all Americans equal justice.
11. People believed in him and his message.
12. He gave people renewed hope in democratic ideals.
13. Many people still pay him respect and honor.
14. A torch burns continuously at his grave.
15. Kennedy worked for a better America.
16. He offered many people a new and better life.

C. Supplying Indirect Objects Add an indirect object to each sentence. Write the sentence.

17. I read _____ a story.

MODEL> I read Sam a story.

18. Our teacher read _____ *The Yearling.*
19. She gave _____ permission to choose our own books.
20. My father lent _____ a book to bring to school.
21. My classmates gave _____ their opinions of the book.
22. I promised _____ my opinion on another book.
23. I lent _____ *Old Yeller.*
24. The book gave _____ a good feeling.
25. The class gives _____ the chance to review books.

UNIT 4

4 Predicate Nominatives *pages 182 – 183*

A. Identifying Predicate Nominatives Write the predicate nominative in each sentence.

1. Impressionism is art that gives an impression of a scene.
MODEL〉 art
2. An Impressionist painting is not a realistic rendering.
3. Impressionists were artists of the nineteenth century.
4. They became students of light and shadow.
5. Most Impressionists were painters of landscapes.
6. Camille Pissarro was a landscape painter.
7. He became a friend of Corot.
8. Corot seemed a major influence on Pissarro.
9. Renoir was an Impressionist who painted people.

B. Distinguishing Between Predicate Nominatives and Direct Objects Write the underlined word in each sentence. Identify it as a *predicate nominative* or as a *direct object*.

10. I am a <u>student</u> of art.
MODEL〉 student—predicate nominative
11. I have always admired the <u>style</u> of Edouard Manet.
12. Manet may have been the first <u>artist</u> to experiment with light.
13. At first the public rejected Manet's <u>paintings</u>.
14. Claude Monet became a close <u>friend</u> of Edouard Manet.
15. Monet was the <u>father</u> of true Impressionism.
16. He painted <u>landscapes</u> in the open air.
17. Boudin was the first <u>artist</u> to influence Monet.
18. Boudin encouraged <u>Monet</u> to paint landscapes.

C. Completing Sentences with Predicate Nominatives Add a predicate nominative to each sentence. Write the sentence.

19. My friend is _____.
MODEL〉 My friend is an artist.
20. My favorite painter is _____.
21. The painting I like best is _____.
22. My favorite building is _____.
23. The most beautiful colors may be _____ and _____.
24. The color of the sky at sunset appears _____.
25. At night the sky becomes _____.
26. Clouds are _____ that sail in the sky.

5 Transitive and Intransitive Verbs *pages 184 – 185*

A. Identifying Transitive and Intransitive Verbs   Write the verb in each sentence. Identify it as *transitive* or *intransitive*.

> **1.** My book contains poems by Robert Frost.

MODEL⟩ contains—transitive

> **2.** Many people like poems by Robert Frost.
> **3.** He reflects on life and human nature.
> **4.** Something in a scene may suggest past experiences.
> **5.** A poem about a road is also a poem about life.
> **6.** Like all other poets, Frost wrote from his own experiences.
> **7.** The countryside is the inspiration for many poems.
> **8.** A poem may describe two roads or a patch of snow.

B. Identifying Transitive Verbs and Their Direct Objects   Write the transitive verb and the direct object in each sentence.

> **9.** Poets express complex feelings.

MODEL⟩ express—transitive verb; feelings—direct object

> **10.** Carl Sandburg wrote many fine poems.
> **11.** His poems celebrate America's spirit.
> **12.** Sandburg writes poems about the prairie and the city.
> **13.** Some poems create small pictures.
> **14.** Lyric poems often evoke moods.
> **15.** Sandburg sees the small details of everyday life.
> **16.** His poems show us the importance of things around us.

C. Adding Direct Objects and Predicate Nominatives to Sentences   Complete each sentence with a direct object or a predicate nominative. Identify each verb as *transitive* or *intransitive*.

> **17.** I read _____.

MODEL⟩ I read "Birches."—transitive

> **18.** My favorite poet is _____.
> **19.** Some poems depict _____.
> **20.** Someday I will write _____.
> **21.** My favorite poem is _____.
> **22.** For English class I memorized _____.
> **23.** Last year I recited _____.
> **24.** Some poets are _____.

6 Active and Passive Voice *pages 186 – 187*

A. **Identifying Active and Passive Voice**   Write each sentence. Underline each verb or verb phrase. Write whether the verb is in the *active* or the *passive* voice.

   1. Young people share many concerns.
   MODEL⟩ Young people <u>share</u> many concerns.   active
   2. Friends give each other moral support.
   3. Many concerns can be discussed openly.
   4. Occasionally a person's ideas may be rejected.
   5. School can make people feel special.
   6. Some students may be overwhelmed by a large school.
   7. We are often supported by our friends.
   8. Individual talents need recognition.

B. **Writing Active and Passive Voice**   Change each verb in the active voice to the passive voice. Change each verb in the passive voice to the active voice.

   9. I call.
   MODEL⟩ I am called.
   10. He saw.   **15.** You were told.
   11. I will tell.   **16.** We have been asked.
   12. You call.   **17.** I had been called.
   13. It has frozen.   **18.** You will have been heard.
   14. We have followed.   **19.** It is filled.

C. **Writing Sentences with Active and Passive Voice**   Complete each sentence with the verb and voice in parentheses ( ). You may add helping verbs and choose your own tense.

   20. Adolescents _____ childhood behind.   (leave—active)
   MODEL⟩ Adolescents leave childhood behind.
   21. Some things _____ you proud.   (make—active)
   22. Music _____ by most people.   (like—passive)
   23. Marsha _____ by the song.   (cheer—passive)
   24. Many students _____ to sports.   (draw—passive)
   25. Relatives sometimes _____ encouragement.   (offer—active)
   26. Daydreams often _____ people.   (help—active)
   27. Teenagers _____ varied experiences.   (need—active)
   28. Hard work _____ Jamal.   (help—active)
   29. An interesting job _____ by Nikki.   (find—passive)

EXTRA PRACTICE

7 Easily Confused Verb Pairs *pages 188 – 189*

A. Using Verbs Correctly Write each sentence. Use the correct verb from each pair in parentheses ( ).

1. (Lie, Lay) the package on the table.
   `MODEL` Lay the package on the table.
2. I love to watch the sun (set, sit).
3. (Let, Leave) me enjoy the sight before we work.
4. I could (learn, teach) you to enjoy it, too.
5. (Lie, Lay) on the sand and watch it with me.
6. You can (sit, set) here on the blanket.
7. I will (let, leave) enough room.
8. You can (take, bring) it back tomorrow.

B. Writing Verbs in Sentences Complete each sentence with a verb from the word box. Some verbs will not be used.

> lie lay sit set let leave
> learn teach take bring

9. _____ me tell you my idea.
   `MODEL` Let me tell you my idea.
10. If you _____ to sew, you won't be bored.
11. You shouldn't _____ in the house all day.
12. Why don't you _____ me how to ride a skateboard?
13. Sherry offered to _____ us use her skateboard.
14. She will _____ it to school just for us.
15. We can _____ it home after school.
16. We can _____ our cares behind for the day.
17. I will _____ in a comfortable position in the chair.
18. We will _____ aside our work for just one day.

C. Writing Sentences Add words to form complete sentences. Use the verbs from the box in **B**.

19. when we camp
    `MODEL` We sit around a fire when we camp.
20. in the mountains
21. around the campfire
22. songs
23. firewood
24. sleep soundly all night
25. together under the trees
26. the food on the table
27. the smoke from the fire
28. sounds of the forest
29. home in spirit

UNIT 5

1 Pronouns *pages 224 – 225*

A. Identifying Pronouns Write the pronoun or pronouns in each sentence.

1. You and I can work in the garden.
`MODEL` You, I
  2. Mother plants flowers, and she tends the garden.
  3. It is beautiful, especially in the spring.
  4. We in the family think of her as Mother Nature.
  5. She makes things grow, and it pleases all of us.
  6. When winter is over, I look for crocuses.
  7. In the spring we wait for the blossoms on the trees.
  8. They burst forth in full color.

B. Writing the Person, Number, and Gender of Pronouns Write each underlined pronoun. Identify its person, number, and, wherever possible, its gender.

  9. The yard is bare in winter, but <u>it</u> will bloom in spring.
`MODEL` it—third person, singular, neuter
 10. <u>I</u> like the garden best in early summer.
 11. <u>You</u> seem to like irises and daffodils, Marcia.
 12. Geraniums are popular because <u>they</u> are colorful.
 13. Tom, do <u>you</u> know that impatiens blooms in the shade?
 14. Kay says that <u>she</u> will plant petunias.
 15. Friends tell <u>her</u> they want to see the onion patch.
 16. <u>They</u> are thinking of the words to an old song.
 17. Mr. Elias says that <u>he</u> can grow almost anything.

C. Writing Pronouns in Sentences Complete each sentence with the correct pronoun in parentheses ( ).

 18. The clerk at the garden center helped (we, us).
`MODEL` The clerk at the garden center helped us.
 19. Ed bought a cherry tree and planted (it, them).
 20. (He, Him) wanted to see it bloom and grow.
 21. Jan came to see (it, they).
 22. (She, Her) admired the new tree.
 23. The colorful blossoms delighted (she, her).
 24. Birds will come, and (they, them) will build nests.
 25. (I, Me) will wait for the eggs to hatch.
 26. Call (I, me) as soon as you see a nest.
 27. Ed promised to call (she, her).

UNIT 5

2 Pronouns and Antecedents *pages 226 – 227*

A. Identifying Pronoun Antecedents   Write each sentence. Draw an arrow from the underlined pronoun to its antecedent.

1. The seventh-grade classes study bees, and <u>we</u> like them.

> MODEL ⟩ The seventh-grade classes study bees, and we like them.

2. Ms. Ramos teaches Fred and helps <u>him</u> learn.

3. This is a butterfly, and <u>it</u> lives in gardens.

4. Female butterflies die after <u>they</u> lay their eggs.

5. The eggs lie underneath a leaf until <u>they</u> hatch.

6. Caterpillars wriggle from their shells and eat <u>them.</u>

B. Replacing Nouns in Sentences with Pronouns   Write the sentences, replacing the underlined nouns with pronouns.

7. A fully grown caterpillar has a hairy body. <u>The body</u> is divided into 13 segments.

> MODEL ⟩ A fully grown caterpillar has a hairy body. It is divided into 13 segments.

8. Jan and I observe, and <u>Jan and I</u> learn more.

9. Caterpillars' eyes are small, and <u>caterpillars</u> cannot see well.

10. Jan and I watch, and suddenly the caterpillar surprises <u>Jan and me.</u>

11. The caterpillar stops eating, and <u>the caterpillar</u> crawls away to a safe place.

12. The skin of the caterpillar begins to split. <u>The split skin</u> reveals a shiny green case.

C. Writing Pronouns in Sentences   Complete each sentence or sentence pair with a pronoun. Write the sentences.

13. The caterpillar is now a chrysalis. A silk thread holds _____ to the leaf.

> MODEL ⟩ The caterpillar is now a chrysalis. A silk thread holds it to the leaf.

14. Jan and I study the chrysalis. _____ learn more.

15. The chrysalis is like a shell, and the emerging butterfly splits _____ open.

16. Its wings are soft, and _____ are crumpled.

17. Newly emerged butterflies are tired. We watch _____.

18. The wings take shape slowly, but _____ are soft.

EXTRA PRACTICE

3 Subject and Object Pronouns *pages 228 – 229*

A. Identifying Subject and Object Pronouns Write the pronoun or pronouns in each sentence. Identify each one as a *subject pronoun* or as an *object pronoun*.

  1. Babies want us to notice them.
  MODEL⟩ us—object pronoun; them—object pronoun
  2. Babies are fascinating to the people watching them.
  3. They are not as helpless as people once believed.
  4. If I stroke little Bobby's palm, he grasps a finger.
  5. Little Lisa is sensitive, and she responds to a touch.
  6. A baby explores the surroundings and responds to them.
  7. Little Bobby smiles when Mother plays with him.
  8. Little Lisa wants attention, and we give it to her.

B. Identifying How Pronouns Are Used Write whether each underlined pronoun is in the *nominative case* or the *objective case*. Explain how it is used in the sentence.

  9. The baby saw me.
  MODEL⟩ objective case—direct object
  10. When he is calm, Jon's movements are smooth.
  11. A slamming door can startle him.
  12. At two months, Jon will give you a smile.
  13. You will be delighted to smile back.
  14. He wants daytime feedings every four hours.
  15. Brothers and sisters can give him a bottle.
  16. Jon will gladly take it.

C. Writing Pronouns in Original Sentences Add words to each word group to form a sentence.

  17. I am
  MODEL⟩ Somehow the baby knows when I am near.
  18. I listen
  19. for me
  20. give her
  21. you said
  22. to them
  23. we hope
  24. brought us
  25. with her
  26. it is I
  27. are they

UNIT 5

4 Possessive Pronouns *pages 230 – 232*

A. Identifying Possessive Pronouns   Write each possessive pronoun and the possessive noun it replaces.

1. June finds that her moods change.
MODEL⟩ her—June's
   2. Teenagers find their moods changing frequently.
   3. Mary says that her confidence sometimes falters.
   4. Jared boasts, but his boasting conceals his fears.
   5. "I like my new self," says Betty.
   6. "Insecurity is a problem, but it is not mine."
   7. "Yours is a good attitude, Betty," says Tanya.
   8. Liz and Eli are conquering their fear of the water.
   9. "Ours is not an unusual fear," they say.
 10. "The lifeguard says our progress is admirable."
 11. "What is your secret, Liz?"

B. Supplying Possessive Pronouns   Write each sentence, adding an appropriate possessive pronoun. Write the number and, wherever possible, the gender of each pronoun you add.

 12. We struggle for _____ autonomy.
MODEL⟩ We struggle for our autonomy.—plural
 13. Two-year-old Lauren expresses _____ independence.
 14. It is difficult for _____ parents to accept.
 15. Sometimes _____ patience is stretched to the limit.
 16. Lauren goes to the TV and pushes _____ buttons.
 17. Would you remain calm if it were _____ new TV?
 18. Two-year-old Adam also shows _____ determination.
 19. "I want _____ cup," he says.
 20. "That is _____," he says, pointing to a toy truck.
 21. He is right; the truck is _____.
 22. We make it _____ job to help children become independent.

C. Writing Sentences with Possessive Pronouns   Add words to these word groups to make complete sentences. Write the sentences.

 23. our house
MODEL⟩ It is fun to have company at our house.
 24. my idea   **29.** its aroma
 25. your skill   **30.** their fun
 26. his and my game **31.** is ours
 27. yours and mine   **32.** was not theirs
 28. his or her turn

5 Reflexive, Intensive, and Demonstrative Pronouns *pages 233 – 235*

A. Identifying Reflexive Pronouns and Their Antecedents   Write each sentence, underlining each reflexive pronoun once and its antecedent twice.

1. You can see yourself improve in sports.

MODEL⟩ You can see yourself improve in sports.

2. Many students teach themselves new athletic skills.

3. Mimi signed herself up for soccer camp.

4. "I can see for myself what I am learning," she said.

5. "Challenge yourselves," the leader told the girls.

6. We can see for ourselves how important that is.

7. Ted and Leo drove themselves to a baseball clinic.

B. Identifying Demonstrative Pronouns and Their Antecedents   Write each demonstrative pronoun and its antecedent.

8. This is an overnight camp.

MODEL⟩ This—camp

9. This is a good place to learn independence.

10. These are cabins with few luxuries.

11. That is an old bed.

12. Those are racks for duffel bags and suitcases.

13. This must be the darkest night of the year.

14. Those are certainly strange calls from the forest.

15. That is only a hoot owl calling.

C. Writing Sentences with Intensive Pronouns   Use these words to write original sentences. Use pronouns that end with *self* and *selves* as intensive pronouns.

16. I, myself, challenge

MODEL⟩ I myself knew that I could accept this challenge.

17. campers, themselves, see

18. Conrad, himself, found

19. children, themselves, reward

20. director, speaks, herself

21. this, challenge, ourselves

22. that, is, himself

23. these, were, herself

24. those, exhausting, ourselves

UNIT 5

6 Indefinite Pronouns *pages 236 – 237*

A. Identifying Indefinite Pronouns   Write the indefinite pronoun in each sentence.

1. Everyone I know is looking for a job.

MODEL Everyone

2. A job is something that can help you grow.
3. No one is unchanged by a work experience.
4. Some learn more than others on the job.
5. There is always something you can do to earn money.
6. One job or another will come your way if you look.
7. Perhaps several will become available at the same time.
8. Few will turn out to be lifetime careers.
9. Many will offer valuable training.
10. Is there anyone who has a job for me?
11. Something is waiting for you right now.

B. Writing Indefinite Pronouns in Sentences   Write an indefinite pronoun that correctly completes each sentence.

12. _____ has found a new job.

MODEL Someone

13. Is there _____ who wants to walk dogs after school?
14. _____ will surely pay for such a service.
15. Our neighbor is looking for _____ to run errands.
16. Can you think of _____ you would be reluctant to go?
17. José has several jobs, but _____ satisfy him.
18. _____ give him more satisfaction than others.
19. Almost _____ can baby-sit on weekends.
20. _____ with imagination can create jobs.
21. _____ require special training or equipment.
22. Look for _____ you would enjoy doing.

C. Writing Original Sentences   Use these words to write complete sentences. Use an indefinite pronoun in each one.

23. I went

MODEL I went somewhere I had never been before.

24. for a great vacation
25. when I want to relax
26. after school
27. a special excursion
28. in all my life
29. at the beach
30. on the lake
31. of my hobbies
32. of my friends
33. whenever I can

UNIT 5

7 Interrogative Pronouns *pages 238 – 239*

A. Identifying Interrogative Pronouns Write the interrogative pronoun in each sentence.

1. Who has changed the most in your class?

MODEL〉 Who

2. What is the most important topic of conversation?
3. Which is your favorite school subject?
4. Whose are these awards?
5. On whom do you rely for support?
6. Which is more often discussed, homework or curfews?
7. With whom in the class do you identify?
8. Do you know which is your future vocation?
9. Can you tell me whose this photograph is?
10. Do you know who is the class leader?
11. Whom do you call for help?

B. Adding Interrogative Pronouns Complete each sentence with an interrogative pronoun. Write the sentence.

12. _____ is the road to success?

MODEL〉 Which is the road to success?

13. _____ is the happiest person you know?
14. _____ do you most admire?
15. _____ do you want for a career, business or finance?
16. _____ is more important, money or happiness?
17. _____ can answer such a question?
18. _____ is the correct answer?
19. _____ can tell me?
20. To _____ do you tell your concerns?

C. Writing Sentences with Interrogative Pronouns Add words of your own to each word group to form a sentence. Write the sentence. Use an interrogative pronoun in each one.

21. sports or music

MODEL〉 Which interests you more, sports or music?

22. is your hero
23. can I rely for inspiration
24. this dream
25. do you know
26. speaks for you
27. your wish
28. was this
29. is realistic
30. was possible
31. will give you answers

UNIT 6

1 Adjectives *pages 268 – 269*

A. Identifying Adjectives   Write the adjectives in these sentences. Do not write the articles.

1. A trip to the movies is a favorite pastime.
MODEL⟩ favorite
2. A feature picture usually runs two hours.
3. Ninety-minute pictures are for a younger audience.
4. Some companies now make movies for television.
5. More movies are made for television than for theaters.
6. A special innovation of television has been videotape.
7. Many programs are now on tape rather than on film.
8. Videotaping is a cheaper process than that of making a movie.

B. Supplying Adjectives   Write each sentence and supply an appropriate adjective for the words in parentheses ( ).

9. (What kind) sounds come from the theater.
MODEL⟩ Joyful sounds come from the theater.
10. (Indefinite article) packed audience saw the new film.
11. I try to see at least (how many) movies a month.
12. For my (which one) birthday I want to have a theater party.
13. I found out it will cost about (how many) dollars for tickets and refreshments.
14. I can't wait to see the (what kind) looks on my friends' faces.
15. Unfortunately, my birthday is almost (indefinite article) year away.
16. By that time I may have a (what kind) idea.

C. Writing Sentences with Adjectives   Write sentences about a real or imaginary park you have visited. Add appropriate adjectives and other words to each word group.

17. the park
MODEL⟩ We heard many wonderful things about the new park.

18. the afternoon	24. were running around
19. we saw	25. laughed and shouted
20. the first person in line	26. drew cheers and applause
21. feature attraction	27. wanted a ride
22. a crowd	28. waited in line
23. movie star	29. parents watched

UNIT 6

2 *This, That, These, Those* pages 270–271

A. Identifying Demonstrative Adjective. Write the demonstrative adjective in each sentence.

1. That tale is a fanciful one.
MODEL〉 That
2. In this town, volunteer storytellers tell us stories.
3. These storytellers come to our school once a month.
4. On that particular day, we wait for their arrival.
5. Some of us have made a list of those story topics we like best.
6. Others of us just want to hear these special people talk.
7. On Wednesday the first story began: "This story is about a lost city."
8. "Is that city Atlantis?" I wondered to myself.

B. Using *This, That, These, and Those* Write each sentence, and add *this, that, these,* or *those.* Write *adjective* or *pronoun* to tell how the word is used in the sentence.

9. _____ students are very attentive.
MODEL〉 Those students are very attentive.—adjective
10. _____ new books belong in the library.
11. Most people like fables, tall tales, or _____ stories that teach a lesson.
12. How many books can _____ carry?
13. _____ new library hours are convenient for me.
14. I don't know if I like _____ better than the stories they told last month.
15. The storytellers memorized a list of _____ books that they thought we would like.
16. I want to finish writing _____ before the end of the day.

C. Writing Sentences with Demonstratives Use each word group to write a sentence containing one or two demonstratives.

17. school, students, books
MODEL〉 The students at this school use those books.
18. pens, stories, write
19. teacher, assignment, homework
20. legends, myths, tall tales
21. storytellers, poems, books
22. newspapers, magazines, record
23. contest, poetry, Monday
24. writers, school, lecture
25. bookmobile, children, read

3 Other Parts of Speech as Adjectives *pages 272 – 273*

A. Identifying Modifiers Write each sentence. Underline once each word that modifies a noun. Underline twice the noun that is modified. Do not underline the articles.

1. Tribal customs teach about ancient people.

MODEL▷ Tribal customs teach about ancient people.

2. Indian legends tell about old customs.

3. Indian villages were built along the Hudson River.

4. Tribes claimed land for hunting rights.

5. Animal ways were familiar to tribe members.

6. To these valley dwellers, everything was alive.

7. Mountain lions and various birds were familiar to them.

8. All lakes and mountains possessed living spirits.

9. Longhouse villages were homes for many tribes.

B. Using Other Parts of Speech as Modifiers Use each word from the list to write two sentences. Use the word as a noun or a pronoun in the first sentence. In the second sentence, use the word as an adjective.

10. city

MODEL▷ Gabriel lives in the city.
Gabriel is a city person.

11. treasure	14. sand	17. student
12. school	15. police	18. geography
13. birthday	16. house	19. forest

C. Writing Sentences Using Other Parts of Speech as Adjectives Add words to each set to make a sentence. Use the given words as adjectives. Write the sentence.

20. This, sea

MODEL▷ This area is famous for its sea breezes.

21. country, few	25. some, animal	29. lively, party
22. bird, tree	26. several, city	30. eager, summer
23. street, favorite	27. field, fence	31. dark, night
24. guitar, pleasant	28. porch, night	32. cattle, grass

EXTRA PRACTICE

UNIT 6

4 Predicate Adjectives *pages 274 – 275*

A. Identifying Predicate Adjectives   Write the predicate adjective in each sentence.

1. The program looks interesting.

MODEL> interesting

2. Talented dancers are happy to perform here.
3. Some of the dancers seem taller than average.
4. That girl in the red shorts is outstanding.
5. Her twirls are so beautiful that we applaud her.
6. She seems dedicated to the company.
7. She could be famous anywhere.
8. The dancers seem intense even as they have fun.
9. The spirited competition, nevertheless, remains good-natured.
10. After an intense performance, the dancers look tired.
11. However, they feel invigorated by the evening.

B. Writing Predicate Adjectives   Complete each sentence with a predicate adjective.

12. A career in dance is _____.

MODEL> A career in dance is challenging.

13. Dancers remain _____ because they enjoy their jobs.
14. Some of them sound _____ whenever they talk.
15. Years later their pupils stay _____.
16. Instructors seem _____ to their students and the company.
17. Some have been _____ for many years.
18. Whatever their preference, the dance is _____ for them.
19. A good performance will always feel _____.
20. Rehearsals seem either _____ or _____.

C. Writing Sentences with Predicate Adjectives   Add words to each pair of adjectives to make a sentence. Use one adjective in each pair as a predicate adjective. Write the sentence.

21. competitive, challenging

MODEL> Competitive sports always seem challenging.

22. outstanding, satisfied
23. ready, long-distance
24. anxious, several
25. proper, critical
26. fit, serious

27. strenuous, helpful
28. regular, preferable
29. brisk, beneficial
30. talented, trim
31. amateur, happy

5 Comparisons with Adjectives *pages 276–277*

A. Identifying the Degrees of Adjectives Write the adjective in each sentence, and identify its degree. Do not write articles.

1. Lisa has an interesting job this year.
MODEL〉 interesting—positive
2. Lisa is working at a large theme park.
3. Her job is more interesting than mine is.
4. She guides groups through the complex park.
5. She is happier now than when she worked in an office.
6. The theme park is the nicest one in the country.
7. Her friends think she has the most enviable job of all.
8. Unusual attractions draw visitors to the park.
9. Which exhibit do you think is the most unusual?

B. Writing Comparisons with Adjectives Write each sentence, using the correct degree of the adjective in parentheses ( ). Identify the degree you formed.

10. The park is (crowded) at night than by day.
MODEL〉 The park is more crowded at night than by day.—comparative
11. The band music is (festive) now than before.
12. The director is (talented).
13. The uniforms are (colorful) than they were last year.
14. This is the (loud) song the band has played all night.
15. The crowd seems (happy) now than before.
16. The fireworks display is (big) than last year's.
17. It is the (elaborate) display I've ever seen.
18. It is probably also the (noisy).
19. You seem (enthusiastic) than I am.

C. Writing Sentences Using Degrees of Comparison of Adjectives Add words to each noun and adjective to make a sentence. Write the sentence.

20. airplanes, louder
MODEL〉 Airplanes are louder than boats.
21. parachutes, most unusual
22. balloons, most colorful
23. gliders, more graceful
24. helicopters, noisier
25. jets, sleekest
26. canoes, most maneuverable
27. sailboats, brightest
28. motorboat, least peaceful
29. ferry, less vulnerable
30. yacht, most expensive

6 Irregular Forms of Comparison *pages 278 – 279*

A. Identifying Adjectives with Irregular Comparisons   Write the adjective with an irregular comparison in each sentence. Identify the degree of comparison.

1. Ms. Baker is the best English teacher I ever had.
MODEL> best—superlative
2. This is the best history course I've ever taken.
3. The art program here is better than at other schools.
4. The science experiment today was the best I have seen.
5. I have less trouble learning than before.
6. I can always go to the instructor for more help.
7. The new language lab is better than the old one.
8. The worst lab of all was at my old school.
9. There are more motivators here than at other schools.
10. We are encouraged to pursue more knowledge.

B. Writing the Correct Forms of Adjectives   Write the form of the adjective in parentheses ( ) that correctly completes each sentence.

11. This computer game is (good) than that one.
MODEL> better
12. This game gives me (little) trouble than that one.
13. I think this is the (good) computer game of all.
14. I have the (much) fun of all when I play it.
15. This receiver has (little) interference than others.
16. It also gets (much) use than others.
17. It gets the (much) use on weekends.
18. My friend thinks this game is (good) than any other.
19. My parents are (bad) at these games than I am.
20. My sister will probably be the (good) player of all.
21. I feel (well) of all after I have won these games.

C. Writing Sentences That Make Comparisons   Use each pair of words to write a sentence that makes a comparison.

22. best, time
MODEL> I have the best time of all on weekends.

23. better, deal	26. least, difficulty	29. best, training
24. further, progress	27. feel, better	30. feel, best
25. highest, level	28. least, interest	31. less, energy

UNIT 6

7 Adverbs *pages 280 – 282*

A. Identifying Adverbs and the Words They Modify   Write the adverb or adverbs in each sentence. Then write the word each adverb modifies.

1. Sometimes I visit an imaginary place.
MODEL⟩ Sometimes—visit

2. I walk quietly to the end of the road.

3. High hills surround a magically hidden town.

4. I found the town accidentally.

5. The entrance is almost covered by shrubs.

6. Once a boy my age appeared mysteriously on the road.

7. His clothes obviously came from a much earlier time.

8. He pointed toward the town and took me there.

B. Writing Adverbs   Write each sentence and supply an adverb that answers the question in parentheses ( ).

9. I (how) followed Jon beyond the hill.
MODEL⟩ I quickly followed Jon beyond the hill.

10. I (how) wanted to see this boy's town.
11. I looked (where) and saw old-fashioned stone houses.
12. Then Jon stopped by a tiny house and took me (where).
13. (when) I was saying hello to Jon's mother and father.
14. They were (to what extent) gracious to me.
15. "We (when) see strangers in this town," they said.
16. Jon's parents were (to what extent) skillful musicians.

C. Writing Sentences with Adverb Modifiers   Add words to these word groups to make sentences with adverb modifiers. Write the sentences.

17. often, tells, imaginary
MODEL⟩ My friend often tells imaginary stories.

18. sometimes, skeptically, listen
19. others, await, eagerly
20. extensively, here, narratives
21. plots, quickly, see
22. inside, everyone, stories

23. weaves, elaborately, often
24. easily, summon, wonderfully
25. brightly, themes, simple
26. call, occasionally, happier
27. now, wistfully, recall

UNIT 6

8 Placement of Adverbs in Sentences *pages 283 – 284*

A. Identifying Placement of Adverbs   Write each sentence. Draw an arrow from each adverb to the word it modifies.

   1. My sister vividly creates imaginary stories.

   MODEL▷ My sister vividly creates imaginary stories.

   2. Erin's stories always seem real to her.

   3. She tells them so convincingly, they seem real to us.

   4. Recently Erin created a new teacher called Mr. Otat.

   5. Mr. Otat is extremely kind and is rarely angry.

   6. Only occasionally does he have to scold the children.

   7. Daily Erin eagerly prepares for school.

   8. It does not bother her that she has never gone.

B. Writing Adverbs in Sentences   Complete each sentence with an appropriate adverb. Write the sentence.

   9. Writers _____ discuss children's attitudes.

   MODEL▷ Writers frequently discuss children's attitudes.

   10. Children's dreams are _____ simple.

   11. Children act out their feelings _____ in play.

   12. The magic of fairy tales can be _____ discussed.

   13. Children _____ identify with fairy-tale heroes.

   14. _____ children make fairy stories their own.

   15. Most fairy tales begin in a _____ realistic way.

   16. Children are _____ overwhelmed by everyday events.

C. Writing Sentences with Adverbs   Write sentences about fairy tales you remember. Use adverbs as directed.

   17. Use an adverb at the beginning of the sentence.

   MODEL▷ Sometimes I felt sorry for Cinderella.

   18. Use an adverb before the verb it modifies.

   19. Use an adverb that modifies a verb before the subject.

   20. Use an adverb before the adjective it modifies.

   21. Use an adverb before the adverb it modifies.

   22. Use an adverb that modifies a verb at the end of the sentence.

   23. Use an adverb that modifies a verb phrase between verb parts.

9 Comparisons with Adverbs *pages 285–287*

A. Identifying Degrees of Comparison of Adverbs Write each adverb, and identify it as *positive, comparative,* or *superlative.*

1. The students carefully painted pictures.

MODEL⟩ carefully—positive

2. Shannon stood thoughtfully by the easel.
3. She worked more slowly than the other students.
4. Jamal paints the most carefully of any of the children.
5. His pictures are more realistically drawn than Tara's.
6. Soon Jamal will take private lessons.
7. He paints better than anyone else in the class.
8. Eddie paints the least of any child in the art class.
9. He works best when he is alone.

B. Writing the Correct Degree of Comparison Write the form of the adverb in parentheses ( ) that correctly completes each sentence.

10. Some writers work (hard) than others at their craft.

MODEL⟩ harder

11. Some writers write fiction (easily) than nonfiction.
12. Of all writers, my favorite writer works (quickly).
13. When he works quickly, the plots develop (fast) of all.
14. Fantasy writers work (hard) of all to make real plots.
15. The stories I enjoy (little) are tall tales.
16. I liked stories about Paul Bunyan (well) of all the tall tales.
17. I read fables (recently) than tall tales.
18. They are among the (early) known fantasy stories.
19. We listen to stories (eagerly) than we read them.

C. Writing Sentences Using Degrees of Comparison of Adverbs Add words to these word groups to write sentences using degrees of comparison of adverbs.

20. most surprisingly, eagle, high

MODEL⟩ Most surprisingly of all, the eagle took us high in the air.

21. best, remote, airborne
22. rarely, sight, more beautiful
23. less, sky, alone
24. treetops, touch, most seldom
25. balloon, clouds, most often
26. amazingly, colorful, view
27. nearest, sun, climb
28. sooner, you, I
29. better, ride, bumpy
30. less, dark, find

EXTRA PRACTICE

UNIT 6

10 Negatives *pages 288 – 289*

A. Identifying Negative Words   Write the negative word in each sentence.

1. No one should live without dreams.
   MODEL⟩ No one
2. Some people don't know the importance of daydreams.
3. They barely allow themselves the luxury of daydreaming.
4. No one who daydreams has to be lonely.
5. There is nothing extraordinary about having daydreams.
6. I can't believe that you reject daydreams.
7. There would hardly be any magic without them.
8. You can never dream too many dreams.

B. Writing Sentences Using Negatives   Write each sentence, using the correct word in parentheses ( ).

9. I don't know (anyone, no one) in the park today.
   MODEL⟩ I don't know anyone in the park today.
10. I haven't (ever, never) seen so many bubbles.
11. You won't find (nothing, anything) prettier than this.
12. Don't go (nowhere, anywhere) else this afternoon.
13. No one (can, can't) believe how beautiful this is.
14. You (will, won't) scarcely believe your eyes.
15. (Nobody, Anybody) else blows bubbles like these.
16. They don't go (nowhere, anywhere) but up into the sun.

C. Writing Sentences with Negatives   Follow the directions to write 10 original sentences using negatives.

17. Tell someone not to litter.
    MODEL⟩ Don't litter, please.
18. Tell about something you have never done.
19. Tell about something you can scarcely believe.
20. Tell about something no one knows.
21. Tell about something you can't find.
22. Tell about someone you barely know.
23. Tell about somewhere you have never traveled.
24. Tell about something you might want.
25. Tell about someone who has no fear.
26. Tell about someone who never listens.
27. Tell about something you don't want.

11 Adverb or Adjective? *pages 290 – 291*

A. Choosing Adjectives and Adverbs   Write the adjective or adverb in parentheses ( ) that correctly completes each sentence.

1. Toy makers use their imaginations (free, freely).

MODEL> freely

2. Do you think it would be (easy, easily) to design toys?
3. You might find it (challenging, challengingly).
4. You would work (creative, creatively) at your job.
5. You could play (happy, happily) with toys you made.
6. Some toys are (beautiful, beautifully).
7. They are often (beautiful, beautifully) made.
8. This doll is (fine, finely) crafted.
9. These blocks (real, really) spark the imagination.
10. Creators of toys work (imaginative, imaginatively).
11. I would be (happy, happily) in such a job.

B. Using Adverbs and Adjectives   Write each sentence, adding an adjective or an adverb to each blank. Write *adjective* or *adverb* to identify the word you added.

12. _____ the children approach the toy store.

MODEL> Happily the children approach the toy store.—adverb

13. Children look _____ around the toy store.
14. Their _____ faces reveal their joy.
15. One girl holds a _____ truck.
16. She _____ pictures herself as the driver.
17. A boy takes a magic set from the _____ shelf.
18. He can _____ wait to learn the new tricks.
19. A _____ craft kit attracts a young shopper.
20. What _____ items can be made with this?
21. _____ children browse in this store.
22. They respond _____ to the creative playthings.

C. Writing Sentences   Write an original sentence using each adjective/adverb pair.

23. large, carefully

MODEL> The large sailboat carefully slips into port.

24. tall, gracefully	28. dreamily, peaceful
25. beautiful, eagerly	29. quietly, still
26. magically, wonderful	30. energetically, enthusiastic
27. unusual, restlessly	31. colorful, lazily

EXTRA PRACTICE

UNIT 7

1 Prepositions and Prepositional Phrases

pages 322 – 324

A. **Identifying Prepositions and Their Objects**   Write each sentence. Underline each preposition once and its object twice.

1. These pictures show life at an earlier time.

MODEL> These pictures show life <u>at</u> an earlier <u>time</u>.

2. The piano was an important source of entertainment.
3. Many textile mills were built beside rivers.
4. Many women worked in factories in New England.
5. At seven o'clock the workers left for the evening.
6. Immigrants lived inside crowded urban tenements.
7. Shaky stairways led to one large room.
8. Two miles of millionaires lived along Fifth Avenue.

B. **Completing Sentences with Prepositional Phrases**   Complete each sentence with a prepositional phrase that makes sense. Write the sentence.

9. The plains of Kansas are covered _____.

MODEL> The plains of Kansas are covered with tall grass.

10. Immigrants settled _____.
11. Windmills brought water _____.
12. Settlers used sod _____.
13. From Russia came winter wheat that grew _____.
14. _____ there would have been no crop.
15. Kansas farmers struggled _____.
16. _____ was a town with stores for the farmers.
17. _____ were schools, churches, and a bank.

C. **Writing Sentences with Prepositional Phrases**   Use each prepositional phrase in an original sentence about some imaginary photographs you found.

18. in boxes

MODEL> We found old photographs in boxes under the eaves.

19. inside these albums
20. beside the car
21. between two friends
22. during the summer
23. through the year
24. along the street
25. beyond the houses
26. without these pictures
27. into the past
28. among my treasures

UNIT 7

2 Prepositional Phrases Used as Adjectives *pages 325 – 326*

A. Identifying Adjective Phrases   Write each sentence. Underline the prepositional phrase once and the noun or pronoun it modifies twice.

1. The history of colonial America is a colorful one.

MODEL⟩ The history of colonial America is a colorful one.

2. You know the story of the nation.
3. Colonists from England sought new opportunities.
4. The first English colony in the New World was Jamestown.
5. The Chesapeake Bay area became a land of opportunity.
6. The Maryland colony granted freedom of worship.
7. The Puritans built a city on a hill.
8. The English claimed all the land along the Hudson.

B. Writing Prepositional Phrases as Adjectives   Rewrite each sentence, changing the underlined adjective to a prepositional phrase.

9. This <u>colonial</u> house is a historical treasure.

MODEL⟩ This house from colonial days is a historical treasure.

10. The <u>wooden</u> beams are the original beams.
11. This <u>metal</u> pot hung over the fire.
12. That <u>corner</u> bed is an antique.
13. A <u>cotton</u> quilt covers the old bed.
14. <u>Patchwork</u> quilts are carefully designed.
15. That <u>pewter</u> bowl could tell a wonderful story.
16. A <u>yarn</u> rug resembles crewelwork.

C. Writing Sentences with Adjective Phrases   Use these prepositional phrases as adjectives in your own sentences.

17. by the river

MODEL⟩ The house by the river is old.

18. of a restored village	23. of wood
19. by colonial workers	24. near the forest
20. in a colonial house	25. above the fireplace
21. with historical significance	26. on the large bed
22. from the American colonies	27. for the family

EXTRA PRACTICE

3 Prepositional Phrases Used as Adverbs *pages 327 – 328*

A. **Identifying Adverb Phrases**   Write each sentence. Underline the prepositional phrase once and the word or words it modifies twice.

1. Anna is preparing for her future.

MODEL⟩ Anna is preparing for her future.

2. She pictures herself in space travel.

3. She knows she must work steadily for many years.

4. She has studied technology in great depth.

5. Research shows that careers will be available in space.

6. Doctors may find new opportunities in the space age.

7. Space technology will be helpful in Anna's work.

8. This knowledge is already being utilized by industry.

B. **Writing Adverb Phrases**   Write each sentence, adding an adverb phrase to modify the underlined word or words.

9. The rocket <u>soars</u>.

MODEL⟩ The rocket soars into space.

10. Rockets <u>travel</u> at incredible speed.

11. Unmanned spacecraft <u>have been launched</u>.

12. Moon landings <u>have been made</u>.

13. Communications satellites are the <u>most useful</u>.

14. Satellites can broadcast Olympic games <u>live</u>.

15. They <u>can</u> also <u>view</u> the entire surface of the earth.

16. Spacecraft <u>have probed</u> beyond the earth.

17. The earliest moon <u>probes crashed</u> when they <u>landed</u>.

18. Later probes landed <u>softly</u> and sent back pictures.

C. **Writing Sentences with Adverb Phrases**   Use these prepositional phrases as adverbs in your own sentences.

19. into space

MODEL⟩ One day I will travel into space.

20. beyond the earth's orbit

21. around the moon

22. to Venus

23. from Mercury

24. on Mars

25. through the asteroid belt

26. through the galaxy

27. above the orbital plane

28. to the outer planets

29. about the sun

EXTRA PRACTICE

UNIT 7

4 Using Prepositions Correctly *pages 329 – 330*

A. Choosing the Correct Prepositions   Write the preposition in parentheses ( ) that correctly completes each sentence.

1. I traveled back (at, to) the turn of the century.

MODEL> to

2. I looked around (to, at) people's houses.

3. (In, To) the houses things looked different to me.

4. I discovered differences (between, among) then and now.

5. No one had electricity (in, into) their homes.

6. (Beside, Besides) a chair was a candle stand.

7. There were other differences (beside, besides) these.

8. Generations gathered together (in, into) their homes.

9. People stayed (at, to) home together for recreation.

B. Completing Sentences with Prepositional Phrases   Complete each sentence with a prepositional phrase that begins with *at, to, between, among, in, into, beside,* or *besides.*

10. I like to travel _____.

MODEL> I like to travel to new places.

11. Some places exist only _____.

12. There are several ways to get _____.

13. _____ you might find a museum or a specialty shop.

14. To go _____ you must walk through a special door.

15. You will find the entrance _____.

16. You can walk _____.

17. _____ you will also find novelties.

18. You can choose _____.

19. Go _____ for special surprises.

C. Writing Sentences with Appropriate Prepositional Phrases   Use these words and words of your own to write sentences about your favorite place. Use prepositional phrases in your sentences.

20. walk, in, me

MODEL> Walk in the park with me.

21. at, see, wonderful

22. to, excitement, come

23. in, absolutely, previously

24. into, unusual, obviously

25. among, various, well

26. between, two, distinguish

27. beside, you, often

28. besides, also, promises

29. among, three, carefully

30. into, only, prepared

UNIT 7

5 Conjunctions *pages 331 – 333*

A. Identifying Conjunctions   Write the conjunction in each sentence. Write *coordinating* or *correlative* to identify the type of conjunction.

1. Ida Wells had four brothers and four sisters.
$\boxed{\text{MODEL}}$ and—coordinating
2. Her father was a carpenter, and her mother was a cook.
3. Both her father and her mother valued education.
4. Her parents died, but Ida kept the family together.
5. Neither Ida nor her brothers had finished school.
6. Ida would get a job, or the family would be separated.
7. She took the teaching examination and passed it.
8. She either wrote or edited articles for a newspaper.

B. Completing Sentences with Conjunctions   Complete each sentence with an appropriate conjunction or conjunctions.

9. Concha Meléndez was a writer _____ a critic.
$\boxed{\text{MODEL}}$ Concha Meléndez was a writer and a critic.
10. She studied _____ in Puerto Rico _____ New York.
11. She had a mild _____ real influence on many writers.
12. Was she known more for her poems _____ her criticism?
13. _____ Doña Concha _____ her husband directed Hispanic studies.
14. She was _____ a student _____ a teacher for years.
15. Her lectures were popular, _____ her poetry was outstanding.
16. Have you read _____ her first _____ her second book?

C. Writing Sentences with Conjunctions   Follow the directions to write sentences with conjunctions.

17. Use *both/and* in a sentence about two people.
$\boxed{\text{MODEL}}$ Both my brother and I like to read about heroes.
18. Use *either/or* in a sentence about two activities.
19. Use *both/and* in a sentence about two friends.
20. Use *neither/nor* in a sentence about two pests.
21. Use *and* in a sentence about two summer activities.
22. Use *but* in a sentence about two opposing wishes.
23. Use *or* in a sentence about two winter activities.
24. Use *but* and *and* in a sentence about a big city.
25. Use *or* and *and* in a sentence about the country.
26. Use *but* and *or* in a sentence about sports.

UNIT 7

6 Interjections *pages 334 – 335*

A. Identifying Interjections Write the interjection in each sentence. If there is none, write *no interjection.*

1. Oh, look at these amazing brochures.
   MODEL〉 Oh
2. Wow! There are hundreds of career opportunities today.
3. Sometimes the number seems overwhelming.
4. My goodness, how do you choose a career?
5. Well, you should first think of your own interests.
6. Aha! That's a good point!
7. You can find a job that uses your skills and talents.

B. Adding Interjections to Dialogue Add an interjection to one sentence in each pair. Write the sentence with the interjection you added.

8. The car is out of gas.
   I'll have to run to catch the bus.
   MODEL〉 Oh dear, the car is out of gas.
9. The dog ran out of the house.
   Catch him before he gets too far.
10. The wind just knocked over the vase.
    It smashed into a thousand pieces.
11. It's not easy taking care of a home.
    There are always so many things going on.
12. I cannot remember a more confusing day.
    It isn't over yet.
13. After today I'm taking a vacation.
    I think you deserve it.

C. Writing Sentences with Interjections Follow the directions for writing each sentence with an interjection. Punctuate each interjection correctly.

14. Write a sentence telling about something you forgot to do.
    MODEL〉 Oops! I forgot to feed the dog!
15. Write a sentence describing a great surprise.
16. Write a sentence describing something beautiful.
17. Write a sentence describing a powerful natural force.
18. Write a sentence telling about an unexpected package.
19. Write a sentence about finding a valuable object.
20. Write a sentence expressing intense joy.
21. Write a sentence expressing your love for music.
22. Write a sentence describing someone who impressed you.

UNIT 8

1 Phrases and Clauses *pages 382 – 383*

A. Identifying Phrases and Clauses   Write *phrase* or *clause* to identify each word group.

1. In Puerto Rico.

MODEL⟩ phrase

2. Roberto Clemente was a proud man.
3. With a great performance in the World Series.
4. He hit two home runs.
5. Although the Pirates lost the first two games.
6. Clemente was a leader of the Pirates.
7. In the seventh game.
8. He hit the first pitch for a home run.
9. José Antonio Pagan drove in a second Pirate run.

B. Identifying Subordinate and Independent Clauses   Write *independent* if a clause expresses a complete thought. Write *subordinate* if it does not.

10. Since he was a baseball superstar.

MODEL⟩ dependent

11. When Clemente was born in Puerto Rico in 1934.
12. Roberto was the youngest of five children.
13. Because of the depression that occurred in the 1930's.
14. Roberto's family was comfortable and friendly.
15. When an earthquake struck the city of Managua.
16. Clemente led a Puerto Rican relief drive for Nicaragua.
17. After the plane took off.
18. Roberto Clemente proved his love for others.

C. Writing Phrases and Clauses   Follow the directions to write sentences containing phrases, independent clauses, or subordinate clauses.

19. Use a subordinate clause beginning with *since*.

MODEL⟩ Since I read about Roberto Clemente, I have become a fan.

20. Use a subordinate clause beginning with *although*.
21. Use a phrase beginning with *after*.
22. Use an independent clause beginning with *I*.
23. Use a subordinate clause beginning with *because*.
24. Use a phrase beginning with *at*.
25. Use an independent clause beginning with *today*.
26. Use a subordinate clause beginning with *when*.
27. Use an independent clause beginning with *you*.
28. Use a phrase beginning with *to*.

2 Complex Sentences *pages 384 – 385*

A. Identifying Types of Sentences   Write *simple, compound,* or *complex* to identify each sentence type.

1. Although she was shy, Eleanor Roosevelt entered politics.
   MODEL⟩ complex
2. When Franklin Roosevelt got polio, he left politics.
3. Louis Howe asked Mrs. Roosevelt for help, and she agreed.
4. She invited politicians to her home.
5. They convinced Franklin that his career was not over.
6. After he returned to politics, he ran for governor.
7. When he became President, Mrs. Roosevelt spoke to the press.
8. She became as well known as her husband.

B. Using Subordinating Conjunctions in Complex Sentences   Write an appropriate subordinating conjunction to begin the subordinate clause in each sentence.

9. _____ Maggie Mitchell watched her mother work, she learned from her how to save money.
   MODEL⟩ As
10. She graduated from college _____ she was fifteen.
11. _____ she wanted a career, few were open to her.
12. Maggie became a teacher _____ she graduated.
13. _____ Maggie liked numbers, she wanted a bank job.
14. _____ she completed school, she applied to the bank.
15. _____ she worked hard, the directors listened to her.
16. She hired women for banking jobs _____ she could.
17. _____ she earned her degree, she founded a bank.

C. Writing Complex Sentences   Write each sentence with a subordinate clause. Use the conjunction in parentheses ( ).

18. I have goals.(because)
    MODEL⟩ Because I have goals, I work hard to achieve them.
19. You work hard. (because)
20. You strive for success. (whenever)
21. People admire you. (wherever)
22. Work is sometimes difficult. (although)
23. People rarely succeed. (unless)
24. You like your job. (even though)
25. You learn new skills. (while)

EXTRA PRACTICE

3 Adjective and Adverb Clauses *pages 386 – 387*

A. Identifying Adjective and Adverb Clauses Write the subordinate clause in each sentence. Write *adverb clause* or *adjective clause* to identify the type of clause.

1. Daedalus was in prison with Icarus, who was his son.
MODEL⟩ who was his son—adjective clause
2. Because he was clever, Daedalus planned their escape.
3. He made wings that were fashioned of feathers in wax.
4. When they were done, Daedalus showed them to Icarus.
5. The wings that the men wore could be melted by the sun.
6. Since he was concerned, Daedalus warned his son.
7. Avoid the hot son, which can melt the wax.
8. When Icarus flew close to the sun, his wings melted.

B. Completing Subordinate Clauses Complete each sentence with a suitable pronoun or conjunction. Write what question the clause answers.

9. Theseus, _____ was the son of King Aegeus, arrived in Athens.
MODEL⟩ Theseus, who was the son of King Aegeus, arrived in Athens.   Who?
10. _____ it was not required, Theseus sailed to Crete.
11. _____ the ship set sail, it had black sails.
12. The ship _____ sailed to Crete carried fourteen men.
13. Ariadne asked for help _____ she could save Theseus.
14. Daedalus gave her a magic ball of thread _____ would help Theseus find his way.

C. Combining Sentences with Adverb and Adjective Clauses Combine each sentence pair into a complex sentence, using the italicized word in parentheses ( ) to begin each subordinate clause.

15. Jason sought the Golden Fleece. He was strong.   (adjective clause—*who*)
MODEL⟩ Jason, who was strong, sought the Golden Fleece.
16. Jason's father had taken him to the Centaur. Jason was young.   (adverb clause—*when*)
17. Jason was raised to be a hero. He was skilled in all sports.   (adverb clause—*since*)
18. The goddess Hera was paying a visit to Earth. She saw Jason.   (adjective clause—*who*)
19. Hera made a promise to Jason. She would keep it.   (adjective clause—*that*)

UNIT 8

4 Misplaced Modifiers *pages 388 – 389*

A. Identifying Correctly Placed Modifiers Write the sentence in each pair that contains correctly placed modifiers.

1. With his camera John snapped a photo of a bear.
   John snapped a photo of a bear with his camera.
   MODEL With his camera John snapped a photo of a bear.
2. We saw the dancers leaping gracefully from the balcony.
   From the balcony we saw the dancers leaping gracefully.
3. The radio with loose wires was repaired by a student.
   The radio was repaired by a student with loose wires.
4. The ape was photographed by Elena swinging from a tree.
   The ape swinging from a tree was photographed by Elena.
5. When he glanced from his tent the moose scared Alex.
   The moose scared Alex when he glanced from his tent.
6. Peering through my binoculars, I saw a deer.
   I saw a deer peering through my binoculars.

B. Rewriting Sentences with Misplaced Modifiers Rewrite each sentence by changing the placement of the modifier.

7. We saw the Gateway Arch landing at the airport.
   MODEL Landing at the airport, we saw the Gateway Arch.
8. Taped to the wall we saw a travel poster.
9. Strung with colored lights, the mayor launched a ship.
10. The baby that was 200 years old wore a silk dress.
11. Sylvia watched the moon rise sleepily.
12. From his perch on the roof Bob saw the bird leap.
13. I watched the bear lumber away smiling.
14. Wearing a red suit, the bull charged Charlie.

C. Writing Sentences with Correctly Placed Modifiers Follow the directions to write each sentence with a modifier.

15. Write a sentence about a quest. Use an adverb clause.
    MODEL Because he was adventurous, Sam wanted to scale the mountain.
16. Write a sentence about a hero's dream. Use an adverb clause.
17. Write a sentence about a hero's setback. Use a prepositional phrase.
18. Write a sentence about a hero's plans. Use an adjective clause.
19. Write a sentence about a hero's success. Use an adverb clause.
20. Write a sentence about a hero's welcome. Use an adjective clause.

UNIT 8

5 Participles and Participial Phrases *pages 390–391*

A. Identifying Participles   Write the participle in each sentence. Then write the noun the participle modifies.

1. Oozing water passes through the earth's crust.

MODEL⟩ Oozing—water

2. Cracked limestone splits and dissolves.

3. Down through the limestone trickles the seeping water.

4. Moving streams push rocks underground as they flow.

5. Streams and rivers constantly change living caves.

6. Live caves have flowing rivers and damp ceilings.

7. The dripping water creates unusual cave formations.

B. Completing Sentences with Participles   Write a participle or a participial phrase to complete each sentence. Then write the noun each one modifies.

8. _____ a cave, scientists found cave pictures.

MODEL⟩ Studying—scientists

9. People _____ caves learn more about the earth.

10. Scientists and other _____ people enjoy this hobby.

11. The _____ wind might create a cave in a mountainside.

12. Waves _____ against seaside cliffs create wave caves.

13. Those _____ cave exploration are called *spelunkers*.

14. Sea caves, _____ with unusual fish and plants, are wonderful to explore.

15. Some caves were hollowed out by _____ liquid rock.

16. Ice caves, _____ in glaciers, are constantly moving.

17. Waterfalls, _____ in place by the cold, make a fantastic sight.

18. _____ through the ice caves, cold winds alter shapes.

C. Writing Sentences with Participles and Participial Phrases   Use each word group to write a sentence about mountain climbers. Include a participle or a participial phrase in each one.

19. snow, fell, mountain

MODEL⟩ The snow, lashed by a strong wind, fell on the mountain.

20. mountain, hikers, stop

21. shelter, cave, rested

22. animal, noise, scurried

23. passerby, notice, figures

24. they, awoke, sleep

25. determination, explorers, continued

26. returned, home, weather

27. victorious, greeted, friends

6 Gerunds and Gerund Phrases *pages 392 – 393*

A. Identifying Gerunds Write the gerund in each sentence. Write *subject, direct object, predicate nominative,* or *object of preposition* to tell how the gerund is used.

  1. People have always dreamed of flying.
  MODEL⟩ flying—object of preposition
  2. All summer we looked forward to riding in a balloon.
  3. Floating in the air was a new sensation.
  4. We enjoyed looking down at the treetops.
  5. My newest interest is ballooning.
  6. Traveling by balloon is unpredictable but pleasant.
  7. My friend helps me by tracking our path.
  8. Locating the balloon is not always easy.
  9. However, he enjoys tracking it across the land.
  10. The best part is drifting slowly over the countryside.
  11. Climbing out of the balloon left me saddened.

B. Differentiating Between Gerunds and Participles Make a list with two columns headed *Participles* and *Gerunds*. Write each participle/participial phrase and gerund/gerund phrase in the correct column.

  12. Exploring underwater is a thrill.

  MODEL⟩ Participles   Gerunds
  _____   _____
                    Exploring underwater
  13. A new experience may be walking underwater.
  14. Wearing proper clothing makes diving easier.
  15. The people dressing the diver work quickly.
  16. Weighed down by his clothes, the diver sits patiently.
  17. Supplying air to the diver is of critical importance.
  18. Working underwater, divers talk on a telephone line.
  19. Walking on the ocean bottom requires practice.
  20. A diver's task may be recovering a safe from a ship.

C. Writing Sentences with Gerunds and Gerund Phrases Use the gerunds and gerund phrases in original sentences by adding word groups of your own.

  21. skin diving
  MODEL⟩ Skin diving has become popular.   27. exploring reefs
  22. protecting his eyes   28. swimming underwater with a camera
  23. flying above the ocean floor   29. supervising the underwater
  24. scuba diving   photographers
  25. breathing through a mouthpiece   30. locating objects below the surface
  26. swimming around in any direction 31. skin diving and scuba diving

7 Infinitives and Infinitive Phrases *pages 394 – 395*

A. Identifying Infinitives   Write the infinitive in each sentence.

1. Emilio wanted to learn about smoke jumpers.

MODEL⟩ to learn

2. Thousands of men and women are called to fight fires.
3. To reach some fires by road is impossible.
4. Smoke jumpers are asked to go to these fires.
5. Lookouts try to spot fires before they grow too large.
6. Then there is time to put them out before they spread.
7. A spotter is required to pinpoint the location.
8. A plane is sent to carry firefighters and equipment.
9. Firefighters race to the area to attack the fire.
10. It is hazardous to be a smoke jumper.
11. A spotter tells the firefighters when to jump.

B. Differentiating Between Prepositional Phrases and Infinitive Phrases   Each sentence includes either a prepositional phrase beginning with *to* or an infinitive phrase beginning with *to*. Write the phrase and identify which kind it is.

12. Firefighters were sent to extinguish a wharf fire.

MODEL⟩ to extinguish a wharf fire—infinitive phrase

13. The chief looked for people to train as fire divers.
14. Trainees are sent to a special school for instruction.
15. They must learn to float for a long time.
16. They also train to stay underwater for long periods.
17. Scuba divers were sent to the location of the fire.
18. A diver went to retrieve equipment from the water.
19. The divers tied hose lines to pilings under a wharf.
20. A buddy is assigned to each firefighter.
21. It is dangerous for fire divers to work alone.

C. Writing Sentences with Infinitive Phrases   Add words to each infinitive phrase to form a sentence. Change each phrase so the modifier does not split the infinitive.

22. to sincerely improve myself

MODEL⟩ I try sincerely to improve myself.

23. to eventually work
24. to further challenge myself
25. to somehow find excitement

26. to actually find the best job
27. to often go to new places
28. to always look for excitement

EXTRA PRACTICE

1 Capitalization and End Punctuation in Sentences *pages 428 – 429*

A. Identifying Kinds of Sentences Identify each sentence as *declarative, interrogative, imperative,* or *exclamatory.*

1. What is the most important Japanese holiday?
MODEL⟩ interrogative
  2. New Year's Day is the most important Japanese holiday.
  3. I wonder who will make the special rice cakes.
  4. Put sweet bean paste into some of the rice paste.
  5. Oh, the cakes will be delicious!
  6. What is the significance of these symbols?

B. Capitalizing and Punctuating Sentences Write each sentence, using correct capitalization and end punctuation.

7. is April a month of festivals and flowers
MODEL⟩ Is April a month of festivals and flowers?

  8. on April 8 many Japanese people celebrate Buddha's birthday

  9. what a happy month April is

10. the cherry blossom is the national flower of Japan

11. how beautiful are the blossoms in April

12. oh, but they last only a few short days

13. does your community hold a Cherry Blossom Festival

C. Writing Sentences Follow the directions to write each kind of sentence.

14. Write a question about a holiday.
MODEL⟩ What is your favorite holiday?
15. Tell how you celebrate a favorite holiday.
16. Give a command to a friend to join you.
17. Exclaim over the beautiful festivities.
18. Ask a question about the origin of certain customs.
19. Write an indirect question about the entertainment.
20. Invite a friend to participate in the entertainment.
21. Tell the significance of a special symbol.
22. Exclaim about the joy of the day.

2 Commas Within Sentences *pages 430–431*

A. Identifying the Use of Commas   Write *A* if commas are used to separate items in a series; write *B* if a comma precedes a coordinating conjunction; write *C* if a comma follows an introductory word or phrase; write *D* if commas are used to set off interrupters; write *E* if commas are used to set off words in direct address.

1. You will be interested, I think, in this story.
MODEL> *D*
2. Famine came to Ireland, and people came to America.
3. They built houses, streets, and factories.
4. Tara, do you know that your ancestors were Irish?
5. You should know, I think, that the people worked hard.
6. Indeed, they worked on the canals and on the railroads.
7. Workers came on boats, and contractors hired them.
8. They took jobs in mills, or they worked in mines.
9. Irish girls were maids, nursemaids, and housekeepers.

B. Using Commas in Sentences   Write each sentence, adding commas where they belong.

10. Oh, my listen to this song.
MODEL> *Oh, my, listen to this song.*
11. The Irish fought poverty prejudice and ignorance.
12. Molly do you recall Grandfather's stories?
13. The immigrants were poor and they took any work.
14. Irish immigration rose and Irish political power grew.
15. Irish communities formed in New York Boston and Philadelphia.
16. The communities were I think close-knit groups.
17. You know Kevin that many of your relatives still live in Ireland.
18. Here Al Smith lost a bid for President but John Kennedy won.

C. Writing Sentences with Commas   Add words to the word groups below to write original sentences. Add commas wherever necessary.

19. Manhattan/Brooklyn/Staten Island
MODEL> *In New York many Irish immigrants settled in Manhattan, Brooklyn, and Staten Island.*

20. shamrock/clay pipe/the color green
21. Everyone/I think
22. Corned beef/cabbage/potatoes

23. music/dancing/storytelling
24. in my opinion
25. they worked/they played

3 Other Punctuation Within Sentences

pages 432 – 434

A. Identifying Reasons for Using Punctuation   Explain why semicolons, colons, and hyphens are used in these sentences.

1. Indonesia is an old land; it has a long history.
   MODEL⟩ The semicolon separates the two clauses of a compound sentence.
2. People worked for freedom; they looked back with pride.
3. One heard several tongues: Arabic, Chinese, and Persian.
4. When the Hindus ruled Java, the kings had almost god-like status.
5. Java had a regional culture; it had a national culture.
6. Sumatra, Bali, and Borneo had rich cultural traditions that eventually gave way to the rule of Java.
7. Java was a powerful kingdom; it became the cultural center of Indonesia.
8. *Bahasa Indonesia* replaced the languages of many individual islands: Sumatra, Bali, Borneo, and Java.
9. Mataram was once only a rice-growing island.

B. Using Punctuation Correctly   Write each sentence, adding semicolons, colons, and hyphens as necessary.

10. The Midwest was a center of German American im migration in the United States.
    MODEL⟩ The Midwest was a center of German-American im-migration in the United States.
11. Many of the German immigrants were farmers they were drawn to the rich farmland of the Midwest.
12. Many German farmers worked forty acre farms in America.
13. In the heartland the German American community grew.
14. The new German citizens respected the land they prac ticed ecology before it was common.
15. By 1850 German Americans had settled in several Mid western cities Milwaukee, St. Louis, and Cincinnati.

C. Writing Sentences   Write ten sentences about immigrants. Include a semicolon, a colon, or a hyphen in each sentence.

MODEL⟩ 16. The ships to America were crowded; most immigrants had very little space to themselves.

UNIT 9

4 Capitalization of Proper Nouns, Proper Adjectives, and *I* *pages 435 – 437*

A. Capitalizing Proper Nouns and Proper Adjectives Write the words in each list. Add capital letters where necessary.

1. street, valley road, new york thruway

MODEL⟩ street, Valley Road, New York Thruway

2. my brother, the marx brothers, dwight d. eisenhower

3. mine, i, my, me

4. our country, dallas, texas, the southwest

5. mississippi river, ocean, greenwood lake

6. chinese-american, vietnamese, asia

7. george washington bridge, jefferson memorial, the fort

8. bill of rights, treaty, bylaws

B. Capitalizing Proper Nouns and Proper Adjectives in Sentences Write each sentence, capitalizing proper nouns and proper adjectives.

9. The spaniards claimed indian land for spain.

MODEL⟩ The Spaniards claimed Indian land for Spain.

10. Americans of mexican descent call themselves Chicanos.

11. They began with the mayas, the toltecs, and the aztecs.

12. The children of spanish and indian people are Mestizos.

13. Many mexican families crossed the rio grande.

14. Trails in the southwest became united states highways.

15. In congress mexican americans work for all citizens.

C. Writing Proper Nouns in Sentences Write a proper noun for each common noun. Use each proper noun in a sentence about a trip you might take.

16. ocean

MODEL⟩ Atlantic Ocean—Our trip will begin at the Atlantic Ocean.

17. day and month	**20.** city	**23.** document
18. monument	**21.** holiday	**24.** title with abbreviation
19. state	**22.** natural feature	**25.** street or highway

5 Letters and Envelopes *pages 438 – 440*

EXTRA PRACTICE

A. Capitalizing and Punctuating Letter Parts Write each letter part, using the correct capitalization and necessary commas.

1. atlanta georgia 30303
MODEL> Atlanta, Georgia 30303

2. dallas texas

3. september 16 1990

4. dear sis

5. sincerely yours

6. 17 orange street

7. san diego california

8. dear sabra

9. dear mrs nieves

10. 220 lexington avenue

11. p o box 222

B. Punctuating Parts of a Letter Write each letter item with correct capitalization and punctuation. Use postal abbreviations as if you were addressing envelopes.

12. 212 east 79th street
MODEL> 212 East 79th Street

13. 21 church street

14. south orange new jersey 07079

15. may 21 1991

16. visitors' group

17. iowa development commission

18. 600 east court suite a

19. des moines iowa 50309

20. dear sir or madam

21. very truly yours

22. laverne wilson

C. Writing Letter and Envelope Parts Follow the directions to write these letter parts. Capitalize and punctuate correctly.

23. Write today's date.
MODEL> January 21, 1995

Friendly letter and envelope:

24. Write your street address.

25. Write your city, state, and ZIP code.

26. Write a greeting to a friend.

27. Write a closing.

28. Write the receiver's envelope address.

Business letter:

29. Write the name of a visitors' bureau.

30. Write the street address.

31. Write the city, state, and ZIP code.

32. Write a formal salutation.

33. Write a closing.

UNIT 9

6 Titles *pages 441 – 442*

A. Writing Titles Write each title, using correct capitalization, underlining, and quotation marks.

1. one hundred years of solitude   (book)

MODEL〉 One Hundred Years of Solitude

2. dreams in the dusk   (poem)

3. america the beautiful   (song)

4. the new york times   (newspaper)

5. the fortune seekers   (book chapter)

6. the morning show   (TV series)

7. orient express   (train)

8. the six rows of pompons (short story)

9. laocoön   (work of art)

B. Writing Titles in Sentences Write each sentence. Use correct capitalization, underlining, and quotation marks.

10. I read a book called the Hawaiian kingdom.

MODEL〉 I read a book called The Hawaiian Kingdom.

11. Frederic García Lorca wrote the book a gypsy ballad.

12. I read that article in the atlantic monthly.

13. We saw a play called if five years pass.

14. This book's first chapter is called welcome home.

15. I saw an article called newcomers in the united states.

16. You will enjoy the performance of firebird suite.

C. Writing Sentences with Titles Answer each question with a sentence that includes a title.

17. What good movie played in your town?

MODEL〉 The movie Big played in our town.

18. What book would you recommend to a younger child?

19. What poem would you read to a younger child?

20. What is your favorite song?

21. What is a title of a short story you might write?

22. What is the name of your local newspaper?

23. What play would you like to see?

24. What magazine is in your library?

25. What work of art hangs in a museum?

7 Outlines and Bibliographies *pages 443 – 445*

A. Identifying Parts of an Outline   Identify each item in an outline. Write *main topic, subtopic,* or *supporting detail.*

  1. I. Coming to a new land
  MODEL⟩ main topic
  2. I. Settlers in a new land
  3.   A. Settlements
  4.   1. Farming
  5.   2. Sheepherding
  6.   B. Conflicts
  7.   1. Aztecs
  8.   2. Anglos
  9. II. Community of Mexican Americans

B. Writing an Outline   Write the information in correct outline form.

  10. immigrants from the orient
  MODEL⟩ Immigrants from the Orient
  11. I. gold in California
  12. a. merchants
  13. 1. silk
  14. 2. tea
  15. b. gold miners
  16. 1. work crews
  17. 2. chinese towns

C. Reading a Bibliography Entry   Use the information in the bibliography entries to answer each question.
"Asia in America." *Bulletin of Concerned Asian Scholars.* Special issue, Fall 1972.
Meltzer, Milton. *The Chinese Americans.* New York: Thomas Y. Crowell, 1980.
"Oriental Americans." *Academic American Encyclopedia.* Vol. 14, 441 – 443.
    Danbury, Connecticut: Grolier Incorporated, 1984.

  18. Who wrote *The Chinese Americans?*
  MODEL⟩ Milton Meltzer
  19. What issue of the magazine carried "Asia in America"?
  20. What is the title of the encyclopedia article?
  21. When was *The Chinese Americans* published?
  22. In what city and state was "Oriental Americans" published?
  23. Which bibliography entry is the most recent?
  24. Which bibliography entry is for a book?

8 Direct Quotations and Dialogue *pages 446 – 447*

A. Identifying Quotations Read each quotation. Write *direct* or *indirect* to identify the type of quotation.

1. "What have we learned?" I asked.
MODEL⟩ direct
  2. "We have learned," said Alma, "about our heritage."
  3. Aaron told me that his grandparents were immigrants.
  4. "Many people," said Mr. Erich, "came to find freedom."
  5. Rosa asked her grandparents why they had come.
  6. Luis said, "Many people want to visit their homelands."
  7. "Can we make the trip?" asked Rosa.
  8. I asked Jason if people came for economic reasons.
  9. "Of course," Jason answered.

B. Writing Quotations Write each quotation, using quotation marks, commas, end punctuation, and capital letters where they are needed.

10. This picture said Carl shows Ellis Island.
MODEL⟩ "This picture," said Carl, "shows Ellis Island."
  11. Did Tara ask you about your home in Ireland I asked
  12. I've told her so many stories said Grandmother
  13. Tomorrow she added she will be asking more questions
  14. Why is she suddenly so curious I asked
  15. She has a school project said Grandma I'm sure of it
  16. Look at these pictures said Tara excitedly
  17. I wonder who the tall woman is said Grandma
  18. Tara exclaimed why, she looks like you

C. Writing Direct and Indirect Quotations Write the following direct and indirect quotations.

19. an indirect quotation about immigration
MODEL⟩ Mom said she wondered who the new immigrants are.
  20. a direct quotation in which a father addresses his son
  21. a divided direct quotation giving a son's answer to his father
  22. an indirect quotation containing the mother's comment
  23. an indirect question asked of the mother
  24. a direct quotation that is an imperative sentence

WRITER'S HANDBOOK

Contents

Sentences

- A **sentence** is a group of words that expresses a complete thought.

  The three best runners competed in the race.

  sentence

- There are four kinds of sentences: *declarative, interrogative, imperative,* and *exclamatory.*

- A **declarative sentence** makes a statement and ends with a period.

  Elena taught herself to play the piano .

  declarative sentence

- An **interrogative sentence** asks a question and ends with a question mark.

  When will you hear the results of the test ?

  interrogative sentence

- An **imperative sentence** gives a command or makes a request and ends with a period. The subject of an imperative sentence is *you* (understood). *You* is understood, not actually written.

  (*you*) Help me fasten my bicycle lock .

  imperative sentence

- An **exclamatory sentence** expresses strong feelings and ends with an exclamation point.

  What a beautiful sunset that is !

  exclamatory sentence

- A **simple sentence** contains one subject and one predicate. A simple sentence may have a compound subject, a compound verb, or both.

  The engine started.
  Tim and Bob are mechanics.
  The old truck sputtered and shook.

  simple sentence

- A **compound sentence** contains two or more related simple sentences joined by a comma and a conjunction or by a semicolon.

  simple
  ⌐ sentence ⌐   ⌐ simple sentence ⌐
  The sun rose , and the darkness gave way to dawn.

  compound sentence

```
┌ simple sentence ┐  ┌──────── simple sentence ────────┐
```

The sun rose ; the darkness gave way to dawn.

complex
sentence

- A **complex sentence** consists of an independent clause and at least one subordinate clause.

```
┌──── subordinate clause ────┐┌──── independent clause ────┐
```

Although he prefers rye, Jason ordered whole wheat bread.

subject

- The **subject** of a sentence names someone or something. The subject is the part of a sentence about which something is being said.

Athletes must eat properly.

complete
subject

- The **complete subject** is all the words in the subject part of the sentence.

The three best runners competed in the race.

simple subject

- The **simple subject** is the main word or key word in the complete subject.

The three best runners competed in the race.

compound
subject

- A **compound subject** is two or more subjects that have the same verb.

Mercury , Venus , and Mars are the planets closest to Earth.

predicate

- The **predicate** of a sentence tells what the subject is or does.

Timothy lived in Japan for three years .

His father was a pilot in the Air Force .

complete
predicate

- The **complete predicate** contains all the words in the predicate part of the sentence.

Rebecca studied German for two years.

simple predicate

- The **simple predicate** is the verb in the complete predicate. It may be one verb or a verb phrase.

Rebecca studied German for two years.

She is planning a trip to Bavaria.

compound
predicate

- A **compound predicate** is two or more verbs that have the same subject.

The jet rose and turned toward the east.

- When a sentence has **natural word order,** the subject comes before the verb.

> Twelve buses are behind the auditorium.

- When a subject has **inverted word order,** the verb comes before the subject.

> Behind the auditorium are twelve buses .

- A **complement** is the part of a sentence that completes the thought started by the subject and the verb. A sentence complement may be a direct object, an indirect object, a predicate adjective, or a predicate nominative.

- A **direct object** receives the action of the verb. To find the direct object, ask *whom* or *what* receives the action.

> The manager hires students for the summer.
>
> **hires whom? students**
>
> The custodian cleaned the rooms and the halls .
>
> **cleaned what? rooms, halls**

- An **indirect object** tells to or for whom or what the action of the verb is done. A sentence must have a direct object to have an indirect object. The indirect object is a noun or a pronoun. It is always placed after the verb and before the direct object in a sentence.

> V   IO   DO
> The coaches gave the players their trophies.
>
> V   IO   IO   DO
> My father built my sister and me a treehouse.
>
> V   IO   DO
> Larry told him an interesting story.

- A **predicate nominative** is a noun or a pronoun that follows a linking verb and renames the subject.

> Sally is a girl with a bright future.
>
> My favorite desserts are apple pie and Boston cream pie .
>
> The captain of the cheerleading squad is she .

- A **predicate adjective** is an adjective that follows a linking verb and describes the subject of the sentence.

> Our neighbors are friendly .
>
> Emily is quiet and shy .

Nouns

noun • A **noun** names a person, a place, a thing, or an idea.

Rita went to Chicago on a bus for a vacation .

singular noun • A **singular noun** names one person, place, thing, or idea.

My friend walked to the store to buy a new kite .

plural noun • A **plural noun** names more than one person, place, thing, or idea. Add *s* to form the plural of most nouns. For help with the spelling of plural nouns, see the *Spelling* section of this **Writer's Handbook.**

The two teams will play tomorrow.

common noun • A **common noun** names any person, place, thing, or idea.

The small child watched the bird in the tree .

concrete noun • A **concrete noun** names something that can be seen, smelled, tasted, felt, or heard.

The smoke from the burning wood made my eyes water.

abstract noun • An **abstract noun** names an idea, a quality, or a feeling that cannot be experienced with the senses.

His goal was to win their trust .

collective noun • A **collective noun** names a group of persons, animals, or things.

The fleet set sail toward the new colony.

proper noun • A **proper noun** names a particular person, place, or thing. A proper noun always begins with a capital letter. For help with the capitalization of proper nouns, see the *Mechanics* section of this **Writer's Handbook.**

Dr. J. S. Levin opened his office on Mill Street on Thursday .

Elizabeth is going to Paris after Thanksgiving .

possessive noun • A **possessive noun** shows ownership or possession.

• To form the possessive of a singular noun, add an apostrophe and *s*.

My brother's tape recorder is broken.

Tess's goal is to become a doctor.

- To form the possessive of a plural noun that ends in *s*, add only an apostrophe.

    We visited the Laughlins' house on Saturday.

- To form the possessive of a plural noun that does not end in *s*, add an apostrophe and *s*.

    Aunt Sue wants to start a women's club in her neighborhood.

- An **appositive** is a noun or pronoun that identifies or renames the noun or pronoun that precedes it.

    appositive

    Mrs. Mayer, the principal, spoke to the parents and teachers.

Pronouns

- A **pronoun** takes the place of a noun or nouns. Pronouns can be singular or plural, and they can be masculine, feminine, or neuter. They can be in the nominative or the objective case. The pronouns that are used most frequently are called **personal pronouns.**

    pronoun

    Mr. Robbins was a sergeant in World War I, and he received a medal for bravery.

    The girls brought two cameras with them .

- The **antecedent** is the noun to which a pronoun refers. A pronoun should agree with its antecedent in number, person, and sometimes gender.

    antecedent

    Hannah thought she would like to go shopping.

    Larry and Mabel missed their ride to school.

- A **subject pronoun** is used as a subject of a sentence. Subject pronouns are in the nominative case.

    subject pronoun

    She cast the deciding vote in the election.

Nominative Case		
	Singular	**Plural**
First Person	I	we
Second Person	you	you
Third Person	he, she, it	they

pronoun-verb agreement

- A pronoun used as a subject should agree with the verb in number.

    She raises prize geraniums.

    They raise award-winning cattle.

predicate nominative

- A pronoun used as a predicate nominative is in the nominative case.

    The winner of the writing contest is she .

object pronoun

- An **object pronoun** can be used as a direct object, an indirect object, or an object of a preposition. Object pronouns are in the objective case.

    My classmates elected her by a landslide.   **direct object**

    Please give us a ride to the game.   **indirect object**

    It is all right with me if you come along.   **object of preposition**

Objective Case		
	Singular	**Plural**
First Person **Second Person** **Third Person**	me you him, her, it	us you them

relative pronoun

- A **relative pronoun** connects a group of words to a noun or pronoun antecedent. The words *that, which, who, whom,* and *whose* can be used as relative pronouns.

    Basil is the spice that you need for this recipe.

possessive pronoun

- A **possessive pronoun** is a pronoun that shows ownership or possession.

    That portrait is our most prized possession.

- Possessive pronouns have one form when they are used before a noun or noun phrase and another form when they are used alone.

Before Nouns		Alone	
Singular	**Plural**	**Singular**	**Plural**
my your his, her, its	our your their	mine yours his, hers	ours yours theirs

- A **reflexive pronoun** refers to the subject of a sentence. The words *myself, yourself, himself, herself, itself, yourselves, ourselves,* and *themselves* can be reflexive pronouns.

reflexive pronoun

> Lucia saw herself in the tarnished mirror.

- An **intensive pronoun** emphasizes a noun or a pronoun. The words *myself, yourself, himself, herself, itself, yourselves, ourselves,* and *themselves* can be intensive pronouns.

intensive pronoun

> Lucia herself placed each cassette in its proper slot.

- A **demonstrative pronoun** points out a particular person, place, thing, or idea. Demonstrative pronouns are *this, that, these, those.*

demonstrative pronoun

> This is my stamp collection.

> These are my most valuable stamps.

> That is where I keep them.

> Those are my brother's books of coins.

- When *this, that, these,* and *those* are used before nouns, they are adjectives, not pronouns.

> I want to buy this book for my brother.

- An **indefinite pronoun** is a pronoun that does not refer to a particular person, place, thing, or idea.

indefinite pronoun

> Everyone is eligible for the team.

Indefinite Pronouns				
Singular			Plural	
all	everybody	no one	all	most
another	everyone	nothing	any	none
any	everything	one	both	several
anybody	most	some	few	some
anyone	much	somebody	many	more
anything	neither	someone		
each	nobody	something		
either	none	such		

- When indefinite pronouns are used before nouns, they are adjectives, not pronouns.

> Each musician performed a solo routine.   adjective

> Each picked a selection to perform.   pronoun

- The indefinite pronouns *all*, *any*, *most*, *none*, and *some* are plural when they refer to things that can be counted. They are singular when they refer to things that cannot be counted.

  All of the teams *have* arrived.   can count teams

  All of the paint *has* dried.   cannot count paint

interrogative pronoun

- An **interrogative pronoun** is used to ask a question. The five interrogative pronouns are *who, what, whose, which,* and *whom.*

  Who is going to make the sandwiches?

  What are you going to prepare?

  Which do you want?

  Whose turn is it to wash the plates?

  Whom did you invite to join us?

Verbs

verb

- A **verb** expresses action or being.

  Ed ran in the fifty-yard dash.

  His father was an Olympic medalist.

action verb

- An **action verb** expresses physical or mental action.

  The dancer leaped over the scenery.

  Carla understood the problem.

linking verb

- A **linking verb** connects the subject of a sentence to a word or words in the predicate. Linking verbs are forms of the verb *be* or verbs that express being, such as *seem, appear, become, look, feel,* and *remain.*

  Your report is the best one so far.

  Greg seems confident that he can win.

verb phrase

- A **verb phrase** is made up of a main verb and one or more helping verbs.

  I could have been ready an hour earlier.

  Pauline is learning to play the piano.

- The **main verb** is the most important verb in a verb phrase.

main verb

Helen could help you with your homework.

- A **helping verb** works with the main verb to express action or being.

helping verb

Millions of people will watch the Olympics.

helping verb

That telephone has been ringing for five minutes.

- A subject and its verb must agree in number. For help with subject-verb agreement, see the *Usage* section of this **Writer's Handbook.**

A rose grows rapidly in a warm, moist climate.

Roses grow in many parts of the country.

- The **principal parts** of a verb are the *present*, the *present participle*, the *past*, and the *past participle*. The principal parts express the time of a particular action or state of being.

Present	Present Participle	Past	Past Participle
march	marching	marched	marched
plan	planning	planned	planned
create	creating	created	created
try	trying	tried	tried

- The **tense** of a verb shows time. Verb tenses change to indicate that events happen at different times. The six verb tenses are the *present*, the *past*, the *future*, the *present perfect*, the *past perfect*, and the *future perfect*.

- The **present tense** expresses an action that takes place now.

The players follow the marching band onto the field.

- The **past tense** expresses an action that took place at some time in the past.

Jeremy completed the assignment yesterday.

future tense • The **future tense** expresses an action that will take place in a time to come.

Kim will represent our school at the state competition.

present perfect • The **present perfect tense** expresses action that began at some time in the past and continues to the present. Form the present perfect with the helping verb *have* or *has* and the past participle.

The people have celebrated this holiday for
more than five centuries.

past perfect • The **past perfect tense** expresses action that started and ended before another action in the past. Form the past perfect with the helping verb *had* and the past participle.

My great-grandfather had purchased this land
long before I was born.

future perfect • The **future perfect tense** expresses an action that will begin and end before a particular time in the future. Form the future perfect with the helping verb phrase *will have* and the past participle.

By tomorrow I will have finished the book.

progressive verb • A **progressive verb** expresses action that continues. Each of the present, past, and future tenses has a progressive form. To make the progressive form of a verb tense, always use the present participle as the main verb with a form of the verb *be* as a helping verb.

Progressive Verb Forms

Present: They are walking to town.

Past: They were walking at dawn.

Future: They will be walking next week.

Present perfect: They have been walking for two months.

Past perfect: They had been walking until the accident.

Future perfect: In June, they will have been walking every
morning for one year.

principal parts of irregular verbs • An **irregular verb** does not have *ed* or *d* added to the present to form the past and the past participle. Most irregular verbs follow one of these five patterns.

Present	Present Participle	Past	Past Participle
come	coming	came	come
begin	beginning	began	begun
bring	bringing	brought	brought
burst	bursting	burst	burst
forget	forgetting	forgot	forgotten

- The verbs *be, have,* and *do* are irregular verbs.

Be Principal parts: be, being, was, been			
	Present	**Past**	**Future**
I	am	was	will be
he, she, it	is	was	will be
we, you, they	are	were	will be
	Present Perfect	**Past Perfect**	**Future Perfect**
I	have been	had been	will have been
he, she, it	has been	had been	will have been
we, you, they	have been	had been	will have been

Have Principal parts: have, having, had, had			
	Present	**Past**	**Future**
I, we, you, they	have	had	will have
he, she, it	has	had	will have
	Present Perfect	**Past Perfect**	**Future Perfect**
I, we, you, they	have had	had had	will have had
he, she, it	has had	had had	will have had

Do Principal parts: do, doing, did, done			
	Present	**Past**	**Future**
I, we, you, they	do	did	will do
he, she, it	does	did	will do
	Present Perfect	**Past Perfect**	**Future Perfect**
I, we, you, they	have done	had done	will have done
he, she, it	has done	had done	will have done

contraction ● A **contraction** is a shortened way of writing a verb and a pronoun or a verb and the word *not*. Use an apostrophe in place of the letters that are left out when you write a contraction.

he will—he'll	they have—they've	you would—you'd
is not—isn't	were not—weren't	would not—wouldn't
cannot—can't	should not—shouldn't	

transitive verb ● A **transitive verb** has a direct object.

The coach threw the javelin.

intransitive verb ● An **intransitive verb** does not have a direct object.

The coach shouted .

active voice ● A transitive verb is in the **active voice** when the subject performs the action.

Maya sang two songs in the show.

passive voice ● A transitive verb is in the **passive voice** when the subject receives the action.

Two songs in the show were sung by Maya.

Adjectives

adjective ● An **adjective** modifies a noun or a pronoun. Adjectives answer the question *what kind, which one, how many,* or *how much.*

Little Monica is wearing a lavender scarf.

proper adjective ● A **proper adjective** is created from a proper noun. Proper adjectives are always capitalized.

I like Mexican food.

article ● The words *a, an,* and *the* are special adjectives called **articles.** *A* and *an* are **indefinite articles.** *The* is a **definite article.**

The fisherman caught a perch and an eel.

- A **demonstrative adjective** points out the noun it modifies. The words *this, that, these,* and *those* are demonstrative adjectives when they point out specific persons, places, things, or ideas.

demonstrative adjective

> This spot looks all right for a picnic.

> The home economics class provided these sandwiches.

> That boat just disappeared over the horizon.

> The ball landed somewhere in those trees.

- A **predicate adjective** is an adjective that follows a linking verb and describes the subject of the sentence.

predicate adjective

> Angela seems satisfied with her schedule of classes.

> By the end of the hike, we were exhausted and hungry .

- Adjectives can be used to compare nouns. Many adjectives have forms, or degrees, to show comparison. These forms are **positive, comparative,** and **superlative.** For help with the spelling of comparative and superlative adjectives, see the *Spelling* section of this **Writer's Handbook.**

adjectives that compare

- The **positive** form is used when no comparison is being made.

positive

> I decorated my room in bright colors.

- The **comparative** degree is used when two things are compared. Form the comparative degree by adding *er* to most one-syllable adjectives and some two-syllable adjectives.

comparative

> A brighter light will help your eyes.

- The **superlative** degree is used when more than two things are compared. Form the superlative degree by adding *est* to most one-syllable adjectives and some two-syllable adjectives.

superlative

> It was the brightest star in the western sky.

- For some two-syllable adjectives and most three-syllable adjectives, form the comparative degree by using *more* or *less.* Form the superlative degree by using *most* or *least.*

more, most, less, least

Positive	Comparative	Superlative
beautiful	more beautiful	most beautiful
expensive	less expensive	least expensive

> This book will be helpful for you.

> Would it be more helpful if Sam tutored you?

> Maria's idea was the most helpful .

irregular comparisons • Some adjectives have irregular forms of comparison.

Positive	Comparative	Superlative
good, well	better	best
bad	worse	worst
much, many	more	most
little (small amount)	less	least

Luis has a good understanding of music.

He is better at reading music than I am.

His sister is the best singer in the neighborhood.

Adverbs

adverb • An **adverb** modifies a verb, an adjective, or another adverb.

The lion roared mightily . **modifies verb**

I have waited a very long time. **modifies adjective**

We arrived too late. **modifies adverb**

• Adverbs answer the questions *when, where, how, how often,* and *to what extent.*

When?	now, soon, late, then, tomorrow
Where?	up, here, there, inside, over
How?	slowly, quickly, easily, hard, fast
How often?	twice, never, often, seldom, once
To what extent?	very, almost, nearly, too, terribly

adverbs that compare • Some adverbs have three forms, or degrees, of comparison: **positive, comparative,** and **superlative.**

positive • The **positive** degree is used when no comparison is being made.

My dog can run fast .

- The **comparative** degree is used when two things are compared. Form the comparative degree by adding *er* to most one-syllable adverbs and some two-syllable adverbs.

comparative

> Jimmy's dog can run faster .

- The **superlative** degree is used when more than two things are compared. Form the superlative degree by adding *est* to most one-syllable adverbs and some two-syllable adverbs.

superlative

> Alicia's dog runs fastest of the three.

- For most adverbs ending in *ly,* form the comparative degree by adding *more* or *less* before the adverb. Form the superlative degree by adding *most* or *least*.

more, most, less, least

Positive	Comparative	Superlative
quickly diligently	more quickly less diligently	most quickly least diligently

> Eddie can assemble the puzzle quickly .
>
> Two people can assemble the puzzle more quickly than one.
>
> We can assemble the puzzle most quickly if everyone helps.

- Some adverbs have irregular forms of comparison.

irregular comparisons

Positive	Comparative	Superlative
well	better	best
badly	worse	worst
much	more	most
little	less	least
far	farther	farthest

- A **negative** is a word that means "no" or "not." Common negative words are *no, neither, nothing, hardly, none, nobody, nowhere, barely, not (n't), no one, never,* and *scarcely*.

negatives

double negative ● A **double negative** is a statement that uses two or more negatives. Two negative words should not be used together.

> incorrect: No one said nothing to the speaker.

> correct: No one said anything to the speaker.

Prepositions

preposition ● A **preposition** relates a noun or a pronoun to another word in the sentence. Some prepositions consist of more than one word.

> The teacher will help you with your science project.

Some Common Prepositions				
about	below	from	of	throughout
above	beneath	in	off	to
across	beside	in back of	on	toward
after	besides	in front of	onto	under
against	between	in place of	out	underneath
along	beyond	in spite of	out of	up
among	by	instead of	outside	upon
around	down	into	over	with
at	during	like	past	within
before	except	near	since	without
behind	for	next to	through	

object of the preposition ● A preposition is always followed by a noun or pronoun known as the **object of the preposition.**

> Three classes will be going to the museum .

prepositional phrase ● A **prepositional phrase** is made up of a preposition, the object of the preposition, and all the words in between.

> Three classes will be going to the museum .

> I left my bike in front of your house .

- A prepositional phrase that modifies a noun or a pronoun is an **adjective phrase.** An adjective phrase answers the question *which one, what kind, how much,* or *how many.*

adjective phrase

> The new headquarters will have columns of marble . modifies *columns*

- A prepositional phrase that modifies a verb, an adjective, or an adverb is an **adverb phrase.** An adverb phrase tells *when, where, how, how often,* or *to what extent.*

adverb phrase

> The orange sun sank in the west . modifies verb
>
> The sand was warm to the touch . modifies adjective
>
> The surfer walked down to the water . modifies adverb

Conjunctions

- A **conjunction** connects words or groups of words in a sentence. Conjunctions connect words that are equal in importance and share the same function in a sentence.

conjunction

- Common conjunctions are *and, or,* and *but.* These are called **coordinating conjunctions.**

coordinating conjunctions

- To show similar ideas, use *and.*

> The campers chose a spot and set up their tent.

- To show contrast between ideas, use *but.*

> They found firewood, but it was too wet to use.

- To show a choice between ideas, use *or.*

> They can wait until it dries or move to another spot.

- Some conjunctions are made up of pairs of words. These pairs are called **correlative conjunctions.**

correlative conjunctions

Some Common Correlative Conjunctions

neither/nor	Neither the pitchers nor the hitters played well.
either/or	Either they were ill or they had a bad day.
both/and	Both the coaches and the fans were upset.
whether/or	They must decide whether to practice or to rest.

WRITER'S HANDBOOK • Grammar

Interjections

interjection
- An **interjection** is a word or group of words that expresses feeling or emotion. It is not related grammatically to the rest of the sentence.

  Hey! Watch out for that car!

- When an exclamation point follows an interjection, the interjection shows strong feeling.

  Oh! What an amazing shot that was!

- When a comma separates an interjection from the sentence that follows, the interjection shows mild feeling.

  Oh, I meant to tell you what happened yesterday.

- Some common interjections are *oh, wow, whew, hurray, ah, alas,* and *oops.*

Verbals

verbal
- A **verbal** is a verb form that functions as a noun, an adjective, or an adverb. Participles, gerunds, and infinitives are the three types of verbals.

participle
- A **participle** is a verb form that is used as an adjective. Most participles end in *ing* or *ed.*

  My grandfather has some used furniture for sale.

  The visiting team was introduced first.

gerund
- A **gerund** is a verb form ending in *ing* that is used as a noun.

  Many people enjoy sailing .

infinitive
- An **infinitive** is a verbal consisting of the present-tense form of a verb preceded by *to.* An infinitive can be used as a noun, an adjective, or an adverb.

  Our team hates to lose . **as a noun**

  Golf is a sport to learn at a young age. **as an adjective**

  Stephen went to Germany to visit his uncle. **as an adverb**

Phrases and Clauses

- A **phrase** is a group of words that does not contain a verb or its subject. A phrase is used as a single part of speech.

    Sarah lives around the corner .

phrase

- A **participial phrase** consists of a participle and its related words. A participial phrase is used as an adjective.

    Elated by the news , the crowd of people cheered.

participial phrase

- A **gerund phrase** consists of a gerund and its related words. A gerund phrase is used in the same way as a noun.

    Helping others in need is a noble pursuit.

gerund phrase

- An **infinitive phrase** consists of an infinitive and its objects and modifiers. An infinitive phrase can be used as a noun, an adjective, or an adverb.

    The police promise to investigate thoroughly .   **as a noun**

    The police need evidence to use in the case .   **as an adjective**

    They searched the house to look for clues .   **as an adverb**

infinitive phrase

- A **clause** is a group of words that has a subject and a verb.

clause

- An **independent clause** has a subject and a verb and expresses a complete thought. An independent clause can stand alone as a simple sentence.

    We returned home after the thunderstorm was over.

independent clause

- A **dependent,** or **subordinate, clause** has a subject and a verb but does not express a complete thought. A subordinate clause cannot stand on its own and is used with an independent clause to form a complex sentence.

    We returned home after the thunderstorm was over .

subordinate clause

- An **adjective clause** is a subordinate clause that modifies a noun or a pronoun. Like an adjective, an adjective clause answers the question *which one, what kind, how much,* or *how many*. It often begins with a relative pronoun (*who, whom, whose, that, which*).

    Introduce me to the artist whose painting won the prize .

adjective clause

WRITER'S HANDBOOK • Grammar

- An **adverb clause** is a subordinate clause that modifies a verb, an adjective, or an adverb. An adverb clause answers the question *how, where, why,* or *to what extent.* It begins with a subordinating conjunction.

The driver turned when he saw the street sign .

Common Subordinating Conjunctions		
after	before	until
although	if	when
as	since	whenever
as if	so that	where
as long as	than	wherever
as soon as	though	while
because	unless	

- A **misplaced modifier** is a modifier incorrectly placed in a sentence so that the meaning is unclear or distorted. A modifier should be placed as close as possible to the word or words it modifies.

incorrect: Sleeping on the roof , I saw the neighbor's cat.

correct: I saw the neighbor's cat sleeping on the roof .

incorrect: I'll check your report when you finish for accuracy .

correct: I'll check your report for accuracy when you finish.

Capitalization

- Capitalize the first letter of the first word in a sentence.   sentences

    T he debating team won a prize.

- Proper nouns, such as people's names, place names, and holidays, always begin with a capital letter.   proper nouns

people	H elen T homas, J osé S anchez
titles	M ayor Gray, D r. Sarah Miles, M rs. Fein
months and days of the week	M arch, F riday
events, holidays	S uper B owl, T hanksgiving D ay, V eterans D ay
historic events and periods	C ivil W ar, F rench R evolution, I ndustrial R evolution, R enaissance, M iddle A ges
roads	M aple S treet, I nterstate 95
cities, states	O gden, U tah; D allas, T exas
countries	I taly, S weden
continents	A sia, S outh A merica
heavenly bodies	M ars, E arth, S aturn, U rsa M ajor Exceptions: sun, moon. The word *earth* is capitalized only when it refers to the planet Earth.
geographical terms	A leutian I slands, the S outhwest, I ndian O cean, R ocky M ountains
buildings and bridges	M etropolitan M useum, S ears T ower, G olden G ate B ridge
monuments	W ashington M onument, M ount R ushmore
institutions, clubs, and organizations	H enderson M iddle S chool, E l P aso G lee C lub, U nited F und, G irl S couts of A merica
companies	R ontrex C ompany; CMN , I nc.
brand names	S undrop C ola, F reewheeler tires
government bodies	C ongress, H ouse of R epresentatives
documents	U . S . C onstitution, B ill of R ights

languages	**C** hinese, **G** erman, **D** utch
races and nationalities	**I** ndian, **M** exican, **C** aucasian
religious names and terms	**C** hristianity, **J** udaism, **I** slam, **G** od, **J** ehovah, **A** llah
awards	**P** ulitzer **P** rize, **C** ongressional **M** edal of **H** onor

abbreviations • An **abbreviation** is a shortened form of a word. Many abbreviations are capitalized and followed by a period.

titles of people	Mister— **M** r., Mistress— **M** rs., Doctor— **D** r., Junior— **J** r., Senior— **S** r., Captain— **C** apt., Sergeant— **S** gt., Professor— **P** rof.
addresses	Street— **S** t., Road— **R** d., Boulevard— **B** lvd., Circle— **C** ir., Avenue— **A** ve., Lane— **L** n., Drive— **D** r., North— **N** ., South— **S** ., Post Office— **P.O.** , Rural Delivery— **R.D.**
states	Alaska— **AK** , Vermont— **VT** , Alabama— **AL**
businesses	Company— **C** o., Corporation— **C** orp., Incorporated— **I** nc.
organizations	North Atlantic Treaty Organization— **NATO** , Parent-Teacher Association— **PTA**
calendar items	Saturday— **S** at., Thursday— **T** hurs. August— **A** ug., January— **J** an. Exceptions: May, June, July
time	midnight to noon— **A.M.** noon to midnight— **P.M.**
units of measure	quart—qt., kilogram—kg, pound—lb., mile—mi., feet—ft., kilometer—km, inch—in., miles per hour—mph

proper adjectives • Proper adjectives are always capitalized.

S wedish meatballs, **S** panish architecture, **A** ustralian football

I • The pronoun *I* is always capitalized.

My brother and **I** are planning to go to the same school.

WRITER'S HANDBOOK • Mechanics

- When writing a letter, capitalize the first words of the greeting and the closing, and the term used to identify the receiver of the letter.

parts of a letter

    D ear S ir or M adam:

    Y ours truly,

- Capitalize the first word, the last word, and all important words in the titles of books, stories, newspapers, magazines, movies, and songs. Do not capitalize short or unimportant words, such as articles, coordinating conjunctions, or prepositions, unless they come at the beginning of the title.

titles

    I n the H eat of the N ight is an interesting book.

    Lemont enjoyed reading " T o B uild a F ire."

- Capitalize the first word of a direct quotation.

direct quotation

    Erika said, " H elp me find the right gift for Rena."

- A direct quotation can be divided into parts. When the second part of the quotation is a continuation of the same sentence, begin it with a lowercase letter.

    " M y brother," said Erika, " i s taking flying lessons."

- When the second part of a quotation begins a new sentence, begin it with a capital letter.

    " T hat's great," Jeff replied. " M aybe he'll take me flying."

- Use a capital letter for the first letter of the first word of headings and subheadings in an outline. Use Roman numerals for main ideas. Use capital letters to indicate subtopics. Capitalize the first letter of each entry.

outline

    I . G overnment

    A . R oman

    B . G reek

- Capitalize the author's last and first names, the publisher's name, the title of the book or magazine, and the place of publication in a bibliography entry.

bibliography

    L ane, E leanor. L ane's G uide to F lowers.

    N ew Y ork: H andy P ress, 1989.

Punctuation

end marks
- End every sentence with a period, a question mark, or an exclamation point.

> Our class visited the fire department .
>
> What is your favorite color ?
>
> That was a wonderful book !

period
- Use a period at the end of a declarative or an imperative sentence.

> It is still snowing on top of the mountain .
>
> Please pass the relish tray .

- Use a period after an initial that stands for a person's name.

> E . B . White   R . K . Chen

- Use periods after most abbreviations.

> Capt . Sims, 1:00 P . M ., Mon ., Jan . 10

- Use a period after a Roman numeral in a main topic and after a letter in a subtopic of an outline.

> I . Government
>
> A . Greek
>
> B . Roman

- The period that ends a direct quotation is written inside the end quotation mark. End each sentence of a direct quotation with the proper end mark.

> The tour guide said, "Take your time looking at the
>
> exhibits. We will be in this area for one hour . "

comma
- Use a comma to separate three or more words in a series. Write a comma after each item except the last.

> Gold , platinum , and silver are precious metals.

- Use a comma before a coordinating conjunction that joins the clauses of a compound sentence.

> The river was cold , but my hiking boots kept my feet warm.

- Use a comma after an introductory word or phrase. An introductory word can be a noun of direct address.

> Kristin , where are your writing assignments?

> All in all , it was a most productive meeting.

- Use commas to set off most appositives. Do not use commas to set off appositives that are necessary to identify the nouns they follow.

> Rita , our team captain , is from Kansas.

> I enjoy swimming , the most complete exercise.

> My friend Tim plays chess.

- Use a comma to separate the clauses of a complex sentence if the subordinate clause comes first.

> When the storm arrived , we were playing soccer.

- Use a comma to set off interrupters. **Interrupters** are noun phrases, nouns of direct address, or parenthetical expressions that are added to a sentence for emphasis or clarity. An interrupter can be removed from the sentence without changing its meaning. An interrupter can be placed at the beginning, middle, or end of a sentence.

> In my opinion , she is the best qualified for the job.

> She is , in my opinion , the best qualified for the job.

> She is the best qualified for the job , in my opinion.

- Use a comma after two or more prepositional phrases at the beginning of a sentence.

> In the summer of 1988 , we had a devastating drought.

- Use a comma after a participial phrase at the beginning of a sentence.

> Looking out the window , Linda saw a rabbit.

- Use a comma between the city and the state and between the day and the year.

> Princeton , New Jersey   March 1 , 19——

- Use a comma after the greeting in a friendly letter and after the closing of any letter.

> Dear Amanda ,

> Sincerely yours ,

- Use a comma between a quotation and the rest of the sentence unless the quotation ends with a question mark or an exclamation point.

> "I'll meet you at the bus stop," said Maria.
>
> "Is the bus still running?" Julian asked.

semicolon
- Use a semicolon to join two independent clauses in a compound sentence when you do not use a coordinating conjunction.

> Mars is making its closest pass to Earth ; it should
> be a spectacular sight through my telescope.

colon
- Use a colon to set off a list of items when the list is preceded by a noun or a noun phrase to which the list refers.

> Our astronomy class has studied the following
> planets : Mars, Venus, Mercury, and Saturn.

- Use a colon to separate the hour and minutes in numerals to indicate time.

> 7 : 30 A.M.   9 : 15 P.M.

hyphen
- Use a hyphen to separate syllables at the end of a line.

> The observatory installed a sophisticated new tele -
> scope at its mountaintop location.

- A hyphen can separate parts of compound words.

> Its high - powered lens is amazing.

parentheses
- Use parentheses to enclose explanatory material that is not necessary to the meaning of a sentence.

> My enjoyment of astronomy (the study of the stars)
> would increase with a telescope like that.

dash
- Use a dash to signal a sudden break in thought within a sentence.

> I saw Mars — except for when the clouds covered it —
> in more detail than I had thought possible.

- Add an apostrophe and *s* to a singular noun to form a possessive noun.

> The dog's collar looks too tight.
>
> Tess's dog won first prize in the contest.

- Add only an apostrophe to a plural noun ending in *s* to form a possessive noun.

> All the contestants' dogs were well behaved.

- Form the possessive of plural nouns that do not end in *s* by adding an apostrophe and *s*.

> This is the children's waiting area.

- Use an apostrophe to form contractions of some verbs and the adverb *not*.

> Mr. Maynard couldn't get through on the telephone.

- Use an apostrophe to form contractions of pronouns and helping verbs.

> After the rainstorm, we'll go hiking.

- When a speaker's exact words are written down, they are enclosed in quotation marks. A period or a comma at the end of a quotation always goes inside the quotation marks.

> The announcer said, " Everyone who participated in today's competition was a winner. "

- If the quotation is a question or an exclamation, the question mark or exclamation point goes inside the quotation marks.

> " How many movies have you seen recently ?" asked Joe.
>
> " That was a great movie !" cried Mrs. Anderson.

- When a quotation contains several sentences that are not interrupted, use one set of quotation marks.

> He then said, " First prize goes to Luis Rojas.
>
> Marie Devereau is the first runner-up. Third prize goes to Jackie Evans. "

- Place quotation marks around the titles of stories, articles, poems, songs, and chapters in books.

> We sang " America the Beautiful " at the meeting.

• If you are writing or typing, underline titles of long works. Use underlining with the following kinds of titles:

books	<u>The Pearl</u>
magazines	<u>Newsweek</u>
newspapers	<u>Chicago Sun-Times</u>
plays	<u>Cats</u>
movies	<u>Who Framed Roger Rabbit</u>
television shows	<u>Live at Five</u>
works of art	<u>The Blue Boy</u>
musical compositions	<u>Rhapsody in Blue</u>
planes, trains, ships	<u>Titanic</u>

Troublesome Words

altar, alter • Use *altar* when you mean "a table or stand in a church." Use *alter* when you mean "to change."

Flower arrangements covered the altar .

Ask the tailor to alter the sleeves on the jacket.

capitol, capital • Use *capitol* when you mean "building." Use *capital* to refer to a city as the seat of a government.

The Capitol dome loomed in the distance.

What is the capital of your state?

course, coarse Use *course* when you mean "a path of action," "part of a meal," or "a series of studies." Use *coarse* when you mean "rough" or "crude."

Our school offers a course in woodworking.

The coarse cloth irritated my skin.

amount, number • Use *amount* when you refer to a quantity thought of as a unit. Use *amount* with a singular word. Use *number* when you refer to a quantity thought of as several things. Use *number* with a plural word.

The amount of food served at the banquet was awesome.

We sampled a number of different foods.

- Use *like* to introduce a prepositional phrase.
  Use *as* to introduce a subordinate clause or a prepositional phrase.

> The metal box sank like a stone.

> Our parents waved as the boat left the dock.

> As a child Anita loved the sea.

- Use *then* as an adverb that tells when.
  Use *than* as a conjunction.

> Dave did his homework; then he ate dinner.

> Homework takes longer now than it did last year.

- Use *fewer* to refer to items that can be counted.
  Use *less* to refer to a quantity that cannot be counted.

> We have had fewer days of rain this year than last year.

> The skies have been less overcast lately.

- Use *accept* when you mean "to receive."
  Use *except* as a verb that means "to leave out" or as a preposition that means "excluding."

> Dan was chosen to accept the award for our school.

> Everyone except Susan will be in the audience.

- Use *their* when you mean "belonging to them."
  Use *they're* when you mean "they are."
  Use *there* when you mean "in that place."

> Our neighbors planted a tree in their front yard.

> They're planning to leave on September 30.

> Place your writing folders there .

- Use *too* when you mean "also."
  Use *two* to indicate the number.
  Use *to* when you mean "in the direction of."

> Our school will be at the meet too .

> Breakfast cost me two dollars.

> My brother and I walked to the shopping center.

Easily Confused Verb Pairs

lie, lay • Use *lie* when you mean "to recline or rest."
Use *lay* when you mean "to place or to put something down."

I love to lie in the hammock.

Don't lay your bikes on the grass.

rise, raise • Use *rise* when you mean "to get up or to move upward."
Use *raise* when you mean "to lift or to bring up."

The sun will rise at five o'clock.

Raise the shade to let in some light.

sit, set • Use *sit* when you mean "to seat oneself or to rest."
Use *set* when you mean "to place or put something down."

Let's sit by the waterfall.

Set those packages on the kitchen counter.

let, leave • Use *let* when you mean "to allow" or "to permit."
Use *leave* when you mean "to go away from" or "to allow to remain behind."

Let me help you with that suitcase.

It's time for the train to leave .

learn, teach • Use *learn* when you mean "to gain knowledge."
Use *teach* when you mean "to instruct."

People learn best by doing.

Teach me how to do that dance step.

lend, borrow • Use *lend* when you mean "to give something that must be given back."
Use *borrow* when you mean "to take something that must be given back."

May I borrow a pencil?

I don't have one, but Nick will lend you one.

- Use *take* when you mean "to carry something away from a place."
  Use *bring* when you mean "to carry something to a place."

take, bring

> Please `take` those away before I eat them all.

> What did you `bring` to me?

Pronouns

- Use *its* when you mean "belonging to it."
  Use *it's* when you mean "it is."

its, it's

> The volcano suddenly blew `its` top.

> `It's` too bad you will not be here for the party.

- Use *your* when you mean "belonging to you."
  Use *you're* when you mean "you are."

your, you're

> Is this `your` folder?

> `You're` going to be one of the few in attendance.

- Use *I* as a subject of a sentence or as a predicate nominative. Use *me* as a direct object, an indirect object, or an object of a preposition.

I, me

> `I` entered the essay contest.   **subject**

> It was `I` who wrote the winning essay.   **predicate nominative**

> Duane chose `me` to be on his football team.   **direct object**

> On the last play he threw `me` the ball.   **indirect object**

> It was a sign of acceptance for `me` .   **object of preposition**

- Use *this, that, these,* and *those* as demonstrative pronouns to take the place of nouns.

this, that, these, those

> `This` is my vegetable garden.

> `These` are radishes.

> `That` is my neighbor's rose garden.

> `Those` are his prize-winning roses.

- Use a subject pronoun as a subject of a sentence or as a predicate nominative. A subject pronoun is in the nominative case.

subject and object pronouns

WRITER'S HANDBOOK • Usage

She broad-jumped 16 feet at the track.   subject

It was she who set the new school record.
predicate nominative

- Use an object pronoun as a direct object, an indirect object, or an object of a preposition. An object pronoun is in the objective case.

My mother and father took us to lunch.   direct object

Lunch cost us eighteen dollars.   indirect object

The waitress stopped to chat with us .   object of preposition

who, whom, whose

- Use *who* as a subject.
  Use *whom* as an object.
  Use *whose* as an interrogative pronoun or as a possessive pronoun.

Who can provide the answer?

To whom did you give the tickets?

Whose is this?   interrogative pronoun

Whose raincoat is that?   possessive pronoun

Adjectives

this, that, these, those

- Use *this, that, these,* and *those* as adjectives when they precede a noun. They point out specific persons, places, things, or ideas.

This car is dependable.

I would like to test-drive that car.

These convertibles are new.

Those cars behind the fence are not for sale.

irregular forms of comparison

- The adjectives *good, bad, many, much,* and *little* have irregular forms of comparison. Study the chart on the next page.

Positive	Comparative	Superlative
good	better	best
bad	worse	worst
much/many	more	most
little	less	least

The storm caused little damage.

It caused less damage than the storm we had last week.

In fact, it caused the least damage of any storm this summer.

Adverbs

really, real

- Use *really* as an adverb; use *real* as an adjective.

Stan is really worried about his test score.

The cabinet is made of real oak.

well, good

- Use *well* as an adverb; use *good* as an adjective.

She performed well in the preliminary rounds.

That was a good idea.

badly, bad

- Use *badly* as an adverb; use *bad* as an adjective.

Things turned out badly for the island village.

We had only one day of bad weather.

surely, sure

- Use *surely* as an adverb; use *sure* as an adjective.

You will surely win a medal.

I am sure you will win a medal.

- The adverbs *well, badly, much, little,* and *far* have irregular forms of comparison.

Positive	Comparative	Superlative
well	better	best
badly	worse	worst
much	more	most
little	less	least
far	farther	farthest

Jim plays the trumpet well .

Jim plays better this year than last year.

Mr. Simon said that Jim is the best of all his students.

Prepositions

at, to
- Use *at* to indicate that someone or something is already in a certain place.
Use *to* to show movement toward a place.

Both teams were waiting at the stadium.

Yolanda ran all the way to the stadium.

in, into
- Use *in* when you mean "already inside."
Use *into* when you mean "moving from the outside to the inside of something."

A capacity crowd waited in the theater.

The long line of fans filed into   the theater.

between, among
- Use *between* when you refer to two things.
Use *among* when you refer to three or more things.

The secret is between you and me.

The trophy was passed among the team members.

- Use *beside* when you mean "at the side of."
  Use *besides* when you mean "in addition to."

beside, besides

> We rented a summer cabin beside the river.

> No one besides my brother fishes in the river.

Agreement

- A verb must agree with its subject in number. The number of a word refers to whether that word is singular or plural. In a sentence a subject and verb must both be singular or must both be plural.

subject-verb agreement

> Lee spends too much time on the phone.

> The Raiders practice more than other teams.

- Use a plural verb with most compound subjects joined by *and*.

subject-verb agreement with compound subject

> The painters and the sculptors show their work.

- Use a singular verb with compound subjects that are normally thought of as a unit.

> Strawberries and cream is my favorite summer snack.

- If a compound subject contains both a singular and a plural noun joined by a conjunction other than *and*, make the verb agree with the subject closer to the verb.

> Either the students or Mrs. Lewis wins first prize.

> Either Mrs. Lewis or the students win first prize.

- Collective nouns can be singular or plural. If a collective noun refers to a group as a whole, it is singular. If it refers to individuals in the group, it is plural.

verb agreement with collective noun

> The chorus has won many awards.

> The chorus have voted twelve to three to buy new uniforms.

- A noun that states the time of day is singular. A noun that states a block of time can be singular or plural.

verb agreement with time and money nouns

> Nine o'clock is the best time to meet.

> Two hours is (are) not enough.

- A noun that states a sum of money is singular unless individual units are described.

> Ten dollars **is** all I have left.

> There **are** **ten dollars** in the treasury.

organizations • The proper name of an organization is singular. If individual members of an organization are referred to, the noun is plural.

> The **Tri-County team** **is** undefeated.

> The **Tri-County team** **are eating** their lunches now.

titles • The title of any work, even if plural in form, is singular and takes a singular verb.

> *The Borrowers* **was** the most popular book

> in our class last year.

irregular noun plurals • Some nouns that are singular in meaning but written as plurals take plural verbs.

> Those **trousers** **are** too long for you to wear.

- Some nouns are written as plurals but take singular verbs.

> The **mumps** **is** a common childhood disease.

subject pronoun and verb • A verb should agree with a pronoun when the pronoun is the subject of a sentence. The form of a subject pronoun changes, depending on whether it is singular or plural.

> **He** **plays** right field for the Cardinals.

> **They** **play** tomorrow for the championship.

pronoun and antecedent • A pronoun should agree with its antecedent in number and gender.

> The **girls** compared **their** research papers.   number

> **Ginny** saw that **her** typing needed improvement.   gender

Paragraph

- A **paragraph** is a group of sentences that tell about one main idea. A paragraph often begins with a topic sentence. The **topic sentence** expresses the main idea of the paragraph. It tells what all the other sentences in the paragraph are about. The other sentences in a paragraph are called detail sentences. **Detail sentences** add information about the topic. They help the audience understand the main idea.

paragraph

Writer's Guide: Paragraph
1. Write a topic sentence that clearly expresses the main idea of your paragraph.
2. Indent the first line of the paragraph.
3. Write detail sentences that support the main idea in your topic sentence.

Today the Nanuet Knights won their fifth consecutive football game, defeating their opponents, the Edgemont Eagles, 42 to 0. Michael Lopez, wide receiver, made a 72-yard reception. Chris Rajib, star quarterback, made five touchdown passes. Mark Lin, defensive end, couldn't be budged. All the other team members also performed well. With today's win, the Nanuet Knights are now in fourth place in the league. If they win their next two games, they will definitely play in the championships in November.

topic sentence

detail sentences

How-to Paragraph

- In a **how-to paragraph** a writer gives directions or explains a process.

Writer's Guide: How-to Paragraph

1. Write a topic sentence that identifies the process you are explaining.
2. Write a detail sentence that lists the materials needed to complete the process.
3. Write detail sentences that explain the steps of the process in the order in which they need to be done.
4. Indicate the order of steps with time-order words such as *first, next, then,* and *last* or *finally.*

---

topic sentence —

materials —

detail
sentences —

steps in time
order —

steps in time
order —

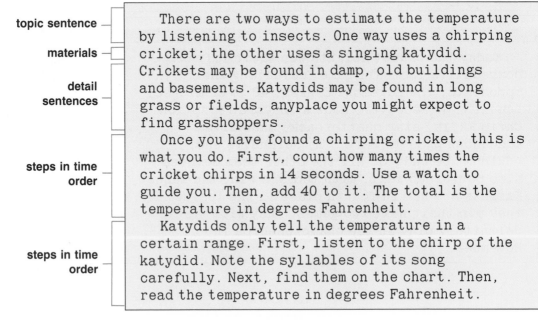

There are two ways to estimate the temperature by listening to insects. One way uses a chirping cricket; the other uses a singing katydid. Crickets may be found in damp, old buildings and basements. Katydids may be found in long grass or fields, anyplace you might expect to find grasshoppers.

Once you have found a chirping cricket, this is what you do. First, count how many times the cricket chirps in 14 seconds. Use a watch to guide you. Then, add 40 to it. The total is the temperature in degrees Fahrenheit.

Katydids only tell the temperature in a certain range. First, listen to the chirp of the katydid. Note the syllables of its song carefully. Next, find them on the chart. Then, read the temperature in degrees Fahrenheit.

Paragraph of Comparison

- In a **paragraph of comparison** a writer shows ways in which two subjects are alike. The subjects may be people, places, or things.

Writer's Guide: Paragraph of Comparison

1. Think of three ways in which your subjects are alike.
2. Write a topic sentence that identifies the two subjects and, if possible, names the qualities you will compare.
3. In the detail sentences, give examples that clearly explain the qualities the subjects have in common.
4. Write about the qualities in the same order in which you introduced them in the topic sentence.

    Middle school is like elementary school in
many ways. In both schools you study the same
basic subjects: reading, math, science, social
studies, language arts, art, music, and physical
education. The schools begin and end at the same
time. In both you have a regular schedule of
classes. There are field trips in middle school
once a month, just like elementary school.

— topic sentence

detail sentences that express similarities

Paragraph of Contrast

paragraph of contrast

- In a **paragraph of contrast** a writer explains the key differences between two subjects. The subjects may be people, places, or things.

Writer's Guide: Paragraph of Contrast
1. Think of three ways in which your subjects are different.
2. Write a topic sentence that identifies the two subjects and, if possible, names the qualities you will contrast.
3. In the detail sentences, give examples that clearly explain the differences between your subjects.
4. Write about the differences in the same order in which you introduced them in the topic sentence.

topic sentence

detail sentences that express differences

    In some ways, of course, middle school differs
from elementary school. There are new courses
such as computer, industrial arts, and home
economics, and this makes your schedule a little
more complicated. You have more homework each day
than you did in elementary school. The student
council in middle school allows students to have
more of a voice in school affairs than they did in
elementary school. It is more fun!

WRITER'S HANDBOOK • Composition

Cause-and-Effect Paragraph

- In a **cause-and-effect paragraph** a writer focuses on a cause that results in certain effects or on an effect that can be traced back to its causes. This type of paragraph can begin with either the cause or the effect.

cause-and-effect paragraph

Writer's Guide: Cause-and-Effect Paragraph

1. Begin paragraphs that focus on effects with a *cause*. Write a topic sentence that tells what happened. The detail sentences should all discuss *effects*.
2. Begin paragraphs that focus on causes with an *effect*. Write a topic sentence that identifies the effect. The detail sentences should all discuss *causes*.
3. Write detail sentences in the order in which the effects or the causes happened.

Ever since computers were introduced, they have become increasingly smaller, more powerful, and less costly. As a result, computers have become more common both in the workplace and at home. Many business and government organizations rely heavily on computers to handle a major portion of their workload. Their compactness and continuing lower cost also contribute to the use of computers in the home. In many households, the adults use computers to keep track of family finances, and the children use them for schoolwork and entertainment. With so many people using computers, a knowledge of their parts and uses is almost a necessity today.

topic sentence that states a cause

detail sentences that state effects

Persuasive Essay

- In a **persuasive essay** a writer states an opinion on an issue and attempts to convince the audience to agree with it. The reasons, or **appeals,** that support the opinion are given in order of importance.

Writer's Guide: Persuasive Essay
1. Form an opinion on an important issue.
2. Find information to support your opinion.
3. Arrange the information in order of importance.
4. Use language convincing to your particular audience.

opinion —

support —

I believe that a group of seventh-grade students can benefit our city. I am serving my second term as president of the Young Detectives' Club at Hazell Middle School. In the four years since we started, under the sponsorship of our science teacher, Ms. Christie Hubbard, we have shown unflagging interest in learning the techniques of crime detection. Our guide is The Young Detective's Handbook by William Vivian Butler.

support —

In his book Mr. Butler says, "In England, Scotland Yard runs a television show called Junior Police 5. It encourages young people to be crimestoppers." We think that our community can benefit from a program of this kind. By organizing a group of junior crimestoppers, you will give students our age a useful purpose. We will become better citizens.

support —

There is good evidence that such a program can really help a community. Our city would be the first in this part of the state to sponsor such a program. All of us, needless to say, are willing to undertake any training you require. We hope you will consider our idea and will support us in our desire to donate our time to our community. We hope that soon we will be junior detectives.

Description

- In a **description** a writer describes a person, place, thing, or event by giving **sensory details,** words that appeal to the senses. In doing this, the writer encourages the audience to see, feel, hear, and sometimes taste and smell what is described.

Writer's Guide: Description

1. Write a topic sentence that identifies your subject.
2. Write detail sentences that give specific information about it.
3. Choose details that set the tone, or mood, you want to create.
4. Use sensory details to help the audience visualize your subject.

I was struck when I first studied <u>Starry Night</u> by Vincent van Gogh, and I decided to give the picture more attention. I was drawn into the peaceful countryside. I first noticed the beautifully illuminated houses, their yellow lamps glowing like stars in the blue background. Then, I let my eye travel up and to the right.

My attention then focused on the vertical lines. I saw the steeple reaching into those clouds, connecting heaven and earth. The greenish-black cypress forced my eye up.

The violent movement of the night sky makes a sharp contrast with the calm village below. The stars burst out of the night like firecrackers. A moon as brilliant as the sun lights the scene from the upper right-hand corner. Giant waves—perhaps the blazing trail of a comet or the movement of a great galaxy—blow across the sea—sky. If the people in those cozy houses knew what this night was like, they would be out here with me, gazing breathless at <u>Starry Night</u>.

- topic sentence
- detail sentences with sensory details
- topic sentence
- detail sentences
- topic sentence
- detail sentences

WRITER'S HANDBOOK • Composition

Dialogue

• In a **dialogue** a writer tells the exact words that one person says to another.

Writer's Guide: Dialogue

1. Place **quotation marks** before and after the exact words of a speaker.
2. Use a comma to separate a quotation from the rest of the sentence unless a question mark or an exclamation point is needed.
3. Begin a new paragraph each time the speaker changes.
4. Be sure that the dialogue sounds like real people talking.
5. Use words such as *said, called, answered, whispered*, and *shouted* to show how the speaker says the words.

---

first speaker

second speaker, new paragraph

> "Look! Isn't that amazing?" cried Astronaut Brown, staring out into space.
>
> "What's amazing, Brown?" asked Astronaut Diaz, looking up from her control panels.
>
> "The planet Earth!" exclaimed Brown. "Isn't it fantastic to be up here looking down at our planet?"
>
> "You're absolutely right," Diaz agreed. "We must be the luckiest people on Earth—or rather, <u>off</u> Earth."

Journal Entry

journal entry

- In a **journal** a writer records a day's significant events and expresses his or her thoughts and feelings about them. Each daily record is called an **entry.** Writers often use journals as idea banks.

Writer's Guide: Journal Entry

1. Begin each entry with the date.
2. Describe the important events of the day.
3. Tell *who, what, when, where, why,* and *how* about each event.
4. Describe your thoughts and feelings about the day's events, or record any special ideas that you might have.

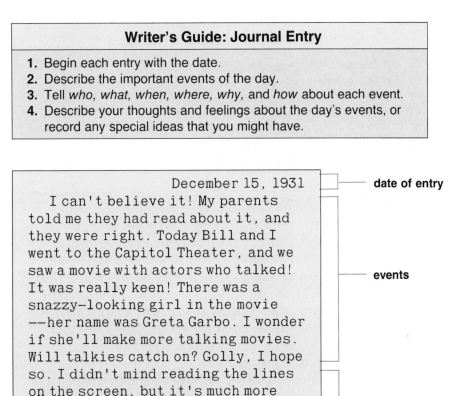

December 15, 1931 — **date of entry**

I can't believe it! My parents told me they had read about it, and they were right. Today Bill and I went to the Capitol Theater, and we saw a movie with actors who talked! It was really keen! There was a snazzy-looking girl in the movie ——her name was Greta Garbo. I wonder if she'll make more talking movies. Will talkies catch on? Golly, I hope so. — **events**

I didn't mind reading the lines on the screen, but it's much more fun to see actors up there actually talking to each other. What's next? Maybe some movies in color! — **feelings**

Personal Narrative

personal narrative

- In a **personal narrative** a writer shares a significant experience in his or her life.

Writer's Guide: Personal Narrative
1. Write from the first-person point of view.
2. Write a catchy beginning.
3. Tell the events that happened in time order.
4. Write a satisfying ending.

catchy beginning

events in time order

satisfying ending

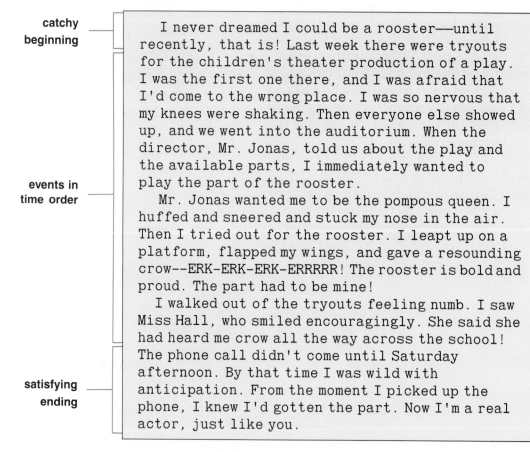

I never dreamed I could be a rooster—until recently, that is! Last week there were tryouts for the children's theater production of a play. I was the first one there, and I was afraid that I'd come to the wrong place. I was so nervous that my knees were shaking. Then everyone else showed up, and we went into the auditorium. When the director, Mr. Jonas, told us about the play and the available parts, I immediately wanted to play the part of the rooster.

Mr. Jonas wanted me to be the pompous queen. I huffed and sneered and stuck my nose in the air. Then I tried out for the rooster. I leapt up on a platform, flapped my wings, and gave a resounding crow--ERK-ERK-ERK-ERRRRR! The rooster is bold and proud. The part had to be mine!

I walked out of the tryouts feeling numb. I saw Miss Hall, who smiled encouragingly. She said she had heard me crow all the way across the school! The phone call didn't come until Saturday afternoon. By that time I was wild with anticipation. From the moment I picked up the phone, I knew I'd gotten the part. Now I'm a real actor, just like you.

Story

- In a **story** a writer tells about one main idea. A story has an introduction, a complication, and a resolution.

Writer's Guide: Story
1. Present the main character and the setting in the introduction.
2. Tell the challenge the main character faces in the complication.
3. Write dialogue between the main character and other characters.
4. Write a resolution. Show how the problem is solved.
5. Write an interesting title for your story.

Hector Helps Out

"I don't like sitting next to Hector," Sally complained. "He doesn't have any feelings."

"Probably not," Lil said. "Hector's an android."

"He buzzes and squeaks when he moves," Sally said, "and he eats synch jello for lunch! I don't see what he's doing in school. They could program him to know everything that they want a machine to know."

"It's an experiment," Lil said. "They want to know if he can learn new things if they start him out with only the basic program."

That afternoon there was a sudden blizzard. No one could get out of the school, and the electricity and furnace went off. "I'm freezing!" Sally cried. Then the principal called Hector out of the room, and soon Sally could feel that the heat was back on.

"Hector's down in the basement," Lil explained. "He's transferring his energy to the furnace to keep it running. They're carrying synch jello to him by the bucketful. Want to help by taking him some?"

The girls found Hector standing with his hand on the big motor. He looked at Sally with pale gray eyes, and she could see that he was getting very weak.

"He can't last long," Lil whispered to Sally.

Soon the lights came back on. A helicopter brought food and blankets, and some people carried Hector away on a stretcher. "They're taking him back to the factory that made him," Lil said. As he came past Sally, Hector just managed to raise one hand. He smiled a weak smile and waved a small goodbye.

"Oh," Sally said, her eyes filling with tears, "he <u>does</u> have feelings. I hope they fix him quickly."

Mystery Story

• In a mystery story a writer uses believable characters and an ordinary setting to tell a suspenseful tale. The **plot** has three parts. An **introduction** presents a problem, the **complication** shows efforts to solve it, and the **resolution** settles the mystery.

Writer's Guide: Mystery Story

1. Use a story map for the introduction, complication, and resolution.
2. Use characterization and dialogue to set the mood.
3. Reveal the solution at the end of the story.

The Mystery of the Missing Coin

As Jenny pulled into the driveway, she wondered why Mr. Van der Horne had called her. When he greeted her at the door and escorted her into the elegant living room, Jenny knew at once that something was wrong.

"Jenny, I'm so glad to see you. I've been so upset since I found that my most valuable gold coin has been stolen," Mr. Van der Horne said.

"Exactly what happened?" Jenny asked anxiously.

"I was reviewing my collection just before I went to my neighbor's for lunch," Mr. Van der Horne explained. "At lunch my neighbor mentioned my collection. It was then that I realized I hadn't shut the safe before I left. When I rushed home, I found the safe closed, but when I opened it, I found the coin gone!"

"Where is the safe?" Jenny asked.

"Behind that portrait."

"Was anyone else here at the time of the burglary?" Jenny continued.

"The only people who were on the estate were my cook and my gardener," Mr. Van der Horne answered.

"Kevin, the gardener, is right outside——you can see him

through the picture window. I believe he is in money trouble, because he recently asked for a large raise, which I refused to give. The cook, Maggie, of course, is in the kitchen. She is an excellent cook but bitter and sullen. She could be the blackmailing type."

Jenny hurried out to the garden. She introduced herself to Kevin and asked if he could spare a moment.

"Sure," he said, brushing the dirt from his worn pants.

"This afternoon one of Mr. Van der Horne's coins was stolen. Can you shed any light on the problem?" Jenny asked.

"Hmm, I think I may have a clue," he said. "At about one o'clock, I was outside the picture window planting petunias and saw Maggie heading toward the safe."

"Thank you," Jenny said, smiling as she left.

As she entered the kitchen, she saw a dark-haired woman with her back turned, busily mixing something in a bowl.

"What do you want?" Maggie said as she turned around.

"One of Mr. Van der Horne's coins was stolen today, and . . ."

"Well, I certainly didn't do it, and I don't like being accused of robbery!" she snapped angrily.

"Thank you," Jenny said shortly and left.

When Jenny returned to the living room, Mr. Van der Horne asked curiously, "Do you really know who stole my coin?"

"Yes," Jenny said.

"How in the world did you find out so quickly?" he asked in astonishment.

"You said that no one besides you knew about the safe, but when I talked to Kevin he said that he saw Maggie heading toward it. Unless he knew where it was, he wouldn't have said that. He also knew when the theft occurred. I think, while gardening, Kevin saw you open the safe and glimpsed the gold coins. When you left, he saw the perfect chance to get the money he so desperately needed. He came into the house, took the coin, and was out before you returned," Jenny explained. "He carefully closed the safe and replaced the other coins. If you hadn't remembered leaving the safe open, it might have been weeks or months before you discovered the theft."

Play

- In a **play** a writer tells a story that is intended to be acted out by performers. A play has characters, one or more settings, and a plot. The conversation between characters in a play is called **dialogue.** The writer includes **stage directions** that tell the actors how to move, act, and speak.

Writer's Guide: Play
1. Use dialogue to tell the story. Let the characters' conversations show how the plot develops. In a play, do not use quotation marks to show what the characters say.
2. Write clear stage directions that tell the actors exactly how to move, act, and speak.
3. Stage directions are written in parentheses and are underlined or in italic type.
4. Be sure your play has interesting characters, dialogue development, and a plot.
5. Give your play a title.

title
stage directions
dialogue
characters' words that advance the plot

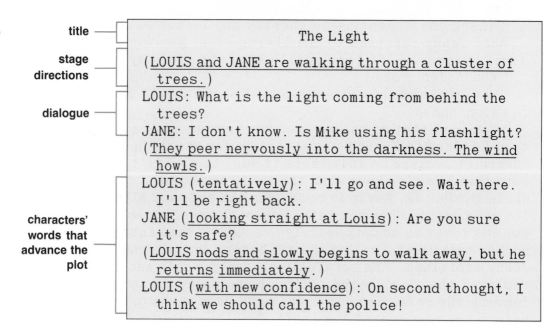

The Light

(LOUIS and JANE are walking through a cluster of trees.)

LOUIS: What is the light coming from behind the trees?

JANE: I don't know. Is Mike using his flashlight?

(They peer nervously into the darkness. The wind howls.)

LOUIS (tentatively): I'll go and see. Wait here. I'll be right back.

JANE (looking straight at Louis): Are you sure it's safe?

(LOUIS nods and slowly begins to walk away, but he returns immediately.)

LOUIS (with new confidence): On second thought, I think we should call the police!

WRITER'S HANDBOOK • Composition

Lyric Poem

lyric poem

- In a **lyric poem** a writer expresses feelings, usually in a songlike manner. Rather than tell stories about people, places, or things, the writer describes them. A lyric poem often has a definite rhyme and rhythm. To help the audience see and feel as the writer does, a poem often contains **figures of speech.** Similes and metaphors are figures of speech. In a **simile** a writer makes a comparison between two unlike things using the word *like* or *as.* In a **metaphor** a writer also makes a comparison but does not use *like* or *as.*

Writer's Guide: Lyric Poem

1. Use strong and colorful descriptive words to describe your subject.
2. To help make your feelings clear to the audience, use similes and metaphors.
3. Use rhyme and rhythm to develop feeling in your poem.
4. Give your poem a title.

The Song of the Percussionist

The percussionist plays
  On the timpani,
Being extra careful
  When she tunes the key.
Boom Bim Boom—Bim—Boom

The percussionist taps
  On the cymbals of brass
And clashes them together
  With a big resounding crash!
CLANG Ting Ting—Ting—Ting

The percussionist rolls
  On the drum called snare,
And her wrists beat tattoos
  As she ruffles the air
Dug—uh Dug—uh BRUM—BRUM—BRUM

The percussionist's melodic
  On the xylophone,
The marimba and the chimes
  And the vibraphone.
La—Dee—Da—Dee Doo—Dee—Doe—Dee
Ding—Dang—Dong!
And that's the end of my
percussionist's song.

Character Sketch

- In a **character sketch** a writer describes a person. The writer shows both the subject's appearance and personality.

Writer's Guide: Character Sketch
1. In the topic sentence, identify the person and try to capture the audience's interest by stating an interesting detail.
2. In detail sentences, describe how the person looks and moves.

My Sister Elizabeth

When I think of Elizabeth, I think of our stairs—not that they are unusual. They are narrow and covered with mottled green carpeting. It was on these stairs that Elizabeth staged her big revolt at the tender age of three. At age three, this child weighed only 35 pounds, but 34½ of those pounds were pure stubbornness.

This is what happened. Elizabeth's friend Mary lent Elizabeth her stuffed yellow duck. When Elizabeth went to Mary's house to play, she returned the duck, but she refused to say thank you. Mom explained that we should show our appreciation when someone lends us something. Elizabeth was silent. Mom warned Elizabeth that if she refused to thank Mary she would have to go straight home. Elizabeth shrugged and began to hum. Mom took Elizabeth home and told her to sit on the stairs until she was ready to say thank you. The battle had begun.

It wasn't until the next day that Elizabeth finally gave in. By that time I was begging Mom to let up. I told her that I would have cracked after one boring half hour. Wasn't it cruel to treat a baby this way? Mom pointed out that Elizabeth enjoyed her own company more than I did mine. She predicted that Elizabeth would not be so stubborn in the future and would learn to be courteous. I, for one, didn't believe it. But you know what? Mom was right! It was a memorable lesson. When Elizabeth is asked to say thank you now, she says it. We are all glad she learned her lesson, and we learned to respect her toughness.

News Story

- In a **news story** a writer provides information about a person, a group, an event, an object, or an issue. A news story has three parts: the lead, the body, and the headline. The **lead** is the first paragraph of a news story. It tells *who, what, when, where, why,* and sometimes *how* about something that happened. The rest of the news story is the **body.** It adds details about the lead. The title of a news story is a **headline.**

news story

Writer's Guide: News Story
1. Write a lead that answers the six news-gathering questions.
2. Give more details about the lead in the body of the news story. Write the most important details first.
3. Write a short, interesting headline. Use a strong verb to attract the attention of the audience.

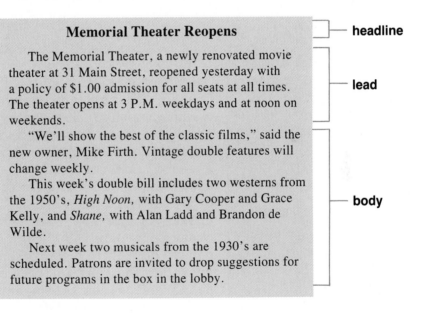

Memorial Theater Reopens — headline

The Memorial Theater, a newly renovated movie theater at 31 Main Street, reopened yesterday with a policy of $1.00 admission for all seats at all times. The theater opens at 3 P.M. weekdays and at noon on weekends. — lead

"We'll show the best of the classic films," said the new owner, Mike Firth. Vintage double features will change weekly.

This week's double bill includes two westerns from the 1950's, *High Noon,* with Gary Cooper and Grace Kelly, and *Shane,* with Alan Ladd and Brandon de Wilde.

Next week two musicals from the 1930's are scheduled. Patrons are invited to drop suggestions for future programs in the box in the lobby. — body

WRITER'S HANDBOOK • Composition

Book Report

- In a **book report** a writer summarizes the important events in a book. The writer also gives his or her opinion of the book.

Writer's Guide: Book Report

1. In your first sentence, give the title of the book and the name of the author. Remember to underline the title of the book.
2. Write a summary of the important events. Include the main idea, the names of the main characters, and some interesting details. Do not tell the ending.
3. Tell why a person might or might not like the book, or give your opinion of the book. Support your opinion with reasons.

---

title/author

Ash Road, an Australian novel by Ivan Southall, is about three boys, Graham, Wallace, and Harry, who begin a January school holiday by camping in the wilderness for a week. The boys relish their independence and freedom. However, the hot, dry weather spells danger for the inexperienced campers, and a huge brush fire, not unlike a major American forest fire, breaks out. How the three friends behave during this dangerous event provides the fuel for this story. The author describes their reactions to the fire, to each other, and to the local residents.

summary

opinion

I enjoyed reading Ash Road. Not only is the story exciting, but it is also unusual. The author makes the fire a major "character" in the novel, and I was drawn into the boys' complex responses to it.

reasons

Research Report

- To write a **research report**, a writer gathers information from several sources, takes notes from the sources, and organizes the notes into an outline. Then he or she writes the report based on the notes and outline.

research report

Writer's Guide: Research Report

1. Use your notes and outline to write your research report.
2. Write an introduction that identifies your topic. Include interesting sentences to capture the attention of the audience.
3. Write one paragraph for each subtopic in your outline.
4. Follow your outline to write details about your topic.
5. Give your research report a title.

The Development of the Draft Horse — title

Draft means "used for pulling." Because draft horses are the strongest, heaviest, and tallest of all horses, they are especially suited to pulling loads. They are short-legged and heavily muscled work animals with big hooves. These horses were first bred in the Middle Ages after the Crusades ended. They are still used today. This is the story of how they were developed. — introduction

The horse from which all modern horses come is called the Mongolian wild horse. Ten thousand years ago, these horses were short, stocky, and about 13 hands (or 62 inches) high. As they migrated from Asia, they adapted as a result of their new environment. Differences in size, color, hair thickness, and other characteristics appeared. The wild horses of northern Europe were noticeably larger than their Asian counterparts.

Horses were bred to a large size to pull war chariots. Large horses became desirable to carry knights in armor in the Crusades. A large, muscular breed called "Great Horses" was bred to carry enormous weights. Only a large, strong horse could carry a knight and armor weighing 400 pounds.

— detail paragraphs from outline subtopics

WRITER'S HANDBOOK • Composition

After the Crusades it was natural to look for another occupation for the Great Horses. As a result of the invention of horseshoes and of a new kind of horse collar, these strong horses could plow the damp clay soil of northern Europe. Consequently, their use led to great improvements in agriculture.

final details Draft horses have played an important role in history. They were important in the clearing and cultivation of land in North America. Today, they are still used to plow, plant, log, and pull loads. People are abandoning machinery and are again using these patient, hardworking animals. Draft horses have become an important part of our American heritage.

Friendly Letter

- In a **friendly letter** a writer sends informal greetings or news to a friend or relative. A friendly letter has five parts.

Writer's Guide: Friendly Letter
1. Write the heading in the upper right corner.
2. Start the greeting at the left margin.
3. Use paragraph form in the body. Tell personal news, and ask your friend or relative questions.
4. Think about your reader and your purpose, and choose words accordingly.
5. Write the closing and your signature in line with the heading. Capitalize only the first word in the closing.

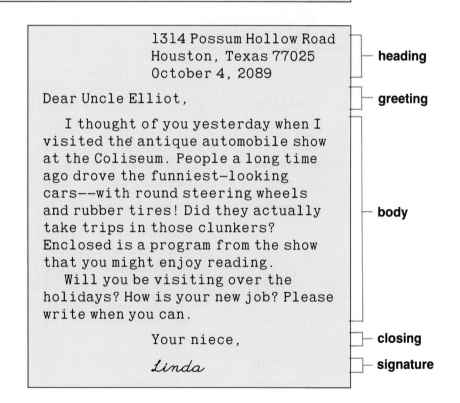

1314 Possum Hollow Road
Houston, Texas 77025
October 4, 2089 — **heading**

Dear Uncle Elliot, — **greeting**

   I thought of you yesterday when I visited the antique automobile show at the Coliseum. People a long time ago drove the funniest-looking cars—with round steering wheels and rubber tires! Did they actually take trips in those clunkers? Enclosed is a program from the show that you might enjoy reading.
   Will you be visiting over the holidays? How is your new job? Please write when you can. — **body**

     Your niece, — **closing**

     Linda — **signature**

WRITER'S HANDBOOK • Composition

Business Letter

business letter • In a **business letter** a writer usually makes a request or places an order for something. A business letter has six parts.

Writer's Guide: Business Letter

1. Write the heading in the upper right corner.
2. Write the inside address at the left margin.
3. Start the greeting at the left margin. If you know your reader's full name, use it. Be sure to precede it with a title (*Mr./Mrs./Ms.*) and follow it with a colon.
4. Write the body in paragraph form.
5. Be polite and brief, but be sure to include all necessary information.
6. Align the closing with the heading. *Yours truly* and *Sincerely* are appropriate closings. Sign your full name in ink under the closing. Type (or print) your full name under your signature.

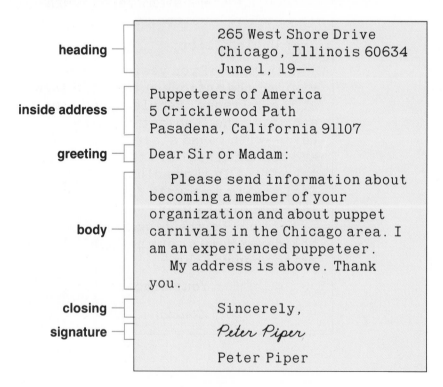

heading
265 West Shore Drive
Chicago, Illinois 60634
June 1, 19--

inside address
Puppeteers of America
5 Cricklewood Path
Pasadena, California 91107

greeting
Dear Sir or Madam:

body
   Please send information about becoming a member of your organization and about puppet carnivals in the Chicago area. I am an experienced puppeteer.
   My address is above. Thank you.

closing
   Sincerely,

signature
   Peter Piper
   Peter Piper

Invitation

invitation

- In an **invitation** a writer invites someone to come to a party or other event or to do something. An invitation has the same five parts as a friendly letter.

Writer's Guide: Invitation

1. Be sure to include a heading, a greeting, a body, a closing, and a signature.
2. In the body, tell *who* is invited and *what* the invitation is for.
3. Tell *when* and *where* the activity or event will take place and any other special information your guest must know.

The Wing School
432 Wing Road
Galveston, Texas 77550
March 15, 19-- }— **heading**

Dear Ms. Frankel, }— **greeting**

　　You are invited to attend the seventh grade's Third Annual International Fair in the gymnasium of The Wing School, Saturday, April 10, at 1:00 P.M.
　　Students will offer songs, dances, music, and stories from their families' native lands. Posters and photographs will show guests what those countries look like. Traditional snacks from some of the countries will be available.
　　We hope you'll come. }— **body**

　　　　　　Sincerely, }— **closing**

　　　　　　Mindy Vega }— **signature**

　　　　　　Mindy Vega
　　　　　　Class Secretary

WRITER'S HANDBOOK • Composition

Thank-You Note

- In a **thank-you note** a writer expresses thanks or appreciation for a gift or a special favor. A thank-you note has the same five parts as a friendly letter.

Writer's Guide: Thank-You Note

1. Be sure to include a heading, a greeting, a body, a closing, and a signature.
2. In the body, tell why you are thanking the person.
3. If you have been a visitor somewhere, tell why you enjoyed yourself.
4. If you received a gift, tell how you are using it.
5. If someone has done a special favor for you, express your appreciation and explain why it was important to you.

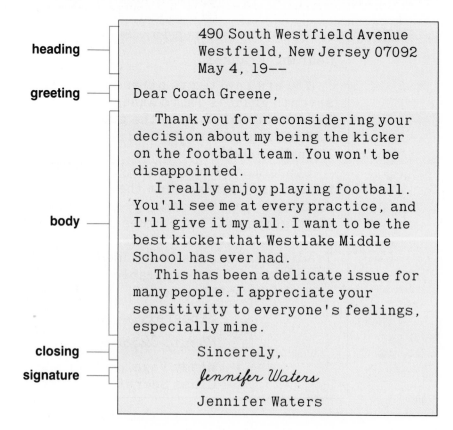

heading

490 South Westfield Avenue
Westfield, New Jersey 07092
May 4, 19--

greeting

Dear Coach Greene,

body

Thank you for reconsidering your decision about my being the kicker on the football team. You won't be disappointed.

I really enjoy playing football. You'll see me at every practice, and I'll give it my all. I want to be the best kicker that Westlake Middle School has ever had.

This has been a delicate issue for many people. I appreciate your sensitivity to everyone's feelings, especially mine.

closing

Sincerely,

signature

Jennifer Waters

Jennifer Waters

Envelope

- An **envelope** is used to send a letter or a note.

- The **mailing address** is the address of the person who will receive the letter. It is written toward the center of the envelope.

- The **return address** is the address of the person who writes the letter. It is written in the upper left corner.

- **Postal abbreviations** are used for state names.

- The **ZIP code** is written after the state abbreviation.

envelope

mailing address

return address

postal abbreviations

ZIP code

Alan Stone
320 East Third Street
New York, NY 10001

return address

Dr. William Williams
Old Tappan Hospital
435 Main Street
Old Tappan, NJ 07675

mailing address

Postal Abbreviations

Alabama	AL	Kentucky	KY	North Dakota	ND
Alaska	AK	Louisiana	LA	Ohio	OH
Arizona	AZ	Maine	ME	Oklahoma	OK
Arkansas	AR	Maryland	MD	Oregon	OR
California	CA	Massachusetts	MA	Pennsylvania	PA
Colorado	CO	Michigan	MI	Puerto Rico	PR
Connecticut	CT	Minnesota	MN	Rhode Island	RI
Delaware	DE	Mississippi	MS	South Carolina	SC
District of		Missouri	MO	South Dakota	SD
Columbia	DC	Montana	MT	Tennessee	TN
Florida	FL	Nebraska	NE	Texas	TX
Georgia	GA	Nevada	NV	Utah	UT
Hawaii	HI	New Hampshire	NH	Vermont	VT
Idaho	ID	New Jersey	NJ	Virginia	VA
Illinois	IL	New Mexico	NM	Washington	WA
Indiana	IN	New York	NY	West Virginia	WV
Iowa	IA	North Carolina	NC	Wisconsin	WI
Kansas	KS			Wyoming	WY

WRITER'S HANDBOOK • Composition

- A **base word** is a complete word that cannot be divided into smaller parts and still retain its meaning. Other word parts may be added to a base word to form new words.

root

- A **root** is a word part to which prefixes, suffixes, base words, or other roots are added to form words.

Root	Meaning	Example
auto	self	automobile
bio	life	biography
dic, dict	say	dictation
gram, graph	write	telegram
meter	measure	kilometer
micro	small	microscope
photo	light	photograph
scope, scopy	see	microscopic
tele	distant	telephone
therm, thermo	heat	thermal

prefix

- A **prefix** is a word part that is added to the beginning of a base word or a root to change its meaning or part of speech.

Prefix	Meaning	Example
de	down, from	detour
dis	opposite of, not	distrust
ex	out of, former	external
extra	outside of, in addition to	extraordinary
fore	before, in front	forehead
inter	between, among	intersect
over	too much, above	overcrowded
post	after	postdate
pre	before	prehistoric
re	back, again	retrace

People crowded around the subway door.

I don't think we'll board that overcrowded car.

San Antonio has many places of historic interest.

Are all fossils prehistoric ?

The police are trying to trace the missing man.

Two detectives will retrace his path.

- A **negative prefix** can mean "not," "opposite of," or "wrongly."

Prefix	Meaning	Example
il	not	illogical
im	not	improbable
in	not	incorrect
ir	not	irresponsible
mis	wrongly, badly	misjudge
non	not	nonstop
un	not, opposite of	unbelievable

A responsible driver wears a seat belt.

An irresponsible driver can cause an accident.

Can you judge the depth of the pool?

You could be injured if you misjudge it.

Mindy's excuse for missing the bus was believable .

Steve told an unbelievable tale about being kidnapped

by Martians.

- A **suffix** is a word part that is added to the end of a word. It usually changes the way a word is used in a sentence. Sometimes a suffix changes the meaning of a word. It may also change a word's part of speech.

Adjective-forming Suffix	Meaning	Example
able, ible	able	enjoyable
al	belonging to, of	seasonal
en	made of, like	wooden
ful	full of	harmful
ish	like	reddish
ive	tending to	massive
less	without	restless
y	showing, having	snowy

Wood from an oak tree is very hard.

My wooden desk is fifty years old.

Tara is behaving like a child .

It is childish to pout.

The snow fell softly.

We all stayed home that snowy night.

Noun-forming Suffix	Meaning	Example
ance, ence	act, state	insistence
er, or	doer	builder
ion, tion	state, action	donation
ity, ty	quality	equality
ment	action, result	arrangement
ness	state, quality	thickness

We insist on leaving early.

Your insistence was wise.

Jay donates blood often.

His donation is a useful gift.

Can you arrange to fly to Ohio?

That arrangement is fine.

Verb-forming Suffix	Meaning	Example
en	become, make	frighten
ify, fy	cause, make	notify
ize	cause to be, make	mobilize

The scary movie filled me with fright .

Did the movie frighten you?

Send a note to the neighbor.

How will we notify your uncle?

WRITER'S HANDBOOK • Vocabulary

The sergeant has a mobile radio.

Captain Smith said to mobilize the troops.

- A **synonym** is a word that has a meaning similar to that of another word.

    Bob's idea was a good one.

    It was an original concept .

synonym

- **Antonyms** are words with opposite meanings.

    It is an honor to compete in the Olympics.

    It is a shame that all countries do not participate.

antonym

- **Homographs** are words that are spelled alike but have different meanings and sometimes different pronunciations.

    May I borrow your new record ?

    I will record this song on a cassette.

homographs

- **Homophones** are words that sound alike but have different meanings and spellings.

    My uncle peddles vacuum cleaners door-to-door.

    The pedals on my bicycle are broken.

homophones

- A **clipped word** is formed when one or more syllables are dropped from a long word.

    Would you like to see the photo of my sister?

    (clipped from the word *photograph*)

clipped word

- A **blended word** is formed when parts of two words are combined into one.

    The smog covered the city like a blanket.

    (*smoke* combined with *fog*)

blended word

- An **acronym** is a word formed from the first letters of a compound term or title.

    He is a member of a scuba club.

    (<u>s</u>elf-<u>c</u>ontained <u>u</u>nderwater <u>b</u>reathing <u>a</u>pparatus)

initialism • An **initialism** is an acronym in which each of the letters is pronounced.

The president of the NCAA visited our school.

(National Collegiate Athletic Association)

multiple-meaning word • A **multiple-meaning word** has specialized meanings in more than one field or subject.

I opened a savings account at the bank .

We left the picnic basket on the bank of the river.

Watch as the two jets bank to the left.

My computer has the information in its memory bank .

On my last camping trip I learned how to bank a fire.

Study Steps to Learn a Word

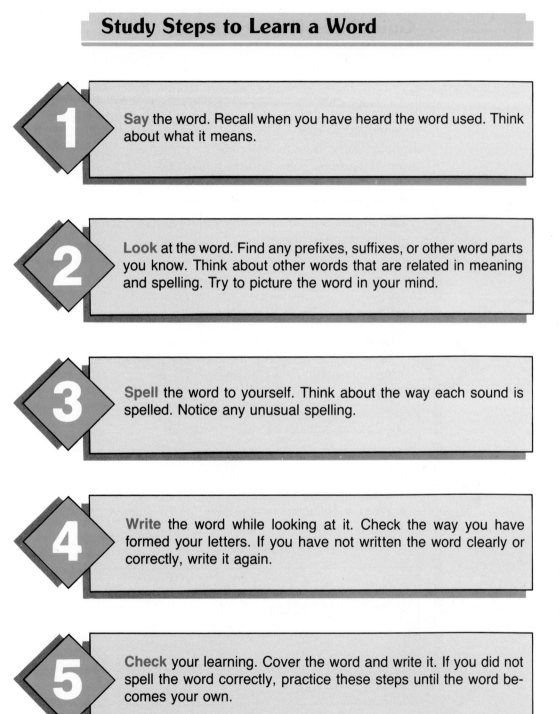

1 **Say** the word. Recall when you have heard the word used. Think about what it means.

2 **Look** at the word. Find any prefixes, suffixes, or other word parts you know. Think about other words that are related in meaning and spelling. Try to picture the word in your mind.

3 **Spell** the word to yourself. Think about the way each sound is spelled. Notice any unusual spelling.

4 **Write** the word while looking at it. Check the way you have formed your letters. If you have not written the word clearly or correctly, write it again.

5 **Check** your learning. Cover the word and write it. If you did not spell the word correctly, practice these steps until the word becomes your own.

Guidelines for Creating a Spelling Word List

You may want to keep your own spelling word list in a notebook. You can organize your spelling word list alphabetically, by subject areas, by parts of speech, or by other categories. Follow these guidelines.

1. Check your writing for words you have misspelled. Circle each misspelled word.

My dog is an (inteligent) animal.

2. Find out how to spell the word correctly.
- Look up the word in a dictionary or a thesaurus.
- Ask a teacher or a classmate.

intelligent
My dog is an (inteligent) animal.

3. Write the word in your notebook.
- Spell the word correctly.
- Write a definition, a synonym, or an antonym to help you understand the meaning of the word.
- Use the word in a sentence.

intelligent--smart, bright
Dogs are <u>intelligent</u> animals.

4. When you write, look at your spelling word list to check your spelling.

That game is for intelligent people.

Frequently Misspelled Words

accepted	doubt	losing	somewhere
accidentally	elementary	luckily	special
advice	embarrassed	might	specific
anywhere	emergency	mirror	stepped
apologize	enforce	misbehave	straight
apologized	errands	mischievous	studying
assign	especially	necessary	supposed
attitude	everybody	neither	surprise
audience	everyday	normally	surprised
barely	everywhere	nowhere	themselves
beginning	excitement	opposing	therefore
bottom	excuse	opposite	throat
bridge	excused	ourselves	tomorrow
business	experience	paid	totally
carry	explaining	planned	tough
carrying	extremely	practiced	tournament
championship	government	principal	trophy
collision	headache	probably	uncomfortable
comfortable	immediately	received	upside
concentrate	incident	referral	usually
congratulated	instance	remembered	visitors
crowds	interested	routine	whatever
daily	involved	safety	whenever
difference	knocked	scene	wherever
disappointed	lecture	separate	whether
discipline	limit	sincerely	whistle
disturbance	lonely	situation	whose

Vowel Sounds

short vowel sounds
- The short vowel sounds /a/, /e/, /i/, /o/, and /u/ are usually each spelled with one letter.

  /a/ is spelled **a**, as in *map*
  /e/ is spelled **e**, as in *expect*
  /i/ is spelled **i** or **y**, as in *miss* or *lyric*
  /o/ is spelled **o**, as in *odd*
  /u/ is spelled **u** or **o**, as in *lunch* or *love*
  Note: /e/ is sometimes spelled **ea**, as in *ready*.

long vowel sounds
- Here are eight ways to spell /ā/.

  a, as in *navy*
  a-consonant-e, as in *brake*
  ai, as in *complain*
  ay, as in *tray*
  ey, as in *whey*
  eigh, as in *sleigh*
  ei, as in *vein*
  ea, as in *steak*

- Here are eight ways to spell /ē/.

  e, as in *equal*
  e-consonant-e, as in *concede*
  ee, as in *sheet*
  ea, as in *eager*
  y, as in *lazy*
  ey, as in *key*
  ei, as in *deceive*
  ie, as in *piece*

- Here are five ways to spell /ī/.

  i, as in *idea*
  igh, as in *high*
  i-consonant-e, as in *rice*
  y, as in *deny*
  ie, as in *pie*

WRITER'S HANDBOOK • Spelling

- Here are seven ways to spell /ō/.

  o, as in *over*
  oa, as in *goat*
  o-consonant-e, as in *rope*
  ow, as in *below*
  ou, as in *shoulder*
  oe, as in *toe*
  ough, as in *although*

- Here are nine ways to spell /o͞o/.

  oo, as in *shoot*
  ew, as in *threw*
  o, as in *to*
  oe, as in *shoe*
  u-consonant-e, as in *rude*
  ui, as in *suit*
  ou, as in *soup*
  ough, as in *through*
  o-consonant-e, as in *move*

Letter Combinations

- Usually when *i* and *e* are combined in a word, they make the sound /ē/ spelled *ie*. *ie, ei*

  relief   grieve

  Exceptions: Words with the sound /ē/ after the letter *c*

  receive   conceive

  Words with the sound /ā/

  vein   skein

- Here are three ways to spell /ər/ at the end of a word. final /ər/

  ar, as in *molar*
  er, as in *mister*
  or, as in *tractor*

- Here are four ways to spell /l/ or /əl/ at the end of a word. final /l/ or /əl/

  al, as in *naval*
  el, as in *nickel*
  le, as in *candle*
  il, as in *evil*

Syllable Divisions

syllable
- A **syllable** is a word or part of a word. Each syllable in a word has one vowel sound. Knowing how to divide a word into syllables can help you pronounce the word correctly. Correct pronunciation, in turn, can help you spell a word correctly. Some rules for dividing words into syllables are listed below.

- When a word has two consonants between two vowel sounds, divide the word between the two consonants. However, do not divide a consonant digraph.

  mon·key   mat·ter   leath·er

- When a word has one consonant sound between two vowel sounds and the first vowel sound is long, divide the word before the consonant.

  vi·tal   ri·val

- When a word has one consonant sound between two vowel sounds and the first vowel sound is short, divide the word after the consonant.

  mod·el   viv·id

- When a word has two vowel sounds between two consonant sounds, divide the word between the two vowels.

  pri·or   buy·er

- When a word ends with a consonant followed by *le*, divide the word before the consonant.

  bus·tle   cra·dle

- When a word has a one-syllable prefix or suffix, divide the prefix or suffix from the base word.

  un·tie   re·do·ing

Verbs

past tense
- Add *ed* to form the past tense of most verbs.

  laugh—laughed   yell—yelled   talk—talked

- To form the past tense of verbs that end in *e*, drop the *e* and add *ed*.

  involve—involved   dare—dared   decide—decided

- To form the past tense of one-syllable verbs that end with a short vowel sound and a consonant, double the final consonant. Then add *ed*.

  trip—tripped   pat—patted   mug—mugged

- To form the past tense of verbs that end in a consonant and *y*, change the *y* to *i* and add *ed*.

  pry—pried   worry—worried   rally—rallied

- Add *ing* to form the present participle of most verbs.

  hatch—hatching   see—seeing   help—helping

present participle

- To form the present participle of verbs that end in *e*, drop the *e* and add *ing*.

  arrive—arriving   grade—grading   involve—involving

- To form the present participle of one-syllable verbs that end with a short vowel sound and a consonant, double the final consonant. Then add *ing*.

  trip—tripping   hop—hopping   beg—begging

Plurals

- Add *s* to form the plural of most nouns.

  scene—scenes   treasure—treasures   storm—storms

plurals

- Add *es* to form the plurals of nouns ending in *ss, s, z, x, sh,* or *ch*.

  match—matches   moss—mosses   relish—relishes

- Add *s* to form the plural of a noun that ends in a vowel plus *y*.

  toy—toys   tray—trays

- To form the plural of a noun that ends in a consonant plus *y*, change the *y* to *i* and add *es*.

  pastry—pastries   tapestry—tapestries

- Add *s* to form the plurals of nouns that end in a vowel plus *o*.

  radio—radios   video—videos

- Add *s* to form the plural of most nouns that end in a consonant plus *o*.

  piano—pianos   solo—solos

- To form the plural of some nouns ending in *f,* change the *f* to *v* and add *es.*

  scarf—scarves   half—halves

- Add *s* to form the plural of words ending in *ff.*

  puff—puffs   muff—muffs

- Some nouns have irregular plural forms.

ox—oxen	goose—geese
man—men	child—children
woman—women	mouse—mice

- Some nouns are spelled the same in the singular and in the plural forms.

sheep—sheep	deer—deer
fish—fish	moose—moose

Compound Words

compound word

- A **compound word** is made up of two or more words that together form a new word.

  text + book = textbook   play + ground = playground

- A **closed compound** is two words written as one.

  landslide   lifeboat   steelworker

- An **open compound** is two words written separately.

  ice cream   baking soda   hot dog

- A **hyphenated compound** is two or more words joined by one or more hyphens.

  sister-in-law   one-third   cross-examine

Contractions

- A **pronoun contraction** is a shortened form of a pronoun and a verb. An apostrophe replaces the letters that are omitted.

  I + will = I'll   he + has = he's   we + are = we're

pronoun contraction

- A **verb contraction** is a shortened form of a verb and the word *not*. Write an apostrophe in place of the letter *o* in *not*.

verb contraction

  has + not = hasn't   did + not = didn't   is + not = isn't
  Exceptions: will + not = won't
               can + not = cannot or can't
               shall + not = shan't

Possessive Nouns

- Form the possessive of a singular noun by adding an apostrophe and *s*.

singular possessive noun

  doctor's office   Carol's purse   horse's saddle

- Form the possessive of a plural noun that ends in *s* by adding an apostrophe.

plural possessive noun

  the students' attention   the Taylors' house

- Form the possessive of a plural noun that does not end in *s* by adding apostrophe and *s*.

  oxen's harness   men's lockers   women's shoes

Adjectives That Compare

- Add *er* and *est* to one-syllable adjectives and some two-syllable adjectives to form the comparative and superlative degrees.

er, est

  high—higher—highest   simple—simpler—simplest

- Double the final consonant in a word with a short vowel sound before adding *er* or *est*.

  big—bigger—biggest

WRITER'S HANDBOOK • Spelling

- Change the final *y* to *i* in a word that ends in a consonant plus *y* before adding *er* or *est*.

dirty—dirtier—dirtiest

- Drop a final *e* before adding *er* or *est*.

nice—nicer—nicest

Adverbs That Compare

er, est
- Add *er* and *est* to one-syllable adverbs and some two-syllable adverbs to form comparative and superlative adverbs.

fast—faster—fastest

- Drop a final *e* before adding *er* or *est*.

late—later—latest

WRITER'S HANDBOOK • Spelling

Sentence Diagramming

- A **sentence diagram** shows how the parts of a sentence work together.

sentence diagram

- The **simple subject** is the main or key word in the complete subject. The **simple predicate** is the verb in the complete predicate.

simple subject and simple predicate

subject	verb

Birds sang.

Birds	sang

- A sentence is in **inverted word order** when the verb comes before the subject. When you diagram a sentence with inverted word order, place the subject before the verb and capitalize any words that are capitalized in the sentence.

inverted word order

subject	verb

Were birds singing?

birds	Were singing

- These diagrams show the simple subject and simple predicate of each kind of sentence.

four kinds of sentences

Declarative: Susie plays chess.

Susie	plays

Interrogative: Does José play chess?

José	Does play

Imperative: Play with José next.

you (understood)	Play

Exclamatory: She plays a wonderful game!

She	plays

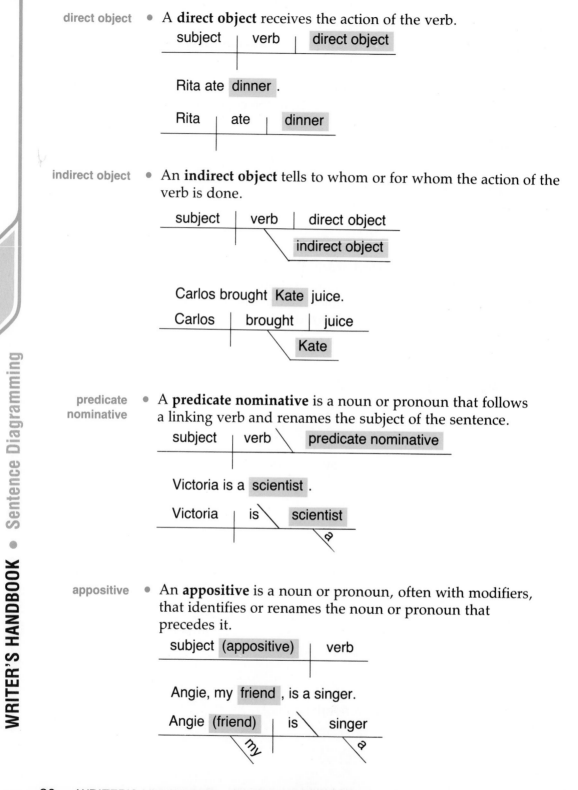

direct object • A **direct object** receives the action of the verb.

subject | verb | direct object

Rita ate dinner .

Rita | ate | dinner

indirect object • An **indirect object** tells to whom or for whom the action of the verb is done.

subject | verb | direct object
indirect object

Carlos brought Kate juice.

Carlos | brought | juice
Kate

predicate nominative • A **predicate nominative** is a noun or pronoun that follows a linking verb and renames the subject of the sentence.

subject | verb \ predicate nominative

Victoria is a scientist .

Victoria | is \ scientist
a

appositive • An **appositive** is a noun or pronoun, often with modifiers, that identifies or renames the noun or pronoun that precedes it.

subject (appositive) | verb

Angie, my friend , is a singer.

Angie (friend) | is \ singer
my | | a

- An **adjective** modifies a noun or a pronoun.

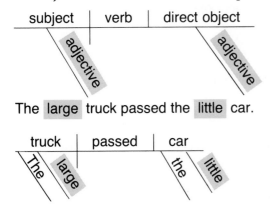

The large truck passed the little car.

- **Possessive nouns** and **possessive pronouns** precede nouns to show ownership or possession. The **articles** *a, an,* and *the* always signal that a noun will follow.

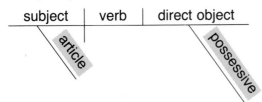

The runner won her race.

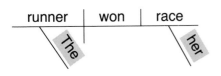

- A **predicate adjective** follows a linking verb and describes the subject of the sentence.

```
subject  |  verb  \  predicate adjective
```

The doctor was grateful .

```
doctor  |  was  \  grateful
    \ The
```

● A **participle** is a verbal used as an adjective.

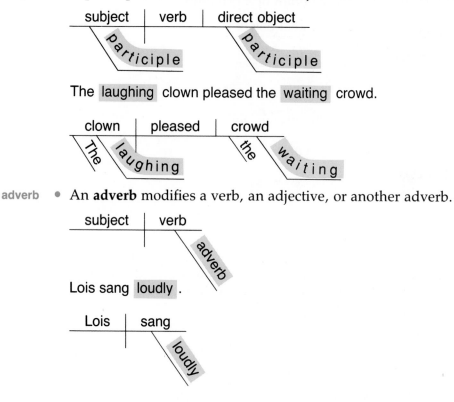

The laughing clown pleased the waiting crowd.

● An **adverb** modifies a verb, an adjective, or another adverb.

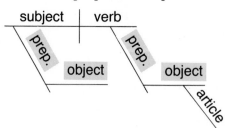

Lois sang loudly .

● A **prepositional phrase** is made up of a preposition (prep.), the object of the preposition, and all the words in between. The object of the preposition is the noun or pronoun at the end of the prepositional phrase.

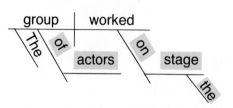

The group of actors worked on the stage .

- An **infinitive** is a verbal consisting of the present-tense form of a verb preceded by *to*. An infinitive can be used as a noun, an adjective, or an adverb.

Infinitive used as a noun:

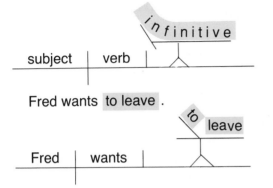

Fred wants to leave .

Infinitive used as an adjective:

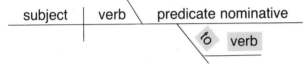

That is the bus to take .

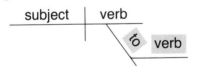

Infinitive used as an adverb:

We read to learn .

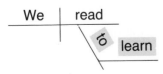

gerund
- A **gerund** is a verbal used as a noun.

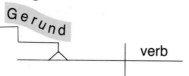

	verb

Swimming is good exercise.

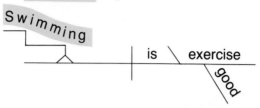

conjunction and an adjective series
- An **adjective series** consists of three or more adjectives that modify one noun or one pronoun. Notice how a conjunction (conj.) is diagrammed in the following example.

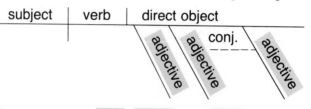

The team wears red , white , and blue uniforms.

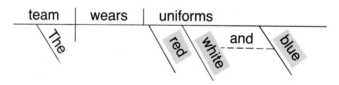

conjunction and a compound subject
- A **compound subject** is made up of two or more subjects that have the same verb. The subjects are joined by a conjunction.

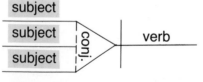

Sue , Ed , and Ellen visited Washington.

- A **compound verb** is made up of two or more verbs that have the same subject. The verbs are joined by a conjunction.

conjunction and a compound verb

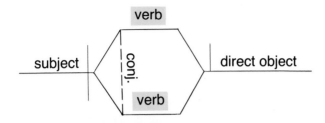

Hilda chased and caught the ball.

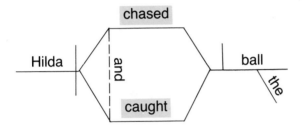

- A **compound sentence** contains two or more related simple sentences joined by a comma and a conjunction or by a semicolon.

conjunction and a compound sentence

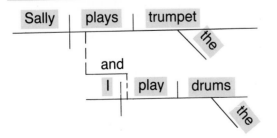

Sally plays the trumpet , and I play the drums .

complex sentence with an adjective clause

- A **complex sentence** consists of an independent clause and at least one subordinate clause. If the subordinate clause functions as an adjective, diagram the sentence in this way.

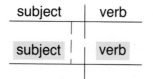

The teacher who leads the band is Mr. Gomez.

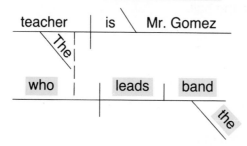

complex sentence with an adverb clause

- If the subordinate clause in a complex sentence functions as an adverb, diagram the sentence in this way.

Ruth helps us when she can.

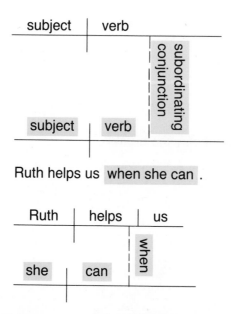

GLOSSARY

Contents

Composition Terms

AUDIENCE *the reader or readers for whom a composition is written* The students and faculty of Hamilton School are the audience for this article in the school newspaper.

> **Cartoonist to Speak at Hamilton School**
> Adam Lee, the famous cartoonist, will be the special guest of our school at next month's assembly.

CLARITY *the preciseness with which information, ideas, and intent are expressed in a composition* Notice the precise words used in this example.

> The two gigantic male elk, their antlers locked in combat, crashed down the muddy riverbank.

COHERENCE *the orderly arrangement of information and ideas in a composition* The sentences in this passage have been rearranged to make their sequence more logical and thus improve coherence.

> The right kinds of sunglasses can help protect your eyes from ultraviolet rays. Sunglasses should be more than fashionable accessories. Make sure the pair you buy screens out these harmful rays.

DRAFTING *the actual writing of a composition, beginning with a first copy* This boy is using his prewriting outline to compose his first draft.

EDITOR'S MARKS *standard symbols used to indicate revising or proofreading changes* Notice that each of these example symbols is used to mark a specific type of change.

Use these marks when you revise.

∧ Add something.	↻ Move something.
✗ Cut something.	⌃ Replace something.

Use these marks when you proofread.

≡ Capitalize.	ⱽⱽ Add quotation marks.	◯ Spell correctly.
⊙ Add a period.		⊓ Indent paragraph.
∧ Add something.	✗ Cut something.	/ Make a lowercase letter.
⋏ Add a comma.	⌃ Replace something.	
	～ Transpose.	

FINAL DRAFT *the finished version of a composition, ready for publication* This is part of a final draft.

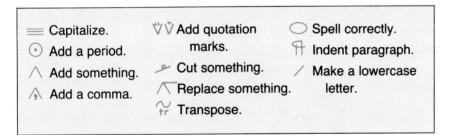

The library was built in 1915 of limestone and marble. It is three stories tall and sits in a rose garden.

FIRST DRAFT   *the rough version of a composition, in which a writer's ideas are first written in paragraph form*   Notice the unfinished quality of the writing in this example.

> In 1066 William the conquorer a norman invade England with his troops across the english chanel.

PREWRITING   *the first stage of the writing process, in which the writer gathers ideas and information and begins to organize them*   This girl is researching a composition topic in the library.

PREWRITING STRATEGIES   *the activities that a writer uses to choose and organize ideas or information*   The following are examples of prewriting strategies.

- **brainstorming**   *any activity that encourages the contribution of ideas from an individual or a group*

- **charting**   *a visual process that helps an individual or a group to classify and organize ideas and information*

Major Rivers of the World		
Asia	**Africa**	**North America**
Chang Jiang Huang He	Nile Congo	Mississippi Missouri

- **clustering**   *a visual technique that helps a group or an individual to brainstorm*

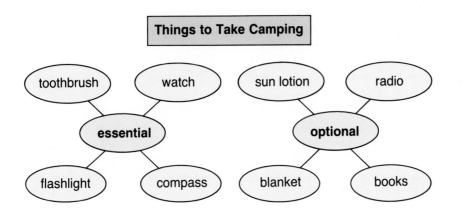

- **diagramming**   *a visual technique for putting information in space order or time order*

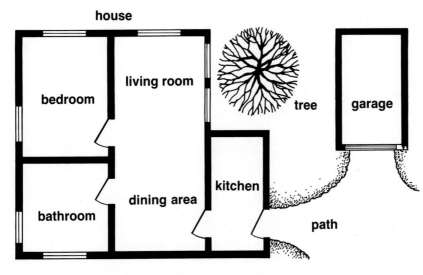

- **using an inverted triangle** *a technique used for narrowing a topic or organizing ideas*

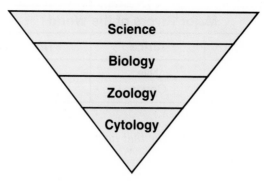

- **list making** *writing, on paper or on the chalkboard, ideas brainstormed by a group or an individual*

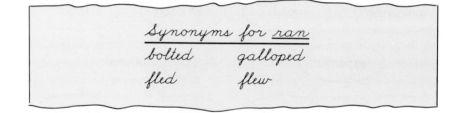

- **mapping** *a visual technique for recording or organizing information*

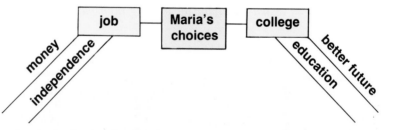

- **slotting** *brainstorming by an individual or a group to find words or word groups to complete a sentence*

The forest was a _____.

pattern of light and shade
cool refuge from the sun
hidden world of surprises

PROOFREADING *reviewing a composition to correct errors in capitalization, punctuation, usage, grammar, and spelling* Corrections in this example are indicated with Editor's Marks.

before you all leave call gregs' Mother

PUBLISHING *making public a final draft of a composition by reading it aloud, submitting it to a school newspaper or literary journal, displaying it on a bulletin board, and so on* This student is giving a speech at a school assembly.

PURPOSE *the reason a composition is written—for example, to inform, narrate, describe, or persuade* This passage was written to describe.

The jagged branches of the ancient tree were silhouetted eerily against the purple sky.

RESPONDING *a revising activity in which the writer and a partner or a small group ask and answer questions about a composition* Here, a writer questions her partner about her composition.

Have I made my point clearly? *You might add one more example.*

RESPONSE GROUP *a group of students who help revise each other's work by asking and answering questions about it* This group member is responding to a question about style.

I think your language could be more vivid.

REVISING *the process of rethinking ideas, looking for errors in organization and language* Reading written work aloud, as this boy is doing, is a useful revising technique.

—no, that's not correct.

"and everyone took their turn..."

STYLE *the use of interesting language and sentence structure to create a particular tone* Compare the style in these two letters.

> Dear Dr. Valdez,
>   Our class congratulates you on your new discovery.

> Dear Dr. Valdez,
>   Our class offers you its heartiest congratulations on your remarkable discovery.

TASK *the assignment or the undertaking of a particular type of composition* A class was given the task of writing a speech to introduce the new principal.

>   Faculty and fellow students, we have been awaiting this moment with great curiosity.

TONE *the language and sentence structure a writer uses to express an attitude toward the subject or audience—for example, formal, informal, humorous, angry, enthusiastic, or critical* In this passage from a book review, the tone is approving.

> Not only did the author develop the characters into real human beings, but he also created a plot that was thrilling and fantastic!

TOPIC *the subject of a composition* The subject of this passage is stated in the first sentence.

> My brother hates camping. He is used to two showers a day and easy access to a refrigerator. Bugs drive him nuts, and he's scared of the dark.

UNITY *the presentation of details that support the main idea of a composition, producing an effect of completeness* Part of this passage was cut to strengthen its unity.

> Being a guidance counselor is a rewarding career. Guidance counselors help solve problems for students and intervene in disputes. ~~Some counselors have problems of their own.~~ It must feel good to help others make wise decisions.

WRITING PROCESS *the ongoing process of prewriting, drafting, responding and revising, proofreading, and publishing a composition* A writer can go back and forth among these stages until the final draft is completed.

GLOSSARY

Literary Terms

ALLITERATION *the repetition of an initial sound, usually a consonant, in two or more nearby words* Notice the alliteration in this description.

> **The vessel sailed across the satiny sea.**

ASSONANCE *a near rhyme between words with similar vowel sounds but different consonants* Notice how *father* and *ladder* are used in these lines from the poem "The Rescue."

> **Up on a big branch stood**
> **his father,**
> **His mother came to the**
> **top of the ladder, . . .**

CHARACTERIZATION *a writer's creation and development of believable characters by describing them physically, recording their actions or speech, revealing their thoughts, or commenting on them directly or through other characters* In this example, Ray Bradbury brings a character to life by telling what she did.

> **She had laid linoleum, repaired bicycles, wound clocks, stoked furnaces, swabbed iodine on ten thousand grievous wounds.**

CHARACTERS *the people (or animals) in a story, a novel, a play, or a poem* The most important are the **protagonist** (the main character) and the **antagonist** (the protagonist's opponent). The protagonist is sometimes called the *hero* or *heroine.*

FICTION *a story invented by a writer* Works of fiction range in length from one-page fables, tales, and short stories to long novels with complicated plots, well-developed characters, and complex themes. **Historical fiction,** although based on true events, includes invented characters and incidents. **Fantasy** may be set in a real or a made-up world, but its characters do impossible things and the plots are highly imaginative. In **science fiction** the action is usually set in a future world, which may be reached by time or space travel.

FIGURATIVE LANGUAGE *words used in unusual, rather than in literal or expected, ways* Similes, metaphors, and personification are three common types of figurative language. In a **simile,** the word *like* or *as* is used to compare two very different things, as in this example: *She slept . . . as relaxed as a white glove to which, at dawn, a brisk hand will return.* A **metaphor** implies a comparison by saying that one thing *is* another, as in this example: *Laing seemed to wear the sea. It was a comfortable coat never discarded.* In **personification,** an object, animal, or idea is given human qualities or abilities, as in this example: *Even his spectacles reached out to welcome the friend.*

FLASHBACK *the introduction of a scene or incident that occurred before the beginning of a story* A writer often uses a flashback to give background information, as in this character sketch.

GLOSSARY

Would she be as I remembered her? The picture that filled my mind made me smile.

I saw a short, thin girl with green-gray eyes, a color that reminded me of the ocean on a stormy night.

FORESHADOWING *a technique used by an author to offer hints about future developments in a story* In this dialogue from a play, we hear a clue about the true identity of Arthur.

SIR ECTOR: Son, you say you withdrew this sword from the anvil? In that case you are the true king of England and should have no trouble placing it back in the anvil again.

IMAGERY *the use of images, or word pictures, in writing* Authors often use descriptive language to make experiences of the senses or emotions more vivid for the reader. In these lines, Ray Bradbury uses imagery to describe an elderly woman facing death.

Looking back on thirty billions of things started, carried, finished and done, it all summed up, totaled out; the last decimal was placed, the final zero swung slowly into line. Now, chalk in hand, she stood back from life a silent hour before reaching for the eraser.

NONFICTION *any writing that accurately describes something that actually happened or that presents information or gives an opinion* Among the forms of nonfiction are **biography,** (the story of a person's life) and **autobiography** (the story of the author's own life). **Exposition** is nonfiction writing that presents or explains information.

ONOMATOPOEIA *the use of words that imitate actual sounds or suggest by their sound what the word means* Notice how in "African Dance" Langston Hughes has used the onomatopoetic word *tom-toms* in these lines.

And the tom-toms beat.
And the tom-toms beat.

PLOT *the action in a story* The most important element in a plot is **conflict,** or the protagonist's struggle against opposing forces. A writer plans a sequence of events around the conflict to hold the reader's attention. In the **introduction,** the setting, characters, and conflict are presented. The problem becomes more apparent in the **complication,** leading the plot to its **climax.** Here the conflict must be faced and worked out. How this is done is told in the **resolution,** or ending, of the story.

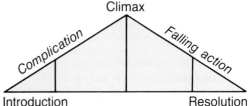

GLOSSARY

POINT OF VIEW   *the perspective from which a story is told, depending upon the author's choice of a narrator*   If an author uses the **first-person** point of view, the narrator is a character in the story. This character sees events only from his or her perspective. To indicate this, the character regularly uses the word *I*. In the **third-person objective** point of view, the narrator is not part of the story, and all characters are referred to as *he, she, it,* or *they*. This narrator only records events and does not offer opinions or reveal the thoughts of characters. When the narrator is an outsider but is able to tell the reader what the characters are thinking or feeling, the **third-person omniscient** point of view is being used.

RHYME   *the repetition of syllable sounds, especially at the ends of lines of poetry*   Below, the rhyming sounds at the ends of the lines are labeled with letters to describe the poem's rhyme scheme. This passage from a Lewis Carroll nonsense poem has an *ABAB* rhyme scheme.

'Twas brillig, and the slithy toves	*A*
Did gyre and gimble in the wabe;	*B*
All mimsy were the borogoves,	*A*
And the mome raths outgrabe.	*B*

RHYTHM   *the pattern of stressed and unstressed syllables, especially in poetry*   A poem may have a regular rhythm, or meter, or the rhythm may change within the poem. Compare the regular rhythm of the first example below with the irregular meter of the second.

A farmer boy,
  His hoe in hand,
Went out to hoe
  His Maryland.
   *   *   *   *

A Beetle, a Bat, and a Bee
Were wrecked on the Isle
  of Boree,
   With a barrel of gum
   And a tom-tom drum
And a hammock for each of
  the three.

SETTING   *when and where a story takes place*   In most longer works of fiction, the action is divided into distinct segments, or **scenes**—for example, an encounter between characters, a conversation, or a fight. The setting often changes with each new scene.

STAGE DIRECTIONS   *instructions given by the author of a play to direct the movements and attitudes of the performers*   At the beginning of these lines of dialogue, the playwright indicates how the lines should be spoken.

SIR ECTOR (*Sternly yet tenderly*): You? Why, Son, you are not yet even a knight!

STANZA   *a group of lines in a poem that are read as a unit and are similar to a paragraph in a work of prose; a verse*   A poem's rhyme scheme and meter usually, but not always, remain the same in each stanza. One common form of verse is the **couplet,** with two lines in each stanza.

> **Abou Ben Adhem (may his**
> ** tribe increase!)**
> **Awoke one night from a**
> ** deep dream of peace.**

Another common stanza form is the **quatrain,** with four lines.

> **Whose woods these are**
> ** I think I know.**
> **His house is in the village**
> ** though;**
> **He will not see me stopping**
> ** here**
> **To watch his woods fill up**
> ** with snow.**

Finally, there is the **cinquain,** with five lines.

> **Listen, my children, and**
> ** you shall hear**
> **Of the midnight ride of**
> ** Paul Revere,**
> **On the eighteenth of**
> ** April, in Seventy-five;**
> **Hardly a man is now alive**
> **Who remembers that famous**
> ** day and year.**

TONE   *an attitude toward a subject, or a particular mood conveyed by a writer through language and sentence structure* The tone of a story, play, or poem may be formal or informal, solemn or humorous, sentimental or critical. In these lines of poetry, Lewis Carroll's tone is comic.

> **"You are old, Father**
> ** William," the young man**
> ** said,**
> **"And your hair has become**
> ** very white;**
> **And yet you incessantly**
> ** stand on your head—**
> **Do you think, at your age,**
> ** it is right?"**

WRITER'S THESAURUS

Contents

What Is a Thesaurus?

A **thesaurus** lists words and their synonyms. Like a dictionary, a thesaurus lists words in alphabetical order. Each of these words is called an **entry word.** A list of synonyms follows the entry word. Sometimes a thesaurus lists antonyms.

Look at the parts of this thesaurus entry for the word *funny.*

The **entry word** is in color. It is followed by the part of speech and a definition. An example sentence shows how the word can be used. ▶

> **funny** *adj.* Amusing; comical. That comedian is so **funny** that I laugh even before he says a word.

Synonyms for the entry word are in italics. Each synonym is followed by a definition and an example sentence. ▶

> *amusing* Causing amusement or fun; laughable. He chuckled at some of the speaker's *amusing* remarks.
> *comical* Causing laughter; funny. Some clowns are *comical* all the time.

If an **antonym** is given, it is printed in dark letters. ▶

> **ANTONYMS:** heartbreaking, mournful, serious, sober, tragic

How to Use Your Writer's Thesaurus

Suppose you are writing a report about the clowns you saw on a recent trip to the circus. When you read your first draft, you realize that you have overused the word *funny*. You open your **Writer's Thesaurus** to find some synonyms. Here are the steps you should follow.

1. Look for the word in the Index to Thesaurus. The Index lists every word in the **Writer's Thesaurus.**
2. Find the word in the Index.

funny *adj.*

You know that *funny* is an entry word because it is printed in color.

3. Turn to the page in your **Writer's Thesaurus** on which *funny* is printed in color. Read the entry carefully. Not every synonym may express exactly what you want to say. Choose the synonym that makes the most sense in your report.

Remember: Not every synonym will have exactly the meaning you want. Look at the entry for *funny* on page 14. Which synonym fits your work best?

◆ Sometimes a word is listed in the Index like this:

amusing **funny** *adj.*

This means that you will find *amusing* listed as a synonym under the entry word *funny*. Since *amusing* is not printed in color, you know that it is not an entry word.

◆ You will also see some lines in the Index that look like this:

tragic **funny** *adj.*

This means that *tragic* is listed as an antonym under the entry word *funny*.

Index to Thesaurus

depressed happy *adj.*

descend fall *v.*

detach join *v.*

detect find *v.*

dialogue conversation *n.*

dilapidated old *adj.*

direct lead *v.*

directions instructions *n.*

disappointing enjoyable *adj.*

disconnect join *v.*

discussion conversation *n.*

disgusting enjoyable *adj.*

disinfect clean *v.*

disprove prove *v.*

division group *n.*

drop catch *v.*

dull bright *adj.*

E

earlier later *adv.*

ecstatic happy *adj.*

effect cause *n.*

elated happy *adj.*

enemy friend *n.*

enjoyable adj.

episode event *n.*

establish prove *v.*

even rough *adj.*

event n.

eventually later *adv.*

evil bad *adj.*

exaggerate v.

exceptionally very *adv.*

exhausted tired *adj.*

expected sudden *adj.*

expensive adj.

explain v.

express say *v.*

extraordinary unusual *adj.*

extremely very *adv.*

F

factor cause *n.*

fall v.

fatigued tired *adj.*

fearful courageous *adj.*

fearsome scary *adj.*

feeling opinion *n.*

fierce scary *adj.*

final first *adj.*

find v.

find out learn *v.*

finer better *adj.*

finery clothes *n.*

finish begin *v.*

first adj.

fly v.

foe friend *n.*

follow lead *v.*

footwear shoe *n.*

fracture break *v.*

free hold *v.*

friend n.

frolic play *v.*

funny adj.

G

gallant courageous *adj.*

gallop run *v.*

gape look *v.*

garb clothes *n.*

gentle scary *adj.*

gigantic big *adj.*

glance look *v.*

gleaming bright *adj.*

glide fly *v.*

go v.

good bad *adj.*

gorgeous beautiful *adj.*

grace beauty *n.*

gracelessness beauty *n.*

gradual sudden *adj.*

gray bright *adj.*

group n.

guide lead *v.*

H

handsome beautiful *adj.*

happy adj.

harm v.

harmful bad *adj.*

hat n.

have hold *v.*

hazy bright *adj.*

headdress hat *n.*

heartbreaking funny *adj.*

heartbroken happy *adj.*

helmet hat *n.*

help harm *v.*

hence then *adv.*

heroic courageous *adj.*

hide find *v.*

hideous beautiful *adj.*

high tall *adj.*

hold v.

homeliness beauty *n.*

hook catch *v.*

house n.

hurdle jump *v.*

I

important big *adj.*

improved better *adj.*

impulsive sudden *adj.*

incident event *n.*

independently alone *adv.*

individuals people *n.*

inexpensive expensive *adj.*

infant child *n.*

initiate begin *v.*

injure harm *v.*

insignificant big *adj.*

instructions n.

J

jagged **rough** *adj.*
jalopy **car** *n.*
join *v.*
jump *v.*
juvenile **child** *n.*

K

keep change *v.*
know learn *v.*

L

large **big** *adj.*
last first *adj.*
later *adv.*
laugh cry *v.*
launch **begin** *v.*
lead *v.*
leading **first** *adj.*
learn *v.*
leave **go** *v.*
link **join** *v.*
litter clean *v.*
little big *adj.*
loafer **shoe** *n.*
look *v.*
loose tight *adj.*
lose find *v.*
loud *adj.*
luminous **bright** *adj.*

M

magnify **exaggerate** *v.*
main **first** *adj.*
maintain change *v.*
mansion **house** *n.*
many *adj.*
mar **harm** *v.*
massive **big** *adj.*

master **learn** *v.*
mature **old** *adj.*
mess clean *v.*
mild bad *adj.*
milestone **event** *n.*
minimize exaggerate *v.*
miserable happy *adj.*
miss catch *v.*
monstrous beautiful *adj.*
motive **cause** *n.*
mournful funny *adj.*
move *v.*
murmur cry *v.*
mystify explain *v.*

N

next to **beside** *prep.*
nice bad *adj.*
noisy **loud** *adj.*
nominate **choose** *v.*
normal unusual *adj.*
notion **opinion** *n.*
now later *adv.*

O

obey lead *v.*
obscure explain *v.*
occasion **event** *n.*
old *adj.*
opinion *n.*
orders **instructions** *n.*
origin **cause** *n.*
originate **begin** *v.*
outcome cause *n.*
outfit **clothes** *n.*
overstate **exaggerate** *v.*

P

pal **friend** *n.*

particularly **very** *adv.*
peer **look** *v.*
people *n.*
perplex explain *v.*
pick **choose** *v.*
planned sudden *adj.*
play *v.*
pleasurable **enjoyable** *adj.*
plummet **fall** *v.*
pollute clean *v.*
population **people** *n.*
possess **hold** *v.*
practically **almost** *adv.*
preserve change *v.*
pretty **beautiful** *adj.*
primary **first** *adj.*
proceed **move** *v.*
prove *v.*
public **people** *n.*
purge **clean** *v.*

Q

quite **very** *adv.*

R

raucous **loud** *adj.*
reassuring scary *adj.*
refute prove *v.*
relaxed tight *adj.*
release catch *v.*
release hold *v.*
remain move *v.*
remark **say** *v.*
remarkable **unusual** *adj.*
remove bring *v.*
renewed tired *adj.*
repair harm *v.*
repulsive beautiful *adj.*
residence **house** *n.*
resounding **loud** *adj.*

rest move *v.*
rested tired *adj.*
result cause *n.*
retreat go *v.*
return go *v.*
revived tired *adj.*
rise fall *v.*
romp play *v.*
rough adj.
run v.

S

sad happy *adj.*
sail fly *v.*
sandal shoe *n.*
saunter walk *v.*
savage scary *adj.*
save harm *v.*
say v.
scary adj.
scour clean *v.*
scream cry *v.*
screech cry *v.*
seamless rough *adj.*
seize catch *v.*
select choose *v.*
serious funny *adj.*
several many *adj.*
severe bad *adj.*
shack house *n.*
shatter break *v.*
shelter house *n.*
shiny bright *adj.*
shoe n.
short tall *adj.*
silky rough *adj.*
single-handedly alone *adv.*
singular unusual *adj.*
slack tight *adj.*
small big *adj.*
small tall *adj.*
smooth rough *adj.*
snare catch *v.*
sneaker shoe *n.*
snug tight *adj.*

soar fly *v.*
sober funny *adj.*
solo alone *adv.*
soothing scary *adj.*
source cause *n.*
spoiled bad *adj.*
spring jump *v.*
sprint run *v.*
stampede run *v.*
startle surprise *v.*
sterilize clean *v.*
stop move *v.*
stretch exaggerate *v.*
stride walk *v.*
strut walk *v.*
stun surprise *v.*
substantiate prove *v.*
sudden adj.
superior better *adj.*
supply bring *v.*
surprise v.

T

take away bring *v.*
talk conversation *n.*
tall adj.
taut tight *adj.*
teach explain *v.*
teenager child *n.*
tell explain *v.*
terminate begin *v.*
then adv.
therefore then *adv.*
thrilled happy *adj.*
throw catch *v.*
thunderous loud *adj.*
tight adj.
timid courageous *adj.*
tiny big *adj.*
tired adj.
together alone *adv.*
topple fall *v.*
tot child *n.*

tote bring *v.*
towering tall *adj.*
toy play *v.*
tragic funny *adj.*
transportation n.
trudge walk *v.*

U

ugliness beauty *n.*
ugly beautiful *adj.*
ultimate first *adj.*
underplay exaggerate *v.*
understate exaggerate *v.*
unexpected sudden *adj.*
unhappy happy *adj.*
unimportant big *adj.*
unique unusual *adj.*
unpleasant enjoyable *adj.*
unremarkable unusual *adj.*
unusual adj.

V

various many *adj.*
vary change *v.*
vault jump *v.*
vehicle car *n.*
vehicle transportation *n.*
verify prove *v.*
very adv.

W

wail cry *v.*
walk v.
weary tired *adj.*
whisper cry *v.*
wound harm *v.*

Y

yell cry *v.*

WRITER'S THESAURUS

A

again *adv.* One more time. Rewind the music box and play the song **again**.

afresh Again; in a fresh or new way. The problem may seem simple if we tackle it *afresh* tomorrow.

anew Once more; in another way. Let's forget the past and become friends *anew*.

almost *adv.* Just about. We are **almost** ready to land, so fasten your seat belt.

approximately Close to; nearly. Mars is expected to become visible at *approximately* 8 P.M.

practically Almost, but not exactly. My cat is *practically* human.

alone *adv.* By oneself or itself; without help. A hermit lives **alone**.

independently Without support; on one's own. That library is private and operates *independently*.

single-handedly Without aid; through one's own efforts. She *single-handedly* saved the company from bankruptcy.

solo Alone. Not every pilot would be willing to fly *solo* to France.

ANTONYMS: accompanied, cooperatively, together

B

bad *adj.* Not good; wrong. That idea is **bad** because someone might get hurt.

evil Purposely bad; very bad or immoral. In some fiction, one character is an *evil* villain.

harmful Damaging. Pesticides are sometimes *harmful* to crops as well as to insects.

severe Harsh. Treat a *severe* cold with bed rest and plenty of fluids.

spoiled Ruined; damaged; rotten. If that chicken salad has been in the sun for hours, it must be *spoiled*.

ANTONYMS: benevolent, good, mild, nice

beautiful *adj.* Extremely lovely; delighting the senses or the mind. That colorful rainbow is one of the most **beautiful** I have seen.

comely Pleasing to look at. You look quite *comely* in your new dress.

gorgeous Magnificent; very beautiful. Your jeweled cape is *gorgeous*.

handsome Good-looking. You don't have to be *handsome* to be an actor.

pretty Pleasant to look at, in a delicate way. Nedra has a collection of very *pretty* seashells.

ANTONYMS: hideous, monstrous, repulsive, ugly

beauty *n.* A quality that is pleasing to see or hear; someone or something beautiful. The painting called the Mona Lisa has a haunting **beauty**.

charm A pleasing, attractive quality. Everyone was enchanted by the hostess's great *charm*.

comeliness Pleasing appearance. She was very taken with the young man's *comeliness* and his manners.

grace Delicacy of body, spirit, motion, or gesture. He moved with exquisite *grace* on the dance floor.

ANTONYMS: gracelessness, homeliness, ugliness

begin *v.* To start. Many tasks that look difficult become easy if you **begin** slowly and take things one step at a time.

initiate To give the first experience of. We will *initiate* two new members into our club.

launch To get something underway. My teacher is scheduling a field trip to *launch* our new science unit.

originate To bring about or come into being. A successful invention may *originate* with a crazy idea.

ANTONYMS: conclude, finish, terminate

beside *prep.* Next to; to one side of. The small painting looks tiny **beside** that huge one.

alongside Side by side with. I walked *alongside* my friend on the busy street.

by Next to; near. There is a nice park *by* our apartment complex.

next to Beside; at the side of. Park your bike *next to* mine.

better *adj.* Having more good qualities; higher; more useful. You will be a **better** pianist than I because you practice more.

finer More exquisite or elegant; of better quality. I'll take the *finer* copy with the leather cover.

improved Made better. Your *improved* story is much more exciting than your original.

superior Higher; much better than average. Chefs insist that fresh spices are *superior* to dried ones.

big *adj.* Large; sizable. We soon learned what caused the **big** commotion.

considerable Of a large or significant size or amount. The man gave a *considerable* sum of money to the animal shelter.

gigantic Enormous; giant. California redwoods are *gigantic* trees.

important Very significant; having a great deal of influence. Jim is an *important* man in local government.

large Big in size or amount. A *large* part of Australia is thinly populated.

massive Tremendous; broad; weighty. Allosaurus was a *massive* dinosaur.

ANTONYMS: insignificant, little, small, tiny, unimportant

break *v.* To make unusable by damaging. If you drop that cup, it will **break**.

crack To damage in such a way that a narrow line or opening appears. I hope I didn't *crack* that mirror when I hit it with my umbrella.

fracture To break, especially a hard surface such as a bone. The quarterback may *fracture* a leg on that play.

shatter To break into many pieces. This windshield cannot *shatter*, because it is made of special glass.

WRITER'S THESAURUS

bright *adj.* Gleaming; shining. The moon is **bright** because of the sun's reflected light.

brilliant Shining brightly; glowing; sparkling. A diamond becomes more *brilliant* after it has been polished.

gleaming Shining, as light reflected on a surface. The ocean is *gleaming* because the noonday sun is strong overhead.

luminous Full of light; glowing. You will see that my watch is *luminous* if you take it into the dark closet.

shiny Bright; gleaming. I'd like to keep my shoes as *shiny* as they are now.

ANTONYMS: dull, gray, hazy

bring *v.* To carry to a place. Ask Tom to **bring** his camera to the zoo.

deliver To carry and hand over. If you will *deliver* my groceries, I will give you a nice tip.

supply To provide what is asked for or needed. Every guest will *supply* one dish for the party.

tote To carry or haul, especially in one's arms or on one's back. In films, the cowboy hero would always *tote* a gun.

ANTONYMS: remove, take away

C

car *n.* Any vehicle used to transport people or things, especially an automobile. The **car** moved slowly up the mountain road.

automobile A small vehicle with four wheels and an internal engine. A seat belt may save you from harm if the *automobile* stops suddenly.

jalopy An old, beat-up automobile; a clunker. You can hear that old *jalopy* from a block away.

vehicle A means of taking people or things from place to place. Do you need a special license to drive a *vehicle* of that size?

catch *v.* To stop and take hold of someone or something. **Catch** the egg before it hits the floor.

capture To catch and keep by force. The police are offering a reward for information to help them *capture* the criminal.

hook To catch, as a fish in the water. You can't *hook* a fish without bait.

seize To grab. Water-skiers must *seize* the towrope firmly.

snare To trap or trick. The salesperson used charm to *snare* buyers.

ANTONYMS: drop, miss, release, throw

cause *n.* The reason that something happens. No one knows the exact **cause** of the explosion.

factor One of the things that contributes to an outcome; one part of a cause. Exercise is one *factor* that leads to good health.

motive The reason for someone's behavior. His *motive* for dieting is to fit into his new outfit.

origin The start, or first cause, of something. Scientists have different theories about the *origin* of the universe.

source Someone or something from which something else begins. The *source* of the fire may have been a faulty wire.

ANTONYMS: effect, outcome, result

change *v.* To make or become different. People have tried unsuccessfully to **change** other metals into gold.

adjust To rearrange to make fit. Please *adjust* your schedule so you can come earlier.

alter To make different. The tailor can *alter* the garment to make it fit better.

convert To change from one shape or function to a different one. Many people want to *convert* their gas heating to a solar heating system.

vary To become or make somewhat different. My cooking was predictable, so I decided to *vary* the menu.

ANTONYMS: keep, maintain, preserve

child *n.* A person from birth to physical maturity. That **child** looks about seven years old.

infant A baby. An *infant* learns new things every day.

juvenile A young person. If you are a *juvenile*, you can't see this movie without an adult.

teenager A person between thirteen and nineteen. A *teenager* is neither a child nor an adult.

tot A small child. This game is good for a *tot* but too easy for an older child.

choose *v.* To pick from more than one. In a fine restaurant, it can be hard to **choose** from among the items on the menu.

decide To weigh the possibilities and arrive at a conclusion. A good driver must be able to quickly *decide* how to act in an emergency.

nominate To name someone as a candidate. *Nominate* Terry for class president.

pick To choose; to select. *Pick* the dog you want to adopt.

select To single out from among more than one. It's hard to *select* someone to hire when everyone seems equally qualified.

clean *v.* To remove dirt and stains. **Clean** the room before you go out.

disinfect To destroy germs that cause disease. The nurse used hydrogen peroxide to *disinfect* the wound.

purge To eliminate impurities. *Purge* your mind of any thoughts of breaking your diet.

scour To clean by rubbing hard with something rough. You can use steel wool to *scour* that dirty pot.

sterilize To destroy germs or bacteria. Before the invention of disposable syringes, doctors had to *sterilize* needles.

ANTONYMS: litter, mess, pollute

clothes *n.* Articles of dress worn by people; clothing. Because styles change, some **clothes** soon become outdated.

attire Clothing, especially of good quality. Judging by his *attire*, he is a rich person.

finery Elegant or showy clothing. People wore their *finery* to the gala event.

garb Style of dress. He wore professional *garb* to the interview.

outfit Clothing of two or more matched pieces. Amy's black skirt and white blouse made a nice *outfit*.

conversation *n.* an informal exchange of information and ideas. The old friends sat down and enjoyed a long **conversation**.

chat A casual conversation. We had a nice little *chat* about our families.

dialogue A conversation between at least two speakers; a talking together to understand each other's point of view. The angry partners sat down and attempted a *dialogue* to try to settle things.

discussion An exchange of ideas and opinions. After the lively *discussion*, the club members went out for a snack.

talk An informal speech. Eric's mother came to school with his raincoat and wound up giving a *talk* on microbiology.

courageous *adj.* Willing to face danger. The **courageous** firefighters made sure that no one remained in the burning building.

audacious Very bold. To save the people, the hero made an *audacious* move.

brave Acting in the face of possible danger. The *brave* pioneers faced adversity with great spirit.

gallant Brave and courteous. I read a story about a *gallant* knight who rescued a princess.

heroic Acting with great courage. *Heroic* men and women are inspiring.

ANTONYMS: cowardly, fearful, timid

cry *v.* To make loud sounds, often expressing grief or fear. The trapped kittens **cry** for help.

scream To let out a loud, piercing cry, as in fear or pain. During a horror film, the audience may *scream* in terror.

screech To give a harsh shriek. The owls *screech* in the evening.

wail To make a long, sad cry. They could hear the wind *wail* through the trees outside.

yell To make a loud scream; to shout. If you lose your way, just *yell*.

ANTONYMS: laugh, murmur, whisper

E

enjoyable *adj.* Pleasant; satisfying. The day at the park was extremely **enjoyable**.

delectable Delightful; delicious. I'd like a second helping of that *delectable* dessert.

delightful Very pleasing. On such a hot day, a cool swim would be *delightful*.

pleasurable Pleasant. Rocking must be *pleasurable* for a baby.

ANTONYMS: annoying, disappointing, disgusting, unpleasant

event *n.* Something that takes place; a special happening. That meteor shower was an exciting **event**.

episode A single event that is part of a larger story or experience. I hate to miss a single *episode* of that show.

incident A minor event. The witness said she had no memory of that *incident*.

milestone A major event, either in a person's life or for society. The day Judy graduated from law school was a *milestone* in her career.

occasion One particular time; a special event. Scott wore a tuxedo for the *occasion*.

exaggerate *v.* To say something is greater than it really is. You **exaggerate** when you claim to be the fastest runner around.

magnify To make something seem larger or more important than it is. Don't *magnify* minor flaws.

overstate To say in words that exaggerate. This critic tends to *overstate* the bad parts of a movie.

stretch To extend; to strain. Harry is sometimes happy to *stretch* the truth if he has something to gain.

ANTONYMS: minimize, underplay, understate

expensive *adj.* Having a high price. The fact that something is **expensive** does not guarantee its quality.

costly Costing a lot. That experiment was *costly* in terms of both money and time.

dear Expensive; precious. If an item is rare and greatly in demand, it is probably also quite *dear*.

ANTONYMS: cheap, inexpensive

explain *v.* To make clear. Can you **explain** how a microwave oven works?

clarify To make pure; to make understandable. A lawyer may be able to *clarify* that law for you.

demonstrate To show or prove by actions, examples, logic, or evidence. The surgeon planned to *demonstrate* a new procedure to the medical students.

teach To help someone learn something. Mr. Klein can *teach* you a lot about European history.

tell To inform. Form groups and *tell* each other your ideas.

ANTONYMS: bewilder, confuse, mystify, obscure, perplex

F

fall *v.* To drop to a lower place or level. In autumn, the leaves **fall** from the trees.

descend To go down. Please *descend* the stairs carefully.

plummet To fall straight down; to drop sharply. She watched the damaged kite *plummet* to the ground.

topple To fall over, as if unbalanced. If you add one more block, the tower will *topple* to the floor.

ANTONYMS: ascend, climb, rise

find *v.* To discover; to locate. You will **find** your other shoe under the couch.

come across To find accidentally or in passing. If you *come across* my notebook, please let me know.

detect To discover something hidden or hard to notice. I *detect* a look of guilt on his face.

ANTONYMS: hide, lose

first *adj.* Before all others. To make an omelet, the **first** thing you must do is break some eggs.

chief Most important. The *chief* reason I work is that I like being busy.

leading Belonging before all others; most outstanding. Dr. Tubbs is the *leading* authority on organ transplants.

main Principal; most essential. The *main* switch is on the left.

primary First. Our *primary* concern is for the passengers' safety.

ANTONYMS: final, last, ultimate

fly *v.* To travel through the air. Even hundreds of years ago, people wanted to be able to **fly**.

glide To move in a downward slant without using power, as a model airplane. The eagle seems to *glide* effortlessly.

sail To move, glide, or float in the air. Just let the kite *sail* on the breeze.

soar To rise high into the air; to fly high. It must have been thrilling to see the first rocket *soar* into space.

friend *n.* A person one knows well and likes. A good **friend** is someone you can rely on for help.

chum A close friend or companion. My mother had lunch with an old college *chum* today.

companion A comrade; a person who accompanies another. Samantha considers her cat a *companion*.

pal A friend; a chum. Mickey has always been my most loyal *pal*.

ANTONYMS: adversary, enemy, foe

funny *adj.* Amusing; comical. That comedian is so **funny** that I laugh even before he says a word.

amusing Causing amusement or fun; laughable. He chuckled at some of the speaker's *amusing* remarks.

comical Causing laughter; funny. Some clowns are *comical* all the time.

ANTONYMS: heartbreaking, mournful, serious, sober, tragic

G

go *v.* To move along; to proceed; to move from one place to another. **Go** quickly to school.

depart To go away; to leave. Don't *depart* without saying good-bye.

leave To go away from or go away without. I did not mean to *leave* my homework on the bus.

retreat To withdraw; to fall back. When they ran out of ammunition, the cavalry had to *retreat*.

ANTONYMS: arrive, come, return

group *n.* A set of persons or things that have something in common. At the YMCA, Ann joined the beginners' swimming **group**.

bunch Several similar things together. A *bunch* of children sat together.

cluster A group of things close together. This *cluster* of grapes looks inviting.

collection A set of things that are purposely gathered together. The museum has an impressive *collection* of minerals.

division A part of a company, government, or department. Diane works in a new *division* of the bank.

H

happy *adj.* Having positive feelings; satisfied. Rick was **happy** to hear that he had made the swim team.

content Satisfied. The citizens reelected the mayor because they were *content* with things as they were.

ecstatic Full of great happiness or delight. The parents were *ecstatic* at the birth of their first child.

elated Filled with joy or pride, as over success or good fortune. The scientist was *elated* when she made the breakthrough.

thrilled Feeling great emotion or excitement. I was *thrilled* with the beauty of the symphony.

ANTONYMS: depressed, heartbroken, miserable, sad, unhappy

harm *v.* To hurt. The frost might **harm** the tomato plants.

damage To injure or break. You may borrow the book if you promise not to *damage* it.

injure To harm or wound. Be gentle with the kitten so you won't *injure* it.

mar To hurt the way someone or something looks. Bad posture can *mar* anyone's appearance.

wound To hurt a living creature, either physically or emotionally. Harsh words can *wound* a friend.

ANTONYMS: benefit, help, repair, save

hat *n.* A covering for the head. Omar wears a fur **hat** with ear flaps on cold winter days.

cap A close-fitting hat, sometimes with a brim in the front. The doorman always tipped his *cap*.

headdress A decorative covering for the head. Before starting the ritual, the chief put on a *headdress*.

helmet A hard covering that protects the head. When you bike, remember to wear a *helmet*.

hold *v.* To carry, as in one's arms or hands, or to have possession of. My mother once could **hold** me in the crook of her arm.

clutch To hold tightly. The children *clutch* their parents' hands.

have To own; to hold. I *have* the answer to your question.

possess To own, as a trait or as property. Three members of her family *possess* artistic talent.

ANTONYMS: free, release

house *n.* A residence or dwelling. Many families can live in an apartment **house**.

mansion A big, stately house. Several servants were required to maintain the *mansion* and its grounds.

WRITER'S THESAURUS

residence A place where people live; a home. Should I send the package to your office or your *residence*?

shack A small, simple house or cabin, often made of wood. The *shack* was a welcome retreat from the city.

shelter A place that gives protection. There is a *shelter* at every bus stop so people won't get wet when it rains.

instructions *n.* Guidelines for doing something. It is important to follow the doctor's **instructions**.

commands Orders given by someone in charge. The guide dog was trained to obey several *commands*.

directions Step-by-step procedures for doing something. Either these *directions* are incorrect or we made a wrong turn.

orders Commands; instructions from one's superiors. My *orders* were to report directly to the captain.

J

join *v.* To put together. The electrician decided to **join** the two ends of the wire with special tape.

attach To join to something. Use a chain to *attach* the bike to a post.

connect To join things or ideas. Through careful investigation, the detective could *connect* the clues.

link To connect or join. I had each child *link* hands with a partner.

ANTONYMS: detach, disconnect

jump *v.* To rise quickly off the ground by bending then straightening the legs. Try to **jump** for the ball.

hurdle To jump over something. Ben saw the thief *hurdle* the fence and race off.

spring To jump up or straight ahead quickly. The dog is trained to *spring* at intruders.

vault To leap over, as with the aid of a pole. The winner will be the one who can *vault* over the highest bar.

L

later *adv.* Sometime in the near future. I will fix it **later**, not now.

eventually After some time; in the end. I will learn this *eventually*, but it may take a while.

ANTONYMS: earlier, now

lead *v.* To be in charge; to show the way. Felicia knows this part of town, so she should **lead**.

conduct To manage. There is a proper way to *conduct* a meeting.

direct To lead or point the way. The man at the information desk will *direct* you to the electronics department.

guide To help by showing where or how. An experienced scout was hired to *guide* the group.

ANTONYMS: follow, obey

learn *v.* To find out about something; to become informed; to gain knowledge or skill. The only way to **learn** to juggle is to practice.

ascertain To find out. Try to *ascertain* the scientific name for this species of grasshopper.

find out To discover. You can *find out* whether people like your writing if you invite them to read it.

know To have the facts; to have a particular skill. Dan's goal was to *know* as much as he could about physics by the time he graduated.

master To become skilled in the use of something; to have control over. If you *master* the rules, I'll be willing to play chess with you.

look *v.* To use the eyes to see or attempt to see. The optometrist had me **look** directly into the light.

gape To stare with an open mouth, as if surprised. She could do nothing but *gape* at the incredible sight.

glance To take a hurried look. Drivers often *glance* at the rearview mirror.

peer To take a close, careful look. I will *peer* into the dark room and try to make out the various shapes.

loud *adj.* Not quiet; noisy. The carpet reduces **loud** noises so the downstairs tenant isn't bothered.

boisterous Wild and noisy. The students were told not to be *boisterous* on the bus.

noisy Filled with noise. A constantly *noisy* environment can damage a person's hearing.

raucous Harsh-sounding. Today's music strikes me as *raucous*.

resounding Making a loud sound; echoing. *Resounding* applause filled the theater.

thunderous Making a loud sound like thunder. His *thunderous* voice boomed out a stern command.

M

many *adj.* A large number of; numerous. **Many** books have been written by celebrities.

countless Too many to count. *Countless* birds migrate south each winter.

several More than two or three, but not many. Elephants fascinated Joe, and he went to the zoo *several* times on his vacation.

various More than one; several. You can see the work of *various* sculptors in Rome.

move *v.* To change position; to progress. As the season went on, my favorite hockey team began to **move** ahead in the ratings.

advance To move forward or ahead from one point to another; to make progress. Once you have taken algebra, you can *advance* to trigonometry and calculus.

proceed To go forward or onward, especially after an interruption. Now that the sirens have stopped, let us *proceed* with the meeting.

ANTONYMS: remain, rest, stop

O

old *adj.* Not young; worn. I've had these **old** boots for ten years.

aged Elderly; advanced in years. The community center runs a recreation program for the *aged*.

decaying Decomposing; rotting; wasting away. That *decaying* log has been sitting there for months.

WRITER'S THESAURUS

dilapidated In partial ruin or disrepair. Frank buys *dilapidated* cars, fixes them up, and sells them at a profit.

mature Fully developed; grown-up. Voting for the first time made Mike feel *mature*.

opinion *n.* Something a person believes to be true but cannot prove. In my **opinion**, there are just too many automobiles.

belief Something believed or thought to be true or good. The men shared a *belief* in people's basic goodness.

feeling An opinion or emotion. My *feeling* is that it's time to adjourn this meeting.

notion An opinion or belief, sometimes an unusual one. Sara entertains the *notion* that there is another planet more highly developed than Earth.

P

people *n.* Human beings; women, men, and children. **People** watched the first lunar landing on TV.

individuals Particular persons. A few *individuals* will be chosen to accompany the President on his peace mission.

population All the people living in one region; a particular group. The nonsmoking *population* is delighted with the recent ban on smoking.

public People referred to as a group for a specific purpose. Book covers are meant to attract the reading *public*.

play *v.* To do an activity just for fun. You should **play** as hard as you work.

cavort To have fun by skipping or jumping around playfully. Dolphins love to *cavort* in the water.

frolic To cavort. The nursery-school teacher put on a record and watched the children *frolic* around the room.

romp To play energetically. The puppies *romp* in the backyard.

toy To play; to entertain oneself by tinkering. On weekends, Jerry liked to *toy* with the engine of the antique car.

prove *v.* To demonstrate that something is true by giving information or evidence or using logic. There are ways to **prove** that heat rises.

confirm To make sure of. Call the airport to *confirm* your plane reservation.

establish To prove to be true. Can you *establish* beyond doubt that this necklace belongs to you?

substantiate To prove by finding or presenting evidence. You will need to *substantiate* your claim to the gold.

verify To give proof that something is accurate. The bank teller must *verify* your signature.

ANTONYMS: disprove, refute

R

rough *adj.* Bumpy; not smooth. One disadvantage to taking the scenic route is that you may hit a **rough** stretch of road.

choppy Short and rough; jerky. The boat tossed in the *choppy* waters.

coarse Not fine; made with rough or loosely woven material. This burlap shirt is *coarse* and itchy.

jagged Having sharp, pointy edges. The knife with the *jagged* edge is good for cutting meat.

ANTONYMS: even, seamless, silky, smooth

run *v.* To move ahead by taking fast steps. **Run** and answer the phone before it stops ringing.

bolt To run away suddenly. A deer will *bolt* when people approach.

dart To move abruptly and quickly. Young children sometimes *dart* into the street without thinking.

gallop To run quickly. That foal could *gallop* at an early age.

sprint To run very fast, as in a short race. Jim won't *sprint* in the race, since it is 10 miles long.

stampede To rush forward without thinking, as in a panicking crowd. Yelling "fire" in a theater can cause people to *stampede*.

S

say *v.* To utter aloud. Kindly **say** what you mean.

declare To state purposefully. She will *declare* the winner of the race.

express To tell in words. I wish I could *express* my feelings.

remark To notice and comment aloud about something. Jon will probably *remark* that your hair is much shorter than it was when he saw you last.

scary *adj.* Causing terror or fear. When you are alone at night, ordinary noises can be very **scary** especially to young children.

fearsome Frightening; capable of causing great fear. The monster in that fairy tale is truly *fearsome*.

fierce Cruel, violent, savage, or angry. The *fierce* winds uprooted many palm trees.

savage Wild, untamed, and often fierce. A *savage* storm ripped along the coast of Florida.

ANTONYMS: benign, gentle, reassuring, soothing

shoe *n.* A covering for a person's foot, usually made of leather or canvas. The lace on my left **shoe** broke just as I crossed the busy street.

boot A shoe that goes partway up the leg. Do you wear a special kind of *boot* to go horseback riding?

footwear Coverings for the feet. My idea of a relaxing vacation is spending a week without using any *footwear*.

loafer A casual leather shoe that has a sole and heel and that slips onto the foot. A *loafer* is easy to slip on but isn't as dressy as an oxford.

sandal A shoe with straps to hold the sole onto the foot. My foot is tan between the straps of my *sandal*.

sneaker A rubber-soled canvas or leather shoe with laces or self-sticking straps. A *sneaker* is a nice, springy shoe to wear when you run or jump.

sudden *adj.* Taking place quickly and unexpectedly. The snowstorm was quite **sudden**.

abrupt Sudden, without warning. Pulling the emergency brake caused the train to make an *abrupt* stop.

impulsive Doing something all at once, without thinking. She offered her favorite shirt to her friend in a burst of *impulsive* generosity.

unexpected Not expected; without warning. We had an *unexpected* change of plans at the last minute.

ANTONYMS: deliberate, expected, gradual, planned

surprise *v.* To catch without warning, as by being unexpected or unusual. If you want to **surprise** Aunt Lydia, you should plan the party secretly.

astonish To surprise very much; to fill with wonder; to amaze. The magician was able to *astonish* her audience with her tricks.

astound To stun with amazement. Stories of his adventures may *astound* you.

startle To frighten, surprise, or excite suddenly. Tiptoe so you won't *startle* the birds.

stun To shock; to astonish. This news bulletin will *stun* everyone.

T

tall *adj.* Above average in height. The Empire State Building is not as **tall** as the World Trade Center.

high Extending far up. At the top of the *high* mountain, the air gets uncomfortably thin.

towering Tall; like a tower. They gazed at the *towering* redwood tree.

ANTONYMS: short, small

then *adv.* As a result; it follows that. If all dogs are mammals, **then** our dog, Sparky, must be a mammal.

consequently So; as a result. Our team won; *consequently*, we celebrated.

hence For this or that reason. Carmen is ill; *hence*, she will not be able to come to the party tonight.

therefore Consequently. The market had a big sale on detergent; *therefore*, I bought enough boxes to last a year.

tight *adj.* Close-fitting. I ate too much, and now my belt is too **tight**.

crowded Too full of people or things. They searched for each other across the *crowded* room.

snug Having just enough room. My jeans shrank and now they are *snug*.

taut Pulled tight. Both teams pulled the rope until it was *taut*.

ANTONYMS: loose, relaxed, slack

tired *adj.* Without energy. Tom was **tired**, so he decided to go to sleep early.

exhausted Extremely tired. The children were *exhausted* after a long day at the circus.

fatigued Very tired, especially from working hard. Mowing the enormous lawn left Elsa *fatigued*.

weary Tired or bored. The machine operator grew *weary* of the same old routine day in and day out.

ANTONYMS: renewed, rested, revived

transportation *n.* A way of carrying from place to place. Boats are basic **transportation** in Venice, Italy.

conveyance Something used to transport. In San Francisco the trolley is a charming as well as practical *conveyance*.

vehicle A means of taking people or things from place to place. Do you need a special permit to drive a *vehicle* of that size?

U

unusual *adj.* Uncommon or rare; not ordinary or usual. That **unusual** creature in the photograph resembles a unicorn.

extraordinary Remarkable; surprising. Einstein had an *extraordinary* mind.

remarkable Worthy of notice; striking; amazing. It is *remarkable* that you can balance cards like that.

singular One of a kind; uncommon. Babe Ruth's *singular* ability as a hitter won the hearts of baseball fans everywhere.

unique Unlike anything or anyone else. I know this shirt is *unique*, because I designed it myself.

ANTONYMS: banal, common, normal, unremarkable

V

very *adv.* To a great degree. Henry is **very** pleased about his grade on the final exam.

exceptionally Unusually. August 10 was an *exceptionally* hot day.

extremely Much more than is usual; very. Our team played *extremely* well last night.

particularly More than most; especially. I enjoyed the whole play, but I *particularly* liked the last scene.

quite Very. Homegrown fruits and vegetables can be *quite* delicious.

W

walk *v.* To go forward, one foot at a time, without running. Please **walk** with me to the store.

amble To walk in a slow, easygoing way. A racehorse that likes to *amble* along will not be a winner.

saunter To stroll. On Sunday, we like to *saunter* along the promenade.

stride To walk with long steps. Since they both had long legs, Melanie and Amy would *stride* along together on the beach.

strut To walk in a self-important way, as if wanting to be noticed. To see a peacock *strut*, you would think it knows how beautiful its tail is.

trudge To plod; to walk in a slow, tired way. After working in the fields all day, the tired man would *trudge* home to a good dinner.

INDEX

INDEX

EP = Extra Practice
G = Glossary
WH = Writer's Handbook
WT = Writers Thesaurus

A

Abbreviations, 84–85, 96, 100, 436–440, EP14
Abstract nouns, 80–81, 100, EP12, WH6
Active voice. *See* Transitive verbs; Verbs.
Addresses. *See* Proper nouns; Nouns.
Adjectives, 249–251, 267, 268–269, 272–273, 290–291, 294, 295, 296, 297–298, 316, EP42–47, EP52, WH34–35. *See also* Usage.
　adjective clauses, 386–387, 402, 460–461, EP61, WH21
　adjective phrases, 325–326, 342, 460, EP54, WH19
　articles, 268–269, WH14
　comparisons with, 276–277, 278–279, 298, 459, EP46, EP47, WH15, WH77–78
　demonstrative, 270–271, 297, EP43, WH15
　nouns as, 272–273, EP44
　predicate, 274–275, 298, EP45, WH5, WH15
　pronouns as, 272–273, EP44
　proper, 268–269, 297, 435–437, 454, EP69, WH14
Adverbs, 249–251, 267, 280–282, 290–291, 294, 295, 298, 316, EP48–50, EP52, WH16–18, WH35–36. *See also* Usage.
　adverb clauses, 386–387, 402, 460–461, EP61, WH22
　adverb phrases, 327–328, 342, 460, EP55, WH19
　comparisons with, 285–287, 299, 459, EP50, WH17, WH78
　placement within sentences, 283–284, 298, EP49
Agreement of subject and verb. *See* Sentences; Subject; Verb.
Alliteration, G10
Analyzing
　character sketch, 62–63, 98
　comparison/contrast composition, 206–207, 244
　descriptive paragraph, 306–307, 340

how-to paragraph, 110–111, 150
mystery story, 364–367, 400
personal narrative, 14–15, 50
persuasive essay, 158–159, 194
poem, 250–251, 252–254, 296
research report, 410–411, 452
Antecedents, 226–227, 246, 458, EP36, WH7
Antonyms, 94–95, 97, 101, WH67
Apostrophe, 90–91, 97, 105, 142–143, WH29
Appositives, 73, 92–93, 96, 101, 105, 345, EP18, WH7
Art, 124
Articles, 268–269, WH14
Assonance, G10
Audience for writing, 21, 23, 33, 37, 39, 41, 43, 45, 70, 72, 81, 85, 87, 93, 116, 117, 119, 129, 131, 136, 138, 140, 165, 167, 169, 174, 177, 179, 183, 185, 210, 214, 215, 217, 225, 227, 232, 245, 258, 259, 261, 284, 293, 312, 313, 315, 324, 330, 333, 371, 372, 374, 380, 385, 389, 418, 419, 421, 426, G2

B

Base words, 190–191, 193, 197, WH64
Bias, 166, 169
Bibliographies, 443–445, 455, 468, 479, EP72
Blended words, 396–397, 399, 403, WH67
Book parts, 467–468
Brainstorming. *See* Thinking processes and skills.
Business letters, 175, 438–440, 454, 484–485, EP70, WH60

C

Calkins, Virginia, 405–409
Capitalization, 428, EP66, EP69, WH23–25
　of abbreviations and initials, 84–85, 100, EP14, WH24
　in addresses, 438–440, EP70
　in bibliographies, 443–445, EP72, WH25
　of first word in sentence, 30–31, 49, 428–429, 453, EP66

INDEX

INDEX

J

L

M

N

O

INDEX

INDEX

F
G
H
I
J

continued from page IV

Rieu. Copyright by E. V. Rieu. Published by Methuen & Company, Ltd.

Sandra M. Simons, on behalf of Ashley Simons: "The Mystery of the Missing Coin" by Ashley Simons.

José Garcia Villa: "To Become an Archer" from *Selected Poems and New* by José Garcia Villa. Copyright © 1958 by José Garcia Villa.

Walker and Company: From pp. 38–39 in *THE AUTOMOBILE: Inventions That Changed Our Lives* by Barbara Ford. Copyright © 1987 by Barbara Ford.

The H. W. Wilson Company: Entry from "COMPACT DISCS" in *Reader's Guide to Periodical Literature,* August 1988. Copyright © 1988 by The H. W. Wilson Company.

Art Acknowledgments

Anthony Accardo: 451; Alex Bloch: 16, 57–61, 65, 149, 205, 242, tap logo (3); Suzanne Clee: 451; Cathy Diefendorf: 221, 262; Anthony Giamas: 10–13, 63, 112, 316, 394, 411; Don Dyen: 48; Simon Galkin: 96, 109, 111, 113, 290, 302–305, 406–409; Meryl Henderson: 148; Loretta Lustig: 243; James Needham: 294; Sue Parnell: 149; Susan Spellman: 250, 251; Gary Undercuffler: 218; Robert Villani: 156–157; Fred Win kowski: 192; Kit Wray: 352–362.

Cover: Tom Vroman

Production and Layout: Blaise Zito Associates

Photo Acknowledgments

PHOTOGRAPHS: Pages 3, HBJ Photo/Rob Downey; 6(t), HBJ Photo/Charlie Burton; (b), HBJ Photo/Rob Downey; 7(t), HBJ Photo/Rob Downey; (b), HBJ Photo/Rob Downey.

UNIT 1: 8, HBJ Photo/Jerry White; 9, George August Studio; 18, HBJ Photo/Rodney Jones; 25, HBJ Photo/Rob Downey; 27, HBJ Photo/Rob Downey; 30, David Weintraub/Photo Researchers.

UNIT 2: 54, HBJ Photo/Jerry White; 55, International Portrait Gallery/New York Public Library Picture Collection; 66, HBJ Photo/Rob Downey; 75, HBJ Photo/Rob Downey.

UNIT 3: 106, HBJ Photo/Jerry White; 114, HBJ Photo/Rob Downey; 122, HBJ Photo/Rob Downey.

UNIT 4: 154, HBJ Photo/Charlie Burton; 163, HBJ Photo/Rob Downey; 166(t), HBJ Photo/Rodney Jones; (b), HBJ Photo/Rodney Jones; 172(l), HBJ Photo/Rob Downey; (r), HBJ Photo/Rob Downey; 173, HBJ Photo/Rob Downey; 176, Diane Wicks, OSF/Taurus Photos.

UNIT 5: 202, HBJ Photo/Richard Haynes; 211, HBJ Photo/Rob Downey; 220(l), HBJ Photo/Rob Downey; (r), HBJ Photo/Rob Downey; 224, HBJ Photo/Peter Burg.

UNIT 6: 248, Focus On Sports; 249(c), Eyre de Lanux; (r), Culver Pictures; 256, HBJ Photo/Rob Downey; 264, HBJ Photo/Rob Downey; 268, Arthur Tress/Magnum Photos.

UNIT 7: 300, HBJ Photo/David Phillips; 301, New York Public Library Picture Collection; 310, HBJ Photo/Rob Downey; 311, The Granger Collection; 318(l), HBJ Photo/Rob Downey; (r), HBJ Photo/Rob Downey.

UNIT 8: 350, Momatiuk/Eastcott/Woodfin Camp & Assoc.; 368, HBJ Photo/Rodney Jones; 377(l), HBJ Photo/Rodney Jones; (r), HBJ Photo/Rodney Jones; 378, HBJ Photo/Rodney Jones.

UNIT 9: 404, HBJ Photo/Richard Haynes; 415, HBJ Photo/Rob Downey; 424(l), HBJ Photo/Rob Downey; (r), HBJ Photo/Rob Downey.